American Governr

The essence of the story of American politics and government is the relationship between liberalism and democracy. *American Government* demonstrates that the tensions and complementarities between liberalism and democracy are crucial for understanding each and all of the central governing institutions and political elements of American public life. The book provides all the information and breadth of coverage required of an introductory text but does so in a manner that highlights the drama of politics. It shows that the crucial features of the American political system were established through difficult decisions made under enormous pressure and often agonizing, even bloody, conflict. By placing such critical choices in specific times throughout American history, it is the first textbook to adopt an American political development approach.

Marc Landy is Professor of Political Science at Boston College, Co-Director of Boston College's Initiative on Constitutional Democracy, and Faculty Chair of the Boston College Irish Institute. He has a B.A. from Oberlin College and a Ph.D. in government from Harvard University. He and Sidney Milkis previously co-authored *Presidential Greatness* (2000). He is an author of *The Environmental Protection Agency: Asking the Wrong Questions: From Nixon to Clinton* (1994) and *Civic Environmentalism in Action: A Field Guide to Regional and Local Initiatives* (1999). Landy has been an editor of six books, including *The New Politics of Public Policy* (1995) and, most recently, *Creating Competitive Markets: The Politics of Regulatory Reform* (2007). In addition to teaching undergraduates and graduate students, he regularly teaches public officials from Ireland and Northern Ireland about American politics through a series of executive programs run by the Irish Institute. He is also Director of Encountering John Adams: Braintree and Boston, a Landmarks Workshop for Community College Teachers sponsored by the National Endowment for the Humanities.

Sidney M. Milkis is the White Burkett Miller Professor of Politics and Assistant Director for Academic Programs at the Miller Center of Public Affairs at the University of Virginia. He has a B.A. from Muhlenberg College and a Ph.D. in political science from the University of Pennsylvania. His books include *The President and the Parties: The Transformation of the American Party System since the New Deal* (1993); *Political Parties and Constitutional Government: Remaking American Democracy* (1999); *Presidential Greatness* (2000), co-authored with Marc Landy; and *The American Presidency: Origins and Development, 1776–2007*, 5th edition (2007), co-authored with Michael Nelson. He is co-editor with Jerome Mileur of three volumes on twentieth-century political reform: *Progressivism and the New Democracy* (1999); *The New Deal and the Triumph of Liberalism* (2002); and *The Great Society and the High Tide of Liberalism* (2005). During the 2005–2006 academic year, he served as the President of the American Political Science Association's Politics and History Section.

American Government

Balancing Democracy and Rights

Second Edition

Marc Landy
Boston College

Sidney M. Milkis
University of Virginia

CAMBRIDGE
UNIVERSITY PRESS

CAMBRIDGE UNIVERSITY PRESS
Cambridge, New York, Melbourne, Madrid, Cape Town, Singapore,
São Paulo, Delhi, Dubai, Tokyo, Mexico City

Cambridge University Press
32 Avenue of the Americas, New York, NY 10013-2473, USA

www.cambridge.org
Information on this title: www.cambridge.org/9780521681285

First published 2008
Reprinted 2010

A catalog record for this publication is available from the British Library.

Library of Congress Cataloging in Publication Data

Landy, Marc Karnis.
American government : balancing democracy and rights / Marc Landy, Sidney M. Milkis. – 2nd ed.
    p.   cm.
Includes bibliographical references and index.
ISBN 978-0-521-86275-2 (hardback) – ISBN 978-0-521-68128-5 (pbk.)
1. United States – Politics and government. I. Milkis, Sidney M. II. Title.
JK276.L36   2008
320'973–dc22   2007024846

ISBN 978-0-521-86275-2 Hardback
ISBN 978-0-521-68128-5 Paperback

We dedicate this book to our teachers at Oberlin College, Muhlenberg College, Harvard University, and the University of Pennsylvania, who kindled and sustained our interest in American politics and government and instilled in us the desire to pass their wisdom on to a new generation.

Brief Contents

Contents

Part Three: Governing Institutions

10. Bureaucracy   500

Case Study: American Foreign Policy: Empire of Liberty or Merely Empire?   556

Part Four: Political Forces

11. Parties and Elections   564

12. Public Opinion and Political Participation   630

Case Study: The Dog That Did Not Bark: No Child Left Behind and Advocacy Politics   686

13. Conclusion: Liberalism and Democracy in the Twenty-first Century   692

Preface

The Story of the Book: The American Political Development Approach

Encouraged by the response to the first edition of *American Government: Balancing Democracy and Rights*, we have undertaken a second edition with three major objectives in mind. First, we wanted to take account of the important developments that have taken place since the publication of the first edition, especially the 2004 and 2006 elections, the Iraq War and its difficult aftermath, and the intense partisan conflict that has characterized George W. Bush's second term. Second, we wanted to refine the writing and analysis throughout the book. In doing so, we have made a special effort to better connect the conceptual framework and historical narrative to contemporary developments in American politics. Third, we wanted to incorporate new scholarship and our own revised thinking about American political development. Most important, having stressed the decline of traditional patronage-based parties in the first edition, we have added a lot of new text in the second edition that takes account of the emergence of a "new" national programmatic party system, allied to broader changes in ideas, institutions, and policies, which has led to major changes in contemporary American politics and governance.

The hard work that went into accomplishing these tasks reaffirmed our commitment to the objectives that informed the first edition of this book. It grew out of a friendship that developed from a deep intellectual affinity. We met in 1984 when we were put on the same panel at the American Political Science Association meeting. We found that we were both preoccupied by the New Deal. Sid was trying to understand how it gave rise to the modern administrative state. Marc was trying to figure out how Franklin Roosevelt both embraced the labor movement and staved off the transformation of the Democratic party into a British-style Labour party. Soon after, Sid came to Brandeis University, where Marc had become a Fellow of the Gordon Public Policy Center. We had adjoining offices at the center and were able to continue our conversations over lunch and coffee and at the center's seminars. We discovered that our common interests were not limited to Franklin Roosevelt and the New Deal; we had both come to believe that the study of political science had been severed from its historical roots and that our job was to graft the study of contemporary politics back on to those roots. Both of us were already doing this in our American politics teaching with very good results. We saw that students developed a much keener and firmer grasp of current matters when they became aware of the intellectual and institutional connections that the contemporary issues and events had with the past. Sid applied this approach to his book *The President and Parties* and to the textbook he co-authored with Michael Nelson, *The American Presidency: Origins and Development.* Marc applied the approach to essays about the labor movement's impact on the development of American politics. Together, we drew on the American political development framework in our investigations for our book *Presidential Greatness.* In the meantime, our devotion to connecting past and present came to appear less eccentric; many other scholars also began to find greater meaning and interest in bringing history to bear on the study of American politics. American political development (APD) has now established itself as one of the most active and intellectually vibrant movements within political science.

This book reflects our understanding of what the APD approach means and how it can best be deployed to educate students about the fundamentals of American politics and government. It is premised on the principle that the structure and dynamics of contemporary politics and government can best be made intelligible by an examination of their origins and the transformations they have undergone. We greatly admire the work of historians, but this book is about political science, not history. Despite its extensive discussions of the past, its central objective is to explain and clarify the political present.

This book provides the full array of information about contemporary American government and politics that students need to know, but it does so in a developmental context that makes that information more comprehensible and meaningful. For example, we do not simply discuss public opinion in terms of the current, and therefore transitory, state of opinion on various issues of the day. We examine how the very idea of public opinion came into being in reaction to the Federalist efforts to limit political participation and how this concept was understood and used by Lincoln and subsequently transformed by the Progressives. Thus, students do not merely learn about current public opinions, which may well have shifted by the time they read this book; they also learn about the efforts to restrict and expand the role of public opinion that have affected the political institutions and dynamics with which they live. Likewise, the discussion of the media's role in politics is informed by an understanding of how that role has evolved, beginning with the creation of a party press in the 1790s. The discussion also includes Theodore Roosevelt's use of the newly created mass circulation national newspapers to popularize his messages to Congress, Franklin Roosevelt's mastery of radio in his fireside chats, and John F. Kennedy's ingenious use of television to expand the audience for his news conferences – to appeal over the heads of journalists and speak directly to the tuned-in public.

Balancing Liberty and Democracy

Like the hangman's noose, writing a textbook concentrates the mind. It forces one to focus on the essentials. What do students absolutely·need to know, and what is the fundamental set of questions that an introductory text must address? As we contemplated the complex interrelationships between ideas, institutions, and political forces that constitute APD, we decided to organize our presentation of these diverse matters around the theme of the central task of American government: balancing liberalism and democracy. Each chapter traces the political development of some specific aspect of American political life in terms of the interplay between *liberalism*, which champions individual liberty and natural rights over community, and *democracy*, which stresses the importance of self-governing political communities that shape the moral character of individuals and provide for the common good. We give equal weight to both the compatibilities and the tensions between these two powerful political principles. We make clear that liberalism supports democracy through its commitment to equal opportunity, and that democracy rests on liberal principles that ensure the liberty of each citizen to actively participate in civic life. But we also stress liberalism's tendency to elevate rights above duties and individual liberty above majoritarianism, and we acknowledge that democracy values obligation to the community more than individual autonomy and the well-being of the whole above the rights of the individual.

As we make clear repeatedly throughout the book, this relationship between liberty and democracy is not the only important dynamic in American politics. We do not shy away from discussing those powerful forces that are neither liberal nor democratic, most notably racial, religious, and sexual bigotry. But we maintain that the core principles and institutions that shape American political culture work against beliefs and practices that are both illiberal and antidemocratic. As Abraham Lincoln and Martin Luther King, Jr., showed, the Declaration of Independence and the Constitution appeal to the American sense of justice. This is not to say that these charters of freedom triumph automatically over prejudice and oppression. In fact, the authors of both the Declaration and the Constitution sought to sidestep, rather than condemn, the institution of slavery. Like any ideals worth preserving, the principles of liberty and democracy cannot prevail without militant champions and jarring struggles. A major aim of this book is to depict the words and deeds of those champions and the epochal character of those struggles.

Narrative Style

A great advantage of the APD approach is that it lends itself to a narrative style that is livelier than the topical style of most textbooks. Politics is not just storytelling, but it is largely about arguments and conflicts that are inherently vivid and dramatic. We try to capture the drama of political life without sacrificing analytic rigor. The essence of drama is choice. The narrative approach highlights the crucial choices that have shaped America's politics. For example, our chapter on the Constitution pays careful attention not only to the arguments of the Federalists, who championed the Constitution, but also those of the Anti-Federalists, who opposed it. We do so to show just how rich the array of alternatives were for the design of American political institutions and how the particular choices made by the Constitution's Framers were therefore fraught with great consequences. The critical episodes discussed in Chapter 4 – Jefferson's Revolution of 1800, the Jacksonian period, the Civil War, the Progressive Era, and the New Deal – focus on the stakes involved and the powerful arguments offered by the contending parties.

Religion and Localism

Framing the book in terms of the tension between liberalism and democracy is particularly helpful for illuminating the political importance of two key features of American political life that contemporary political science too often neglects: religion and localism. For example, Chapter 2 describes how the Puritans conceived of America as a country with a special mission, a "city upon a hill" whose utopianism and democratic zeal were at odds with the view of America as a secular nation dedicated to individual rights. Chapter 6 describes the religious roots of the Populist attack on laissez faire as symbolized by William Jennings Bryan's evocation of the "Cross of Gold." Chapter 12 discusses the religious sources of abolitionism and the impact of the social gospel movement on Progressivism. Several chapters consider the importance of the Christian Right in contemporary politics and how religion currently animates conflicts over abortion, stem cell research, and same-sex marriage.

The book shows how the centrality of local self-rule to the idea of American democracy, rooted in the relationship between size and democracy, has created greater resistance to the centralization of power in the United States than in other nations that have representative governments. Chapter 4 discusses the Jeffersonian and Jacksonian eras in terms of their intertwined commitments to localism and democracy. Chapter 5 explains that because the Constitution does not fully clarify the dividing line between state and federal power, disputes over what the government *ought* to do frequently turn into disputes over *where* the decision should be made, with decisive implications for both the protection of individual rights and the exercise of majority rule.

Outline of the Book

We adhere to a conventional table of contents that devotes a separate chapter to each of the most important topics that a basic textbook needs to cover. The three chapters of Part 1, "Formative Experiences," provide the general intellectual framework of the book with regard to political culture, development, and institutional design. The two chapters of Part 2, "Pivotal Relationships," look at two of the most important consequences of the liberal doctrine of limited government – federalism and the free economy. The four chapters of Part 3, "Governing Institutions," examine the three branches of national government and the bureaucracy as well. The two chapters of Part 4, "Political Forces," focus on the most important political phenomena that exist outside the formal governing structures and on how these forces shape political debate and governmental decision making. These forces include political parties, social movements, interest groups, and the media.

In preparing this edition, we added an essay at the end of each major section on an important contemporary event, each of which illustrates the connection between the larger themes of that section and current developments in American government. "Formative Experiences" (Part 1) ends with a discussion of the so-called culture war that purportedly divides Americans today. The "Pivotal Relationships" (Part 2) section is capped by an essay on Hurricane Katrina that sheds light on the enduring challenges of maintaining America's federal democracy. "Governing Institutions" (Part 3) ends in a discussion of how current controversies in foreign policy, especially the War on Terror, extended with such profound consequences to Iraq, provide a new test of the enduring challenge of balancing national security, civil liberties, and self-government. "Political Forces" (Part 4) concludes with a discussion of advocacy politics, considering how partisan competition combined with the rights revolution to bring about major education reform in 2001, the No Child Left Behind Act, which has transformed the politics of education in the United States.

The first and last chapters of the book highlight the foundational principles and never-ending struggles that animate America political life. Chapter 1 clarifies the key concepts that the book employs, most especially liberty and democracy; it explains why these two profound principles are often in tension, and it acquaints the students with the APD approach. Chapter 13 reviews the central aspects of the American constitutional order to highlight its enduring strengths and grave weaknesses. It ends by returning to the question that Benjamin Franklin asked more than two hundred years ago: can a republic such as ours endure?

The book offers separate chapters on immensely important and interesting subjects that are rarely treated comprehensively in other textbooks. To provide a theoretical framework, a set of reference points, and a common analytic vocabulary for later chapters, Chapter 4 focuses on the major points of transition that have occurred since the constitutional founding. It argues that the Jeffersonian Revolution of 1800, Jacksonian democracy, the Civil War, and the New Deal are truly refoundings that engaged citizens in debate and conflict about the meaning of the Declaration and the Constitution and required citizens to reexamine key questions about the relationship between liberty and democracy.

We devote an entire chapter to political economy (Chapter 6). If war is too important to leave to the generals, then an understanding and appreciation of the interaction between economics and politics is certainly too important to leave to the economists. As the name implies, this chapter highlights the political forces that have shaped the institutional and legal framework in which economic activity takes place. It aims to show students how all the critical aspects of economic life are affected by the tensions between liberty and democracy. In the other chapters, students are made aware that what they are learning in their history courses complements their political science understanding, and vice versa. Chapter 6 shows them how the study of economics and of political science inform one another as well.

This book contains no separate chapters about civil rights, civil liberties, or public policy because these subjects are so integral to American politics that we wanted them to permeate the entire book. In addition to extensive discussions of all three topics in the chapter narratives, each chapter contains "Contemporary Politics" boxes that address current civil rights, civil liberties, and public policy issues. These boxes help students to understand the continuing relevance of key historical debates and conflicts by providing contemporary examples of these same issues and conflicts. Additional boxes, labeled "Nuts and Bolts," enable us to provide the full range of necessary factual information about the operations of contemporary politics and government without disturbing the chapter narrative or simply tacking on all this vital information at the chapter's end.

Each chapter begins with a chapter overview. Following the overview, a short vignette depicts a dramatic political moment, a lively political conflict, or a vivid symbolic action. Some vignettes are very prosaic. For example, the bureaucracy chapter (Chapter 10) begins with a story of a young driver who gets a parking ticket. Some stories are memorable. Chapter 1 opens with a description of Martin Luther King's "I Have a Dream" speech. Some are dramatic. The chapter on Congress (Chapter 7) starts by relating Senator James Jeffords's decision to leave the Republican party in May 2001, thereby handing control of the Senate to the Democrats. In all chapters, these vignettes are designed both to capture the student's attention and to link the topic of the chapter and the pervading theme of the book. In each chapter, the vignette is followed by a narrative that elucidates the major arguments and themes of the chapter developmentally, extending through the present to account for contemporary developments and emerging trends. The conclusion of each chapter reconsiders the themes presented in the beginning in light of the information and ideas presented in the narrative and the boxes. Each chapter ends in a summary that reviews the major developments that have been covered, a list of major concepts that have been highlighted, and a number of suggested readings that allow students to explore the subject further.

How to Use This Book

The organization of each chapter suggests a way to use this book as a teaching tool. For example, the vignette itself can serve as a basis for class discussion, or the instructor can ask students to come up with their own concrete examples of how issues of liberty and democracy are provoked by the ideas, institutions, or political forces that form the subject matter of the chapter. Likewise, the boxes can be used as topics for research assignments and for further class discussions that are enriched by the added knowledge the students have acquired on their own. Because the organization of each chapter is essentially the same, the instructor can encourage the students to compare similar stages of historical development across different chapters, which helps to integrate students' understanding of how various political forces and institutions are developing simultaneously. The essays that appear at the end of each major section of the book also can be used to help students understand the unifying themes and general trends of different developments in American government.

The strong thematic stance of this book invites challenge and dissent in a way that a less consistent and insistent approach does not. The suggested readings at the end of each chapter include writings that challenge the book's point of view and can therefore be used to encourage a lively debate about how central liberalism and democracy really are and what alternative ways of thinking about APD might be more persuasive.

Changes for the Second Edition

We have made several changes in the second edition that should enhance the use of this book by students and instructors. Greater attention has been given to basic information and contemporary issues in the "Nuts and Bolts" and "Contemporary Politics" boxes. In addition, the cross-chapter cases that appear at the end of each section clarify the major themes of the book and link them more effectively to contemporary issues. Finally, we have added chapter overviews and chapter summaries to help students understand the major arguments and developments of each chapter. These changes link the conceptual framework of the book to more contemporary issues and make the book more student-friendly.

Companion Website

The companion website for this textbook is available for students. It contains a range of review and self-study material. Visit the site at: www.cambridge.org/landymilkis.

Acknowledgments

We deeply appreciate the sage counsel and generous support of our editor, Ed Parsons of Cambridge University Press. His commitment to this project and patience with its authors resulted in a much stronger volume than we otherwise would have produced. We received splendid help from Cambridge's editorial assistants Faith Black and Bonnie Lee. Alison Smith of Boston College provided invaluable help with charts, tables, and figures. Jesse Rhodes of the University of Virginia offered energetic research support and insightful suggestions during the preparation of the second edition of the text. The following readers offered thoughtful and keen commentary on the first edition of the book, helping us immeasurably in preparing this version: Thomas Baldino, Hugh Heclo, Philip Klinkner, G. Roger McDonald, Lucas Morel, Michael Nelson, Peter Ubertaccio, and McGee Young.

Credits

Chapter 9 Page 450: Library of Congress, Prints & Photographs Division [LC-USZ62–8499]; page 462: © Granger Collection, New York; page 471: © AP/Wide World Photos; page 474: © AP/Wide World Photos; page 479: © AP/Wide World Photos; page 493: Supreme Court of the United States, 2006.

Chapter 10 Page 506: © Granger Collection, New York; page 517: Library of Congress, Prints & Photographs Division [LC-USZ62–12825]; page 524: Library of Congress, Prints & Photographs Division [LC-USW3–057017-C]; page 547: © AP/Wide World Photos.

Case Study Page 562: © NewsCom.

Chapter 11 Page 566: © NewsCom; page 590: © Granger Collection, New York; page 613: © NewsCom.

Chapter 12 Page 657: © AP/Wide World Photos; page 664: Library of Congress, Prints & Photographs Division [LC-USZ62–109643]; page 674: © AP/Wide World Photos.

Case Study Page 687: © NewsCom.

Chapter 13 Page 699: © AP/Wide World Photos; page 713: © AP/Wide World Photos.

American Government

1 Introduction

American Government: Rights and Democracy, Consensus and Conflict

Chapter Overview

This chapter focuses on:

☆ The view that ideas about rights and democracy and the struggles that have taken place over the meaning of rights and democracy are the very heart of American political life

☆ The meaning of classical liberalism and the Constitution as the concrete embodiment of that political philosophy

☆ The role of religion and localism in nurturing democracy

☆ The different meanings of the words *liberal* and *conservative*

☆ The distinctive approach to studying politics and government called American political development

"I Have a Dream"

On August 28, 1963, 250,000 people marched on Washington to protest discrimination against African Americans and to celebrate the rise of the Civil Rights Movement. Race relations in the South were dominated by so-called Jim Crow laws, enacted at the end of the nineteenth century, which imposed racial segregation in all aspects of life. In *Brown v. Board of Education of Topeka* (1954), the Supreme Court declared the so-called "separate but equal" doctrine in education policy unconstitutional. Nonetheless, many Southern schools remained segregated. Not since the turbulent Reconstruction Era that followed the Civil War had the South been so alienated from the rest of the country.

When civil rights demonstrations broke out throughout the South to protest this racial caste system, local police brutally repressed efforts to break down what the distinguished African-American sociologist W. E. B. Du Bois had called the "color line." When African-American students tried to enter Little Rock High School, a crowd of white parents cursed and threatened them as the governor of Arkansas, Orval Faubus, blocked the door. A particularly ugly confrontation took place in Birmingham, Alabama, where one of the Civil Rights Movement's most important leaders, Martin Luther King, Jr., was jailed. President John F. Kennedy had been reluctant to take on civil rights, arguing that it was up to local officials to enforce the law. After Birmingham, however, Kennedy gave his support to a comprehensive civil rights bill making racial discrimination in hotels, restaurants, and other public accommodations illegal and giving the attorney general the power to bring suits on behalf of individuals to speed up lagging school desegregation. The measure also authorized agencies of the federal government to withhold federal funds from racially discriminatory state programs.

When this bill ran into stubborn opposition in Congress, civil rights leaders organized the largest single protest demonstration in American history. King's speech at the Lincoln Memorial was its climax. Late in the afternoon, the summer heat still sweltering, King appeared at the microphone. The crowd, restlessly awaiting King's appearance, broke into thunderous applause and chanted his name. King began by praising Lincoln's Emancipation Proclamation as "a great beacon of hope to millions of Negro slaves who had been seared in the flames of withering injustice." But,

> [O]ne hundred years later, we must face the tragic fact that the Negro is still not free. One hundred years later, the Negro is still sadly crippled by the manacles of segregation and the chains of discrimination. One

Martin Luther King, Jr., called upon Americans to practice the political and social ideals of the Declaration of Independence.

hundred years later, the Negro lives on a lonely island of poverty in the midst of a vast ocean of material prosperity. One hundred years later, the Negro is still languishing in the corners of American society and finds himself an exile in his own land. So we have come here today to dramatize an appalling condition.

This litany of oppression might have elicited anger; indeed, some of King's followers had been growing impatient with his peaceful resistance to Jim Crow and its brutish defenders. But King, an ordained minister, spoke the words of justice, not revenge: "Let us not seek to satisfy our thirst for freedom by drinking from the cup of bitterness and hatred." A reverend might have been expected to invoke the warnings of the biblical prophets in calling America to account; however, in the wake of a century's scorn, King appealed to America's charters of freedom:

> When the architects of our republic wrote the magnificent words of the Constitution and the Declaration of Independence, they were signing a promissory note to which every American was to fall heir. This note was a promise that all men would be guaranteed the unalienable rights of life, liberty, and the pursuit of happiness.

King lamented that America had not lived up to those famous words. Even after the Brown case had interpreted the Constitution so as to fulfill the promise of the Declaration of Independence, segregationists prevailed. The "check" that promised freedom had come back marked "insufficient funds."

Still, he counseled continued faith in the promise of American life. African Americans should "refuse to believe that the bank of justice is bankrupt." At the same time, King warned, their faith in American justice could not last much longer; the time had come "to make real the promises of Democracy." "Now is the time to rise from the dark and desolate valley of segregation to the sunlight path of racial justice." His indictment went beyond the South. "We can never be satisfied as long as a Negro in Mississippi cannot vote and a Negro in New York believes he has nothing to vote for." The crowd shouted and clapped in cadence with him. Inspired by this surge of feeling, King abandoned his prepared text; but even as he spoke "from his heart," in words that would make this address memorable, King's sermon had a familiar ring, drawing again on the Declaration of Independence:

> I say to you today, my friends, that in spite of the difficulties and frustrations of the moment, I still have a dream. It is a dream deeply rooted in the American dream. I have a dream that one day this nation will rise up and live out the true meaning of its creed: "We hold this truth to be self-evident, that all men are created equal".... When we let freedom ring, when we let it ring from every village and every hamlet, from every state and every city, we will be able to speed up that day when all of God's children, black men and white men, Jews and gentiles, Protestants and Catholics, will be able to join hands and sing in the words of the old Negro spiritual, "Free at last! Free at last! Thank God almighty, we are free at last!

As King's inspiring speech made crystal clear, African Americans were not fighting just to get more economic and political power, they were fighting for their *rights* – the inalienable rights promised to all Americans by the Declaration of Independence. A right is a claim that belongs to an individual *naturally*; natural rights cannot be violated by any person or society. The Constitution provides a list of rights, among the most hallowed of which are freedom of speech, assembly, and religion; equal protection of the law; and freedom from being deprived of one's property without due compensation. The Declaration calls these rights *unalienable* to emphasize that they cannot be taken away, even by the majority. But as the whole history of African Americans makes dreadfully clear, their rights had been *alienated* and not by a king or a tyrant but by the actions of their fellow Americans. Several clauses that protected slavery were included in the original Constitution that was ratified by the people of the original states. The state legislatures that passed the Jim Crow laws and the governors who obstructed school desegregation were all popularly elected.

Like the word *rights*, the word *democracy* is cherished by Americans. We insist that our laws and the actions of our representatives reflect the people's will. But as the civil rights story shows, rights and democracy can come into terrible conflict. Indeed, such tension will arise whenever individuals or minorities claim that the majority is depriving them of their rights.

The challenge of this book is to convince the reader that the most essential ideas for understanding how Americans act politically are ideas about rights and democracy and that struggles over the meaning of rights and democracy are the very heart of American political life. The need to balance the two arises precisely because they are both such highly cherished values. They are both desirable, but they are not identical, and sometimes they pull in opposite political directions. Indeed, the book will show that much of the conflict and tension in American politics is attributable to the inherent clash between rights and democracy.

Rights

The problem of how best to secure rights dominated the thinking of the authors of the Declaration of Independence and the Constitution. After proclaiming the existence of "unalienable rights," the Declaration of Independence explains that "to secure these rights, governments are instituted among men." Thus government exists solely for this crucial but limited purpose. The deepest conviction that the Founders held about government is that it should be limited. In their minds, securing rights and limiting government were synonymous.

Originally developed by the great English political philosophers Thomas Hobbes and John Locke, this rights-based approach was a sharp departure from earlier political philosophical traditions. Those had stressed the duties and obligations individuals owed to the political community rather than the rights and freedoms of individuals. Hobbes and Locke influenced the American Founders to believe that individuals have these rights by nature and therefore the community may not trample on them. This new stress on individuals was as radical as the stress on rights. Traditionally, people conceived of themselves as members of a greater whole – a clan, a tribe, a city – not as solitary persons. Of course, Americans still recognize their ties to family, community, and nation, but Hobbes's and Locke's theories regarding the primacy of the individual have had a profound effect. Rarely do people disregard their own interests and desires simply because they recognize that they also belong to a larger whole. Americans are not taught to think of themselves merely as parts of a larger organism. It is considered legitimate and acceptable for Americans to pay a lot of attention to what is best for them as individuals and what rights they have on an individual basis. In recognition of John Locke's crucial role in developing this new understanding of the primacy of the individual, this philosophical perspective is often referred to by scholars as Lockean Individualism.

The principles of Lockean Individualism just described are also often referred to by political theorists and historians as classical liberalism. This use of the term *liberal* should not be confused with the one popular in contemporary American politics. When *conservative* politicians criticize their opponents by calling them "tax-and-spend liberals," they are not talking about classical liberalism. The classical liberal tradition is simply the rights-based perspective embraced by the authors of the Declaration of Independence and the Constitution.

The Framers of the Constitution believed that the greatest threat to inalienable individual rights came from the tyranny of the majority. They feared that, by dint of superior numbers, a majority would grab the reins of government and use that power to deprive others of their rights. Checks on the powers of government are designed to prevent a majority, or a minority for that matter, from behaving tyrannically. Government secures life, liberty, and the pursuit of happiness by establishing the rule of law to ensure that law-abiding citizens are protected from assault by the lawless. It also protects against foreign attack by providing for the common defense. Pursuit of happiness is the most difficult of the three inalienable rights to define and comprehend. Almost all the colonial charters referred to "life, liberty, and property." Yet in drafting the Declaration, Jefferson substituted "pursuit of happiness" for "property." It appears that this phrase is supposed to guarantee a right to property and more, but what more? It does not promise happiness itself, but only the right to "pursue" that dream. The difficulties that have arisen from this complex formulation are so profound that we devote an entire chapter, entitled Political Economy, to tracing how disputes about what government should and should not do to secure the pursuit of happiness have repeatedly been a source of conflict in American political life.

Illegal Immigration

Tens of thousands marched in the 2006 Great American Boycott and Immigration Rights Rally in New York City to protest proposed reforms of U.S. immigration laws.

The Census Bureau estimates that each year 500,000 people come to the United States illegally. Of the 33.1 million foreign-born residents of the United States, roughly 9 million are illegal immigrants. Clearly, the millions of illegal immigrants who risk their lives to come to the United States do so in the "pursuit of happiness" – abandoning their homes, friends, and often their families in order to try to make a better life. For the most part, they work hard and live frugal lives in order to send money back to those they have left behind. But because they are not citizens, they are not entitled to the rights of citizens. They cannot vote, obtain valid driver's licenses, obtain Social Security cards, or enjoy many of the other benefits that citizens enjoy. And they live under the constant threat of being deported.

Many advocates for illegal immigrants would like to eliminate these disadvantages and narrow the distinction between who is a citizen and who is not. They would grant amnesty to those illegals who are already here and make it much easier for illegal immigrants to become citizens and to partake of all the various education, health, welfare, and other benefits that citizenship confers.

Those who oppose such changes do not deny that a right to pursue happiness exists but rather believe that this right is meaningless in the absence of a government strong enough to protect it. An essential power of such a rights-ensuring government is the ability to distinguish between who is and who is not a citizen of that government and who is entitled to the full measure of its protection. Therefore, the advocates of stricter control of illegal immigration support stricter border control, including building a fence along the border with Mexico. They also oppose providing greater public benefits to illegal immigrants on the grounds that to do so is to reward criminal behavior.

The dispute over illegal immigration is but the first of many examples in this book of how different understandings of rights arise in practical political circumstances and how such differences are dealt with democratically.

In declaring that "all men are created equal," the Declaration implies that the "pursuit of happiness" requires some form of democratic government. Believing that democracies are more likely to protect rights than other forms of government, especially the sort of monarchy against which the American colonies revolted, the Declaration required that governments derive their "just powers" to secure rights from the "consent of the governed." Therefore, no matter what a governing scheme looks like, it is legitimate only if it has gained the approval of the people. That is what is meant by the term *popular consent*, the democratic principle underlying the commitment to inalienable rights. In theory, the Declaration calls for limited democratic government that will protect natural rights; in practice, maintaining a balance between popular rule and individual rights has been an enduring challenge.

The Constitution

The Constitution gives concrete governmental form to the principles of limited government, securing rights, and popular consent. Ratified by the thirteen states that formed the original republic, the Constitution divides power among three separate branches of the national government and between the national government and the states. The legislative branch, called Congress, is composed of two separate bodies, the House of Representatives and the Senate. The executive branch is headed by the president. The judicial branch consists of three levels of federal courts with the Supreme Court as the highest level. Each of these three branches is treated in a separate chapter.

Some of the Constitution's most essential features, which we will discuss in Chapter 3, were purposely intended to protect rights by limiting majority rule. For example, Supreme Court justices are appointed for life, meaning that elected representatives cannot remove them except through the impeachment process. Because they are not beholden to popular opinion, judges are expected to give greater care and attention to the rights of minorities. Every state elects two senators regardless of its population. Therefore, even though today California has more than thirty times as many people as Wyoming, both those states have the same number of senators. This was done to ensure that the states with large populations did not threaten the rights of the citizens of the smaller ones.

In fact, the constitutional system of checks and balances, which regulates the relationships among the legislative, executive, and judicial branches, is designed especially to filter the voice of the people, to moderate the intemperate passions that inevitably well up from time to time in a democratic society. The House of Representatives, elected directly by the people, was expected to be more responsive to such passions. But as the most important architect of the Constitution, James Madison, noted, the Senate, executive, and judiciary would be more independent of public opinion and, therefore, capable of expressing "the cool and deliberate sense of the community." Madison hoped that Americans would support the Constitution, even though its complex system of "filtrations" would not respond directly or immediately to the people's collective concerns. This hope, resting in the people's deep and abiding commitment to individual rights, would be fulfilled. Indeed, the Constitution, along with the Declaration of Independence, became the object of religious devotion, a principal symbol of America's civic religion. The reverence that Americans developed for the Constitution has made it much more than a plan of government. It has become the guiding star of American political life. When Americans argue about serious political questions, the argument often turns to constitutional questions. Does the Constitution permit the president to pursue a war against terrorism without obtaining a Declaration of War from Congress? Did the Supreme Court really have the constitutional authority to determine the outcome of the 2000 presidential election by siding with George W. Bush, and against Al Gore, in the legal contest over disputed votes in Florida?

To understand the role the Constitution plays in American political life requires more than an explanation of its specific features. It requires an explanation of *constitutionalism*. This term indicates that the Constitution is more than the sum of its parts. It is the embodiment of the people's claim to govern. If Americans had not become constitutionalists, the idea of popular sovereignty, that the people are the ultimate source of political authority, would ring hollow. Anyone can see that the people do not run the government. At most, they vote for those who do. Nonetheless, as the preamble to the Constitution states, "We the People . . . ordain and establish" the set of governing structures and principles that the Constitution contains. Those structures and principles only remain in force because the people consented to them. Thus, the people do not govern, but the authority of the government ultimately rests with them. This is what the Framers meant by a republic. In their minds, a republic was a complex constitutional creature established by popular consent, combining democratic principles with respect for rights. It was the best form of government because it was accountable to the people, paid attention to their wishes, and protected their liberty. It provided an opportunity for the people to participate in government, but only indirectly, by electing representatives and the chief executive. Electing one's rulers is what is meant by representative democracy. But it also smoothed democracy's rough edges and checked its excesses, making it more responsible and more competent. It was designed to give the people a part in governing while warding off demagogues, ruthless and ambitious politicians who usurp power by stirring up popular passions.

Individual Rights Protected by the Constitution

The Constitution accords many different kinds of rights to individuals. This box groups those rights, which are scattered throughout the amendments to the Constitution, together on the basis of what kind of rights they confer, thus providing a composite image of the rights enjoyed under the Constitution. *Civil rights* refer to fundamental questions of human liberty. *Political freedoms* refer to those freedoms deemed necessary to enable citizens to govern themselves and render their government accountable. Notice that the right to bear arms is listed as a political freedom because its intention was to enable citizens to form a militia for the purpose, among others, of resisting government tyranny. *Religious freedom* is precisely what its name implies. *Criminal rights* refer to the rights enjoyed by those accused of a crime. The final category is something of a miscellany containing various other restraints on what government can do to an individual. The specific place that each right is to be found among the amendments to the Constitution is in parentheses. This list is not complete. For the full enumeration of rights see the copy of the Constitution in Appendix 2.

Civil Rights – All persons are entitled to equal protection of the law, to due process of law (Fourteenth Amendment), and to not be held as slaves (Thirteenth Amendment).

Political Freedoms – Persons enjoy the right to free speech, to assemble in public, and to petition the government regarding their grievances (First Amendment). Citizens cannot be denied the right to vote on the basis of race (Fifteenth Amendment) or age as long as they are older than 18 years (Twenty-sixth Amendment). Citizens have the right to own and bear arms (Second Amendment).

Religious Freedom – Individuals have a right to freely exercise their religion. Government is forbidden from privileging one religion above the others (First Amendment).

Criminal Rights – Persons have a right to a trial, to be judged by a jury, to confront witnesses, to the assistance of counsel, to not be tried for the same crime twice (Sixth Amendment), and to reasonable bail (Eighth Amendment).

Protection from Government Control, Supervision, and Oppression – The government may not force people to house troops in their homes (Third Amendment), search homes or seize property without reasonable cause (Fourth Amendment), or take property for public use without just compensation (Fifth Amendment).

Equality and Democracy

As the Declaration and the preamble to the Constitution claim, the rights tradition accommodates democracy because it understands liberty to be a natural and equal endowment of all humans – no one can claim to be fit to rule over anyone else. Based on the principle of popular sovereignty, as embodied in the phrase "We the People," the Constitution provides for elections of legislators and the president. Even the members of the judiciary, nominated by the president and confirmed by the Senate, as Madison insisted, "derived [their] powers . . . indirectly from the great body of the people." But this vital accommodation cannot eliminate the tensions that arise between a rights-based preoccupation with preventing tyranny of the majority and the democratic determination to promote majority rule.

From the very beginning, the Constitution was criticized for being insufficiently democratic. Sounding a complaint that would be echoed throughout American history, the opponents of the Constitution, the so-called Anti-Federalists, argued that it placed too many barriers in the path of the majority. Then and now, advocates of greater democracy have never claimed to oppose inalienable rights. Rather, they have insisted that the rich and powerful exploit the Constitution's protection of rights to protect their privileges. Such critics have wondered why the few have so much and the many have so little. Whatever the letter of the Constitution, they have not believed that the vast inequalities in living conditions, wealth, and educational opportunity that have persisted in the United States are consistent with its claim that it is based on the consent of the people. Indeed, the earliest conflicts in the new republic, over the payment of debts and the creation of a national bank, were between those defending property rights and those who believed that such claims were a smoke screen by which a privileged few were benefiting at the expense of the many. As the economy industrialized and

The Founders signed the Declaration of Independence as a commitment to the self-evident truths of life, liberty, and the pursuit of happiness.

agriculture became increasingly commercial, farmers and workers came to believe that the unbridled liberty of the railroads and corporations was being exploited to create a vast economic tyranny that was crushing them. They demanded that the majority exercise its will to limit those abuses of freedom.

Champions of business have often claimed that the "pursuit of happiness" is best served by preventing government from doing anything at all to limit lawful efforts to accumulate property, pass it on to one's children, and enjoy its fruits. But over time, the voters have pressured the government to intervene. It collects inheritance taxes, which take away part of what one leaves to one's children. It maintains a graduated income tax, which takes proportionately more from a rich person than from a poorer person. And, it offers financial aid to qualified students who would otherwise miss out on a college education for lack of funds. Much of the stuff of American politics is composed of the clash between an understanding of the "pursuit of happiness" that emphasizes the rights of property, including the right to have more of it than other people, and a more democratic – egalitarian – understanding that would limit property rights in order to enable everyone to participate in what Abraham Lincoln called "a fair race of life."

The concern to curb inequality is one element of the democratic tradition; no less important has been the concern to enhance political participation. Since the birth of the republic, the celebration of rights and constitutionalism has had to compete with the view that popular sovereignty requires more than elections and institutional checks and balances. As we will see in Chapter 3, the Anti-Federalists attacked the Constitution's checks on democracy, claiming these innovations would not refine but mute public views. Champions of democracy have long bridled against the constitutional constraints on majority rule, favoring popular participation in and influence on government. If representation was necessary in a large country, the Constitution's critics insisted, then representatives should be numerous enough and selected in a fashion so that those in government would "possess the same interests, feelings, opinions, and views the people would were they all assembled." Moreover, substantial representation should be combined with short terms and rotation in office, allowing for a significant portion of the citizenry to participate meaningfully in public affairs.

The democratic critique of the Constitution has endured throughout American history. Indeed, since the beginning of the twentieth century, reformers have argued that the best cure for the injustices of political life in the United States is more democracy. As our discussion of political participation in Chapter 12 will show, over the past 100 years there has been a steady movement toward increasing use of methods such as referenda, recalls, and initiatives that attempt to involve voters directly in the governance of their states and localities. Ardent democrats have rarely rejected rights claims outright; but they have insisted that liberty cannot survive without a vigilant citizenry, nurtured by active involvement in politics and government. Political participation, as one prominent Anti-Federalist put it, is the only means by which "people are let into the knowledge of public affairs" and are "enabled to stand as the guardians of each other's rights."

Religion

Two features of American political life that have nurtured democracy coexist uneasily with the emphasis on individual rights. The first is religion. Although the Constitution provides for a separation between church and state, spiritual devotion has nurtured a sense of obligation and community that challenges individualism. Religion was at the heart of the original founding of the country. The Puritans conceived of America as a country with a special mission. They likened America to a "city upon a hill," a high place visible to the "lowly" of Europe who would see it as an example to follow. To provide the proper example, they sought to be as pure in their everyday lives as they were in their religious practice. The persistence of this view accounts for much American utopianism and democratic zeal. It is at odds with the view of America as a secular nation, a place that prizes individual liberty above civic obligation and moral purity. Instead, it perceives that the country was founded as part of a sacred covenant, as "the world's best hope," as Lincoln put it, to secure self-government on a grand scale. Religion has been at the heart of many of the nation's most ambitious and successful reform efforts including Abolitionism, Populism and Progressivism, and the Civil Rights Movement. Ironically, the great influence that religion has had, and continues to have, in buttressing a sense of community in American life is itself predicated on an inalienable right, freedom of religion. As the First Amendment to the Constitution asserts, in the United States, people are free to practice any religion they choose and no one religion will be favored over any other. In theory, religious freedom is supposed to create, as Jefferson put it, a "wall of separation" between government and religious organizations. In practice, however, as our example of Martin Luther King well documents, religious devotion has aroused political organizations and social movements that have inspired Americans to pursue reforms that have profoundly affected political life. In religion, as in so many other areas of American life, democracy and rights both exert enormous influence.

Localism

The second feature is localism. Direct democracy, in which people do not rely on representatives but govern themselves, is only possible in small places. The larger the political unit the greater the sophistication needed to govern and the lesser the amount of trust and intimacy among the citizenry. As boundaries expand, ordinary people are forced to rely on representatives to govern in their stead. Direct democracy thrived in the small towns that were the political centers of early American life, encouraging citizens to become attached to their local government, which they saw as close to their concerns and accessible to their influence.

The Framers of the Constitution worried that local government was indeed too accessible, too prone to dominance by potentially tyrannical majorities. Their fears were heightened by the excesses of democratic zeal that took place in the wake of the War of Independence, leading in some cases to violence and mob rule.

Federalism

The Framers sought to strengthen the national government against the states and localities, "to form a more perfect Union" as a bulwark of

The recent Ten Commandments monument controversy, in which an Alabama Supreme Court judge defied federal orders and refused to remove the overtly religious symbol from government property, demonstrates both the ongoing tension between America's founding religious convictions and its commitment to secular governance and the tension between states' rights and national interests.

individual freedom. But the system of federalism established by the Constitution retained key virtues of local self-rule. Federalism attempts to marry the best features of local with the best of national government. The national government was given responsibility to take care of those few and well defined problems that affected the whole nation, for example, national security, interstate commerce, and taxation. The states and localities were asked to take on, as Madison put it, the "numerous and indefinite" matters that did not require national attention such as the local economy, education, road maintenance, and providing law and order.

Madison assumed that for practical purposes these state responsibilities would actually be carried out by local governments. The Framers recognized that the line between the one national community and the many local communities would never be perfectly clear; each would be tempted to encroach on the other's authority. The Constitution, in fact, invites and encourages competition between America's national aspirations and her local foundations. As the term "We the People" implies, the Framers placed their ultimate reliance on the people to determine the proper balance between national and state power. Over time, especially since the

1930s, this competition has worked in the national government's favor. But the centrality of local self-rule to the idea of American democracy, rooted in the relationship between size and democracy, has created uncommon resistance to the centralization of power in the United States as compared to other nations that have representative governments. As Chapter 5 will show, the struggle between centralization and local self-rule is ongoing. In recent times, state governors and attorneys general have fought to return more power to the states with some important success. A new generation of mayors and other municipal officials has revived local government as well.

Box Three: Nuts and Bolts

Foundations of American Government: Perspectives, Principles, and People

This box provides a brief definition of some of the most important terms used in this chapter, which are frequently used throughout the book.

Popular Sovereignty is the idea that the people are the ultimate source of government's authority.

Natural Rights are those things that a human has simply because one is human. As the Declaration of Independence says, they are "unalienable," meaning they cannot be taken away: "among these [rights] are life, liberty and the pursuit of happiness."

Classical Liberalism is a theory of politics that stresses political and economic liberty and is based on the principles of natural rights, private property, and popular sovereignty. Two Englishmen, John Locke (1632–1704) and Thomas Hobbes (1588–1679), were among the greatest thinkers who worked to devise this theory.

Lockean Individualism is a term used to stress the importance that John Locke gave to the freedom of the individual. It is often used to refer to the importance of that idea in American political development.

The *Framers* were the individuals who actually went to the Constitutional Convention in Philadelphia in the summer of 1787. Two men, John Adams and Thomas Jefferson, who did not attend had so much influence on those who did that they are counted among the Framers.

The *Liberal Tradition* began in the seventeenth century with the classic writings of Hobbes and Locke and was perpetuated in America through the writings of the Framers. Later, it was upheld by such important thinkers and leaders as Abraham Lincoln and Martin Luther King.

The *Democratic Tradition* can be traced back to the congregational politics of the American Puritans and has been continued by such important political movements as the Anti-Federalists, the Jacksonian Democrats, the Labor Movement, and the Civil Rights Movement.

Modern Liberalism is often used to refer to the political outlook of those who favor more egalitarian public policies and a more active government. This form of liberalism came into being during the Progressive Era and the New Deal and should not be confused with classical liberalism.

Liberals and Conservatives in Contemporary American Politics

Before explaining how this book is organized and why it takes the particular approach to understanding the interplay of rights and democracy that it does, it is first necessary to clear up a confusion that is likely to bedevil any beginning student of American government and politics. The confusion regards the meaning of *liberal* and *conservative*. Today, *liberal* is often used by the media and politicians alike to describe someone who favors a more activist government and greater equality between rich and poor. It is contrasted with the term *conservative*, which describes someone who favors less government and less redistribution of wealth and income. The Democrats are considered the more liberal party and the Republicans the more conservative one. As recently as the 1920s, those favoring bigger and more egalitarian government did not call themselves liberals, they called themselves *progressives*. In recent years, as fewer and fewer Americans identify themselves as liberals, many Democratic party politicians and activists have gone back to calling themselves progressives. As more voters identify themselves as conservatives, many Republicans who used to reject the conservative label have come to embrace it. To make matters even more complicated, prior to the 1930s the term *liberalism* was identified with the individualistic, rights-based theories of Hobbes and Locke, hence the term Lockean Liberalism. Thus an eighteenth- or nineteenth-century liberal, a devotee of John Locke, would today more likely be viewed as a conservative.

There is no easy way out of this complexity. Politics necessarily involves changes in, and conflicts over, the meaning of political labels. When engaged in politics, people choose and define words in such a way as to make their case seem most convincing. The best one can do in order to keep the meaning straight is to carefully explain oneself when using evolving words like *liberal* and *conservative*. The contemporary meaning of liberalism and conservatism was born of the New Deal, which was the political order that arose from the economic and international crises of the 1930s and 1940s. To create a link between core American values and the idea of a more expansive government, President Franklin D. Roosevelt and his New Deal allies appropriated the term *liberalism*. The political success of the New Deal, which dominated American politics for nearly half a century, led to a redefinition of liberalism, one that supported not only an expansion of rights, but also an expansion of the national government's role in American society. Indeed, the very success of New Deal liberalism and its novel interpretation of rights led champions of limited government to stop calling themselves liberals and to adopt the name conservatives instead. They did so reluctantly, knowing that they were conceding a very popular word to the supporters of big government. In time, however, critics of big government came to embrace the conservative label, as big government liberalism lost favor in the United States.

A good example of the connection between classical liberalism and contemporary conservatism is provided by the continuing controversy over gun control. Many American cities and states have passed laws banning the possession of handguns and assault weapons. Opinion polls show that these laws are often supported by large majorities. But this display of majority sentiment has not put an end to the dispute over gun control in those places. Opponents of gun control are usually conservatives. They do not deny that they are in the minority. Rather, they claim that their rights are being violated. The Second Amendment to the Constitution declares a "right to bear arms." It does not place any limits on that right. Indeed, the amendment justifies the right to bear arms on the grounds that this right is necessary to the existence of a "well regulated Militia [which is] necessary to the security of a free State." The right to possess guns is thus not fundamentally about hunting turkeys or taking target practice, or even protecting oneself against intruders. It is about the ability of free citizens to organize themselves to protect their republic, either against outside invaders or against tyranny imposed from within. For such a force to be militarily viable, it needs real weapons, hence the opposition to banning any type of gun even those primarily intended to shoot humans. But contemporary conservatives are not always on the side of rights and contemporary liberals are not always on the side of democracy. Liberals tend to favor granting full rights to homosexuals including the right to marry. Conservatives tend to oppose gay marriage. In the summer of 2003, the Massachusetts Supreme Court decided that homosexuals could marry in that state. In November 2004, seventeen states voted to ban gay marriage. National opinion polls reveal that a majority of Americans oppose gay marriage. In this case, it is liberals (for the most part) who favor gay marriage and believe homosexuals have a right to marry. Conservatives argue that their opposition to gay marriage is validated by the strong majorities that have been marshaled against it.

To say that liberals and conservatives are both capable of "flip flopping" when rights and democracy are pitted against each other is not to call them hypocrites. Rather, it is a stark reminder that in America rights and democracy are both such cherished values that it almost always makes sense to try to appeal to one or the other or both when trying to win a political contest. The best way to think about what today we call liberals and conservatives is to see each of them as embodying a distinctive combination of ideas about rights and democracy. The content of those combinations changes over time and therefore so does the meaning of particular political labels such as *liberal* and *conservative*.

American Political Development

Each of the chapters that follow takes up the close yet conflict-ridden relationship between rights and democracy from a different vantage point. Although each one concentrates on a separate major topic in American politics and government, they all proceed historically. This approach to political science is known as American political development. It enables students to fully appreciate that nothing about the way we govern ourselves is inevitable. If, at critical moments in the past, leaders and citizens had made different choices, what now seems most natural and unavoidable about American politics would indeed be very different. Imagine if the states had voted not to ratify the Constitution, or if the South had been allowed to secede from the Union. These were real political options that enjoyed widespread support at the time.

As these examples demonstrate, the critical choices shaping American politics have taken place at various times throughout American history. Understanding how and why these choices were made and how they relate to one another is a necessary step for making sense of current political realities. The nuts and bolts of contemporary political life are fully presented, but they are put in a developmental context that makes them more comprehensible and meaningful. Studying the political development of the American nation uses the past to illuminate the present and the future. It is also a critical reminder that debate, discussion, and conflict are the essence of politics. Political development is not something that happened only in the past; it is the continuing process of political decision-making that is happening now and will continue into the future.

The most dramatic episodes of change in America show how rights and democracy are not simply rival traditions. Each major political transformation has allowed our citizens and their representatives the opportunity to revisit the fundamental principles of the Declaration of Independence and reset the terms of constitutional government in light of this return to, and conflict over, the meaning of its core principles. Each one of these moments involves a democratic contest over the meaning of rights – they breath new life into our collective political life by engaging the American people in debate, conflict, and resolution about what those supposedly "self-evident" truths actually mean.

The popular upheavals of constitutional politics have not weakened people's reverence for the Constitution; rather, these episodes have renewed people's faith in the fundamental principles and laws that govern them. This was even true of the slavery controversy, which had to be resolved by bullets rather than by ballots. It marked, as Lincoln said in the Gettysburg Address, a "new birth of freedom." So it has been with all great episodes of reform; America's finest and most dangerous historical chapters have allowed each generation, as Franklin Roosevelt exclaimed, to have its own "rendezvous with destiny."

When the Frenchman and great political thinker Alexis de Tocqueville came to America in the 1830s, he feared that the most serious threat to individual rights in America was not revolution, but the temptation of the people to become absorbed completely by their own concerns, to live in their own "tiny private universes." If "citizens continue to shut themselves up more and more narrowly in the little circle of petty domestic interests," he warned, "there is a danger that they may in the end become practically out of reach of those great and powerful public emotions which do indeed perturb peoples but which also make them grow and refresh them." In preventing the people from falling into rank apathy, American democracy has kept the principles of the Declaration vital and the American Constitution alive. As Jefferson hoped, the Constitution has "belonged to the living."

An examination of political development helps explain the mundane as well as the extraordinary aspects of American politics and government. Much of political life is routine. One's political behavior is often best predicted by discovering what one did in the past. Therefore, it is only by delving into the past that the origins of such behavior can be discovered and it becomes possible to explain why those rules and rituals that people follow uncritically and even unconsciously came about in the first place.

Path Dependency

History is important not only because it highlights the pivotal choices of the past, but also because the weight of history drives current events. Political scientists call this phenomenon *path dependency*, meaning that once an important course of action has been embarked upon, considerable inertia develops that encourages the continuation of that course.

A striking everyday example of path dependency is typewriting. When inventor C. L. Sholes built the first commercial typewriter prototype in 1868, the keys were arranged alphabetically in two rows. But the metal arms attached to the keys would jam if two letters near each other were typed in succession. So, Sholes rearranged the keys to make sure that the most common letter pairs such as "TH" were not too near each other. The new keyboard arrangement was nicknamed QWERTY after the five letters that form the upper left-hand row of the keyboard. QWERTY's original rationale has disappeared because keyboards now send their messages electronically. Many typing students find it very hard to master. Despite its shortcomings, QWERTY remains the universal typing keyboard arrangement simply because it is already so widely used and so many people have already taken pains to master it. Future typists might benefit from a change, but they do not buy keyboards; current typists do. Many political institutions and practices are just like QWERTY. Although their original purposes no longer exist, people are used to them and the costs of starting afresh are just too high.

There are countless examples of path dependence in American politics. Perhaps the single most important example is the way in which the United States is carved up into individual states. State boundary lines exist for all sorts of peculiar historical reasons. On the East Coast, they represent, for the most part, the grants given by Britain to specific individuals and groups to establish colonies. On the Pacific Coast and in the Southwest, they represent the boundaries of colonies obtained from Spain. In the Great Plains, they often represent little more than the preference of surveyors for drawing squares and rectangles. One can imagine many good reasons for adjusting state boundaries to accommodate practical realities. Why should Kansas City be split between Kansas and Missouri? The suburbs of northern New Jersey and southwestern Connecticut are dominated culturally and to a large measure economically by New York City and yet they remain part of other states. But there have been very few changes in state boundaries over the entire course of American history.

This bias in favor of the status quo is not simply because people are creatures of habit, though indeed they are. It is also because, as a rule, those who benefit from an existing policy will fight harder to keep the policy in place than those who might benefit from a change will fight to alter it. This difference in intensity is explained by the word *might*. Beneficiaries of existing policies know what they have and what they stand to lose if policies change. Potential beneficiaries can only estimate the benefits that a policy change might bring them. Therefore, politically speaking, fear of loss is a more powerful motivator than hope of gain. Kansas City, Kansas; Bergen County, New Jersey; and Fairfield County, Connecticut, provide valuable tax revenues and other tangible benefits to the governments of their respective states. Acutely aware of how much is to be lost, the governors and state legislatures of Kansas, New Jersey, and Connecticut are much more willing to expend political energy to keep them than their counterparts in New York or Missouri are to acquire them.

Of course, many other factors may intervene to hamper the defense or aid the offense. Indeed, the American constitutional system dedicated to rights and establishing a complex system of checks and balances to secure them was deliberately designed to enhance the odds in favor of those resisting change. For example, Article IV, Section 3 of the Constitution protects existing state boundaries by providing that they cannot be changed "without the Consent of the Legislatures of the States concerned as well as of the Congress." Periodically, social and political movements emerge to exert democratic pressure on these inertial forces. Change does take place but the bias of the governing system stacks the odds against it. Looking at the origins and early development of contemporary policies and institutions enables one to understand how those odds are set and why, sometimes, the odds are beaten.

The Plan of This Book

This book is divided into four parts. The first, "Formative Experiences," contains Chapters 2, 3, and 4, which focus respectively on political culture, constitutional design, and critical episodes in American political development. Chapter 2 examines the formation and meaning of the core beliefs that Americans profess, especially as they relate to rights and democracy. It shows how those beliefs coalesce to form what Tocqueville called "habits of the heart," an enduring political culture shaping the political opinions and actions of Americans. Chapter 3 looks at the Constitution: the political debate its creation provoked; the conflicts between rights and democracy that it settled, and those that it left unsettled. It explains why it is so important that the American government was erected on the basis of an original and carefully designed blueprint and how that conscious plan both reflects American political culture and has helped to shape it. Chapter 4 focuses on the major points of transition that have occurred since the constitutional founding.

Part 2, "Pivotal Relationships," looks at two of the most important consequences of the Lockean liberal doctrine of limited government – federalism and the free economy. The Tenth Amendment to the Constitution explicitly announces what virtually all the Founders understood, that those matters not delegated to the national government remain the province of the states. Because the Constitution restricts the powers of the federal government, state governments remain very influential and federalism remains an important means for checking national power. Because "pursuit of happiness" implies a qualified right to property, the American economy has remained free of government intervention to an extent unmatched by any other major industrial nation. This protection is enshrined in the Fifth Amendment guarantee that no private property will be taken for public use without just compensation.

Just as the Constitution does not establish fixed boundaries between national and state governmental power, so it does not clearly demarcate property rights and government regulation. The disputes provoked by these uncertain boundaries have proven to be among the most hotly contested controversies in all of American political life and have given it much of its distinctive style and substance. As we shall see, those who fight for greater national power as well as those who resist either in the name of states rights or property rights all invoke the principles of rights and democracy to support their side.

The four chapters that form Part 3, "Governing Institutions," each examine one of the three branches of national government – the Congress, the presidency, and the federal judiciary – enumerated in the Constitution, as well as a fourth, the bureaucracy, which developed outside of formal constitutional arrangements. These chapters describe how those institutions operate now and how they have changed over time. The great debates over the structure and purposes of these institutions demonstrate how political arguments and political decisions shape and alter the "nuts and bolts" of government.

Part 4, "Political Forces," focuses on the most important political phenomena that exist outside of the formal governing structures and how they shape political debate and governmental decision making. These include political parties, social movements, interest groups, and the media. All of these political actors have been discussed extensively earlier in the book but always in supporting roles. It would be impossible to have full-fledged discussion of any of the topics in Parts 1 through 3 without paying due attention to their mighty influence. Here they gain center stage. The spotlight is on their development and dynamics and how they have embodied and exemplified key questions of liberty and democracy.

This chapter, and each chapter to follow, contains boxes labeled "Contemporary Politics" and "Nuts and Bolts." These boxes provide important supplementary information that does not fit neatly into the chapter's narrative flow. The Contemporary Politics boxes give vivid illustrations of how concepts included in the chapter apply here and now. The Nuts and Bolts boxes supply crucial information about how different political and governing institutions are organized and how they actually work.

An Invitation

This book encourages an appreciation as well as an understanding of political life. Because no person is an island, politics is inescapable. We must live with the collective decisions made in our midst whether we choose to participate in them or not. Inescapable yes, tedious no. Politics combines the suspense of sports with the colorful array of characters found in great literature. What follows is a comprehensive account of American politics and an invitation to savor its richness, its dramatic intensity, and its capacity to surprise.

Chapter Summary

☆ The struggles over the meaning of rights and democracy are the very heart of American political life.

☆ The problem of how best to secure rights dominated the thinking of the authors of the Declaration of Independence and the Constitution.

☆ The Constitution gives concrete governmental form to the classic liberal principles of limited government, securing rights, and popular consent.

☆ Advocates of greater democracy do not oppose inalienable rights. Rather, they insist that the rich and powerful exploit the Constitution's protection of rights to protect privilege.

☆ Religion and localism nurture democracy but coexist uneasily with rights.

☆ Federalism attempts to marry the best features of local with the best of national government.

☆ The terms *liberal* and *conservative* each embody a distinctive combination of ideas about rights and democracy. The content of those combinations change over time and therefore so does the meaning of the political labels *liberal* and *conservative*.

☆ American political development is an approach to the study of politics and government that proceeds historically in order to illuminate how the past affects the present and future.

Major Concepts

checks and balances
conservative

constitution
constitutionalism
democracy
direct democracy
equality
equality of opportunity
equality of result
federalism
liberal
liberalism
limited government
majoritarianism
path dependency
popular consent
popular sovereignty
progressives
representative democracy
republic
rights
tyranny of the majority

Suggested Readings

Bryce, James. *The American Commonwealth*. Indianapolis, IN: Liberty Fund, 1996.

Chesterton, G. K. *What I Saw in America*. New York: Dodd Mead, 1923.

Croly, Herbert. *Progressive Democracy*. New York: Transaction, 1998.

Du Bois, W. E. B. *The Souls of Black Folk*. New York: Penguin, 1996.

Hamilton, Alexander, James Madison, and John Jay. *The Federalist Papers*, ed. Charles Kesler. New York: Mentor Books, 1999.

Hartz, Louis. *The Liberal Tradition in America*, 2d ed. New York: Harvest Books, 1991.

Landy, Marc, and Martin Levin, eds. *The New Politics of Public Policy*. Baltimore, MD: Johns Hopkins University Press, 1995.

Lowi, Theodore. *The End of Liberalism*, 2d ed. New York: W. W. Norton, 1979.

McWilliams, Wilson Carey. *The Idea of Fraternity in America*. Berkeley: University of California Press, 1973.

Morone, James. *Democratic Wish: Democratic Participation and the Limits of American Government*, rev. ed. New Haven, CT: Yale University Press, 1998.

Orren, Karen and Stephen Skowronek. *The Search for American Political Development*. New York: Cambridge University Press, 2004.

Pierson, Paul. *Politics in Time: History, Institutions, and Social Analysis*. Princeton, NJ: Princeton University Press, 2004.

Smith, Rogers M. *Civic Ideals: Conflicting Visions of Citizenship in the United States*. New Haven, CT: Yale University Press, 1999.

Storing, Herbert, ed. *The Complete Anti-Federalist*. Chicago: University of Chicago Press, 1981.

Tocqueville, Alexis de. *Democracy in America*, ed. Harvey Mansfield and Delba Winthrop. Chicago: University of Chicago Press, 2000.

PART ONE

Formative Experiences

2 Political Culture

This chapter focuses on:

☆ The seminal contributions of the Puritans and of seventeenth-century liberal thought to the development of American political culture

☆ The Declaration of Independence as a statement of the American political creed

☆ The role of slavery in challenging and undermining the creedal devotion to liberty and democracy

☆ The growing conflict during the 1780s between the champions of unfettered democracy and those who sought to curb democracy to better preserve liberty

The Declaration of Independence does not say "all Americans are created equal." It extends the promise of equality and of the inalienable rights attached to it to all men, meaning all people. In a series of speeches in the days and weeks following September 11, 2001, President George W. Bush argued that the terrorist attacks on the World Trade Center and Pentagon were not merely acts of senseless destruction but direct challenges to the universal principles of human freedom that the Declaration defined.

Three days after the attack, speaking at a prayer service at the National Cathedral, the president explained that the War on Terror was about nothing less than the future of human freedom and that defending freedom was America's oldest responsibility and greatest tradition: "In every generation, the world has produced enemies of human freedom. They have attacked America, because we are freedom's home and defender. And the commitment of our fathers is now the calling of our time."

The following week, addressing a joint session of Congress, he explained why America in particular had been the target of the attacks: "Why do they hate us? They hate us for what we see here in this chamber – a democratically elected government. Their leaders are self-appointed. They hate our freedoms – our freedom of religion, our freedom of speech, our freedom to vote and assemble and disagree with each other."

He told the members of Congress that the War on Terror was not merely to protect American lives and property but to defend the universal principles at the heart of the American creed: "Freedom and fear are at war. . . . The advance of human freedom now depends on us."

In early November, President Bush addressed the United Nations to impress upon the peoples of the world that America's fight was their fight as well because the natural rights at stake belonged to everyone.

> . . . the dreams of mankind are defined by liberty, the natural right to create and build and worship and live in dignity. . . . These aspirations are lifting up the peoples of Europe, Asia, Africa and the Americas, and they can lift up all of the Islamic world. We stand for the permanent hopes of humanity, and those hopes will not be denied.

In his January 2002 State of the Union address, he spoke of how America was once again being called upon to play a "unique role in human events," a role first recognized by John Winthrop when he announced that the New World was "a city upon a hill," a beacon of freedom beamed at a world threatened by despotism.

There are many different approaches that Bush could have chosen for explaining to the American people what the problem was and how the government would respond. His decision to so strongly emphasize issues of human freedom and natural rights provides an important clue to just how deeply embedded such ideas are in what this chapter calls *American political culture*. Political culture refers to the core beliefs in a society, what the French author Alexis de Tocqueville referred to as "the habits of the heart." These central beliefs forge a people – "We the People," as the preamble to the Constitution reads – from a large and diverse society.

The first part of the chapter goes back to the origins of the American colonies to show how American political culture was forged as a zesty broth of democratic, religious, and liberty-loving principles tainted by the poison of slavery. Then it expands upon the previous chapter's discussion of the Declaration of Independence and the meaning of Republican government. It explains how and why the Declaration established itself as America's *political creed*. It describes how conflicts emerged between the creed's dual commitment to liberty and equality, provoking a search for a republican solution capable of preserving the essentials of both.

The Origins of "We the People"

Many accounts of the American political system assume that the founding of the nation happened in 1787, when the Constitution was written. Abraham Lincoln pointed to 1776, when the Declaration of Independence was written, as the nation's real birthday. But the author of *Democracy in America*, the Frenchman Alexis de Tocqueville, marked the settling of the New England colonies in the early seventeenth century as the true beginning of the American people. No sooner had the *Puritans* landed in Massachusetts than they formed a *covenant*, pledging the new settlers "to combine together into a body politic" for the "better ordering and preservation, and furtherance" of a new society. This act left a legacy of "habits, ideas, and mores" that allowed a republic dedicated to natural rights to grow and flourish. "When I consider all that has resulted from this first fact, I think that I can see the whole destiny of America contained in the first Puritan who landed on those shores, as that of the whole human race in the first man," wrote Tocqueville.

The terrorist attacks of September 11, 2001, were viewed as attacks upon the American creed. President George W. Bush told a joint session of Congress, "They hit our freedoms."

Sources of American Political Culture: Puritanism

The Puritans acquired their name because they sought to purify the Church of England. Unlike the Pilgrims, they did not separate from that church but rather devoted themselves to reforming it, seeking to return it to the pure state it enjoyed in the time of Christ and his disciples. Even their departure to the New World was predicated on the idea that they would be a "city upon a hill" that served as a beacon of inspiration to their fellow Englishmen. They sought to remove all vestiges of what they took to be the idol worship that dominated the Roman Catholic Church and that was becoming increasingly prevalent in the Church of England. They objected to ostentatious robes, elaborate ceremonies, and magnificent artwork, all of which diverted worshippers from concentrating on their devotion to God.

Puritan religious understanding was grounded in the thought of the great theologian John Calvin (1509–1564), who was born a Frenchman but who lived most of his life in Geneva. Calvinism's defining principle was that because humankind was so deeply sinful, individuals could not, on their own, redeem themselves in the eyes of God and bring about their own salvation. Salvation was something that only God could bestow. One of Calvin's greatest criticisms of the Roman Catholic Church was its acceptance of the idea that through confession, penance, and good works a person could be saved and expect to go to heaven.

One might imagine that a rejection of good works would cause Calvinists to become selfish and self-indulgent, but the Puritans' interpretation of the impossibility of saving themselves led in just the opposite direction. They determined to create a covenant with God in which they would pledge to act as righteously as possible and to be single minded in their devotion to him. A covenant is not a contract. It put God under no obligation. The totality of the Puritan commitment came with no strings attached. Individuals did not enter the covenant; it was entered into by the entire congregation, hence the origin of the term *congregationalist*. This communal pledge required that each member of the congregation accept some measure of responsibility for the behavior of every other member. And, because any one member could destroy the covenant, it implied that each member was as important as everyone else. The idea of the covenant was therefore a very powerful glue binding the lives of all the members of a Puritan congregation and is one of the great sources of the strong grassroots democracy that emerged in the early New England towns.

The Puritans did not need to come to America to discover the principle of rights. The colonists were "Anglo Americans," as Tocqueville put it, who sought to give new meaning to values they brought with them from England. England was the "mother country" – the colonists' political principles, commercial relations, and educational practices all were closely tied to Great Britain. In fact, most state charters, issued at the king's discretion but closely overseen by the British parliament, guaranteed the colonist the "rights of Englishmen." The Seal of Massachusetts, for example, showed an "English American" holding a copy of the Magna Carta and a sword. The Magna Carta, issued in 1215, enumerated the fundamental rights and privileges of the English people. Considering the religious persecution they had suffered in England, the Massachusetts colonists, and those in other colonies as well, meant to protect these rights against the king more vigilantly than had the British parliament.

The Anglo-Americans emphasized the more democratic side of the English tradition. Tocqueville noted in awe that their migration to a new continent made them "born equal." Cut off from the feudal tradition that linked kings, noblemen, and commoners in a hierarchical chain, Americans enjoyed a fresh start, spawning a society shaped by an unprecedented "equality of conditions." This did not mean that Americans were politically and economically equal, but that they were equally entitled to enjoy rights, such as freedom of religion, association, and property.

Cultural Strains

The absence of a feudal tradition in the United States nurtured a strong sense of individual rights against the claims of society and government. America celebrated social equality and therefore appeared to be a democracy; but the will of the majority was tempered by a strong sense of individual entitlement. It was a liberal democracy, in which individual rights strained the bonds of collective authority. As Tocqueville described this novel sense of independence:

> Aristocracy links everybody, from peasant to king, in one long chain. [American] Democracy breaks the chain and frees each link.... As social equality spreads, there are more and more people who, though neither rich nor powerful enough to have much hold over others, have gained or kept enough wealth and enough understanding to look after their own needs. Such folks owe no man anything and hardly expect anything from anybody. They form the habit of thinking of themselves in isolation and imagine that their whole destiny is in their hands.

The extraordinary independence encouraged by social conditions in America could easily go too far. Tocqueville warned that Americans might become so self-centered as to ignore everything but their own affairs. Individualism in the United States might then deteriorate into "egoism," an "exaggerated love of self." Not only does American democracy "make men forget their ancestors," but it also clouds their view of their descendents and isolates them from their contemporaries. "Each man is forever thrown back on himself alone, and there is danger that he may be shut up in the solitude of his own heart."

The self-absorption that stems from the liberal emphasis on individual rights continually threatens to eat away at social cohesion and political solidarity. But this is not the whole American story. Religion in particular has provided a check on self-interest and cultivated community ties, helping to foster the idea of a national democratic community. As Tocqueville observed, the special character of American politics owes much to the interweaving of the spirit of religion and the spirit of freedom, which were both present from the beginning.

Religion, Localism, and Freedom

The Puritans came to America to advance an idea of free religious expression that fostered a sense of congregational solidarity. In a speech entitled *A Model of Christian Charity*, John Winthrop, the first governor of Massachusetts, gave voice to this mission, suggesting that England would soon take heed of what they were accomplishing in the New World: "For we must consider that we shall be as a city upon a hill, the eyes of all people are upon us." The stakes were great, he admonished, for "if the lord shall be pleased ... he shall make us a praise and glory."

The strong sense of community that Winthrop exalted was made practical by local self-government – "the mainspring and lifeblood of American freedom," as Tocqueville put it. Because the government of his native France was highly centralized, Tocqueville was especially impressed with the vitality of New England's town government, which was spreading to other parts of the country as well. By the time the Constitution was ratified in 1788, the commitment to decentralized administration was well established. Immense political authority rested not only in the states, but also in the localities.

The vitality of townships and counties followed from the same obsession with individualism that made the colonists reject the hierarchical approach to religion followed by both the Roman Catholic Church and the Church of England. Tocqueville observed that strong local self-government derived from the premise that "each man [was] the best judge of his own interest and best able to satisfy his private needs." Leaving townships and counties in charge of their "special interests," in turn, cultivated civic attachments by giving each individual "the same feeling for his country as one has for one's family . . . a sort of selfishness made [one] care for the state . . . patriotism grew out the provinces."

Nurtured by localism and religion, the American people had a sense of participating in a special, even providential task. Winthrop's sermon resonated well beyond his time: future generations have kept returning to the exalted image of "a great experiment unfolding in America, with the rest of the world – all eyes – waiting on the outcome." Even today, when individualism, now expressed through a multitude of racial and ethnic identities, threatens to destroy America's image as a "city upon a hill," Winthrop's vision still stirs the embers of American patriotism and gets quoted by politicians across the political spectrum. Figure 2.1 shows that Americans consider religion to be more important than do citizens of comparable European nations.

To be sure, the American community has not always been tolerant. Religious persecution was not uncommon in the colonies; indeed, Winthrop's "city upon a hill" could not abide a complete separation of church and state. Roger Williams's dissent from Puritan orthodoxy led to his banishment from Massachusetts in 1636. In 1644, he obtained a charter from the English parliament to establish the colony of Rhode Island. Like Massachusetts, Rhode Island's government was relatively democratic, but all religions were tolerated in Williams's colony, and church and state were rigidly separated.

The tension between Winthrop and Williams illustrates the uneasy fit between American individualism and the idea of community in the United States. The concept of a special American mission could be cruel to those who were not considered part of it. As we will see in subsequent chapters, the right to define the meaning of that mission has led to periods of intolerance in local, state, and national politics that have denigrated the concept of American individualism.

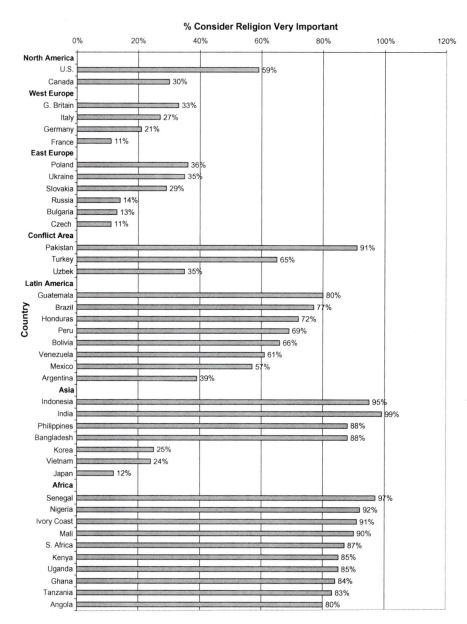

Figure 2.1. Religious Belief in America and Europe. Religion is far more important to Americans than to citizens of comparable wealthy European nations. Almost 60 percent of Americans say that religion is "very important," as compared to only a third of Britons, a fifth of Germans, and hardly more than 10 percent of French.

Source: Pew Global Attitudes Project, 2002.

Slavery

Although liberalism and democracy, and the uneasy relationship between them, explain most features of American *political culture*, they do not explain everything. As political scientist Rogers Smith has noted, many persons have been denied personal and civil liberties on the basis of what he calls ascribed characteristics – race, ethnicity, gender, and even religion. Slavery was the most glaring example. In fact, forced servitude was no less deeply rooted in American soil than was the Puritan idea of justice.

Virginia was the first of the English colonies, founded in 1607. Unlike Massachusetts, it was founded by seekers of gold and silver, not religious freedom. No sooner had it been settled than it began to deprive men and women of the fruits of their labor. Introduced in 1620 by a Dutch ship that landed twenty Africans on the banks of the James River, slavery was destined to exert immense influence on the South in particular and the rest of the country as well.

Virginia's leaders would eventually absorb many features of the New England liberal political tradition. Indispensable figures in the founding of the nation, George Washington, Thomas Jefferson, and James Madison, practiced politics there. But, this liberal political order coexisted uneasily with a labor system based on race and forced servitude. Just as the first Puritan who stepped ashore gave birth to an idea of America as a "city upon a hill," so the first slave who came ashore bequeathed a legacy of oppression that would badly compromise the nation's commitment to liberty and equality.

Still, it is important to recognize that the core principles and institutions that shape American political culture work against illiberal beliefs and practices. As Abraham Lincoln and Martin Luther King showed, the Declaration of Independence and the Constitution appeal to the American sense of justice. This is not to say that these charters of freedom triumph automatically over religious, racial, and sexual bigotry. In fact, the authors of both the Declaration and Constitution sought to sidestep, rather than condemn, the institution of *slavery*. Like any ideals worth preserving, the principles of liberal democracy cannot prevail without militant champions and jarring struggles.

The Civil War, in which nearly a million Americans lost their lives, showed just how precarious the hold of liberalism and democracy was in America. But the antislavery forces did emerge victorious. In American political life, the moral high ground belongs to liberal democratic reformers. Unlike their opponents, they do not have to rewrite or impose perverse interpretations on the Declaration and Constitution in order to prevail.

America's Creed: The Declaration of Independence

American political development has involved conflict among liberal ide-als, democratic values, and bigotry. It has entailed great contests of opin-ion and occasionally bloody conflicts over the meaning of rights in the United States. The American Revolution resulted in the first efforts of the American people to clarify and to justify their experiment in self-rule.

Relations between England and the colonies had been deteriorating since 1763, when the expenses incurred by the mother country in the French and Indian War encouraged the king and parliament to impose higher taxes on the colonies and tighter regulation over their trade. Particularly controver-sial were the Townshend Duties, a series of levies on glass, lead, paper, and tea imported into the colonies. These acts stirred resistance in America, giving rise to the famous slogan, "No taxation without representation."

But the leaders of the colonies were reluctant to turn that resistance into a full-scale rebellion against British rule. Even as the prominent Philadel-phia lawyer John Dickinson insisted that the English parliament had no right to tax the colonies, he encouraged his fellow Americans to "behave like dutiful children, who have received unmerited blows from beloved par-ents." "Where shall we find another Britain," he pleaded. "Torn from the body to which we are united by religion, liberty, laws, affections, relation, language, and commerce, we must bleed from every vein."

Common Sense

It was not Thomas Jefferson, the author of the Declaration of Indepen-dence, who first challenged the American people to break their ties with Great Britain. It was Thomas Paine, a newly arrived English corset-maker and civil servant turned pamphleteer. The publication of Paine's pamphlet *Common Sense* in January 1776 had a tremendous impact on public opinion in the colonies, arousing strong sentiment not only against King George, but also against the idea of monarchy itself. *Common Sense* proclaimed that the time had come for Americans to grow up. It attacked the Crown and vilified monarchy, calling King George a "Royal Brute," "the hardened sullen tempered Pharaoh of England." Urging Americans to declare their independence, Paine appealed to their pride, insisting that their cause "was in great measure the cause of mankind. . . . We have it in our power to begin the world all over again. . . . The birth-day of a new world is at hand, and a race of men perhaps as numerous as all of Europe contains, are to receive their portion of freedom from the event of a few months."

Common Sense was an appeal to America's democratic tradition. It not only conveyed a revolutionary message, but also featured a new style of writing that deliberately sought a wider reading public. It was written in simple and direct language shorn of the flowery trappings characteristic of late eighteenth century political writing. It succeeded spectacularly in its objective: about 150,000 copies were sold in the critical period between January and July 1776.

Paine called for a democratic representative government with power concentrated in a large national popular assembly. Elections would be frequent, terms short, and rotation in office required. Paine opposed the creation of any independent executive power. The Congress should choose the president from its own members, Paine recommended; moreover, a new president from a different state should be selected every year. Everything possible should be done to prevent the national government from developing a sense of independence from popular opinion. As the size of America grew, so should its assembly, assuring a strong relationship between the people and their representatives.

Paine did not defend unlimited majority rule, however. Like Winthrop, Paine saw the New World as especially blessed. But Paine viewed *natural rights*, not community, as sacred. Since the Middle Ages, political science had supported the view that individual freedom was subordinate to religious and political obligation. Paine, reflecting the liberal understanding we discussed in Chapter 1, rejected that view. He believed that the founding of America signaled humanity's emancipation from the limits of nature and the duties of community. In America, individuals served their fellow citizens by pursuing gain and increasing the general prosperity.

Paine's view of natural rights implied a sharp distinction between government and society and an unyielding defense of limited government.

> Society is produced by our wants, and government by our wickedness; the former promotes our happiness positively by uniting our affections, the latter negatively by restraining our vices. . . . Society in every state is a blessing . . . but government even in its best state is but a necessary evil.

The popularity of *Common Sense* suggests that it appealed to a deep belief that *natural rights* united the colonists as a people. This principle required the establishment of a liberal, not a pure, democracy, one that would cultivate beliefs and habits reconciling majority rule and individual rights. Such marriage between equality and natural rights could not rest on sentiment alone. Paine predicted that as Americans surmounted the first difficulties of immigration that held them together, they would indulge their passion for material security and "begin to relax in their duty and attachment to each other." Government was needed, therefore, "to supply the defect of moral virtue."

Government's influence on society had to be restrained by law. Anticipating the Constitution, Paine suggested it would have to be a higher form of law not alterable by the regular course of politics. Law must become America's king.

Paine's ideas were not entirely novel. Similar words had been spoken at the Continental Congress, which first met in Philadelphia, in September 1774. Formed at the suggestion of Massachusetts, which called for a meeting of delegates from the colonies to consider common action (only Georgia failed to send representatives), the Congress passed a declaration of grievances that amounted to a complete condemnation of Britain's actions since 1763. The delegates also endorsed Massachusetts's proposal that the American people take up arms to defend their rights against Britain's violation of them.

As the historian Pauline Maier has argued, "Paine wanted to shift the focus of public debate from evaluations of British rulers and the prospects for reconciliation to deciding how an independent America should be governed." His great contribution was to argue the case for independence in a form that reached beyond political leaders in Congress and the various states and persuaded popular opinion of its righteousness. His idea that Americans had the power, indeed the duty, to form an independent republic appealed not only to their discontent with British rule but also to their pride in being a people that had come to America, as he put it, "to begin the world over again." Box 2 discusses a contemporary political question about America's democratic obligations.

Box Two: Contemporary Politics

Exporting Democracy

A key aspect of the controversy surrounding the war in Iraq centers upon the degree to which America is obliged to help spread liberty and democracy to those places in the world that do not currently have it.

The speeches of George W. Bush have resounded with a faith in freedom and a belief that the United States must do what it can to enable others to enjoy it. In his second inaugural speech, Mr. Bush declared "complete confidence in the eventual triumph of freedom because freedom is the permanent hope of mankind, the hunger in dark places, the longing of the soul." He told an Arab-American audience, "No matter what your faith, freedom is God's gift to every person in every nation." In another speech he proclaimed, "We believe that freedom can advance and change lives in the greater Middle East." Once Saddam Hussein was overthrown, the United States devoted great effort to organizing free elections that would place the Iraqi government on a democratic footing.

Critics charge that President Bush overestimates the ease with which democracy and freedom can be implanted. In a *New York Times* editorial of December 19, 2006, Harvard sociology professor Orlando Patterson contested the idea that every person desires freedom: "Freedom is neither instinctive nor universally desired...most of the world's peoples have found so little need to express it that their indigenous languages did not even have a word for it before Western contact. It is, instead, a distinctive product of Western civilization, crafted through the centuries from its contingent social and political struggles and secular reflections, as well as its religious doctrines and conflicts." Critics like Patterson argue that because freedom is so difficult to establish, any effort to do so needs to be modest and carefully crafted. Simply removing a dictatorship and holding free elections is not enough. They point, for example, to the 2006 Palestinian elections that gave a known terrorist organization, Hamas, a majority of the seats in parliament. They insist that every time an overly optimistic and simplistic effort to establish democracy fails, it becomes that much harder for later efforts to succeed.

Supporters of Bush's view, such as the prominent Soviet dissident Natan Sharansky, claim that dictatorships in the Middle East and elsewhere survive because the Western democracies appease them and fail to come to the aid of democratic challengers. They argue that the failure to create a stable democratic regime in Iraq has less to do with a cultural or religious antipathy to democracy and more to do with the support that terrorists and death squads in Iraq receive from neighboring authoritarian governments in Syria, Saudi Arabia, and Iran and the refusal of powerful countries like France, Russia, and China to join in the British-U.S. effort to sustain the Iraqi democracy.

The Great Declaration

When the members of the Second Continental Congress met in Philadelphia, in May 1776, they recognized the powerful appeal of Paine's words. Many, in fact, sent copies to their home constituencies. The tone of the debate in the national legislature and the country changed dramatically as Paine's call to arms took effect. On June 7, 1776, Richard Henry Lee introduced a resolution in the Continental Congress on the instructions of the Virginia convention:

> RESOLVED: That these United Colonies are, and of right ought to be, free and independent States, that they are absolved from all allegiance to the British Crown, and that all political connection between them and the State of Great Britain is, and ought to be totally dissolved.

The Continental Congress did not want to take such a dramatic step until it had achieved a strong consensus, and some colonies, most notably Maryland and Pennsylvania, were still reluctant to break all ties with the mother country. The champions of independence decided to give the reluctant colonies time to accept a break with Great Britain that, gradually, was becoming inevitable. Congress appointed a committee to prepare a declaration of independence. That committee had five members: Thomas Jefferson of Virginia, John Adams of Massachusetts, Benjamin Franklin of Pennsylvania, Roger Sherman of Connecticut, and Robert R. Livingston of New York. The committee asked Jefferson, who was the most gifted writer of the group, to prepare a draft. The result, with a few amendments made by Franklin and Adams and some moderating changes in language the whole Congress insisted on, was officially adopted by the delegates on July 4, 1776, two days after the actual break with Great Britain had been approved by the legislature.

Americans do not celebrate the Continental Congress's resolution of July 2 that declared the colonies independent of Great Britain. Instead, they established a national holiday to celebrate the document that justified the colonies' action. The Declaration of Independence did include a lengthy indictment of the "injuries and usurpations" of George III. But the condemnation of the British king's actions was allied to a statement of general principles justifying the right of any people to revolt against tyranny and to form a government based on the consent of the people. The Declaration would rival the Constitution as the civil religion of America; indeed, as we noted in Chapter 1, these two documents – one laying out America's creed, the other the laws that embodied it – would eventually become inseparable. Significantly, the date that was set aside as a day of national celebration was July 4, not September 17, the day the Constitution was signed.

The Liberal Origins of the Declaration

The Declaration established Jefferson as an icon of American democracy, but its ideas were not original with Jefferson. They appeared in many other contemporary writings, including *Common Sense*. Paine and Jefferson both drew on the social contract theory expressed by John Locke, the English liberal political philosopher.

Locke's *Second Treatise on Government* argued that individuals had natural rights that all legitimate governments were obligated to protect. Indeed, there was nothing legitimate about government, or political life, per se. Political life was justified only because a properly organized government better protected the individual's rights than did the "state of nature," which "however free, is full of fears and continual dangers." Locke's views were especially influential in the colonies, which, cut off from Europe's feudal past, came close in their isolation to duplicating the conditions of the state of nature.

Americans believed that they had an equal right to pursue happiness as each individual defined it. Americans were therefore unwilling to tolerate English inheritance laws, such as *primogeniture* (establishing an exclusive right of inheritance for the oldest son), which tended to perpetuate a landed aristocracy. Nor were they likely to defer very much to political authority. Social and political equality was an article of faith in the colonies, one which made Paine's radical attack on monarchy appear to be but "common sense"; and one which made the Declaration's justification of an equal, inalienable right to pursue happiness appear "self-evident."

Box Three: Nuts and Bolts

Of Contracts and Covenants

Locke's idea of the social contract was starkly different from the Puritans' notion of covenant:

1. Like any contract, the social contract rested on promises made by each of the contracting parties. According to Locke's theory, people lived completely freely, on their own, until they chose to

make a contract with one another to form a government. They each promised to give up their natural freedom to do exactly as they wished in return for the protections that only a government could provide. By contrast, the Puritan covenant was a one-way promise, made by the congregation to God. God made no promise in return.

2. When a contractual promise is broken, the contract is null and void. Thus, in Locke's view, if the government failed to secure the rights of those who contracted for it, the contractees were free to break the contract and return to the state of nature. Since God made no promises, there was no way for him to break the covenant. Therefore, the requirements the covenant placed on the congregation were everlasting.

3. Locke's social contract was entered into by individuals. The covenant was entered into collectively. The purpose of the social contract was to protect individual rights. The purpose of the covenant was to commit to collective obligations.

The attraction such leading Framers as Jefferson felt toward the social contract idea would have been impossible if they adhered to the Puritan understanding of God and of the covenant. But they did not. They were attracted to an alternative religious understanding that was grounded in science and reason. They did not deny the existence of a supreme being, but unlike the Puritans they believed that everything important about religion and about God could be understood on the basis of historical evidence and human experience. They believed that science was a far more accurate guide to knowledge than was the Bible. Thus when Jefferson invoked the deity in the Declaration of Independence, he refers to him as "Nature's God." The Puritans would have considered it heretical to attach any modifier to God, especially "nature," since God created nature.

Having reduced the scope and importance of God, Jefferson believed that he was free to think about politics on the basis of what was best for humans. He rejected the Puritan view that humans were inherently sinful. He believed they were essentially good. This did not mean that they could flourish in the absence of government. Nature, though benevolent, was still a risky place for humans to thrive in. Jefferson agreed with Locke that people voluntarily renounced their natural state of complete freedom, what Locke had called "the state of nature," to enter into a social contract that remedied the inconveniences that living free created. The contract created a government whose sole purpose was to protect an individual's rights. It provided laws protecting each individual's personal security, freedom, and property and provided policemen to enforce those laws. If government did anything to endanger individual rights, the social contract was broken and individuals returned to the state of nature.

Social contract theory, and the new religious understanding that it depended on, did not replace Puritan congregationalism among Americans. The two outlooks coexisted in a state of dynamic tension. The rational-scientific view of religion and the contract view of society were most popular among the educated classes from which the Founders came. The older view was much more strongly held among ordinary people who trusted more in their fellow religious congregants than in reason and science and who were more prone to view humans as sinful. But many individuals were torn between the two outlooks, reflecting the tension between the concern for righteousness and community solidarity, on the one hand, and individual liberty, comfort, and security, on the other, that continues to pervade American life.

The Constitutional Stature of the Declaration

Jefferson's contribution was to state compellingly what most Americans already believed. Paine urged the colonies to have the courage of their republican convictions; Jefferson dignified what Paine had aroused. As Jefferson wrote many years later, the essential thing was

> not to find new principles, or new arguments, never before thought of, not merely to say things which had never been said before; but to place before mankind the common sense of the subject, in terms so plain and firm as to command their assent. . . . Neither aiming at originality of principles or sentiments, nor yet copied from any particular and previous writing, it was intended to be an expression of the American mind.

Jefferson did far more than merely take account of the American mind, however. With the help of the drafting committee and the Continental Congress, he transformed political orthodoxy into an exalted cause – one that condemned monarchy and justified popular sovereignty. As edited and approved by the Continental Congress, the Declaration was not just a statement of commonly accepted truths, but a *constitutional document*. No less than the Constitution itself, adopted some ten years later, it was a state document that concerned the fundamental authority of government. Significantly, all the members of the legislature signed the Declaration, even though it officially required only the signature of the Congress's president, John Hancock. Hancock's signature was the largest to appear at the end of the Declaration – to save King George III the trouble, he noted cheekily, of putting on his reading glasses. The other members of Congress, embracing their president's rebellious spirit, added their names. After all, the Declaration was no mere official document, but "an avowal of revolution."

In making their signatures part of such a dangerous state paper, the members of the Continental Congress took a solemn oath as citizens of a new government. They gave the first official display of the American political community. As the dramatic last sentence of the document read, "for the support of this declaration, with a firm reliance on the protection of divine providence, we mutually pledge to each other our lives, our fortunes, and our sacred honor."

The gravity of this pledge was demonstrated by the manner in which the Declaration was publicized. It was read before groups of people in public ceremonies. The mobilization of British soldiers on American soil for the purpose of suppressing the incipient rebellion added solemnity to these occasions. With this menace in mind, Congress directed that the Declaration should be proclaimed not only in all the colonies but also by the head of the army.

On July 9, General George Washington ordered officers of the Continental Army brigades stationed in New York City to obtain copies of the Declaration from the Adjutant General's Office. Then, with the British soldiers "constantly in view, upon and at Staten-Island," as one participant recalled, the brigades were "formed in hollow squares on their respective parades," where they heard the Declaration read. The event, Washington hoped, would "serve as a free incentive to every officer, and soldier, to act with Fidelity and Courage, . . . knowing that now the peace and safety of his Country depends (under God) solely on the success of his arms."

The Revolution and Social Reform

The Continental Army itself revealed the significance of the break with Great Britain – and feudal Europe. Although drawn mostly from the poorest ranks of society and often facing the most desperate military and economic conditions, the Continental soldiers displayed a revolutionary independent spirit. When the Continental Congress ignored their needs, they threatened mutinies until their grievances were addressed. Baron Von Steuben, a Prussian who assisted Washington in trying to instill discipline, observed that American soldiers behaved differently from European soldiers, following orders only if their officers explained the logic of commands to them. The Revolutionary forces "turned the world upside down," or so English aristocrats feared, by sensing their power and asserting a real measure of personal independence.

The states eliminated the remnants of feudalism, abolishing primogeniture and *entail* (the right of an owner of property to prevent heirs from ever disposing of it). It became customary in the colonies to reject any practice that smacked of aristocracy. When a group of army officers, including the esteemed George Washington, founded the Society of Cincinnati, it was widely denounced: many citizens found alarming the mere existence of an organization of army officers, especially one with a hereditary membership, passed on from a member to his eldest son.

The former colonies also attacked religious privilege, depriving established churches, such as the Anglican Church in Virginia, of the special status they enjoyed under the original English charters. Jefferson also took great pride in having written the 1786 Virginia Statute of Religious Liberty establishing a "wall of separation" between church and state, inspiring similar legislation throughout the colonies. It declared, "Our civil rights have no dependence on our religious opinions, any more than our opinions in physics or geometry. Truth is great and will prevail if left to herself." Therefore, "no man shall be compelled to frequent or support any religious worship, place, or ministry... nor shall otherwise suffer on account of his religious opinions or belief."

The notion that religious beliefs were mere "opinion" would have astounded both worshipers and atheists in Great Britain and Europe. Such a view, as we have noted, also diverged critically from John Winthrop's vision of a Puritan Commonwealth. Despite Jefferson, religious life would continue to have a special place in American society. But Jefferson's determination to create an impenetrable barrier between church and state resonated with most Americans because they believed that individuals had a right to worship in a place of their own choosing. Hence, no one church should be singled out for government support. Americans opposed giving the clergy a special title to their authority because it imported an important element of aristocratic life to American soil.

The disdain for social and economic privilege the American Revolution spawned did not lead to a radical egalitarian assault on social and economic inequalities as the French Revolution did. State governments almost always seized the property of *Tories*, those who did not support the Revolution, but not in order to redistribute wealth or give land to the poor. Although some Tory estates were broken up and sold to small farmers, most passed to wealthy individuals or groups of speculators. The free pursuit of life, liberty, and happiness did not require that all individuals share equally in the goods of society. As Lincoln would later stress, it only required that they engage in a reasonably fair "race of life." Chapter 6 discusses how the free enterprise system – capitalism, as Marx would later call it – allowed, indeed required, inequalities of wealth.

The Declaration and Slavery

Ironically, the principal author of the declaration proclaiming the equality of all men owned slaves. This contradiction was not lost on Jefferson. Contemplating the hypocrisy of Americans asserting the "unalienable" rights to "life, liberty, and happiness" while maintaining a system of forced servitude, he wrote, "I tremble for my country when I reflect that God is just." In truth, Jefferson's views on slavery were highly conflicted. Although he claimed that slavery was wrong, he advanced the "suspicion" that "blacks, whether originally a distinct race, or made distinct by time and circumstances, are inferior to the whites in the endowments both of body and mind." This tortured ambivalence about African Americans and their forced bondage also affected many of Jefferson's fellow citizens; and it would endure, leaving to reformers of other centuries the task of reconciling the American creed with the reality of political life in the United States.

Even the deliberations over the Declaration gave some hint of how difficult that struggle was likely to be. Although the Declaration made no explicit mention of slavery, Jefferson did attempt to address the slave trade in the original draft. In a long paragraph, which John Adams admiringly called "the vehement philippic against Negro slavery," Jefferson charged King George III with waging "cruel war against human nature itself, violating its most sacred rights of life and liberty in the persons of distant people who never offended him, captivating and carrying them into slavery in another hemisphere, or to incur miserable death in their transportation thither."

Jefferson accused the British of compounding their crime by sowing seeds of rebellion among slaves. His uncharacteristically venomous prose was aimed at the "Christian king of Great Britain," who, through his subordinates in America,

> was now exciting these very people to rise in arms among us, and to purchase that liberty of which he deprived them, by murdering the people upon whom he also obtruded them; thus paying off former crimes committed against the liberties of one people, with crimes which he urges them to commit against the lives of another.

Slavery was a uniquely American problem, and the Founders' failure to deal with it properly would haunt the discourse of rights and freedom for the next century.

Congress eliminated all discussion of the slave trade in the final draft, acquiescing to South Carolina and Georgia, who sought to perpetuate the slave trade, and to many in the North who profited from the transportation of slaves.

Jefferson's diatribe against the king's role in the slave trade was misguided. Slavery was an American problem, not one of the king's making. More fundamentally, Jefferson's failed effort to address the slave trade in the Declaration of Independence revealed a clash of cultures in America, in which the country's liberal aspirations and its commitment to natural rights competed with traditions of prejudice and bigotry that tarnished its civic religion.

The deep roots of this conflict, dating back to the very first colonial settlement at Jamestown, made clear to Jefferson just how difficult it would be to live up to the promises of the Declaration. "Justice cannot sleep forever," he prophesized. But it was "impossible to be temperate" on such a subject, to pursue it "through the various considerations of policy, of morals, of history natural and civil." Those who saw the Declaration as a condemnation of slavery "must be contented to hope" that its principles would gradually force their "way into every one's mind."

The words of the Declaration would indeed become an important weapon against slavery. In the first decades after the Declaration, one Northern state after another abolished slavery. Appropriately, New York's act to emancipate slaves gradually was approved on July 4, 1799, and New Jersey's on the same day five years later. The Southern states resisted emancipation (see Figure 2.2). Even gradual abolition would have violated the "property rights" of thousands of influential men, including Jefferson, and left the South with the unwanted task of devising a new labor system. Moreover, the South was afraid that a large population of free blacks would exact retribution, perhaps violently. Jefferson would write in 1820:

> I can say with conscious truth that there is not a man on earth who would sacrifice more than I would to relieve us from this heavy reproach in a practical way. . . . But as it is, we have the wolf by the ears, and we can neither hold him, nor safely let him go. Justice is in one scale, and self-preservation on the other.

Jefferson's fears were tragically realized by the violent slave uprising led by Nat Turner, which originally was planned to begin on July 4, 1831. The revolt actually began on August 22, when a band of eight slaves led by Turner killed five members of the Travis family in Southampton, Virginia. During the next three days, the ranks of the rebels swelled to between sixty and seventy and they killed an additional fifty-eight whites in Jerusalem, Virginia. Militias caught most of the rebels within a few days, and Turner was captured on October 31. He was executed on November 11, 1831.

Still, the Declaration ensured that *abolitionists*, not defenders of slavery, would be able to claim the moral high ground. John C. Calhoun of South Carolina, one of slavery's most effective champions, admitted as much in the late 1840s. He lamented that the Declaration had "spread far and wide, and fixed itself deeply in the public mind." The Declaration became a revered document, not just because its message was "popular," as Calhoun thought, but also because it confirmed the American creed. Frederick Douglass, a former slave who had escaped bondage to become an eloquent defender of emancipation, made clear to America in his famous July 4,

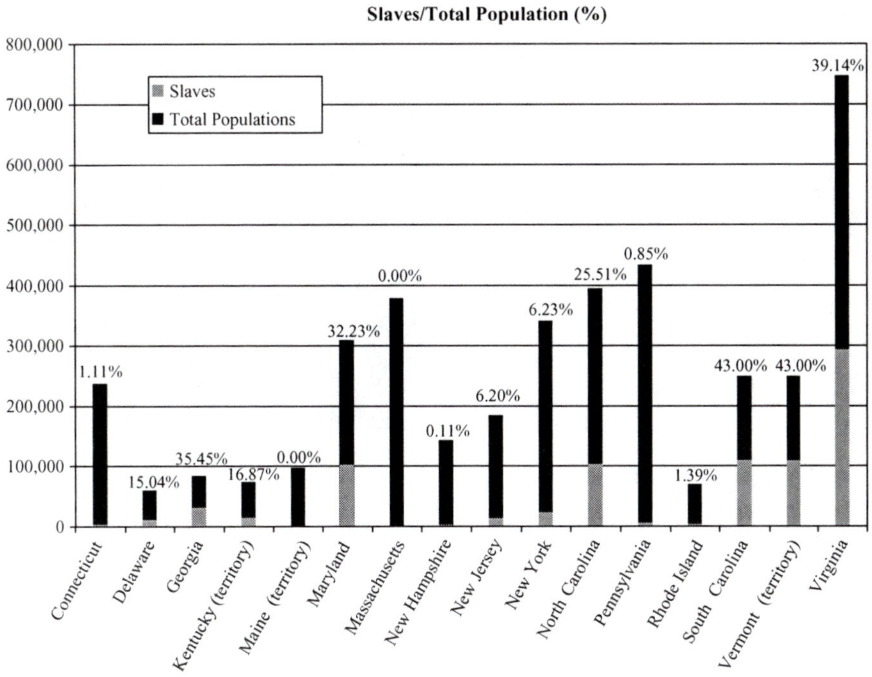

Slaves/Total Population (%)

Figure 2.2. Slaves as Percentage of State Population, 1790.
Source: Data from U.S. Census Bureau, 2000.

1852, oration that the United States could not enslave African Americans and still be true to its deepest beliefs:

> What to the American slave, is your 4th of July? I answer; a day that reveals to him, more than all the other days in the year, the gross injustice and cruelty to which he is the constant victim. To him your celebration is a sham; your boasted liberty an unholy license; your national greatness, swelling vanity; your sounds of rejoicing are empty and heartless; your denunciations of tyrants, brass fronted impudence; your sermons and thanksgivings, with your religious parade, and solemnity, are, to him, mere bombast, fraud, deception, impiety, and hypocrisy – a thin veil to cover up crimes which would disgrace a nation of savages.

Like Abraham Lincoln and Martin Luther King, Douglass made clear that slavery robbed the Revolution of its true meaning. The fight for independence was not about separating from Great Britain alone; it was a critical step in fulfilling a special mission – a duty, as Winthrop had preached – that inspired political life in the United States. Some Americans might resist such an argument; but they could not ignore it.

The organizers of the Seneca Falls Convention in 1848 were veterans of the antislavery movement and used the words of the Declaration of Independence to indict political and social practices that excluded women from full citizenship rights.

The Declaration and the Rights of Women

The Declaration and the Revolution also led many people in the United States to challenge the subjugation of women. For example, it became somewhat easier for women to obtain divorces in the aftermath of the struggle for independence. During the colonial period, divorces were rare, but easier for men to obtain than for women. The difference did not vanish after the Revolution, but it did diminish. Before independence, no Massachusetts woman was known to have obtained a divorce on the grounds of adultery; thereafter, wives were more likely to sue errant husbands successfully.

As with racial inequality, changes in sexual relations were limited. When Abigail Adams urged her revolutionary husband John and his fellow rebels to "remember the ladies," or the women would "foment a revolution of their own," he did not take his wife's plea seriously. Politics, he insisted, was "not the Province of the ladies." In truth, Abigail Adams was not advocating political rights; she was advocating fairer treatment for women in the household. "Do not put such unlimited power into the hands of husbands," she wrote. "Remember all men would be tyrants if they could."

The Revolution brought important change in educational opportunity for women. The New Englander Judith Sargent Murray urged the cultivation of women's minds to encourage self-respect and "excellency in our sex." Her fellow reformer, Benjamin Rush, gave political expression to this view: only educated and independent-minded women, Rush argued, could raise the informed and self-reliant citizens that a republican government demanded.

This emphasis on "republican motherhood" and its potential to bestow dignity on the democratic individual had a dramatic influence on female literacy. Between 1780 and 1830, the number of colleges and secondary schools, including those for women, rose dramatically. Women's schools and colleges offered a solid academic curriculum. By 1850, there were as many literate women as men. Nonetheless, American women remained excluded from participation in political life. Most Americans considered the female's rightful place to be in the home. But like opponents of slavery, advocates of women's rights found the Declaration a powerful text to enlist on behalf of their cause.

The organizers of the first convention for women's rights, in 1848 at Seneca Falls, New York, were veterans of the antislavery movement. In preparing the convention's statement of principles and demands, Elizabeth Cady Stanton invoked the Declaration. "We hold these truths to be self-evident," the proclamation declared, "that all men and women are created equal." The Seneca Falls proclamation went on to submit "facts" to a "candid world" to prove "the history of mankind is a history of repeated injuries and usurpations on the part of man toward woman, having in direct object the establishment of an absolute tyranny over her."

Even some of the convention's leaders, such as Lucretia Mott, felt that the right to vote was too advanced for the times and would lead to ridicule of the nascent women's movement. But, Frederick Douglass, one of thirty men brave enough to attend the Seneca Falls gathering, argued convincingly that political equality was essential if women were to enjoy true freedom. The convention adopted the suffrage resolution by a small majority. The Seneca Falls Statement of Principles, as Stanton observed, "would serve three generations of women" in their fight for natural rights promised by the Declaration (see Figure 2.3).

Political Scripture

Although hardly an apostle of equal rights for African Americans or women, Jefferson hoped that the words he inserted in the Declaration would pose hard challenges to other illiberal political practices and institutions, such as the effort of one generation to politically bind the next. Each should have the right "to change their laws and institutions to suit themselves." Only Jefferson's generation, the revered Founding Fathers, constrained future Americans, for as the principal author of the Declaration claimed, only "the inherent and unalienable rights of man" were "unchangeable."

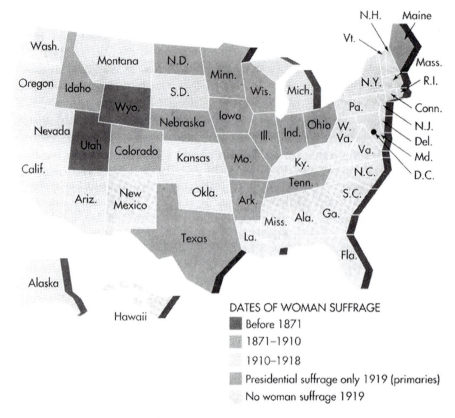

DATES OF WOMAN SUFFRAGE
- ▓ Before 1871
- ▓ 1871–1910
- 1910–1918
- ▓ Presidential suffrage only 1919 (primaries)
- No woman suffrage 1919

Figure 2.3. Women's Suffrage. The disparity in women's suffrage from state to state was constitutionally amended in 1919 to grant all eligible American women a right to vote.

Toward the end of his life, Jefferson himself embraced the Declaration of Independence as political scripture. He came to believe that only through the periodic clash between the ideals it propounded and the practices that fell short of them could the United States avoid the insidious spread of a shallow and selfish materialism. In the last letter he wrote before he died, Jefferson waxed hopefully about the global significance of the Declaration: "May it be to the world...the signal of arousing men to burst the chains under which monkish ignorance and superstition had persuaded them to bind themselves, and to assume the blessings and security of self government." In the end, Jefferson believed, the Declaration would confirm the "palpable truth, that the mass of mankind has not been born with saddles on their backs, nor a favored few booted and spurred, ready to ride them legitimately by the grace of God."

Jefferson died on July 4, 1826, the fiftieth anniversary of the Declaration of Independence, just a few minutes before his great collaborator in drafting America's scripture, John Adams. This remarkable coincidence only deepened the country's reverence for the Declaration and its author, a slaveholder, yet enshrined as the "greatest democrat ever to spring from American democracy."

Toward the Constitution

The Declaration did not specify the institutional forms that would best protect the rights it proclaimed. The ex-colonies still had to decide how to govern themselves. To be sure, the Declaration pronounced the equality of all men, claimed that this self-evident truth required that government rest on the consent of the governed, and claimed that government was obligated to protect the inalienable right of individuals to life, liberty, and the pursuit of happiness. But the leaders of the revolution disagreed about whether a government based on consent of the people had to operate by means of their consent, that is, by democratic institutions. John Locke had argued that the people could consent to place the hands of government in a monarchy (rule of one), aristocracy (rule of few), or democracy (rule of the many). He believed that a mixed government – one in which powers were shared among different institutions representing different interests – best protected individual liberty.

As we have noted, Thomas Paine and John Adams shared a passion for independence, but disagreed about the form of government that would fulfill the Declaration's promise to protect natural rights. Paine prescribed a complete departure from the British system, with its clashes among the king, the House of Lords, and the House of Commons. America should be governed by a popular assembly and organized to express the sentiments of the people. In contrast, Adams encouraged the national and state governments to adapt the British system of separated powers. Perhaps the united colonies should not have a king, but they needed a strong executive who would share power with separate legislative and judicial institutions. "Without three orders and an effectual balance between them," he wrote in 1786, America "must be destined to frequent unavoidable revolutions."

State Constitutions

For a time, Paine's idea of "simple" popular government prevailed. From the perspective of 1776, the most important task in forming new state and national governments was to constrain executive power. In the wake of the Declaration, and its charges against King George III, most of the states wrote constitutions that sought to ensure that executive power would not threaten popular liberty. In some states, the executive office, an outpost of royal administration during the colonial period, was eliminated entirely. Where an executive was provided for, governors were often given little power. They had no authority to convene or dissolve the legislature; nor could they exercise a veto over laws passed by the assemblies. They were not allowed to appoint state officials or to manage executive branch activities.

Following Paine's advice, the states vested vast authority in popular assemblies. The great Boston patriot Samuel Adams declared, "[E]very legislature of every colony ought to be the sovereign and uncontrollable Power within its own limits of territory." To ensure that legislatures were truly popular, state constitutions put them on a very short leash. They called for annual elections and required candidates to live in the districts they represented. Many states went so far as to assert the right of voters to instruct the men in office how to vote on specific issues and to elect judges. No state granted universal manhood suffrage, but most substantially reduced the size of the property requirements for voting that had previously been in place.

As Adams warned, the decisive rejection of the British system of mixed government enabled legislatures to become as oppressive as the royal governors had been. But in the wake of independence, there was little support for institutional checks and balances. The revolutionary struggle, aroused by pamphlets like *Common Sense*, made political leaders more conscious of the power of the people. Political leaders competed with each other in demonstrating their sympathy for the people – and in so doing, greatly expanded their public audience.

The emergence of democratic sentiments actually preceded the Revolution. In 1766, for example, the Massachusetts House of Representatives erected a public gallery for the witnessing of its debates – "a momentous step," according to the historian Gordon Wood, "in the democratization of the American mind." The Pennsylvania Assembly followed reluctantly in 1770, and eventually other legislatures followed suit, usually provoked by revolutionary leaders, who were anxious to build popular opposition to Great Britain. Although attention to public opinion began prior to the Revolution, the fight for independence intensified the celebration of "the People." Consequently, the line between "gentlemen" and the rest of the society, never as clear in the colonies as it was in the mother country and Europe, was radically blurred by the revolution and its aftermath.

Amid this democratic clamor, constitutional barriers were not likely to offer much restraint. For example, the Virginia Constitution called for three separate branches of government. But its first governor, Thomas Jefferson, admitted that only the legislature had real power. Both *Common*

Sense and the Declaration, celebrating Americans' dedication to a new idea of individualism, had papered over the possible tension between popular rule and inalienable rights. Watching the dominance of legislative power over executive authority in Virginia, Jefferson came to doubt the compatibility of majority rule and the self-evident truths of the Declaration. It was no comfort to know that the powers of a popular assembly "will be exercised by a plurality of hands, and not by a single one. One hundred and seventy three despots would surely be as oppressive as one." Anticipating the effort to form "a more perfect Union" in Philadelphia six years later, Jefferson scolded,

> An elected despotism was not the government we fought for; but one which should not only be founded on free principles, but in which the powers of government should be so divided and balanced among several bodies of magistry as that no one could transcend their legal limits without being effectively checked and restrained by the others.

Religion's Impact

The democratic tradition was not created by the Revolution – it was deeply rooted in the religious experiences and local self-government of the colonies. Because the American colonies had been a haven for religious dissenters, no one church dominated life in the colonies. The Continental Congress did not attempt to establish a single official American church. The separation of church and state strengthened religious influence on American society. Freedom of religion cultivated the belief that churches did not threaten individual liberty, as was the case in feudal Europe, but protected it. This relationship gave the clergy significant influence over rights-conscious Americans. Shorn of state sponsorship, churches became strong, independent institutions that contributed significantly to the emergence of a distinctive American culture. The Anglican Church in America, painfully weaned from government support, became the Episcopal Church. After the Revolution, Roman Catholics previously under the administration of the vicar apostolic of England came under the authority of Father John Carroll of Baltimore, named in 1789 the first American Roman Catholic bishop. Winthrop's Congregational Church, no longer the established Church of Massachusetts, thrived as a private, more decentralized institution.

Religious life helped to cultivate a sense of civic responsibility, even as it ingratiated itself into secular society. Tocqueville observed, "While the law allows the American people to do everything, there are things which religion prevents them from imagining and forbids them to dare." Winthrop's vision of a "city upon a hill" endured, moderating rights talk in the colonies with a sense of political community. American religion did not become a tool of elites for imposing order on unruly majorities. The commitment to religious expression went hand in hand with post-revolutionary reforms eliminating the vestiges of privilege. Freedom of religion came to be viewed as an entitlement similar to the natural right to self-government.

Box Four: Contemporary Politics

Religion, Liberty, and Democracy

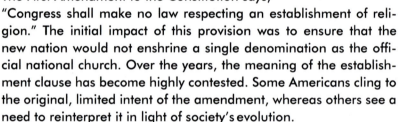

The First Amendment to the Constitution says, "Congress shall make no law respecting an establishment of religion." The initial impact of this provision was to ensure that the new nation would not enshrine a single denomination as the official national church. Over the years, the meaning of the establishment clause has become highly contested. Some Americans cling to the original, limited intent of the amendment, whereas others see a need to reinterpret it in light of society's evolution.

When the Constitution was written, virtually all Americans were Christians and the vast majority were Protestants. The establishment clause was aimed at preventing government from recognizing one Protestant denomination in preference to the others. But now America is home to large numbers of non-Christians: Buddhists, Hindus, Jews, Muslims, and others. Some Americans now object to the display of non-denominational but overtly Christian religious symbols, such as those relating to Christmas and Easter, in schools and other public buildings because such displays imply an official preference for Christianity. In the contemporary world, many people view themselves as secular, and they consider any government sanction of religion to impinge on their right to have no religion. But taken to an extreme, relentless exclusion of religion from the public sphere also threatens to violate the establishment clause by indicating a government preference for atheism. Also, many people hold beliefs that seem religious in nature but are not associated with the established world religions. Should the schools ban "save the whales" posters because some of those people who seek to protect these aquatic mammals do so because they believe that all species have a sacred right to exist?

Political conflict over the relationship of religion to liberty and democracy takes place on a variety of other fronts as well. In the city of Cleveland, for example, many poor parents are able to use state funds to pay for their children to attend religious schools. Proponents argue that this program gives the poor the same freedom as the rich to enjoy an alternative to public schools that they deem inadequate. Opponents argue both that it is illiberal to provide government subsidy to a religious endeavor and that it is undemocratic for taxpayers to support educational institutions over which they have no control.

President George W. Bush declared that a faith-based initiative was to be a central element of his "compassionate conservative" domestic policy agenda. This initiative was intended to lend greater government support for religiously oriented private social service programs. Many such programs claim that they have greater success in rehabilitating drug addicts, preventing teenage pregnancy, and lowering criminal recidivism rates than do their purely secular counterparts. Although private religious organizations can already receive government assistance under many circumstances, the purpose of the initiative was to create a level playing field and clear away many of the hurdles that religious organizations had to overcome to prove that they were not spending public money for religious purposes. Critics of the initiative claimed that it threatened First Amendment freedoms. For example, in its original form it would have permitted a faith-based program to discriminate by refusing to hire job applicants who were not of that particular faith. In June 2007, a closely divided Supreme Court ruled in *Hein v. Freedom from Religion* that taxpayers did not have "standing" to challenge the discretionary spending of the Bush White House's Office of Faith-Based and Community Initiatives. The 5–4 majority thus refused to hear the charge of an atheist and agnostic group from Wisconsin that claimed the Bush administration had given churches and religious groups an unfair advantage in access to federal grant programs.

The Articles of Confederation

As Tocqueville recognized, local self-government reinforced political community and democratic participation. Decentralization of power in the United States encouraged individuals to think of government as their own, as protecting their rights and encouraging their participation in politics.

And yet, the celebration of localism made the creation of the new nation a delicate business. Paine had urged the various states to develop a greater sense of *nationalism*, to tighten "the Continental belt." Indeed, the motto of the new nation was *e pluribus unum* – "from many one." Patrick Henry gave early expression to this ideal in 1774: "The distinction between Virginians, Pennsylvanians, New Yorkers, and New Englanders are no more. I am not a Virginian, but an American." But like all political rhetoric, Henry's oratory stretched the truth; in fact, even after the Revolution succeeded, he believed that Virginia should govern itself. Like other members of the revolutionary generation, he identified deeply with his home state and even more deeply with his home county and township.

Allegiance to states and localities, not the Union, dominated the first efforts to form a national government in the United States. In fact, the Declaration of Independence referred explicitly not to the United States but to these "free and independent states." It envisioned not one large republic, which revolutionary leaders feared would render popular rule impractical, but a loose federation of thirteen. The first national government after the Revolution, formed after the Articles of Confederation ratified in 1781, embodied this desire to retain the full independence of the states.

The Articles provided for a national legislature modeled on the Continental Congress. It remained the creature of the state legislatures, which chose its members, had the power to remove them at any time, and paid their salaries and expenses. It had the authority to declare war, conduct diplomacy, coin money, regulate Indian affairs, appoint military officers, and requisition men from the states. But it had little power to fulfill these responsibilities. It could neither levy taxes nor regulate trade. The states retained the power of the purse, as well as the ultimate authority to make and administer laws.

The national government had no distinct executive branch. The president was a figurehead, a delegate chosen to preside over congressional sessions. Executive power, such as it was, rested with congressional committees, constantly changing in their membership. With no means for carrying out policies of finance, war, and foreign policy, the national government's power was extremely limited.

The lack of centralized authority stemmed from the democratizing influence of the Revolution. Just as the state constitutions were written to keep representatives closely tied to popular opinion, so the Articles of Confederation took pains to broaden citizen involvement in national affairs. It provided that members of Congress be annually elected and forbidden to serve in the national legislature more than three years in any six-year span.

The Continental Congress had also relied on the states, but its dependence occurred during wartime, which made the states relatively willing to provide men and money for the common defense. But a loose alliance of states proved far less practical during peacetime. From 1781 to 1786, for example, Congress requested 15 million dollars to carry out its foreign and domestic responsibilities but received only 2.5 million.

The absence of national power also weakened national security. No sooner had the 1783 treaty ending the Revolutionary War been signed than British ministers, seeking to exploit the new weak alliance of colonies, surreptitiously instructed the Canadian colony to maintain its forts and trading posts, so they could serve as bases for raids and espionage against the United States. Trouble also developed in the Southwest where the Spanish closed the Mississippi River to American navigation in 1784. The Confederation's weak response prompted settlers along the western frontier to consider seceding from the Union and joining Spain's empire.

Chaos ensued from the Confederation's inability to control commerce among the states and with foreign nations, which aggravated the economic hardship that the war had wreaked. The states imposed competitive duties and tariffs aggravating interstate rivalries and fought with each other over foreign trade. These squabbles enabled Britain to engage in a policy of divide and conquer. British merchants got around the regulations of states that sought to restrict their goods by bringing their products in through states that did not.

Britain expanded exports to America while holding imports to a minimum. The Confederation lacked the authority to retaliate.

Debtors and Creditors

Economic depression and the unfavorable balance of trade led to increased pressure on states to make life easier for debtors, especially for small farmers who were well represented in the democratic state legislatures. They demanded that more paper money be printed to expand the money supply, making it cheaper for them to repay their debts. More than half the states yielded to this pressure between 1785 and 1786. Rhode Island printed so much money that creditors fled the state to avoid being paid in worthless currency. Although this case was extreme, many states experienced the ironic spectacle of debtors hunting down creditors, who hid for fear of being paid!

State legislatures that maintained a sound currency fared no better. Massachusetts's decision to maintain a tight money supply led to an armed rebellion. In the summer of 1786, mobs in its western communities tried to halt farm foreclosures by taking up arms and forcibly closing the debtor courts. The rebellion's leader was Daniel Shays, a war hero who had fought at Bunker Hill. The Massachusetts governor appealed to Congress, but the national government had no legal authority to put down rebellions in the states. When the state government finally mobilized its own troops, with funds raised by frightened private merchants, and sent them to squash the uprising, the rebels attacked the Springfield arsenal. Shays was defeated and fled to Vermont, but the Massachusetts legislature did respond to the rebels' plight by providing some debt relief.

Shays's Rebellion greatly strengthened the hand of leaders, such as George Washington, Alexander Hamilton, and James Madison, who believed stronger national government was needed to solve the international and domestic troubles experienced under the Articles of Confederation. Still, there were many Americans, including prominent patriots such as Patrick Henry and Samuel Adams, who resisted efforts to convene a constitutional convention for the purpose of tightening "the buckle of the continent." Indeed, to do so might jeopardize the democratic spirit aroused by revolution and agitated by economic crisis.

Jefferson, as a champion of American democracy, considered active engagement in politics critical to the protection of rights. From Paris where he was serving as ambassador, he wrote Madison urging him not to overreact to the Massachusetts uprising. Democracy has "its evils," he acknowledged, and the acts of Shays's band were "absolutely unjustifiable." But such popular rebellions, although "evil," were "productive of the good." They prevented "the degeneracy of government" and nourished "a general attention to the public affairs. . . . I hold it that a little rebellion now and then is a good thing, and as necessary in the political world as storms in the physical."

Washington and Madison disagreed with Jefferson. "What, gracious God, is man! that there should be such inconsistency and perfidiousness in his conduct," the usually stoic Washington declared after hearing of the Massachusetts riots. "We are fast verging to anarchy and confusion." Still, the supportive response of the Massachusetts legislature to the rebellion showed that Jefferson's sentiments were not merely the musings of a patriot abroad. After all, Shays's rebels were not radicals, calling for a redistribution of property, they were former soldiers and respected citizens trying to protect their property.

From Democracy to Republican Government

The disagreement between Jefferson and Washington about Shays's Rebellion highlights the uneasy relationship between democracy and liberalism.

It challenges the notion that equality and rights, both celebrated in the Declaration, were truly compatible. During the process of creating and ratifying the Constitution that followed this dispute, the American people displayed a remarkable ability to rise to that challenge.

Shays's Rebellion impelled all the states, except Rhode Island, to send representatives to a convention in Philadelphia in the summer of 1787 to redress the weaknesses of the Articles of Confederation. The delegates were not quite "an assembly of demi-gods," as Jefferson gushed. Their genius was practical. Their experience in state and national politics had confirmed their nationalism, strengthening their belief in the need for a stronger central government.

Many great patriots, like Patrick Henry and Samuel Adams, refused to attend. They viewed the convention as an effort to weaken local self-government. Even among the nationally minded representatives who did attend the Constitutional Convention, there were strong disagreements about just how much centralization of power the country could endure and still operate democratically.

Nationalizing Factors

The creation of the Constitution and the ratification contest that followed in the states will be discussed in detail in the next chapter. Here we consider the nationalizing factors that gave rise to it. A crucial intellectual influence was John Adams's three-volume work, *A Defense of the Constitutions of Government of the United States*. Adams's decision to write it was provoked by Shays's Rebellion: "The commotion in New England alarmed me so much that I have thrown together some hasty speculations upon the government."

Fearful that the country might adopt the simplistic centralizing schemes of Paine, Adams defended a republican form of separated and divided powers: He proposed a two-chamber legislature – one popularly elected, the other based more on aristocratic principles – and a strong, impartial executive who could veto acts of the legislature. The whole system was to be overseen by an independent judiciary. Such a constitution would moderate the sort of raw and disruptive conflict between rich and poor that the Massachusetts uprising portended.

Volume I appeared just as the Constitutional Convention was assembling. "Mr. Adams book has excited a great deal of attention," Madison informed Jefferson in June 1787. "It will probably be much read, particularly in the Eastern States, and contribute with other circumstances to revive the predilections in the Country for the British Constitution . . . and become a powerful engine in forming public opinion."

Those who saw the need for a stronger national government appealed, as Paine once had, to national pride. Noah Webster was particularly effective in making the connection between a growing sense of nationalism and the imperative of strengthening the central government. Webster would become famous later for his American dictionary; but during the 1780s, his *Spelling Book* made him a household name. The *Spelling Book* emphasized American, as distinct from British, language. Its preface urged Americans to appreciate and further develop their own literature. Webster's *Reader*, published soon thereafter, included selections from the speeches of revolutionary leaders whom Webster praised as orators the equal of Demosthenes and Cicero. Both of Webster's books sold several million copies and remained bestsellers through the nineteenth century.

Webster considered a strong sense of nationality vital to the preservation of the Union. Americanism was not just a matter of political principles and governing institutions. A true spirit of nationality could develop only from distinctiveness in the daily life of the people. It was intimately associated with everyday matters of dress, speech, manners, and education. Cultural independence was the "mortar for the stones of union.... An American ought not to ask what is the custom of London and Paris, but what is proper for us in our circumstances and what is becoming our dignity."

In an influential 1785 tract, Webster joined his appeal to America's sense of national identity to a defense of stronger union. The Articles of Confederation was too "feeble to discharge its debts" and was, therefore, unworthy of a rising nation. It encouraged Americans to think small, clinging to "provincial views and attachments" that arrested the country's development. Some form of allegiance to states and localities was necessary. Provincial liberties were an important part of Americans' sense of themselves as citizens. But the country would only reach its fulfillment if people in the various states recognized and embraced their shared sense of mission: "The citizens of this new world should enquire not what will aggrandize this town or this state, but what will augment the power, secure the tranquility, multiply the subjects, and advance the opulence, the dignity, and the virtues of the United States." Only in this way would American individualism transcend narrow, destructive selfishness.

The Ordinance of 1787

Webster's celebrity indicates that the people's sense of national identity grew during the 1780s, preparing the country to accept a stronger national government. The Ordinance of 1787, enacted while the Confederation was still in existence, reveals this impulse toward a stronger national constitution. This legislation established rules for the Northwest Territory, which included the present day states of Ohio, Indiana, Illinois, Michigan, and Wisconsin. These states were carved from territory that once belonged to the original colonies, who ceded them to the national government. The western lands, which just a few years before had encouraged conflicts among the states, became a force for unity once they were given to the national government.

Jefferson sought to limit this nationalist force. In 1774, before he departed for France, he drafted the first version of the ordinance. This early version displayed the same decentralizing tendencies that gave rise to the Articles. It divided the Northwest Territory into ten states, each to be admitted into the Union on equal terms as soon as its population reached the same level as that of any existing state. In the meantime, Jefferson's draft ordinance provided for democratic self-government of each territory by all free adult males. Notably, Jefferson included a provision that prohibited slavery in the Northwest Territory, upholding his view, and that of many members of the founding generation, that slavery was a necessary evil, and should be confined to the South.

As finally enacted, the Ordinance was more nationalistic. It provided for an interim period in which Congress held sway in the territory through its appointees – a governor, secretary, and three judges. When the population reached 5000 free adult males, a legislature was to be established, yet its laws required the governor's approval. When the population reached 60,000, the inhabitants might apply for statehood, but the whole Northwest Territory was to be divided into no less than three or more than five states. The Ordinance of 1787, then, fell short of Jefferson's democratic principles. But it guaranteed basic rights – freedom of religion and trial by jury – and provided for support of public education. No less important, Congress maintained Jefferson's prohibition on slavery throughout the territory, enabling westward expansion to occur in conformity with the inalienable rights of the Declaration.

As we point out in Chapter 4, Abraham Lincoln used the Ordinance of 1787 to show that the Founders condemned slavery and sought its ultimate extinction. The ordinance also marked a shift from an emphasis on democratic experimentation to a stronger sense of the Union. Western expansion would take place according to a national idea of rights, giving the growing country a sense of principled unity.

American Heroes

America's first national heroes embellished this continental feeling. The Philadelphia printer and inventor, Benjamin Franklin, became the toast of the nation – and the Western world. Already celebrated for his tribute to common sense, *Poor Richard's Almanac*, and the invention of the Franklin stove, Franklin became still more famous as a statesman bravely championing the cause of independence. He celebrated America as a "party of virtue." Its unique immunity from the orthodoxies that bred intolerance in Europe and Great Britain made it possible to combine a strong sense of country and a respect for individual rights. He helped draft the Declaration of Independence and negotiated France's support of the American Revolution. As the historian John Garraty has observed, Franklin "demonstrated, to Europeans and to Americans themselves, that not all Americans need be ignorant rustics."

George Washington was the "chief human symbol of common Americanism." Washington won fame not only for his leadership of the Continental Army, but also for the way he carried himself. Washington was dubbed the "Father of His Country" before the War of Independence was over. Most important, he appeared to embody a new kind of republican leader, one who achieved a following not through title but through disinterested service to his country.

Washington's greatest attribute was his ability to exercise power while displaying an extraordinary willingness to give it up. At the height of his influence, after the successful conclusion of the Revolution, he voluntarily returned to private life. His retirement from power had a profound effect everywhere in the Western world. The greatest English military heroes such as Cromwell, William of Orange, and Marlborough had sought political rewards commensurate with their political achievements. In contrast, Washington was sincere in his desire for all the soldiers "to return to our Private Stations in the bosom of the free, peaceful and happy country." This unprecedented display of restraint gained Washington worldwide fame and eased the American people's fear of a powerful leader and strong government. Washington was not a brilliant military tactician, but he embodied virtues that defined an emerging nation, and his leadership was indispensable in holding the American forces together.

Franklin and Washington were true national heroes, because they combined great stature with deference to the country's fear of centralized power. They understood the uneasy but critical relationship between equality and rights, between American democracy and American liberalism. When these two heroes of the revolution agreed to attend the Constitutional Convention in Philadelphia, they bestowed those proceedings with invaluable legitimacy. Washington, in fact, agreed to serve as the president of the convention, to preside over what was sure to be a contentious debate over the country's future. His unifying presence in Philadelphia did not discourage that debate, but it surely gave it more prestige and enhanced the prospect that the final document would receive a fair hearing from the American people.

George Washington and Benjamin Franklin represented an emerging national culture that added support and dignity to the cause of creating "a more perfect Union."

Conclusion: The Meaning of the American Republic

The conflicts and debates of the 1780s raised the fundamental question of whether liberalism could best survive without democracy. What role should citizens play in protecting their rights? Did the preservation of liberty require an active and competent citizenry or was it safer to create a governmental system that limited political participation in order to preserve liberty? In the next chapter, we shall see how the Framers of the Constitution chose to protect liberty by limiting democracy. But as this chapter has shown, the roots of American political culture have been nourished by democratic as well as liberal nutrients. Religion, localism, and the great writing of Paine and Jefferson created a commitment to democratic principles that has continued to flourish. Jefferson believed that only an engaged people would be alert enough to defend their liberties. In the face of an apathetic populace even a well constructed government, which balanced ambition against ambition, would dissolve into a cabal, with "separate and distinct interests from the people." This point of view remains alive in American politics, in no small measure because of the veneration given to his masterpiece, the Declaration of Independence.

As Abraham Lincoln and Martin Luther King taught us, the Declaration of Independence is as much a founding document of the American republic as is the Constitution. It is the Old Testament of America's civic religion even as the Constitution is the New. The Declaration celebrates individual rights but also calls the American people to arms to protect those liberties. Martin Luther King's appeal to American democracy, as he stood beside the Lincoln Memorial, showed that the Revolution did not absolve future generations from the responsibility to debate the meaning of their rights or the relevance of the Declaration and the Constitution to their own freedom. Like Lincoln, King showed that liberalism was not something that simply existed, it had to be won in a democratic struggle. Therein lies the challenge of the Founding Fathers to future generations. How could America make the law its king, protecting people against their own selfishness, bigotry, and tunnel vision, while still preserving the dignity of the democratic individual and the maintenance of an active and public-spirited citizenry?

Chapter Summary

☆ Cut off from feudal, hierarchic Europe, Americans enjoyed a fresh start. The culture they developed was shaped by an unprecedented equality of condition and a strong sense of individual rights to be exercised against the claims of society and government.

☆ Religion in particular has provided a check on self-interest, by cultivating community ties and helping to foster the idea of a national democratic community.

☆ Despite the powerful influence of liberty and democracy, many persons have been denied personal and civil liberties on the basis of ascribed characteristics – race, ethnicity, gender, and religion. Slavery was the most glaring example. Forced servitude was no less deeply rooted in American soil than was the Puritan idea of justice or the liberal principle of rights.

☆ The Declaration of Independence draws heavily from the social contract theory of John Locke, the seventeenth-century English liberal political philosopher. Locke's *Second Treatise on Government* argued that individuals had natural rights that all legitimate governments were obligated to protect. Indeed, there was nothing legitimate about government per se. Government was justified only because, properly organized, it better protected an individual's rights than did the "state of nature."

☆ In the 1780s, leading political thinkers such as John Adams became increasingly concerned about the threat to liberty and stability posed by unchecked democracy. Adams sought to curb democratic power by establishing a system of separate and divided powers overseen by an independent judiciary.

☆ Those who saw the need for a stronger central government appealed to national pride.

☆ In order for America to take its rightful place as a great nation, it needed a government powerful enough to protect it from foreign foes. The growth of national identity was much enhanced by the creation of America's first national heroes, Benjamin Franklin and George Washington. When these two great heroes agreed to attend the Constitutional Convention in Philadelphia, they bestowed those proceedings with invaluable legitimacy.

Major Concepts

abolitionists
covenant
entail
nationalism
natural rights
political creed
political culture
primogeniture
Puritans
slavery
Tories

Suggested Readings

Almond, Gabriel, and Sidney Verba. *Civic Culture: Political Attitudes and Democracy in Five Nations*. Princeton, NJ: Princeton University Press, 1963.

Du Bois, W. E. B. *The Souls of Black Folk*. New York: Penguin, 1996.

Franklin, Benjamin. *The Autobiography of Benjamin Franklin and Other Writings*, ed. Ormond Seavey. New York: Oxford University Press, 1998.

Garraty, John. *The American Nation; a History of the United States*. New York: Harper and Row, 1968.

Hartz, Louis. *The Liberal Tradition in America*, 2d ed. New York: Harvest Books, 1991.

Howe, Daniel Walker. *The Political Culture of American Whigs*. Chicago: University of Chicago Press, 1984.

Kloppenberg, James. *The Virtues of Liberalism*. Cambridge, MA: Harvard University Press, 2000.

Maier, Pauline. *American Scripture: How America Declared Its Independence from Britain*. New York: Random House, 2002.

McWilliams, Wilson Carey. *The Idea of Fraternity in America*. Berkeley: University of California Press, 1973.

Meyers, Marvin. *The Jacksonian Persuasion*, rev. ed. Stanford, CA: Stanford University Press, 1990.

Miller, Perry. *The New England Mind: The Seventeenth Century*. Cambridge, MA: Belknap Press, 1983.

Morone, James. *Hellfire Nation: The Politics of Sin in American History*. New Haven, CT: Yale University Press, 2003.

Oates, Stephen B. *Let the Trumpet Sound: The Life of Martin Luther King, Jr.* New York: Harper and Row, 1982.

Paine, Thomas. *Common Sense*. New York: Penguin, 1976.

Smith, Roger M. *Civic Ideals: Conflicting Visions of Citizenship in the United States*. New Haven, CT: Yale University Press, 1999.

Tocqueville, Alexis de. *Democracy in America*, ed. Harvey Mansfield and Delba Winthrop. Chicago: University of Chicago Press, 2000.

Wood, Gordon. "The Democratization of Mind in America." In *The Moral Foundations of the American Republic*, 2d ed., ed. Robert H. Horowitz. Charlottesville: University Press of Virginia, 1979.

_____.*The Creation of the American Republic, 1776–1787*. Chapel Hill: University of North Carolina Press, 1998.

3 Contesting the Constitution

A Lovers' Quarrel

This chapter focuses on:

☆ Debates between the Federalists and Anti-Federalists about the nature of the Constitution and the Bill of Rights

☆ The leadership of George Washington, James Madison, and Benjamin Franklin during the Constitutional Convention

☆ The Great Compromise that established the House of Representatives and the Senate, and the Dreadful Compromise that maintained toleration of slavery

☆ The system of checks and balances created by the Constitution

☆ Ratification of the Constitution

Benjamin Franklin remarked at the 1787 Constitutional Convention that the President's chair depicted a "rising sun and not a setting sun," indicating his high hopes for the fledgling U.S. government.

While the last members were signing [the Constitution] Doctor Franklin, looking towards the President's Chair, at the back of which a rising sun happened to be painted, observed to a few members near him, that painters had found it difficult to distinguish in their art a rising sun from a setting sun. "I have … often and often in the course of the session, and the vicissitudes of my hopes and fears as to its issue, looked at that [sun] behind the president without being able to tell whether it was rising or setting: But now at length I have the happiness to know it is a rising sun and not a setting sun."

Benjamin Franklin spoke these famous words at the Constitutional Convention while the delegates who labored during the summer of 1787 to draft the Constitution were coming forward to sign their names to the document. Franklin's remarks expressed the grave doubts that even the most optimistic Founders felt about whether the people would approve the new Constitution. Even if they did, would the result, as the preamble promised, "form a more perfect Union"? Franklin himself confessed that "there are several parts of this constitution which I do not at present approve." It was, after all, the product of many compromises, made necessary by the diverse interests represented at the convention. Moreover, the Constitution – embodying an attempt to serve the competing traditions of liberalism and democracy – represented a novel experiment in self-rule, one that was bound to be controversial.

As the oldest man at the convention, Franklin was aware of just how daunting a task it was to launch not only a new government but also a new way of governing. The Framers of the Constitution had invented the large-scale federal democratic republic. Before the establishment of the United States, the idea of democracy had been applied only to small places, such as ancient Athens and the small American states under the Articles of Confederation. Large places were governed by kings or queens. But Americans celebrated the dignity of the democratic individual. Franklin shared with his fellow delegates the hope that this novel attachment to individualism – to the inalienable rights championed by the Declaration of Independence – would make possible what had previously only been a political dream: self-governing individuals joined together in a massive collective enterprise. Only such a bold attempt at self-rule on a grand scale could make Americans' obsession with rights compatible with their passion for equality.

In spite of his doubts, Franklin saw the sun rising over America because he believed that the Constitution gave institutional form to the values that aroused the Revolution and pushed the country toward the creation of a national community. Today, more than 200 years later, Americans have reason to share Franklin's sense of accomplishment and possibility. Despite dim and dark moments, the sun has never set on the American experiment in large-scale constitutional democracy.

This chapter focuses on the process of invention that took place at the Constitutional Convention held in Philadelphia in the summer of 1787. It dwells on what happened at the beginning, because at the beginning nothing could be taken for granted. None of the participants knew for sure what would work and what would not. Therefore they had to carefully consider a wide variety of alternative institutional forms and principles. That consideration, reflected both in the debates at the Constitutional Convention and in the subsequent debates over ratification, was the fullest and freshest exploration of how best to organize a free government that has ever taken place. All the critical tensions between the competing traditions of natural rights and democracy were on display. Those initial debates and controversies offer the best starting place for an understanding of how American institutions are structured, how they work, and how they fail to work.

Virtually all the questions that continue to bedevil American democracy were raised during the debates over the Constitution. Fear that a strong executive would become too powerful worried the delegates in Philadelphia just as it informs debates in Washington today. Whether to limit the number of terms that a member of Congress could serve was a topic of controversy at the Constitutional Convention just as it is now. How to keep organized interests from dominating the government preoccupied the Founders as much as it does contemporary reformers. Because these issues have not gone away, we dare not confine our consideration in this book only to the winners of the constitutional debate. As brilliant and farsighted as the winners' proposals have proven to be, many of the most serious criticisms levied against them have also proved telling. Only by examining the arguments of the opponents as well as the supporters of the Constitution can students of American government fully appreciate the enduring conflicts that animate the American democratic experiment.

The first section in this chapter describes a constitutional debate that was grounded in conflicting views of rights and equality. The next section looks at the complex combination of theoretical and practical political considerations that led to the writing of the Constitution. Then the chapter examines the key debates and compromises that took place during the writing of the Constitution and the subsequent ratification process. We conclude with a look at how the Constitution has affected those issues of liberty and democracy about which both its supporters and opponents were most concerned.

Democracy, Liberalism, and the Constitution

The debate over the Constitution resembled a "lovers' quarrel," because the two sides shared so much in common, most especially a deep and abiding love of country and of freedom and an understandable pride for having thrown off the yoke of British rule. But as lovers sometimes do, the two sides argued fiercely, and their disputes were about the things dearest to their hearts and minds. The debate over the Constitution, which included a spirited exchange at the convention and a more rough-and-tumble battle during the ratification process, marked the culmination of an ongoing struggle between two rival political theories about how to make popular rule work. Although the proponents of the Constitution, called *Federalists*, believed in popular government, they sought to establish principles and institutions that would restrain popular passion in order to protect liberty. Even though the Constitution's critics, the *Anti-Federalists*, cherished liberty, they believed that its preservation depended primarily on the constant vigilance of a democratic people. The depth and passion of this lovers' quarrel resulted from these two different understandings of how democracy affected liberty.

The Federalists and the Extended Republic

The contest over the Constitution was waged not only indoors, in the Philadelphia convention and state ratifying conventions, but "out-of-doors" as well, through the media. Many newspaper essays, although written in the heat of political battle, provided a continuing commentary on the virtues and flaws of the Constitution. The New York ratification contest led to the most famous Federalist defense of the Constitution. The eighty-five separate essays that compose *The Federalist Papers* – written by John Jay, James Madison, and Alexander Hamilton using the pseudonym Publius (a Roman statesman who championed the cause of the people) – are among the best American writing on political life.

In "Federalist No. 10," Madison laid out the principle that most clearly separated the Federalists from the Anti-Federalists ("Federalist No. 10" is reprinted in Appendix 3 of this book). Madison insisted that the American Constitution's restraints on majority rule preserved popular government; indeed, he claimed it beheld a republican government that better protected natural rights than a "pure democracy . . . , a society consisting of a small number of citizens, who assemble and administer the government in person." He refuted the Anti-Federalist belief, shared by all previous republican thinkers, that a *good* republic was a *small* republic. He argued that a large republic was better suited for maintaining liberty because it discouraged the creation of a single majority faction capable of dominating the minority and depriving it of its rights. Madison understood faction to be the following:

> A number of citizens, whether amounting to a minority or majority of the whole, who are united by some common impulse of passion, or of interest, adverse to the rights of other citizens, or to the permanent and aggregate interests of the community.

Because he knew that Americans would insist on popular rule, Madison feared majority tyranny more than he did minority tyranny. In his concern, he resembled the great republican thinkers of the past. But Madison and his fellow Federalists parted company with the tradition of republican thinking by denying that the problem of majority tyranny could best be solved by abolishing faction. Madison's analogy was that liberty bears the same relationship to faction that air does to fire. It is possible to snuff out a fire by depriving it of air but then the people cannot breathe either. Likewise, faction can be destroyed, but only at the price of snuffing out liberty for everyone.

According to Madison, previous thinkers had failed to appreciate that a large republic deals with faction better than a small one does. The larger the republic is, the more separate factions it will contain. As factions multiply, they become less able to coalesce into a stable and coherent majority capable of tyrannizing others. Size and diversity, traditionally the enemy of republics, turn out to be its dearest friends:

> Extend the sphere and you take in a greater variety of parties and interests; you make it less probable that a majority of the whole will have a common motive to invade the rights of other citizens; or if such a common motive exists, it will be more difficult for all who feel it to discover their own strength and to act in unison with each other. Besides other impediments, it may be remarked that, where there is a consciousness of unjust or dishonorable purposes, communication is always checked by distrust in proportion to the number whose concurrence is necessary.

Madison's remedy for factionalism revealed his fear that any majority – even one composed of citizens who professed deep and abiding faith in individual rights – might impose its will on society. As we pointed out in Chapter 2, Madison's concerns about unreliable majorities were not merely theoretical. During the 1780s, while the country was governed by the Articles of Confederation, several state legislatures, in their effort to ease debt, caused the value of money to fluctuate wildly and made the most routine commercial transactions risky. Madison shared the widespread concern that such clashes between debtor and creditor, which culminated in Shays's Rebellion, risked dangerous class conflict.

Madison's impressive discussion of factions suggests how the republican government created by the Constitution will moderate majority rule but leaves unclear what will hold the nation together. Can a society of individuals, separated into a multitude of diverse interests, agree about very much, for very long? Might such a divided people be easily dominated by the government, by rulers who become a separate class from the people? Indeed, Madison acknowledged that factions might become even more of a problem within government than among the public at large, because government officials have their hands on the levers of power.

The Federalist Papers revealed how the Constitution, to keep any governmental faction from tyrannizing over society, built on John Adams's idea of *checks and balances*. No single part of the government would enjoy a monopoly of power. Each of the three branches – the president, Congress, and the judiciary – would be granted some power to meddle in the affairs of the other branches as a means of ensuring that government power remained dispersed.

The Federalists, then, put little faith in the virtue of the citizens or their representatives. Instead, they thought it more practical to depend on institutional arrangements that could, as Madison put it, compensate for "the defect of better motives." Perhaps, in a "nation of philosophers [a] reverence for the laws would be sufficiently inculcated by the voice of an enlightened reason. But a nation of philosophers is as little to be expected as the philosophical race of Kings wished for by Plato." In fact, Madison's doubts about the possibilities of virtuous action even extended to philosophers. Calling for the creation of a national legislature that would be limited in size, he wrote: "In all very numerous assemblies, of whatever characteristics composed, passion never fails to grasp the scepter from reason. Had every Athenian citizen been a Socrates, every Athenian assembly would still have been a mob."

This rather startling observation follows from the Founders' "new science of politics." The passions of democratic life, the clash of factions, could only be controlled by a novel and ingenious arrangement of institutions. Madison stated this view in a famous passage from "Federalist No. 51" (see Appendix 4):

> Ambition must be made to counteract ambition. The interest of the man must be connected with the constitutional rights of the place. It may be a reflection of human nature that such devices should be necessary to control the abuses of government. But what is government itself but the greatest of all reflections on human nature? If men were angels, no government would be necessary. If angels were to govern men, neither external nor internal controls on government would be necessary. In framing a government which is to be administered by men over men, the great difficulty lies in this: you must first enable the government to control the governed; and in the next place oblige it to control itself.

The Anti-Federalists' Defense of the Small Republic

The Anti-Federalists feared that the "new science of politics" would destroy rather than reform popular rule. They were led by some of the greatest heroes of the Revolution, including Samuel Adams and Patrick Henry, who warned that the Constitution would destroy the "Spirit of '76" and drain the country of the popular enthusiasm for politics that the fight for independence had inspired. In the minds of the Anti-Federalists, the creation of a large republic, even one whose governing institutions were intended to check and balance each other, would inevitably re-create the tyrannical rule they had shed blood to escape.

The Anti-Federalists viewed the large republic as inherently undemocratic. Small size was necessary for democracy, they believed, because all self-government relies on friendship and trust among the citizens. Anti-Federalists also feared tyranny of the majority, but sought to avoid it by nurturing ties of mutual affection and common interest among the community as a whole rather than by multiplying faction. If democratic citizens knew and trusted each other well enough, a majority of them would not tyrannize the rest even if it had the chance. But such civic ties, they argued, could never be cultivated in the extended republic that the Federalists proposed to form. The Anti-Federalist writing under the pseudonym Cato, most likely George Clinton, warned: "Enlarge the circle of political life as far as conceived by the Constitution...[and] we lose the ties of acquaintance, habits, and fortune, and thus, by degrees, we lessen our attachments, till, at length, we no more than acknowledge a sameness of species."

To trust and empathize with another person, one has to know that person's character. Such knowledge is possible only in small places. As anyone who lives in a small town knows, not everyone has to be on a first name basis with everybody else. But there can be no real strangers. By consulting a friend, or the friend of a friend, one can obtain a rich assessment of the character of a person that one does not know personally. This knowledge does not imply that everyone likes and trusts one another. Even in the smallest of towns, one is likely to make enemies. But because there is so much knowledge of one another, one knows whom to trust and whom not to trust. Although grudges and feuds are bound to develop, their importance in the overall scheme of things is likely to be small compared to the sense of mutual responsibility, affection, and solidarity that small places instill.

In a large place, people remain anonymous and are therefore incapable of disciplining one another. Small places are nosy and gossipy. This lack of privacy can be aggravating, but because people are so knowledgeable about each other, they can anticipate political problems before those problems mushroom into open conflict. The Anti-Federalists counted on the capacity of citizens in small republics to exercise mutual vigilance to nip the formation of oppressive faction in the bud.

Small republics are also better at political education. The Anti-Federalists denied that such instruction could take place in schools. Schools, they claimed, made citizens literate, a necessary but not a sufficient condition for political education. Democracy, more than other forms of governance, required active participation in the affairs of state. As Cato put it, democracy worked best when it was "well-digested," that is, when it gave citizens meaningful opportunities to rule as well as be ruled. A government that valued participation

> affords to many the opportunity to be advanced to the supreme com-
> mand, and the honors they thereby enjoy fill them with a desire of
> rendering themselves worthy of them; hence this desire becomes part
> of their education, is mastered in manhood, and produces an ardent
> affection for their country.

The Federalists believed that large republics can rely on representatives to govern. The Anti-Federalists countered that popular rule must resemble the "pure democracy" that Madison scorned in "Federalist No. 10." They recognized that practical circumstances often required some sort of representative scheme; but to delegate as much responsibility to a small number of citizens as the Constitution allowed made popular sovereignty impractical. The Anti-Federalists recognized that in such circumstances, only a very small percentage of the population would have an opportunity to govern; most citizens would be robbed of the critical education that only governing affords. The Anti-Federalists considered citizenship to be like a muscle: it could only become strong through exercise. Only by partaking in the myriad tasks of local governance could people learn the hard lessons of citizenship: how to speak in public; how to listen carefully to others; how to know when to hold fast to principle and when to compromise. The passivity bred of relying too much on representatives yielded political impotence. Only active involvement in local affairs, as provided for in the Articles of Confederation, afforded one the chance to become knowledgeable enough to know how to protect one's liberty. This commitment to democracy also made the Anti-Federalists skeptical about relying on checks and balances. Preserving and nurturing the capacity of citizens, not creating complex forms of institutional competition, was the way, they believed, to keep a republic free.

Because Anti-Federalists counted on the people themselves to preserve and protect the republic, they were much more concerned than the Federalists were about the character and outlook of citizens. The Federalists praised the character of the American people, claiming that the Revolution showed their capacity to embrace a novel democratic experiment that would "preserve our liberties and promote our happiness." Yet Cato warned that this very pride in bold experimentation might lead to the creation of a constitution and laws that paid insufficient attention to moral character. Left to themselves, the American people would retreat to private concerns,

The Constitution represented a unique political experiment: to serve the
competing traditions of liberalism and democracy.

especially since the Constitution would spawn a large, diverse society whose
commercial bent

> begets luxury, the parent of inequality, the foe to virtue, and the enemy
> to restraint; and that ambition and voluptuousness, aided by flattery,
> will teach magistrates where limits are not explicitly fixed to have
> separate and distinct interests from the people.

Believing that corrupt and decadent people were incapable of being good
citizens, the Anti-Federalists favored the use of public sanctions to encourage virtue and discourage vice. Because religion is such a powerful source
of good conduct and also a potential source of terrible factional discord,
the Anti-Federalists believed that government had to both support and
regulate it. Some Anti-Federalists favored the establishment of an official
church and the punishment of religious dissent. They believed that successful democracy required the limitation of some forms of personal liberty,
and they were prepared to pay that price.

The framework for the new American government created by the Constitution both did and did not settle the lovers' quarrel between Federalists
and Anti-Federalists. On the whole, the Constitution was a victory for the
Federalist side, a triumph of liberalism. Its central premise, the creation

of a strong national government, ensured that America would be a large republic that emphasized natural rights and placed obstacles in the path of majority rule. Key aspects of the Constitution – most notably the Senate and the Supreme Court – were adopted despite telling criticisms about how antidemocratic they were. But the Constitution did not close the door on democracy. Under Anti-Federalist pressure, the Federalists reluctantly agreed to the *Bill of Rights*, the first ten amendments to the Constitution, as a powerful guarantor of free political life.

Significantly, the Bill of Rights as first enacted was viewed not as a list of individual entitlements but instead as a constraint on the power of the national government – as a bulwark of local self-rule. The Anti-Federalists' ability to shape the Constitution thus helped ensure that the new national government did not destroy the existing forms of local and state politics that the Anti-Federalists cherished as the home of popular rule.

Leadership and Deliberation at the Constitutional Convention

Although the Constitution is a true original – the first written set of ground rules for governing an entire nation – it did not appear out of the blue. Thirteen separate states did not defeat the British; the United States of America did. As we noted in Chapter 2, the specific terms governing that union were set out in the Articles of Confederation, adopted by the Continental Congress in 1781. The legal transformation of the colonies into states was done on the basis of rules set out by the Articles. It is therefore literally true that the United States of America is older than the states themselves. But the Articles were not a constitution; they did not fully set out a blueprint for national governance.

The weakness of the Articles of Confederation was that they reflected the hope that no strong central government would be needed to govern the Union. Most important public problems were to be dealt with by the states. Issues requiring national attention, such as interstate and foreign commerce, were to be handled by Congress in such a way that the individual states would gladly comply voluntarily or would be shamed into complying. Coercion by the national government would not prove necessary.

The creators of the Articles of Confederation were not naive. They understood the risks associated with a weak central government. But they had just freed themselves from an empire. They preferred to take those risks rather than endure the loss of liberty that they were certain would result from a powerful central government. Those Founders who had always favored a strong central government – a minority that included George Washington, Alexander Hamilton, and James Madison – bided their time.

Their best hope was to allow the Continental Congress to try, and fail, to cope with pressing issues of nationwide import. Their patience was rewarded. The conflicts and anxieties spawned by the weak system for dealing with debt and taxes, highlighted by Shays's Rebellion, created a political atmosphere favorable toward the building of a strong national government.

In response to this shift in public mood, the Congress agreed to allow a convention to be called in Philadelphia to propose changes to the Articles that would remedy its defects. There was no discussion of, or permission to write, a wholly new document. Washington, Madison, Hamilton, and their key allies first had to convince the other delegates to violate the letter of their instructions and adopt a new constitution, and then they had to sell the new document to a skeptical and cautious citizenry.

The views of those Founders who would later oppose the Constitution were underrepresented at Philadelphia because most had not favored such a gathering in the first place and had no desire to participate in it. Nonetheless, the Federalists had to anticipate that even though the Anti-Federalist point of view would be muted at the convention, it would surface during the ratification debates.

But the Federalists had another problem as well. Even those who favored a stronger national government in principle had ample reason for differing about what a specific draft constitution should contain. Inevitably, a change in the governmental ground rules would benefit some interests at the expense of others. In particular, a stronger central government would threaten those views that were held by a majority of citizens in a single state but that were held by a minority of the nation as a whole. It is not surprising, therefore, that many of the representatives who came to Philadelphia tempered their enthusiasm for creating a new and better government with the realization that they would have to fight to protect the interests of their particular states. These anxieties were felt most keenly by delegates from small states, who expected the largest states – those containing great population centers such as New York, Boston, and Philadelphia – to dominate a national government. Even New York was sharply divided between friends and foes on the subject of forming an energetic union. Strongly influenced by Governor George Clinton, who would become an important Anti-Federalist, the New York state legislature sent a delegation to Philadelphia that flanked Alexander Hamilton with two opponents of federal power – John Lansing, Jr., and Robert Yates – who, according to the historian Ron Chernow, "would smother [Hamilton's] influence" at the convention. Perhaps the most daunting challenge to a successful convention was posed by representatives from slave states, many of whom feared that a national majority would eventually favor the abolition of slavery. On many important issues, Madison conceded, "the states were divided into different interests not by their difference of size, but principally from their having or not having slaves." Some of the most enduring elements of the Constitution, such as the Senate, resulted in part from efforts to placate such fears among those who were, on the whole, supporters of a strong national government. The most repugnant elements of the Constitution, that is, the protections granted to slavery, were also included for this reason. The Constitution is not simply a blueprint, it is a *political* blueprint. It is based both on principles that express the idealistic commitments of those who designed it and on practical compromises necessary to win sufficient support to gain its adoption.

The success of the Philadelphia convention beat the odds. Not only did its delegates embrace rival theories of democracy, but they came from very different states and regions with widely varying opinions and interests. What is more, many members of this distinguished group had their own favorite ideas about how best to organize the government. The most likely outcome of the convention was stalemate. Remarking on the difficulties of assembling a number of men whose "joint wisdom" might have been obscured by "their prejudices, their passions, their errors of opinion, their local interests, and their selfish views," Franklin confessed he was "astonished" to find the Constitution "approaching so near perfection as it does."

Nearly 200 years later, the historian Catherine Drinker Bowen used the term *miracle* to describe the success of these would-be architects in agreeing on a single constitutional blueprint. But the miraculous events in Philadelphia were distinctively practical, the result of political debate, compromise, and decision. The convention succeeded because most of the delegates displayed a great talent for deliberation, and a few showed a great talent for leadership. Studying the Philadelphia convention allows students to see the workings of these two key political principles – leadership and deliberation – that are so central to the success of a large, complex republic.

Deliberation

Deliberation is the art of reasoning together. Political deliberation is the application of this art to public decision making. It is not enough to have good talks; political deliberation is successful only when an assembly comes to a decision about whatever public issue is at stake.

Political deliberation involves a complex set of skills and attitudes. The key attitude is open-mindedness. Whatever one's preconceived ideas, one must be open to changing one's mind. This may not happen often. But if one remains close-minded, the other debaters will see that efforts at persuasion are hopeless and they too will be tempted to close their minds. The deliberation will turn into irreconcilable conflict. If the constitutional deliberation had degenerated into a stalemate, it would have been a contest with no winners. Those delegates who sensed they were losing the debate would have diverted their energies either to sabotaging the convention or to convincing the voters in the several states not to ratify the document that was produced. Because delegates allowed themselves to be influenced by other delegates, creative solutions were found to problems that at first seemed intractable. Today's government was born out of the painstaking and imaginative political deliberation engaged in by the men who wrote the Constitution and worked for its ratification.

Secrecy

To encourage deliberation, the convention delegates took the drastic step of adopting a secrecy rule: nothing spoken within Philadelphia's convention hall was "to be printed, or otherwise published or communicated without leave." The convention took place without visitors, journalists, or even public discussions by the delegates in earshot of non-participants. Citizens who suspected that the convention would strengthen the central government beyond what a democracy could tolerate complained that such a "Dark Enclave," as Patrick Henry put it, could only be the work of conspirators.

Even Thomas Jefferson, in Paris at the time, who thought the convention "an assembly of demigods," complained of the "abominable...precedent...of tying up the tongues" of the delegates. His criticism expressed the principle that democracy is strengthened by, as Woodrow Wilson would later put it, "open covenants, openly arrived at." Public deliberations, these men believed, allow citizens to judge representatives and the arguments brought to bear in support of their positions. Moreover, public debates educate and improve public judgment.

Still, the convention delegates adopted the secrecy rule easily and never wavered from their decision to hold meetings behind closed doors. Reflecting on that hot summer in Philadelphia many years later, Madison insisted that "no Constitution would ever have been adopted by the convention if the debates had been public." The secrecy rule encouraged the delegates to take controversial positions, discuss them freely, and work out compromises without fear of challenging received wisdoms, such as the sovereignty of the states, and without temptation to play to any gallery save that of posterity.

Leadership

The enduring union that the Constitution achieved required more than the luxury of secret deliberations; it also required leadership. Madison, Washington, and Franklin provided that crucial leadership. Each had his own gifts and style, but collectively they gave the convention a sense of direction. Like most serious deliberations, the Constitutional Convention risked having to consider too many options in too little time. Madison, Washington, and Franklin controlled the agenda to ensure that the initial choices that were made would shape and guide later choices. They provoked the other delegates when the deliberation became listless, and they calmed their colleagues when it became overheated. They took initiative when others were timid and suggested compromise when others were intransigent.

George Washington made his greatest leadership contribution simply by showing up. As we noted in Chapter 2, he was the most famous and celebrated man in America. He had led the Continental Army to victory, and in the wake of that victory, he refused to help disgruntled army veterans overthrow the feckless national government and make him king. Having seen Washington's commitment to republican rule, no citizen could believe that he would use the convention for selfish political purposes. At no other time in American history has one person towered over all others in terms of public affection and respect. His presence at the convention ensured that it would be viewed as a serious and auspicious occasion.

It was a foregone conclusion that Washington would chair the convention. As the presiding officer, he was called not chairman but president. Although Washington spoke little at the convention, he determined who would speak when, which issues would be brought up, and in what order. Washington was known to favor a strong national government. By presiding over the convention, he was able to push the deliberations in the direction he favored. By attending the convention and signing the Constitution, Washington proclaimed to the country at large that its leading citizen had given his seal of approval.

If Washington was the Constitutional Convention's lion, Madison was its fox. He complemented Washington's nobility and sobriety with his intelligence and cunning. He was the only participant to devise a broad strategy for ensuring that the convention produced what he wanted it to produce, and to do so in advance. The most crucial decision made by the delegates in the first days of the convention had to do with setting the agenda. What issues were they going to consider, and in what order? Because Madison was the only delegate ready to propose a comprehensive plan, his so-called

James Madison provided the intellectual force for the new Constitution. He called for a radical strengthening of the national government at the Constitutional Convention.

Virginia Plan, which called for a radical strengthening of the national government, was placed at the top of the agenda and dominated the convention deliberations from beginning to end. The Constitution that was finally adopted bears a striking resemblance to that plan.

Franklin was the sheepdog of the convention, bringing the delegates back into the fold when they threatened to stray. Franklin's fame as an inventor and writer as well as a statesman made him second only to Washington in prestige. The convention was dominated by young men in their twenties and thirties. Franklin, at eighty-one, was the oldest. He would die three years later. Weak and ill at the time of the convention, he marshaled his strength for the moment of greatest crisis. After several weeks of debate, the delegates seemed on the verge of quitting. They were particularly troubled by the question of representation in the Congress, an issue that, as we explain later in this chapter, aroused fierce territorial loyalties. Should each state be represented equally, according to the principles of the Articles of Confederation? Or, befitting a "more perfect Union," should congressional representation be based on population? Delegates from large states, such as Virginia, favored basing representation on population. Small states, such as New Jersey, favored equal territorial representation.

Franklin had long been passionately committed to a unicameral legislature. But instead of immersing himself in these quarrels, he spoke to remind the delegates of their higher calling. At the beginning of the war with Britain, the Continental Congress had daily prayed for divine protection. If that continual effort to seek God's guidance had worked to win independence, was it not even more vital for determining how to govern wisely? Franklin implored the delegates to think and act for a cause greater than themselves. If not, he warned,

> We shall be divided by our little partial local interests, our projects will be confounded and we ourselves shall become a reproach and a by-word down to future generations. And, what is worse, mankind may hereafter from this unfortunate instance, despair of establishing government by human wisdom and leave it to chance, war and conquest.

The delegates did not accept Franklin's proposal to open each session with prayers. Sons of the Enlightenment, the Framers believed that reason would be a sufficient guide for resolving this sticky problem. But Franklin's appeal to heaven reminded them of their common commitments and enabled the delegates to resume reasoning together. In fact, as the historian Gordon Wood has noted, Franklin's appeal to a higher calling was joined to a practical appreciation of the diversity and clashing interests in America. He had come to realize during years of public service that "when you assemble a number of men, to have the advantage of their joint wisdom, you inevitably assemble with those men all their prejudices, their passions, their errors of opinion, their local interests, and their selfish views." Franklin's efforts to bring the delegates together drew them back into a deliberative mood, calming them down and shifting their attention away from petty territorial squabbling. Within a few days, a committee had been appointed to seek a compromise on the issue of representation. Franklin, appointed to the committee, introduced the committee's compromise resolution – which called for representation according to population in the first legislative branch and an equal vote for each state in the second. The resolution passed, albeit by a very close vote. From then on the success of the convention was never really in doubt.

The Ties That Bound

In the final analysis, the Philadelphia convention succeeded because most delegates were more strongly devoted to what they had in common than to what divided them. The debates over the Constitution took place within this context of shared beliefs and attachments. In Chapter 1, we described several key terms vital to an understanding of America's political tradition. Now we return to those key terms, and add a few more, to describe what those delegates had in common.

The strong mutual affections that made the debate over the Constitution a lovers' quarrel were most clearly embodied in the Declaration of Independence. North and South, small states and large, were united in their dedication to the principle of *natural rights*, the core principle of liberalism, as expressed in that hallowed document. The willingness of some delegates, especially those from states such as Georgia and South Carolina, to overlook the fact that such rights should apply to slaves does make them hypocrites. But hypocrisy is not so uncommon among lovers. Because the attachment to these principles was so deep and their articulation by the Declaration so clear and pithy, there was no need to restate them in the Constitution. But supporters and opponents alike agreed that the most important test of the Constitution's merit was whether it improved on the Articles of Confederation in securing those rights that humans were entitled to by their very nature.

There was also virtually universal commitment to the principle of *popular sovereignty*, the core of America's democratic tradition. Government was to be considered legitimate only if it rested its authority in the consent of the people. Delegates favored many specific practical means for restraining the power and influence of ordinary people, and those means are found in the Constitution. Among them are life tenure for Supreme Court justices and the indirect election of the president by an electoral college. But underlying these limitations on popular rule was the principle stated in the first words of the Constitution's preamble. "We the People" had consented to these restrictions on democracy. By amending the Constitution, the people could assert their right to change those restrictions.

The compromise between liberalism and democracy was cemented by the Framers' commitment to *limited government*. Government was to be restricted to only those situations and problems that people could not cope with on their own. If public intervention was necessary, it should be provided by local government. If local government was inadequate to the task, people should then look to their states. National government intervention was a last resort. In England and on the European continent, government held the upper hand; governments could act unless expressly forbidden from doing so. For all their differences, both Federalists and Anti-Federalists agreed on the need to reverse that presumption. Both sought to make government subordinate to a constitution, even if they disagreed on exactly what that constitution should say.

Federalists and Anti-Federalists were all *constitutionalists*, meaning that they believed the government should be subservient to a set of fundamental governing principles and procedures. One crucial governing principle was the concept of *enumerated powers* – that the government would be restricted to only those powers that the Constitution specifically granted to it. This principle was therefore a critical means for ensuring limited government. The longest and most detailed part of the Constitution is Article I. It spells out the powers granted to Congress. The Framers expected Congress to be the single most powerful part of the government because it had the power to write laws. As the English philosopher John Locke, who had such a profound influence on America, had argued, a free society necessarily depended on a body of "settled, standing laws." For this very reason, the Framers explicitly limited Congress's powers to those expressly stated in this section. Box 1 discusses the most difficult to interpret of the national government's enumerated powers, interstate and foreign commerce.

Box One: Nuts and Bolts

The Commerce Clause

Of the various enumerated powers of Congress, the one that has proven hardest to define and therefore most contentious is the Commerce Clause. Article I, Section 8 grants Congress the power "to regulate Commerce with Foreign Nations, and among the several States and with the Indian Tribes." But what is "commerce"? Initially, the Supreme Court adopted a narrow and literal meaning of the term and limited federal government intervention to matters involving the actual trading and/or transporting of goods between states or overseas. In the twentieth century, the court extended the definition to include manufacturing, thus enabling the federal government to intervene to break up monopolies. During the New Deal, the definition was further expanded to include virtually any form of economic activity. Since the New Deal, the Commerce Clause has been used to justify environmental and safety regulations as well. Between the New Deal and the mid-1990s, the Supreme Court refused to overturn any national government intervention justified on the basis of the Commerce Clause; therefore, the very principle of enumerated powers was losing its meaning. However, as we discuss in Chapter 5, in *Lopez v. the United States* (1994), the court overturned a federal law banning the carrying of handguns in schools on the grounds that such an activity had nothing meaningful to do with interstate commerce and therefore could not be subject to federal action.

Constitutional government did not rest on enumerated powers alone, however. It also depended on the *separation of powers*. The three essential governmental functions – legislation, execution, and adjudication – should each be assigned to a distinct branch of government. Both sides agreed that to enable the same persons who made the laws to execute them as well, or to adjudicate cases that arose under those laws, was an express route to tyranny. Article II established the organization and powers of an independent, energetic executive; Article III framed an independent judiciary.

The delegates also shared an unsentimental view of their fellow humans. Human corruption and frailty encouraged majorities to deprive minorities of their inalienable rights. Therefore, Federalists and Anti-Federalists agreed that *tyranny of the majority* was the gravest threat to liberty. Because they believed in popular sovereignty, the delegates could not prevent tyranny of the majority in the old-fashioned way, by vesting power in a king. It had to be accomplished in a manner that still left the people in charge.

Finally, the two groups shared a sense of common *nationality*. In most instances, the delegates' deeper loyalty was to their states, but the sacrifices made during the Revolution and their mutual adherence to the great principles articulated in the Declaration of Independence instilled in the delegates feelings of solidarity that transcended state borders.

Agenda Setting, Conflict, and Compromise

The delegates were slow to arrive in Philadelphia. Eleven days elapsed between the scheduled start of the convention on May 14, 1787, and its actual opening on May 25, when enough delegates had finally arrived to produce the minimum number of seven states required for official business to begin. Because Madison insisted, the Virginia delegation, including Washington, arrived on time. Madison had more than punctuality on his mind. He used the spare eleven days to work with the Virginia delegation to gain its united support for his plan. The session opened with Virginia's plan as the only one on the table and with a Virginia delegate as the presiding officer. Under these favorable circumstances, the Virginia Plan became the framework for the convention's subsequent discussions. The Virginia delegation agreed that the convention should ignore its mandate to revise the Articles and instead construct a whole new scheme that provided for a strong national government. When Virginia governor Edmund Jennings Randolph, the delegation's official spokesman, rose to introduce the plan, he pressed for a strong national government. Then he outlined the Virginia Plan's strategy to create such a powerful national entity.

The Virginia Plan

If all the delegates had arrived on time, there would have been no fully formed proposal to claim first place on the agenda. The delegates may well have chosen to begin with a broad discussion of the state of the country and wrangled about how best to revise the Articles. Such a meandering discussion might have produced only minimal changes or resulted in no agreement at all. Instead, the *Virginia Plan*, which clearly and self-confidently challenged Congress's instructions, put the delegates on the spot. They would immediately have to decide whether to violate their instructions and write a new and powerful constitution. Because the choice was posed so starkly and because the Virginia Plan was so comprehensive and compelling, the delegates made their most decisive choice first, to face the full challenge of constituting a national government.

The heart of the Virginia Plan was contained in a resolution that Randolph proposed on May 30 "that a national government ought to be established consisting of a supreme legislature, judiciary, and executive." The words national and supreme left no doubt about the proposal's sweep. To accept it was bold but to reject it would be to give up any hope of thoroughgoing improvement and to make the convention a waste of time. Had the delegates been able to avoid such a stark choice so early in the convention, a majority might have chosen to do so. But faced with an either-or decision, they chose to accept Randolph's challenge, and his resolution passed easily. For the next several weeks, the deliberations of the convention focused on the Virginia Plan. Although many of its specific elements were changed or rejected, there was no retreat from the principles encapsulated in Randolph's May 30 resolution. The fork in the road heading toward a new constitutional order had been taken.

On June 15, the opponents of the Virginia Plan finally introduced a plan of their own. The so-called *New Jersey Plan* differed from its rival in that it was framed as a series of amendments to the Articles of Confederation and called for a revision, not a transformation, of the existing governmental plan. It left intact the one state-one vote legislature and made no broad claim about national supremacy. Had this scheme served as the initial basis of discussion, the convention's product might have been far less revolutionary. It is a testament to the political skill of the Virginians – Washington and Madison in particular – that the New Jersey Plan now seemed, by comparison to their plan, excessively tame, even though it did include proposals to give Congress power to tax and regulate commerce, to establish a supreme court, and to create an executive authorized to compel states to obey federal law. Three weeks earlier these same proposals would have appeared to many delegates as bold indeed.

In the midst of the debate about the two plans, Alexander Hamilton rose to offer yet a third plan. Because the convention chose to decide issues on a state-by-state basis, Hamilton's vote was nullified throughout by his fellow two delegates. Indeed, Hamilton rarely spoke during the first three weeks of the proceedings. When he broke silence, Hamilton broached a radical plan. To counterpoise a democratic House of Representatives, he proposed a president and Senate that would be elected but would then serve during "good behavior." Resting in the principle that there must be a "permanent will" to balance the untrustworthiness of public opinion, the proposal was especially distinctive in the powers it delegated to an independent executive, who, for all intents and purposes, would be an "elective monarch." Hamilton's plan was so radically nationalist and antirepublican that it received no discernable support from the delegates. But by its very extremism, it had the political effect of making the Virginia Plan appear moderate by comparison. Delegates who might have been intrigued but frightened by the nationalizing implications of the Virginia Plan could now console themselves that by supporting it they were adopting the "middle way."

No tangible evidence exists to prove that Hamilton was acting in cahoots with Madison and Washington. As Chernow writes, "Of all the founders, Hamilton probably had the gravest doubts about the wisdom of the masses and wanted elected leaders who would guide them." But Hamilton must have recognized that his plan was too extreme for most of the delegates.

Indeed, after delivering his thoughts, Hamilton left the next day for New York to attend to personal business and did not return to the convention until early September. It was as if he recognized that his initial proposal had stamped him as such a radical that anything he endorsed was likely to be defeated. Why would he put himself in such an unpopular position unless he was intentionally presenting an extreme case in order to make his friends look more moderate? Hamilton had been Washington's closest aide during the war and would later serve as his secretary of the treasury. Madison would later become Hamilton's enemy and rival, but in the months after the convention they would collaborate to produce the most celebrated of all the defenses of the Constitution, *The Federalist Papers*. In fact, no one fought harder or more effectively for the new Constitution than did Hamilton; and although he consistently interpreted its language in support of a strong executive, Hamilton never wavered in his support for the Constitution.

Conflicts

Although the Virginians had succeeded in framing the overall debate around their vision of a truly national government, some delegates had specific concerns so pressing that they would vote against any plan that did not address those concerns. In addition to the deep divide between delegates who favored a strong central government and those who opposed it, two other profound political divisions existed among the delegates. Those from the small states feared that if government was nationalized and consolidated, the views and interests of the large states – Massachusetts, Pennsylvania, and Virginia, in particular – would prevail. Slaveholders feared that the new nation's non-slaveholding states would try to persuade Congress to inhibit slavery.

Even if delegates from small states and from slave states agreed in principle that the United States was a full-fledged union, not merely a compact of states, they recognized that reserving strong powers for the individual states was still the best way to protect their specific interests. They were not persuaded by the argument that the states would be adequately protected because the new national government was to be one of strictly enumerated powers. In principle, the idea of strict enumeration ensured that all matters not delegated to the national government would be reserved to the states, but the small-state delegates realized that such delegations of authority would never be entirely clear-cut. The national government would always be tempted to interpret its power in the most expansive manner possible. Indeed, nationalists could draw on general language, such as the final clause of Article I, Section 8, which authorized Congress "To make all Laws which shall be necessary and proper for carrying into Execution the foregoing Powers," to consolidate their influence. Therefore, at a minimum, the small-state delegates wished to make sure that states would enjoy a powerful political role within the national government itself.

The Virginia Plan made no provision for state representation in the national government. It provided for a Congress consisting of two houses, that is, a bicameral legislature. Members of the first branch would be chosen by popular election. Members of the second branch would be chosen by the members of the lower chamber from lists of nominees provided by state legislatures.

The Great Compromise

The most dramatic moment of the entire proceedings occurred on July 16, 1787, when a majority of delegates were persuaded to support the compromise over representation in the bicameral legislature, a plan based on Benjamin Franklin's motion. Franklin's plea for "the assistance of Heaven" had helped to restore a deliberative atmosphere in which the delegates could consider the most difficult issue confronting them.

The Great Compromise provided for two houses. The lower house, called the House of Representatives, would provide representation proportional to each state's population. In order to provide some tilt in importance to this lower house, it was stipulated that all bills relating to the raising of revenue would have to originate there. The upper house was called the Senate, and its members would be chosen by the states. Each state, regardless of its size, would be entitled to two senators. As a result of this compromise, the bicameral legislature came to embody the two opposing views of what role states should have in the new constitutional order. In the Senate, the states would continue to be represented as distinct and equal political societies, whereas in the House they would be reduced to nothing more than the sum of the representatives that were allotted to them.

The Great Compromise took two weeks of hard negotiations. Its ultimate success depended on five delegates who mediated between the champions of nationalism and the champions of states' rights: John Dickinson, a highly respected statesman from the country's smallest state, Delaware; Franklin, whose prestige and leadership were indispensable to the delegates' acceptance of the negotiated settlement; and the three members of the Connecticut delegation, whose steady role in the process led some delegates to dub the deal the Connecticut Compromise. The compromise passed by a majority of only one vote. Madison remained adamantly opposed to the compromise because he saw it as a surrender to narrow state interests. So small was the margin that the nationalists considered pushing ahead without the small states. But a brief recess allowed cooler heads to prevail, with the Constitution makers among them willing "to yield... and to concur in such an act, however imperfect and exceptionable."

William Samuel Johnson of Connecticut was the first to recognize the compromise as something more than a jury-rigged solution. He pleaded with both sides to see the virtues of forming not a centralized nation or a fragmented confederation but rather a federal republic of a people who are unwilling to live solely as one or as many communities. He reminded states' rights advocates that the country was, for many purposes, "one political society" made up of individuals who viewed themselves as Americans. He urged Madison and the other nationalists to remember that the states were not merely "districts of people," but also "political Societies," with "interests" of their own to protect.

Ironically, James Madison, the most stubborn of nationalists, would be the first to publicly celebrate this "invention" of American federalism as a beneficial compromise between small and large government. In "Federalist No. 39," Madison claimed that the convention, liberated by the Great Compromise, created a Constitution that was "in strictness neither a national nor a federal Constitution, but a composition of both."

A similar compromise was adopted when the delegates created a two-stage process for presidential elections. The first stage was governed by the principle of population. States were assigned a number of presidential electors based on the number of representatives they had in Congress. If one candidate received a majority of electoral votes, that candidate became president. But if no one received a majority, only the top five vote getters survived to enter the second stage. The second stage – in which each state had an equal voice regardless of its size – called for the choice to be given to the House of Representatives. However, House members would not cast individual votes; instead, all the members from a given state would meet together and the majority would decide which candidate received the state's votes. The candidate receiving a majority of state votes would become president. Thus, the states were provided with a direct role in the choice of the executive as well as in the choice of one half of the legislature.

Born of compromise, federalism in general and the Senate in particular proved critical for a reconciliation of liberalism and democracy. These institutional innovations enabled the country to reconcile the need for a national government that was expansive and powerful enough to protect people's rights with the equally important objective of enough local and regional autonomy to make active citizenship possible.

The Dreadful Compromise

The other major compromise, involving the toleration and protection of slavery, did not display this same happy mix of principle and practicality. Because slavery deprives humans of their liberty and treats them as property, it is profoundly illiberal. The compromise sustaining it marked a major exception to the lovers' quarrel among liberals typical of the constitutional debates.

How could such otherwise ethically progressive and sophisticated people abet this evil? The question is all the more perplexing because so many of them, including some slave owners, recognized the evil of slavery. They acquiesced because they feared that to oppose slavery would foment a greater evil, the dissolution of the Union. Slavery's advocates, a majority in all the slave states, had made it clear that they would oppose the Constitution if they perceived that it would threaten either the present or the future of slavery. Therefore, even those delegates most opposed to slavery were obliged to consider what life would be like if that threat were carried out. Their willingness to compromise with slavery came from their considered conclusion that to do so was the lesser of two evils.

Their willingness to compromise was partly rooted in their feelings of loss at being politically separated from so many of their revolutionary allies, especially the great Virginians – Washington, Jefferson, and Madison. But more important was their recognition that the Union had almost no chance of survival if the Southern states left. Already the young fragile nation faced a hostile power, Britain, on its northern border. West of the Mississippi lay the French and Spanish empires. If the South seceded, the Union would be reduced to little more than a strip of coastline that extended southward only as far as Pennsylvania (Delaware would remain a slave state until the ratification of the Thirteenth Amendment in 1865). And it would share a long southern border with what would then be a hostile country. To make matters worse, the easiest route west went through the South. The North was hemmed in by the Appalachian Mountains and powerful, hostile Indian nations. The most active western settlement was occurring in the slave-owning territories of Tennessee and Kentucky. In the near future, the South was likely to become larger and more powerful than the North. Therefore, the Northern delegates recognized that they had no practical choice but to appease the South on the issue that it regarded as most important, namely, slavery.

The Constitution contains three clauses protecting slavery. The first dealt with how slaves were to be counted for purposes of apportioning congressional districts. The Southern states contained relatively few white people. Therefore, in order not to be outvoted by the North in the House of Representatives, the Southern states required that slaves be counted in the census, on which the apportionment of seats in the House would be based. Ironically, this demand forced them to admit that slaves were indeed human beings, but they were prepared to live with this awkwardness for the sake of protecting their political strength. The opponents of slavery were unwilling to count slaves on an equal basis with non-slaves, but they compromised by allowing each slave to be counted as three-fifths of a person for the purposes of congressional apportionment.

The second proslavery clause guaranteed the continuation of the importation of slaves for a period of twenty years. To ensure that this protection would not be abridged, this clause was declared non-amendable. This provision was politically the most complex because it did not have the unified support of all slaveholders. States, such as Virginia, that already had more slaves than were needed to run their plantations would have been happy to ban the importation of slaves as a way to increase the value of their slave property. But states, such as South Carolina and Georgia, that needed more slaves for their plantations had strong interests in continuing the international slave trade in order to keep the price of slaves down. In the end, the greater intensity of feeling on the issue among the deep Southerners enabled them to prevail.

The third provision, and the one that was to cause the most enduring controversy, was the fugitive slave provision. This provision required all states, including those that prohibited slavery, to return escaping slaves to their owners.

The fugitive slave provision in the Constitution states, "No person held to service or labor in one state, under the laws thereof, escaping into another, shall, in consequence of any law or regulation therein, be discharged for such service or labor, but shall be delivered up on claim of the party, to whom such service or labor may be due." The original proposal from the South Carolina delegation required "slaves and servants to be delivered up like criminals." The final version makes no reference either to slaves or criminals, only to persons "held to service or labor." Another version required that fugitive persons be delivered up to the person "justly claiming" their labor. The final version makes no reference to the justice of the claim. Instead of "justly claiming," it substitutes "to whom such service or labor may be due" and therefore ignores the issue of whether that claim is just. And the convention's committee on style changed the definition of a fugitive from one "legally held to service or labor" to a person held "to service or labor in one state, under the laws thereof." This wording thereby removed any direct constitutional endorsement of the legality of the practice of slavery. If indeed a promise to return fugitive slaves was a necessity, it is difficult to imagine how such an endorsement could have been worded to offer less support for slavery in principle.

The fugitive slave provision of the Constitution represents the fine line the Framers walked between codifying slavery and denying its moral legitimacy. As dreadful as these concessions and compromises with slavery were, they could have been worse. While allowing the continuation of slavery and even abetting it by promising to help catch fugitive slaves, the Constitution ostentatiously refrains from providing slavery with a moral stamp of approval. The term *slavery* is never even mentioned in the document. The embarrassed delegates resorted to euphemisms such as "persons held to service," a tacit acknowledgment of their feelings of shame in acquiescing to it.

One cannot entirely exonerate the antislavery delegates, because it is impossible to say for sure that their willingness to go along with these three provisions was indeed the absolute minimum degree of cooperation required to placate the proslavery delegates. After all, quitting the Union would have exacted a high price from the South as well; the South too had an incentive to compromise to keep the Union intact. But if one accepts the premise that abiding with slavery was necessary to preserve the Union, then the Northerners may be given credit for not making a far worse deal, one that indicated positive approval for slavery and provided it with moral legitimacy.

Obviously, scrupulous attention to the wording of proslavery provisions provided no solace for those doomed to remain in chains. But the Constitution's wording, which deprived the defenders of slavery of any additional moral ground to stand on, provided later opponents of slavery with a crucial moral advantage. If the document had directly endorsed slavery, Abraham Lincoln would not have been able, decades later, to claim that the cause of the Union, a cause rooted in the Constitution, required that slavery be curtailed. The convention's insistence on treating slavery as a necessary evil, rather than a positive good, enabled Lincoln to argue that the Framers intended to confine slavery in the expectation that it ultimately would die. This expectation, Lincoln insisted, demonstrated their belief that "a house divided against itself could not stand"; and it justified Lincoln's position that a defense of the Constitution required that slavery was wrong and must ultimately be abolished.

Slavery was officially ended by the Thirteenth Amendment to the Constitution. Box 2 explains the process by which the Constitution can be changed.

Box Two: Nuts and Bolts

Amending the Constitution

The Framers wanted it to be both possible and difficult to amend the Constitution. They knew that they could not completely account for all the future needs of the nation and therefore it was necessary to allow for changes in the plan of government. But, for the most part, they hoped that change would be accomplished through legislation and would not require tampering with the fundamental principles and designs the Constitution embodied. The more the people came to view those fundamentals as permanent the more they would come to cherish and revere them. Article V of the Constitution establishes a process for amending the Constitution, a difficult and complicated process.

Actually, Article V sets out two alternate methods for amending the Constitution. If two-thirds of the states demand it, Congress must call a convention for proposing amendments. This has never happened. Instead, all the twenty-seven amendments enacted thus far have been adopted as a result of the other method, which requires Congress to pass a proposed amendment by a two-thirds majority in each house. Then the amendment must be passed either by three-quarters of the state legislatures or three-quarters of state ratifying conventions, whichever method Congress chooses to require. In practice, this has meant three-quarters of the state legislatures. Perhaps, someday, the states will demand that a new Constitutional Convention be held. If so, one can only hope that the delegates chosen exhibit the same spirit of patriotism, compromise, and concern for the long run that their original counterparts displayed.

A Strong Executive

For the most part, the completed Constitution was based on the initial Virginia Plan as modified by the defenders of the states and of slavery. But there is one enormous exception to this description. Neither Madison nor his Anti-Federalist critics envisaged the establishment of a strong executive branch of government as provided for in Article II of the Constitution.

This part of the Constitution most owes its existence to the deliberative activity of the convention itself. In the end, the delegates agreed to create a powerful presidency that almost none of them would have been willing to accept beforehand. It was only as a result of continual debate over executive power that they came to accept this radical and uncomfortable idea.

The Virginia Plan was quite vague about the executive. It allowed for *either* an individual *or* a committee. Whatever it was, it would be elected by the legislature. This decision to keep it captive of the legislature reflected Madison's deep fear of despotism. Independence had come in a war against a king. Madison, like most of the other delegates, even those who favored a strong national government, feared creating another king. In fact, before the Constitution was written, the conventional wisdom held that strong executive power and democracy did not mix. Initially, Madison preferred to rely on the Senate to perform those tasks normally assigned to an executive. A few delegates, most notably Alexander Hamilton, Gouverneur Morris, and James Wilson, favored a strong and independent executive. But early on, they were a distinct minority. Hamilton's proposal for an "elective monarch" only served to distract the delegates from the challenge of creating a republican president.

The initial opposition to a strong executive melted slowly. The gradual change in mood took place as the delegates faced up to just how complex and difficult it would be to run a country that extended from Massachusetts to Georgia. They came increasingly to recognize that the decision to *have* a strong national government directly implied the creation of a strong executive able to administer it.

Several specific controversies dominated convention debate about the executive. Should it be single or plural? Should it be chosen by the legislature or in some other fashion? And should the chief executive be eligible for reelection? Although the discussions continued for many weeks, these questions remained unresolved. But the longer the convention lasted, the greater the momentum built for a strong and independent executive.

As the overall shape and format of the national government became clearer, the majority of the delegates began to recognize that such a bold effort needed a single identifiable person in charge as well as the means to make that person accountable and responsible. Thus, the delegates agreed to a single person rather than a committee because no one would be able to figure out whom to hold responsible if several different people participated in an executive decision. Allowing the executive to run for reelection gained favor because it provided a means for holding an incumbent accountable.

The final piece of the puzzle was resolved with the invention of the Electoral College. On the one hand, allowing the legislature to choose the president would violate the principle of checks and balances between the branches. The delegates had come increasingly to view this means of preventing tyranny by any one governing institution as a key to preserving liberty. On the other hand, direct election by the people would allow a demagogue to win – a popular but unscrupulous leader who would make false promises and exploit prejudices to gain power. Moreover, delegates from smaller states feared that the larger states would dominate such a process. The Electoral College provided that each state would choose its own electors, in proportion to their representation in Congress, and that

The final result

Each state is sized according to the number of votes it has in the electoral college

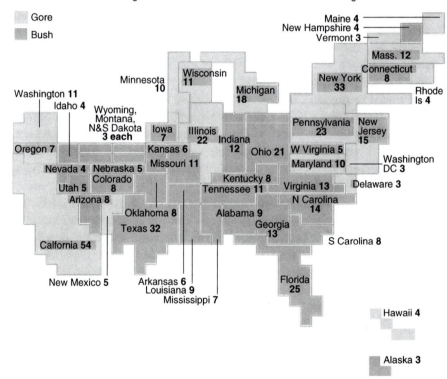

Figure 3.1. Electoral Votes per State for 2000 Presidential Election. The Electoral College magnifies the role of small states in presidential elections. This illustration shows states in proportion to their number of electoral votes. *Source:* electoral-vote.com, 2000.

the electors would choose the president (see Figure 3.1). This solution gave separate representation to each state in the electoral process, thereby reassuring the smaller states that they would indeed play a role in the choice. The indirect nature of the election empowered the people but also created a buffer – the electors – between the people and the choice of president. Proponents of election by the Congress were appeased because if no presidential candidate obtained an electoral vote majority, the choice among the leading candidates was to be made by the House of Representatives.

Box Three: Contemporary Politics

Was the 2000 Presidential Election a Popular Loss?

The 2000 presidential election marked the first time since 1888 that a candidate won the presidency while losing the popular vote. This result sparked calls by prominent American politicians – including Hillary Clinton, senator from New York and former First Lady – for the abolition of the Electoral College. Abolition was defended in the name of majoritarian democracy: the candidate who gets the most votes should win. The current rules enable a candidate to obtain narrow majorities in enough states to secure an Electoral College majority while losing other states by such wide margins as to lose the overall popular vote. Al Gore's popular-vote majority was accounted for in large measure by his landslide victories in two of the three most populous states, California and New York. Opponents of the current system also argue that this system discourages candidates from spending time and money in states that they know they cannot win. They concentrate their efforts on the close states, treating voters in "safe" states as if those votes did not count.

Supporters of the Electoral College acknowledge that it creates unfairness but argue that the cure is worse than the disease. They defend their support on the basis of the complex blend of liberal and democratic arguments that underlie American federalism. Federalism protects the interests of the smaller, less populous states against the bigger ones, and the Electoral College is a bulwark of that protective mechanism. If candidates needed to win individual votes rather than whole states, they would spend their time and money where those votes could be obtained most efficiently. They would saturate the largest metropolitan areas, which also constitute the largest media markets, with personal appearances and advertising. More sparsely populated places, especially those outside the major media markets, would be ignored. Furthermore, the need to win states requires candidates to pay attention to issues of concern to individual states. Otherwise, presidential campaigns would appeal to voters on other grounds – on the basis of their ethnicity, social class, or something else – but not on the basis of their status as citizens of a particular state.

The clamor for Electoral College reform that arose in the immediate aftermath of the 2000 presidential election vanished as quickly as it appeared. Americans are reluctant to tinker with the Constitution, even when they do not approve of a particular part of it. But the chorus of protest was also muted by the recognition that a constitutional amendment to alter the Electoral College had no chance of passing the Senate. Too many small, remote states would be disadvantaged by such a change, and those states each had the same number of senators as the big states did. Obtaining a two-thirds Senate majority was simply out of the question. Thus one pillar of the federal system intended to give states power over national policy, the Senate, protected another pillar of the federal system, the Electoral College.

Although these various elements of the executive were considered during the course of the entire convention, they were assembled into a single package only at the last minute by a committee appointed to propose final solutions for the important matters that the convention deliberations had left unresolved. When the overall proposal was presented to the delegates, they approved it overwhelmingly. In the course of a few months, most of them had traveled an enormous political distance, from opposing any independent executive to endorsing one that had a single person in control, was elected independently of the legislature, and was eligible for reelection. On no other question was the cumulative impact of all that deliberating so great.

Regardless of whether one adopted Madison's view of a strong executive as a restraining hand on an impetuously populist House of Representatives or Gouverneur Morris's view of the executive as the "general guardian of the national interests," the position of president emerged from the delegates' deliberations far stronger than any of the delegates could have imagined on the opening day of the convention. The delegates were all too aware that any plan for a strong executive would invite the enemies of the Constitution to condemn it as a monarchy. But they undoubtedly took considerable comfort from the knowledge that George Washington would be the first president. The powers of the president were "full great," Pierce Butler of South Carolina wrote the following year to a relative in England, "and greater than I was disposed to make them." They would not have been so formidable, Butler admitted, "had not many of the members cast their eyes toward General Washington as President; and shaped their ideas of the powers to be given a President, by their opinions of his virtue."

The New Science of Politics

The convention's adoption of novel institutional devices such as federalism and the presidency revealed just how open the architects of the new Constitution were to innovation. The Declaration of Independence, announcing the country's commitment to unalienable rights, had already signaled a novel experiment in combining democratic accountability and the dignity of the individual. Encouraging Americans to display equal daring in ratifying a new Constitution, Madison asked:

> Is it not the glory of the people of America that, whilst they had paid a decent regard to the opinions of former times and other nations, they have not suffered a blind veneration for antiquity, for custom, or for names, to overrule the suggestions of their own good sense, the knowledge of their own situation, and the lessons of their own experience.

The boldness of the convention's enterprise announced itself in the opening sentence of the preamble, "We the People of the United States." Its very first words signaled the Constitution's most revolutionary change: a loose agreement among the several states was to be transformed into a covenant between a single large national government and the individuals who composed it. Although the original United States, composed of the thirteen colonies that had rebelled against Britain, was very small by modern standards, it was by far the largest country that had ever attempted to govern itself according to the will of the people. Up to that time, all the impressive republics – Athens, Sparta, Venice – had been city-states. Once the Founders embraced the idea of a large republic, they recognized that they would have to invent a "new science of politics" in order to understand how to make it work. The fundamental concepts of the new science they invented form the foundation of American liberalism.

Size and Representation

The sheer arithmetic of large republics dictates that the actual work of government will be carried out not by the people themselves but by their representatives. In "Federalist No. 10," Madison took representation to be the very essence of what a republic is and the key to making it work effectively. Representation is what enables popular government both to remain popular and to avoid the otherwise inescapable difficulties posed by popular rule. Caught up, as they inevitably are, in the task of earning a living and tending to their families, subject to prejudice and passion, ordinary people are simply not capable of assuming the burdens of governance. At best, they can make reasonably good choices about who should govern for them and whether the record of those who govern is worthy of their continuing support.

Properly structured, the process of electing representatives enables ordinary people to hold their government accountable but does not place unreasonable burdens on them. Here again, size comes to the rescue. Bigger electoral districts are better than small ones because they contain a larger number of individuals fit to assume the mantle of leadership. They provide voters with a richer array of talent from which to choose. The keys to the new science of politics are therefore size and representation.

The republic must be of a sufficient size to ensure a great multiplicity of faction. It must also establish a representative system capable of balancing the legitimate concerns of citizens to hold representatives accountable with the representatives' need for freedom from excessive meddling by those who lack the expertise and the temperament to govern.

Designing the representative system is therefore a matter of creating the right blend of autonomy and accountability. Article I, establishing the Congress, provides the recipe. Its most important ingredient is *bicameralism*. The legislative branch of government consists of two separate houses. One house is more accountable, the other more autonomous. But since they both must agree in order for a bill to become a law, the overall legislative process ensures that accountability and autonomy are both sufficiently in the mix.

The House of Representatives was intended to be the more popular of the two houses. Its members would be kept relatively close to the people because they would have to run for election frequently, every two years, most likely from districts that were relatively small. (The Constitution does not mention district elections for the House, and they were not mandated by law until 1842). By contrast, senators, two from each state, would be elected for six-year terms. Once the delegates reached the Great Compromise – signaling their intention to define a middle ground between the

impotence of confederation and the danger of excessive centralization –
most also agreed that they wanted a Senate that might perform the role
of an "upper house." The Senate would not simply uphold states' rights
but would also check the excesses of the more popular House. Six-year
terms would insulate senators somewhat from the ebb and flow of popular
passions. The system of staggered elections, by which only one-third of
the Senate could change in any given election, would further enhance the
ability of its members "to refine and enlarge the public views." Those senators from the bigger states would be especially free from popular pressure.
The large size of their constituencies meant that they would represent a
diverse set of interests and would not slavishly serve any one narrow point of
view.

Because they enjoyed freedom from constituency pressure and because
their house was of manageable size, senators would be able to consider
public questions in a "cool and deliberate" fashion. They could be calm
and reasonable in ways that members of the House could not, providing
them, in Madison's view, with a special responsibility:

> Stimulated by some irregular passion, or some illicit advantage, or
> misled by the artful misrepresentations of interested men, [the people]
> may call for measures which they themselves may afterwards be the
> most ready to lament and condemn. . . . [At such times, they need] the
> interference of some temperate and respectable body of citizens . . . to
> check . . . the blow mediated by the people against themselves, until
> reason, justice, and truth can regain their authority over the public
> mind.

Checks and Balances

In addition to blending the virtues of accountability and autonomy, the
creation of a two-house Congress embodied the principle of checks and
balances. Each house of Congress would exert an independent check on the
other. The Founders assumed that people who entered politics were the sort
to push their ambitions to the utmost. Such ambitious people were desirable
recruits because they had the talent necessary to govern a large republic.
But if that ambition were not curbed, it would bubble over into tyranny.

To prevent the tyranny of a governing clique, the Founders not only
bisected the legislature but also set up an independent executive and judiciary. When they created these independent branches of government, the
Founders gave each branch sufficient power – and involvement in each
other's affairs – so that each branch's own ambitions would act to stalemate
the ambitions of the others. In the words of "Federalist No. 51":

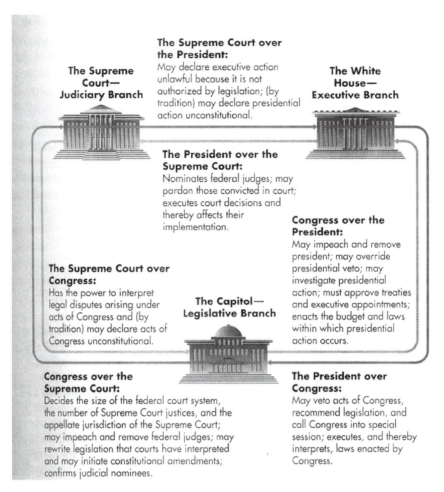

The Supreme Court over the President:
May declare executive action unlawful because it is not authorized by legislation; (by tradition) may declare presidential action unconstitutional.

The Supreme Court— Judiciary Branch

The White House— Executive Branch

The President over the Supreme Court:
Nominates federal judges; may pardon those convicted in court; executes court decisions and thereby affects their implementation.

Congress over the President:
May impeach and remove president; may override presidential veto; may investigate presidential action; must approve treaties and executive appointments; enacts the budget and laws within which presidential action occurs.

The Supreme Court over Congress:
Has the power to interpret legal disputes arising under acts of Congress and (by tradition) may declare acts of Congress unconstitutional.

The Capitol— Legislative Branch

Congress over the Supreme Court:
Decides the size of the federal court system, the number of Supreme Court justices, and the appellate jurisdiction of the Supreme Court; may impeach and remove federal judges; may rewrite legislation that courts have interpreted and may initiate constitutional amendments; confirms judicial nominees.

The President over Congress:
May veto acts of Congress, recommend legislation, and call Congress into special session; executes, and thereby interprets, laws enacted by Congress.

Figure 3.2. The System of Checks and Balances. The system of checks and balances was designed to ensure that ambition would not turn into a tyranny of the majority.

[T]he great security against a gradual concentration of the several powers in the same department consists in giving to those who administer each department the necessary constitutional means and personal motives to resist encroachments of the others.... Ambition must be made to counteract ambition. The interest of the man must be connected with the constitutional rights of the place,... [so] that the private interest of every individual may be a sentinel over the public rights.

Figure 3.2 shows how the system of checks and balances works. Congress checks the other two branches through its role in judicial and executive appointments and its power of impeachment. The Senate has final approval over the president's choices for judges, members of the Supreme Court, and members of the cabinet. If no presidential candidate garners a majority of the Electoral College, the House of Representatives elects the president. The House determines whether a judge, an executive official, or the president should be subject to an impeachment trial. If the House impeaches, then the Senate decides whether to remove the impeached person from office. Any treaty negotiated by the president with a foreign power must be ratified by a two-thirds vote of the Senate.

The president's greatest power over Congress resides in the ability to veto legislation. This power is far from absolute, however, because Congress can override that veto by a two-thirds vote of each house. The president also appoints the members of the Supreme Court and other federal courts and members of the cabinet, all subject to Senate approval. The importance of the president in making the complex system of representation work further reveals the Founders' objective of moderating democracy. The Founders' intention was that the presidency was to be a great national office that would draw strong leaders – those who would not be content merely to respond to public opinion but would seek to leave an enduring record of achievement.

The judiciary would also draw ambitious, talented individuals to its offices. Like the president, federal judges would be inclined to establish a record that resisted the momentary whims and destructive factionalism on the part of democracy.

The Constitution was not explicit in providing checks for the judiciary over the other two branches. Indeed, as we describe in Chapter 9, the issue of whether the Supreme Court had the power to declare acts of Congress unconstitutional remained hotly contested even after the Constitution was adopted. In "Federalist No. 78," however, Alexander Hamilton argued that the court did have such power and that its ability to declare laws unconstitutional was a crucial aspect of the checks and balances system. Because even a presidential veto could be overridden by Congress, the court needed this authority in order to prevent congressional despotism. Hamilton recognized that granting such great power to judges appointed for life was highly undemocratic. But he argued that because the judiciary was inherently the weakest branch of government, it was not in a position to abuse that power.

> The judiciary . . . has no influence over the sword or the purse. . . . It may truly be said to have neither Force nor Will, but merely judgment; and must ultimately depend upon the aid of the executive arm even for the efficacy of its judgments.

Checks and balances ensure that all three branches of government are interdependent and cooperative. President George W. Bush (executive) nominated Samuel Alito to the Supreme Court (judicial), whose nomination was then approved by Congress (legislative).

Hamilton further argued that judges alone had the knowledge and institutional means to uphold the law. Only they were fully competent to interpret the Constitution, and their lack of executive authority meant that they would not do so in a dictatorial fashion.

The Compound Republic

In addition to the checks and balances among the institutions of the federal government, the Constitution provided the overarching check of states' rights. The system of federalism made for a "compound republic," Madison observed, in which "the power surrendered by the people is first divided between two distinct governments, and then the apportion allotted to each subdivided among separate and distinct departments." The system of federalism thus ensured "a double security" in protecting "the rights of the people."

Madison, and most Federalists, generally understood that the powers of the national government were limited to those specifically enumerated in the Constitution. The states retained sole power over all legitimate governmental activities that the Constitution did not grant to the national government. Although the exact extent of that grant was ambiguous, it was understood to be limited to those matters that spilled over state boundaries, most prominently interstate and foreign commerce and national defense. All the rest – the routine but critical matters that affected the daily lives of people, such as education, policing, and road maintenance – were left to the states.

Furthermore, in spite of opposition by Madison and other ardent nationalists, the Constitution granted the states a good measure of influence within the national government itself. The president was to be elected by the Electoral College, whose members were chosen by the states and whose votes were cast on a state-by-state basis. The Senate gave equal representation to each state, and in the original Constitution, the senators were actually chosen by the individual state legislatures.

Finally, Article V of the Constitution gave the states an important role in the amendment process. Constitutional amendments, which required approval by two-thirds of both the House and Senate, also had to be ratified by three-fourths of the states. The Constitution also provided an alternative amendment method by which two-thirds of the states may call for a constitutional convention that would have the authority to propose amendments (see Box 2).

The new Constitution appeared to embody the natural rights tradition. It claimed to rest ultimate authority in people, but beheld institutional arrangements that would place many critical decisions, especially those relating to the economy and foreign affairs, at a great remove from ordinary citizens. Did this document go so far to protect individual rights that it failed to provide for an active and competent citizenry? Equally troubling, did the rights it ordained, which ignored the humanity of slaves, reduce the promises of the Declaration to a narrow, illiberal protection of property? These questions, turning on whether the new Constitution fulfilled or betrayed the principles of the Declaration, roiled the ratification contest in the states.

Ratification

In order for the draft Constitution to go into effect, it had to be adopted by nine states. After the convention ended its deliberations on September 17, 1787, and the Continental Congress agreed to abide by the ratification procedure that the document contained, the focus of political attention shifted to the states. The outcome of the state-by-state voting was by no means certain. All the states had prominent Anti-Federalists.

Anti-Federalist Objections

As the Anti-Federalist Patrick Henry forcefully argued at the Virginia ratifying convention, the opponents of the Constitution rejected the wording "We, the People" in favor of "We, the States." They recognized that the Constitutional Convention had gone against the instructions issued by the Continental Congress and that the very first words of the preamble had revolutionary consequences. Their preference was to marginally strengthen the national government without a major alteration of the Articles of Confederation. Anti-Federalists favored expanding national power sufficiently to remedy the specific grievances that had necessitated a constitutional convention in the first place. But they had no intention of departing from the essential principle of the Articles, which were that the United States was a compact of member states and that the essential loyalty of its citizens was to their individual states.

Despite their preference for direct citizen involvement, the Anti-Federalists did recognize the need for political representation. Even state capitals were too far away to enable most citizens to participate in state government. They also grudgingly acknowledged the need for some form of national government. But their innate distrust of representation led them to take a very different view of national government than did the Federalists. The Anti-Federalists' goal was to minimize the separation, both physical and psychological, between representative and constituent. They wanted the former to serve as a mirror of the latter. Therefore, they believed, representative districts should be as small as possible, enabling the representative to stay in touch with each constituent. Elections should be held yearly, giving constituents frequent opportunity to oust an incumbent who did not adequately reflect their concerns. No matter that the result would be a House of Representatives so large as to be unwieldy and whose members would serve such brief terms that they would not have a chance to become knowledgeable and competent. The loss of effectiveness and deliberative capacity, argued the Anti-Federalists, were small prices to pay to preserve democratic accountability.

The Federalists had seen a great opportunity in the existence of a relatively small representative body, the Senate, because it could serve as a classroom for mutual instruction among the representatives. For the same reason, the Anti-Federalists loathed the Senate. They recognized that its small size and infrequent election would encourage a strong sense of collegiality among its members. This was not the type of classroom or the kind of mutual instruction they favored. Anti-Federalists took the word *represent* literally. The task of the representative was to *re-present* the views of constituents to the representative body. The Anti-Federalists envisaged representatives returning home frequently to districts small enough to enable them to instruct constituents about the events taking place at the national capital and to receive instruction about how best to represent their constituents.

The Anti-Federalists similarly feared and loathed the proposed presidency. Having severed from a king, why now voluntarily succumb to a monarch? They opposed not only a commander-in-chief, but also the very idea of a standing army available for such a commander to lead. They admitted that the Union might face military danger, but they much preferred placing responsibility for defense in citizen militias, mobilized by the states, whose sole purpose was to respond to a military emergency. When the emergency passed, the militias would disband, and the country would not then have to worry about how to cope with the threat inevitably posed to its freedom by a standing army led by a powerful commander.

The Federalists recognized the practical advantages of a strong central government for a republic that might well grow to continental proportions. They favored those sorts of institutions that a strong central government required – a Senate, an executive, a standing army. The Anti-Federalists believed that republican liberties and virtues required the rejection of such inherently antidemocratic institutions regardless of their practical value. Anti-Federalists placed their trust in decentralized political institutions – the towns, the states, the militias. Whatever the practical defects of such institutions, argued the Anti-Federalists, they were far more amenable to popular control and therefore more compatible with freedom.

Ironically, Anti-Federalists attacked the Constitution both for protecting and inadequately securing slavery. Southern Anti-Federalists, such as Patrick Henry, savaged the proposal for a new government not only because its powerful executive would expose the country to an elected despotism; Henry also warned that a strong centralized government made possible the abolition of slavery, which would cripple the South's economy. Conversely, the Massachusetts Anti-Federalist, Consider Ames, who had participated in Shays's Rebellion, indicted the new Constitution for sanctioning and protecting an institution that denigrated the core principle of the Declaration. Just as Henry feared emancipation, so Ames feared the extension of slavery into free states like Massachusetts, which had outlawed slavery by judicial decree just a few years earlier. As the political scientist David Siemers has noted, "If Congress could pass whatever laws it thought necessary and proper, as the Anti-Federalists believed it could and those laws automatically trumped state laws, then the gradual nationalization of slavery policy was likely and both [Henry and Ames] feared the results of nationalization."

Federalists Triumph

The battle over ratification of the Constitution was fought out during the winter of 1787 and spring of 1788. In June of 1788, New Hampshire became the ninth state to ratify the document. Although technically New Hampshire's action was sufficient to put the new constitution into effect, the actual fate of the process was not clarified until ratification was approved by the two crucial states of Virginia (June 25) and New York (July 26). North Carolina chose to put off a vote, waiting to see whether the first Congress would follow through on proposing a bill of rights. Rhode Island did not take any action. Congressional and presidential elections took place early in 1789. George Washington received all the electoral votes and was inaugurated in New York in April of 1789.

The debates that preceded the ratification votes were long and heated. What ultimately enabled the Federalists to triumph was the same advantage they possessed in the Philadelphia convention: they had a specific, comprehensive, and detailed plan for governing the nation, and their opponents had none. Therefore, the Anti-Federalists were continually on the defensive, criticizing this or that feature of the Constitution but offering no broad alternative for how the new nation would sustain itself into the future.

The Federalists had a second advantage, which they obtained courtesy of their critics at the convention. Thanks to the compromises made to achieve the support of wavering delegates, the Constitution contained many important concessions to the Anti-Federalist point of view. In the debates over ratification, the Federalists were politically astute enough not to trumpet the radical innovations that the document contained but rather to emphasize its fundamental compatibility with the ideas and principles that Anti-Federalists held dear. This shrewd combination of arguments is shown to best advantage in *The Federalist Papers*, written, as we have noted, for the express purpose of gaining support for the Constitution in the politically

volatile state of New York. Each paper concentrated on either a particular reason for seeking change in the status quo, a particular advantage
offered by the new Constitution, or a refutation of some criticism about
the Constitution levied by the Anti-Federalists.

Taken as a whole, *The Federalist Papers* provided a systematic and comprehensive case for the necessity of revamping the Articles and for adopting a strong central government. They also persuasively argued that the
new government would preserve the most essential features and virtues of
the existing system, most important, the power and influence of the states.
Then, as now, a political campaign is usually won by whoever can most successfully appeal to the undecideds. The Federalists won because they could
convince citizens in the middle that their plan was both radical enough to
solve the problems posed by the weakness of government under the Articles of Confederation and conservative enough to protect the sovereignty
of the states.

A Bill of Rights

The Federalists found it wise to make an additional concession during the
ratification debates. They pledged that if the Constitution were adopted,
they would support the addition of a bill of rights, in the form of a series
of constitutional amendments. Many state constitutions already contained
bills of rights. In some cases, these rights were listed in the preamble of the
state constitution, as if to show that the details of institutional design that
followed should be viewed as the specific devices by which the goals set out
in the bill of rights were to be achieved.

The leading architects of the federal Constitution, including Madison
and Hamilton, had opposed including a bill of rights. They claimed to
oppose it because such a list was unnecessary for a government whose
authority was expressly limited to its enumerated powers. But this argument
cannot be taken at face value because in various parts of the Constitution
this principle of relying on enumeration is violated and specific protections
against government excess are provided. The deeper reason the Federalists
opposed a bill of rights may have been that the government they were
trying to put in place would not be strong enough and that its enemies
would make use of a bill of rights to weaken it still further.

Supporters of a bill of rights saw it as an essential means for explaining
to citizens what the purposes of the new government were and how the
public should judge it. This explanation was especially important to wavering Anti-Federalists who acknowledged the need for a stronger union but
found the proposed constitution devoid of any clear statement about how
it was to serve the greater goal of protecting liberty. They feared that later

generations would not fully realize that behind the Constitution lay the Declaration of Independence. In their minds at least, the Constitution was worthless if its various institutional contrivances were not explicitly dedicated to "unalienable rights." Therefore, they insisted that the Constitution be amended to enumerate the most essential components of those rights to ensure that future generations would be fully informed about what it was that their government had been established to protect.

Box Four: Nuts and Bolts

The Bill of Rights

Passed by Congress in 1789, only months after it came into session, and ratified by the states by the end of 1791, the Bill of Rights consisted of ten amendments to the Constitution. The First Amendment forbids Congress to establish a particular religion, to prohibit the free exercise of religion, or to abridge the freedom of speech, press, assembly, or petition to redress grievances. The Second Amendment ensures the right to keep and bear arms. The Third Amendment states that soldiers can be quartered in private homes only during wartime in "a manner prescribed by law." The Fourth Amendment protects against unreasonable searches and seizures. The Fifth Amendment forbids summary trials, double jeopardy, self-incrimination, and confiscation of private property without just compensation, and it guarantees due process of law. The Sixth Amendment guarantees a speedy trial, an impartial jury, the right to confront witnesses, and the right to be represented by counsel. The Seventh Amendment extends the right to trial by jury to civil cases. The Eighth Amendment protects against excessive bail and cruel and unusual punishment. The Ninth Amendment declares that the enumeration of specific rights in the Constitution does not imply that the people do not have other rights as well. The Tenth Amendment declares that those powers not delegated to the national government by the Constitution, nor specifically prohibited by it, are reserved by the states and the people.

The enduring importance and success of the Bill of Rights, its special place in the hearts of Americans, proved that its supporters were right. It is fitting that the lovers' quarrel among Americans over adoption of the

Constitution should have led in the end to such a critical improvement in the nature of their relationship.

Conclusion: The Enduring Contest

The Bill of Rights is one demonstration of the critical role played by the Anti-Federalists as well as the Federalists in founding the new government. The quarrels between these rivals were mostly resolved in favor of the Federalists. Not only did they succeed in convincing the convention to do more than amend the Articles of Confederation, but they also prevailed over the Anti-Federalists on two of the most contentious issues – the extended republic and the establishment of a direct connection between citizens and federal government. But the Anti-Federalists' enduring contribution both to the creation of the Constitution and to the subsequent development of American politics and government should not be underestimated. Even at the convention itself, where their ranks were thin, delegates with Anti-Federalist sympathies succeeded in forcing the Federalists to provide a much more powerful role for the states than delegates such as Madison or Washington were initially inclined to accept.

The inclusion of a Senate elected by and with equal representation of the states was a compromise forced on Federalists. Likewise, giving the states such a prominent role in the amendment process and providing for the election of the president by an electoral college organized on a state-by-state basis were also grudging concessions made to win over the support of wavering delegates with Anti-Federalist sympathies. These specific provisions add up to the creation of a new form of federalism that represented one of the Constitution's most imaginative and daring innovations.

In order to win passage of the Constitution in several undecided states, the Federalists made an additional public concession to the Anti-Federalists. They promised to cooperate in establishing a bill of rights in the form of a set of amendments to the Constitution and to do so as quickly as possible. Americans have come to view the Bill of Rights as an integral and cherished part of the Constitution, and they have the Anti-Federalists to thank for it.

Although the more extreme Federalists, such as Hamilton, had hoped to use the Constitution to enshrine the dominance of centralized national authority, they did not succeed. The Constitution itself left the relationship between central and local politics in a purposefully ambiguous tension. Sadly, this ambiguity would eventually result in civil war. But it also provided the opportunity for democratic politics to survive and thrive within a constitutional context. As the American republic developed in the nineteenth century, the national government remained small and relatively insignificant while state and local politics flourished. State constitutions were rewritten to permit and encourage democratic participation to an extent that would have warmed the hearts of Anti-Federalists (see Chapter 5). Democratic impulses gained a far greater grip on the national imagination than the Federalists expected or hoped. The key success in the framing of the Constitution was not to settle the conflict between liberalism and democracy but rather to create a strong and resilient framework within which these two indispensable aspects of the American creed could continue to fruitfully collide and coexist.

Chapter Summary

☆ The principles and sentiments that the Federalists and the Anti-Federalists shared were more important than those that divided them.

☆ The deepest division between Federalists and Anti-Federalists occurred with regard to the relative merits of the large and the small republic.

☆ The key principles that define American constitutionalism are popular sovereignty, natural rights, limited government, enumerated powers, and the separation of powers.

☆ The success of the Constitutional Convention was due to the political capacities of the delegates – their capacity to deliberate, to compromise, and to understand how specific decisions about the design of the government would affect the ability of that government to endure.

☆ The two most controversial issues at the convention were the differing views about representation held by the large states and the small states, and the insistence by the slave states that slavery be protected. These differences resulted in compromise. The Senate was designed to protect the interests of the small states and several specific protections were inserted to safeguard slavery.

☆ After much hesitation, the convention accepted the principle of a strong, unitary executive chosen indirectly by the people.

☆ In order to reconcile the need to make the legislature accountable and to enable it to deliberate, the convention established two houses of the legislature – the House of Representatives, which was highly accountable, and the Senate, which enjoyed a greater degree of autonomy.

☆ In addition to separating power among the three branches of government, the convention gave each branch some specific means for intervening in the affairs of the other two, thus providing for a system of checks and balances.

☆ In addition to checks and balances between the branches, the convention created a federal system in which the states and the national government check the power of one another.

☆ The Bill of Rights was adopted to dispel Anti-Federalist fears of tyranny and also to make crystal clear to the people that the Constitution was dedicated to the preservation of liberty.

Major Concepts

Anti-Federalists
bicameralism
Bill of Rights
checks and balances
constitutionalists
enumerated powers
Federalists
nationality
natural rights
New Jersey Plan
separation of powers
slavery
Virginia Plan

Suggested Readings

Bailyn, Bernard. *The Ideological Origins of the American Revolution.* Cambridge, MA: Harvard University Press, 1992.

Bowen, Catherine Drinker. *Miracle at Philadelphia: The Story of the Constitutional Convention, May to September, 1787.* New York: Book of the Month Club, 1966.

Chernow, Ron. *Alexander Hamilton.* New York: Penguin Books, 2004.

Fallon, Richard. *The Dynamic Constitution: An Introduction to American Constitutional Law*. New York: Cambridge University Press, 2004.

Farrand, Max, ed. *The Records of the Federal Convention of 1787*, 4 vols. New Haven, CT: Yale University Press, 1966.

Hamilton, Alexander, James Madison, and John Jay. *The Federalist Papers*, ed. Charles Kesler. New York: Mentor Books, 1999.

Jensen, Merrill. *The Articles of Confederation*. Madison: University of Wisconsin Press, 1963.

McDonald, Forrest. *The Formation of the American Republic*. New York: Penguin, 1967.

Rakove, Jack. *Original Meanings: Politics and Ideas in the Making of the Constitution*. New York: Knopf, 1997.

Rossitor, Clinton. *1787: Grand Convention*. New York: Macmillan, 1966.

Siemers, David. *The Anti-Federalists: Men of Great Faith and Forbearance*. Lanham, MD: Rowman and Littlefield, 2003.

Storing, Herbert, ed. *The Complete Anti-Federalist*, 7 vols. Chicago: University of Chicago Press, 1981.

_____. *What the Anti-Federalists Were For*. Chicago: University of Chicago Press, 1981.

Wood, Gordon. *The Creation of the American Republic*. New York: W. W. Norton, 1982.

_____ *The Americanization of Benjamin Franklin*. New York: Penguin Books, 2004.

4 Political Development

Crucial Episodes

Chapter Overview

This chapter focuses on:

☆ The crucial episodes of American political development and how each sought to balance democracy and rights

☆ The idea of a *constitutional refounding* and how it was central to each crucial episode

☆ The role of race and religion in American political development

☆ The persistence of limited, decentralized government in the nineteenth century

☆ The expansion of national government and national administrative power during the twentieth century

On August 9, 2001, President George W. Bush delivered the first prime-time special presidential address of the twenty-first century. Surprisingly, he did not speak about issues that had dominated the 2000 campaign and the first seven months of his presidency – issues such as taxes, Social Security, healthcare, and relations with China and Russia. Rather, he spoke about his decision to allow the federal government to fund embryonic stem cell research. These cells come from the excess embryos that result during medical efforts to implant embryos in women. Embryonic stem cell research offers promise for treating Alzheimer's disease, Parkinson's disease, diabetes, and spinal cord injuries.

Bush posed two fundamental questions. Were embryos human life? And, because the embryos were otherwise going to be destroyed, shouldn't they be used instead for research that had the potential to save lives? These questions entailed debate not only about scientific ethics but also about the proper relationship between church and state. Many religious conservatives viewed stem cell research as a form of abortion. When President Bush visited the Vatican a few weeks before his speech, the Pope urged him to "reject practices that devalue and violate human life at any stage from conception, until natural death." But most Americans, and most Catholics, supported stem cell research, viewing it as a scientific and medical issue beyond the church's jurisdiction. Before President Bush made his decision, several conservative Republicans, including former first lady Nancy Reagan and Utah senator Orrin Hatch, urged him to support federal funding. Mrs. Reagan had witnessed her husband's devastating experience with Alzheimer's. Which side, after all, was pro-life?

President Bush tried to bridge the two sides of the debate by allowing federal funds only for research that used embryos that had already been donated by fertility clinics, embryos that were already doomed to destruction. But he prohibited the national government's support of research that involved the creation or destruction of additional embryos. "As your president . . . I have an important obligation to foster and encourage respect for life. . . . Human life is a sacred gift from our creator."

Stem cell research did not arouse the same passionate debate abroad. Great Britain and Japan treated it as a technical policy decision, left to expert commissions and the bureaucracy. Even Italy, which is 95 percent Catholic, did not engage in heated parliamentary debate, treating it instead as an administrative matter. President Bush's predecessor, Bill Clinton, had relied on guidelines issued by an expert administrative agency, the National Institutes of Health, which permitted embryonic stem cell research.

But Bush claimed that America's strong commitment to democracy and religion made such an administrative approach unacceptable. The Clinton administration's guidelines, Bush said, aroused "a national debate and dinner table discussions" that required Bush to submit them to more careful public scrutiny. But he did not call on the nation's representative assemblies – the Congress and the state legislatures – to debate the issue. Rather, Bush established his own commission of experts to consider the question and issue a report. By doing so, he was tacitly acknowledging that the question was not suitable for democratic deliberation. Like so many scientifically and technically complex policy issues, the issue of stem cell research was simply too difficult for ordinary people, or even their representatives, to resolve meaningfully. Thus, the public's role in the stem cell debate was left as uncertain as it had been before. If public debate over stem cells was truly required, why should the issue be resolved by experts? What was the democratic significance, if any, of the president taking the trouble to think hard, pray, and consult his cabinet, friends, even the Pope?

In the end, the immense appeal of medical progress made it impossible for the Bush White House to resolve the stem cell controversy administratively. The debate fell dormant for a time after September 11, 2001, when the country's attention shifted to the war on terrorism. By 2004, however, a growing demand for stem cell lines, evidence that stem cell research had blazed ahead in other countries, and a new wave of pressure from activists, scientists, and Congress, renewed the debate over embryonic stem cells. The issue was dramatically injected into the 2004 presidential campaign when Ronald Reagan, Jr., gave an address to the Democratic convention appealing on behalf of his family for the restoration of federal funding. Bush's re-election, which turned principally not on "social" issues but rather on homeland and national security, did not settle the stem cell debate. Encouraged by the ongoing support of Nancy Reagan and public opinion, Congress, anticipating a competitive midterm election, took up stem cells seriously in 2006.

Undeterred by the threat of a presidential veto, which would be the first of the Bush presidency, the Republican leadership in the House and Senate supported legislation that would restore federal funding of stem cell research. Senator Arlen Specter, a Republican from Pennsylvania, and chairman of the Senate Judiciary Committee, which had primary responsibility for stem cell legislation, likened President Bush to those who scorned Columbus, imprisoned Galileo, and rejected anesthesia, electricity, vaccines, and rail travel. Specter's position was hardly surprising. A moderate, he frequently jousted with the White House. But Bush's stem cell position was also opposed by conservative Republican leaders in both chambers of Congress. Their close collaboration with the White House had allowed the president to avoid a direct confrontation with the legislature for the first five years of his presidency. Bush's frail hope of preempting a full legislative hearing was dashed by Senate Majority

Leader, Bill Frist (R-TN), a former transplant surgeon, who owed his position in no small measure to the White House's influence. Rescinding his earlier support for the Bush policy, Frist now insisted that "stem cells offer hope for treatment that other lines of research cannot offer."

In July 2006, Congress passed a bill to lift funding restrictions on human embryonic stem cell research. Although the bill passed in both chambers by comfortable margins, it did not have the two-thirds majority necessary to override Bush's veto. Nonetheless, Democrats kept the stem cell controversy alive politically – indeed, they made the demise of the popular measure an issue in the fall elections.

The stem cell controversy is a powerful reminder of the continuing tension that exists between democracy and liberalism. A free, secular society grounded in sacred truths and inalienable rights is the epitome of America's liberal tradition. In the previous chapter, we explained how the Framers devised institutional arrangements to buttress this tradition. The Constitution did not create a "pure" democracy but rather a "republican" democracy, with a strong president, a Senate, and an independent judiciary to moderate popular rule. One aim of creating so much space between the government and the people was to discourage great contests of opinion over the sort of profound religious and ethical issues raised by the stem cell question. But, as we have pointed out in all previous chapters, American liberalism's dominance is not complete. It has been influenced by, and sometimes competed with, a democratic tradition that is nurtured by religious beliefs and local self-government. As we discussed in Chapter 3, the Federalists did not have their own way in Philadelphia. At both the Constitutional Convention and the state ratifying assemblies, the Anti-Federalists exercised considerable influence. As a result, the Constitution, complemented by the Bill of Rights, provided more balance between the states and the national government and preserved a far more participatory local government than defenders of a strong union would have liked. The opponents of the Constitution joined Thomas Jefferson and other allies to fight for an even more democratic constitutional order. The great contest of opinion that ensued, culminating in Jefferson's election in 1800, showed that the Constitution could not always succeed in preventing public debate about divisive issues, including the very meaning of republican government. Indeed, such debates have recurred throughout American history.

The first section of this chapter connects Chapter 3's study of the Constitution with the critical political episodes that form the core of this chapter. The five subsequent sections focus on those episodes that are central to the development of the American nation: Thomas Jefferson's "revolution" of 1800, Andrew Jackson's *mass democracy*, the Civil War, and the New Deal. These major points of developmental transition each involve public debate and conflict about fundamental questions of American political life: the meaning of rights and how government can best protect them. These episodes reveal that liberalism and democracy can combine to reinvigorate constitutional government. Each episode was a *refounding* that engaged citizens in conflict and resolution about the meaning of the Declaration and Constitution for their own time. The final section of this chapter looks at contemporary politics in terms of the impact of all the various refoundings, especially the New Deal. The conclusion of this chapter revisits the question of whether the expansion of government during the twentieth and twenty-first centuries has undermined the capacity for self-rule and has made democratic deliberation over profound issues like stem cell research impossible. Our answer will be informed not only by contemporary public controversies like stem cell research that challenge what Jefferson characterized as the "wall of separation" between church and state, but also by a historical record that reveals American democracy's extraordinary resilience.

The Constitutional Founding

Americans tend to view the Constitution as the uncontested law of the land and to express pride in its enduring place in their politics. With the ratification of the Constitution, conventional wisdom has it, the foundation of American politics and government was solidly established. The Constitution has sustained the economic and political development of the United States for more than 200 years. Even critics of American politics tend to admire the Constitution's success. It has been so dominant, they lament, that the radical egalitarian movements it was designed to inhibit have never built up much steam. Critics attribute the American welfare state's arrested development, compared to other representative democracies, to the energy-sapping complexity of the constitutional system of checks and balances. Political scientist James Morone argues, "If the United States had been playing by parliamentary rules, it would have had [national health insurance] in 1949 (after Truman campaigned on the issue) – more or less on the same schedule as the [parliamentary democracies]."

Americans living at the time of the Constitutional founding would have been surprised by these views. They saw the Constitution as fragile and controversial. No sooner had it been ratified than Americans began to fight over its meaning. This contest led to the emergence of two fiercely divided parties, the Federalist party and the Republican party, that became engaged in a heated contest of principle. To a point, this contest was bounded by the liberal tradition. The Federalists, led by Alexander Hamilton, and the Republicans, led by Thomas Jefferson, both spoke the language of rights and accepted the "self-evident" truth that government existed to protect property and free enterprise. But the two parties disagreed fundamentally about the relationship between liberalism and democracy and about whether rights were best protected by limiting or by encouraging active citizen participation. Federalists believed that republican government rested in the deliberations of political representatives held at a considerable distance from popular opinion. Republicans championed the view, as Jefferson put it, that political authority "could be trusted nowhere but with the people in mass."

A Commercial Republic

A constitutional struggle broke out during George Washington's first term, thwarting his desire to place the presidency and the Constitution above partisan conflict. Washington's two most brilliant cabinet ministers – Alexander Hamilton, secretary of the treasury, and Thomas Jefferson, secretary of state – differed over Hamilton's program to strengthen government's finances. At the request of the first Congress, Hamilton issued a series of reports between 1790 and 1791 that called on the legislature to pay off the national debt, assume the war debts of the states, encourage manufacturing through the creation of a system of tariffs, and create a national bank. Jefferson opposed the national bank because he feared it would establish an unhealthy concentration of power in the national government, creating a dangerous tie between the capital and the country's wealthiest citizens, and because it was unconstitutional. Jefferson believed that democracy required a predominant agricultural sector, comprising small landholders of roughly equal wealth. Hamilton's commercial republic, Jefferson claimed, would breed inequality and moral decay, thus destroying the moral foundation of a free society.

Hamilton and his allies, identifying themselves as the respectable defenders of constitutional order, called themselves Federalists. Washington refused to adopt the label but tilted toward Hamilton. The Jeffersonians rejected the name Anti-Federalist and instead called themselves Republicans, sentinels of liberty standing against the Federalist threat. Republicans did not want to destroy the Constitution but did want to restore its balance between rights and popular rule, between liberalism and democracy. They opposed the expansion of national government authority because Congress would be forced to delegate more responsibility to the executive branch. The Republicans believed that such an "administrative republic" would make the more decentralized and popular institutions – Congress and the states – subordinate to the executive, would frustrate popular sovereignty, and would push the United States toward a British-style monarchy.

Foreign Policy and Executive Aggrandizement

France and the United States enjoyed a special relationship as a result of their 1778 alliance. Americans remained deeply grateful for the indispensable aid France gave during the independence struggle. The French Revolution in 1789 led to a further outpouring of American sympathy and support. But the French Revolution's radical turn in 1792, including the execution of the French king, divided Federalists and Republicans.

The Federalist Hamilton envisioned a dominant role for America's president in foreign relations. A great nation, he argued, must be a great empire. The Constitution gave the president more foreign authority than domestic authority; what is more, Hamilton claimed, only the executive was equipped to manage foreign affairs successfully. The war that took place between Britain and France in 1793 was a critical test of Hamilton's view.

Seeing the French Revolution as democracy running amok, Hamilton sought to ally with Britain. He pushed Washington to issue the Neutrality Proclamation of 1793 requiring the United States to disregard its existing treaty obligations to France. The Republican Jefferson lamented that abandoning republican France denigrated the American spirit of liberty. He believed that America's greatness did not come from imperial ambition but, as we pointed out in Chapter 2, from John Winthrop's vision of America as "a city upon a hill" and from Thomas Paine's vow that by dedicating itself to aspirations for individual freedom, America would "begin the world over again." France's revolution and subsequent adoption of republican government seemed to show that Paine and Winthrop's expectations were being realized.

Washington's Neutrality Proclamation had been issued without congressional consent. Republicans viewed the document as a declaration of no war and therefore the constitutional equivalent of a declaration of war, which could only be issued by Congress. Because the Constitution did not justify such an enlarged view of executive power, on what grounds could the Washington administration defend it? As Madison put it, "The powers of making treaties and the power of declaring war are royal prerogatives in the British government and are accordingly treated as executive prerogatives by British commentators." Republicans feared that Washington was copying the British by asserting his *prerogative*, that is, his right to act unilaterally whenever he deemed such action to be necessary.

Pro-British Federalists viewed pro-French Republicans as agents of a radical revolution whose aim was to destroy constitutional republicanism and replace it with the instability and fanatical egalitarianism of "pure" democracy. Whereas Republicans hoped that the democratic spirit embodied by the Declaration would inoculate the Constitution from monarchy, Federalists expected that Americans' devotion to individual rights would prevent republican government from degenerating into mob rule.

The First Refounding: Jefferson's Democratization of the Constitution

The first refounding of the nation was provoked by the deep difference of opinion that emerged during the Washington administration, and it reached fruition between 1800 and 1808, during Thomas Jefferson's two terms as president. The first refounding promoted democracy by endorsing and nurturing those political institutions and constitutional principles that Jefferson and his followers considered to be most democratic in character, such as free speech, legislative supremacy, and a powerful defense of states' rights.

The 1798 Sedition Act prohibited false accusations against the president or Congress, inciting further partisan debate over the relationship between free citizens and their elected government.

A Partisan Press and Free Speech

The first refounding was inextricably connected to two new forms of political communication and conflict: a popular press and political parties. The Republican attack on the Washington administration was not confined to the councils of government; it was also communicated directly to the public through newspapers. In early 1791, Hamilton helped start the *United States Gazette*. Jefferson and James Madison aided in the establishment of a competing Republican newspaper, the *National Gazette*, which appeared in October 1791. As the political struggle between the Republicans and Federalists intensified, the number of newspapers expanded dramatically, from fewer than 100 in 1790 to more than 230 in 1800. By 1810, Americans were buying 22 million copies of 376 newspapers annually, the largest newspaper circulation in the world.

Madison's essays in the *National Gazette*, published in 1791 and 1792, illustrated his opposition to the Federalists' concentration of executive power. Previously, Madison's fears of majority tyranny led him to support the Constitution's institutional arrangements for dividing and filtering the voice of the people. But now he sought to arouse a "common sentiment" among citizens in the various states against the consolidation of government power. Formerly a defender of nationalism, Madison became a champion of the states as agents for mobilizing public opinion against excessive consolidation. By working with Jefferson to organize the Republican party, Madison championed *political* centralization as a way of defending state and local interests against *governmental* centralization. He hoped to unite former Anti-Federalists, jealously attached to their states, with democratically inclined supporters of the Constitution who were more nationalist in outlook.

Previously, Madison had opposed Jefferson's notion that the "Constitution belongs to the living." He had warned against frequent public appeals about constitutional issues, fearing that popular contests over them would "carry an implication of some defect in the government" and thus "deprive the [Constitution] of that veneration which time bestows on everything." Continual constitutional discord would prevent the Constitution from becoming the American political religion. But Madison now believed that the Federalists had undermined the Constitution's system of checks and balances and had created a struggle between the many and the few. Now, Madison decided, it was necessary to provoke just the sort of popular constitutional debate he had previously opposed.

The terms of this debate were illustrated by the different ways in which Republicans and Federalists chose to celebrate the Fourth of July, which became a national holiday during the 1780s. The Federalists emphasized nationalism and made few, if any, references to the Declaration of Independence, whose anti-British character embarrassed the Federalists who now sought economic and political reconciliation with the mother country. Also, to claim that "all men were created equal" seemed too democratic. Federalists preferred to celebrate the Constitution – whose "more perfect Union" was dedicated to moderating America's democratic impulses – rather than to praise Jefferson's handiwork. Federalists took no comfort from remembering that President John Adams, a Federalist, had been an influential member of the Declaration's drafting committee.

Republicans, by contrast, celebrated the Declaration as a "deathless instrument," written by "the immortal Jefferson." They eagerly invoked its indictments of the British monarchy and recalled America's great debt to its sister republic, France. Republicans stressed above all the Declaration's opening paragraphs – proclaiming that all men were "created equal" with "unalienable rights"– which they celebrated as America's creed. The essence of that creed, one Republican newspaper claimed, was not to be celebrated merely "as affecting the separation of one country from the jurisdiction of another; but as being the result of rational discussion and definition of the rights of man, and the ends of civil government."

The Federalists tried to stifle the recurring constitutional debate that Madison was now advocating. The *Sedition Act* of 1798 made it a crime, punishable by fine or imprisonment, to make false accusations against the president, Congress, or the government. The debate over enforcement of the act marked a crucial turning point in the development of American democracy. Federalists claimed that they were not restricting free speech through the act but were suppressing malicious opinions that undermined respect for the Constitution and for republican government. The Republicans replied that in the heat of political battle, malicious falsehood would be confounded with legitimate dissent. Jefferson insisted that unlimited public debate was necessary to nourish republican principles and that false opinion could be safely tolerated so long as "reason is left free to combat it."

Pushed through Congress by Federalists and signed into law by Washington's successor, John Adams, the Sedition Act incited partisan intimidation, including attacks on leading Republican newspapers, and inspired twenty-five arrests, fifteen indictments, and ten convictions. In 1799, the resolutions that Madison wrote denouncing the arrests were adopted by the Virginia legislature. Jefferson wrote another set that was adopted by the Kentucky legislature. The positions that Madison and Jefferson staked out became a virtual party platform for the 1800 Republican campaign. The Sedition Act gave the Republican party a perfect opportunity to defend "the rights of man" and reclaim the "Spirit of '76."

Madison defended the Virginia Assembly's right to declare the Sedition Act unconstitutional and called on other state legislatures to join in resisting the offensive statute for the purpose of "leading to a change in the legislative [Congress's] expression of the general will." The reference to a general will invoked Jean-Jacques Rousseau, the eighteenth-century French philosopher who defended democracy as indispensable to a free society. It reflected Madison's revised understanding of the Constitution as relying not merely on effective institutional arrangements but also on national opinion, cultivated by civic associations in the states and localities.

Democratic Results

The Republican triumph over the Federalists in the 1800 election strengthened the democratic character of the Constitution. This shift toward democratic principles did not dismantle republican government, but it did put an end to Federalist efforts to restrain popular opinion and to secure ordered liberty through the creation of an administrative establishment in the nation's capital. Jefferson was the first president to invoke the authority of the "will of the majority." He denied that the president, not to mention the judiciary, could claim authority that did not rest ultimately with "the people in mass."

"Absolute acquiescence in the decisions of the majority," Jefferson declared in his first inaugural address, "is the vital principle of republics, from which there is no appeal but force, the vital principle and immediate parent of despotism." Representatives' views, even those of presidents, should not be privileged over ordinary Americans, for when the voices of democratic citizens were added together they represented the ultimate sovereign. These combined voices represented *public* opinion – a concept that would soon come to dominate American political culture.

The *Revolution of 1800* was not dedicated to strengthening mass opinion as it is understood in contemporary America, however. Rather, its objective was to strengthen the decentralizing and more democratic institutions of the Constitution – the states and the House of Representatives. The Republicans sought to limit the scope of central government authority so that it rarely touched people's lives. They cut taxes and spending. Jefferson pardoned everyone (mostly Republican newspaper editors) convicted under the recently expired Sedition Act. The decentralized republic that Jefferson bequeathed remained so until the Civil War. Box 1 shows that even today, despite its immense size, the United States retains a degree of local self-government, commitment to the rights of individuals, mistrust of elites, and lack of centralized rule unique among modern democracies.

The Scope of American Government in Comparative Perspective

In every European country, the cop on the corner is an agent of national, not local government. Typically, European school curricula are set by the national education department not a local school board. The government provides preschool education and pays for everyone's healthcare. Many people live in government-owned housing and, in some countries, work for government-owned companies.

In the United States, some aspects of crime, education, and health policy are set by the national government, but, for the most part, these areas of life are dominated by state or local government or by no government at all. Government regulates business, but, with the exception of the generation of electric power, it engages in very little productive economic activity. Public housing does exist but only a small percentage of the population lives in it. The United States has the highest percentage of family home ownership in the world. To summarize, the American national government is involved in a wide variety of activities but it plays a less dominant role in the life of the citizenry than its European allies do.

Republican faith in democracy was not absolute. Office was sought as a matter of honor, on the basis of accomplishments and service to one's country, not through active campaigning. Full citizenship rights, including the vote, were limited to men with property. Property qualifications were relatively modest – about two in three white males could vote in America compared to one in four in England – but most Republicans considered property to be an important barometer of independence and responsibility. Republican moderation was also evident in the decision to leave some important elements of the Federalists' economic program intact. The National Bank remained until 1811, when its charter expired. In 1816, after the War of 1812 with Britain made clear the need for some sort of currency control, the Republicans chartered a second bank.

Jeffersonians did not advocate a permanent mass party system. The Republican party was a temporary expedient for defeating the Federalists and restoring balance to the constitutional order. Having accomplished those tasks, it could safely wither away, restoring the non-partisan character of the Constitution. Jefferson's first inaugural address made overtures to Federalists, promising constitutional continuity and political moderation: "every difference of opinion is not a difference of principle. . . . We have all called by different names brethren of the same principle. We are all republicans – we are all federalists."

The demise of the Federalists ushered in the so-called Era of Good Feelings and appeared to restore the non-partisan character of the Constitution. By 1816, the Federalists had grown so weak that they stopped fielding a national ticket. In 1820, Republican president James Monroe was reelected without opposition. This restoration took place on Republican terms. The presidency became more accountable to public opinion and the national government more beholden to the states and localities.

Empire of Liberty

The Jeffersonian refounding did not end tensions between America's liberal and democratic traditions. Those tensions reemerged over westward expansion. Federalists feared it as a threat to order and stability. By contrast, Jefferson predicted that westward expansion would transform the United States into "an empire of liberty," which he hastened into being by purchasing the Louisiana Territory from France in 1803. It doubled the country's size, adding some 830,000 square miles. The Constitution made no provision for acquiring foreign territory and incorporating it into the Union. But constitutional niceties were overlooked so that this vast southwest territory could be added to "make room for the generations of farmers yet unborn," strengthening the rural and therefore the democratic character of the republic.

But this rural republic would soon be plagued by deep divisions over slavery, pitting differing understandings of liberty and democracy against one another. As we explained in Chapter 2, the Northwest Ordinance of 1787 banned slavery in those territories that would eventually become the states of Ohio, Illinois, Wisconsin, Michigan, and Indiana. This prohibition conformed to the Founders' view that slavery was a necessary evil to be confined to Southern states and condemned to ultimate extinction. But by 1803, antislavery sentiment had declined sufficiently to prevent an antislavery article from being written into the Louisiana Purchase treaty. When Missouri, part of the Purchase territory, applied to become a state in 1820, the status of slavery in the Southwest threatened to become a full-blown crisis. Jefferson, by then a private citizen, lamented, "This momentous question, like a fire-bell in the night, awakened and filled me with terror. I considered it at once the death knell of the Union."

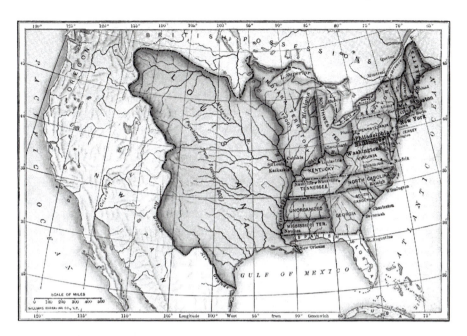

Thomas Jefferson believed that westward expansion would transform the United States into an "empire of liberty." To achieve this goal, Jefferson doubled the size of the country with the Louisiana Purchase of 1803.

Congress postponed the crisis by enacting the Missouri Compromise. Unlike the Northwest Ordinance, this legislation enshrined the sectional cleavage over slavery by drawing a clear geographical line between slave and free states. It banned slavery from all western territories north of Missouri's southern border, but admitted Missouri into the Union without any restrictions. Slavery supporters appealed to democracy in claiming that Missourians should be permitted to make their own decision about slavery. Opponents of the compromise argued that it effectively nullified the constitutional guarantee of "the full privileges and immunities of citizens in the several states" because African-American citizens lost their citizenship privileges upon entering Missouri soil. Thus, in the name of protecting local democracy, the compromise failed to protect inalienable rights as promised by the Declaration.

The Second Refounding: Jackson's Mass Democracy

Tensions over slavery simmered for several decades, but during the remainder of the 1820s and into the 1830s, they were subordinated to demands for more democracy for whites. Andrew Jackson, who was elected president in 1828 and reelected in 1832, was a powerful symbol of these democratic aspirations. Like the Jeffersonians, Jackson and his political allies sought to strengthen the democratic tradition that the Constitution had sought to tame. But the Jacksonians' political philosophy encouraged a much bolder assault on the principles and institutions of republican government that were dedicated to harnessing majority rule than the Jeffersonians had undertaken. By the 1830s, the word *democracy* had largely supplanted *republicanism* as a description of American government. Indeed the Jacksonians changed their party's name from Republican to Democrat. This change followed from the Jacksonian celebration of majority rule. The constitutional battles between Republicans and Federalists obscured their agreement about the need to moderate democracy through institutional checks and balances. The Jacksonians sought to reverse this equation and make the Constitution and its institutional arrangements servants of public opinion. Democracy did not displace liberalism in the Age of Jackson. Rather, Jacksonians sought to capture liberalism for the people. Thereafter, demands for rights would have to come to terms with a highly mobilized, competitive, and locally oriented democracy.

A leading Jacksonian journalist, John O'Sullivan, dismissed the Founders' fears of democracy: "We are opposed to all self-styled 'wholesome restraints' on the free action of popular opinion and will." He believed in a system of checks and balances, which prevented "precipitate legislation," but not "on any such forms of representation as, by length of tenure of delegated power, tend to weaken that universal and unrelaxing responsibility to the vigilance of public opinion." The historian and loyal Jacksonian George Bancroft wrote in 1826: "The popular voice is all powerful with us. . . . This is our oracle; this, we acknowledge, is the voice of God."

Andrew Jackson embodied this version of democracy. He was the first "outsider" president. His predecessors were highly educated and had undergone extensive apprenticeships in national politics and diplomacy. A self-made man, Jackson had little formal education, only brief experience in Congress, and no experience in the executive branch. In his first inaugural address, he stated the matter forthrightly: "the majority is to govern."

With Jackson championing the "will of the people," pressure mounted to open up the political process. By the late 1820s, most states had eliminated property qualifications for office holding and had expanded suffrage to include all adult white males. These reforms contributed to the rise of a new type of politician, a professional who sought office not for honor or duty, but to make a living. A leading Jackson loyalist, Martin Van Buren of New York, epitomized this new breed. The son of a New York tavern keeper, he lacked great oratorical skills or a magnetic personality. But he was a master organizer and tactician. His abilities carried him to the Senate, Jackson's cabinet, the vice presidency, and eventually the White House, where he succeeded Jackson in 1836.

Although the form of politics that Van Buren represented was less elevated than the great contest between Federalists and Republicans, it brought elections and government closer to the people. Symbolizing this easy familiarity, Jackson was nicknamed Old Hickory. Van Buren, from Kinderhook, New York, was called Old Kinderhook, abbreviated "OK." Eventually, OK became the common expression for "all right," signifying the great comfort and confidence that Americans came to have in their new democratic politics. Voter turnout soared. In 1824, only 27 percent of the eligible voters bothered to go to the polls. Four years later, when Jackson was elected, turnout doubled to 56 percent. In 1840, 78 percent of eligible voters cast ballots, a remarkable rate of participation that did not decline until the end of the nineteenth century.

A Party System

Political parties gave energy to American democracy. The Republicans had viewed their party as a temporary expedient for defeating the Federalists' program of "consolidation." Their successors, the Democrats, defended not just parties but a *party system* as a critical extraconstitutional device to make democracy work (see Chapter 11). Parties were the only means for cultivating strong attachments between the people and the fundamental law. "Political parties are the schools of political science," a Jacksonian newspaper editorialized, "and no principal can be safely incorporated into the fabric of national law until it has been digested, limited, and defined by the earnest discussions of two parties. . . . [Parties] diffuse knowledge, cultivate the popular mind, and as they tend to give the people larger liberties, prepare them for enjoyment."

The Democratic party organized voters on the basis of decentralizing principles and practices. Jackson sought to establish the president, rather than Congress, as the principal agent of popular rule. But as historian Marvin Meyers has written, Jackson "mobilized the powers of the government for what was essentially a dismantling operation." The federal budget was cut, road projects were vetoed, and most significantly, Jackson vetoed renewal of the Bank of the United States, which the Jeffersonians had learned to live with. The bank was killed, and its deposits reinvested in selected state banks.

Viewed through the lens of contemporary mass democracy, in which attacks on "big government" are carried out in the name of protecting personal property and privacy, the Democrats' dismantling operation might appear to have been radically individualistic, pandering to what Alexis de Tocqueville called "egoism" (see Chapter 2). In fact, the Democrats were more committed than the Jeffersonians to preserving the integrity of local communities and to collective assertions against the rich and powerful. The Democratic party itself embodied these decentralizing principles. During the Jeffersonian era, national politics centered on the congressional caucus, which had the power to nominate candidates for president and vice president. As we point out in Chapter 8, the Democrats replaced "King Caucus" with national nominating conventions dominated by state party conventions whose delegates sprang directly from the rank and file. To extend this grassroots politics into government, the Jacksonians were committed to rotation in government office, using the president's appointment and removal power to give jobs to partisan loyalists. New York senator William Marcy, a militant Jacksonian, described the credo of the new patronage system: "to the victors belong the spoils of the enemy."

By the end of the nineteenth century, reformers would attack the *spoils system* as a corrupting influence on government. But patronage politics was conceived originally to extend the people's control over the executive branch, to confirm the transformation from republican government to democracy. The Democrats' commitment to limited and decentralized government made it possible to claim that federal officeholders, many of whom served in widely scattered custom houses and post offices, could safely be recruited from the rank-and-file citizenry. As Jackson put it in his first annual message to Congress, "The duties of all public officers are, or at least admit of being made, so plain and simple that men of intelligence may readily qualify themselves for their performance."

Patronage did not always serve democratic principles well. The lust for government jobs could exalt party organization as an end-in-itself – to the detriment of firm attachments to principles and programs. Nonetheless, the mechanism of periodic replacement of a substantial part of the government established the material basis for a mass party that mobilized large turnouts in presidential elections and thus counteracted "general indifference" to political life, which Tocqueville identified as the greatest threat to liberty in a *commercial republic* like the United States. Prior to the 1830s, the spoils of office usually referred to the benefits that legislators bestowed on their constituents. Following the rise of the Democratic party, spoils came to refer to the perquisites that party leaders lavished on campaign workers. As the historian Richard John has written, "Rather than something to fight for, the spoils became . . . something to fight with."

Decentralist, patronage-based democracy became so dominant that the *Whigs*, the opposition party formed against Jackson's bank veto, also committed themselves to it. They too claimed descent from Jefferson and praised his celebration of the dignity of the democratic individual. Desperate to escape the Federalists' fate, the Whigs did not attempt to construct a strong executive. To avoid appearing elitist, Whig leaders such as Henry Clay of Kentucky and Daniel Webster of Massachusetts sought to convey the impression that they were less well educated and privileged than they actually were.

The Whigs set the precedent for how an opposition ought to behave in a party system. They did maintain and express important political differences from the Democrats. They believed in a much stronger federal government than did the Jacksonians. They supported a federally controlled national banking system and federal funding of roads, canals, and other forms of internal improvements. They also sought to strengthen Congress and keep a stronger check on the executive. But in the midst of these differences, they did not challenge the core Jacksonian commitment to local self-government. Nor did they question the legitimacy of the other party, tacitly admitting that both they and the Democrats were loyal supporters of the Constitution.

Democratic Nationalism

This bipartisan celebration of decentralization raised the question of whether a strong, centrally governed union was necessary at all. In 1832, South Carolina's legislature summoned a state convention to force the federal government to bow to its demands for a lower *tariff*, that is, the tax imposed on imported goods. The convention passed an ordinance forbidding tariff collections in the state and threatening to secede if the federal government responded by blockading Charleston harbor or other use of force.

South Carolina's action was inspired by its leading statesman, Vice President John Calhoun, whose *nullification doctrine* held that a state could declare any federal law it deemed unconstitutional to be inapplicable within its borders. Calhoun sought to gain credibility by linking nullification to Jefferson's Kentucky resolution that defended a state's right to declare acts of Congress unconstitutional.

Calhoun's invocation of Jackson's hero, Jefferson, had no effect on Jackson, who issued a proclamation vigorously rejecting South Carolina's nullification, labeling it unconstitutional. Jackson placed the responsibility to defend the Union squarely on the president's shoulders. Jackson thus gave voice to the rising spirit of democratic nationalism, which sustained and strengthened the Union in the face of sectional conflicts over the tariff and slavery. The final pages of the proclamation, imploring the

South Carolinians to embrace the nation, were a hymn to the glories of American democracy: its growing worldwide reputation; its success in preserving liberty; and its advancements in commerce, arts, science, and religion. The Whigs shared this vision of democratic nationalism; Daniel Webster proclaimed, "Liberty and Union, now and forever, one and inseparable!"

Ultimately, this faith in democratic nationalism united Democrats and Whigs. Even as they battled over the constitutional and policy questions involved in the bank controversy, both parties agreed that the matter should be settled democratically, in the court of public opinion. Consequently, the 1832 election was a *national* partisan contest over Jackson's veto. His overwhelming defeat of Whig nominee Henry Clay convinced even his political opponents that the veto had been sustained. Jackson's triumph thus transformed the Democratic doctrine of local self-government into a *national* creed. Because the partisan battle was fought within the confines of the Declaration of Independence and Constitution, a peaceful resolution was possible. The bank fight was not really the sort of class conflict between rich and poor that Madison feared. Both Democrats and Whigs spoke the language of rights, including the protection of property, and fought for constitutional interpretations and policies that supported their understanding of those rights.

Jacksonians believed that destroying the bank did not threaten a free economy but instead honored it. They hoped to unleash the commercial spirit from the shackles of government-created monopolies such as the bank, which favored idle speculators over the productive members of society: farmers, laborers, and mechanics. The clarion call of Jacksonian democracy, "equal rights to all and special privileges to none," promised political and economic independence to the producing "bone and sinew of the country." Similarly, this independence required local self-government, a deep and abiding effort, as the Democratic governor of New York, Horatio Seymour, put it, "to distribute each particular power to those who have the greatest interest in its wise and faithful exercise."

Popular Sovereignty

By the 1830s, what made America most distinctive was its faith in popular sovereignty. Its commitment to collective political action and economic independence established a common identity, creating a sense of nationalism in a country otherwise separated by sectional, religious, and ethnic differences. Walt Whitman, the self-styled "poet of democracy," boasted of America's "[g]rand common stock!... [that] planted the standard of freedom" and would "test the capacities of men for self government."

Other commentators, especially European visitors, viewed American democracy less romantically. They acknowledged the robust nature of political participation and the economic prosperity of Jacksonian democracy but disdained American provincialism and its mean-spirited, materialistic culture. "No stigma attaches to the love of money in America," Tocqueville wrote, "and provided it does not exceed the bounds imposed by public order, it is held in honor." Even the English philosopher Adam Smith, famed as the apostle of capitalism, viewed American individualism as indifferent to moral concerns and criticized the country's "unnecessary and excessive enterprise."

But it was slavery, not greed, that Europeans viewed as America's greatest sin. It gave the lie to the Jacksonian claim that popular sovereignty was compatible with natural rights and to the boast that America was the "Land of Liberty." "For the first time in my life," the English aristocrat Thomas Hamilton wrote, "did I bless God for the whiteness of my skin." From the perspective of Europeans, slavery showed most clearly how Americans were content to turn everything, even human beings, into a commodity. Slavery defiled America as a "city upon a hill," an inspiration for the rest of the world.

Religion's Role

Neither Whigs nor Democrats sought to engage Americans in a contest of opinion over slavery. Both were *national* parties, and their leaders feared that such a sectional struggle would fracture the Union. But the party system could not long suppress such a profound moral issue. Fittingly, the movement against slavery grew out of the churches. Evangelical Christianity, today considered a conservative force, was then a powerful reform agent. Animated by the religious revival efforts of the 1830s, called the *Second Great Awakening*, religious groups organized Sunday schools, spread the Gospel, opposed drinking, worked for peace, and fought slavery.

Abolitionists sought to extend their influence through religious societies. There were forty-seven abolitionist societies in 1833, and more than 1000 by 1837. Antislavery preachers moved from town to town, organizing new chapters and enlisting reform-minded church members, especially women, in petition drives to place antislavery motions before Congress. Although abolitionists operated outside regular political channels, they benefited from the spread of mass democracy. Appealing to a public already accustomed to following national political debates, the abolitionists flooded the country with newspapers, pamphlets, tracts, and pictures calculated to arouse African Americans, free and slave, and Northern public opinion against forced servitude.

Slavery and Free Debate

The Jacksonian Democrats sought to repress abolitionism. In his 1835 annual message to Congress, President Jackson, whose hero, Jefferson, had fought against censorship, called for a national law barring "incendiary" materials from the mails. When Congress did not pass the law, Jackson imposed it administratively, ordering postmasters to remove antislavery material from the mails. Jackson's action drew little opposition from the political establishment. Even in the North, most Democratic and Whig newspaper editors viewed abolitionism as a threat to peace and union. But Jacksonian democracy had unleashed popular forces beyond its leaders' control. Hundreds of petitions with tens of thousands of signatures poured into Congress, pressing for the abolition of slavery in the nation's capitol and asking that neither Florida nor Texas be added to the Union as slave states.

In a last, desperate attempt to stifle debate, House leaders proposed a "gag rule" that prohibited the House from discussing or even mentioning the antislavery petitions. The gag rule passed in 1835 with Jackson's strong support and was tightened in 1840 during the term of his successor, Martin Van Buren. This affront to democracy was turned to the advantage of the antislavery forces by Jackson's old political rival, John Quincy Adams, who had been elected to the House in 1834. Adams adroitly exploited reverence for the Declaration of Independence and popular rule to defeat the gag rule. In January 1842, Adams presented an antislavery petition from a town in his district and ordered the House clerk to read the Declaration of Independence – reminding the House that popular rule rested on unalienable rights that slavery defiled. Adams exploited the gag rule controversy to remind white people that the basic right of free speech was also under attack. Thus, he was able to enlist support from Americans who, regardless of their views on slavery, believed that the House should remain a free and open arena for democratic debate. The House repealed the gag rule in 1844.

The Third Refounding: Civil War and the Reconstruction of the Union

The third refounding took place in response to the slavery controversy, which reached a fever pitch during the 1850s and which threatened to dissolve the Union. Even before becoming president in 1860, Abraham Lincoln defined the terms of this refounding. It entailed not only a decision to keep the Union intact but also a rededication of the Union to the principles of the Declaration of Independence. On these principles was fought the greatest challenge to the viability of the American constitutional order: the Civil War.

The Debate over the Meaning of Democracy

A national debate over slavery exploded with the enactment of the 1854 Kansas-Nebraska Act. Sponsored by Senator Stephen Douglas and supported by President Franklin Pierce, the act repealed the Missouri Compromise and enabled the Kansas and Nebraska territories to adopt slavery. The bill represented the corruption of Jacksonian democracy by slavery and the spoils system. It passed Congress because of Pierce's heavy-handed use of patronage and was justified as a logical extension of the Democrats' commitment to local self-government (the resident voters would decide whether the new territories should enter the states as free or slave states). In his debates with Abraham Lincoln during the 1858 Illinois senatorial election, Douglas justified Northern Democratic defense of "popular sovereignty" on the grounds that government in the United States was "formed on the principle of diversity in the local institutions and laws, and not on that of uniformity.... Each locality having different interests, a different climate, and different surroundings, required different local laws, local policy and local institutions, adopted to the wants of the locality."

The new Republican party, which had replaced the Whigs in the wake of the Kansas-Nebraska controversy, believed that Douglas's position defiled the Declaration of Independence. Lincoln mocked the idea that "if one man would enslave another, no third man should object," insisting that it was the height of hypocrisy to call that position "popular sovereignty." He granted that the national government had no right to interfere with slavery where it was already established. But he was unwilling to tolerate its extension into the territories, which would undermine the best features of American political culture by depriving the Constitution of its moral foundation, the Declaration of Independence.

Drawing on a verse from the Bible's Book of Proverbs – "A word fitly spoken is like apples of gold in pictures of silver" – Lincoln praised the Declaration's principle of "liberty to all" as the essence of American political life. "The assertion of this principle, at the time was the word 'fitly spoken' which has proven an 'apple of gold' to us. The Union, and the Constitution, are the pictures of silver, subsequently framed around it. The picture was made, not to conceal, or destroy the apple, but to adorn and preserve it."

Before Lincoln, Thomas Jefferson and Daniel Webster had invoked the Declaration as the nation's creed and had shown the link between its moral principles and the institutional arrangements of the Constitution.

But Republicans were less willing to compromise this relationship than Jefferson or the Whigs had been. As historian Daniel Walker Howe has observed, Lincoln reinterpreted Jefferson to make "the proposition that all men are created equal... a positive goal of political action, not simply a pre-political [or *natural*] state that government should preserve by inaction." The Declaration, Lincoln maintained, "did not mean to assert the obvious untruth, that all were actually enjoying that equality, nor yet, that they were about to confer it immediately upon them. They meant simply to declare the *right*, so that *enforcement* of it might follow as fast as circumstances should permit." The principles of the Declaration, therefore, were to be "constantly looked to, constantly labored for, and even though never perfectly attained, constantly approximated."

Douglas insisted that the "signers of the Declaration had made no reference to the Negro whatever, when they declared all men to be created equal," instead reserving such equality for whites. Lincoln retorted that denying African Americans a share in the Declaration threatened to transform slavery from a necessary evil into a positive good, a moral right, and thus risked "a gradual and steady debauching of public opinion." In the United States, where popular sovereignty was everything, the consequences of such a change in the public mind would be devastating. Douglas's impropriety was compounded in 1857 by the *Dred Scott* decision (see Chapter 9). Authored by Roger Taney, chief justice of the United States and a militant Jacksonian, the decision declared any act of Congress or territorial legislatures that abolished slavery to be unconstitutional.

In part, the debate between Lincoln and Douglas involved a struggle for the soul of Jacksonian democracy. Douglas supported the worst side of Jacksonianism, the commitment to white supremacy; Lincoln championed the best side, commitment to the rights of the common American. Like his hero Jefferson, Lincoln sought to engage the American people in another refounding, one that went further than Jefferson's Revolution of 1800 or than Jackson's mass democracy, one that truly reconciled rights, or liberalism, and democracy.

The Role of Rhetoric

The importance that Lincoln and his political allies placed on a revolutionary transformation of public opinion caused them to focus their attention on rhetoric. Lincoln was perhaps the greatest political orator in American history; much of his political power derived from his mastery of words and his ability to make them justify political action. His speeches endowed the Union with a religious aura, incorporating the principles of the Declaration into America's political and constitutional practices. Lincoln's impressive

Abraham Lincoln's address at the site of the
Gettysburg battlefield in 1863 established
the Declaration of Independence, not the
Constitution, as the nation's founding
document.

debates with Douglas did not win him the 1858 Senate election. As provided for in the original Constitution, the Illinois state legislature, not the voters, determined the outcome, and it chose Douglas. But Lincoln's impressive campaign did not go unnoticed. Indeed, it laid the foundation for Lincoln's election as president over Douglas two years later.

Lincoln's presidency was consumed by the Civil War. He took actions during the war, such as the suspension of habeas corpus, that were highly controversial (see Chapter 8). But as the Massachusetts senator Charles Sumner said in his 1865 eulogy for the slain president, Lincoln's words were more important and enduring than the battles that determined the outcome of the contest between North and South.

Lincoln's rhetoric did not invoke the image of military glory. In his 1863 Gettysburg Address, Lincoln defined the war's aim as a preservation of America's constitutional heritage, a devotion that required the country to adopt a steady, measured course toward a new founding. Its opening lines, "Four score and seven years ago our forefathers brought forth on this continent a new nation, conceived in Liberty, and dedicated to the proposition that all men are created equal," established the Declaration, not the Constitution, as the nation's founding document. In 272 carefully chosen words, he expressed the larger purpose of the sacrifices made on the hallowed Gettysburg battlefield:

> From these honored dead we take increased devotion to that cause for which they gave the last full measure of devotion – that we here highly resolve that these dead shall not have died in vain – that this nation, under God, shall have a new birth of freedom – and that government of the people, by the people, for the people, shall not perish from the earth.

From Scripture to Obligation: The Thirteenth, Fourteenth, and Fifteenth Amendments

As we explain further in Chapter 8, Lincoln matched his words with deeds, pressing for adoption of the Thirteenth Amendment to the Constitution, which prohibited slavery. Thus, Lincoln began the task of imbedding the Declaration into the Constitution. As political theorist Wilson Carey McWilliams has pointed out, Gettysburg established a storyline for the development of the nation. Americans were not "born free"; rather, their rights depended on an honored past and a collective will to fight for those rights. The American story that Lincoln told at Gettysburg thus honored not only the Founders and those soldiers who died there but also the dignity of democratic individuals willing to acknowledge their debts to the people they had wronged, the enslaved Americans who had been denied "the fruits of their own labor."

Lincoln's magnificent rhetoric proclaimed that Americans were not merely dedicated to material satisfaction; they were also part of a moral community with mutual obligations. As legal scholar George P. Fletcher has written, the Gettysburg Address "repeated regularly in school assemblies and preserved in stone at the Lincoln memorial . . . became the secular prayer" of post–Civil War America, giving new prominence to the Declaration's self-evident truths as the foundation of a new constitutional order. Because the Constitution protected slavery, leading abolitionist William Lloyd Garrison condemned it as a "covenant with death . . . an agreement with Hell." The Thirteenth Amendment transformed America's scripture, the Declaration of Independence, into a formal constitutional obligation.

That obligation was further extended by the Fourteenth Amendment, ratified in 1868, which granted all Americans the "privileges or immunities of citizens of the United States," "due process," and "equal protection of the laws." The Fifteenth Amendment, added in 1870, proclaimed that the "right of citizens of the United States to vote shall not be abridged by the United States or any State on account of race, color, or previous condition of servitude." The three Civil War amendments changed the course of constitutional development and expanded government's obligation to protect the rights of the common citizen. As Lincoln told a special session of Congress in July 1861, the amendments aimed "to lift artificial weights from all shoulders – to clear the paths of laudable pursuit of all – to afford all an unfettered start, and a fair chance, in the race of life."

The Limits of the Constitutional Transformation

Lincoln neither expected nor intended that emancipation would secure the rights of black Americans quickly. He sought to realize his constitutional revolution in a lenient fashion, preferring to address the prejudices of Americans with persuasion rather than force. But his assassination, and his bigoted successor Andrew Johnson, severely limited Lincoln's constitutional refounding. The presidential election of 1876 effectively ended Reconstruction, the attempt of the national government to restructure government in the former confederate states and to protect the rights of the former slaves. The Democrat, Samuel Tilden, won the popular vote, but if the Republican, Rutherford B. Hayes, carried the electoral vote of four disputed states – South Carolina, Louisiana, Florida, and Oregon – he would win the election. Unlike the 2000 election, which was decided by the Supreme Court, the 1876 election was resolved by an electoral commission consisting of eight Republicans and seven Democrats. The commission awarded the election to Hayes on a straight party vote. To make this controversial decision acceptable to the Democrats, Hayes agreed to remove military troops from the South. This agreement enabled white majorities in Southern states to enact Jim Crow laws, a system of forced segregation that prevented enforcement of the Fourteenth and Fifteenth Amendments and that denied African Americans a full share of American citizenship for nearly a century. Thus, a debased form of Jacksonian local self-determination returned to American politics.

Prelude to the Fourth Refounding: The Promise and Disappointments of Progressive Democracy

We call this section on the Progressive Era a "prelude" because the Progressive Era did not constitute a full-fledged refounding on the order of those we have already examined. But it did generate political ideas and precedents that have remained critically influential ever since. It began the process of national government expansion that proved to be the most crucial political development of the twentieth century. Therefore, the Progressive Era is the place for students to begin to understand both the benefits that this expansion offered to liberty and democracy and the price it exacted. The Progressive Era had no official beginning or end. But its influence began to be felt in the1890s. It lost direct political influence when Warren Harding, a conservative Republican, was elected president in 1920, but its ideas remained influential throughout the 1920s. Progressivism formed a crucial part of the fourth refounding, the New Deal, that began in 1933.

The Birth of Progressivism

The reform assault on the post–Civil War, decentralized republic was motivated by indignation against economic injustice, not racial prejudice. The U.S. population doubled between 1870 and 1900. Urbanization and immigration increased at rapid rates and were accompanied by a shift from local, small-scale manufacturing and commerce to large-scale factory production and mammoth national corporations. Technological breakthroughs and frenzied searches for new markets and sources of capital caused unprecedented economic growth. From 1863 to 1899, manufacturing production rose by more than 700 percent. But this dynamic growth also generated profound economic and social problems that challenged the capacity of the decentralized republic to respond.

By the turn of the century, economic power had become highly concentrated, threatening the security of employees, suppliers, and customers. Many Americans believed that great business interests had captured and corrupted government. Those people who fought to reform the economy and the government became known as Progressives. No event so aroused their ardor as the nationwide celebration, in 1909, of the 100th anniversary of Lincoln's birth. A Progressive magazine editorial rejoiced:

> Coming as it did in the flood tide of the most dangerous and determined reaction from fundamental democratic ideals and principles that have marked our history, it has given a new inspiration and hope to thousands who were all but despairing of the success of popular rule in the presence of the aggressive, determined and powerful march of feudalism and privileged wealth, operating through political bosses and money controlled machines, and the pliant tools of predatory wealth in state, press, school and church.

Yet this celebration of Lincoln went hand in hand with an attack on the decentralized republic that he had supported. Forgetting that Lincoln and the Republicans had defended localized parties as critical agents of "government of the people, by the people, for the people," Progressives scorned party leaders as servants of special interests and usurpers of the Constitution. They championed the creation of direct mass democracy, of "government at first hand: government of the People, directly by the People."

In their attack on intermediary organizations such as political parties and interest groups, Progressives supported women's suffrage; the *direct primary*, in which voters, not party leaders, would choose candidates; and direct election of senators. They also championed methods of "pure" democracy, such as the *initiative*, by which a bill could be forced to the attention of legislatures by popular petition, and the *referendum*, which allowed the electorate to overrule decisions of state legislatures (see Figure 4.1). Especially controversial was the idea of subjecting constitutional questions to direct popular control, including referenda on laws that state courts had declared unconstitutional. Direct democracy became the centerpiece of the insurgent Progressive party campaign of 1912, which pledged a "covenant with the people," making the people "masters of their constitution."

Progressives blamed the celebration of property rights for the perversions of the industrial age. Consequently, they stressed collective responsibilities and duties rather than rights. Despite their reverence for Lincoln, they did not emulate his devotion to the Declaration of Independence. Instead, they invoked the preamble of the Constitution to assert their purpose of making "We the People" effective in strengthening the national government's authority to regulate the society and economy.

Like previous champions of democracy, the Progressive reformers' idealism owed much to religion. Many of them, including Raymond Robbins of the Men and Religious Forward Movement and *Outlook* editor, Lyman Abbot, owed allegiance to the *social gospel movement*. They saw the Progressive party and other reform associations as political expressions of the movement to promote Christian social action. An official publication of the Progressive party proclaimed that it represented "a splendid idealism in the field of practical achievement," offering a "fitting medium through which the fervor, the enthusiasm, the devotion of true religion can utter itself in terms of social justice, civic righteousness and unselfish service." The Progressives' celebration of national democracy dovetailed with the social gospelers religious devotion, which downplayed, if it did not scorn, particular theological doctrines and denominations. "We have been a wasteful nation," argued Walter Rauschenbusch, the esteemed social gospeler, in a speech praising the Progressive party. "We have wasted our soil, our water, our forests, our childhood, our motherhood, but no waste has been so great as our waste of religious enthusiasm by denominational strife. The heed of

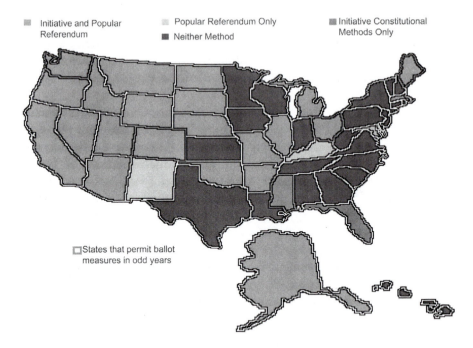

Figure 4.1. Referendum/Initiative Map. One legacy of Progressivism is referenda or initiatives, which are forms of direct popular control over public policy making.
Source: *The Book of the States, 2000–2001* (Lexington, KY: The Council of State Governments, 2000), 233.

social service is seen in the fact that as the social spirit rises the sectarian spirit declines." The social gospelers thereby invested religious fervor in Progressivism's crusade for a new form of politics that would transform the religion of America into a national democracy.

Whereas Jeffersonian democracy and the principles set forth in the Declaration of Independence dominated the nineteenth century, a popular, idealistic version of Hamiltonianism, dedicated to realizing the nationalist potential of the Constitution, has prevailed since the beginning of the twentieth century. In the words of the first Progressive president, Theodore Roosevelt (TR), "I have never hesitated to criticize Jefferson; he was infinitely below Hamilton; I think the worship of Jefferson a discredit to my country." Yet TR was no blind disciple of Hamilton. Unlike Hamilton, who supported an energetic executive in order to curb popular influence, TR viewed the president as the visionary champion of social and economic reform. In the words of the reformer Herbert Croly, the aim of progressive nationalism was "to give democratic meaning and purpose to the Hamiltonian tradition and method."

Progressive Divisions

One reason that Progressivism did not generate a constitutional refounding was that it was too internally divided. These divisions were revealed in the three-way 1912 presidential election. The Republican incumbent William Howard Taft, running as the candidate of the rule of law, came in third. Former president Theodore Roosevelt, candidate of the Progressive party, calling himself a *New Nationalist*, proposed to control the trusts by creating a powerful national regulatory agency. The victor, Democrat Woodrow Wilson, embraced a *New Freedom* version of Progressivism that was less trusting of centralized authority and that emphasized antitrust measures and state regulations as alternatives to expanded administrative power.

Like Lincoln, Wilson believed that local "prejudices" could not be remade by administrative decree. But Wilson lacked Lincoln's faith in the natural rights philosophy embodied by the Declaration of Independence. He shared the New Nationalists' view that history, not nature, supplied the standard of rights. "If Jefferson were alive today," Wilson insisted, "he would see that the individual is caught in a confused nexus of all sorts of complicated circumstances, and that to let him alone is to leave him helpless as against the obstacles with which he has to contend. . . . " The central government thus had to intervene to preserve the people's freedom against the highly centralized trusts: "Freedom today is something more than being left alone. The program of government of freedom must in these days be positive, not only negative."

Once elected, Wilson supported national economic control initiatives, such as the creation of a federal trade commission with broad responsibilities for overseeing business practices, much like the one TR had proposed. Wilson also supported creation of the Federal Reserve system to administer the national banking and currency system (see Chapter 6).

Administrative Management

This partial establishment of a national administrative state revealed a contradiction between the Progressives' celebration of direct democracy and their desire to cope with economic problems and inequalities by means of a more powerful and independent bureaucracy. In fact, Progressive reforms made government services less connected to elected officials and more tied to administrative agencies and bureaucracies over which the voter at the polls had little control. Progressive reformers tended to believe that the most popular branches of government – state and national legislatures – were also the least capable and most corrupt. They were convinced that the exacting new tasks of government were too demanding for untrained legislators, who often sat only a few months at a time and who lacked policy expertise. The most extreme version of this resort to expertise was the city manager form of government, which supplanted elected mayors with appointed administrators. This movement mirrored reforms that efficiency expert Frederick W. Taylor was advancing for private industry – systematic and "scientific" forms of management from the head office to the shop floor. To bring such reform to government, Taylor urged the president to put an efficiency expert in the cabinet.

Progressives never carried the idea of non-political service to the same lengths that other modern democracies did; for example, civil service reform was far more extensive in France and Great Britain. But by the end of TR's two terms in office, the merit system had begun to supplant the spoils system; Wilson, especially in his second term, built on TR's commitment to professional administration. Presidential leadership, previously dependent on patronage-seeking state and local party machines, now required careful attention to administrative management, sometimes to foster economy and efficiency and sometimes to bolster the power of the increasingly active federal government.

Despite Progressivism's championing of mass democracy, its mix of attack on political organizations and commitment to administrative management conspired to make American politics and government seem more removed from the everyday lives of citizens. Civil service reform and the decline in monetary and social rewards for political activity significantly reduced the individual's incentive to participate in campaigns and elections. Thus Progressive democracy actually decreased voter turnout, which was lower in 1920 and 1924 than at any time since the emergence of mass democracy in the 1830s. "Early in the 19th century, soaring turnout among white men reinforced the impression of the People governing," Robert Wiebe has observed; "early in the 20th, falling turnouts reinforced the impression of people being governed."

Progressive Democracy and Liberalism

The Progressive faith in majoritarian democracy dealt severe blows to the liberal principle of equal rights. TR and Taft tolerated racial segregation in the South because they acknowledged its political popularity. Woodrow Wilson, a native Virginian elected to the White House in large part because of white Southern support, allowed his administration to actively promote it. He permitted a number of federal departments to segregate their employees in Washington and to demote or fire their black federal workers in the South.

Progressive indifference to individual rights was not limited to Southern issues. The Progressive movement, for all its moral fervor, tended to view social differences skeptically, if not disdainfully. Immigration restrictions and racial segregation were often supported by "reformers," who viewed the growing diversity of America as a threat to national unity. By 1920, to disenfranchise immigrants, nine Northern states passed literacy tests for voting and eleven states repealed older laws permitting aliens to cast ballots once they pledged to become citizens. The United States and Japan reached a so-called gentlemen's agreement in 1907 that excluded Japanese immigrants. In the same year, Congress appointed a commission to study the immigration question. Two years later, the commission issued a forty-one volume report advocating immigration restrictions. In 1920, Congress passed the most restrictive immigration bill in the nation's history. Nativist sentiment – which scorned beer drinking as a vice of German, Irish, and Italian immigrants – led to the 1919 ratification of the Eighteenth Amendment to the Constitution, which prohibited the manufacture, sale, and transportation of intoxicating liquors. As the political scientist James Morone has written, "Prohibiting liquor looked like one more progressive social amelioration, blending easily into the movement's disdain for inferior people and corrupt politics."

Progressive Democracy and War

The repressive tendencies of Progressive democracy were revealed dramatically during World War I. President Wilson's war aim was to make the "World Safe for Democracy." To convey the message to the American people, Wilson formed the Committee on Public Information (CPI), which enlisted 75,000 speakers to "persuade" the public that the war was a crusade for freedom and democracy against the Germans, a barbarian people bent on world domination. Most Americans supported the war. But a significant minority opposed it, including German and Irish Americans, whose ethnicity caused them to doubt the cause of the Allied powers, and Progressive reformers such as the prominent social worker Jane Addams, who thought American democracy would be corrupted by the necessities and cruelties of total war. The CPI and a number of self-styled "patriotic groups" sought to discourage, and sometimes repress, this dissent. People who refused to buy war bonds were often exposed to public ridicule and even assaulted. People with German names, scorned as hyphenate Americans, were prosecuted indiscriminately. Some school boards outlawed the teaching of the German language.

Wilson's Progressive democracy did not deter this oppression. Indeed, his view that the war was a moral crusade – to "make the world safe for democracy" – inspired intolerance. Wilson signed the Espionage Act of 1917, which imposed fines of up to $10,000 and jail sentences ranging to twenty years on persons convicted of aiding the enemy or obstructing military recruitment. He banned seemingly treasonable or seditious material from the mails. In May 1918, he signed the Sedition Act, which made it a crime to "utter, print, write, or publish any disloyal, profane, scurrilous, or abusive language" about the government, the Constitution, or the uniform of the Army and Navy, or "say anything" to discourage war bond purchases. Socialist leader Eugene V. Debs was sentenced to ten years in prison for making an antiwar speech. Thus, the Progressives, many of whom idolized Alexander Hamilton, showed themselves to be as indifferent to civil liberties as Hamilton and the Federalists had been in the 1790s.

The Fourth Refounding: The New Deal and the Triumph of Liberalism

With the Progressive movement in disarray after World War I, the nation was left with two major parties dominated by conservatives. Republican Warren Harding's 1920 campaign slogan, "Return to Normalcy," which promised a less intrusive federal government, captured the fancy of the country and helped send him to the White House. In the Democratic party, conservative Southerners were similarly hostile to an expanded federal role that might jeopardize their region's "way of life." Northern urban bosses, fixated on local patronage, also had little use for the national government.

The "return to normalcy" was shattered in 1929 by the Great Depression, the worst economic cataclysm in American history. Out of its ruins rose the *New Deal*, the defining episode of the twentieth century. The New Deal built on the two pillars of Progressive democracy: mass politics and national administration. But, unlike the Progressive Era, the New Deal was a full-fledged constitutional refounding. Grounded in a new understanding of rights, it marked a critical departure in governing principles, political alignments, institutional arrangements, and public policy.

New Deal Liberalism

Until the New Deal, the American liberal tradition was associated with natural rights and limited government. But Franklin Delano Roosevelt (FDR) was the first president to call himself a liberal, adding the word to the common political vocabulary. In doing so, he reworked – or, as his political enemies claimed, "perverted" – the elements of the old liberal faith drawn from the Declaration of Independence.

The Progressives' dream of national community promoted an unvarnished majoritarianism that undermined the Constitution's promise to protect individual freedom against the whims and passions of mass opinion. By the late 1920s, the Progressive philosopher John Dewey, struggling to reconcile individualism and Progressive ideals, embraced a new version of liberalism that accepted government interference with private property in order to guarantee social and economic welfare. Earlier Progressives such as TR and Herbert Croly advocated replacing individualism with a greater commitment to social responsibility. Dewey sought a new understanding of individualism. He called on the national government not only to create the conditions in which individuals could realize their full potential but also to advance social welfare policy and foster community participation in the "cause of the liberty of the human spirit."

Borrowing from Dewey, FDR termed his philosophy "Liberalism" rather than "Progressivism," but FDR's version was more in keeping with the American constitutional tradition. FDR asserted a connection between nationalism and rights. In his 1932 Commonwealth Club address and at each key rhetorical juncture thereafter, FDR stated that the purpose of modern government was "to assist in the development of an economic declaration of rights, an economic constitutional order."

A New Declaration of Independence

To FDR, the Great Depression made painfully obvious what should have been clear three decades earlier, that it was necessary to rewrite the social contract to take account of a national economy remade by industrial capitalism and economic concentration. This new contract would establish a stronger national state to countervail concentrated economic power. As FDR put it, "The day of enlightened administration has come." The traditional emphasis on self-reliance should give way to a new version of the social contract in which government guarantees individuals protection from the uncertainties of the market. Security was to be the new self-evident truth of American political life.

The triumph of the New Deal was greatly aided by the Great Depression. When FDR took the oath of office on March 4, 1933, about a third of the workforce, 15 million workers, were unemployed. In thirty-two states, all banks were closed; in sixteen more, banking operations were severely curtailed. That morning, the New York Stock Exchange closed its doors. But the New Dealers looked beyond the immediate crisis; their principal objective was not economic recovery but enduring political reform. American politics could not be remade unless the New Deal was interwoven with traditional constitutional principles. FDR gave legitimacy to Progressive

Franklin D. Roosevelt's New Deal offered a new social contract of the government's role in aiding Americans during the Great Depression, when one-third of American workers were unemployed.

ideas by imbedding them in the language of constitutionalism and interpreting them as a fulfillment rather than a subversion of natural rights. The task of statesmanship, FDR insisted, was to redefine the rights of the Declaration in terms of a "changing and growing social order."

The new understanding of the Declaration and Constitution was the principal message of FDR's reelection bid in 1936, and his success was the decisive triumph that established the Democrats as the majority party in American politics for a generation. Lincoln, as this chapter has pointed out, defended the Declaration as America's founding document, claiming that the centrality of the rights it proclaimed justified a "new birth of freedom."

The 1860 Republican platform championed the Declaration of Independence as America's founding document. The 1936 Democratic platform, drafted by FDR, was written as a pastiche of the Declaration and thus emphasized the need for a fundamental reconsideration of rights. "We hold this truth to be self-evident," it said, "that government in a modern civilization has certain inescapable obligations to its citizens." Among these new responsibilities was "to erect a structure of economic security for its people, making sure that this benefit shall keep step with the ever increasing capacity of America to provide a high standard of living for all its citizens."

The 1936 election appeared to sanction FDR's redefinition of the social contract. He won every state but Maine and Vermont. The 1936 Republican platform declared that "America is in peril" and dedicated the party to "the preservation of ... political liberty," which "for the first time" was "threatened by government itself." But FDR successfully defended the New Deal in terms of enhancing liberty. Harking back to the American Revolution, FDR defined his opponents as "economic royalists" who

> have conceded that political freedom was the business of government, but they have maintained that economic slavery was nobody's business. They granted that the Government could protect the citizen in his own right to vote, but they denied that government could do anything to protect the citizen in his right to work and his right to live. ... If the average citizen is guaranteed equal opportunity in the polling place, he must have equal opportunity in the marketplace.

Former president Herbert Hoover, who had been FDR's opponent in the 1932 election, insisted that the Republican party, with its historical commitment to preserving a large sphere of private action, was "the true liberal party." The New Deal, he warned, was a "false liberalism that regimented men and extended bureaucracy." But Americans chose to link the term liberal with FDR's New Deal instead. After 1936, therefore, the term came to signify an active national government working to secure prosperity and meet large domestic and international responsibilities. New Deal liberalism dominated American politics until the late 1970s and is still central to American political life.

Enlightened Administration and Programmatic Rights

The New Deal refounding, which was built on the Progressive prelude, was the first to emphasize national administrative power. Previous refoundings occurred within the parameters set by private property rights, limited government, and administrative decentralization. Even the Civil War, the most serious constitutional crisis of American history, did not lead to a departure from this consensus. As we explain in Chapter 8, FDR managed to push through Congress political reforms that led to the creation of the White House office, the hub of the executive office of the president. The reconstituted executive office deprived party leaders of the very tasks that gave them status and influence: linking the president to interest groups, staffing the executive branch, developing policy, providing campaign support, and linking the White House to public opinion. Moreover, New Deal political reforms were directed not just at creating presidential government but also at embedding progressive programs – which were considered tantamount to rights – in a bureaucratic structure that would insulate reform and reformers from party politics, conservative presidents, and even, to a point, public opinion.

The most important of these new *programmatic rights* was Social Security. The 1935 Social Security Act provided old age insurance, unemployment insurance, and Aid to Families with Dependent Children (AFDC), popularly known as welfare. Unlike old age insurance, unemployment compensation and AFDC were jointly administered by the national and state governments. Social Security was carefully nurtured by FDR to appear as a right, the cornerstone of the economic constitutional order. He insisted that it be financed by a payroll tax rather than by general revenues: "We put those payroll contributions there so to give the contributors a legal, moral right, and political right to collect their pensions. With those taxes in there, no damn politician can scrap my social security program."

And none did. By the 1950s, Social Security was the "third rail" of American politics, bringing political death to those who challenged it. By European standards, the Social Security program was quite limited. It did not include any support for healthcare, and its levels of welfare spending were low. It left considerable discretion and funding responsibility to the states, which dealt out social justice unevenly. Nevertheless, the program marked a watershed in the national government's assumption of the responsibility to protect individuals from the uncertainties of the market. Its programs, especially old age pensions, grew over the years, so that Social Security became the largest of all federal programs.

Expanding Rights

The 1935 *National Labor Relations Act* established another economic right, that of unions to bargain collectively. The act created a National Labor Relations Board (NLRB) to ensure fair collective bargaining elections, a move that transformed American society and economy (see Chapter 6). When the New Deal began, few factory workers belonged to labor unions, which left them vulnerable to workplace abuses and business cycle uncertainties. By the late 1930s, industrial unionism was firmly in place.

In his 1944 State of the Union message, FDR called for a new bill of rights that provided adequate food, clothing, recreation, employment, housing, and education to all, "regardless of station, race, or creed," and that provided protection from the economic fears of old age, sickness, and accident. These new rights did not officially become part of the Constitution, but they formed the foundation of a new public philosophy that redefined the role of the national government. The previous understanding of rights – which was dedicated to limiting government – gradually gave way to a more expansive understanding that presupposed the creation of a large and powerful executive establishment.

Civil Rights

As World War II neared, the New Deal approach to civil rights changed. As the political scientist Ira Katznelson has noted, "During Jim Crow's last hurrah in the 1930s and 1940s, when Southern members of Congress controlled the gateways to legislation, policy decisions dealing with welfare, work, and war either excluded the vast majority of African Americans or treated them differently from others." The 1938 Federal Housing Administration Act, for example, had required the home mortgages that it insured to have racially restrictive covenants. But only two years later, the Roosevelt administration established the Fair Employment Practices Commission (FEPC), which was charged with eliminating discrimination in the employment of workers in the defense industry or in government because of "race, color, creed, or national origin." As the wartime internment of Japanese Americans and the continued racial segregation of the armed forces showed, this action did not mark a sea change in racial attitudes. Nor was the FEPC an adequate response to racial discrimination. Nevertheless, it was the first federal government effort since Reconstruction that was specifically aimed at alleviating racial discrimination.

These administrative efforts were joined to judicial politics. At FDR's behest, his attorney general, Frank Murphy, set up the Civil Liberties Section of the Justice Department in 1939. Later called the Civil Rights Section, this office played a critical part in bringing and successfully adjudicating Supreme Court cases that challenged white supremacy in the South. The most important case, *Smith v. Allwright*, decided in 1944, declared the white primary, a critical foundation of Jim Crow electoral practices, unconstitutional.

FDR's successor, Harry Truman, went further. His 1948 executive order demanded that "there shall be equality of treatment and opportunity in the Armed Services without regard to race, color, or national origin."

Liberal Internationalism

Progressives championed internationalism that would make the world safe for democracy; New Deal rhetoric stressed international rights. As FDR put it in his famous 1941 Four Freedoms speech, the traditional liberal freedoms of speech and religion were to be supplemented by two new freedoms. "Freedom from want" was a commitment to "economic understandings which will secure to every nation a healthy peace time life for its inhabitants." "Freedom from fear" was dedicated to "a world-wide reduction of armaments to such a point and such a fashion that no nation will be in a position to commit an act of physical aggression against any neighbor."

In his draft of the 1941 *Atlantic Charter*, FDR committed the Allies to "respect the right of all peoples to choose the form of government under which they will live" and "to see sovereign rights and self-government restored to those who have been forcibly deprived of them." Believing that rejection of imperialism was crucial to defeating the Axis powers, FDR persuaded a nervous Winston Churchill to endorse the charter even though the language might be, and eventually was, used against the British Empire.

Of course, FDR's idealism frequently gave way to practical considerations. In his negotiations with Stalin toward the end of the war, FDR failed to prevent Soviet dominion over Eastern Europe. Likewise, the internment of Japanese Americans in concentration camps revealed all too clearly that New Deal rights did not provide ironclad protection for minorities against xenophobic hysteria. Still, liberal internationalism proved more resilient than did the Progressive ambition to make the world safe for democracy. World War I stifled Progressive domestic reform and fueled nativist attitudes. World War II strengthened the sense of entitlement, thereby justifying New Deal reforms, and advanced an inclusive popular nationalism and a readiness to use the federal government to secure prosperity and meet important domestic and international needs. As Lincoln showed, words are more important than battles. After the war, the rights rhetoric that FDR pioneered was used effectively against imperialist and discriminatory impulses.

Just as New Deal liberalism made the national government an enduring presence in domestic affairs, FDR's liberal internationalism made it difficult for America to retreat from the world stage. Indeed, domestic and international commitments merged to enhance the influence of modern liberalism on American life. For example, in 1944, Congress enacted the

The expansion of rights during the New Deal was not universal. During World War II, xenophobic fears prompted the government to force Japanese Americans to abandon their properties and live in internment camps.

GI Bill of Rights that entitled war veterans to home loans, business loans, unemployment compensation, and subsidies for education and training. This legislation did not provide the broad security and employment programs that FDR championed in his 1944 second bill of rights speech, but it did greatly expand the economic and educational benefits available to a very large and significant portion of the population, returning veterans and their families.

The Impact of New Deal Liberalism on Contemporary Politics

The New Deal's two most characteristic features – a readiness to use the federal government to deal with domestic and foreign problems and an inclusive popular nationalism – are hallmarks of contemporary America. Nonetheless, the enduring importance of the New Deal has not been unchallenged or uninterrupted. Some critics have charged that it was too conservative a response to potentially revolutionary conditions and that it failed to sustain a vital labor movement. Unlike British reformers, FDR and the New Dealers made no effort to build on the labor movement to create a labor party that was committed to nationalizing industry and redistributing wealth. These socialist principles have never appealed to a large number of Americans. But a less socialistic, more democratic critique of New Deal liberalism did resonate widely among postwar Americans.

A Great Society

In the signature speech of his presidency, a May 1964 commencement address at the University of Michigan, Lyndon Baines Johnson (LBJ) pointed to the New Deal's promise to end poverty and racial justice as "just the beginning." Challenging the students and parents to embrace more ambitious goals for America, LBJ described his vision of "a Great Society... where the city of man serves not only the needs of the body and the demands of commerce but the desire for beauty and the hunger for community."

John Dewey had prophesied that Progressive reforms would reach fulfillment in a "Great Community" that would "order the relations and enrich the experience of local associations." Reformers in the 1960s hoped that the *Great Society* would produce the same thing. Their ambitions were fueled by the success of the Civil Rights Movement. This movement called not merely for a fulfillment of rights promised African Americans but also for direct action to overcome the bureaucratic inertia of the New Deal state. Its success "demonstrated not only the power and possibility of organized protest, but the unsuspected fragility of resistance to liberating changes," claimed Richard Goodwin, who drafted LBJ's University of Michigan speech.

Indeed, the Civil Rights Movement was a model for the social movements that grew out of the 1960s, including organized opposition to the Vietnam War, feminism, consumerism, and environmentalism. In the early days of the Great Society, LBJ and influential aides like Goodwin supported these movements (except for the antiwar protests), viewing their clarion call for participatory democracy as paving the way for a new generation of reform.

The Great Society's deepest ambitions were never realized. Its important achievements in civil rights, environment, consumer protection, and education did not increase participatory democracy. Steeped in the rights talk popularized by FDR, it led rather to a rights revolution, an explosion of new entitlements proclaimed by groups competing with one another for recognition and for government programs to remedy the historic injustices they had suffered. Rights of women, gays and lesbians, the disabled, consumers,

Michael Leavitt, Secretary of the U.S. Department
of Health and Human Services, urged people to
sign up for Medicare Part D in May 2006.
Medicare is a federal healthcare program for the
elderly that is central to the debates over citizens'
rights and the discretionary use of national
administrative power.

and welfare recipients followed logically from the New Deal idea of a just
society. The New Deal promised security in the face of the uncertainties
of the business cycle and the unintended hazards created by a dynamic
capitalism. The rights revolution expanded on those ideas to encompass
protections against the prejudices of private citizens, the risks of congenital
disabilities, and the consequences of poverty and family decomposition.

Counterrevolution

The rights revolution ignited opposition among many people who felt that
the government was doling out too many entitlements at their expense.

This growing hostility culminated in Ronald Reagan's 1980 election to the White House. Reagan's message as candidate and president was but a variation of the theme he first developed in a nationwide address on behalf of the 1964 Republican presidential candidate, Barry Goldwater. Reagan invoked Paine, Jefferson, and Jackson as he proclaimed that citizens must not be denied the means of exercising their right of rebelling against government.

The New Deal state, Reagan argued, gave an especially pernicious turn to government oppression, cloaking its intrusiveness in the language of the Declaration. By acting "outside of its legitimate function," Reagan insisted, "natural unalienable rights" were presumed to be a "dispensation of government," which stripped people of their self-reliance and their capacity for self-government. "The real destroyer of liberties of the people," said Reagan, "is he who spreads among them bounties, donations, and benefits." In his inaugural address, the first in more than fifty years to appeal for limited government, he sounded the same theme: "In the present crisis, government is not the solution to our problem; government is the problem." Reagan promised to shrink government and restore the vitality of a democracy based on limited government and decentralized politics.

But the *Reagan revolution* did not redefine the New Deal social contract and therefore did not constitute a refounding. Despite his antigovernment rhetoric, Reagan managed only to halt the expansion of programmatic rights. He had little success in cutting back *middle-class entitlements* such as Social Security and *Medicare*, a healthcare program for the elderly created in 1965. Reagan's efforts to loosen regulatory standards for civil rights, environment, and consumer protection were successfully resisted by public interest groups and their allies in Congress and the courts.

Box Two: Contemporary Politics

Pollution: Rights versus Risk

Much political deliberation consists of discussion about the relative merits of "less" and "more." The absolute nature of rights makes "rights" an inappropriate topic for a discussion that tries to assess relative costs and benefits. Therefore, it is most essential to determine whether a particular policy issue really involves "unalienable" rights. This question is the essence of the contemporary debate about air and water pollution.

Economists, risk scientists, and polluting businesses argue that any choice about how much to improve air or water quality should be about the relative merits of less and more. How much does society benefit from one additional life saved or sick day prevented compared to the cost of reducing pollution enough to produce that marginal benefit? Environmentalists argue along Rooseveltian lines that everybody has a right to clean air or clean water and that therefore a sufficient amount of pollution protection must be provided to secure that right.

Political scientist Martha Derthick has explained that the architects of Social Security purposely promised it as a right in order to keep future generations of legislators from tampering with it. Social Security was purposely designed to be uncontrollable. It was expected to grow as the number of people entitled to it grew. Contemporary debate over air and water pollution policy is essentially about whether a similar irrevocable commitment is appropriate in the environmental sphere.

In fact, the Reagan administration upheld many aspects of the New Deal, especially its commitment to liberal internationalism, which had lost much support among Democrats since the Vietnam War. Ironically, Reagan's greatest accomplishment may have involved an act of perpetuation. Finishing what Harry Truman began, Reagan prosecuted the Cold War to a successful conclusion. The demise of the Soviet Union occurred for many reasons, but Reagan's tough talk – he dubbed the Communist power an "evil empire" – steered American policy away from detente, the position of accommodation that had prevailed since the early 1970s. Reagan returned to containment as pursued by Presidents Truman, Eisenhower, Kennedy, and Johnson. This rhetorical hard line justified the extensive arms buildup that put great technological and economic pressure on the Soviet Union and contributed to its ultimate collapse.

Even when championing "conservative" causes, Reagan defended an activist presidency that belied his promise to "get the government off our backs." The conservative movement that helped bring him to power was aroused in no small part by the abortion controversy, which led Reagan and many of his supporters to defend the rights of the unborn in a way that required extending the power of government. Posed in opposition to the rights of pregnant women as championed by the women's movement, the Reagan administration contemplated prohibiting women from having abortions, or in certain cases, even getting counseling from birth control clinics. For example, in early 1988, the Department of Health and Human

Services issued a regulation declaring that federal funds could not go to clinics that provided abortion counseling. The merits of this position aside, it shows that in the post–New Deal era, when conservatives challenge liberal policies, they do so in the name of new rights that presuppose discretionary use of national administrative power.

Conservative Liberalism

Bill Clinton, elected in 1992 – the first Democrat to occupy the White House in sixteen years – appeared to ratify the "Reagan revolution." Indeed, he proclaimed that "the era of big government is over." This pronouncement was not made without provocation – it followed the disastrous defeat of his ambitious plan to establish a comprehensive healthcare program. When the Republicans, led by the militant conservative Newt Gingrich, won control of both houses of Congress in 1994 – the first time this had happened in forty years – Clinton signed a welfare reform bill that vastly reduced the number of persons receiving public assistance and constructed a bipartisan coalition in support of a balanced budget.

Yet Clinton revived his presidency and fended off the aggressive leadership of Speaker of the House Gingrich by defending New Deal and Great Society programs. Clinton was reelected in 1996, the first time a Democratic president had been returned to office by the voters since FDR. The crux of his reelection campaign was his dedication to perpetuating Medicare, Medicaid (a healthcare program for the disadvantaged), education spending, and stringent environmental regulation. Clinton – not his opponent, Kansas senator Robert Dole – was the real conservative in this campaign, because he fought to preserve the status quo, the programmatic rights that were the legacy of FDR and the New Deal, from Republican efforts to scale it back.

Box Three: Nuts and Bolts

Major Twentieth-Century Public Policies

The twentieth century ushered in a vast expansion of the American national government. The following is a list of the most important national public policies adopted during the three great waves of public policy expansion during the twentieth century – the Progressive Era, the New Deal, and the Great Society. The list provides a brief explanation of the purpose of each policy and the name and date of the law enacting it.

Progressive Era
Regulation of railroads (Hepburn Act of 1906)
Regulation of food and drug purity (Pure Food and Drug Act of 1906)
Expanded efforts to fight industrial monopoly and oligopoly (Federal Trade Commission Act of 1914)
Establishment of a national banking system (Federal Reserve Act of 1913)

New Deal
Pensions for the elderly (Social Security Act of 1935)
Regulation of the buying and selling of stocks and bonds (Securities Act of 1933)
Insurance for bank deposits (Glass-Steagall Act of 1933)
Subsidies for farmers (Agricultural Adjustment Act of 1938)
Collective bargaining rights for workers (Wagner Act of 1935)
Minimum wages for workers (Fair Labor Standards Act of 1938)
Unemployment insurance (Social Security Act of 1935)
Regulation of gas and electric companies (Public Utilities Act of 1935)
Welfare for the disabled and for poor single-parent families (Social Security Act of 1935)

The Great Society
Healthcare for the elderly (Medicare) (Social Security Act of 1965)
Healthcare for the poor (Medicaid) (Social Security Act of 1965)
Desegregation of public facilities (Civil Rights Act of 1964)
Enforcement of voting rights for African Americans (Voting Rights Act of 1965)

Important new policies were also initiated in the periods between these great waves and after the last one. For example:

Education benefits for military service (GI Bill of Rights of 1944)
Creation of the interstate highway system (Federal Aid Highway Act of 1956)
Air pollution control (Clean Air Act of 1970)
Water pollution control (Federal Water Pollution Control Act Amendments of 1972)
Worker health and safety (Occupational Safety and Health Act of 1970)
Welfare reform (Personal Responsibility and Work Opportunity Reconciliation Act of 1996)

The Legacy of New Deal liberalism

Twentieth-century reform began with an effort to strengthen democracy in order to check the economic oppression spawned by the Industrial Revolution. Ultimately, reform came not in the form of a purified democracy but in the guise of new rights. Some critics cried foul, claiming that the New Deal arrested the most generous impulse of Progressivism, that is, to create a more socially conscious America. Instead, critics claimed, the New Deal turned Jeffersonian democracy, rooted in individual responsibility, locality, and natural rights, into a suburban republic dedicated to individual achievement, global awareness, and programmatic rights. This outlook risked confounding rights and interests, and it exposed the post–New Deal state to the relentless, selfish claims of interest groups.

As political scientist Hugh Heclo has argued, this era is one in which each right-sponsoring group goes its own way, with no overall vision holding things together and "no philosophical foundation on which to rest the rickety edifice of right piled upon right." The expansion of rights deepens the tension between liberalism and democracy. New Deal liberalism has made the sense of common citizenship more fragile. "Our rights talk, in its absoluteness," writes legal scholar Mary Ann Glendon, "promotes unrealistic expectations, heightens social conflict, and inhibits dialogue that might lead toward consensus, accommodation, or at least the discovery of common ground."

In the wake of FDR's revolution, important public questions are propounded as rights, purporting to confer constitutional status on liberal and conservative policies alike. The blurring of the line between rights and interests, between entitlement and policy, tends to turn contemporary political battles into legal contests that scorn democratic politics. There are exceptions. Despite a clash of rights claims, the abortion dispute has engendered intense and lively political debate. But for the most part, the New Deal allied rights and administration in a fashion that made rights talk routine and democratic politics less important. Political parties and local governments, the institutions that nurture an active and competent citizenry, languish. Political debates tend to take place in bureaucratic agencies and courts, which weakens representative democracy.

The strengths and weaknesses of the New Deal follow from its attempt to expand the possibilities of individual freedom by grafting a national administrative apparatus and activist public philosophy onto a rights-based constitutional system and political culture. This new understanding of liberalism proved effective in coping with economic insecurity at home and despotism abroad. But can it sustain a vital civic culture? Can the more centralized, bureaucratic political conditions it gave rise to support a nation of individuals capable of pursuing happiness with dignity and responsibility?

Conclusion: Religion, Homeland Security, and the Renewal of Party Conflict in American Political Development

This chapter began with a discussion about President Bush's attempt to lead the debate over stem cell research. His speech may be viewed as an effort to snatch this conflict from the bureaucratic agencies and courts that have often been the center of post–New Deal political life. People have engaged in moral and religious questions as they struggled over the proper understanding of the "pursuit of happiness," and the debate over stem cell research, closely associated with the abortion dispute, raises the most fundamental questions about individual rights. Indeed, the conflict between a secular and traditional understanding of the right to life echoed themes that divided the country in the 2000 election. Bush supporters tended to adhere to traditional moral standards. Gore supporters were more open to newer, more relativistic moral views. Income was a poorer predictor of voting patterns than church attendance was.

And yet, President Bush's speech did not put the issue before Congress or the people in a manner reminiscent of the great democratic debates over slavery or civil rights. Instead, he created the President's Council on Bioethics "to recommend appropriate [stem cell] guidelines and regulations, and to consider all the medical and ethical ramifications of biomedical innovation." That the president gave this authority to a board of experts appeared to affirm the loss of faith in public deliberation and judgment that formed part of the New Deal legacy.

But the stem cell controversy could not be managed away. It resurfaced in the 2004 election campaign and returned to the headlines two years later during congressional debate and enactment of a bill to lift the restrictions that Bush had placed on federally funded human embryonic stem cell research. President Bush's veto of this bill became an issue in the 2006 elections, which saw the Democrats reclaim control of the House and Senate. In June 2007, Congress once again passed legislation to ease restrictions on stem cell research; once again, the President used his veto to prevent a challenge to the expansion of federal support for research using stem cells. For the time being, legislative challenges to Bush's controversial policy position came to an end. But the conflict between the president and Congress ensured that the public controversy would continue and testified to the enduring conflict in the United States over the boundary between church and state.

That boundary was further tested by the emergence of same-sex marriage as an important national issue, a controversy aroused by the Massachusetts Supreme Court decision in November 2003 declaring restrictions on same-sex marriage unconstitutional. Hoping to build on the political momentum they thought this highly publicized case engendered, some pro-gay marriage local officials took provocative administrative action. For example, the San Francisco mayor, Gavin Newsome, ordered city clerks to violate California state law by issuing marriage licenses to gay couples. Opponents of gay marriage reacted by placing proposed amendments on the ballot in thirteen states during the 2004 election that prohibited same-sex marriage; the Bush White House and Republican leaders put a similar constitutional amendment before Congress. In both red and blue states, voters overwhelmingly supported proposals to outlaw same-sex unions. Although Congress failed to enact a constitutional amendment, opposition to gay marriage continued to roil local and state politics. Since 1998, twenty-six states have banned gay marriage.

Speculation abounded that issues like stem cell research and gay marriage contributed to mounting partisan rancor and the slight but decisive edge that Bush and the Republican party gained in the 2004 election. Bush defeated his Democratic opponent, Senator John Kerry of Massachusetts, in the popular vote 51 to 48 percent, and the Republicans strengthened their majorities in both the House and Senate (see Chapter 11). Considerable evidence showed, however, that Bush and his party's victory was attributable not principally to social issues but, rather, to the attack of September 11, 2001, and the war on terrorism that followed. This is not to deny that the Bush campaign's emphasis on wartime leadership was skillfully tied to national security and traditional values that appealed to Republican partisans. Indeed, the White House's aggressive response to terrorism, pursued with such controversy in Iraq, confirmed the support of conservatives for and liberals against Bush and the Republican party. Republicans and Democrats instigated a serious partisan dispute in 2004 that captured the attention of the American people and mobilized the largest turnout in a presidential election since 1968. In turn, popular disaffection with the Iraq War, which led to a dramatic decline in support for Bush among independents and moderate Republicans, reenergized Democrats and enabled them to capture the House and Senate in the 2006 elections.

Pundits and scholars lament the divided state of American democracy. Yet, cast against the polarizing episodes to expand popular sovereignty during the first three decades of the twentieth century, the conflagration over slavery, the disruptive conflicts aroused by industrial capitalism during the turn of the century, the divisive struggles to come to terms with the Great Depression, and the explosive battles waged over civil rights and Vietnam during the sixties, the present partisan rancor seems pretty tame. In spite of the important differences between Democrats and Republicans on a number of important issues, both parties currently have accepted big government as a central part of contemporary political life in the United States.

Bush, in fact, has tried to distinguish himself from the Reagan administration's antigovernment posture by calling for a "compassionate conservatism" that would employ activist government for conservative ends. In part, the moral commitment Bush envisioned would be served by empowering non-profit institutions that worked outside of government. For example, he proposed changes in federal and state regulations that would allow private, "faith-based" charitable organizations to play a larger role in providing government services to the poor. But the national government would play an important role in sustaining moral values as well. The Reagan administration, although it expressed hostility to big government, also made use of national administrative power; however, the Bush administration was prepared to take big government conservatism much further. Although Reagan and his conservative allies once talked of eliminating the Department of Education, Bush proposed to make the public schools more accountable to the department by linking federal aid to national standards of learning. Social conservatives had long sought to advance morality by opposing abortion. Bush, as the stem cell controversy showed clearly, professed to be staunchly "pro-life," but he called for more incremental attacks on abortion. More important, he proposed to buttress conservative religious values with affirmative government efforts to help the poor, promote marriage, and ensure that "every child will be educated."

The efforts to consolidate a conservative administrative state on Bush's watch may represent, to use the political scientist E. E. Schattschneider's phrase, a "displacement of conflict," in which the struggle between champions and opponents of big government has given way to a battle between liberals and conservatives for its services. This battle, as the partisan conflict over Iraq reveals, has been extended to foreign affairs. Nonetheless, the renewal of partisanship in America has not yet undermined strong agreement on core beliefs and institutional arrangements. The war on terrorism, in fact, confirmed, even strengthened, the two pillars of modern liberalism: a broad, inclusive cultural nationalism and a readiness to use federal programs and deficit financing when necessary to secure prosperity and meet large domestic and international needs. Although some hate crimes against Muslim Americans took place after September 11 and although the government did initiate a widespread investigation that caused many citizens and aliens of Middle Eastern descent to be held for questioning, the signs of intolerance were fewer than in past national crises. As the *National Journal* reported in October 2002, "Even after the deadliest-ever attack on American soil . . ., not one prominent politician is calling for martial law or an Alien and Sedition Act, or for internment of an ethnic minority group."

Indeed, the cultural divide that separated Bush and Gore supporters in the 2000 election was rendered insignificant as Americans reacted to the terrorists' expressed hatred of their way of life. After September 11, the journalist David Brooks observed, Americans rediscovered the source of their unity, printed on every penny and dollar bill: *e pluribus unum*, "from many, one." Unity stemmed from a mutual commitment "to the idea that a person is not bound by his class, or by the religion of his father but is free to build a plurality of connections for himself. We [all] are participants in the same striving process, the same experimental journey."

The conflicting evidence about the health of the nation one sees by comparing the brave and generous response to September 11 with the partisan rancor that divides Democrats and Republicans in the nation's capital indicates that this journey remains difficult. But, as the political scientist Morris Fiorina has argued, raw and disruptive partisanship, although a real and perhaps a pernicious phenomenon, is limited on most issues to a relatively small circle of political activists and members of Congress. Significantly, most Americans still support initiatives and programs that protect individual men and women from the uncertainties of the marketplace and foreign threats. It is not surprising, therefore, that rather than curtail New Deal and Great Society entitlements, as the Reagan administration promised, and ultimately failed, to do, Bush and his political allies have sought to give them a conservative image. It is significant, too, that the current White House's efforts to fundamentally change these popular programs have backfired. Bush's program to add a prescription drug benefit to the Medicare program, albeit in a way that gave considerable discretion to the pharmaceutical and insurance industries in administering it, has been very unpopular. Furthermore, the Bush White House's more ambitious effort to remake Social Security by "privatizing it" – that is allowing those under fifty-five years of age to invest some of their benefits in personal savings accounts – was met with indifference, if not avowed hostility by Democratic and Republican legislators alike.

Even as Americans continue to support the pillars of the modern liberal state, the question that remains is how can a state that is expansive and powerful enough to protect its citizens' rights provide for an active and competent citizenry? In the nineteenth century, Americans sought answers to this dilemma in a *natural rights* version of liberalism that celebrated local communities. Born of Jeffersonian and Jacksonian support of local self-government, traditional party organizations and newspapers compensated for the Constitution's insufficient attention to civic matters. But the "golden age" of parties sometimes yielded an intolerant democratic politics. Progressive and New Deal reformers had good reasons to view the foundations of the decentralized republic – the right to property and localized democracy – as obstacles to justice for the dispossessed, African Americans, and women.

The new constitutional order spawned by the New Deal has introduced more centralized bureaucratic politics that emphasize rights – entitlements to domestic and international security – to the detriment of the mainsprings of America's democratic tradition: local community, decentralized parties, and political participation. This "rights revolution" weakened the civic bonds that spawn passionate democratic engagement. Still, as the events of September 11 show, there can be no return to weak national government. There was little political opposition to the Bush administration's creation of a new Department of Homeland Security, or to his imposition of tighter restrictions on airports, or to his embrace of deficit spending to ease the economic disruptions caused by the terrorist attack. Although he has been deeply committed to strengthening the Republican party, Bush found himself justifying the War on Terror in a manner reminiscent of FDR. "Freedom and fear are at war," he told a joint session of Congress on September 20, 2001. "The advance of human freedom, the great achievement of our time, and great hope of every time, now depends on us. Our nation, this generation, will lift a dark threat of violence from our people and our future. We will rally the world to this cause by our efforts, by our courage. We will not tire, we will not falter, and we will not fail."

Built in response to the Great Depression, World War II, and the threat of communism, the modern American state is obligated to tackle problems such as discrimination at home and terrorism abroad. It remains to be seen whether the heartfelt signs of patriotism and unity that followed the unspeakable horrors of September 11 mean that "freedom from want" and "freedom from fear" can now be achieved without sacrificing common deliberation and public judgment, the means to sustain a vital civic culture. Rather than lamenting debate and conflict over issues like stem cell research and the war in Iraq, we should perhaps accept such controversy as a hopeful sign that the contemporary obsession with security – the lodestar of the modern liberal state – has not caused Americans to lose all interest in political affairs, the sort of indifference that Tocqueville considered the greatest threat to liberty in a commercial republic like the United States. Still, it is unlikely that the tension between liberalism and democracy can ever be resolved. The tension between individual rights and rule of the people is at the heart of the political development of the American nation.

☆ Each great political episode in American political development was a *refounding* that engaged citizens in conflict and resolution about the meaning of the Declaration and Constitution for their own time.

☆ The first two great political parties, the Federalists and the Republicans, disagreed fundamentally about the relationship between liberalism and democracy and about whether rights were best protected by limiting or by encouraging active citizen participation.

☆ The first refounding, which took place during the presidency of Thomas Jefferson, promoted democracy by endorsing and nurturing such democratic principles as free speech, legislative supremacy, and a powerful defense of states' rights.

☆ The second refounding, during the presidency of Andrew Jackson, greatly expanded upon the democratic impulses of the first and established a party system in which presidential leadership played a critical part.

☆ The third refounding, during the presidency of Abraham Lincoln, took place in response to the slavery controversy. It entailed not only a decision to keep the Union intact but also a rededication of the Union to the principles of the Declaration of Independence.

☆ The Progressive Era did not constitute a full-fledged refounding. But it did generate new political ideas and precedents regarding national government expansion, direct democracy, and expertise in government that have remained critically influential ever since.

☆ The fourth refounding, during the presidency of FDR, rewrote the social contract to establish a stronger national state to countervail concentrated economic power and to supplement political rights with programmatic economic rights.

☆ The Great Society, propounded by President Lyndon Baines Johnson, failed in its effort to increase participatory democracy but succeeded in greatly expanding the definition of programmatic rights.

☆ Ronald Reagan halted the expansion of programmatic rights but did not reduce them. He was unable to redefine the New Deal social contract and rein in the national administrative state.

☆ The expansion of rights that has occurred since the New Deal deepens the tension between liberalism and democracy.

Major Concepts

Atlantic Charter
commercial republic
constitutional refounding
direct primary
empire of liberty
executive aggrandizement
Great Society
initiative
mass democracy
Medicare
middle-class entitlements
National Labor Relations Act
New Deal
New Freedom
New Nationalist
nullification doctrine
party system
prerogative
programmatic rights
Progressive movement
Reagan revolution
referendum
Revolution of 1800
Second Great Awakening
Sedition Act
social gospel movement

spoils system
tariff
Whigs

Suggested Readings

Ackerman, Bruce. *We the People: Foundations*. Cambridge, MA: Harvard University Press, 1991.

_____. *We the People: Transformations*. Cambridge, MA: Harvard University Press, 1998.

Bensel, Richard. *Yankee Leviathan: The Origins of Central State Authority in America, 1858–1877*. Cambridge: Cambridge University Press, 1990.

Burnham, Walter Dean. *Critical Elections and the Mainsprings of American Politics*. New York: W. W. Norton, 1971.

Derthick, Martha. *Policymaking for Social Security*. Washington, D.C.: Brookings Institution, 1979.

Eisenach, Eldon. *The Lost Promise of Progressivism*. Lawrence: Kansas University Press, 1994.

Gerstle, Gary. *American Crucible: Race and Nation in the Twentieth Century*. Princeton, NJ: Princeton University Press, 2002.

Jaffa, Harry. *Crisis of the House Divided: An Interpretation of the Issues in the Lincoln-Douglas Debates*, with a new Preface. Chicago: University of Chicago Press, 1982.

_____. *A New Birth of Freedom: Abraham Lincoln and the Coming of the Civil War*. Lanham, MD: Rowman and Littlefield, 2000.

Keller, Morton. *Affairs of State: Public Life in Late Nineteenth Century America*. Cambridge, MA: Belknap Press, 1977.

Kennedy, David. *Freedom from Fear: The American People in Depression and War, 1929–1945*. New York: Oxford University Press, 1999.

Landy, Marc, and Martin Levin, eds. *The New Politics of Public Policy*. Baltimore, MD: Johns Hopkins University Press, 1995.

Lowi, Theodore. *The End of Liberalism: The Second Republic of the United States*, 2d ed. New York: W. W. Norton, 1979.

McConnell, Grant. *Private Power and American Democracy*. New York: Vintage Books, 1970.

McMahon, Kevin J. *Reconsidering Roosevelt on Race: How the Presidency Paved the Road to Brown*. Chicago: University of Chicago Press, 2004.

Mettler, Suzanne. *Soldiers to Citizens: The G. I. Bill and the Making of the Greatest Generation*. New York: Oxford University Press, 2005.

Milkis, Sidney M. and Jerome Mileur, eds. *The New Deal and the Triumph of Liberalism*. Amherst: University of Massachusetts Press, 2002.

Milkis, Sidney M. *The President and the Parties: The Transformation of the American Party System since the New Deal*. New York: Oxford University Press, 1992.

Morone, James. *The Democratic Wish: Popular Participation and the Limits of American Government*. New Haven, CT: Yale University Press, 1998.

_____. *Hellfire Nation: The Politics of Sin in American History*. New Haven, CT: Yale University Press, 2003.

Patterson, James. *Grand Expectations: The United States, 1945–1974*. New York: Oxford University Press, 1996.

Sanders, Elizabeth. *The Roots of Reform: Farmers, Workers, and the American State, 1877–1917*. Chicago: University of Chicago Press, 1999.

Skocpol, Theda. *Protecting Soldiers and Mothers: The Political Origins of Social Policy in the United States*. Cambridge, MA: Harvard University Press, 1992.

Skowronek, Steven. *Building a New American State: The Expansion of National Administrative Capacities, 1877–1920*. New York: Cambridge University Press, 1982.

_____. *The Politics Presidents Make: Leadership from John Adams to Bill Clinton*. Cambridge, MA: Harvard University Press, 1993.

Young, James Sterling. *The Washington Community: 1800–1828*. New York: Columbia University Press, 1965.

Case Study: Is There a Culture War in America?

Although they debate its depth and severity, political scientists, historians, sociologists, public intellectuals, and pundits tend to agree that American politics and government have become more polarized over the past twenty-five years. Partisan rancor has increased; what's more, Republicans and Democrats have become anchored in distinct regions, states, and communities: the Republicans in the Southern, border, and mountain states, especially in small towns and "exurban" enclaves; the Democrats along the two coasts, especially in the major metropolitan areas. Moreover, those pundits and scholars who see party polarization resting in fundamental principles fear that the popular consensus necessary to sustain responsible constitutional government, requiring a citizenry that celebrates individual rights and the separation of church and state, has been eroded by "culture wars"; the "two Americas," they claim, have been divided on issues such as abortion, stem cell research, and gay marriage that defy any meaningful sense of national community. As one high-level Republican political operative has put it, "We have two massive colliding forces. One is rural, Christian, religiously conservative. [The other] is socially tolerant, pro-choice, secular, living in New England and the Pacific coast."

As we noted in Chapter 4, the conflict over gay marriage emerged as a national issue in November 2003, when the Massachusetts Supreme Court issued its controversial ruling in *Goodrich v. Department of Public Health*. Julie and Hilary Goodrich and six other couples filed the lawsuit in 2001 after being denied marriage licenses. The case made its way to the state's highest court, which declared that "barring an individual from the protections, benefits, and obligations of civil marriage solely because a person would marry a person of the same sex violates the Massachusetts Constitution." Despite Massachusetts Republican governor Mitt Romney's efforts to stop them, the first same-sex marriages took place six months later. During the next two years, more than 8000 same-sex couples married in Massachusetts.

Goodrich deeply divided conservative and liberal activists who sought to engage the American people in public debate and resolution of a challenge to one of Western civilizations most sacred institutions. In the aftermath of the *Goodrich* decision, lawsuits backed by the ACLU and gay rights groups were initiated in several other states with the object of persuading the courts to declare that same-sex couples had a right to marry based on state constitutional protections for equality and due process. The groups hoped that this strategy would eventually establish legal precedents that might influence the United States Supreme Court to endorse a constitutional right to same-sex unions nationwide. In the midst of these legal battles, San

Francisco mayor Gavin Newsome issued an executive order that required city clerks to issue marriage licenses to gay couples. National television showed hundreds of gay couples lining up in the rain and waiting through the night to receive marriage licenses from city hall. This highly publicized drama was largely symbolic, as Newsome's decree violated Proposition 22, supported by 61.4 percent of the state's voters in 2000, which defined marriage as solely between a man and a woman. Newsome's executive order thus quickly became part of a lawsuit that slowly worked its way through the California court system.

The campaign to establish same-sex marriage as a fundamental right aroused a strong counteroffensive. Conservative Christians such as Focus on the Family's James Dobson flooded the airwaves urging followers to bury federal lawmakers with calls and letters. The eruption of faith-driven activism prodded Republicans leaders in Congress into drafting the Marriage Protection Amendment, a federal constitutional amendment that would preserve marriage and its benefits for unions between men and women. Lending his support to this amendment, President Bush linked the issue of gay marriage to abortion, thus crafting, according to the *Washington Post*, his most reliable applause line during the 2004 campaign: "I stand for marriage and family, which are the foundations of our society. I stand for a culture of life in which every person matters and every being counts."

Although the proposed constitutional amendment failed in the Senate in 2004, gaining only forty-seven of the sixty-six votes needed, the battle for marriage continued at the state level where, as noted in Chapter 4, ballot measures banning same-sex marriage were successful in thirteen states: two (Missouri and Louisiana) voted earlier in the year; eleven more, including Oregon and Michigan, which supported the Democratic candidate for President, Senator John Kerry of Massachusetts, voted November 2. The results of these state initiatives, combined with an exit poll that appeared to show that social issues significantly influenced voting decisions, led to claims that George Bush's opposition to gay marriage gave him the election. This interpretation gained plausibility by the results in Ohio, the critical swing state in the election, in which 62 percent of the voters approved a ban on same-sex marriage. The gay marriage initiative, many commentators claimed, inspired a heavy turnout of social conservatives whose support proved pivotal to Bush's victory in Ohio, and the nation.

Many pundits and scholars suggested that the gay marriage controversy confirmed that the American polity, once governed by constitutional forms that facilitated compromise and a civic culture that privileged the "vital center," was now polarized by party confrontations over issues that scarred the political landscape with deep schisms. But most evidence showed that national and homeland security, not social controversies like gay marriage, were the most riveting and polarizing issues during the 2004 presidential election. Indeed, gay marriage counted among the least important issues tested in surveys that asked voters to rank their priorities for the 2004 election. Similarly, as noted in Chapter 4, popular disaffection with the Iraq War, which led to a dramatic decline in support for Bush among independents and moderate Republicans, reenergized Democrats and enabled them to capture the House and Senate in the 2006 elections. There was little talk about gay marriage in the midterm campaigns, even though constitutional amendments banning same-sex marriage were on the 2006 ballot in eight states. Voters approved seven of these eight measures (Arizona became the first state to reject a same-sex marriage amendment), but not with any sense of urgency that could counteract the tide that swept the Republicans out of power. Even a New Jersey Supreme Court case, which occurred late in the campaign season, ruling that same-sex couples should enjoy the same legal rights as heterosexual couples, failed to rally the Republican base.

Most of the public, in fact, has expressed great ambivalence about the marriage controversy, especially about efforts to enact a federal constitutional amendment that would ban same-sex unions. The fact that Congress has repeatedly failed to approve such an amendment, most recently in July 2006, testifies to the fact that a significant number of Americans who personally oppose gay marriage do not support a constitutional amendment to ban it.

When cast against the history of civil rights conflicts in the United States, the gay marriage controversy highlights the ongoing tension in American politics between rights claims and majority rule – between the nation's liberal and democratic traditions. As the results of anti-gay marriage initiatives show, a majority of the public (about two-thirds in most polls) feels strongly about reserving the privilege of marriage to unions between men and women. The enduring support for traditional marriage in the United States suggests that it embodies what James Madison's "Federalist No. 63" characterized as "the deliberate sense of the community." The most prominent feature of the gay marriage issue was not polarization or rancorous partisanship, but rather settled agreement.

At the same time, Americans have become much more supportive of rights for gay men and women during the past several decades. Even as they oppose gay marriage, a majority of Americans, including President Bush, express support for civil unions that would provide gay couples many of the same rights as married couples. A July 2006 Pew poll, for example, showed that 54 percent of the respondents favored such unions, an increase from the 45 percent who expressed support for them in 2003. Popular support for economic equality has increased even more dramatically: Gallup

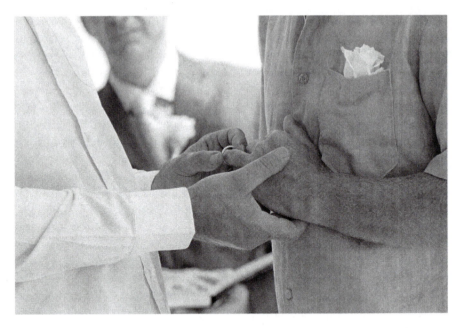

Hot topic issues such as gay marriage highlight not only the importance of social issues to partisan politics but also the tension between rights claims and majority rule.

Polls in 1997 showed that 56 percent of those surveyed supported the idea that homosexual men and women "should have equal rights in terms of job opportunities," while 33 percent did not favor fair job treatment. By 2006, when asked the same questions, 89 percent favored equal treatment while only 9 percent opposed. The discrepancy between Americans' views on gay marriage and other forms of civil and economic rights for homosexuals is demonstrated dramatically by California legal standards. Although Proposition 22 passed overwhelmingly, California is one of the best places in the nation for gays to live: the state offers domestic partner rights that range from adoption to health insurance and provides legal shields against discrimination and hate crime.

According to the noted sociologist James David Hunter, who coined the phrase "culture wars," the success of the gay rights movement is the most recent example of an underlying narrative in American culture about freedom. Just as *Brown v. Board of Education* was ahead of public opinion in many respects and initiated critical changes in deep-rooted American conventions, the *Goodrich* case, Hunter suggests, might push the country down the road to a greater commitment to fundamental rights for gay men and women. Gay rights advocates have tapped into a deep cultural structure very successfully, he claims, "so that when conservatives challenge gay rights, whatever rights they are, it sounds like they're against freedom. And that's a losing proposition."

Yet, as we have shown, the narrative of freedom in the United States has been roiled by conflict that has engaged Americans in contests about the appropriate meaning of their rights. The struggle for civil rights for African Americans and women has not been resolved by judicial or executive decrees. Battles for these entitlements have been waged in the streets, electoral campaigns, state legislatures, and the halls of Congress. On occasion, as in the case of affirmative action, these struggles have been subject to uneasy compromises between the claims of rights and the settled standards of the community. As the controversy over gay marriage played out, some commentators hopefully identified a middle ground that would defy the culture wars waged by liberal and conservative activists: a compromise that would privilege traditional marriage yet provide gay couples a legal structure in which to arrange and manage their domestic lives. As has been the case with the ongoing controversy over affirmative action, however, such a compromise with respect to gay rights is unlikely to end a conflict between the rights claims of a minority and the settled conventions that a majority of Americans embrace. At its deepest level, the fight over gay marriage entails an exalted, ineluctable struggle between the right of homosexuals to share in a sacred institution and majority opinion that seeks to uphold the deepest values of family and faith.

PART TWO

Pivotal Relationships

5 Federalism

This chapter focuses on:

☆ The competition for power between states and the national government that has acted as a driving force in American political development

☆ The claims and counterclaims about liberty and democracy that have shaped the competition for power between states and the national government

☆ The different kinds of relationships between the national government and the states that federalism has incorporated, including dual, cooperative, "strings attached," and unfunded mandates federalism

☆ The current role of the states in making and administering public policy and in influencing national politics and policy

In 1992, a twelfth-grade student arrived at Edison High School in San Antonio, Texas, carrying a concealed .38-caliber handgun and five bullets. He was arrested and eventually charged with violating a federal law, the Gun Free School Zones Act of 1990. In 1995, in the case of *United States v. Lopez*, the U.S. Supreme Court overturned his conviction. The court did not dispute the prosecution's account. Lopez did in fact have a pistol in school. Nor did the court deny that guns in school are a bad thing deserving of punishment. Instead, the court found that the national government did not have the authority to make laws regarding guns in schools. It determined that the Constitution made this issue a state and local one, not a federal one.

In America, disputes over what the government ought to do frequently turn into disputes over where the decision should be made. The gravest crisis in all of American history, the Civil War, was fought both about the issue of slavery and about whether the national government was supreme over the states. One hundred years later, when federal courts imposed crosstown busing as the remedy for racial segregation in the schools, opponents claimed that the federal government had unconstitutionally usurped the power to make education policy. The fight over *what* turns into a fight over *where* because the Constitution does not fully clarify the dividing line between state and federal power.

If all one knew of the Constitution were the preamble's promise to "insure domestic tranquility and promote the general welfare," it would seem perfectly clear that the federal government had the right to put Lopez in jail. Few people would dispute that tranquility and the general welfare are better served when schools are free of guns. However, if all one knew of the Constitution were the Tenth Amendment's requirement that "the powers not delegated to the United States by the Constitution nor prohibited by it to the States, are reserved to the states," Lopez would be set free and a whole range of national government activity would be clearly unconstitutional. Where does the Constitution say that the federal government can set safety standards for drinking water or require colleges to provide equal funding for women's sports?

As we discussed in Chapter 3, this lack of clarity about the limits of national power exists because at the time of the founding the country was divided between those who wanted a strong national government and those who did not. The Constitution is to some extent a compromise between those two colliding points of view. In order to obtain consent for the establishment of a strong national government, its supporters agreed to limit its powers to those that were expressly delegated to it. They also agreed to give the states a direct role in national governance via the Senate and the Electoral College, both of whose members are elected on a state-by-state basis.

From the beginning, the argument about the relative power of the states and the federal government was fought on the basis of appeals to liberty and democracy. Defenders of a strong central government viewed the passionate attachments provoked by states and localities as a crucial threat to liberty, whereas defenders of the states saw those same passionate attachments as wellsprings of democratic energy and as bulwarks of liberty that defended local rights and privileges against centralized despotism. To this day, claims and counterclaims about liberty and democracy dominate debate about federalism.

However, the terms of that debate have shifted. Now, advocates of strong national government most often resort to arguments about democracy, claiming that lower units of government thwart majority will. Such advocates deploy state government to overcome local parochialism and national government to overcome state parochialism. Supporters of decentralization invoke liberty, claiming that the national government would stifle critical personal freedoms in order to homogenize and equalize life in the states and that state governments would be prone to do the same thing to the localities.

The Lopez case provides a strong illustration of the complex relationship between federalism and liberty and between federalism and democracy. Supporters of the decision point to its protection of the liberty of Texans to remain free of central government dictates and to preserve Texas as a democratic political system in which the rules are determined by the majority of its citizens. Opponents of the decision decry the loss of liberty to the students of Texas who must now face a graver threat of being gunned down in school. Opponents also lament the blow to democracy dealt by depriving a national majority, as reflected by the vote of its representatives in Congress, to be able to work its will.

This chapter is divided into five parts. The first looks at the early development of American federalism to explain how and why states and localities came to dominate. The second section examines the struggle for supremacy between states and the national government that culminated in the Civil War. The third section describes the resurgence of local and state power that took place in the war's aftermath. The fourth section explains how, in the twentieth century, federalism was transformed because of the centralizing impact of Progressivism, the New Deal, and the civil rights revolution. The fifth section looks at the current status of the states, indicates how contemporary federalism continues to be subject to both centralizing and decentralizing forces, and discusses the most important trends in state government and politics in that light. The chapter concludes by showing how America's pioneering attempt to govern immense territory in a manner compatible with liberty and democracy now serves as an inspiration for federalizing efforts around the world.

The Decentralized Republic

For the first 150 years of the life of the United States, the states and localities dominated. Indeed, for the first sixty years of the United States' existence, it was not clear that the Union would prevail. That question was
decisively settled only by the Civil War. Even after the Civil War, local
self-government, supported by the more decentralizing institutions of the
Constitution – Congress and the states – remained the most prominent
feature of American political life. The national idea and the constitutional
structure that frames it were preserved in the absence of a powerful central
state. Only in the middle of the twentieth century, as a result of the New
Deal and the Second World War, did Americans come to view national
governance as dominant in their political lives (see Figure 5.1).

This long struggle to create a nation was born of the Constitutional Convention. As we explained in Chapter 3, the key victory that supporters of
the Constitution scored over their opponents was to enshrine the idea of a
large republic. America was to be a great nation that combined the size and
strength of the leading European powers with a dedication to individual
liberty and republican rule that the older nations lacked. Although leading
Americans might have disagreed about how the government of the American nation should be organized, they shared a profound commitment to
the national idea itself as expressed in the Declaration of Independence:
"that all men are created equal, that they are endowed by their Creator
with certain unalienable rights." America was the land where liberty ruled.
Box 1 briefly describes and discusses the most important clauses of the
Constitution that deal with federalism.

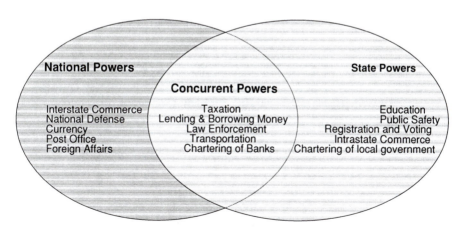

Figure 5.1. Federalism Venn Diagram. Federalism as a governing system:
examples of national, state, and concurrent powers.

Key Constitutional Clauses Relating to Federalism

"We the People" – The preamble to the Constitution boldly states that the constituent element of the Union is the people, not the states. The existence of this clause emboldened Andrew Jackson to suppress South Carolina's attempt to nullify a national law and it also encouraged Lincoln to declare the South's secession unconstitutional.

"The Senate of the United States shall be composed of Two Senators from each state ... " – Article I, Section 3 establishes that the upper chamber of the national legislature shall be composed of representatives of the states, two per state. It also established this clause as unamendable.

"To regulate commerce among the several states ... " – The commerce power enumerated in Article I, Section 8 has been the most frequently used rationale for national government intervention in state affairs.

"No state shall enter into any treaty, alliance or confederation ... " – Article I, Section 10 provides a list of prohibitions on the states. Those prohibitions mirror, for the most part, the powers expressly delegated to the national government.

"Each state shall appoint ... a number of electors equal to the whole number of Senators and Representatives to which that state is entitled ... " – Article IIII, Section 1 establishes that the president will be elected by an Electoral College chosen by the states, proportioned roughly to their population.

"Full faith and credit ... privileges and immunities ... " – Article IVIV, Section 1 and Section 2 declare that each state must respect the laws adopted in the other states and that a citizen of one state enjoys the same rights as those in other states. It does not, however, clarify what happens if two states adopt laws that contradict one another, as in the case of gay marriage where, for example, Massachusetts permits it and Ohio forbids it.

"A republican form of government..." – Article IVIV, Section1 declares that the national government shall ensure that the essential republican character of each state is protected either from subversion or from invasion.

"The powers not delegated..." – The Tenth Amendment restricts the national government to the powers granted by the Constitution, reserving all others to the states or to the people.

"The Judicial power...shall not be construed..." – The Eleventh Amendment prevents the national government from interfering in suits between citizens of different states or between a foreigner and a state.

"Nor shall any state deprive any person of...due process of law...(or) equal protection of the laws..." – The Fourteenth Amendment gives the national government the authority to prevent states from denying individuals these fundamental rights.

"The right of citizens of the United States to vote..." – The Fifteenth Amendment forbids the states from denying citizens the right to vote on the basis of race, color, or previous conditions of servitude. The Nineteenth Amendment forbids them from denying the vote on the basis of sex. The Twenty-fourth Amendment forbids them to deny the vote by reason of failure to pay a poll tax or any other tax. The Twenty-seventh Amendment forbids them from establishing voting age requirements on anyone above the age of eighteen.

Federalists and Federalism

The Federalists believed that preserving and promoting the great American nation required a powerful central government but not an all-powerful one. They accepted the limits on government that were stipulated in the Constitution, especially the concept of enumerated powers (see Chapter 3). But they argued that those enumerated powers provided plenty of support for an active and energetic government. In particular, such a central government had ample authority to protect the nation against foreign threat and to stimulate and direct economic expansion. These crucial goals required a well organized federal bureaucracy, a well staffed professional army and navy, and a court system capable of settling disputes between the states and the national government.

The Federalists were unapologetically elitist. Although they accepted the idea that the people were the ultimate source of authority, they sought to make popular rule as indirect as possible. Because the central government was further removed from the citizenry than were the states and localities, Federalists were more confident that it could be made to function in a stable and reliable manner. They were particularly supportive of its two least democratic elements, the Senate and the Supreme Court.

Republicans and the Compact Theory

The most fundamental difference between Federalists and their rivals, Thomas Jefferson's Republicans, revolved around the very nature of the U.S. Constitution. Did it bind each individual American directly to the national government, or was it a compact entered into by the states? Republicans held to the *compact theory*. They reminded the Federalists that the Constitution had been adopted on a state-by-state basis. They interpreted the phrase "We the People" to mean "we the people of the several states," implying that the federal government was not necessarily superior to the states and could not necessarily make demands on the citizens of a state if the state government opposed those demands. The first serious challenge to federal supremacy occurred in 1798, when the legislatures of Kentucky and Virginia passed resolutions rescinding the national Sedition Act – which punished people who made false accusations against the government – and urging other states to do the same (see Chapter 4). The Kentucky resolution went so far as to claim that each state had the right to nullify, or refuse to obey, acts of the federal government. The other states refused to join in on these acts of defiance. Once Thomas Jefferson took office as president in 1801, he simply allowed the Sedition Act to expire.

An Empire of Liberty

The Republicans, Jefferson's party, believed in majority rule. They viewed the Federalists not merely as elitists but as monarchists in the making. They saw no possibility of preserving constitutionally guaranteed liberties in the face of a strong central state. Their understanding of enumerated powers was much more severe in its limitation on government. They were deeply suspicious of the two least democratic aspects of the constitutional order, the Senate and the Supreme Court.

Jefferson's hostility to central government did not undermine his commitment to the nation. But he was convinced that the greatness of the American nation rested in the beliefs and sentiments of the people, which included a deeply felt aversion to a strong national government. Central government was too ponderous to oversee the expanse of territory that Jefferson envisaged as America's "empire of liberty." This empire would be ruled not by soldiers and bureaucrats but by the shared commitment to the great governing principles of the rights to "life, liberty, and the pursuit of happiness." Jefferson's empire of liberty would be the first in all humankind not to be ruled from a single center. He was committed to preventing New York or Philadelphia from controlling this empire the way Rome, Paris, and London had become the controlling forces of the Roman, French, and British empires.

Respect and affection between the scattered provinces of this empire would be insufficient to hold such a large entity together unless those sentiments were held together by common material interests. If shared reverence for the principles of the Declaration of Independence were the ideological glue for holding the empire of liberty together, the practical adhesive would be commerce. Trading with people in other parts of the country would enable Americans to develop ties of trust, respect, and reciprocity. Because people in different parts of the far-flung nation needed goods produced in other parts, buying and selling provided an avenue for developing a national outlook that politics, an essentially local activity, did not.

In order for commerce to play this crucial integrating role in national life, it needed to be kept free and open. Jefferson's fear of economic concentration and monopoly mirrored his opposition to political centralization. If economic life became dominated by an elite, an economic despotism would emerge that was every bit as destructive of liberty as political despotism was. Indeed, the two worked hand in hand. Economic privilege could flourish only if government power was wielded to establish and protect it. To keep this unholy marriage of economic and political power from being consummated, Jefferson – in his role as George Washington's secretary of state – opposed Secretary of the Treasury Alexander Hamilton's plan to establish a national bank (see Chapter 4). Despite the objections of Jefferson and his allies, Congress approved the First Bank of the United States in 1791. But the Jefferson Republicans refused to renew the first National Bank's charter in 1811 on the grounds that it was unconstitutional. Although the severe economic dislocations of the War of 1812 persuaded President James Madison and the Republicans to charter a second national bank in 1816, they did so with the view that it was a necessary evil that had the potential to corrupt the republic.

Jefferson's presidency enshrined the pattern of federalism that endured in crucial respects until the New Deal of the 1930s. Jefferson rejected the Hamiltonian spirit that had crept into the interpretation of governmental powers during the first twelve years of the new nation. He abandoned the ambitious projects that Hamilton had embarked on; he cut the federal budget; and he made clear that the initiative for domestic public policy making would reside with the individual states. But he left the letter of the Constitution intact. Certain that he and his congressional allies would interpret the Constitution in a manner consistent with states' rights, Jefferson saw no need to embolden the states to adopt the role of super-legislature as he himself had outlined it in the Kentucky resolution.

At the same time that he decentralized policy making, Jefferson spearheaded the greatest territorial extension in American history. As a result of his purchase of the Louisiana territory from France in 1803, the nation more than doubled in size. Although much of the newly acquired territory was thought to be uninhabitable, the sheer magnitude of the additions changed Americans' understanding of themselves from a country dominated by the eastern seaboard to a nation of truly continental proportions. As Jefferson's theory of an empire of liberty dictated, these territories would not become colonies. Each would establish its own government and quickly be absorbed into the vast nation of states. Jefferson acted in the service of this vision, even though he conceded in a letter to Senator John Breckenridge of Kentucky that he did not think the Constitution provided "for our holding foreign territory, still less for incorporating foreign nations into our own union."

Cooperative Federalism

Nor did Jefferson and his Republican allies oppose all forms of federal intervention in state affairs. Although Jefferson did not believe that the federal government should directly undertake such publicly beneficial activities as building roads or establishing universities, he supported the proposal by his secretary of the treasury, Albert Gallatin, to give grants of land to the states for the support of public schools. Over time, land grants to the states would be used to support activities such as higher education, canal and railroad construction, river and harbor improvements, land reclamation, and veterans' benefits. Jefferson did not object to this form of federal involvement in his empire of liberty because he felt that it was cooperative and non-coercive. Land was preferable to cash as a form of subsidy, believed Jefferson, because the federal government owned so much land. This idea of a *cooperative federalism* that enabled states to enjoy federal help for programs they wanted to do anyway remains a key aspect of the state-federal relationship to the present day.

Cooperative federalism was the driving force in the creation of the American system of state universities. The Morrill Act of 1862 gave land grants to states to establish colleges that taught agriculture, mechanical arts, military science, natural science, and classical studies. Whereas only seventeen state universities existed before 1862, the Morrill Act led to the creation of sixty-nine more. Because Congress set such clear and strict standards regarding curriculum, the Morrill Act represents the first important example of federal strings being attached to state grants. Ever since, federal and state governments have differed about how tight and how numerous such strings should be.

Modern agricultural and transportation policy have also been framed by cooperative federalism. The Smith Lever Act, enacted in 1914, created the Department of Agriculture's Extension Service. Rather than impose technical advice on wary farmers, the Extension Service functions as a partnership between the Department of Agriculture and the state land grant colleges. Federal employees work with federally subsidized state specialists to develop programs of technical assistance geared to the specific needs and preferences of local farmers.

Road building is one of the most important but also most politically sensitive responsibilities of government. Decisions about where to put roads and where to locate entrances and exits to limited-access roads can determine which communities prosper and which ones die. Rather than try to make such difficult and politically potent decisions from afar, Washington has, for the most part, restricted its role to providing funds to the states to pursue highway projects. Since the 1920s, federally subsidized road building and repair have been among the most important activities of the states.

However, cooperative federalism's emphasis on unconditional assistance no longer applies. Now, federal aid comes replete with pages and pages of guidelines, timetables, and restrictions. States still enjoy a great deal of discretion in how they spend federal money, but that discretion is never complete or uncomplicated. Figure 5.2 demonstrates the high degree of state dependency on such aid.

The Struggle for Federal Supremacy

The period from the election of Andrew Jackson as president to the end of the Civil War was characterized by intense efforts to decentralize political power, to dissolve the Union, and to preserve it. Ultimately, the Union was preserved and the supremacy of the national government was established, but the states were able to retain a formidable degree of political power.

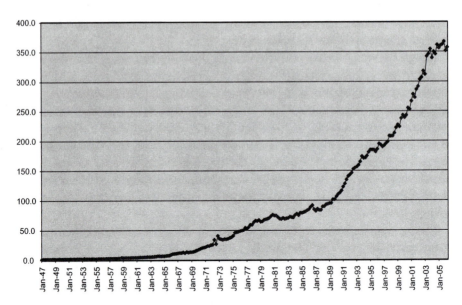

Figure 5.2. Federal Grants-in-Aid to State and Local Governments.
Amounts are in billions of dollars.
Source: U.S. Department of Commerce: Bureau of Economic Analysis.

The Supreme Court, Defender of National Supremacy

The successors to Hamilton and Jefferson as spokesmen for the cause of centralization and decentralization were, respectively, Chief Justice John Marshall of the Supreme Court and President Andrew Jackson. Marshall took the lead both in enshrining the supremacy of the national government and in preventing states from obstructing the free markets and undermining individual property rights. In a series of unanimous decisions over a period of almost thirty-five years, the Marshall Court established the principle of the supremacy of the federal government over the states and limited the states' ability to interfere with economic competition, property rights, and the sanctity of contracts.

As we discuss in Chapter 9, Marshall's opinion in *McCulloch v. Maryland* (1819) clearly established the supremacy of the federal government over the states. In that case, the Supreme Court voided a tax that the state of Maryland had imposed on the Second National Bank of the United States. Marshall asserted that the Constitution was derived from the people, not the states. Although limited to those powers specifically enumerated by the Constitution, the federal government's authority was supreme within those limits. The Constitution does not mention the chartering of a national bank, but according to Marshall, such a financial institution was obviously "necessary and proper" for carrying out the enumerated powers to tax and to regulate commerce. Although states also have the right to tax, they do not have the right to tax federal functions. As the Maryland example demonstrated, such taxes have the power to hamper and indeed to destroy legitimate federal activities. Box 2 describes a contemporary dispute about the right of the states to tax.

Taxing the Internet

In 1998, Congress enacted The Internet Tax Freedom Act, which prohibits states from imposing sales taxes on internet purchases. The temporary ban was later extended through 2007. Exempting internet sales follows the precedent the Supreme Court established in 1992 when, in *Quill v. North Dakota*, it exempted interstate mail order sales from sales taxation.

As internet sales mushroom, many state governors are questioning the wisdom of the internet exemption. States amass much of their revenue from sales taxes. They fear that the exemption will undermine the ability of states to raise necessary revenue and give an unfair competitive advantage to e-commerce and mail order at the expense of stores. Of course, this problem could be resolved by abolishing retail sales taxes altogether but this would only worsen the revenue raising problems that states face. In defending its desire to enable states to tax interstate mail order and the internet, the National Governors Association makes an additional civic argument. It claims that local stores make a distinctive contribution to a community's civic and economic vitality that distant mail order and internet companies do not make and that stores should not suffer the 6 to 8 percent price advantage that sales tax exemption grants to those competitors.

Those who favor the tax exemption argue that, so far, internet sales have not hurt state sales tax collections, which have been continuing to rise at a healthy clip. They worry that the imposition of tax burdens would hinder the huge number of very small entrepreneurs who find the internet to be the lowest cost form of advertising and selling their products. Often these people have very little capital and operate on tiny profit margins. A website is infinitely cheaper to establish and maintain than a store. If the cost of doing business were to rise as the result of taxation, the internet's phenomenal ability to stimulate entrepreneurship would decline.

Both sides may well be correct. As the internet gains legitimacy and credibility, it may well eat into retail store sales hurting both stores and the states that depend on them for sales tax revenue. And, if sales taxes are imposed, small sellers operating on narrow profit margins may well go out of business. An important means for escaping poverty may disappear. Therefore, any decision about imposing sales tax on the internet may pit the well-being of communities and the recipients of sales tax–funded public services against the well-being of low-income people trying to pull themselves up by their bootstraps via the inexpensive merchandising vehicle of the internet.

In *Gibbons v. Ogden* (1824), the court ruled that New York's granting of a monopoly for steamboat service violated the federal government's right to protect the freedom of interstate commerce. Marshall took a broad view of commerce, claiming that it included all aspects of trade, including shipping. He argued that the commerce affected by the New York steamboat monopoly was interstate in character even though the monopoly applied only to the New York portion of waterways. Those waterways, coastal and inland, extended beyond the borders of New York and were therefore aquatic avenues of interstate commerce. It was the constitutional responsibility of the federal government to ensure that trade remained free at all points along those interstate routes.

Marshall's success was based on the power of his reasoning and his self-discipline. He knew that the combined strength of the legislative and executive branch could defeat him by passing constitutional amendments that voided the court's decisions, by impeaching him and his allies, or by defying the court's rulings. Therefore, he picked his opportunities carefully. The court refused to entertain any important cases regarding the two most controversial issues of the time, slavery and the tariff, because feelings about those two issues were so strong that any decision the court might choose to render would risk tearing the country apart. Marshall's court confined itself to cases in which some disagreement existed among its erstwhile opponents, the Republicans. For example, many Republicans were so deeply committed to free enterprise that they shared Marshall's opposition to New York's establishment of steamboat monopoly. Likewise, many Republicans appreciated the positive economic contribution of the Second National Bank and were therefore opposed to the efforts of specific states to hamper its activities. Thus the rulings that the court handed down were relatively uncontroversial; their great importance lay in the precedents they established. Because his political opponents were so preoccupied by the immediate implications of the rulings, they underestimated the long-term implications.

The Democratic Localist Revolution

Whereas the limits of Supreme Court power required Marshall to concentrate on the long term in his efforts to centralize, President Andrew Jackson was able to marshal the considerable powers of the presidency to press for immediate decentralization. Lying on his sickbed in the spring of 1832, Jackson told his vice president, "The bank, Mr. Van Buren, is trying to kill me, but I will kill it."

With that, Jackson set about to veto the rechartering of the Second National Bank of the United States, an act that most vividly symbolized his determination to radically curtail the power of the national government. He objected to the bank on democratic-egalitarian grounds. Jackson was convinced that the bank granted "exclusive gratuities and privileges" that "made the rich richer and the potent more powerful."

The bank controlled the money supply and was the dominant lender in America, making 20 percent of all commercial loans. This extraordinary combination of powers enabled it to crush rival banks by manipulating their reserves and to curry favor with Congress by granting legislators loans at favorable rates. Jackson was not inclined to reform the bank. He was suspicious of the very idea of a national bank, fearing that so much financial power placed in a single institution would inevitably lead to privilege and corruption. Better to abolish it and disperse its functions among state banks, believed Jackson. The best way to make the national government democratic was to give it as little to do as possible.

Jackson's actions were consonant with the growing democratic sentiment of the time and with the principle that democracy could best be encouraged locally. In the1820s and 1830s, many states rewrote their constitutions primarily in order to make them more democratic. Property qualifications for voting were eliminated, thereby expanding the size of the electorate to include virtually all white males. State offices, including judicial offices that had previously been appointed, became directly elected by the people. Just as the national government ceded power to the states, so states devolved powers to localities.

Jackson's decentralist convictions were so thoroughgoing that he opposed some national government projects even if he approved of their aims. In 1830, he vetoed federal aid for construction of the Maysville Road. Although the road was supposed to be a link of the national road, it was to be built entirely within the state of Kentucky. Jackson did not believe that the federal government's interstate commerce powers encompassed a project that was essentially local in nature. The road was probably a good idea, but if the people of Kentucky wanted it, Jackson asserted, they should build it.

Federal Supremacy Challenged

Unlike his idol Jefferson, Jackson did not believe in the compact theory of the Constitution. He took the phrase "We the People" literally. His vision of national power was that its scope of responsibility was very limited, but within that scope it reigned supreme. While attending a dinner in honor of Jefferson's birthday, Jackson was disturbed to hear Robert Hayne, senator from South Carolina, offer a toast to "the Union of the States and the Sovereignty of the States." In his own toast, Jackson responded "Our Federal Union, it must be preserved." Sensing that South Carolina was on the verge of passing a nullification ordinance in which it would refuse to pay federally imposed tariffs, Jackson told a South Carolina congressman:

> "Please give my compliments to my friends in your state, and say to them that if a single drop of blood shall be shed there in opposition to the laws of the United States, I will hang the first man I can lay my hand on engaged in such treasonable conduct, upon the first tree I can reach."
>
> When Senator Hayne asked Senator Thomas Hart Benton of Missouri whether Jackson would really do such a thing, Benton replied, "When Jackson begins to talk about hanging, they can begin to look out for ropes."

Jackson responded to South Carolina's Nullification Ordinance of 1832 with a Nullification Proclamation in which he explained his refusal to accept the ordinance and his willingness to call out federal troops to quell any attempt by South Carolina to enforce it. South Carolina backed down. Although Jackson and Democrats in Congress conceded to a reduction in the tariff, the president succeeded in his objective of teaching his fellow partisans the difference between states rights and nullification of legitimate national policy. Had Jackson failed to defend federal supremacy, it would have disappeared as a premise of American constitutional government and Lincoln's later defense of it would have proved impossible.

Slavery and National Supremacy

Presidential leadership prevented a state rebellion over tariffs, but it could not do so over the expansion of slavery. Beginning with the Missouri Compromise of 1820, every effort to admit new states to the Union provoked a conflict over how the new admission would affect the political balance between slave and non-slave states. The Missouri Compromise had established the latitude line of 36°30' as the dividing line between slave and non-slave states. But as it became apparent that more new states would be established north than south of the line, proslave representatives in Congress abandoned the line as a compromise principle.

Stephen Douglas, senator from Illinois, sought to devise a new compromise principle through the exercise of what he called popular sovereignty: each territory would decide the question for itself. If a majority voted for slavery, then the territory would be admitted to the Union as a proslave state. If a majority voted no, slavery would be banned in that state. The great advantage of Douglas's plan was that it was democratic. New states could determine their own destiny. And it did not require the Congress as a whole to take a position on slavery. The American people could agree to disagree.

Douglas's opponent in the Illinois senatorial election of 1858, Abraham Lincoln, opposed the scheme. He did not deny its democratic virtues, but he saw it as a repudiation of the essential character of the Union. Echoing the Bible, Lincoln asserted that "a house divided against itself cannot stand." The Union could not endure "half-slave and half-free" because a deeper principle than democracy was at stake – the principle of freedom. As he put it so beautifully five years later in the Gettysburg Address, America was "conceived in Liberty, and dedicated to the proposition that all men were created equal." Free men could not choose to deprive others of their freedom, even if they sought to do so democratically. Lincoln built on Jackson's defense of the primacy of the Union vis-à-vis the states by equating the principle of union with the defense of human liberty.

Keeping the Union together required the establishment of a strong and active central government. The American Civil War was the first major war of the industrial age. Railroads and the telegraph became crucial weapons in the fight. A large civil and military bureaucracy was needed to cope with all the administrative and technical complexities involved in modern industrial war including telecommunications, sanitation, mass transportation, munitions manufacture, and food supply.

The Limits to Federal Supremacy

In Lincoln's Gettysburg Address, given on November 19, 1863, the brave soldiers who had died on that battlefield were honored through Lincoln's promise of a "new birth of freedom" and the restoration of "government of the people, by the people, for the people." Lincoln's intention for conceiving this new birth of freedom was the national government. The Civil War had been fought simultaneously over slavery and over the right of individual states to secede from the Union. Ending slavery required an unequivocal establishment of national supremacy.

The Thirteenth, Fourteenth, and Fifteenth Amendments to the Constitution, inspired by the Civil War, removed the stain of slavery from the Constitution and committed the federal government to secure and protect the civil and political rights of all Americans, including former slaves. But for the next 100 years, that commitment was not fulfilled. The success of the Southern states in maintaining racial segregation and in denying voting rights to African Americans continued the nullification battle by means more subtle and non-confrontational than outright secession.

In the immediate aftermath of the war, it appeared that African-American civil and political rights would indeed be secured through the vigorous exertion of national power. The United States established, for the first and only time, a powerful military government to rule on domestic soil. *Reconstruction* involved thousands of troops and was led by thirty-five generals. The South was divided into five military districts. Generals were empowered to void state and local elections; dismiss governors and mayors; and participate in the selection of tax collectors, sheriffs, judges, and other local officials. The military staffed and led the key Reconstruction agency, the Freedman's Bureau, which provided food and medical assistance to both blacks and whites and established schools for 500,000 children. Federal troops maintained law and order while Southern states rewrote their constitutions to provide slaves with full civil and political rights.

But the Reconstruction effort became increasingly halfhearted over time. The number of troops stationed in the South declined, as did the size and ambition of the Freedman's Bureau. Resistance by white Southerners took many forms, including terrorism and murder. The Ku Klux Klan was a powerful symbol and organizational weapon for this resistance.

Reconstruction ended as a result of a deal to resolve the disputed 1876 presidential election. In exchange for granting the presidency to the Republican, Rutherford B. Hayes, Democrats, the party of the white South, exacted Hayes's tacit endorsement for the end of all meaningful federal reconstruction efforts.

Jim Crow

The Supreme Court refused to employ the Fourteenth and Fifteenth Amendments to protect the civil and political rights of African Americans. It refused to overturn the literacy tests that Southern states imposed as a prerequisite for registering to vote despite ample evidence that the tests were being used to prevent African Americans from voting. In *Plessy v. Ferguson* (1896), the court ruled that municipalities could adopt laws and ordinances segregating the races as long as the separate facilities that were provided were "equal" (see Chapter 9 for a further discussion of this case). But it made no attempt to demonstrate that the separate streetcar facilities being provided by the city of New Orleans to African Americans were equal to those available to whites.

The court's inattention enabled Southern states to erect the complex and comprehensive system of racial oppression nicknamed *Jim Crow*. African Americans were prevented from voting and other forms of political participation, forbidden from eating at restaurants or staying at hotels patronized by whites, and relegated to inferior facilities at theaters and on streetcars. They were sent to separate schools and incarcerated in separate prisons and restricted to menial jobs. In the rural South, mobs tortured and hanged African-American suspects with no police interference. The Jim Crow laws, because they required a great deal of intervention by government, were the great exception to the retreat from government activism by the states in the post–Civil War era. For the purpose of maintaining white supremacy, the Southern states deviated from the prevailing liberal principles of limited government and laissez faire to establish an active and interventionist government capable of regulating and scrutinizing virtually every aspect of social and economic life.

Laissez Faire

The resistance to national government power that developed in the wake of the Civil War was not confined to the South or to racial questions. It was propelled by a new theory called *laissez faire* that blamed excessive government intervention for creating and sustaining social ills (see Chapter 6 for a more complete discussion). This dogma found ready acceptance among a war-weary people who yearned to escape the government constraints imposed on them by military necessity and who looked forward to the pleasure of private life after enduring so much hardship. The war had stimulated a vast expansion of economic life, and many Americans felt that a prosperous future lay in store if only the government would leave the economy alone.

JIM CROW LAW.

UPHELD BY THE UNITED STATES SUPREME COURT.

Statute Within the Competency of the Louisiana Legislature and Railroads—Must Furnish Separate Cars for Whites and Blacks.

Washington, May 18.—The Supreme Court today in an opinion read by Justice Brown, sustained the constitutionality of the law in Louisiana requiring the railroads of that State to provide separate cars for white and colored passengers. There was no interstate, commerce feature in the case for the railroad upon which the incident occurred giving rise to case—Plessey vs. Ferguson—East Louisiana railroad. was and is operated wholly within the State, to the laws of Congress of many of the States. The opinion states that by the analogy of the laws of Congress, and of many of states requiring establishment of separate schools for children of two races and other similar laws, the statute in question was within competency of Louisiana Legislature, exercising the police power of the State. The judgment of the Supreme Court of State upholding law was therefore upheld.

Mr. Justice Harlan announced a very vigorous dissent saying that he saw nothing but mischief in all such laws. In his view of the case, no power in the land had right to regulate the enjoyment of civil rights upon the basis of race. It would be just as reasonable and proper, he said, for states to pass laws requiring separate cars to be furnished for Catholic and Protestants, or for descendants of those of Teutonic race and those of Latin race.

Despite the ratification of the Thirteenth, Fourteenth, and Fifteenth Amendments, African Americans in the South were still treated as second-class citizens under the Jim Crow laws that persisted into the 1960s.

Belief in laissez faire shrank state government as well. Many state constitutions were revised to limit the power of state legislatures and reduce the frequency and duration of legislative sessions. As late as the 1930s, forty-two state legislatures were in session only once every two years, and half of those met for a mere sixty days or less. The Alabama legislature met only once every four years.

Laissez-faire doctrines also had a powerful impact on the Supreme Court, which, as we discuss in Chapter 9, became increasingly willing to interpret the Constitution, and the Commerce Clause in particular, as forbidding both federal and state economic regulation.

The Exception to Laissez Faire: Cities

As national and state governments retrenched, local governments came increasingly to dominate political life. Cities, towns, and counties ran the schools, provided police protection, and built and maintained the roads. They raised more taxes and spent more money than the state and federal governments combined. Their impact was particularly pronounced in the large cities that dotted the Eastern seaboard (New York, Philadelphia, Boston, and Baltimore) and in the growing industrial metropolises of the Midwest (Chicago, St. Louis, Cleveland, Minneapolis, Detroit, and Cincinnati), where a whole new form of politics and governance was emerging. These cities were home to hundreds of thousands of immigrants from Eastern Europe, Italy, and Ireland. Immigrants received a harsh welcome from the existing residents of these cities, but they were recognized as valuable new political resources by the political party organizations. Their votes were especially valuable to the Democrats, who had become a minority party in the North in the wake of the Civil War.

For the first time in American political history, government became a big business. These cities coped with their exploding populations by greatly expanding their physical infrastructure and their provision of public services. They built new streets, parks, trolley tracks, courthouses, waterworks, and sewage systems, and they multiplied the number of firefighters, police officers, building inspectors, and bureaucrats needed to regulate and assist life in the increasingly complex and chaotic urban maze.

The word *city* does not even appear in the U.S. Constitution. Technically, cities are creatures of the states and derive their governmental authority from the states. The small-town and rural legislators who controlled state government were skeptical if not hostile to the urban politicians whose ethnic, religious, and cultural backgrounds were so different from their own. Cities also suffered politically because most state senates were apportioned

The first great urban park, Central Park in New York City, was created by Frederick Law Olmsted as a result of joint efforts between social reformers and the powerful political machine, Tammany Hall.

on the basis of territory, not population. Therefore, an entire urban area housing hundreds of thousands of people might have the same number of state senators as a rural area housing a tiny fraction of that number. Defenders of this arrangement pointed out that the U.S. Constitution organized the upper chamber of the Congress in a similarly antidemocratic fashion in order to protect liberty by providing a check on the popular will. The antiurban cast of state legislatures would remain in place until the 1960s, when the Supreme Court ruled that the upper chambers of state legislatures had to be apportioned on the basis of population rather than territory.

Despite political tensions, the cities were the most dynamic and innovative political arenas of the second half of the nineteenth century. In many instances, broad coalitions were formed behind ambitious efforts at civic betterment. For example, the first great urban park, Central Park, was created as a result of the joint efforts of social reformers and the most powerful New York City political organization, Tammany Hall. These two uncomfortable allies bickered throughout the entire period of the park's construction, but their continual disputes never undermined their mutual support for the goal itself. A similar spirit of wary cooperation pervaded other great civic accomplishments, including the building of great bridges and water systems and the establishment of vital cultural institutions such as museums, libraries, and auditoriums. Table 5.1 lists the population of the twenty largest American cities as of 2005.

Suburbs

During this same period, another distinctive form of municipal life, one that would eventually come to dominate the American political landscape, came into being – the suburb. The spread of railroads and trolley lines enabled people to live farther away from their place of work. The first suburban developments were clustered around railroad and trolley stops, enabling their residents to commute to work in the city. As envisaged by such early suburban planners as Frederick Law Olmsted, suburbs would offer the best of both rural and urban life. Suburbanites would live close to nature in a neighborly, uncrowded atmosphere while still enjoying the access to good jobs and the cultural richness of the city. For some city dwellers, suburbs also represented a means of escape from the urban newcomers whose cultural, religious, and political outlook they did not share.

Most suburbs were organized into relatively small governmental units, more like the older small towns that dotted the rural landscape than the big cities that suburbs adjoined. But like the populations of the big cities, the large and growing populations of the suburbs were spread over a relatively small area, and therefore they were underrepresented in the state legislatures, especially the upper chambers. Because the suburbs were expanding so fast, they had a voracious demand for new roads, sewers, and schools. Sharing some traits with the small towns and some with the big cities, the suburbs came to represent a distinctive, new, third force in American state politics. Figure 5.3 shows the growth in the suburban population that occurred between 1910 and 2000.

Federalism Redefined

Starting in the late nineteenth century and continuing throughout most of the twentieth, federalism was transformed. The supremacy of the federal government, established in principle by the Civil War, became a concrete fact. This transformation began with its intellectual roots in Progressive thought and continued with its actual manifestation during the New Deal, the civil rights revolution of the 1960s, and the broader rights revolution that followed during the 1970s. Box 3 describes the different forms of federalism that have arisen at different periods in American history.

Table 5.1. Population of the Twenty Largest U.S. Cities, 1960–2005

Rank	1960 Place	Population	1980 Place	Population	2005[a] Place	Population
1.	New York, N.Y.	7,781,984	New York, N.Y.	7,071,639	New York, N.Y.	8,143,197
2.	Chicago, Ill.	3,550,404	Chicago, Ill.	3,005,072	Los Angeles, Calif.	3,844,829
3.	Los Angeles, Calif.	2,479,015	Los Angeles, Calif.	2,966,850	Chicago, Ill.	2,842,518
4.	Philadelphia, Pa.	2,002,512	Philadelphia, Pa.	1,688,210	Houston, Tex.	2,016,582
5.	Detroit, Mich.	1,670,144	Houston, Tex.	1,595,138	Philadelphia, Pa.	1,463,281
6.	Baltimore, Md.	939,024	Detroit, Mich.	1,203,339	Phoenix, Ariz.	1,461,575
7.	Houston, Tex.	938,219	Dallas, Tex.	904,078	San Antonio, Tex.	1,256,509
8.	Cleveland, Ohio	876,050	San Diego, Calif.	875,538	San Diego, Calif.	1,255,540
9.	Washington, DC	763,956	Phoenix, Ariz.	789,704	Dallas, Tex.	1,213,825
10.	St. Louis, Mo.	750,026	Baltimore, Md.	786,775	San Jose, Calif.	912,332
11.	Milwaukee, Wis.	741,324	San Antonio, Tex.	785,880	Detroit, Mich.	886,671
12.	San Francisco, Calif.	740,316	Indianapolis, Ind.	700,807	Indianapolis, Ind.	784,118
13.	Boston, Mass.	697,197	San Francisco, Calif.	678,974	Jacksonville, Fla.	782,623
14.	Dallas, Tex.	679,684	Memphis, Tenn.	646,356	San Francisco, Calif.	739,426
15.	New Orleans, La.	627,525	Washington, DC	638,333	Columbus, Ohio	730,657
16.	Pittsburgh, Pa.	604,332	Milwaukee, Wis.	636,212	Austin, Tex.	690,252
17.	San Antonio, Tex.	587,718	San Jose, Calif.	629,442	Memphis, Tenn.	672,277
18.	San Diego, Calif.	573,224	Cleveland, Ohio	573,822	Baltimore, Md.	635,815
19.	Seattle, Wash.	557,087	Columbus, Ohio	564,871	Fort Worth, Tex.	624,067
20.	Buffalo, N.Y.	532,759	Boston, Mass.	562,994	Charlotte, N.C.	610,949

[a]Populations for 1960–1980 are Census figures. 2005 figures are population estimates.
Source: U.S. Census Bureau. For 2000 Census figures, see *Top 50 Cities in the U.S. by Population and Rank, 1990, 2000, and 2005.*

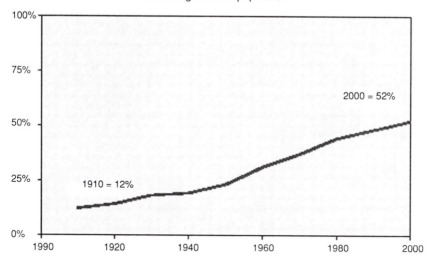

Figure 5.3. Percentage of Population Living in Suburbs.
Source: *Historical Statistics of the United States, Colonial Times to 1970,*
Bicentennial Edition (Washington, D.C.: U.S. Census Bureau, series A 57 and A
69); *Statistical Abstract of the United States* (Washington, D.C.: U.S. Census
Bureau, 1999), table 46.

Box Three: Nuts and Bolts

Forms of Federalism

The relationship between the states and the national
government has taken a variety of forms over time and continues
to do so today. None of the forms that have characterized this relationship have ever entirely disappeared, even as new forms have
been adopted. Today's federalism is an amalgam of all the forms
described below.

Dual Federalism

This form characterized the original understanding of federalism. The
states and the national government would each operate within their
own spheres with little or no overlap. Thus, the national government would exercise the powers enumerated in the Constitution and

use whatever means were "necessary and proper" to achieve those ends. For the most part this understanding limited the national government to issues relating to national security, diplomacy, trade, and currency. All other matters, such as education, morals, public works, and economic issues not directly involved in interstate and foreign trade, were the exclusive domain of the states. Although it is difficult to find an area in which the original dual federal idea functions absolutely, it remains the case that in such areas as civil law, criminal law, and education, state law and policy are far more influential than federal law and policy.

Cooperative Federalism

Cooperative federalism blurred the clear line between state and national responsibility established by the doctrine of dual sovereignty. It enabled the national government to provide aid to the states to carry out activities that both the states and the nation conceived to be in their interest. The earliest example of cooperative federalism was the dredging of harbors performed by the Army Corps of Engineers in the early 1800s. In the first half of the nineteenth century, national aid was given to states and localities to build railroads and canals as well. Two of the most important examples of cooperative federalism involved federal aid to establish state universities and federal aid for road building, an activity that continues to this day.

"Strings Attached" Federalism

The New Deal greatly increased the varieties and amount of federal aid to the states, but much of this aid came with strings attached. In order to qualify for the money, states had to adhere to many specific rules and regulations established by the national government. Most of this aid retained a cooperative dimension. States were very eager to obtain the money and quite willing to adhere to many if not most of the stipulations. But they also resented the sheer amount of paperwork involved in demonstrating to the national government that they were complying with the regulations. And, in some instances, they considered the regulations to be unnecessarily burdensome, or even counterproductive. Strings continue to be attached to current federal aid programs dealing with everything from housing to health to air pollution.

Unfunded Mandates Federalism

Since the 1970s, Congress has continued to use the states and localities to achieve policy goals that it sets. But, in many instances, it
has provided at best a small fraction of the funds that states need
to achieve those goals. Therefore, states have had to carry out
those objectives at their own expense. Among the most expensive
of Congress's unfunded mandates are the requirements that states
and localities retro-fit public buildings to make them handicapped-
accessible and build expensive water treatment plants to meet
national water quality standards. The water pollution example shows
how a cooperative program can morph into an unfunded mandate.
In the 1970s, the national government paid most of the bill for municipal water treatment plants, but to help balance its own budget it
greatly reduced its subsidy for this purpose while keeping the mandate to build such plants in place.

Progressivism

By the late nineteenth century, the prevailing doctrines of social Darwin-
ism and laissez faire began to give way in the face of powerful political
and intellectual forces that pressed for greater government intervention in
economic life. These forces crystallized into what came to be called the
Progressive movement. The changed understanding of politics, government,
and economics that the Progressives brought about would eventually lead
to the transformation of American federalism.

The Progressives pointed out the inadequacies of the prevailing orthodoxies regarding both economic and political decentralization. The great
claim of laissez faire was that it fostered economic liberty and produced
economic progress. The Progressives pointed to the growth of giant corporations and the capacity of those corporations to stifle competition as
proof that the liberty of the ordinary businessperson was being smothered
and the economic well-being of the general populace was being hampered.

Because the powers required to tame the corporations were not enumerated in the Constitution, orthodox political theory would relegate this
responsibility to the states. But in the minds of the Progressives, the states
were incapable of performing this crucial task. The big corporations operated on a multistate basis. In the 1870s and 1880s, some states had tried
to regulate the railroads, the quintessential multistate corporations. But
even before the Supreme Court had overturned many such laws, state

jurisdictional limits had rendered them ineffective. Therefore, the Progressives rejected the doctrine of enumerated powers as it was articulated in Article I of the Constitution and in the Tenth Amendment.

This new way of thinking led to only a modest expansion of national power. An Interstate Commerce Commission was established in 1887 to regulate the railroads. The Pure Food and Drug Act was passed in 1906 to enable the inspection of agricultural products and prevent unsafe drugs from being marketed. The Sherman (1890) and Clayton (1914) Antitrust Acts were passed to prevent corporations from exercising monopoly power. The Federal Trade Commission Act (1914) strengthened the national government's authority to regulate business practices. Progressivism's greatest impact was an educational one. It dominated the thinking of an entire generation of young political leaders who would exert practical political power twenty years later during the New Deal. The New Deal transformed the size and scope of the national government and did so along Progressive lines.

Because state constitutions and municipal charters were far more easily changed than the U.S. Constitution, Progressivism's near-term impact was greater on the state and local levels than at the national level. In order to democratize state politics and governance, the Progressives fought for non-partisan elections, party primary elections, and citizen-initiated referenda, initiatives, and recalls. They sought to replace partisan with non-partisan elections in the hopes that if candidates were shorn of party identification, voters would choose "the best person" rather than the party stalwart. Primary elections substituted the will of party voters for that of political leaders in determining whom the party would nominate for state and federal office. The referendum enabled voters to bypass the state legislature and vote directly for or against specific policy proposals. In the big cities, and many medium-sized ones as well, Progressives tried to build on earlier reform efforts to defeat the immigrant-based political organizations. All three of these Progressive-inspired changes are still in effect. Virtually every state now relies on party primaries to choose candidates for state and national office. Many cities including Boston and Cincinnati choose their mayors and city councilors on a non-partisan basis. Table 5.2 shows which states make use of the initiative and/or the referendum and which do not.

To illustrate the diversity of policy proposals that voters are asked to vote on directly, consider the 2004 elections. One hundred and sixty-two different referenda were on the ballot in thirty-four states. Voters approved same-sex marriage bans in eleven states. California chose to be the first state to publicly fund embryonic stem cell research. Arizona voted to require residents to prove they are U.S. citizens before they can register to vote or receive welfare benefits. Colorado voters declined to repeal limits on

Table 5.2. The Initiative and Referendum States

	Statutes			Constitution	
State	Initiative	Citizen Petition Referendum	Legislative Referendum	Initiative	Legislative Referendum
Alaska	D*	Yes	No	None	Yes
Arizona	D	Yes	Yes	D	Yes
Arkansas	D	Yes	Yes	D	Yes
California	D	Yes	Yes	D	Yes
Colorado	D	Yes	No	D	Yes
Florida	None	No	No	D	Yes
Idaho	D	Yes	Yes	None	Yes
Illinois	None	No	Yes	D	Yes
Kentucky	None	Yes	Yes	None	Yes
Maine	I	Yes	Yes	None	Yes
Maryland	None	Yes	Yes	None	Yes
Massachusetts	I	Yes	Yes	I	Yes
Michigan	I	Yes	Yes	D	Yes
Mississippi	None	No	No	I	Yes
Missouri	D	Yes	Yes	D	Yes
Montana	D	Yes	Yes	D	Yes
Nebraska	D	Yes	Yes	D	Yes
Nevada	I	Yes	Yes	D	Yes
New Mexico	None	Yes	Yes	None	Yes
North Dakota	D	Yes	Yes	D	Yes
Ohio	I	Yes	Yes	D	Yes
Oklahoma	D	Yes	Yes	D	Yes
Oregon	D	Yes	Yes	D	Yes
South Dakota	D	Yes	Yes	D	Yes
Utah	D&I	Yes	Yes	None	Yes
Washington	D&I	Yes	Yes	None	Yes
Wyoming	D*	Yes	No	None	Yes
U.S. Virgin Is.	I	Yes	Yes	I	Yes

Initiative – a law and/or constitutional amendment introduced by the citizens either to the legislature or directly to the voters.

D – Direct Initiative; proposals that qualify go directly on the ballot.

I – Indirect Initiative; proposals are submitted to the legislature, which has an opportunity to act on the proposed legislation. Depending on the state, the initiative question may go on the ballot if the legislature rejects it, submits a different proposal, or takes no action.

D* – Alaska and Wyoming's initiative processes exhibit characteristics of both the direct and indirect initiative. Instead of requiring that an initiative be submitted to the legislature for action (as in the indirect process), they require only that an initiative cannot be placed on the ballot until after a legislative session has convened and adjourned. The intent is to give the legislature an opportunity to address the issue in the proposed initiative, should it choose to do so. The initiative is not formally submitted to the legislature.

Referendum – a process by which voters may express their judgment on statutes and/or constitutional amendments enacted by the legislature.

Source: The National Conference of State Legislatures, 2007.

homeowners' suits against builders for construction defects. Montana voters approved a medical marijuana program. Michigan voters passed a measure requiring voter approval for any new gambling establishments.

In 2002, California's recall provision was the instrument used by Arnold Schwarzenegger, the famous body builder and movie star, to oust the incumbent governor, Gray Davis. After Californians voted to eject Davis in the middle of his term, a special gubernatorial election was held and Schwarzenegger won.

The Administrative State

The vast expansion of national power that took place during the New Deal enhanced rather than diminished the role of the states (see Chapter 4 for a detailed discussion of the New Deal). Most New Deal programs were cooperative endeavors between Washington and the states. The national government lacked the personnel and the administrative capacity to actually run such expensive and ambitious programs, and so it provided incentives for the states to do most of the actual work. Rather than redistribute authority from one level of government to another, the New Deal increased the total amount of government. The most important functions of state government – running the universities and the prisons, building and maintaining state roads – remained squarely within state control.

Although many state governors and legislators were suspicious of Washington, they desperately needed Washington's help and had no choice but to cooperate. Their resentment was fueled by the many strings attached to state aid. For example, states were "blackmailed" into administering the federal unemployment compensation scheme because a 3 percent tax would be levied on all employers in states that did not assume this administrative burden.

Previous federal grant programs had simply given out money to the states on the basis of relative population size or some other measure. Now, New Deal welfare grants required states to provide matching funds and to designate a single agency to be responsible for receiving and spending welfare aid. Many states had no existing agency capable of performing such a task and were compelled to create state welfare departments. Even those that already had welfare departments were required to expand and professionalize the operations of those agencies in order to meet federally imposed standards.

States emerged from the New Deal with many more functions and far greater administrative capacity with which to perform them. But the relationship between the states and the federal government was irrevocably altered. The federal government had become the senior partner. Goals and strategies for an ever-wider sphere of policies were set in Washington. The states were left with the task of implementing those policies according to rules and regulations dictated to them from above.

States responded to their roles as junior partners in different ways. Some sought to make the New Deal programs their own by vigorously endorsing and expanding them. These states created "little New Deals" in which state government took on the same expansive and experimental character that the national government did. Led by Governor Philip La Follette, Wisconsin increased taxes on the rich, expanded aid to education, and reorganized state agencies. Some states sought to resist federal encroachment. In Georgia, Governor Eugene Talmadge actually reduced state spending for highways, daring the federal government to cut highway assistance in response. He also refused to cooperate with the mandates of federal welfare and agricultural assistance programs. The fear that this approach would actually cause the federal government to stop helping Georgians led to Talmadge's defeat for reelection in 1936.

In general, the wealthier industrial states of the East and Midwest tried to cooperate with and even emulate FDR's New Deal, whereas the poorer states, primarily those in the South, resisted change to the extent they could without endangering their access to federal help. Despite the strings it imposed, the New Deal did not succeed in unifying policies across the states. Indeed, the differing state responses to it in many ways served to accentuate the political and policy differences among them.

Local government was even less disturbed by the New Deal. It retained full control of its most important historic tasks: providing education and police protection. The combined impact of the civil rights revolution that began in the 1950s and the Supreme Court's decisions on how states apportioned the voters in state legislative elections radically reduced local autonomy. By the 1960s, national authority had expanded once again, but this time at the expense of state and local authority. Table 5.3 shows how much states received from the federal government for different purposes.

The Civil Rights Legacy

The civil rights struggle was the first serious political conflict to be fully televised. Americans all over the country watched Southern sheriffs and police officers beat and bully well mannered young African-American men and women for the "crime" of ordering food at a whites-only lunch counter. Americans saw Southern governors blocking the schoolhouse doors that African-American children were politely trying to enter. These dramatic

Table 5.3. Federal Grants-in-Aid by Function (outlays; in billions of dollars)

	Actual										Estimate	
	1960	1965	1970	1975	1980	1985	1990	1995	2000	2005	2006	2007
Natural resources and environment	0.1	0.2	0.4	2.4	5.4	4.1	3.7	4.0	4.6	5.9	5.8	5.9
Agriculture	0.2	0.5	0.6	0.4	0.6	2.4	1.3	0.8	0.7	0.9	0.8	0.7
Transportation	3.0	4.1	4.6	5.9	13.0	17.0	19.2	25.8	32.2	43.4	46.7	51.5
Community and regional development	0.1	0.6	1.8	2.8	6.5	5.2	5.0	7.2	8.7	20.2	22.3	21.8
Education, training, employment, and social services	0.5	1.1	6.4	12.1	21.9	17.1	21.8	30.9	36.7	57.2	60.3	57.9
Health	0.2	0.6	3.8	8.8	15.8	24.5	43.9	93.6	124.8	197.8	210.6	216.5
Income security	2.6	3.5	5.8	9.4	18.5	27.9	36.8	58.4	68.7	90.9	93.7	95.0
Administration of justice			0.0	0.7	0.5	0.1	0.6	1.2	5.3	4.8	3.7	4.7
General government	0.2	0.2	0.5	7.1	8.6	6.8	2.3	2.3	2.1	4.4	4.4	4.1
Other	*	0.1	0.1	0.2	0.7	0.8	0.8	0.8	0.9	0.8	0.8	0.9

Source: The White House, 2007.

moments tarnished the image of state and local government in the minds of many Americans. Although they might continue to respect the leadership in their own state, they increasingly came to question whether important policy matters should be left in the hands of states whose own troopers used cattle prods to disperse peaceful civil rights demonstrators.

The initial wave of resistance to integration of school and public facilities and to African-American voter registration efforts seemed to confirm the skepticism of those Americans who doubted that racial attitudes could be changed by federal legislation. But in the face of persistent and aggressive national intervention, the resistance soon crumbled. Although racial politics would continue to roil American politics for many years, schools and facilities in the South were desegregated and African Americans achieved comparability with whites in terms of voter participation.

In 1970, Jimmy Carter was elected governor of Georgia. Among his first acts as governor was to put a portrait of Martin Luther King on display in the State Capitol. By publicly associating himself with the great leader of the Civil Rights Movement, he broke with the tradition that linked Southern governors, and the governments they led, with racism.

The success of the Civil Rights Movement was not lost on other groups and interests wanting political change. In particular, they sought to emulate African Americans by staking their political claims as matters of rights. Rights do not respect state boundaries. If a person has a right to a healthy environment or to a guaranteed income, then that right must be recognized in Maine and Florida as well as California and Minnesota. In the 1970s, these new rights claims led to the extension of national authority to several issues that had previously been the exclusive purview of the states, including pollution control, education, and redistricting of state legislatures.

The democratic momentum created by the civil rights struggle propelled the national government to concern itself with voting rights issues that did not directly involve race. In *Baker v. Carr* (1962), the Supreme Court ordered state legislatures to equalize the voter population in legislative districts according to the principle of "one man, one vote." In *Reynolds v. Sims* (1964), the court extended this dictate to include the upper chambers of state legislatures even when state constitutions expressly established an alternative principle. (See Chapter 9 for further discussions of these cases.)

The Voting Rights Act of 1965, which provided federal protection to African Americans attempting to exercise their right to vote, and the reapportionment decisions have severely limited the ability of states to determine the shape and character of their own political systems. By requiring strict numerical equality among state legislative districts, the Supreme

Court ignored the political reality that nobody lives in a legislative district; people actually live in a place – a neighborhood, a city, or a town. A real place has a name, a past, and a collective identity.

In the name of equality, the court has, in effect, removed locality as an organizing principle for state political representation. Likewise, the perceived need to interpret voting rights on group terms rather than strictly individual terms meant that localities could no longer shape their own political destinies unless their choices met with the approval of the federal government. Here again, those who favored and those who opposed the court decisions appealed to democratic principles. Supporters pointed to the obvious democratic benefits of ensuring that each vote cast would have the same weight. Opponents pointed to the lessening of effective democratic control that occurs when representatives represent no place in particular.

Mandates

In the late 1960s and early 1970s, the rights revolution spread beyond issues of voting to include an entire host of policy issues such as the environment, job safety, mental health, education, and the rights of people who are disabled. Although this rights revolution was inspired by the civil rights crusade, the national government's response to it was critically different. No federal marshals showed up to enforce national environmental or occupational safety and health laws. No dramatic confrontations occurred between state governors and national authorities. Instead, the national government relied, for the most part, on the states to implement the new array of federally imposed mandates.

This state-national relationship resembled the cooperative federalism that had been pioneered in the nineteenth century, but with a crucial difference: the federal restrictions had become tougher and more binding. Although the states rarely disagreed with the broad purpose of the federal mandates, they often adamantly opposed the specific regulations that dictated the pace at which the mandates would be implemented. No longer did Washington simply point the states in a particular policy direction; it now provided detailed timetables for meeting specific objectives and penalties for failing to attain them in the time allotted.

This *federal mandate* approach was particularly appealing to Congress because it enabled the central government to gain the credit for accomplishing popular policy goals, such as cleaner air or better education for the disabled, without having to pay the large costs that such policies incur. Federal statutes established the goals to be accomplished and then required others to pay the cost of meeting them. For example, a pulp mill was expected to pay the costs of new equipment needed to meet tougher federal water pollution standards; a local school system had to pay for the installation of federally mandated elevators that improved accessibility for disabled students. In the mid-1990s, the city of Columbus, Ohio, conducted a study demonstrating that federal mandates were costing the city hundreds of millions of dollars a year.

Environmental policy provides a striking example of this shift in state-federal relations. Prior to the late 1960s, environmental policy was, for the most part, a state and local matter. National involvement was mostly limited to the management of national parks, forests, and other public lands. Each state had its own laws for regulating air and water pollution. Cities and towns were responsible for managing their own solid waste disposal. This decentralized situation was transformed by the environmental movement that gathered steam in the late 1960s. Not only did this movement expose numerous examples of state and local failure to properly deal with pollution problems, but it changed the language in which such problems were discussed. Specifically, environmentalists spoke of the right that Americans have to a safe and healthy environment. Such a right could not be subject to differing state and local policies. The environmental movement contended that like the rights to "life, liberty, and the pursuit of happiness," environmental rights were "unalienable."

This rights-based principle was embodied in the 1970 Clean Air Act, which addressed clean water, toxic substances, hazardous waste disposal, and other environmental matters. This act – the model for a whole host of later statutes – has been amended several times over the past thirty years, but it retains its original central premise that Americans enjoy a right to healthy air. The act establishes national air quality standards that embody the two defining characteristics of a right: the standards are universal, and they are inalienable. Because air quality levels are set sufficiently low to protect "sensitive individuals," meaning those who are most prone to breathing-related illnesses, the standards are universal. They are inalienable because they cannot be revoked for being too expensive; the costs of imposing the standards cannot be taken into account when the standards are set.

As the Clean Air Act has evolved, it has become ever more centralizing. Originally, the states were allowed a great deal of discretion in deciding how to control emissions in order to meet the clean air standards. However, Congress became dissatisfied with the pace at which the states were implementing these changes. In the 1990 revision of the Clean Air Act, the states lost most of the discretion they had previously enjoyed. The revision set specific deadlines and timetables for lowering emissions. The role of the states had been reduced from determining how best to meet the nationally specified objectives to carrying out the nationally specified procedures.

Environmental rights remain highly controversial. They do not have the same status as the political rights embodied in the Bill of Rights. Every effort by the Environmental Protection Agency to set new air quality standards, or to revise existing ones, has been subject to lawsuits charging that those standards are unconstitutionally vague. Some suits are based on the claim that it is impossible to establish a right to environmental safety and health because environmental health science is incompatible with the principle of rights. Any amount of a pollutant in the air is liable to make someone, somewhere, sick. Therefore, environmental risk is relative, and there is no possible way to ensure complete safety and health. Whatever the intellectual merits of this position, it has not been supported by the courts. In 2001, the Supreme Court once again ratified the constitutionality of the Clean Air Act.

A similar rights revolution occurred in what had been the most local of all public services – education. Like environmental policy, education policy also came to be permeated with claims of rights. Local school boards have had to respond to claims for equal treatment regarding not only race but also language and gender as well as physical, mental, and emotional disabilities. These claims often came into conflict with the counterclaims of localities to exercise democratic control over the most vital of all local services. Many of the current controversies that surround education policy pit the desires of majorities in towns and cities against the rights claims of specific individuals backed up by federal courts.

In the past, a school superintendent would have had total discretion in determining a pupil's school assignment. But now, if a superintendent chooses to send a physically disabled student to a school far from that student's home because that school is more handicapped-accessible than the closer one, that decision might well face a court challenge. A federal judge might decide that because the student cannot attend the local school, the student's constitutional right to equal protection of the law has been violated; the court might order the school system to make the local school more handicapped-accessible in order to accommodate the student.

The pressure to centralize education also came from local taxpayers who were increasingly resistant to paying higher school costs. The major tax imposed locally is the property tax. Voters in California and Massachusetts used the referendum procedures that had been created during the Progressive Era to reduce their property tax burdens, thereby placing greater pressure on the states and the national government to fund the schools. Figure 5.4 gives a rough idea of the burden that unfunded mandates impose on the states.

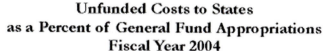

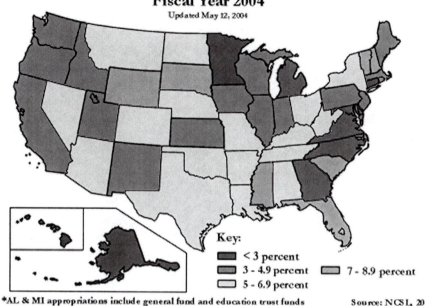

Key:
▪ < 3 percent
▪ 3 - 4.9 percent   ▫ 7 - 8.9 percent
▫ 5 - 6.9 percent

*AL & MI appropriations include general fund and education trust funds   Source: NCSL, 2004

Figure 5.4. Unfunded Mandates.
Source: The National Conference of State Legislatures, 2004.

The High Tide of Process Federalism

The impact of rights-based national intervention extended to virtually every aspect of public policy. Although the national government funded much of welfare policy, states were responsible for administering it and, in the tradition of cooperative federalism, had done so with very little national interference. Until 1996, federal welfare law provided aid to families with dependent children (AFDC). This provision, adopted as part of the Social Security Act in 1935, was intended to provide assistance primarily to poor, single-parent families. What if a parent was absent, but another adult, a boyfriend or girlfriend of the single parent, was living in the house? Some states adopted rules declaring such people to be substitute parents. Because, legally speaking, such a family now had two "parents," it was dropped from the welfare rolls. In *King v. Smith* (1968), the U.S. Supreme Court interpreted the meaning of the term parent differently. It declared that for welfare purposes, only someone with the legal obligations of a parent is a parent and that the states could not deny welfare benefits to such families.

In *Garcia v. San Antonio Metropolitan Transit Authority* (1985), the Supreme Court appeared to give a blanket endorsement to national government intrusions into what had previously been the domain of the states and localities. It adopted a theory of federal-state relations known as *process federalism*, which argues that the meaningful constitutional protections for the states are not provided either by the Tenth Amendment or by the principle of enumerated powers, but by the structure of the national government itself. The most important of these structural protections is the U.S. Senate, whose members are chosen by the states. This opinion implied that the court would not object to any imposition by the national government on the states as long as the Senate approves it.

The Receding Tide of Process Federalism

Garcia proved to be the high-water mark of a tide that has since begun to ebb. Although the essential features of the centralization-through-regulation programs of the 1970s and 1980s remained in place, both Congress and the Supreme Court have acted in recent years to tip the balance of governmental power in the direction of the states. Beginning with *Lopez* in 1995, the case discussed at the beginning of the chapter, the Supreme Court retreated from the process federalism principle of *Garcia*. The majority argued that the very principle of enumerated powers underlying the Constitution meant that the Commerce Clause was intended to exclude *something*. If interstate commerce could be used to justify all manner of congressional activity regardless of how tenuous the connection between the problem at hand and the flow of interstate commerce, then the Commerce Clause was meaningless. (See Chapters 1 and 3 for a complete discussion of the Commerce Clause.)

In 1996 and 1997, the court issued a series of decisions that reinforced the defense of states' rights begun by *Lopez*. The Eleventh Amendment to the Constitution forbids the federal judiciary from entertaining any suit against a state by a citizen of another state. In *Seminole Tribe v. Florida* (1996), the court interpreted the Eleventh Amendment to mean that states enjoy *sovereign immunity*, meaning that the federal courts may not hear a case against a state brought by a citizen of that state. The court did not declare this immunity to be absolute; it is limited by the due process and equal protection guarantees of the Fourteenth Amendment. But if those civil rights protections are not at stake, the federal courts may not intrude in legal disputes between a state and its citizens. In *Printz v. United States* (1997), the Supreme Court invalidated a section of the Handgun Violence Protection Act, popularly known as the Brady Bill, which required local law enforcement officials to conduct background checks on people seeking to buy guns. The Court interpreted the Tenth Amendment to mean that local and state officials cannot be compelled to do the national government's business.

In Congress, the turn toward reducing national centralization occurred as a result of the congressional elections of 1994. For the first time since 1953, the Republicans gained control of the House of Representatives as well as the Senate. A centerpiece of the Republican congressional campaign was a promise to devolve power from Washington to the states. The first fruit of that promise was the 1995 Unfunded Mandates Reform Act, which required Congress to explicitly consider the costs to state and local government of any new regulatory impositions. The act has many loopholes, but since its passage Congress has resisted imposing new and costly mandates on the states and localities.

The single most important act of Congress during the 1990s was welfare reform. The *Personal Responsibility and Work Opportunity Reconciliation Act* of 1996 actually reduced the national role in welfare policy. Although the national government continues to fund welfare, it does so under conditions that more closely resemble the pre-1970s cooperative federalism programs. Money is provided in the form of so-called *block grants* that enable the states to exercise far greater discretion over how the grant money is spent. As a result, states have been able to experiment to find the best combination of work programs, eligibility requirements, and other counseling and education techniques to deal with their own particular welfare-related problems. But this new program is not really cooperative federalism of the old type. In the spirit of post–New Deal centralization, the federal government has imposed strict limits on how long a person may receive welfare, and these limits apply everywhere.

The states and the national government have long been at odds over control of the nation's wetlands. Wetlands are those swampy and marshy areas adjacent to rivers, lakes, and oceans that are often relatively dry but which absorb huge amounts of water during storms. Therefore, they are crucial to preventing flooding and are also the favored habitats of many different animal species. The U.S. Army Corps of Engineers has interpreted the power the 1972 Clean Water Act gives it to regulate the discharge of dredged or fill material into "navigable waters" to mean that it can also control the dredging and filling of wetlands. Critics of this policy have argued that the Corps was making a mockery of the distinction between navigable waterways, which flow among and between states and are therefore a proper object of national regulation, and local waterways like ponds, streams, swamps, and marshes over which the national government should have no regulatory authority. Supporters of the Corps argued that because wetlands play such a vital role in preventing floods and protecting endangered species they are worthy of national protection.

In June of 2006, the Supreme Court ruled in *Rapanos et ux., et al. v. United States* that the Corps had exceeded its authority under the Clean Air Act. In his concurring opinion Justice Kennedy said that the Corps' approach was too open-ended, allowing it to regulate drainage ditches and streams that did not have an impact on "the integrity of an aquatic system." As is often the case, the court provided no clear standard for determining when a wetland's impact is significant enough to require national regulation. Its ruling only indicates that the Corps had gone too far. As in so many arenas of public policy, the proper balance between state and national control of wetlands will remain a matter of dispute and will invite further political and legal controversies.

The New State of the States

States have improved the technical and administrative capabilities needed to make productive use of their newly enhanced responsibilities. As we point out in greater detail in Chapter 10, many of the tasks that government performs are detailed, routine, and technically complex. They require information technology, management systems, and analytic techniques that are similar, and similarly complicated and expensive, to those found in large corporations. State governments were much slower than the private sector to take advantage of the revolution in data processing and information management made possible by modern computing and modern telecommunications. But they took advantage of the prosperous 1990s to invest in information technology and to make other infrastructural improvements as well.

The success of the civil rights revolution also did much to enhance state government, particularly in the South. The caliber of state government employees improved as opportunities at all levels were opened up for racial minorities and women. The image of state government likewise improved as it shed its previous image as a defender of racial segregation. As the links between national and state policy development and implementation became ever tighter, many ambitious policy experts found that at certain points in their careers, they could rise faster and exert more meaningful authority in state than in federal posts. This movement of personnel between state and national government did much to dissolve the atmosphere of mistrust that had so often prevailed in dealings between state and federal officials. These improved relations did not signal a return to true cooperative federalism, but they did create a much closer sense of state-federal partnership in a variety of policy areas.

It is too soon to tell whether an important reaffirmation of American federalism has been generated by the congressional and judicial developments and the improvements in state governing capacity that have been discussed earlier in this chapter. They may be nothing but temporary detours in the path toward greater centralization that public policy has been treading since the New Deal. But for the first time since the 1930s, the philosophical and legal questions that are at the heart of federalism are being discussed and debated in a serious way. Substituting national for state or local authority is no longer an automatic response to a serious public problem. This development coincides with a renewed appreciation of the practical advantages that states enjoy. Compared to the national government, states are relatively small and therefore can be more responsive and accessible to citizen concerns. Compared to localities, states have constitutional authority and operate on a broader geographical scale. This increased importance of state governance – as well as continued competition among national, state, and local authorities – is evident in current policy debates dealing with education and welfare.

Federalism and Education Revisited

Despite the greater involvement of the national government in education since the 1960s, differences in educational achievement among local school districts have become ever more glaring. Unlike the U.S. Constitution, many state constitutions promise a right to education. State courts have insisted that governors and legislatures fulfill that promise. In such states, exclusive reliance on local property taxes, which resulted in far greater education expenditures in rich communities than in poor ones, has given way to a mix of local and state funding aimed at reducing the spending gap.

Many states have adopted uniform curriculum guidelines that serve as the basis for statewide educational testing. In the state of Massachusetts, for example, since 1998 all fourth, eighth, and tenth graders take a set of standardized tests. Students who fail those tests may not progress to the next grade until they pass them. Defenders of the tests view them as powerful weapons for prodding poorly performing schools to improve. The upgrading of weak schools creates greater equality of educational opportunity. Opponents attack these standardized tests on grounds of both liberty and equality. By depriving many students from poorer schools of a chance to graduate on time, the tests stigmatize such students and therefore handicap their chances for future success. By standardizing the curriculum, the tests deprive individual school districts of the freedom to innovate and to adopt curriculum that is responsive to the wishes of parents and children.

In 2001, the federal government acted to push those states that were not already testing to do so. The No Child Left Behind Act supported by President Bush and bipartisan majorities in both houses of Congress requires states to devise statewide standards in reading and mathematics, to test all students annually in grades 3 through 8, and to meet annual statewide progress objectives ensuring that all groups of students reach proficiency within twelve years. Testing, which began as an experiment in a few states, is now the object of the most extensive involvement by the federal government in education policy in all of American history.

Welfare

Many states have taken advantage of the increased flexibility provided by the 1996 welfare reform law to cope more effectively with welfare problems. For example, Wisconsin has gained national recognition for adopting a plan that combines tighter eligibility with more intensive provision of child care and job training. It is now harder to qualify for welfare in Wisconsin, but instead of returning the savings from reduced welfare rolls to the taxpayers, the state spends much of that money to help welfare recipients pay for day care while they learn job skills and then go out and work. Supporters of the Wisconsin plan see it as a useful experiment that other states may choose to emulate. Opponents generally applaud the services that the plan provides but view its eligibility limits as heartlessly restrictive, depriving many needy people of good child care and job training opportunities. Opponents believe that such denials constitute a deprivation of the economic rights that the New Deal promised to secure. Once again, democracy and liberty come into conflict as the majority's desire to lessen the cost of welfare and to discourage dependency clashes with a minority's claim to rights.

Governors and Attorneys General

The revival of state government has benefited from a newfound ability of governors from different states to cooperate with one another and also to initiate innovative policies. Since 1976, all the presidents save one (George H. W. Bush) have been former state governors. They have demonstrated a greater appreciation of the value and importance of state government than

In 1996, President Clinton signed a welfare reform bill into law that gave states increased flexibility to administer welfare programs.

did the non-governors who held the presidency for the preceding thirty years. Since 1976, intergovernmental organizations – as exemplified by the National Governors Association, the Republican Governors Association, the Democratic Governors Association, the National Council of State Legislatures, and the National Municipal Association – have greatly expanded their presence and influence in Washington.

In the mid-1990s, the governors of all the largest states were Republicans. By acting together, they were able to exert great political influence in Washington. For example, the welfare regulation waivers that they demanded from the Department of Health and Human Services led to experiments that propelled the revolutionary changes in national policy contained in the 1996 welfare reform act. The governors also acted in concert to ensure that a governor was chosen as the Republican nominee for president in 2000. Their strong and consistent support for Texas governor George W. Bush enabled him to emerge as the front-runner and to attract the financial and political backing needed to win the nomination. Box 4 looks at the critical role that governors are playing in a complex series of policy innovations aimed at discouraging sprawl.

Smart Growth

States have become deeply involved in questions of land use, acting to preserve farms and parklands and discourage sprawl. States are imperfect instruments for land use planning, because land use patterns do not respect state lines. But there exists no higher constitutionally established form of government, short of the national government itself, for dealing with land use–related problems. The political difficulties inherent in national land use planning have precluded any serious national involvement in such thorny matters as zoning and other means for controlling population density. However, most localities are simply too small to make a meaningful impact on such matters.

The governors of several states, including Maryland, Georgia, Vermont, and Oregon, have attempted to discourage sprawl through "smart growth" initiatives that use various legal powers of the state to discourage growth in rural areas and encourage it in urban areas. Smart growth strives to leave open spaces open and to construct new facilities in places that are already highly developed. State agencies decide where to build new roads and mass transit systems and where to put highway entrances and exits and rail stops. They also choose where to place new state facilities such as community colleges, prisons, and office buildings. As the chief executive, it is up to the governor to make sure that various agencies coordinate with one another so that the sum total of their separate decisions actually discourages sprawl. The smart growth strategy reduces pressure to convert farms and forests into stores, offices, and homes. It also lowers governmental expenditure by lessening the need for new infrastructure, such as sewers, power lines, and water mains. Urban areas already possess such infrastructure, whereas lightly developed rural areas do not.

Smart growth responds to a publicly expressed desire to preserve a diversity of environments and not to homogenize an entire state into one large suburban development and office park. But this strategy is attacked on grounds of personal freedom. Although farmers cherish their land, they may decide that it is in their best interest, or that of their heirs, to sell off some or all of their farms to real estate developers. If state policy discourages them from doing so, it lowers the value of their property. It prevents them from determining how best to provide for their own future and the futures of their children and grandchildren as well. Even if most smart growth initiatives are favored by a majority of people, they are still susceptible to the charge that they violate the liberty of a minority.

In addition to governors, attorneys general from many states are also demonstrating active and coordinated leadership primarily through concerted legal action geared to win huge financial settlements for their states and to influence public policy nationwide. The most successful of these activities has been the Tobacco Settlement of 1998, in which tobacco companies agreed to pour billions of dollars into state treasuries in return for a willingness on the part of the states to renounce their legal claims against the companies. More recently, they have been at the forefront of efforts to reduce the carbon dioxide emissions that most scientists believe contribute to global warming. A group of twelve attorneys general petitioned the U.S. Supreme Court to review a federal appeals court decision that supported the U.S. Environmental Protection Agency's (EPA's) refusal to regulate motor vehicles emissions that they claimed cause the climate to warm. Massachusetts attorney general Thomas Reilly claimed that "this case goes to the heart of EPA's statutory responsibilities to deal with the most pressing environmental problem of our time." The attorneys general did not argue that EPA's failure affected their states in particular; rather, they claimed that their role as legal guardians of their states required them to take action when the national government failed to protect the nation as a whole, of which their states are obviously a part.

In April 2007, the Supreme Court ruled 5 to 4 that the Environmental Protection Agency violated the Clean Air Act by improperly declining to regulate new-vehicle emissions standards to control the pollutants that scientists say contribute to global warming. Although this case, *Commonwealth of Massachusetts et al. v. Environmental Protection Agency et al.*, might eventually further centralize environmental regulation, the ruling might also lend important authority to efforts by the states either to force the federal government to reduce greenhouse gas emissions or to be allowed to do it themselves. For example, New York is leading an effort to strengthen regulations on power-plant emissions; and California has passed a law seeking to cut carbon dioxide emissions from automobiles starting in 2009, an effort that has encouraged many other states to adopt similar regulations.

The Empire of Liberty Reinvigorated

Jefferson's empire of liberty has been reinvigorated by a vast influx of immigration from abroad. During the last decade, not a single state lost population, and almost all made significant gains. Most big cities, which had been steadily losing population for many years, began to gain once more. Although certain rural areas continued to shrink, it is no longer accurate to talk about a stagnant Rust Belt encompassing much of the Northeast, Midwest, and Great Plains. Although the Sun Belt of the Southeast and Southwest sustained its previous dramatic growth, all the other regions grew as well.

Prosperity yielded greater tax revenue and allowed cities and states to raise a great deal more money for roads, sewers, school and university buildings, crime fighting, garbage removal, and park maintenance. For example, New York City's improvement was so dramatic that its image changed from one of an asphalt jungle to the Big Apple, a place where young people want to relocate and a mecca for tourists from throughout the nation and the world. Stimulated by the energies and talents of new residents from Asia and Latin America, states throughout the Midwest and Great Plains likewise rebuilt their infrastructures and revitalized their economies. Jefferson would have rejoiced in the regenerative capacity of states and cities that only a decade earlier had been virtually given up for dead. Although federal policy played a part in this remarkable national success story, it was by no means the dominant factor. As Jefferson hoped, these new Americans responded to the political freedom and economic opportunity to be found here by working hard to make their new homeland more productive and prosperous. Figure 5.5 describes the state share of the U.S. population.

Junior Partners?

The strongest evidence for the continuing and perhaps expanding importance of the states and localities is their increasing role in the overall financing of government. The gap between the two revenue sources has been closing since the mid-1980s. For most of this period, federal expenditure has been shrinking while state and local expenditure has been rising, and the two forms of spending are now more or less equal. The lines first crossed in 2001 and then again in 2003. When the notorious bank robber Willie Sutton was asked why he robbed banks, he replied, "because that is where the money is." If one is asked why states and localities will continue to be critical elements in the overall governing process, one could make the same reply.

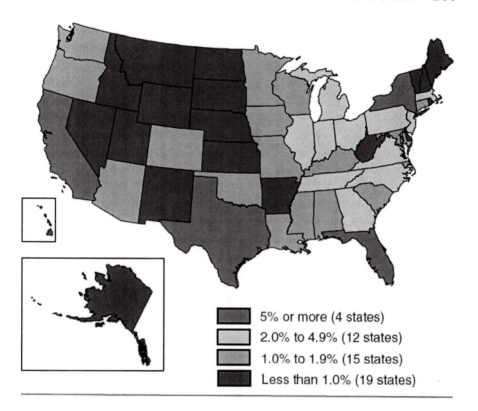

Figure 5.5. State Share of U.S. Population, 2000.
Source: "A Short Retrospective on U.S. Population Change" by John Beal, Indiana Business Review: Spring 2001, 12.

Conclusion

The "empire of liberty" that Jefferson envisaged has not disappeared. An American traveling abroad is struck by how much more intrusive and pervasive government is elsewhere. In many other democratic countries, citizens must carry identity cards. If they move, they must inform the government. Government permission may be required for activities, like laying off a worker, that Americans consider to be matters of strictly private concern.

In New Hampshire, the slogan "live free or die" appears on all the license plates. Texans have a legal right to carry concealed handguns and, as we learned in *Lopez*, the federal government has no right to keep those handguns away from schools. Other countries have national police forces whose jurisdiction extends as far as the nation's borders. In this country, ordinary police work is done by local police forces whose powers cease at the city and county limits. We have all seen movies in which the police have to give up chasing the crook because he gets across the county line. The willingness to put up with this ridiculous outcome is eloquent testimony to how deeply Americans cherish the idea of local government.

France has a national education system. A fourth grader in Marseilles studies the same things and reads the same textbooks as a fourth grader in Lyon or in Strasbourg. In the United States, most school systems are governed at the town or county level. A fourth grader in one school may study something far different from the fourth grader who is just across the road but on the other side of the county line.

The presidential election of 2000 that pitted the Democrat Al Gore against Republican George W. Bush showed the price that Americans pay for their empire of liberty. The electoral vote was so close nationwide that the outcome of the election would be decided by Florida. Florida and many other states allow individual counties to select their own methods of ballot design and vote counting. The presidential election in Florida was, in reality, a series of local elections with different ballot designs, tabulation methods, and recount procedures. In Palm Beach County in particular, the ballot design was sufficiently confusing that many elderly voters who intended to vote for Gore voted for Patrick Buchanan instead. In other counties, failure to fully poke a hole next to the name of the candidate one favored resulted in so-called hanging chads, which made it impossible to tell for sure who the voter had voted for. As initially tallied, the vote was so close that the loser, Gore, refused to acknowledge Bush as the winner. The resulting chaos and confusion encouraged each party to suspect the other of "stealing" the election. Ultimately, the outcome in Florida, and thus in the election as a whole, was decided by the U.S. Supreme Court who declared Bush the winner.

However, state and local discretion also enables Americans to enjoy enormous freedom to pick the style of government that suits them. If they don't like the way things are being done where they live, they have the option of moving. For example, New Hampshire has no state taxes and few statewide land-use regulations. If a citizen wants more state services and more protection of rural open space and if that citizen is willing to pay higher taxes and submit to property rights restrictions, he or she can cross the Connecticut River and live in Vermont instead.

American federalism is no longer of interest only to Americans. As the European countries struggle to determine how best to strengthen and expand the European Union, they have increasingly come to look to American federalism as a source of inspiration. America's form of government organization, which in the wake of the New Deal and the rights revolution seemed destined to disappear, now serves as a model for emulation.

Seen through European eyes, it is federalism's overall success, not its many specific failures, that is most impressive.

America invented republican government on a continental scale. Now, as the Europeans try to form a union of comparable size and even greater diversity, they recognize federalism as the key device for reconciling the governance of immense territory and population with meaningful liberty and democracy. Federalism enabled the United States to become the most powerful nation-state in the world while allowing its component parts the liberty to express meaningful political differences. It has helped Americans possess the security that only great size and strength can provide while still enjoying the democratic participatory opportunities that only small-scale government can offer. Federalism does not resolve the tensions between democracy and liberty, between the rights of the majority and those of minorities, but it does enable those tensions to serve as sources of political energy and strength rather than as seeds of chaos and destruction. As Jefferson recognized, federalism is what saves the "empire of liberty" from being a contradiction in terms.

⭐ The Constitution is a compromise between those who wanted a strong national government and those who did not. In order to obtain consent for the establishment of a strong national government, its supporters made concessions to those who feared a strong national government. They agreed to limit its powers to those that were expressly delegated to it, reserving all other powers to the states. They also agreed to give the states a direct role in national governance via the Senate and the Electoral College.

⭐ Defenders of a strong central government viewed the passionate attachments provoked by states and localities as a crucial threat to liberty. Defenders of the states saw those same passionate attachments as wellsprings of democratic energy and as bulwarks of liberty that defended local rights and privileges against centralized despotism.

⭐ For the first 150 years of the life of the United States, the states and localities dominated American government and politics.

⭐ The issue of the supremacy of the national government was resolved by the Supreme Court in *McCulloch v. Maryland* (1819), but it was decisively settled only by the Civil War.

⭐ As national and state governments retrenched in the aftermath of Reconstruction, local governments came increasingly to dominate political life. They raised more taxes and spent more money than the state and federal governments combined. Cities were the most dynamic and innovative political arenas of the second half of the nineteenth century.

⭐ The beginning of the shift of power from the states to the national government that occurred during the nineteenth century began with the Progressives' campaign to enable the federal government to regulate the activities of multistate corporations, especially the railroads.

☆ Rather than redistribute authority from one level of government to another, the New Deal increased the total amount of government, providing incentives for the states to carry out the programs the president and Congress devised. These incentives came with strings attached, ushering in the modern era of state-federal relations in which states receive federal aid in return for accomplishing federal objectives. Over time, national directives on how the states must implement federal policy have become ever more detailed and specific.

☆ Since the New Deal, the terms of the debate about governmental centralization have shifted. Now, advocates of strong national government most often defend it on democratic grounds, claiming that states and localities thwart majority will. Supporters of decentralization invoke liberty, claiming that the national government stifles personal freedom and discourages diversity.

☆ The illegal and often brutal resistance, which many Southern states displayed during the 1950s and 1960s in the face of demands by civil rights protestors and by the Justice Department to end racial desegregation, badly tarnished the image of state and local government in the minds of many Americans.

☆ During the 1990s, for the first time since the New Deal, Congress and the courts actually reduced the capacity of the national government to displace the states. Several court rulings overruled acts of Congress as being in violation of the Commerce Clause or the Tenth or Eleventh Amendments. Congress passed the Unfunded Mandates Reform Act, which required it to explicitly assess the costs to state and local government of any new regulatory impositions it is considering, and the Personal Responsibility and Work Opportunity Reconciliation Act of 1996, which enabled the states to exercise far greater discretion over how federal welfare aid is spent.

☆ During the last several decades, state government has undergone a significant process of modernization and improvement. Its capacity to manage its affairs has been greatly enhanced by improved data processing and information management, better personnel, and expanded employment opportunities for women and minorities.

☆ Federalism enabled the United States to become the most powerful nation-state in the world while allowing its component parts the liberty to express meaningful political differences. It has helped Americans possess the security that only great size and strength can provide while still enjoying the democratic participatory opportunities that only small-scale government can offer.

Major Concepts

block grants
compact theory
cooperative federalism
federal mandate
Jim Crow
Personal Responsibility and Work Opportunity Reconciliation Act
process federalism
Progressive movement
Reconstruction
sovereign immunity

Suggested Readings

Beer, Samuel. *To Make a Nation: The Rediscovery of American Federalism*, rev. ed. Cambridge, MA: Belknap Press, 1998.

Conlan, Timothy. *From New Federalism to Devolution: Twenty-Five Years of Intergovernmental Reform*. Washington, D.C.: Brookings Institution, 1998.

Derthick, Martha, ed. *Dilemmas of Scale in America's Federal Bureaucracy*. New York: Cambridge University Press, 1999.

_____. *Keeping the Compound Republic: Essays on American Federalism*. Washington, D.C.: Brookings Institution, 2001.

Diamond, Martin. *As Far as Republican Principles Will Admit: Essays by Martin Diamond*. Washington, D.C.: AEI Press, 1992.

Donahue, John D. *Disunited States*. New York: Basic Books, 1998.

Ehrenhalt, Alan. *Democracy in the Mirror: Politics, Reform, and Reality in Grassroots America*. Washington, D.C.: CQ Press, 1998.

Elazar, Daniel. *American Federalism: A View from the States*, 3d ed. New York: Harper and Row, 1984.

Greve, Michael. *Real Federalism*. Washington, D.C.: AEI Press, 1999.

McDonald, Forrest. *States Rights and the Union: Imperium in Imperio, 1776–1876*. Lawrence: Kansas University Press, 2000.

Peterson, Paul E. *The Price of Federalism*. Washington, D.C.: Brookings Institution, 1995.

Walker, David B. *The Rebirth of Federalism: Slouching toward Washington*. New York: Chatham House, 2000.

6 Political Economy

Chapter Overview

This chapter focuses on:

☆ The relationship between economic liberalism and democracy

☆ The crucial conflicts that have taken place about when and how government should intervene in economic affairs

☆ The various protest movements that have arisen to criticize and reform economic liberalism

☆ The political implications of such economic concepts as the corporation, depression, inflation, and taxation

☆ The role of politics and government in the most important contemporary economic issues such as deficits, taxes, entitlements, international trade, and corporate fraud

Wal-Mart is America's most successful retail chain. It offers a wide variety of brand-name products, including clothes, toys, electronics, and pharmaceuticals, at low prices. Even though these stores offer consumers an unusual variety of cheap and good-quality items, many small towns across America have organized Stop Wal-Mart campaigns. These campaigns are partly an effort by local merchants to reduce competition, but that is not the only motivation. In order to provide ample parking and to build on cheap land, Wal-Mart, unless forced to do otherwise, builds its stores on the outskirts of a town, which siphons business from downtown merchants and drains the life out of the downtown area.

The Stop Wal-Mart campaign attracts people who consider a downtown to be what turns a mere aggregate of homes and stores into an actual community. Downtown is where townspeople meet and talk. These critics do not consider that protecting local merchants is an unfair restraint on trade. They defend the downtown merchants on civic grounds, because the local merchants sponsor Little League teams, are high school sports boosters, support local churches, lead charity drives, and sustain civic associations such as the Rotary Club and the Chamber of Commerce.

Of course, these same people enjoy paying less for a better choice of goods. Some might even shop at a Wal-Mart in another town. Because these people believe that, on the whole, free economic competition is a very good thing, they may feel sheepish about fighting Wal-Mart. Even those townspeople who do not participate in the Stop Wal-Mart activities may well be torn between shopping where they choose and keeping their local democracy intact. These conflicting values reveal the tensions that arise between liberal commitments to economic freedom and democratic commitments to political solidarity.

This chapter focuses on the relationship between economic liberalism and democracy. It looks at the constitutional foundation of the liberal economy and examines the critical episodes in the relationship between political development and economic development: the impact of the free labor ideology that developed in opposition to slavery, the rise of laissez faire, the relationship of Progressive politics and economic regulation, and the development of the New Deal insurance state. It discusses the economic consequences of the larger government that the New Deal spawned and the politics surrounding the disillusionment with big government that set in during the 1970s and 1980s. The final section examines economic policy battles of the immediate past and present.

The Creation of Economic Liberalism

When Thomas Jefferson drafted the Declaration of Independence, he borrowed from John Locke's *Second Treatise*, which argued that government

The debates that greet the opening of a new
Wal-Mart store underscore the tensions
between the liberal commitment to economic
freedom and the democratic commitment to
local communities.

could only be legitimate if it rested in the consent of the governed and
protected the "natural rights" of "life, liberty, and estate." But Jefferson
changed "estate," by which Locke meant "property," into "the pursuit of
happiness." This wonderfully enigmatic phrase captures the essence of the
liberal political economic system the Founders envisioned. The phrase is
based on rights, not results. It does not promise happiness but, rather, a fair
chance to pursue that dream. It hints at the complex amalgam of striving,
optimism, and uncertainty that form the distinctively American economic
quest.

The liberal economy that embodies this understanding of the pursuit
of happiness has three essential aspects: private property, competition,
and promise keeping. Jefferson did not want to list property among the
three most essential inalienable rights, but he did not intend to deny its

importance. The right to property enables persons to keep what possessions they have and to know that if they make investments or do work, they can keep the fruits of those risks and labors. The right to property also means that government is obliged to protect people's property against theft and that government itself cannot rob people of their hard-won assets.

The liberal economy is inherently competitive; it depends on producers vying with one another for the patronage of consumers by offering better goods and cheaper prices. The liberal economy is like a track meet in which everyone is given an opportunity to run the race. The competition is not entirely fair, because some runners are better trained, coached, and equipped. But once at the starting line, everyone must obey the same rules or face disqualification. In the economic version of the race, contracts are kept, debts are paid, thieves and counterfeiters are caught and punished, and the list of ingredients printed on the package is accurate. Government officiates; it writes the rules and enforces them.

A liberal economy requires people to keep their word as well as do their work. Such trust cannot develop in an atmosphere of deceit. I lend money to you only if I believe your pledge to repay it. If we sign a contract together, it is because we trust each other to live up to the bargain. Box 1 looks at a recent economic scandal to demonstrate the crucial role that trust and promise keeping play in the modern economy and the dire consequences that result when a major corporation violates the public trust.

Of course, as all the previous chapters have discussed and as the Stop Wal-Mart campaign demonstrates, liberalism is not the whole American story. Democratic and religious principles are also at the heart of the American creed. In the economic realm, these three different principles sometimes coexist harmoniously and sometimes are at odds.

The Constitution and the Liberal Economy

The Constitution, including the Bill of Rights, commits the U.S. government to preserving a liberal economy, the essence of which is the sanctity of private property, free and open competition, and the keeping of promises. Article VI holds the federal government responsible for debts that the previous government under the Articles of Confederation was obligated to pay. The Fifth Amendment forbids government from taking a person's property without just compensation. Article I authorizes Congress to tax, borrow money, coin currency, issue patents and copyrights, and regulate interstate and foreign commerce. Indeed, in the minds of many Framers, federal oversight of interstate and foreign commerce was the most compelling reason for creating the Union in the first place. Lack of such authority under the Articles of Confederation raised such dangerous possibilities as coastal states blackmailing landlocked ones into paying for permission to ship products overseas, or downstream states imposing tariffs on goods shipped from states upstream. But even more important than any of these specific clauses were the overarching constitutional principles of limited government and enumerated powers. These principles kept government from interfering with Americans' freedom to do what they liked with their property and to conduct their business as they pleased so long as contracts were kept and laws were obeyed.

The new Constitution proved effective in keeping interstate and foreign commerce flowing, but it could not avoid great strains arising over debt and taxes. The federal government, for example, instituted a whiskey excise tax that it considered a constitutionally sanctioned revenue-raising device. Western Pennsylvania corn farmers, who were greatly increasing their income by turning their corn into whiskey, saw the excise tax as a threat to their livelihood. President George Washington used an aggressive display of military force to end the 1794 Whiskey Rebellion, but the view of taxation as oppression that the rebellion expressed has proved to be a repetitive theme in American politics.

Box One: Contemporary Politics

The Fragile Underpinning of a Liberal Economy

Because a liberal economy rests on the willingness of investors to make gambles, it is crucial that they have ample and trustworthy information on which to base their investment decisions. In 2001, the largest business failure in all of American history shook this country's faith in the integrity of corporate America. Enron, one of the largest American companies, went bankrupt. It had overstated its profits by more than half a billion dollars and had inflated its worth as a result of 1.2 billion dollars in accounting errors. Before news of the company's desperate plight became public and while its stock prices were still high, several of its top executives sold millions of dollars of their Enron holdings. And just as the stock began to plummet, the company prevented the Enron retirement fund from selling its Enron stock. As a result, when the firm went bankrupt, the value of ordinary Enron workers' retirement savings was drastically reduced.

The Enron scandal revealed serious limitations in how the liberal economy polices itself. The government does not audit corporations. Auditing means reviewing a firm's financial records to make sure they give a true picture of its financial health. Audits are performed by private accounting firms hired by the companies themselves. Enron's auditing firm, Arthur Anderson, had failed to publish negative information about the company's finances and had even shredded documents containing damaging facts. Accounting firms are permitted to do consulting work for firms that they audit. This situation creates a potentially serious conflict of interest. Companies are less likely to award lucrative work to accounting firms whose audits put the company in a bad light. Major accounting firms make more money from consulting than they do from auditing, which worsens the conflict of interest.

Conflict-of-interest problems exist for the president and members of Congress as well. Enron was the single largest contributor to the 2000 Bush presidential campaign; it donated $114,000. Between 1989 and 2001, 187 current House members and seventy-one senators from both parties received more than 1 million dollars from the Enron Political Affairs Committee. In 2000, the Securities and Exchange Commission (SEC), the government agency responsible for regulating the stock market, proposed stricter rules for accounting firm conflict of interest. Congress forced the SEC to back off from its stricter rules. During the 1990s, the Financial Accounting Standards Board (FASB), the industry's own standard-setting organization, suggested several new, stricter accounting methods. Congress pressured the FASB to abandon, moderate, or delay those new guidelines.

In May 2006, former Enron CEOs Kenneth Lay and Jeffrey Skilling were convicted of a total of twenty-nine criminal counts including fraud and criminal conspiracy. In July 2006, Kenneth Lay died of a heart attack.

Debtors and Creditors

To sustain the Revolutionary War against England, the states had taken on huge debts. Many people who bought state bonds to finance the war believed that the bonds would never be repaid, so they sold them at a loss to speculators who gambled that eventually the bonds would be paid in full. Citing the constitutional provision guaranteeing repayment, Secretary of the Treasury Alexander Hamilton produced a plan whereby the national government would redeem the state bonds, paying the bondholders in full. Hamilton argued that the government would be able to borrow in the future only if it maintained an unsullied record for keeping its promises.

Thomas Jefferson and James Madison sympathized with the original bondholders who would now lose money twice, first by selling off their bonds too soon and then by paying additional taxes in order to finance Hamilton's plan to pay off the bonds in full. Many of these original bondholders sold their bonds not because they had lost faith in the government but because they had run out of money while waiting to be repaid. The buyers were not necessarily more patriotic than the sellers were, but they were richer and could afford to wait and see what the government would eventually do. Jefferson and Madison viewed Hamilton's plan not as an effort to show good faith but as a trick played on the poor to benefit the rich. In the end, Madison and Jefferson abandoned their opposition to Hamilton's plan in exchange for Hamilton's support for their proposal to move the nation's capital from New York, the seat of financial power, to Philadelphia, where it would reside for ten years. According to the compromise of 1790, a permanent site for the national capital would be established on land that bordered Virginia, the present District of Columbia.

The Case for Government Intervention

As his support for bondholders showed, Hamilton was an economic liberal who placed great emphasis on people keeping their promises. But he did not believe that the pursuit of happiness could be left entirely to the individual choices made by buyers and sellers. In response to Congress's request for reports on banking and manufacturing, Hamilton launched an enduring debate about American economic policy. How much, he asked, and for what, should a free economy rely on government? How and when should government intervene in the economy, to what ends, and with what means?

Congress had asked Hamilton to investigate manufactures as a way "to render the United States independent of foreign nations for military and other essential supplies." Hamilton argued in his Report on Manufactures that even more than providing essential military supplies, manufactures would help forge the strong sense of national identity that makes a country feel secure. He encouraged trade between South and North as a way to develop closer ties between the two regions and to promote a common sense of nationality. But Southern states would sell their products in the North instead of Europe only if the North could replace Europe as the South's source of manufactured goods. Therefore, argued Hamilton, national security required federal support for manufactures.

In defending manufacturing, Hamilton did not address the democratic argument for agriculture propounded by Jefferson, which stressed the independence and versatility of farmers. Rather, Hamilton pointed out that manufacturing's increased specialization was a great boon to efficiency. The act of encouraging workers to concentrate on doing a single task well would dramatically increase the wealth and therefore the security of the American nation. Whether a worker who is trained to do only one thing can be a competent democratic citizen is not a question that Hamilton chose to raise.

To promote manufacturing, Hamilton supported a national bank, high tariffs on imported manufactures, and a government commission to award bounties for the establishment of new industries and to award prizes for the encouragement of inventions, particularly of labor-saving machinery. Jefferson and his allies opposed Hamilton's plan not only because they were suspicious of manufacturing but also because they believed the plan was unconstitutional.

Hamilton defended the constitutionality of his scheme by referring to the preamble of the Constitution, which gives "We the People" responsibility to "provide for the general welfare." Because manufacturing would improve national security and bring the states into "a more perfect Union," Hamilton believed, it was a legitimate means of providing for the general welfare. His opponents disputed this expansive claim, arguing instead that "general welfare" derived its meaning from the specific provisions of Article I, which enumerated government powers and thus preserved the principle of limited government. Otherwise, opponents argued, any conceivable initiative could claim to improve the "general welfare."

Hamilton defended the proposals in his Report on Manufactures as necessary for the establishment of a nation strong and prosperous enough to secure people's rights. Jefferson and others attacked the proposals for undermining equality of opportunity by privileging one economic sector – manufacturing – and for undermining democratic citizenship by converting family farmers into wage slaves. Jefferson believed that owning one's own farm allowed one to be free to a degree that was impossible if one worked for someone else. This conflict about the meaning of the General Welfare Clause has continued throughout American history. In this first dispute, defenders of the enumerated powers doctrine won.

Hamilton's proposals were defeated, except for the National Bank. Jefferson also opposed the creation of a national bank, even though the creation of such an institution appeared to follow from powers explicitly sanctioned by the Constitution, such as the right to collect taxes, borrow money, regulate trade among the states, and support an army and navy. The "necessary and proper clause" of Article I, Section 8, Hamilton argued, made clear that the national government had "implied powers," that is, all the means necessary to carry out the explicit powers enumerated in the Constitution. Although Jefferson considered Hamilton's constitutional argument a perversion of the "necessary and proper" clause, arguing that a measure had to be not just reasonable but also indispensable to pass constitutional muster, he and his political allies eventually learned to live with the National Bank, as a matter, as Madison put it, of "expediency and almost necessity."

Eventually, even Jefferson acknowledged that national security required America to industrialize. In 1814, reflecting on the terrible damage Britain had inflicted during the War of 1812 and the threat that it continued to pose, Jefferson resorted to a biblical analogy to express his sorrowful acceptance of this awful truth: "Our enemy has indeed the consolation of Satan on removing our parents from Paradise: from a peaceful agricultural nation he makes us a military and manufacturing one."

As time went on, military necessity was supplemented by economic, social, and political pressures to increase government assistance to and regulation of the economy. To encourage settlement and transcontinental transport, railroads were built on lands donated by government. Business tactics and labor conditions came under increasing government scrutiny. By the mid-twentieth century, America became, as Hamilton had hoped, a fully mixed economy of private property, market competition, and high levels of government intervention. Box 2 describes a contemporary example of an industry, the pharmaceutical industry, whose protection from ordinary market forces has been defended largely on Hamiltonian grounds.

Box Two: Contemporary Politics

The Pharmaceutical Industry

The Congressional Budget Office (CBO) reports that, in recent years, growth in prescription drug spending has outpaced every other category of health expenditures. Spending on prescription drugs grew at a real (inflation-adjusted) average annual rate of 14.5 percent from 1997 to 2002, reaching 162 billion dollars in 2002. That rapid growth raised prescription drug spending's share of total health expenditures to 10.5 percent in 2002, compared with 5.8 percent a decade earlier. In 1999, prescription drugs surpassed nursing homes as the third-largest category of personal healthcare expenditures, after hospital and physician services.

Drug companies can set high prices for many drugs because when they discover a new drug they can patent it for a period of between ten and fourteen years. A patent is a form of government subsidy. It commits the government to preventing any one except the patent holder to sell the patented product while the patent is in force. The only limit on the price of a patented drug, therefore, is the willingness of patients' health plans to pay for it, and, if it is truly effective. Patients and government officials will put enormous pressure on health plans to pay. As a result, the pharmaceutical industry is among the most profitable of all industries. In a *Fortune Magazine* survey, it ranked third out of forty-seven industries with a profit-to-sales ratio of 15.8 percent. The median for all industries was 5.2 percent. Its profits-to-assets ratio was 8.1 percent, placing it twelfth out of forty-seven industries. The median for all industries was 4.1 percent.

The pharmaceutical industry defends its patent-protected high prices on the grounds that it needs such high returns to justify the high risk and expenses it incurs in discovering new drugs. Most new compounds never make it to market, and research costs from the many failures are financed by sales from the few successes. For example, late in 2006 a major drug company, Pfizer, had to take a billion dollar loss on a heart drug it had developed called torcetrapib, which failed its clinical trials and therefore had to be abandoned. The CBO cites a study claiming that when all relevant economic costs are taken into account, including costs from unsuccessful compounds, an average of about 800 million dollars in research and development spending is incurred for each internally produced new compound reaching the market.

Critics charge that drug prices are too high. They cite the companies' willingness to charge lower prices in countries where the government runs the healthcare system and insists on a lower price. A few states have even permitted health plans and citizens in their states to buy medicines in Canada, where prices are government controlled and lower than in the United States. In the 2006 congressional campaign, Democrats pledged to require the government-operated Medicare drug plan to negotiate with the drug companies for lower prices for its many millions of subscribers.

The Republicans and the drug industry oppose both these schemes. They point out that the only reason the drug companies are willing to accept lower prices abroad is because they can count on sufficient profits from the high prices in the American market. If the practice of buying abroad became really widespread, the industry would either require the foreign governments to actively prevent resale back to the United States or they would impose the U.S. price abroad on a take-it-or-leave-it basis. Drug companies fear that if government were able set drug prices it would be under excessive public pressure to set prices too low and therefore the industry would have too little incentive to aggressively develop new medicines. It is hard to know in advance whether or not this would really happen. But the risk exists that government would lack either the political flexibility, or simply sufficient knowledge, to set drug prices at a level where consumers would benefit *and* drug companies would maximize their drug research and development efforts.

Hamilton recognized that subsidizing industry would make some people, or in this case companies, inordinately rich. This did not bother him because he believed that the benefits in the form of innovation and efficiency which subsidization produced were far greater than the cost. He would not have been troubled by current drug prices. They have indeed induced a remarkable outpouring of new and useful medications. But even in his own day, Hamilton was opposed by Jefferson and Madison. They were not content to make economic judgments on efficiency grounds alone. They worried about the impact of the economy on the moral character of the citizenry. They doubted that a society could survive in which some were helped by the government to become very rich while others struggled to survive in the face of government indifference. No doubt that they would have been troubled by what they would have considered to be the obscene levels of profit enjoyed by the drug industry and the degree of government complicity in obtaining those profits.

The Attack on Economic Privilege

In 1832, Andrew Jackson declared war on the "monster" Second National Bank, successor to the one created by Hamilton. Although Jackson placed less emphasis on the virtues of agriculture, he was faithful to Jefferson in his opposition to what he took to be unconstitutional government support for a small, parasitic economic elite whose interests diverged from that of ordinary, hardworking people.

Like the earlier debates between Hamilton and Jefferson, the bank war debates exposed tensions within liberalism and strains between liberal and democratic understandings of economic life. Jackson's bitter opposition was rooted in the liberal principle of equal opportunity. The small farmer and the Westerner did not enjoy access to the bank's loans, which went mostly to Eastern commercial and industrial bigwigs. Also, the bank threatened democracy by lavishing money on its political allies and by subverting democratic essentials – honest toil and social solidarity. Its credit manipulation created an artificial economy of phony paper assets and speculation that threatened the health of the real economy, the one based on hard work, honest exchange, and neighborliness.

Jackson vetoed the bank's recharter. By supporting his subsequent reelection, a majority of voters voiced their own qualms about the economy's impersonality and complexity. They too preferred a tangible, manageable economy in which profit and competition blended with affection for customers, confidence in partners, respect for rivals, and trust in coworkers. Jackson called the people who live this kind of economic life – "the farmer, the mechanic, and the laborer" – the "bone and sinew of the country."

The Democratic Defense of Manufacturing

Jackson's opponents in the bank war debates created America's first fully functioning opposition party, the Whigs. Like Hamilton before them, the Whigs believed that government should play an active role in stimulating economic growth. They supported not only the bank but also high tariffs and federal funds for such internal improvements as roads, railroads, and canals. They shared Jackson's belief in democracy, hard work, and honesty but did not believe that those virtues were threatened by government economic promotion. Indeed, the more money that government spent on transportation improvements and loans to business, the better the work opportunities would be for people with the grit and determination to take advantage of them. As the Democrats became ever more ensnared in protecting slavery, support for free labor was increasingly associated with the Whigs, with the Free Soil Party that split from the Democrats in 1848 to field its own presidential candidate, and with these two parties' joint successor, the Republicans. These parties preserved the Hamiltonian defense of industry and government intervention but without its elitist overtones. In his 1830 Fourth of July oration delivered in Lowell, Massachusetts, Whig spokesman Edward Everett eloquently expressed the relationship between political freedom and economic success:

> It is the spirit of a free country which animates and gives energy to its labor; which puts the mass in action; fires its motive and intensity; makes it inventive; sends it off in new directions; subdues to its command all the powers of nature, and enlists in its service an army of machines, that do all but think and talk. Compare a hand loom with a power loom, a barge poled up against the current of a river, with a steamer breasting its force. The difference is not greater between them than between the efficiency of labor under a free or despotic government, in an independent state or a colony.

Thus, the new industrial economy unleashed democratic energies. From the Whigs onward, many advocates of industry and manufacturing would claim that they, not the "backwards looking" farmers celebrated by Jefferson, were the true voice of the people.

The Economic Impact of the Civil War

Edward Everett shared the podium with Abraham Lincoln at Gettysburg. Indeed, his address, not Lincoln's, was the featured one on that memorable day. Americans remember Lincoln, not Everett, because it was Lincoln who attached the free labor principle to the greatest of all American political struggles, abolition of slavery. Although Lincoln was morally opposed to slavery, he knew most Northerners were not. He therefore justified his opposition to territorial expansion of slavery not only on the terrible impact it had on black slaves but also on the harm it would do to the economic opportunity of whites. As he stated in a speech of October 16, 1854,

> We want them [the territories] for homes of free white people. This they cannot be, to any considerable extent, if slavery shall be planted within them. Slave States are places for poor white people to remove from. New free States are the places for poor people to go to, and better their condition.

Lincoln reminded Northerners that whatever their feelings about African Americans, halting the spread of slavery was necessary to keep the North from sinking into the poverty and torpor endured by the non-slaveholding Southern white majority. A successful free labor economy could not survive in the midst of slavery. Indeed, Union commitment to free labor conspired with sheer military necessity to turn the Civil War into a powerful stimulus for economic growth.

Economic Stimulus

In the midst of the Civil War, Congress enacted the *Homestead Act of 1862*, which enabled settlers to claim 160 acres of free, previously unin-habited land on condition they reside there for at least five years. Thus, even the poor could become property owners simply by working the land. By 1880, the federal government had given away 65 million acres to homesteaders.

The extraordinary productivity of Midwestern corn and wheat farms meant that even though the Civil War caused so many young farm-ers to join the army and enlisted so many Union soldiers who needed to be fed, there was still too much grain. Deprived of their South-ern market, farmers accelerated their efforts to sell grain abroad. War's end brought many soldiers back to the farm and made the grain states even more dependent on the world market to absorb ever larger sur-pluses. Between 1870 and 1900, a third of the American wheat crop was exported. The United States became the chief source of food for Western Europe.

The Civil War also accelerated demand for manufacturing production and labor. Armies need uniforms, weapons, ammunition, wagons, cooking utensils, and more. At the same time, taking so many young men away from their jobs drastically reduced the industrial labor supply. To produce more with less, industry invented new labor-saving techniques, including steam-powered equipment and other forms of mechanization.

To ensure the security of war supplies, Congress in 1861 enacted a very high tariff on imported goods. Southern states, fearing that European coun-tries would revenge themselves by imposing similarly high tariffs on their cotton exports, had opposed the protective tariff. But during the war and its aftermath, the South was unable to influence Congress to protect its economic interest. Therefore, high tariffs survived long into the post-war period, increasing the profitability of American manufacturing and greatly accelerating its growth. National security likewise provided a strong rationale for the building of the transcontinental railway. Because it would take years for sufficient freight traffic to develop to make the railway prof-itable, Congress provided enormous subsidies in the form of land grants to the two railroads that were partners in the project.

These same policies, so effective for carrying out the war, aggravated tensions between liberalism and democracy because they encouraged corruption. Prosecuting a war demands haste, so hasty decisions are inevitable. In its rush to stimulate wartime production and railroad expansion, the government could not be overly scrupulous in doling out subsidies or in driving hard bargains for the equipment that soldiers needed to stay warm and dry and to kill the enemy. Corruption and profiteering were rampant. The same war that sent hundreds of thousands of young men to their deaths produced a bumper crop of millionaires who thrived by overcharging for clothing, food, and munitions and by bribing government officials to win profitable contracts.

Fostering Inequality

Former slaves were excluded from the economic bounty that the war created. Efforts to convert them into free laborers were quickly abandoned. The plantation system was replaced by *sharecropping* in which ex-slaves would farm white-owned land and pay the owner a specified share of the harvest. In order to obtain seed and fertilizer, sharecroppers were forced to borrow money from often unscrupulous store owners. Legal bondage was replaced by the economic bondage of debts with huge interest payments that sapped sharecroppers' earnings and that they had no hope of paying off. The economic system of sharecropping proved as significant as the Jim Crow laws in keeping Southern African Americans from becoming fully free citizens.

World War II provided the first significant improvement in African-American economic conditions since slavery's end. Fearful of Southern political opposition, President Franklin D. Roosevelt (FDR) initially made little attempt to include African Americans in the war effort. A. Phillips Randolph, president of the Brotherhood of Sleeping Car Porters, threatened to organize a protest march in June of 1941 that would demand racial integration of the armed forces and the hiring of African Americans for war production jobs. FDR realized that such a protest would undermine his claim that the United States was fighting a world war for freedom. He persuaded Randolph to call off the march, and in exchange, he issued an executive order creating a Fair Employment Practices Committee (FEPC) to combat job discrimination. The FEPC had little direct impact. The great economic improvements for African Americans that took place during this period were mainly the result of the acute labor shortage created by the war. Nonetheless, Randolph's bold threat marked a crucial turning point in the battle for equal employment opportunity. It demonstrated that African Americans could best press for greater equality by publicizing the gap between America's professed love of liberty and its willingness to condone second-class treatment of racial minorities.

This approach permeated the civil rights revolution of the 1960s, during which African-American leaders were continually pointing out America's hypocrisy: it claimed to be leading a worldwide struggle against Soviet totalitarianism while it simultaneously deprived African Americans of their rights. The high point of this effort, the 1963 March on Washington for Jobs and Freedom (see Chapter 2), took place less than a year after the most chilling of all Cold War confrontations, the Cuban Missile Crisis. The march's focus was on jobs as well as freedom, an indication of the economic as well as the political agenda advocated by the Civil Rights Movement.

Laissez Faire and the Attack on Laissez Faire

War always creates economic winners and losers. But the unprecedented scale of the Civil War, in terms of both deaths and industrial production, greatly magnified the political importance of the war's economic consequences. A new cynicism and brazenness entered American politics as many war veterans sullenly contemplated why some citizens who stayed home had grown rich on the back of the veterans' suffering. The strong sense of solidarity and common sacrifice that had been maintained during the war was shattered. People became less willing to tolerate government interference. This national mood created a great receptivity to the political economic theory of *laissez faire*, a French term meaning "leave alone," which we touched on in Chapter 5. If people were only left alone, according to laissez faire, progress and economic liberty would go hand in hand. Laissez faire's appeal was enhanced by its claim to scientific truth. The writings of English philosopher Herbert Spencer popularized the idea that Darwin's theory of biological evolution applied to society as well. Human improvement was based on "the survival of the fittest." Government aid to people who were less fit would undermine the process of natural selection and weaken society as a whole.

Laissez faire served as a rationale for Congress to limit government scrutiny and discipline of business behavior but it was no obstacle to Congress's lavish subsidy of railroads and tariff protections for industry. A government that was hell-bent on economic expansion did not dwell on this logical inconsistency. Even today, government continues to provide billions of dollars in tariff protection, tax breaks, production quotas, and outright subsidies to industries such as agriculture, steel, automobile, tobacco, and oil.

The Creation of Laissez Faire: The Modern Corporation

One of the most important consequences of the rise of laissez-faire ideology was the adoption of general incorporation. Originally, a corporation required a special grant from a state legislature attesting that it performed a public purpose that could not readily be achieved in any other way. For example, in 1785, the Massachusetts legislature created a corporation to build a bridge across the Charles River. By 1837, the Charles River Bridge's high tolls had sufficiently enraged travelers that the legislature granted a charter to another corporation to build and operate a bridge nearby. The Charles River company complained that by incorporating a rival, the legislature destroyed the value of the company's charter. In the landmark case of *Charles River Bridge v. Warren Bridge*, the Supreme Court rejected that argument, thereby discouraging the use of state-chartered corporations as a device to obtain special privileges. As the public ceased to regard corporations as an unfair means for acquiring privilege, it began to recognize that they could serve as mighty engines of economic advancement, provided government did not interfere with their creation and functioning.

The essence of the corporation was the principle of *limited liability*. If a corporation failed, individual stockholders could not be held responsible for paying its debts. Their liability was limited to the amount they had invested. Limited liability meant limited risk. Potential investors could calculate how much money they could afford to lose and limit their stock purchase to that amount.

General incorporation was defended on democratic grounds. The great Massachusetts senator Daniel Webster gave the following explanation as to why limited liability served vital democratic purposes. Industrial expansion provided more jobs and cheaper products, but it was hindered by lack of capital. America lacked a large class of very wealthy people who could afford to take great investment risks. To encourage ordinary people to invest, the system needed to limit their risk by enabling them to calculate in advance how much they could possibly lose. Thereby, limited liability democratized the investment process.

Trust and Antitrust

Echoing Jackson, critics called limited liability corporations "monsters." Not only were these corporations large and powerful, but because their liability was limited, no actual person could be held accountable for the promises they made. At the stroke of a pen, a corporation could go out of business and leave suppliers, customers, and creditors with nobody to hold responsible for what was owed to them.

Railroads were the lightning rods for popular discontent with the new corporate order and the laissez-faire principles on which it rested. Railroads needed government help to acquire property along proposed routes and to subsidize construction costs. To obtain such assistance, they bribed state legislatures and other government officials. Railroads' tentacles crossed state lines, which thwarted a state's ability to discipline them. The great expense of building railroads made the companies quasi-monopolies. Farmers were lucky to have even one railroad nearby; therefore, they could not credibly threaten to ship their crops on a rival line. Farmers might be charged different prices for the same service depending on whether they had alternative transportation options. Such *price discrimination* made economic sense, but it fed the farmers' fear of being held hostage to the whim of the "monster." Ignoring the extent to which they relied on government, railroads tried to evade government regulation and control by arguing that such interference was a violation of their economic freedom.

In the 1880s, ambitious business leaders, most prominently John D. Rockefeller, clung to the letter of laissez faire but evaded the spirit as they sought to bend the free competition rules in order to monopolize key industries. The Ohio charter of Rockefeller's company forbade it from acquiring property outside the state or from merging with other oil companies. Rockefeller circumvented the charter by having the various oil companies he sought to control turn their stock over to a newly created entity called a trust. In return, they each became part owners of the trust. The effect was to enable the trust to control the bulk of the nation's oil output. Similar consolidations occurred in other industries, most notably sugar refining and steel. Between 1898 and 1902, more than 2600 corporate mergers worth more than 6.3 billion dollars took place.

Defenders of trusts pointed to the great *economies of scale* attainable through consolidation. Economies of scale exist whenever an increase in size reduces costs. For example, if an oil refiner increases its oil supply and acquires more customers, it can afford to build bigger refineries. Bigger refineries operate more cheaply than smaller ones. With bigger refineries and fewer competitors, Standard Oil could lower its cost of producing such refined oil products as petroleum and kerosene and increase its profits.

The term *trust* became an epithet for corporate greed and anticompetitive behavior. Corporations were opposed on both laissez-faire and democratic grounds. Because they drove rivals from the market, they stifled competition. Because they were so big and rich, they could bribe

TAKING THE BULL BY THE HORNS

This 1906 cartoon from the *Minneapolis Journal* shows President Roosevelt's strong stance against big, rich trusts that stifled competition, such as the Northern Securities Corporation.

legislators and pass laws that benefited them to the detriment of the public.

Opposition to trusts led to the passage in 1890 of the *Sherman Antitrust Act*, named for its Senate sponsor, Ohio Republican John Sherman. The act was a manifestly liberal rather than a democratic public policy tool. It outlawed efforts to create monopolies, but it did not oppose corporate bigness as such. It relied on the courts to determine whether a particular corporation was truly engaged in anticompetitive behavior. This determination was a very complex one. The cases that the Justice Department brought against the oil, steel, and other trusts remained in the courts for years.

Populism

While lawyers and judges were debating the meaning of the antitrust laws, a grassroots movement known as Populism was taking hold in the American countryside. Populism was devoted to democratic reform of the American economy. Unlike their European counterparts, the Populists were not socialists. Their goal was not to replace private ownership with government ownership but rather to rid free enterprise of its antidemocratic and anti-Christian tendencies. In 1896, the Populist leader William Jennings Bryan was nominated by the Democrats for president (see Chapter 11 for a further discussion). At the nominating convention, Bryan echoed Lincoln's defense of free labor, claiming that the measure of a businessman was not money or property but productiveness, like a farmer who "by the application of brain and muscle to the natural resources of the country creates wealth." Bryan scolded adherents of laissez faire for undemocratically depriving most hardworking Americans of the status they had earned:

> We say to you that you have made the definition of a businessman too limited in its application. The man who is employed for wages is as much a businessman as his employer; the attorney in a country town is as much a businessman as the corporation counsel in a great metropolis; the merchant at the crossroads is as much a businessman as the merchant in New York. . . . We come to speak for this broader class of businessmen.

Bryan recognized that "the broader class of businessmen" were mostly debtors. He sought to take America off a currency standard that was strictly gold and onto a standard that would include silver as well. Since silver was more plentiful than gold, this change would increase the money supply, making money cheaper and debts easier to pay. Bryan transformed this seemingly technical question about currency into a titanic religious struggle by denouncing his opponents in starkly religious terms: "You shall not press down upon the brow of labor this crown of thorns, you shall not crucify mankind upon a cross of gold."

Democrats in favor of the gold standard, nicknamed Gold Democrats or "Gold Bugs," invoked the principle of promise keeping. If borrowers cheapen the value of money when their debt comes due, Gold Democrats claimed, they are cheating on their promise to pay back their debt in full, an action that is both immoral and economically destructive. If creditors doubt that their loans will be fully repaid, they will be less likely to make loans and economic activity will decline. Bryan and the Silver Democrats did not dispute the importance of promise keeping. Rather, they stressed other virtues that the liberal emphasis on promise keeping ignored – justice, forgiveness, and charity. They believed that the farmer who could not pay his loan because his crops failed was not a sinner, but that the banker who called in the loan was, because he ignored the Christian duty to be charitable and the democratic duty to help a neighbor. As this debate points out, liberal economics fits uneasily with democratic ideas of equality, solidarity, and cooperation or with Christian notions that the "last shall be first" and "it is easier for a camel to fit through the eye of a needle than for a rich man to enter the kingdom of heaven."

Organized Labor

In the 1880s, violent strikes occurred in the rail and steel industries. The strikes were organized by labor unions who, like the Populists, sought to rein in laissez faire in the name of democratic solidarity. Denying that employers had a right to pay them whatever the market would bear, workers banded together to collectively withhold their labor and shut their workplaces down. These strikes were broken largely because federal courts interpreted the Sherman Act's antimonopoly provisions to apply to labor. Strikes were deemed illegal efforts to deprive workers of their freedom to determine their own individual conditions of employment. Initially, the Sherman Act did more to suppress unions than to promote competitive industry.

The first national post–Civil War labor organization was the Knights of Labor. Its ineffectiveness led its successor, the *American Federation of Labor* (AFL), to turn its back on the electoral and legislative tactics used by the Knights and to concentrate on organizing workers in individual workshops and construction sites. As the term *federation* in its title implies, the organization was a decentralized one whose real strength lay at the local level.

The first AFL president, Samuel Gompers, once said that he was a trade unionist in America but he would be a socialist in Germany and in Russia a nihilist. He meant that in order to be most effective, workers had to adopt the organizational and political strategy most appropriate to their condition. In Germany, workers could make use of a powerful and effective state. In Russia, they had to resort to violence to bring down a hopelessly corrupt and backward-looking monarchy. In the United States, workers had to adapt to a liberal political economy. The American way was self-reliance;

William Jennings Bryan's 1896 Cross of Gold speech drew attention to the uneasy coexistence of liberal market values and religious values. The speech won him the presidential nomination.

workers needed to rely on themselves, not government. By forming strong organizations based on their common interests and skills, workers could approach management on a businesslike basis, offering to provide their labor on the basis of terms collectively agreed on.

For Gompers, collective bargaining was a decent compromise between the liberal fiction that an individual worker could freely negotiate with a monster corporation and the distinctively illiberal and un-American doctrine that government should dictate terms of employment. Gompers understood that labor unions could not be based solely on liberal, individualistic premises. Collective bargaining was based on the threat of collective action. If some workers failed to support a strike, it was not credible. Therefore unions depended on a degree of mutual reliance and solidarity not attainable solely through appeals to self-interest. Inevitably, some workers would decide that their own interests were better served by making a deal than by going out on strike. Their commitment could only be obtained by appealing to their sense of group loyalty.

Because solidarity was more easily forged among workers with the same skills, the AFL unions tended to be organized on a craft basis. Plumbers, bricklayers, carpenters, and teamsters each had their own *craft union*. Gompers himself was a highly skilled cigar maker and rose up through the ranks of his craft union. To this day, important segments of the labor force, including construction workers, unionize on a craft basis.

Workers were not privy to what was actually discussed behind the closed doors of labor-management bargaining sessions. They *had* to trust their leaders, and therefore they kept their leaders on a short democratic leash. Local, state, and national union leaders were elected for fixed terms. Campaigns for union leadership positions often took on the same degree of intensity and electioneering savvy as did campaigns for public office.

The Federal Reserve

In most respects, the late nineteenth-century economy resembled today's economy more than it did the economy of the 1830s. It was dominated by large corporations, complex systems of production and distribution, robust exports, and a mass domestic consumer market. Its growth during the 1880s and 1890s was staggering. Industrial production quadrupled between 1879 and 1899, and agricultural output increased by 50 percent. But in one crucial area, the turn-of-the-century economy was closer to that of the Jacksonian era – there was no system for regulating the money supply. Thus, in the United States, the principle of laissez faire applied not only to consumer, labor, and capital markets but to the currency market as well. Thanks to Jackson's veto of the Second National Bank in 1832, the United States was the only advanced industrial country with no *central bank*, meaning a bank of issue, one that stood responsible for the currency and operated to control it.

Originally, the great central banks of Europe – including the Bank of England and the Bundesbanke (Germany) – were private institutions, because government was not trusted to control the currency. Government is always tempted to solve its own money problems by printing more, thereby depreciating the value of the currency. A private institution can be required by law to stand behind the currency, to redeem with gold the paper money it issues. Such a monetary monopoly was deemed to be a necessary exception to the competitive norms of a laissez-faire economy because sound money was considered a necessary precondition for such an economy to flourish. But as Jackson's veto of the Second National Bank illustrated, the American democratic spirit resisted granting so much power to a single entity.

As the American economy became ever more complex and as markets became increasingly national and international, the problems caused by lack of monetary control multiplied. The money supply system was too rigid to prevent bank panics, situations when depositors swarmed banks to withdraw their money all at the same time. Banks could not respond because there was no "bankers' bank" to provide cash to tide them over until the panic passed. Small-town banks deposited their extra cash in city banks that placed their cash in big New York banks that used it to finance stock purchases on Wall Street. When a panic broke out, the New York banks could only provide cash by calling in their stock loans. Since the stock market was itself falling in response to the panic, it was extremely difficult to collect on such loans. Therefore, local and small city banks were forced to fold for lack of cash.

In 1907, the third largest New York bank failed. In response to the ensuing panic, Congress proposed a banking federation resembling a European central bank. The Democrats were opposed, but once they regained control of the House of Representatives in 1910, they felt obliged to come up with an alternative. Led by Representative Carter Glass of Virginia, Congress passed a bill that created a decentralized federation of reserve banks, each a private institution owned and operated by its members, which were any individual banks in its region who chose to join. The bill divided the nation into twelve regions, each with its own reserve bank. Each regional reserve bank acquired capital by requiring its members to spend 3 percent of their own capital to buy its stock.

Regional reserve banks had three tools with which to regulate the money supply. First, they could change the *discount rate*, the interest rate that member banks paid to borrow money from them. The higher the discount rate, the more expensive it was for members to borrow money and the higher the rate was that members would charge to lend money to customers. Raising the discount rate made money more expensive, thereby lowering demand for it. Second, regional reserve banks could change the reserve requirements imposed on members. If banks had to keep more assets in reserve, they could make fewer loans, thereby shrinking the amount of money in circulation. Third, reserve banks could engage in *open market operations*, buying and selling government bonds and notes. When the reserve banks sold notes and bonds, the money used to pay for them was taken out of circulation, thereby reducing the money supply. During a panic, a reserve bank might use all three tools – buying bonds and notes, lowering the discount rate, and reducing reserve requirements – to rapidly expand the money supply and make more funds available to threatened banks.

This Federal Reserve Act (passed in 1913) was a distinctively American solution to the problems posed by an inflexible money supply. It created institutions for manipulating money and credit but did not cede control to either Washington or Wall Street. The twelve regional banks were responsive to their members and to the *Federal Reserve Board* (the Fed), whose members were appointed by the president but had staggered terms so that no single president could appoint a majority. The Fed would eventually become a central bank in all but name.

Reining in the Market

By the early twentieth century, the grip of laissez faire on political economic thinking had begun to wane. The public became more sensitive to the failure of unfettered markets to adequately provide safe products and decent working conditions and became more offended by the sheer rapacity and dishonesty of many leaders of industry. During this time, Progressivism began to influence the economic and social changes that were taking place in America (see Chapter 4). Progressivism's greatest impact on the American political economy was to establish a role for government in regulating the economy. Congress passed legislation establishing the *Food and Drug Administration* (FDA) in 1906 to protect consumers from rotten food and impure pharmaceuticals. In 1914, it created the *Federal Trade Commission* (FTC) to provide more effective regulation of unfair business competition by supplementing judicial enforcement with the active intervention of an executive agency. Several states, especially New York, also passed laws limiting working hours and requiring safer working conditions for industrial workers.

The Great Depression, which started in 1929, had a far greater impact on public mistrust of laissez faire. It put one-third of the workforce out of work. In 1933, Congress created the *National Recovery Administration* (NRA), an ambitious effort to substitute planning for competition. The organization set up committees of producers, workers, and consumers to write codes of fair conduct for every industry. These codes fixed prices, set wages, and even established production quotas for individual firms. For a moment, it appeared that the laissez-faire presumption underlying the American economy had disappeared.

But the NRA could not reconcile the diverging goals of the different code-writing participants. Bigger producers in a given industry wanted to reduce competition, depress wages, and raise prices. Smaller rivals sought to limit the monopoly power of bigger firms. Unions tried to improve wages and working conditions. Consumers tried to lower prices. The code-writing committees became just another venue for economic conflict. The codes proved unenforceable and had little practical effect. Even before the Supreme Court declared it unconstitutional in 1935, the NRA was seen as a failure. No similarly comprehensive effort to direct and control American industrial life has ever been tried again.

The Modern Labor Movement

The NRA left two enduring legacies. It spawned the modern labor movement, and it alerted certain industries to the benefits of cooperating among themselves to reduce competition. Because NRA committees included labor, it had to be determined who spoke for workers in a given industry. Except for construction trades and certain other skilled occupations, most workers were not unionized, especially those in the heavy industries such as steel and automobiles that were coming to dominate the American economy. Although the NRA did not require industrial workers to form unions, Section 7a of its enabling law gave workers a right to bargain collectively, which granted unions the legitimacy they had previously lacked.

John L. Lewis, president of the *United Mine Workers of America* (UMWA), which represented coal miners, was determined to exploit Section 7a to launch a major organizing offensive. He dispatched UMWA organizers to unionize automobile and steel factories, instructing them to tell workers that "FDR wants you to join." President Franklin D. Roosevelt had said no such thing; Section 7a permitted but did not require union membership. But if FDR refuted Lewis's claim, he would appear to side with management. The president remained silent, which enabled Lewis's organizers to tell workers that by joining the union they were helping the president. Hundreds of thousands of laborers joined, and most large manufacturing companies became unionized.

The *United Steel Workers of American* (USWA), the *United Automobile Workers* (UAW), and other new unions did not enjoy good relations with the AFL. They called themselves *industrial unions*, not craft unions, meaning that all workers in a factory, regardless of their particular job, belonged to the same union local. The AFL unions, committed to organizing on a skills basis, resented the workplace approach. The industrial unions organized a rival labor federation, the *Congress of Industrial Organizations* (CIO), and elected John L. Lewis president. As the leader of this increasingly large and militant organization, Lewis emerged as one of the nation's most powerful political figures. Unlike the AFL, the CIO became deeply immersed in electoral politics. In 1936, it provided much of the money and the organizing effort for FDR's successful reelection bid and for campaigns by many pro-labor governors and members of Congress as well.

The 1935 Wagner Act, named for Senator Robert Wagner, Democrat of New York, established specific procedures for implementing the promise contained in Section 7a. It created the *National Labor Relations Board* (NLRB) to oversee collective bargaining elections and to ensure protection of workers' rights. If a company's workers sought to organize, they could petition for a collective bargaining election. Once the NLRB certified it, employers had to abide by NLRB election rules. If a majority voted for a union, management had to recognize that union and bargain with it "in good faith."

The Wagner Act did not force workers to join unions nor management to accept union demands. Like the Social Security Act, it declared an economic right, that is, to join a union and to bargain collectively. The success of unions, coupled with the World War II economic expansion, transformed the lives of American workers. The United States became the first nation in history to enable blue-collar workers to enjoy a standard of living previously reserved for the upper middle class. In industrial cities and suburbs throughout America, assembly-line workers were able to buy homes, cars, and television sets and to enjoy excellent medical and retirement benefits. After World War II, the CIO's organizing success coupled with a desire to reduce the costs of running two separate federations, led the AFL to agree to merge with the newer federation. The AFL-CIO occasionally supported pro-labor Republicans such as Senator Jacob Javits of New York, but the bulk of its considerable political power was exercised within the Democratic party. Between 1936 and 1968, all Democrats nominated for president enjoyed enthusiastic AFL-CIO support.

The growth of the modern labor movement relied heavily on compulsory union membership – the so-called closed shop, a provision in union contracts stipulating that union membership be required as a condition of employment. Unions insist that the very nature of collective bargaining requires that if a majority of workers vote to have a union, all the workers must be compelled to join and to abide by all subsequent decisions reached by majority membership vote. Management and those workers hostile to unions favor an open shop that makes union membership voluntary. This tension between the collective rights of unions, on the one hand, and the property rights claimed by business interests, on the other – representing claims of democracy and liberalism, respectively – has been partially ameliorated by federalism. The 1947 Taft-Hartley Act permits states to pass "right to work" legislation that outlaws the union shop, and many states, most of them in the South, have done so. Consequently, unions enjoy different rights depending on what state they are in. This milestone legislation made it much more difficult for unions to expand and sustain their membership. As of 2004, there were 15,472,000 union workers, representing less than 15 percent of the workforce. The decline of unionism is not only attributable to Taft-Hartley, but also to changes in the economy, which, once dominated by producing farmers and laborers, has been remade by the information age and the growing importance of white-collar professionals and service workers.

Cartels

FDR's New Deal programs did not engage in comprehensive government planning and intervention, as did social-democratic governments in Western Europe, but inspired by the NRA codes, the New Deal did assist in forming *cartels* in several industries. Cartel members reduce competition by preventing entry of new competitors, fixing prices, or creating production quotas. They rarely succeed on their own. They need government help to punish members for cheating and to prevent competition from those companies not invited to join.

Only the worst-off industries would accept the close government scrutiny that was required to maintain a cartel. To obtain congressional help, a cartel needed to develop strong internal unity and find a publicly acceptable rationale. The coal and oil industries used the rationale of conservation of natural resources, claiming that free competition would lead to excessive exploitation of those resources. The aviation and shipping industries used national security as a rationale, claiming that competition had to be limited to ensure that successful airlines and shipping companies would be available in time of war. Truckers claimed that highway safety required keeping the decrepit trucks of "fly-by-night" operators off the roads.

Among the most compelling rationales for a cartel was protection of the weak and vulnerable. Farmers, for example, argued that the right to economic security should apply to them as well as to the elderly and disabled. Most Americans no longer lived on farms; still, agriculture was the largest American export and had the highest level of total investment. But agricultural prices had been in decline for a decade, and dependence on world markets deprived farmers of the ability to control their own fate. Indeed, the harder they worked, the larger their harvests, and the lower the prices paid for their crop.

Despite their vaunted independence, farmers were impelled by these deteriorating conditions to become more politically active. Since the mid-1920s, farm leaders had been exploring ways to reduce overproduction. By the early 1930s, the American Farm Bureau Federation (AFBF) had emerged as a very influential political organization. In 1933, Congress responded to AFBF pressure by passing the *Agricultural Adjustment Act* (AAA). Although the Supreme Court declared the AAA unconstitutional in 1935, it was reenacted in 1937 with its most important components intact.

The act enabled farmers to collude by creating county committees that set overall county crop limits; then the farmers divided that quota among themselves. The AAA provided government payments to compensate for lost production, price supports, conservation payments, purchase of surplus crops, and other forms of subsidy and market controls. No other major sector of the economy obtained so much government assistance.

To obtain government support, the AFBF invoked the hallowed Jeffersonian claim that farmers did not just work, they served America. Their vigor and toil put food on America's table; their spirit of independence and patriotism animated American freedom. Farm leaders claimed that they were seeking aid to ensure equal treatment. Farm prices, they said, should be on a par with industrial prices so that the farmers' standard of living would match that of industrial workers. "Parity" became the rural rallying cry. Farming remains the only American commercial activity that is directly and extensively subsidized by government.

In 2001, farmers received 19.3 billion dollars in government payments, plus 5.5 billion dollars in subsidized loans. The more their farms grow, the more the government pays them, up to a total limit, as of January 2002, of $460,000 per farm per year. Farmers also receive payments for keeping environmentally sensitive land out of production. In 1996, Congress passed the Freedom to Farm Act, designed to gradually wean farmers from direct subsidies. But soon thereafter farm prices plummeted and Congress responded by restoring crop payments.

Because payments are tied to quantity of output, the greatest beneficiaries of farm aid are the mammoth wheat and corn farms of the Midwest and the rice and cotton farms of the South. These large enterprises do not fit the Jeffersonian stereotype of the family farmer. They are often owned by corporations headquartered in New York, Chicago, or, perhaps, London or Amsterdam. They are run by salaried managers and they specialize in a single crop. Despite more than sixty-five years of aid that has totaled hundreds of billions of dollars, the percentage of the U.S. population engaged in farming has shrunk to less than 1 percent and the percentage of family-owned farms continues to shrink. But the power of Jeffersonian democratic rhetoric is still in evidence as farm aid supporters continue to defend the program based on the need to protect the family farm and the democratic political virtues it embodies.

Small merchants also demanded federal help to protect them against what they deemed excessive and unfair competition. In the 1920s, chain stores such as Sears endangered local merchants. The automobile destroyed the virtual monopoly of local stores by enabling customers to drive long distances in search of better prices and products. To keep chains out, downtown merchants made the same claims about their superior civic virtue that were later used to discourage the Wal-Mart stores. Merchants also complained that chain stores competed unfairly by forcing suppliers to give discounts based on the huge volume of their purchases.

Volume discounting illustrates the tension between liberal and democratic economic understandings. Small merchants viewed volume discounts as an antidemocratic form of intimidation of suppliers by the monster chain store. But suppliers gained enormous benefits by selling in volume. The cost of billing and shipping one Sears order of a thousand items was much less than that of filling a thousand small orders. *The Robinson-Patman Act* (1936) tried to protect independent retailers without depriving consumers of the opportunity to shop at chain stores. It banned various forms of unfair competitive practices and placed certain restrictions on volume discounting. In its wake, many states provided additional protections to specialty retailers such as drugstores and liquor stores.

As these cartel examples illustrate, Americans were unwilling to choose between the efficiency claims of liberal economics and the democratic claims made on behalf of efforts to rein in the market. Farm subsidies did not revive family farms. Loopholes enabled chain stores to enjoy economies of scale. But the breadth and scope of these protective attempts show the depth of the public's desire to enjoy the civic advantages of small operators and the consumption advantages provided by large ones.

The New Deal Legacy

The most enduring New Deal changes in economic policy avoided tinkering with the market and used other means to redistribute wealth, provide economic security, and promote prosperity. Ever since, economic policy has aimed less at influencing market behavior and more at altering the framework within which market competition takes place. Government now relies on three major forms of policy to frame the private economy: it provides a minimum level of economic security; it taxes people in rough proportion to their level of wealth; and it manipulates the money supply and overall levels of taxing and spending in order to promote steady and ample economic growth.

Economic Security

The Social Security Act in 1935 extended the American understanding of rights to encompass economic rights (see Chapter 4). This fundamental change in economic self-understanding was achieved without impinging on the competitive nature of economic life because it promised to provide old age pensions to economic winners and losers alike.

Two other forms of economic security were explicitly designed to enhance the performance of a competitive economy. The *Federal Deposit Insurance Corporation* (FDIC) provided a government guarantee that depositors could reclaim their bank deposits, up to a certain limit, if a bank failed. The FDIC encouraged them to leave their money in the bank, which bolstered the economy by increasing the amount of capital available for banks to lend. The unemployment compensation program provided income for a period of time to those who lost their jobs. Because unemployed workers knew they had a cushion, they could spend more time finding the right job rather than taking the first one that came along. This government-supported flexibility improved labor market efficiency by emboldening workers to find the best outlet for their talents.

Progressive Taxation

During the New Deal, a progressive income tax was instituted that not only was large enough to constitute the greatest source of federal government revenue but also significantly redistributed income. The tax was called a *progressive tax* because as a person's income increased, so did the percentage of tax paid by that person. In its early phase, the rich were required to pay as much as 75 percent of their income. No one actually paid that much because the government allowed many income deductions, including the deduction for interest paid on home mortgages and for gifts made to charity. Nonetheless, the progressive tax did force the rich to pay a larger share of their income in taxes than those less well off. Box 3 describes this country's income tax in its current form. The progressive tax is organized on the basis of brackets which are income ranges. Everyone in the same income range pays the same amount of tax. The higher the bracket the higher the percentage of income that a person pays in tax. People in higher brackets do not pay the higher rate on their entire income but only on the portion of that income that rises above the limits for each of the lower brackets (Box 3 shows how this bracket system actually works.)

Box Three: Nuts and Bolts

The Current Income Tax

Over time, the income tax has become less progressive. The highest brackets have been eliminated and the amount of income it takes to move to a higher bracket has risen. The figures that we are using here are the tax rates for married couples; the rates for single people are higher.

As of 2006, married couples paid 10 percent on income up to $15,100; 15 percent on income from $15,100 up to $61,300; 25 percent on income from $61,300 to $123,700; 28 percent on income from $123,700 to $188,450; 33 percent on income from $188,450 to $336,550; and 35 percent on income above $336,550.

The income tax is more progressive than the above figures indicate because of the earned income tax credit that is given to low-income taxpayers. The maximum credit can be as much as $4,400 for workers supporting two or more children. A worker with one child can get up to $2,662 with the credit. And $399 is available to a childless eligible employee. A single filer's adjusted gross income must be less than $11,750 if he or she has no children, $31,030 with one child, and $35,263 with two or more kids. Married couples filing jointly are allowed to earn $2,000 more in each category and still claim the credit. Therefore, those who qualify and who have children actually receive more from the credit than they owe in taxes and therefore they have a negative income tax bill.

Opponents of the progressive income tax argue that it has a deleterious effect on economic performance; it discourages richer people from working harder, because for every extra dollar they earn, they will have to give more than 35 cents back to the government. It is very difficult, however, to prove this assertion because the disincentive effect of steep tax rates is counterbalanced by the drive that richer

> people have to earn more income so as to be able to pay those high taxes and still maintain their expensive lifestyle. Whether or not the progressive income tax discourages work effort overall, it certainly does not interfere with the internal dynamics of the free market.

The progressive income tax redistributes income because although the rich pay higher tax rates they do not benefit proportionally from the policies the government provides. Many government programs are geared to help the poor and even more programs provide entitlements for the middle class. Therefore the rich pay more but, at least in direct money terms, they do not get more.

The income tax is not the only tax that most Americans pay. They also pay a separate tax to fund Medicare and Social Security tax. These taxes are not progressive. Everyone whose job qualifies them for Social Security pays 6.2 percent of their wages up to a maximum of $94,200. Employers match this contribution, also paying 6.2 percent of each employee's wage. Employers and employees also pay 1.45 percent of the employee's wage to Medicare. Thus low wage earners who benefit from the earned income tax credit pay much more of their income for Social Security and Medicare tax than they do for income tax, whereas for higher income individuals it is the reverse. Most states also impose a state income tax. These vary, but most are not as progressive as the federal tax. Local governments rely heavily on the property tax. In most localities, residents pay a fixed percentage of the assessed value of their property and therefore this tax is not progressive either. Although, technically, only property owners pay property tax, in fact renters pay it as well because their landlords pass at least some of the tax burden on to them in the form of higher rent.

Macroeconomics

Old age pensions and income taxes had figured prominently in Populist and Progressive political platforms for several decades. The genuinely new idea adopted by the New Deal was macroeconomic policy, often called "Keynesianism" in honor of its inventor, Englishman John Maynard Keynes. *Macroeconomics* is the study of how economies function as a whole, as opposed to *microeconomics*, the study of how the various parts of an economy function and interact with one another.

Keynes saw that the overall performance of an economy was not just the sum of its parts. It depended on the expectations of businesspeople about the future performance of the economy. If expectations were high, businesses would invest in new equipment, add supplies, and hire more workers. If expectations were low – even if business was good at the time – they would reduce inventory, eliminate new investment, and fire workers. Therefore, government's role was not to intervene in particular markets but to encourage positive expectations about the economic future.

Keynes saw that worldwide economic depression made businesspeople pessimistic about the future, which created a self-fulfilling prophecy. To create business optimism, more money had to be put into the hands of the non-rich. If the wealthy were given more money, they might save some of it. The non-wealthy would spend a higher proportion because they had more pressing material wants. Giving the non-rich money, regardless of how, was therefore the most efficient way to stimulate a rise in consumer demand that would encourage businesses to purchase new resources and equipment and hire more workers to satisfy it. As unemployment declined, purchasing power would increase and consumer demand would continue to grow. A new, optimistic, self-fulfilling prophecy would be established.

FDR was reluctant to embrace Keynesianism because it required government to spend money it did not have and therefore to operate at a deficit. Government had engaged in *deficit spending* in the past, but only in wartime. Purposely going into debt in peacetime seemed immoral. Initially, FDR allowed for deficit spending only as an emergency measure. When the economy showed signs of recovery, he cut federal spending to reduce the deficit. The economy declined. When spending was increased because of the imminent threat of World War II, the economy rebounded.

Thus, FDR never embraced Keynesianism in theory but was forced to do so in practice. Keynesianism did not become official government doctrine until 1946, when President Harry Truman signed the *Full Employment Act*, committing government to maintain a growing economy using all available means, including Keynesian tactics. The act created a *Council of Economic Advisors*, professional economists who would provide the president with technical expertise in maintaining high levels of employment and steady economic growth. Table 6.1 shows the government's major executive departments and agencies and the congressional committees involved in each major aspect of economic policy making.

The New Deal also deepened government involvement in macroeconomics by centralizing monetary policy making. The 1935 Banking Act shifted decision-making power from the regional reserve banks to the Federal Reserve Board and its chairman, Mariner Eccles. This change was accompanied by a new understanding of the Fed's mission. It was no longer merely an instrument for adjusting seasonal changes in credit demands and

Table 6.1. The Web of Economic Policy Making

Monetary Policy
  • Federal Reserve Board
Taxing
  • Department of the Treasury
  • House Ways and Means Committee
  • Senate Finance Committee
Spending
  • Office of Management and Budget
  • Congressional Budget Office
  • House and Senate Budget Committees
  • House and Senate Appropriations Committees
Antitrust
  • Justice Department, Antitrust Division
  • Federal Trade Commission
Stocks and Bonds
  • Securities and Exchange Commission
  • House and Senate Banking Committees
Banking
  • Federal Reserve Board
  • Federal Deposit Insurance Corporation
  • House and Senate Banking Committees

for averting bank panics; it was now a full-fledged partner in manipulating the economy to stimulate economic growth. Eccles invoked the Fed's credit-expanding authority because he realized that the stimulative effect of deficit spending would be blunted unless interest rates were kept low. Low interest rates allowed businesses to borrow money in order to expand their production in response to the increased demand for their goods brought on by increased government spending.

During World War II, the Fed worked in tandem with the Department of the Treasury, keeping interest rates low to minimize wartime borrowing costs. But at war's end, the tensions inherent in their relationship burst into the open. The treasury still sought to fund government debt as cheaply as possible by maintaining low interest rates. Although the Fed sympathized with this goal, it became increasingly concerned about the threat to economic stability posed by rapidly rising prices.

Although macroeconomic policy was forged to deal with depression, in theory it was just as applicable for combating the opposite problem – *inflation*. In a free market, prices are supposed to serve as signals for adjustments in supply and demand. Inflation does not represent a rise in a particular price but in prices as a whole. *When inflation runs wild, prices cease to provide clear signals for economic decisions and the economy suffers.* Eccles believed that continuing to pump more money into the economy would drive prices up. Therefore, he opposed the treasury's demand that the Fed continue to work to keep interest rates down.

Initially, President Truman sided with the treasury by refusing to reappoint Eccles as Fed chairman. Still a member of the Fed board, Eccles mobilized allies in Congress. Senator Paul Douglas, Democrat of Illinois, chaired hearings on the dispute and issued a report critical of the Truman administration. Stung by criticism from a fellow Democrat, Truman affirmed the Fed's right to set monetary policy based on its own assessment of the needs of the economy rather than the financial needs of government. Although presidents have often clashed with Fed chairmen about interest rates, the essential principle of Fed independence has never again been seriously challenged.

Because of the close intertwinement between treasury decisions about government bonds and Fed decisions about interest rates, the treasury and the Fed collaborate closely. The treasury secretary and the Fed chairman meet and talk regularly and try to synchronize their actions. But Eccles's none-too-subtle reminder that the Fed is a creature of Congress, not the executive, has in practice enabled the Fed to retain a full measure of independence. Since World War II, that independence has been most aggressively exerted in the fight against inflation, where the interests of the treasury and the Fed are at odds, rather than combating recession, where their interests tend to merge. Although the treasury cares about curbing inflation, it still has an incentive to keep interest rates low so as to minimize the amount of money that the government has to pay to its bondholders. In inflationary periods, the Fed has sought to raise rates in order to dampen overall demand and thus lower inflation.

The Political Economy of Prosperity

America emerged from World War II as the only major industrial nation whose production facilities were intact. Its industry and agriculture could respond – free of foreign competition – to the enormous consumer demand that had built up during the war. The sustained economic boom that lasted until the late 1960s turned America into a nation of suburban homes, appliance-filled kitchens, two-car garages with two cars in them, shopping centers, and national brand advertising. A level of comfort and material well-being was attained that this country had never before experienced on a mass scale. Not every American enjoyed such luxury, but the typical American did. This economic boom extended to blue-collar workers, who, thanks to their union contracts, enjoyed pay levels, job security, and fringe benefits unheard of a decade earlier.

Demand was further stimulated by continued high expenditures on defense that had been induced by the Cold War. Despite the return of U.S. service personnel, labor remained scarce. High demand combined with labor shortages was advantageous to unions. Employers, desperate for workers, could afford pay raises and still make a healthy profit. They preferred to acquiesce to union demands rather than risk work stoppages. The 1950s economy was typified by large corporations, large unions, good pay, and plentiful products.

Prosperity: The Role of Government

Government played a substantial indirect role in producing the post–Cold War prosperity, especially regarding taxes. Normally, workers might be expected to prefer higher wages to fringe benefits such as health insurance or old age pension. But changes in the federal tax codes enacted during World War II exempted benefits from taxes. Because wages were taxed and benefits were not, workers preferred receiving the same amount of additional money in the form of benefits. Employers, with the support of labor leaders, could buy more worker loyalty and contentment per dollar by expanding benefits. Therefore, many workers came to enjoy low-cost healthcare as well as pensions that were far larger than what Social Security provided. Because such benefits are exempt from taxation, they are called *tax expenditures* (see Table 6.2). Tax expenditures likewise subsidized the explosion of home ownership during the 1950s and 1960s because buyers could deduct interest paid on their mortgages from their taxable income.

When the social benefits, mostly in the form of health insurance and old age pensions, that these tax expenditures provide are added to publicly provided Social Security, healthcare, veterans benefit, and welfare, it turns out that the United States spends roughly the same amount on social programs (as a percentage of *Gross Domestic Product* [GDP]) that Europeans spend. As political scientist Jacob Hacker points out, the difference is that the United States provides a lot more social benefits privately, subsidized by tax exemptions, and that the recipients of U.S. social spending come more predominantly from the middle class. For a time, the Taft-Hartley system of trust funds and other forms of government subsidies served unionized workers well; by the late 1980s, however, many plans came under severe financial pressure. The skyrocketing of healthcare costs forced funds to reduce benefits, tighten eligibility requirements, and increase the out-of-pocket expenses for covered workers. The stress of the "private welfare state" contributed significantly to the declining fortunes of the American labor movement.

Table 6.2. U.S. Government Accountability Office Analysis of Office of Management and Budget Report on Tax Expenditures, Fiscal Year 2006

Tax expenditure	Revenue loss estimate (billions $)	Revenue loss estimate as a percentage of sum	Taxpayer group	Budget function
Income tax exclusion of employer contributions to medical insurance premiums and medical care*	$102.3	14.0%	Individual	Health
Deductibility of mortgage interest on owner-occupied homes*	61.5	8.4%	Individual	Commerce and housing credit
Net exclusion of pension contributions and earnings: 401(k)	47.7	6.6%	Individual	Income security
Net exclusion of pension contributions and earnings: employer plans*	47.0	6.5%	Individual	Income security
Deductibility of non-business state and local taxes (other than on owner-occupied homes)*	45.3	6.2%	Individual	General purpose fiscal assistance
Accelerated depreciation of machinery and equipment	44.7	6.1%	Corporate and Individual	Commerce and housing credit
Capital gains exclusion on home sales	29.7	4.1%	Individual	Commerce and housing credit
Deductibility of charitable contributions other than education and health*	27.4	3.8%	Corporate and Individual	Education, training, employment, social services
Exclusion of interest on public purpose state and local bonds*	26.2	3.6%	Corporate and Individual	General purpose fiscal assistance
Capital gains (other than agriculture, timber, iron ore, and coal)*	25.2	3.5%	Individual	Commerce and housing credit
Exclusion of net imputed rental income on owner-occupied homes	24.6	3.4%	Individual	Commerce and housing credit
Step-up basis of capital gains at death	24.2	3.3%	Individual	Commerce and housing credit
Child credit (effect on receipts only)	22.4	3.1%	Individual	Education, training, employment, social services

(continued)

Table 6.2. (*continued*)

Tax expenditure	Revenue loss estimate (billions $)	Revenue loss estimate as a percentage of sum	Taxpayer group	Budget function
Exclusion of interest on life insurance savings*	20.1	2.98%	Corporate and individual	Commerce and housing credit

Source: GAO analysis of OMB budget report on tax expenditures, fiscal year 2006.
*Denotes tax expenditures that have been reported by treasury since 1974.
Note: Some tax expenditures split into additional listings to reflect legislation expanding existing tax expenditures. For example, the treasury began listing the net exclusion of pension contributions and earnings with separate estimates for employer-defined benefits and 401(k) pension plans following 2001 legislation increasing the contribution limits for 401(k) accounts. From year to year, revenue loss estimates may change because treasury updates their estimates for each new budget to reflect legislation enacted, prevailing economic conditions, and the latest taxpayer data available. Although there are substantial revenues forgone for these fourteen large tax expenditures, the estimated amount of federal spending that would be required to provide equivalent assistance is frequently larger than the revenue forgone because this spending could be subject to income tax. For example, the outlay equivalent estimate for the income tax exclusion of employer contributions for medical insurance premiums and medical care is 126.7 billion dollars for fiscal year 2004.

The economy was further enhanced by the GI Bill, enacted in 1944, which entitled war veterans to attend universities and specialized training programs of all sorts at government expense. The skills of the American workforce greatly improved at no cost to employers. Labor remained scarce, but the pool of well educated workers expanded dramatically, improving productivity and increasing the proportion of workers in high-paying jobs. Just as the United States was the first nation in history to enable most young people to go to school, it was also the first to provide mass higher education. Thanks in part to the GI Bill, the number of students enrolled in college jumped from less than 1.5 million in 1941, representing just 16 percent of high school graduates, to almost 2.5 million in 1949, representing 40 percent of high school graduates. Enrollment dipped somewhat in the later 1950s as the number of new veterans declined, but it never again dropped below 25 percent of high school graduates. In 2001, more than 15 million students were enrolled in college, representing 47 percent of high school graduates.

The economic boom of the 1950s and 1960s, unlike subsequent booms in the late 1980s and in the 1990s, was marked by large increases in government spending. This spending had political as well as economic benefits. Although, as Chapter 4 explained, the expansion of "programmatic rights" during the New Deal weakened political associations such as political parties, the GI Bill expanded economic rights in a form that contributed to American democracy. Commentators such as Tom Brokaw, Stephen Ambrose, and Robert Putnam have praised World War II veterans as "the Greatest Generation," celebrating their remarkable commitment to the principles and practices of democracy. As political scientist Suzanne Mettler has shown, this patriotism followed in part from a sense of reciprocal responsibility. Veterans who used the GI Bill's education and training provisions became more active citizens in public life in the postwar years than those who did not use it. Education alone does explain this civic participation; whatever their education and socioeconomic experiences, individuals who benefited from the GI Bill belonged to more civic organizations and participated in more political activities than the nonrecipients.

Although government outlays increased tremendously during these years, the pain of such expenditure was minimized by continued income growth, enabling government to pay for massive defense outlays, benefits to veterans, the interstate highway system, and health insurance for the elderly (Medicare) without tax increases. Revenue raising was also eased by *bracket creep*, a form of undeclared tax increase: inflation rose throughout the 1950s and 1960s, but wages rose faster, which pushed earners into higher tax brackets and required them to pay a proportionally higher percentage of their earnings in tax.

Prosperity's Blind Spots: Pockets of Poverty and Environmental Damage

The excellent overall performance of the economy in the 1950s and 1960s dampened demands for government ownership and radical redistribution of the wealth, demands previously associated with the Populists, with the more radical wing of the labor movement, and with socialist-minded intellectuals. The most influential work of economic criticism appearing in the 1960s was entitled *The Other America*. Its author, Michael Harrington, intended the title to draw attention to the significant minority of poor people who were being ignored because they lived in "poverty pockets," or isolated rural areas and urban ghettoes.

Harrington's book and other well publicized exposés such as Edward R. Murrow's television documentary about migrant workers, titled *Harvest of Shame*, aroused public indignation that such misery could exist in the richest nation in the world and in history. But the term poverty pockets indicated that these embarrassing circumstances did not seem to require systemic change. Rather, a set of specific policy tools was developed: literacy classes, personnel training, preschool education, preventive healthcare, and supplemental nutritional assistance. The War on Poverty instigated in the 1960s by President Lyndon B. Johnson (LBJ) broadened for a brief time the reach of such antipoverty efforts to put more political power in the hands of the dispossessed. But the Democratic majority in Congress, many of whose members came from districts with poverty pockets, quickly curbed those political tendencies and confined the poverty fight to inoffensive education, health, nutritional, and vocational tools.

Affluence as well as poverty revealed shortcomings of the American economy. People who moved to the suburbs to escape urban blight became increasingly discomforted by sprawl, smog, traffic congestion, and filthy waterways. Economists had a ready explanation for these and other types of environmental degradation: *market failure*. Market failure occurs when the costs and benefits of an economic activity are not fully reflected in the price paid for it. Because the air is free, factories use it as a handy way to get rid of noxious pollutants. If a factory had to compensate everyone who suffers from this pollution, its prices would rise and its profits would fall. The company would have incentives to lessen its pollution emissions. Costs such as bad air that are not factored into a market transaction are referred to as *negative externalities* because their ill effects have not been internalized into the selling price. Environmental economists preached that polluters could be made to "internalize" these negative externalities if firms were taxed on the basis of how much pollution they emitted. But environmental organizations and Congress preferred to impose coercive standards on polluters, forcing them to pay fines if their pollution emissions exceeded specified levels.

Disillusionment with Big Government

Economists thought that inflation and unemployment could not rise simultaneously because when people lose their jobs they buy less; thus, overall demand is lowered and inflation is reduced. Nonetheless, both inflation and unemployment did rise during much of the 1970s. The term *stagflation* was coined to describe an economy that is stagnating and inflating at the same time. The perception of stagnation was not entirely accurate. This period produced an enormous expansion of jobs, but not enough to accommodate the large number of baby boomers – people born in the late 1940s and early 1950s – who were reaching working age as well as the increasing percentage of women seeking work. Thus, the unemployment rate rose. Per capita income continued to rise but at a slower rate. Higher unemployment and slower income growth made people feel less secure and optimistic. Their perception of economic stagnation had more to do with their fears about the future than about their current circumstances.

But, as we pointed out in the section on macroeconomics, expectations about the future are more powerful drivers of economic behavior than present experiences are. Pessimism was also fueled by inflation. In 1974, inflation reached 14 percent, the highest level since the end of World War II. As prices and interest rates soared, people worried that they would not be able to keep up. To some extent, these fears were exaggerated because wages and interest on bank deposits were also going up, which gave people more dollars with which to pay their inflated expenses. But people grew increasingly fearful that this uncertain balance would not continue, especially because the unemployment rate was rising and they could well be faced with trying to pay higher prices and interest rates while they were out of a job.

Inflation had two very specific ill effects in addition to building uncertainty. The first was bracket creep. As long as people felt economically secure and hopeful, they barely noticed that inflation was pushing them into higher tax brackets and forcing them to pay a higher percentage of their income to the government. But in the midst of uncertainty, this loss of income was infuriating.

Second, inflation hurt real estate and automobile sales because higher interest rates made such large purchases, paid for with borrowed money, more expensive. Higher borrowing costs forced many people to postpone purchases or settle for smaller houses and cheaper cars. These deprivations might appear trivial compared to the homelessness and hunger experienced during the Great Depression. But for people expecting to live in bigger homes and drive better cars than their parents did, they were painful.

The high inflation, which lasted with varying degrees of severity until 1980, was triggered by LBJ's refusal to raise taxes to pay for the Vietnam War. By contrast, President Truman during the Korean War had raised taxes and interest rates and imposed price controls. LBJ feared that if he raised taxes, the public would demand cuts in non-military programs, which would gut his domestic policy agenda. His decision illustrated the great political vulnerability of Keynesian economics. It was politically painless to incur deficits to fight depression. It was far more painful to raise taxes and reduce spending to counter inflation. Neither LBJ nor his successors were willing to implement the Keynesian solution to inflation by doing so.

The continuation of inflation during the 1970s had many diverse causes. Energy prices rose dramatically when the *Organization of Petroleum Exporting Countries* (OPEC) – which included most of the world's leading oil producers – declared a boycott of oil sales to the United States. Because

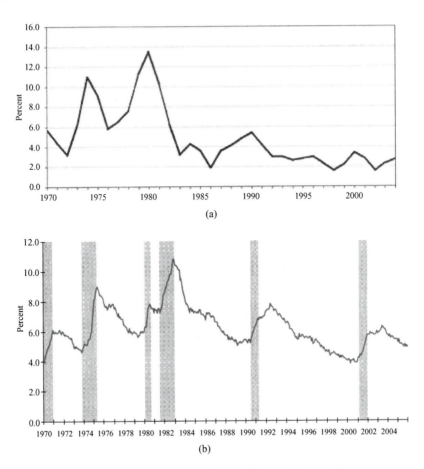

Figure 6.1. (a) **Inflation Rates, 1970–2005.** (b) **Unemployment Rates, 1970–2005.**
Sources: Bureau of Labor Statistics, 2007.

all manufacturing and transportation industries use energy, increases in oil prices led to price increases throughout the economy. Also, because the economy was absorbing so many new and inexperienced workers in such a short amount of time, worker productivity declined for the first time in many years. Furthermore, world food prices rose because of the failure of the Peruvian anchovy crop, the leading source of fertilizer. Economists continue to debate the relative impact of these and other inflationary developments. But regardless of the cause, government proved incapable of sustained inflation reductions. Figure 6.1(a,b) shows the annual change in inflation rates as well as the unemployment rates from 1970 to 2005.

Deregulation

Sustained high inflation during the 1970s led to the most significant reduction in government economic control since the New Deal: the deregulation of the trucking, telephone, and airline industries. Such deregulation had been considered politically impossible because of the combined opposition of the leading firms and unions in the regulated industries. Nonetheless, the defensive advantage enjoyed by these employer-employee coalitions was overcome by the ability of the president, congressional leaders, and professional economists to convince ordinary Americans that they had something at stake in the outcome, namely lower inflation.

Deregulation also took place in the retail sector. Many states' fair-trade laws that limited price competition in pharmaceuticals and alcoholic beverages were repealed; and the Robinson-Patman Act's restrictions on volume discounting, although still a matter of law, were rendered less significant by changes in the interpretation of the antitrust laws by courts and the Federal Trade Commission, which administers the statute. Banks, insurance companies, and investment companies are now much freer to compete with one another as a result of federal legislation allowing them to enter each other's markets. Some states have also promoted electricity deregulation. Farm price supports and subsidies remained because of continued public support for the family farm.

New Regulation

Inflation fears were not sufficient to impede expansion of occupational and environmental regulation. In the 1970s, stringent national limits on air, water, and hazardous waste pollution were imposed, and workers received national protection from dangerous and unhealthy workplaces. In 1970, Congress also passed the *National Environmental Policy Act* (NEPA), which required all large government-financed projects – airports, highways, ship channels, and so on – to produce a report describing the important environmental effects of the project and the specific means proposed to minimize its ill effects.

These environmental regulations had two great political advantages. First, they did not require large public funds. Business purchased the equipment and hired the new employees necessary to meet environmental standards, and it paid for them by raising its prices. Thus, consumers, not taxpayers, paid for environmental improvement, but because most people are both, this distinction was economically meaningless. Nonetheless, the situation created the impression that environmental quality was virtually a free good.

Second, although economists defended environmental regulation on the basis of market failure, it was sold to the voters as an essential means to protect their rights, just as FDR had justified the Social Security Act by proclaiming Americans' right to economic security. The leading congressional environmental spokesman, Senator Edmund Muskie, declared that clean air and water laws were necessary to protect Americans' right to health. These claims that industry was threatening fundamental health and safety rights, coming hard on the heels of the Civil Rights Movement's successful appeal to rights, resonated with the public. Rights claims dominated every subsequent debate over environmental policy and saved the major environmental laws from the Reagan administration's effort to gut them.

The Reagan Revolution

The defining moment in the 1980 election occurred during the first televised debate between Ronald Reagan and President Jimmy Carter, when Reagan looked out at the television audience and asked, "Are you better off today than you were four years ago?" For many voters – enough to give Reagan a decisive victory – the answer was no.

Of course, a dispassionate reading of economics statistics does not provide such a clear-cut answer. But Americans were not taking an Economics 101 exam; they were expressing frustration at high prices, especially of cars and houses, and at the bracket creep that was taking an ever larger portion of their incomes in tax. They had lived through a period of Democratic political domination during which government spending, taxes, and budget deficits had all increased, and yet, inflation, slow economic growth, and unemployment continued to fester. For the first time since the New Deal, conservative Republican arguments for less government and lower taxes became deeply appealing. Voters elected Reagan, who promised to reduce inflation and lessen the burden of government.

Stereotyped as an old-fashioned, penny-pinching conservative, Reagan did not govern in that mode. Instead of first reducing spending and then cutting taxes, thus keeping the budget in balance, Reagan chose a bolder approach. Because the House of Representatives remained in Democratic hands, he could not cut popular domestic programs. And he was committed to increases in defense spending. Therefore, he turned conventional conservative thinking on its head by first pressing for a massive tax cut and only then seeking compensatory reductions in spending. Those spending cuts never came. The budget quickly went into deficit to the tune of more than 100 billion dollars, the largest peacetime deficit in American history. It peaked in 1983 at which time it accounted for 6 percent of the GDP.

Despite the deficit, the inflationary spiral of the 1970s ended painfully. The Fed severely restricted the money supply, making it much harder for business to invest. The ensuing recession created very high unemployment, particularly in the Midwestern industrial heartland. As it worsened, Reagan said he would "stay the course," meaning that he would not try to reduce unemployment at the risk of rekindling inflation. His expression of determination did what his predecessors had failed to do – change employer and employee expectations. Believing that inflation would not return, Americans became less aggressive in raising prices and making wage demands, which in turn lowered inflation.

These changes in outlook happened because people believed that Reagan would keep his word. Reagan took grave political risks in allowing unemployment to rise, especially since the crucial swing states of Illinois, Ohio, and Michigan were hardest hit. But Reagan had shown early in his presidency that his word was good. He had warned that he would not tolerate illegal work stoppages by government employees. When air traffic controllers went out on strike, he fired them all and hired new ones. The air traffic controllers' union had been one of very few to support Reagan in the 1980 election and therefore expected kind treatment from the new president. The wholesale replacement of workers in such a crucial occupation left no doubt about Reagan's credibility.

Contemporary Political Economy

During the administrations of George H. W. Bush (1988–1992), Bill Clinton (1992–2000), and George W. Bush (2000–present), economic policy and the politics surrounding it has been dominated by five issues: deficits, entitlements, taxes, international trade, and fallout from the scandals involving corporate and managerial financial fraud that erupted in the late 1990s and early 2000s.

Deficits, Entitlements, and Taxes

Throughout the 1980s and into the 1990s, much lip service was paid to reducing the deficits created by Reagan's tax cuts, but no budget reductions or tax increases of sufficient magnitude were enacted. In the absence of inflation, both parties preferred deficits to the risk of higher unemployment. But surprisingly, the deficit proved to be a powerful political issue at the grassroots. People resented seeing more of their tax dollar "wasted" on interest payments for rising government debt, and they doubted that such deficits could be sustained in the long term. If an individual went deeply into debt, there were bound to be serious consequences; shouldn't this be true for government as well?

H. Ross Perot's opposition to the deficit was the centerpiece of his remarkably successful 1992 independent presidential campaign. In late spring, he was actually leading both President George H. W. Bush and Bill Clinton in the polls! Perot's popularity began to fade before he mysteriously withdrew from the race in mid-summer, and he was unable to regain his full momentum after reentering the race with only four weeks to go in the campaign. Nonetheless, he still garnered the largest vote outside of the two-party system since Theodore Roosevelt ran on the Progressive ticket in 1912.

President Bill Clinton recognized that if Perot did not run in 1996, he, Clinton, could win a two-person race only if he attracted a substantial majority of 1992 Perot voters. This knowledge impelled him to work hard for deficit reduction. To do so without breaking campaign promises to aid the urban poor and expand national service, he proposed an energy tax. When that failed to pass Congress, he chose to stick with deficit reduction even at the cost of alienating important Democratic constituencies. Throughout his entire tenure in office, Clinton introduced no major spending initiatives. This budget discipline, coupled with the increased tax revenue stemming from the 1990s economic boom, resulted in continual deficit reductions and culminated in a budgetary surplus by the middle of Clinton's second term. Although Perot did run again in 1996, his appeal declined considerably the second time around, in no small measure because the Clinton administration had stolen much of the thunder from his remonstrations against government debt.

The 1990s were extraordinarily successful economically, combining robust growth, rising income, low unemployment, and low inflation. Clinton signaled his resolve to stifle inflation by not criticizing Fed chairman Alan Greenspan's reining in of the money supply. Democrats grumbled about lack of public spending, but by renominating Clinton in 1996, they acknowledged the political wisdom of his conservative economic policies. At this stage, in fact, both parties were committed to budgetary discipline to prevent deficits and to tighten the money supply to prevent inflation. Figure 6.2 can be used to track the course of budget deficits and surpluses between 1960 and 2008.

Clinton made his commitment to preserving and protecting the two largest social insurance entitlement programs, Social Security and Medicare, the centerpiece of his 1996 campaign. He interpreted Republican promises to reform entitlements during the 1994 congressional campaign to be evidence that they would put the economic security of the middle

Federal Budget Deficit (or Surplus), FY 1960–2008
in billions of CONSTANT FY 2003 dollars (President's proposals)

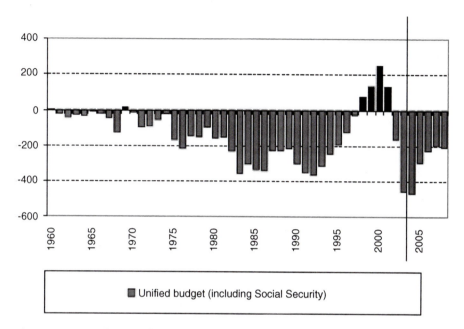

Figure 6.2. Budget Deficits, 1960–2008. Data for fiscal years 2004–2008 are projections based on the president's budget proposals, updated by the Office of Management and Budget's midsession review.
Source: Budget of the U.S. Government, 2004.

class at risk. When the Republicans scored their massive victory in the 1994 elections, Clinton had been declared politically dead. Yet Clinton's fierce battle with the Republican-controlled Congress in 1995 and 1996, during which GOP leaders tried to pressure him to accept their budget priorities by twice shutting down government offices, revitalized his presidency. The president's veto in December 1995 of a sweeping Republican budget bill that not only would have overhauled Medicare, but also remade decades of federal social policy roused popular support for the administration. Clinton's impressive reelection victory in the wake of this confrontation with Congress demonstrated both his enormous political skill as well as the greater faith that the electorate had in the Democrats to protect middle-class entitlements.

The centerpiece of George W. Bush's 2000 presidential campaign was a promise to reduce taxes. Within weeks of his inauguration, he prevailed on Congress to make good on that promise. He stuck to those reductions even when an economic downturn and massive increases in military spending ensured that decreased tax rates would force the budget into deficit. In 2003, he renewed his commitment to tax reduction by proposing to Congress that it end taxation of stock dividends and make permanent the reduced income tax rates that had been adopted only on a temporary basis in 2001. As a result of the recession that began in 2001, reduced tax revenues, the large size of the 2001 tax cuts, and the increase in military and homeland security spending for the War on Terror, budget deficits rose throughout Bush's first term. The deficit reached 413 billion dollars in 2004. This figure represents 3.8 percent of the Gross Domestic Product. In 2005, the deficit fell to 319 billion or 2.6 percent of GDP. In contrast to Clinton's reelection promise to protect middle-class entitlements, Bush's 2004 campaign called not only for a further reduction in taxes but also for a comprehensive overhaul of Social Security. These issues did not dominate the campaign, national security did. Nonetheless, Bush's bold plan to privatize aspects of Social Security formed the (unsuccessful) centerpiece of his 2005 legislative agenda.

As the actions of Clinton and Bush demonstrate, the Democrats remain the party of FDR whereas the Republicans have become the party of Reagan. Although elected as a "New Democrat" pledging to modernize his party, Clinton staked his reelection on a defense of the programmatic rights that FDR had proclaimed a half century earlier. By adhering to the tax cuts, Bush attached himself to the Reagan brand of conservatism that is more committed to reducing tax burdens than to balancing the budget.

Free Trade

In spite of these enduring partisan differences, the leadership of both parties agreed on the most significant economic policy development of the 1990s – expansion of free trade. In 1993, President Clinton endorsed the *North American Free Trade Agreement* (NAFTA), which eliminated tariff barriers and other trade constraints between the United States, Mexico, and Canada. This free trade zone encompassed a 6.5 trillion dollar market containing 350 million consumers. The following year, the United States joined the *World Trade Organization* (WTO), a new international body with extensive powers to settle trade disputes, and endorsed the most recent General Agreement on Tariffs and Trade (GATT). GATT reduced tariffs by 40 percent by phasing out quotas on textiles and apparel and by extending copyright and other forms of protection to intellectual property, including recordings and books.

These major agreements were further steps toward freer trade, a process that had been going on since the end of World War II. During the period between the Civil War and World War II, protectionism prevailed. In 1930, the average tariff on imported goods was 50 percent of their price; by

1951, it had fallen to 12.5 percent, and by the end of the 1990s, it was approximately 5 percent. The lowering of tariffs as well as other forms of trade barriers has continued even as the American position in world trade has become less dominant and as specific sectors of the economy, such as steel, textiles, garments, and toys, have suffered grievously.

After World War II, protectionism no longer pitted the agrarian South against the industrial North. Foreign investment was dispersed throughout the country, forcing members of Congress from every region to pay attention to the arguments against protectionism. Foreign investment has grown considerably in recent decades. Foreign firms and individuals now own approximately 9 percent of U.S. assets and employ 4 percent of total U.S. workers and 10 percent of U.S. workers engaged in manufacturing. Workers employed by foreign firms support trade agreements that make it cheaper for their firms to import parts and supplies from the home country.

Free trade was also encouraged through national security considerations. The United States simply could not enter into military and mutual security arrangements with other nations and then limit import of their goods. Indeed, economic interdependence was viewed as a crucial component of national security, the theory being that countries benefiting from mutual trade were unlikely to fight one another.

Unlike the politics of deficits, taxes, and entitlements, free trade issues reveal deep divisions within rather than between the parties, especially among the Democrats. Clinton's decision to enter into the NAFTA, WTO, and GATT agreements was not supported by a majority of Democratic members of Congress. They would not have passed if a majority of Republicans had not supported them. Trade had become a fractious issue within the Democratic coalition. The labor movement opposed free trade because of fear that American manufacturing jobs would be lost as consumers switched to cheaper foreign goods made with cheap labor. Some segments of the environmental movement opposed it because they believed that competition from countries with weak environmental standards undermined American environmental quality. Corporate Democratic supporters, most notably software and entertainment companies, supported free trade to expand their already substantial exports.

Fraud and Corporate Governance

Beginning in the late 1990s and continuing into the new millennium, financial fraud and manipulation resulted in the demise of such major corporations as Tyco, WorldCom, Global Crossing, and Adelphia. Enron collapsed in December 2000 (see Box 1). By July of 2002, the Dow Jones Industrial Average, a major stock market index, had dropped 25 percent from its

Congressman Michael Oxley (L) and Senator Paul Sarbanes (2nd L) sponsored the bill that President Bush signed, the Sarbanes-Oxley Act of 2002, which improves quality and transparency in financial reporting and independent audits and accounting services for public companies.

historic high in March of 2000. It has been estimated that in this period the stock market lost 7 trillion dollars. This collapse riveted public attention on the variety of accounting techniques that corporations had used to overstate profits, minimize losses, and otherwise exaggerate how economically healthy they were. There were also disturbing revelations about the extent to which the outside accountants hired by corporations to audit the company books had aided and abetted these fraudulent practices. Likewise, it was revealed that stock analysts responsible for making buy and sell recommendations to their investor clients had been bribed by the companies they were supposed to objectively analyze to encourage clients to buy stock in those companies. Ordinary investors came to realize that they could trust neither the information they were given about the financial health of individual companies nor the recommendations they received from their stock brokers.

Initially, Republicans were more reticent than Democrats about supporting major intrusive changes in financial reporting, investment advice, and corporate governance as a means for restoring public confidence in the financial markets. But as new scandals continued to emerge, the Bush administration and the Republican congressional leadership felt it would be too politically damaging to allow the Democrats to emerge as the sole defenders of stockholders. As a result of the widespread participation of ordinary workers in stock owning pension funds and the great increase of mass participation in buying and selling stocks that occurred during the 1980s and 1990s, most Americans were stockholders. Therefore, in 2002, congressional Republicans joined with Democrats to pass the Sarbanes-Oxley Act of 2002, named for the chairs of the Senate and House committees that drafted it, Senator Paul Sarbanes (D-MD) and Representative Michael Oxley (R-OH). It contained the most important changes in securities law and corporate governance since the New Deal.

Sarbanes-Oxley established the Public Company Accounting Oversight Board (PCAOB), a private regulatory body, appointed by and under the oversight of the SEC. Accountants would no longer regulate themselves; instead, they would be subject to federal accounting rules enforced by the PCAOB. The act's greatest innovation was its imposition of federal rules regarding the composition, structure, and operation of corporate boards. Formerly, such matters had been dealt with by state corporation law, and dealt with very loosely. Sarbanes-Oxley required public corporations to appoint an Audit Committee and Compensation Committee composed entirely of independent directors, thus excluding the corporation's own management. At least one auditing committee member had to qualify as a financial expert according to new SEC rules. The law gave the audit committee sole responsibility for hiring, paying, and approving the work of the outside auditors. The independent compensation committee determined how much management was to be paid.

Sarbanes-Oxley also required the Chief Executive Officer (CEO) and the Chief Financial Officer (CFO) to personally attest that the corporation's financial statements were accurate and complied with the accounting rules the new law set in place. The CEO also had to certify that the company's own accounting practices were capable of detecting and preventing fraud. Making corporate CEO and CFO's personally liable for the quality and accuracy of their companies' financial statements inspired a massive reorganization and reform of internal accounting and reporting procedures.

Sarbanes-Oxley has been criticized for imposing excessive regulatory burdens on accountants and corporations. But, whatever its flaws, it has helped avoid what might have been a massive flight of investors away from the stock market due to the cynicism fraudulent accounting and massive financial fraud was instilling in them. Sarbanes-Oxley reduced the liberty of accountants and managers to a democratic purpose, that of restoring the confidence of the ordinary citizen-investor in one of the bedrock elements of the economic order, the stock market.

Conclusion: Economic Liberty, Political Freedom, Religious Scruples

The American economy remains liberal to the core. Free market competition is the preferred means of providing goods and services. Market control has declined from its New Deal heights, but the democratic-egalitarian impulses that sparked the battles against funding the debt in the 1790s and against the Second National Bank in the 1830s are still strong. Although not as steeply progressive as it was a generation ago, the federal income tax redistributes income from the rich to the poor. The rights to economic security first proclaimed by FDR ensure that ordinary people enjoy levels of income security and healthcare previously enjoyed only by the rich.

On the whole, the promise of economic security has served to complement rather than undermine the liberal competitive economy. High-wire acrobats perform more audaciously when they have a safety net to catch them. The promise of a liberal economy is based on risk taking. Investors risk their money on new ventures. Workers risk unemployment when they search for better jobs. Risk taking is encouraged both by the promise of great rewards and by the confidence that comes from knowing that one will not lose everything should one fail. The modern so-called welfare state is mostly an insurance state that encourages risk taking by providing a safety net. As Jacob Hacker has argued, social welfare policy over the past two decades has eroded to a significant degree the "socialization of risk" that the New Deal welfare state embodies. Nonetheless, the failure of the Bush administration's efforts to "privatize" Social Security reveals the enduring commitment to middle-class entitlements. Indeed, the Bush administration, with the support of some moderate Democrats, expanded the Medicare program to include a prescription drug benefit. Although this program has been very controversial and has been condemned by Democrats for conceding too much influence to the pharmaceutical and insurance industries, its enactment makes clear that the promise of the Reagan administration and the Republican Congress empowered by the 1994 elections to roll back the welfare state have been defied by a recognition of liberals and many conservatives that big government is an important reality of contemporary American politics. As Hugh Heclo has noted, Reagan's rhetoric had a serious "blind spot": "His explanation of government growth based on inadvertence, carelessness, and bureaucratic inertia was a partial truth masquerading as a whole. Government also grew to do things that people, in all their variegated ways, really wanted done."

As we showed in the discussion of Wal-Mart that opened this chapter, the safety net does not eliminate all tensions between liberalism and democracy. An owner's decision to close a factory, for example, can be viewed as a liberal decision to do with the property as the owner wants. But if the plant is the sole employer in town, the closing rends the community fabric. It threatens the community's employment and tax base. Schools will close; property values will decline; citizens will leave. A democratic polity withers and dies. In hard times, citizens have organized themselves to oppose plant closings. They have challenged property rights in the name of community solidarity.

Economic liberty also remains in tension with religious convictions. The modern competitive economy is premised on the customer getting what the customer wants. Such a principle rests uneasily with the Christian tradition that scorns greed and materialism. The "cross of gold" refers not only to tight money but also to the sinful seductiveness of money itself. As the Bible's New Testament makes clear, it is the rich man, not the poor one, who has the worse chance of entering the kingdom of heaven. These tensions emerge in practical ways as states and communities debate whether to institute lotteries, legalize casino gambling, or permit suggestive billboard advertising along the highway.

As Jefferson envisioned, the goal of American economic life remains the pursuit of happiness. But for a people seeking simultaneously to be rich, to be free, and to be free from sin, that pursuit is complex indeed.

Chapter Summary

☆ A liberal economy is one that has three essential aspects: private property, competition, and promise keeping.

☆ The Constitution, including the Bill of Rights, commits the U.S. government to preserving a liberal economy.

☆ Thomas Jefferson argued that agriculture promoted a superior way of life, as compared to manufacturing.

☆ Alexander Hamilton argued that manufacturing deserved to be subsidized because it promoted national security and national greatness.

☆ The Jacksonians believed that the greatest danger to economic liberty was the ability of an economic elite to make use of government economic policy for its own benefit.

☆ The essential principle underlying the modern corporation is that of limited liability.

☆ The Populists combined a belief in national government economic regulation with intense religious dedication.

☆ The American labor movement, unlike most of its Western European counterparts, is not socialist.

☆ The New Deal ultimately adopted a view of economics called "Keynesianism," after its inventor, Englishman John Maynard Keynes. Keynesianism focuses on how economies function as a whole. It advocates deficit spending in times of economic contraction and raising taxes when the economy inflates.

☆ Government now relies on three major forms of policy aimed less at influencing market behavior and more at altering the framework within which market competition takes place. It provides a minimum level of economic security; it taxes people in rough proportion to their level of wealth; and it manipulates the money supply and overall levels of taxing and spending in order to promote steady and ample economic growth.

☆ The federal tax code provides strong incentives for employers to provide healthcare and pension benefits for their employees and for people to own their own homes. This is a major reason why home ownership rates are so high in the United States and such a large proportion of pension and healthcare benefits are employer provided.

☆ Contemporary debates over such issues as taxes and entitlements mirror earlier debates about the proper role of government in redistributing wealth and securing individuals against risk.

☆ The modern competitive economy is premised on the customer getting what the customer wants. Such a principle rests uneasily with the Christian tradition that scorns greed and materialism.

Major Concepts

Agricultural Adjustment Act (AAA)
American Federation of Labor (AFL)
bonds
bracket creep
cartel
central bank
Congress of Industrial Organizations (CIO)
Council of Economic Advisors
craft union
deficit spending
discount rate
economies of scale
Federal Deposit Insurance Corporation (FDIC)
Federal Reserve Board (the Fed)
Federal Trade Commission (FTC)
Food and Drug Administration (FDA)
Full Employment Act

Gross Domestic Product (GDP)
Homestead Act of 1862
industrial union
inflation
laissez faire
limited liability
macroeconomics
market failure
microeconomics
National Environmental Policy Act (NEPA)
National Labor Relations Board (NLRB)
National Recovery Administration (NRA)
negative externalities
North American Free Trade Agreement (NAFTA)
open market operations
Organization of Petroleum Exporting Countries (OPEC)
price discrimination
progressive tax
Robinson-Patman Act
sharecropping
Sherman Antitrust Act
stagflation
tax expenditures
United Automobile Workers (UAW)
United Mine Workers of America (UMWA)
United Steel Workers of America (USWA)
World Trade Organization (WTO)

Suggested Readings

Chandler, Alfred Dupont. *Scale and Scope: The Dynamics of Industrial Capitalism.* Cambridge, MA: Belknap Press, 1990.

_____. *The Visible Hand: The Managerial Revolution in American Business.* Cambridge, MA: Belknap Press, 1977.

Derthick, Martha, and Paul J. Quirk. *The Politics of Deregulation.* Washington, D.C.: Brookings Institution, 1985.

Friedman, Milton. *Capitalism and Freedom.* Chicago: University of Chicago Press, 1963.

Gottschalk, Marie. *The Shadow Welfare State: Labor, Business, and the Politics of Health Care in the United States.* Ithaca, NY: Cornell University Press, 2000.

Hacker, Jacob. *The Divided Welfare State: The Battle over Public and Private Social Benefits in the United States.* New York: Cambridge University Press, 2002.

Harris, Richard, and Sidney M. Milkis. *The Politics of Regulatory Change: A Tale of Two Agencies,* 2d ed. New York: Oxford University Press, 1996.

Hawley, Ellis. *The New Deal and the Problem of Monopoly: A Study in Economic Ambivalence.* New York: Fordam University Press, 1995.

Howard, Christopher. *The Hidden Welfare State: Tax Expenditures and Social Policy in the United States.* Princeton, NJ: Princeton University Press, 1997.

McCoy, Drew R. *The Elusive Republic: Political Economy in Jeffersonian America.* Chapel Hill: University of North Carolina Press, 1996.

McCraw, Thomas K. *Prophets of Regulation: Charles Francis Adams, Louis D. Brandeis, James M. Landis, Alfred E. Kahn.* Cambridge, MA: Belknap Press, 1984.

Savage, James. *Balanced Budgets and American Politics.* New York: Cornell University Press, 1988.

Sellers, Charles. *The Market Revolution: Jacksonian America, 1815–1846.* New York: Oxford University Press, 1991.

Stein, Herbert. *Presidential Economics: The Making of Economic Policy from Roosevelt to Clinton,* 3d rev. ed. Washington, D.C.: AEI Press, 1994.

Case Study: Katrina as a Test of Pivotal Relationships

In August of 2005, Hurricane Katrina struck southeast Louisiana, including New Orleans, and the Gulf Coast of Mississippi. It was the worst natural disaster in American history. It caused more than 100 billion dollars worth of damage, killed more than a thousand people, destroyed or damaged at least 850,000 housing units, and forced more than a million people to evacuate. Two years after the hurricane, hundreds of thousands still had not returned home.

The sheer magnitude of the disaster made Katrina a severe test for citizens and government alike as both struggled to deal with the storm's devastation and its aftermath. It placed particular strain on the pivotal relationships between levels of government and between government and the private economy that we discussed in Chapters 5 and 6.

Disaster response poses an especially difficult challenge to federalism because such response requires speed, efficiency, and effective coordination. These qualities are not the strong suits of a three-level system encumbered by a welter of duplicative and competing agencies and governing structures.

Katrina's test of the American form of political economy was equally severe because, as we saw in Chapter 6, there are no clear lines of demarcation between the public and the private economic spheres. An individual's property rights frequently clash with the government's understanding of what it needs to control and regulate in the public interest. Therefore, the questions that Katrina raised about how rebuilding would take place invited arguments about what property owners could decide for themselves and what the government would decide for them. Does a flood victim have a right to aid from the government? Do homeowners have a right to rebuild their flooded properties and to do so in any manner and form they choose? If the city as a whole will be better off if certain properties are not rebuilt, does the good of the whole trump the rights of the individual homeowners? These are but some of the profound arguments about fundamental liberal and democratic principles that this terrible flood brought to the surface.

Historically, individual property owners bore the brunt of the responsibility for coping with natural disasters. After all, it was *their* houses and streets that were being flooded. They relied on their families, friends, and neighbors to help them out. Secondarily, they expected their local governments, especially fire and police departments, to organize protective and relief efforts that were beyond what they could accomplish on their own. The national role with respect to flooding was limited to building flood protection embankments, called levees, a task the Army Corps of Engineers

The devastation of Hurricane Katrina on the Gulf Coast in August 2005 brought to national attention the government's often cumbersome multilevel structure that hindered it from responding with the required efficiency and coordination.

has been performing since the early 1800s. State governments provided extra help in the form of state national guardsmen to help throw sandbags on the levees to raise them above the surging flood waters.

The national role greatly expanded in 1974 when Congress enacted the Disaster Relief and Emergency Assistance Act, known as the Stafford Act in honor of its chief Senate sponsor Senator James Stafford of Vermont. The timing of the passage of this act was not coincidental. As Chapter 5 discussed, during the 1960s and 1970s Congress expanded federal involvement in a whole host of issues previously relegated to states and localities including air and water pollution, hazardous and solid waste treatment and disposal, occupational safety and health, and the education of children with disabilities. But the Stafford Act did not put the federal government in charge, rather it provided for

> an orderly and continuing means of assistance by the Federal Government to State and local governments in carrying out their responsibilities to alleviate the suffering and damage which result from such disasters.

To provide assistance and to coordinate the efforts of other federal departments to help, a new federal agency, the Federal Emergency Management Agency (FEMA), was created.

As the media beamed images of New Orleanians sitting on rooftops, their belongings floating down the flooded streets, federalism was the furthest thing from the public mind. Rather, it wanted and expected *the* government to help. It did not think in terms of different levels or parts of government. For weeks after the flood, public discussion of Katrina – in the media, among the victims, and in the halls of Congress – was dominated by the question of who was to blame for the government's failure. The mayor of New Orleans blamed FEMA and President Bush for the painful slowness with which federal assistance reached his stricken city. Representatives of the Bush administration blamed Louisiana governor Kathleen Blanco for failing to place an official request for federal assistance as required by federal law. Both federal and state officials blamed Mayor Nagin for failing to implement the city's own emergency evacuation plan, especially the part that called for providing buses to remove the tens of thousands who did not have access to an automobile.

As the days passed, help did arrive from a variety of sources including FEMA, the National Guard, the U.S. military, the Red Cross, and hundreds of private volunteer organizations. But the finger pointing continued. Whose fault was it that thousands were stranded in the Superdome without adequate food, water, and sanitation? Ongoing disputes between local, state, and federal government about who was responsible for which aspects of recovery and who should pay for what continued to slow things down. For a representative democracy to function, it is necessary that government officials be held accountable. Weeks and months of congressional hearings and reports from congressional committees and from the White House itself were devoted to detailing the specific errors made by every level of government during the months and years that preceded the storm and in its aftermath.

These exhaustive efforts to pinpoint blame and to propose reforms are likely to have a positive effect. Criticizing and even punishing public officials for their mistakes is a necessary first step to improving future performance. But even as the public and the experts press to bring about improvements, a crucial constitutional lesson needs to be kept in mind. There is no *the* government that responds to natural disasters. There is a trio of governments. This compound system exists not because it is the quickest or most efficient means for coping with the problem, but because the Framers believed that it was the best way to protect liberty and to encourage civic responsibility. Indeed, the trio is really a foursome. Citizen themselves have the prime responsibility for taking care of themselves in event of disaster. Local, state, and federal governments serve to assist the citizens but not to displace them as the primary agents of their own survival and well-being. Since the national government is the most powerful and therefore the most dangerous government, even a disastrous flood is not a sufficient reason to allow its voice to drown out the other members of the quartet.

Though they cursed *the* government for its ineptitude, Katrina's victims still recognized how much help they required from government in order to rebuild. Banks demanded that they first obtain flood insurance in order to qualify for the mortgages they needed to pay the expense of rebuilding. Insurance companies were only willing to offer such insurance if the government first certified which homes had been made sufficiently floodproof to qualify and also subsidized the cost of the insurance. In addition, FEMA and other federal and state agencies provided further help in the forms of grants, technical assistance, and cheap loans.

The availability of all these forms of government help was delayed while FEMA struggled to determine what it would demand in the way of improved building standards to make it less likely that future floods would wreak a comparable level of damage. Finally, after eight months, it released its new elevation guidelines. In most instances, these guidelines required that all new construction as well as rehabilitation of homes that had been substantially damaged would have to elevate the height of their ground floors by three feet. Such a requirement added $20,000 or more to the cost of rebuilding and was greeted with fury by those who felt that the unique circumstances of their home sites made such expensive renovation unnecessary. In very poor neighborhoods where housing values were low and where people had little to spend on rebuilding, $20,000 spent on elevating a house might come close to doubling the cost of the entire project and push construction costs above the house's market value.

Although, initially at least, FEMA's guidelines were only advisory, it was widely assumed that insurance companies would be unwilling to sell flood insurance and banks would be unwilling to give mortgages on properties that violated those rules. The supposedly private insurance and mortgage markets were thus totally dependent upon the standards established by a government agency. Many homeowners saw the FEMA elevation requirements as a violation of their right to do with their property as they wished. But FEMA insisted that such guidelines were necessary to protect the government's considerable recovery investment. Therefore, it saw itself not as depriving a minority of its liberty but as the representative of the legitimate concerns of the great majority of democratic citizens who in their role as taxpayers were spending billions to rescue and assist that minority.

The Katrina story shows just how closely related the two pivotal relationships between different levels of government and between the government and private sector truly are. Both of these relationships seek to balance the democratic demand for accountability with the equally strong impulse to leave people alone and to prevent the growth of centralized government power. These questions will continue to dominate the debate over disaster response and relief as citizens and their representatives struggle to improve the capacity of different levels of government to work together, to encourage citizens to take more responsibility for their own security and safety, and to ensure that the rights of victims to control their own destiny do not put unfair burdens on the nation's taxpayers and do not create excessive risks of future loss of life and property.

PART THREE

Governing Institutions

7 Congress

The First Branch
of Government

Chapter Overview

This chapter focuses on:

☆ The critical questions about representative government that the Framers had to confront when they designed the legislative branch and that continue to challenge the American political system

☆ The liberal and democratic forces that have shaped and animated Congress

☆ The structure and dynamics of Congress that work to reconcile, as well as aggravate, tensions between liberal and democratic forces

☆ The four crucial phases of congressional development

☆ The contemporary partisan conflicts in Congress and the ongoing tensions between Congress and the president

On May 24, 2001, Senator James M. Jeffords, Republican of Vermont, announced he was leaving the Republican party. He would become an independent but would side with the Democrats in decisions about congressional organization and leadership positions. Such conversions are very rare. Jeffords's was especially newsworthy because it tipped the Senate balance of power to the Democrats. The Senate had previously consisted of fifty senators from each party. Therefore, in the case of ties, the deciding vote had been cast by Republican Vice President Richard Cheney, who, as the Constitution prescribes, presided over the Senate. Before Jeffords's shift, as a result of the 2000 elections, Republicans also controlled the White House and the House of Representatives, the first time they had such full command of government since 1954.

Jeffords's decision ended the Republicans' monopoly over the executive and legislative branches. It catapulted Senate Democratic leader Thomas Daschle of South Dakota into the majority leader's post that had been previously occupied by Republican senator Trent Lott of Mississippi. It also gave the Democrats control over all major Senate committees, threatening President George W. Bush's initiatives on such critical issues as energy production and missile defense as well his choices for federal judgeships, which require Senate confirmation.

Jeffords, a moderate, was at odds with conservative Republican congressional leaders regarding such issues as abortion, defense, fiscal policy, and environmental protection. These differences were not new (Jeffords was serving his third term), but the Republican return to the White House increased pressure on him to toe the party line. He insisted that his decision to leave his party was based on fundamental principles. According to the Constitution, he represented Vermont, not the Republicans. His constituents were more moderate than the senatorial Republican leadership. His departure was necessary to enable him to best represent his state and his conscience.

The conflict that Jeffords experienced between his partisan and his state identity reveals a tension between the liberal and democratic traditions as they affect Congress. Congress is the central branch of the national government. Established by Article I of the Constitution, Congress has the final say on national law and policy. Both houses are democratically elected (although the Senate was not originally elected by the people). More than the president and courts, Congress speaks for the national majority. As we point out in this chapter, the discipline that congressional party leadership imposes on its members is a crucial device for pressing individual members of Congress to obey the popular will.

But even when one party controls both the House and the Senate, Congress is not simply the voice of the majority. Because it is organized on a geographical basis – each House member is elected by a district, each senator by a state – Congress speaks with many voices, expressing the diverse, sometimes provincial, interests of localities and states. Majority sentiment at home may be at odds with majority party sentiment or even with the dictates of a member's own conscience. Local pressures often force individual members to vote against party colleagues and, sometimes, against their own better judgment.

Where such conflicting sentiments exist, representatives must choose between two different understandings of their democratic duties: should they represent their local majority or their party majority? But if their own judgment is at odds with either local or national majority sentiment, they are also choosing between democratic and liberal imperatives. The view of representation defended by James Madison, the key architect of the Constitution, was that representatives should show better judgment than those they represent, that representatives should engage in "refining and enlarging" the views of their constituents. They should lead, not simply mirror, their constituents. After all, their constituents still retained the option of punishing them for this show of independence at the next election. In Jeffords's case, these competing obligations were in such great conflict with one another that he chose to abandon his party responsibility in order to fulfill his obligations to his state and to himself.

The complex nature of congressional representation follows from its responsibility in a republican rather than a direct democracy. As we discuss in Chapter 1, direct democracy requires citizens to personally make and administer laws. The American republic delegates those duties to a small number of citizens elected by the rest and extends the government over a large and diverse society. Nearly 300 million people are represented by the 435 members of the House of Representatives and 100 members of the Senate.

As we argue throughout this book, American democracy is brought to life by contests between differing opinions and competing political parties. In representative government, public debate and resolution is filtered through the legislature. Thus, Congress serves the democratic objective of giving the people a loud voice in lawmaking and the republican goal of attaining sufficient distance from popular opinion to act deliberatively.

This chapter examines the liberal and democratic forces that have shaped and animated Congress and discusses how the structure and dynamics of Congress work to reconcile as well as aggravate tensions between those forces. It describes Congress's principal part in shaping the major episodes of American political development, the refoundings described in Chapter 4, that have sustained a vital connection between the national government and the public. In this chapter, we explain how Congress became unsurpassed among the world's legislatures in upholding the rule of law and how that achievement is threatened by the expansion of national administrative power, the extension of rights, and the emergence of national presidency-oriented parties. Senator Jeffords's dilemma reflected a degree of party polarization on Capitol Hill that made life difficult for moderates in both parties. Cast against the historical ground we cover in this book, there is nothing new or unusual about the pattern of sharp partisanship that has affected the past two presidential elections and has aroused raw and disruptive battles in the House and Senate. Party warfare occurred frequently in the nineteenth century and parts of the twentieth century. The relative truce between Democrats and Republicans that lasted for roughly twenty-five years after World War II was an exception to the more normal pattern of intense party conflict. That unusual period of bipartisanship was largely the result of the strong national consensus that formed around Cold War foreign policy and the perpetuation of New Deal entitlement policies. When this bipartisanship broke down beginning in the mid 1960s, renewed party conflict erupted in a manner that threatened to undermine the deepest principles of representative government. The intense partisan conflicts that obsessed Congress often failed to engage the American public. This divergence between the battle of the Beltway and the concerns of ordinary Americans threatened to alienate the public from the "representative" branch of government.

The first section of the chapter examines the crucial questions about representative government that the Framers had to confront when they designed the legislative branch. The subsequent sections look at each crucial phase of congressional development: emergence as the dominant branch of government in the nineteenth century; transformation in response to the rise of activist national government in the twentieth century; Congress's resurgence since the 1970s; and the renewed threat to Congress's institutional integrity posed by the expansion of executive power and party polarization after September 11, 2001. The chapter concludes by showing how the complex story of Congress's evolution helps explain its continuing struggles to fulfill and reconcile its liberal and its democratic responsibilities.

Congress and the Constitution

Article I of the Constitution established Congress as the preeminent branch of government, granting it seventeen legislative powers, including the most important of all governmental powers: taxation, regulation of commerce, and declaration of war. These enumerated powers are followed by the "necessary and proper clause," which makes clear that Congress should have whatever additional powers are necessary to exercise its specific responsibilities. Article I, Section 2 designates the speaker as the principal officer of the House of Representatives; the president of the Senate, who is the vice president, as the presiding officer of the Senate; and a president pro tempore who presides in the absence of the vice president. But unlike the speaker, the two Senate officers rarely are at the center of leadership in their chamber. In part, this difference follows from the distinct qualities of the Senate and the House; the Senate is smaller and composed of more celebrated, independent-minded individuals. The upper chamber is both less in need of and more resistant to strong leadership. Box 1 describes how Congress actually exercises its legislative powers by making law.

Box One: Nuts and Bolts

How a Bill Becomes a Law

Although the Constitution gives Congress the power to make laws, not all, or even most, legislative proposals originate there. When a proposal for a new law is introduced into Congress, it is referred to as a "bill" and assigned a number. If it is first introduced by a senator, to the Senate, the number is given the prefix S. For example, the Energy Policy and Conservation Act of 1975 was first introduced in the Senate and was labeled S622. If a bill is first introduced by a House member, to the House of Representatives, the number is given the prefix HR. For example, a 1990 bill overhauling federal aid for vocational education was first introduced into the House and was labeled HR7. Executive departments also draft bills, as do various lobbying organizations. But no bill becomes a law unless it is passed by both houses of Congress and signed by the president. If the president vetoes the bill, it must be repassed by a two-thirds majority in each house of Congress in order to become a law, a move that is known as a veto override.

The normal pattern is for a legislative proposal to first be assigned to the committee or committees of the House that specialize in the issues addressed by the proposal. Most senators and congressmen keep their same committee assignments from session to session. Since the mid-1970s, the leadership, or chairs, of the committees have been chosen by the members of the party that controls the House and the Senate (the majority party caucus). The committee members of the majority party select the chairs of the subcommittees, where much of the important work of the House and the Senate is carried out. In practice, these procedures for selecting committee and subcommittee chairs give considerable power to the majority party leadership, especially the Speaker of the House.

If the proposal deals with questions that relate to raising revenue, the Constitution requires that the proposal first be considered by the House. If the proposal covers any other topic, the Senate is free to consider it, or alternative proposals, at the same time or even in advance of House consideration. Because the Senate has fewer members, however, it cannot scrutinize as many proposals as the House can. Therefore, the Senate often allows the House to act first, using the lower chamber as a filter to determine which issues really merit further attention. Committees and subcommittees of both chambers hold hearings to garner opinions from a variety of governmental and non-governmental sources such as federal agencies, business groups, and citizen groups.

Congressional committees are typically too large to provide the detailed scrutiny that legislative proposals require. Subcommittees produce drafts of bills that go to the full committee to be voted on. The full committee may also modify the draft as it sees fit. In the House, a bill approved by committee goes to the Rules Committee, which determines when and whether to place the bill before the entire House for debate. The entire House may choose to amend the bill, meaning it can modify what the bill contains, and then either pass or defeat it.

The Senate process is less routinized than the House's, although it normally follows a similar pattern of subcommittee and committee deliberation and then consideration by the body as a whole. Often, each chamber will pass a significantly different version of a bill. To reconcile these differences, the House and Senate leadership each appoint members to a joint conference committee. The conference committee tries to achieve compromises regarding the major issues in dispute. If it succeeds, the conference version goes back to each house to be ratified or defeated. If both houses approve of the compromise bill, it is sent to the president's desk for a signature.

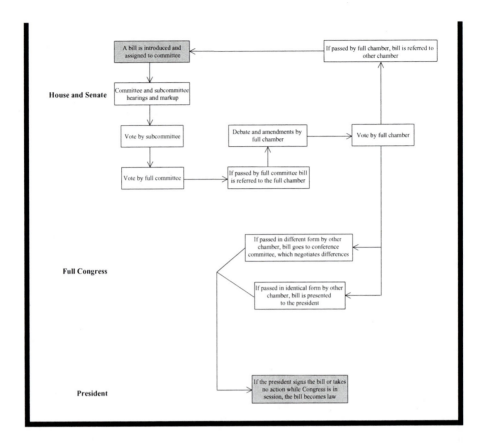

Having granted so much power to the legislature, the Convention delegates were determined to make it act responsibly and sensibly; they sought to avoid the intemperate and irresponsible behavior of their own state legislatures during the currency crisis of 1785. Americans went on such a buying spree after the Revolutionary War – importing such luxuries as clocks, glassware, and furniture from Great Britain – that gold and silver became scarce and the value of money was driven up. Indebted farmers who had left their land to fight for independence and who still had not been paid by the financially destitute national government were able to convince several state legislatures to loosen the money supply by printing vast sums of money. These legislative policies were highly democratic but nearly disastrous for the states' economies (see the section titled "Debtors and Creditors" in Chapter 2).

This irresponsible behavior of state legislatures was aggravated by the impotence of the central government under the Articles of Confederation. The national legislature lacked authority to regulate interstate commerce and could not impose more responsible economic policies on the states.

Members of Congress were chosen by the state legislatures, which paid their salaries and had the power to remove them at any time. Therefore, congressional representatives were afraid to take actions that their state legislatures disapproved of for fear of losing their positions or having their pay reduced. To craft a Congress capable of more enlightened statesmanship and better public policy making than could be found in the state legislatures, the Framers carefully considered methods of selection, overall size, and what checks to establish between House and Senate and between the Congress as a whole and the rest of the government.

Representation: Selection and Size

To select better representatives, the Framers determined to draw them from a bigger pool. House districts would be large; senators would be chosen by entire states. State legislators were often elected for periods of a year or even six months. By creating longer congressional terms – two years for the House, six for the Senate – the Framers hoped to insulate representatives from volatile changes in public opinion.

To promote deliberation, Congress was to be a relatively small body. The House of Representatives would have only sixty-five members and the Senate, twenty-six. By contrast, the legislature of Massachusetts had more than 300 members. Anti-Federalists protested that the small size of the legislature made it insufficiently representative. So intent were the Framers on maintaining distance between House members and their constituents that until the very last day of the Constitutional Convention, they fought to maintain a ratio of one member per 40,000 citizens. Fearing that such a high ratio would offend democratic sentiments, George Washington stepped down from the chair – the only time he did so – to defend reducing the minimum from 40,000 to 30,000. The convention had debated and rejected this proposition several times in the preceding weeks, but once Washington endorsed it, debate ceased and it passed unanimously.

The Anti-Federalists' warning that the House was not sufficiently democratic would continue to haunt American political life. House size did not keep pace with population expansion; today, one representative speaks for almost 700,000 people. The House has not grown since 1911, when its number, based on the 1910 census, increased to 435. In truth, Madison's hope that the House would be sufficiently democratic to win the confidence of the American people would never quite be fulfilled – throughout American history the debate has continued about whether Congress is truly, as the Virginian George Mason prescribed, "the grand depository of the democratic principle of the Government" or, as the Anti-Federalists insisted, a

Table 7.1. Profile of the Members of the 110th Congress

House of Representatives
  Members – 435
  Party – 233 Democrats, 202 Republicans
  Average Age – 56
  Average Length of Service – 10 years (5.07 terms)
  Women Members – 74
  African-American Members – 42
  Hispanic Members – 26

Senate
  Members – 100
  Party – 49 Republicans, 49 Democrats, 2 Independents (aligned with Democrats)
  Average Age – 63
  Average Length of Service – 12.82 years (slightly more than two terms)
  Women Members – 1
  African-American Members – 1
  Hispanic Members – 3

---

pseudo-representative branch that "had very little democracy in it." Table 7.1 provides a profile of the individuals who make up the current Congress.

Bicameralism

The Framers feared that the Anti-Federalists underestimated the democratic character of the House, which, if left to its own devices, would become all too responsive to popular whims and passions. Although they believed that the heated differences of opinion and jarring of parties that would flare up from time to time in the House were necessary to sustain the republican character of the Constitution, the Framers sought, as Madison put it, to refine popular passions by "successive filtrations," by a system of separated powers that would restrain such passionate outbursts. The first line of defense was bicameralism, the creation of two separate houses of Congress. All laws had to be passed by both houses. The House's state delegations were based on population and its members elected directly by the people every two years, thus making it a national representative body. By contrast, each state, regardless of size, would have two senators who would (originally) be selected by the state legislatures for six-year terms, thus establishing the Senate as an important ingredient of federalism.

Not only would authority be divided between states and nation, but also national representation would itself be a compound of national and local interest. The House was larger, had shorter terms, and could turn over its personnel every two years. All revenue bills had to originate in the House. This concession to the House suggested the Framers' commitment to placing principal authority in a democratic assembly.

But the House would be moderated by the more discerning attention of the Senate. The Senate's smaller size, its longer terms, the staggering of its members' terms (only one-third of the body would be up for reelection every two years), and the selection of these members by state legislatures, not the people, encouraged prudence. As befit the chamber's "cool and deliberate sense of the community," the Senate was given a privileged part in foreign affairs and government staffing. It was granted sole authority to ratify foreign treaties, confirm presidential nominations to the executive branch and judiciary, and try public officials impeached by the House.

Separation of Powers

The space between government action and public opinion was further expanded by the separation of powers, in which Congress shared government control with the president and judiciary. In *parliamentary democracies* like Britain and Canada, the representative assembly makes laws and administers them. By contrast, the American system creates an institutional maze that enables all three branches to participate in lawmaking and implementation (see Chapter 3).

By limiting a legislature to a small number of representatives, by drawing those representatives from a large and diverse society, and by restricting the reach of the legislature through a complex scheme of separated powers, the republican government created by the Constitution sought to make popular rule more competent and just.

Congressional Dominance

For the first half of the United States' political development, Congress served as the chief national policy-making body. Congressional opposition to the executive was first aroused by Secretary of the Treasury Alexander Hamilton's reports to Congress in 1790 and 1791, which called on Congress to assume the war debts of the states, enact tariffs, protect infant industries, and create a national bank (see Chapter 4). James Madison, the leading figure in the House, charged that Hamilton's economic plan would make the more democratic institutions – Congress and the states – subordinate to the executive. Madison's concern that the expansion of the national government's responsibilities would lead to an elected monarchy led him to abandon his alliance with Hamilton, a political friendship that had been so critical to the writing and ratification of the Constitution. He joined with Jefferson to form the Republican party, which was dedicated to stemming the expansion of executive authority. Yet his warning proved prophetic. We point out later in this chapter that the expansion of the national government's powers subordinated legislature power to the executive prerogative; indeed, when big government came to America during the twentieth century, it went hand-in-hand with a massive delegation of legislative power to the executive branch, raising concerns about presidential imperialism.

Organizing Congress: The Emergence of the Party Caucus

Chapter 11 describes the Framers' fear of political parties as factions that would incite class, religious, or racial conflict and thereby endanger liberty. The Constitution's system of separation of powers, operating in a large and diverse society, was intended to inhibit the emergence of a strong two-party system. Ironically, it was that very party system that enabled Congress to perform its constitutional responsibilities. In 1800, the Republicans triumphed over the Federalists and installed Thomas Jefferson as the nation's third president. The most important result of this critical election was to empower a party dedicated to constraining the president and strengthening Congress and the states.

In order to perform its democratic function of passing laws that reflect majority sentiment and its liberal function of holding executive power in check, Congress needed a unifying force that, as Jefferson saw, could only be provided by political parties. Presidents can be strong and appear "above party." Congress, however, is a large collection of individuals. Although members of Congress may achieve celebrity and popularity outside of parties – witness the acclaim that greeted Senator Jeffords's defection from the Republican camp, or the public's admiration for the maverick senator John McCain (R-AZ) – Congress as an institution can rival the president's claim to public confidence only if it can be held collectively accountable. Accountability requires that parties reward and punish members based on their adherence not only to collective decisions of the party but also to the tactics adopted by the party leadership for implementation of those decisions.

Unlike Washington and Adams, therefore, Jefferson deemphasized his formal powers and governed instead through his extra-constitutional role as party leader. He helped build a disciplined party organization in Congress and relied on *party leaders* in the House and Senate to advance his program. Jefferson himself sometimes presided over the meetings of the congressional Republican representatives, known as *party caucuses*. Jefferson exercised strong presidential leadership over the Congress, but he presided over the development of party machinery that made possible a radical change in the relationship between the executive and legislature. When Jefferson left office, congressional party leaders assumed command of the national government.

The Rise of the Power of the House Speaker

The Republican congressional caucus assumed control over the nomination of presidential candidates. In 1808, the caucus had to choose between Madison, Jefferson's secretary of state who was generally regarded as his heir apparent, and James Monroe, supported by an anti-Jefferson faction led by John Randolph of Virginia. Madison was nominated and elected, but he had to make concessions to the Randolph faction. Whereas Hamilton's plans risked unbalancing the constitutional order in favor of the president, the dominance of the Republican caucus risked the reverse: executive subordination to congressional president-makers. Indeed, Madison's renomination in 1812 apparently was delayed until he assured the *war hawks* in the congressional caucus that he supported their desire to go to war with Great Britain.

During this same time, Kentuckian Henry Clay's extraordinary power as Speaker of the House confirmed the subordination of the executive to Congress. The speaker's emergence as an important office was not inevitable; the Constitution does not stipulate the position's responsibilities nor was there any significant discussion of it at the Constitutional Convention. Before Clay, the position was largely ceremonial, as indicated by the fact that Clay was elected speaker in 1808, at the beginning of his second congressional term. Yet Clay was able to use the speakership to dominate Congress, and much of the rest of government as well, for the next fifteen years.

Clay first served in the Senate; he was elected by the Kentucky legislature in 1806 to fill an unexpired term. But he found the Senate's "solemn stillness" boring. Elected by state legislatures rather than by popular vote, members of the Senate had the luxury, as the Framers prescribed, of debating issues at a distance from the currents of popular opinion. Their debates lacked the passion and immediacy of those that occurred in the House. Clay quit the Senate after being elected to the House in 1808. In January 1810, he was returned to the Senate; however, in August of that year he was elected once again to the House of Representatives and eagerly returned to the lower chamber, where he resumed his position as speaker in 1811.

Before Clay, party leadership in the House had been shared by several floor leaders, and the speaker acted as merely a moderator. A strong president such as Jefferson could dominate this diffuse congressional leadership. Clay made the speaker the leader of the majority party in the House, and he extended party control over congressional committees, which became, in Woodrow Wilson's celebrated phrase, "little legislatures," meaning that the committees performed the real work of formulating legislation. Like most great legislative leaders, Clay derived his success in large part from his extraordinary personality. John C. Calhoun, a fierce rival, said, "I don't like Henry Clay, he is a bad man, an imposter, a creator of wicked schemes. I wouldn't speak to him, but, by God, I love him."

Clay displaced Jefferson's successor, Madison, as the dominant national political leader during the controversy with Britain that led to the War of 1812. Madison, whose leadership qualities were poorly suited to the presidency, left the pressing issues of the day to the Congress. In the absence of strong presidential leadership, the Eleventh Congress, which met during Madison's first two years in office, was unprepared to resolve foreign policy controversy. Clay resolved that the Twelfth Congress would be different. Unifying the Republican caucus behind him, Clay strengthened the House's capacity to meet its broader legislative obligations by expanding the number and influence of its committees, which enabled each representative to specialize in a specific policy area such as finance or foreign policy. Clay was especially careful to appoint as committee chairs those representatives who shared his views about the crisis with Britain. For example, he appointed New York congressman Peter Porter, a widely known war hawk, as chairman of the foreign affairs committee. Coordination of committee activities by the party's leadership turned the House into an effective legislative body.

Clay forced a reluctant Madison to deliver a war message to Congress. On June 18, 1812, President Madison signed the first war declaration in American history. But this war was Clay's, not Madison's, which signified that the initiative in public affairs now resided with the speaker and his congressional allies. Unfortunately, Congress proved far more eager to declare war than to prepare for it. Traditional Republican hostility to centralized power caused Congress to slash tax revenues and military appropriations, leaving the military both understaffed and undersupplied. Legislative dominance deprived the country of the solid benefits that the Framers expected from a unified and energetic executive. The inability of Congress to match its talent for deliberation and debate with administrative competence would continue to bedevil national governance throughout the nineteenth century.

President versus Congress; Democrats versus Whigs

In pitting the executive against the Congress, the Constitutional Convention sought to reconcile America's liberal and democratic traditions.

Congress's growing strength during the early nineteenth century was a deliberate effort by the Republicans to reinforce popular rule against the threat of executive imperialism. But by 1824, Congress had become so dominant as to threaten popular rule.

As we discuss more extensively in Chapter 11, the 1824 election provoked accusations that Congress had acted undemocratically. In the absence of an Electoral College majority, as the Twelfth Amendment to the Constitution prescribes, Congress was to select the president. It rejected Andrew Jackson in favor of John Quincy Adams even though Jackson had more, but not a majority of, electoral votes. Adams then chose Henry Clay, who had led the fight for him in the House, as his secretary of state. Jackson and his supporters treated what they termed this "corrupt bargain" as an indictment of Congress as a whole. Therefore, they parted with their hero Jefferson to champion the presidency, not Congress, as the legitimate agent of democracy. Looking to the 1828 election, they formed the Democratic party and used it to promote a strengthened executive.

The supporters of Adams and Clay, who like Jackson and his supporters had been Republicans, called themselves Whigs, borrowing the name of the English political party that opposed the power of the king and supported parliamentary superiority. The name was meant to imply that the Democrats were really Tories, that they had abandoned Jeffersonian principles in favor of an elected monarch, Jackson, whom the Whigs dubbed "King Andrew the First." But it was Jackson's message that resonated more with the voters, which led to his victory over Adams in the 1828 election.

In Chapters 4 and 6, we discuss Jackson's veto of the Second National Bank. This victory established the president, rather than the Congress or the states, as the principal agent of the emerging mass party system in the United States. Sustained by his party's far-reaching political network, Jackson became the first president to appeal to the people over the heads of their legislative representatives.

Leading Whigs, including Clay, Daniel Webster, and John C. Calhoun, accused "King Andrew" of popular demagogy that would destroy the republican character of the Constitution. (Calhoun broke with Jackson over the nullification controversy and joined the Whigs in 1833, supporting their opposition to the president's campaign to kill the national bank.) In a partial reversal of constitutional responsibilities, the Whigs looked to Congress, especially the Senate, as the guardian of constitutional forms and defender of the liberal tradition against the encroachments of a popular dictator.

The Whigs were especially alarmed at Jackson's decision to remove the federal government's deposits from the Second National Bank and put them in state banks even before the bank's charter expired. When Secretary of the Treasury William Duane refused to do so, Jackson replaced him with Roger

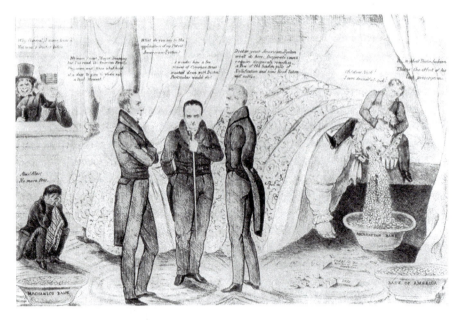

This 1833 cartoon depicts the great debaters Webster, Clay, and Calhoun bemoaning the sad state of the federal bank emptying into smaller banks, as Andrew Jackson gleefully peeks through the window.

B. Taney. Taney's was a "recess appointment," meaning he could serve until the Senate came back from its recess. When it returned, the Senate rejected Taney's nomination, but by that time the deposits had been removed.

In March 1834, the Senate for the very first time voted to censure the president, accusing him of usurping "authority and power not conferred by the Constitution and laws." It refused to enter into the Senate journal Jackson's written protest claiming the censure to be unconstitutional. Although the censure did not remove Jackson from office, it did threaten to undermine his authority and usurp his powers.

Taken together, Duane's dismissal, Taney's removal of public deposits from the national bank, and the Senate's censure of Jackson raised a fundamental question: can the president dictate the proper exercise of a power delegated by Congress to a department head? Whig leaders, notably Clay and Webster, defended Congress's right to vest truly independent authority in the secretary of the treasury. Congress's direct power to constrain the secretary derived from its power over the purse – no more critical authority, they claimed, belonged to the "people's representatives."

Jackson's view was that because the president, not Congress, represented the people's will, the president must maintain control over the executive branch. Like the bank controversy, the Senate censure matter was brought before the voters; it became the leading issue in the next round of Senate elections. Jackson's Democratic allies took control of the upper house in 1837. By a vote of twenty-four to nineteen, the Senate directed its secretary to draw heavy black lines around the censure notation in its 1834 journal, thus formally "expunging" it from the record. Henry Clay, dressed in black to mourn the Constitution, lamented that "the Senate is no longer a place for decent men."

The Whigs exaggerated the degree to which Jackson's two terms expanded the opportunities for unilateral executive action. His extension of executive power was mediated by the party organizations. Jackson's allies, including Senator Martin Van Buren (D-NY), who became vice president in 1833, built the first mass party organization, the Democratic party (see Chapter 11). It not only reached into Congress, as the Jeffersonian party had done, but also penetrated every corner of the nation. Voter turnout grew in presidential and congressional elections, such that nearly 80 percent of the eligible electorate participated in them. (Although turnout in off-year congressional elections declined from those held in presidential election years, the discrepancy between presidential and off-year elections was much less than it tends to be in contemporary American politics.) Jackson's "appeal to the people" in the banking and censure controversies was waged mainly through the party. Therefore, Jackson remained critically dependent on party leaders to maintain his power.

Parties linked both president and Congress more directly to public opinion. The Whigs feared that this development would turn republican government into lawless democracy. But they too were drawn into party campaigns for both president and Congress, which engaged the American people in great contests of opinion. As the bank controversy showed, these contests involved major constitutional disputes – passionate debate about rights and constitutional forms. In these debates, democracy did not eclipse liberalism; rather, the liberal tradition was brought alive by a vibrant democratic politics that strengthened the attachment between the fundamental law and the American people.

The Emergence of the Citizen Legislature

Even with the strengthening of the presidency, Congress remained at the center of American politics and government. Organized by a mass-based, decentralized party system, Congress became a more vibrant institution, one that registered competing democratic voices. Unlike the contemporary Congress, viewed as the keystone of an unresponsive government establishment, the nineteenth-century Congress became a "citizen legislature."

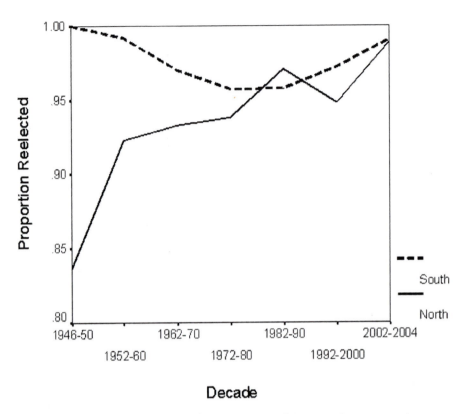

Figure 7.1. Reelection Rates of House Incumbents. In the nineteenth century, there was great turnover in Congress in every election. In the modern era, relatively few incumbents are defeated in their reelection attempts. *Source:* "Incumbency, Redistricting, and the Decline of Competition in U.S. House Elections," by A. Abramowitz, B. Alexander, and M. Gunning, Dept. of Political Science, Emory University, 2005.

The most striking feature of this citizen legislature was the very rapid turnover of its members. For much of the twentieth century, power in the Congress was acquired through *seniority*, which encourages long congressional careers. But in the nineteenth century, the House had 30 to 60 percent turnover at every election. By contrast, turnover in the 2002 election was 15 percent; turnover in 1994 election, uncharacteristically high for today's Congress, was still only 20 percent (see Figure 7.1). The Senate's longer and overlapping terms gives it a more stable membership than the House, but it too saw far more turnover in the nineteenth century than it does today. Like Henry Clay, politicians fled the chamber as soon as another opportunity presented itself. Before the Civil War, members very rarely made the Senate a career. Until the end of the century, the average senator did not even finish one term, completing only three to four years of service.

One cause of the high turnover was the unpleasantness of life in Washington at that time. Unlike the first two capital sites, New York and Philadelphia, Washington lacked culture and creature comforts. Members of Congress felt stranded in this primitive new city, described by the historian Merrill Peterson as "a village pretending to be a capitol, a place with a few bad houses, extensive swamps, hanging on the skirts of a too thinly peopled, weak and barren country." Another disincentive to long congressional service was the limited role that the national government played in the political life of the country. The triumph of the Jacksonians over the Whigs had restored the primacy of state and local government.

Another key characteristic of the citizen legislature was a high level of partisan competition. The two political parties were evenly balanced during most of the nineteenth century, and therefore House elections tended to be close, which threatened reelection prospects. State legislative elections were also close. Because the Senate was chosen by the state legislatures, senatorial elections were likewise highly competitive. State legislative candidates would often run for office pledged to a particular senatorial candidate. This is why the famous 1858 Lincoln-Douglas debates took place all over the state of Illinois. Each candidate was trying to help elect legislative candidates pledged to vote for him.

Partisan competition and member turnover combined to create a lively Congress. Much legislative business was mundane, dealing with appointments to low-level federal government positions. But when the localized parties got caught up in big issues, such as slavery, tariff policy, the bank, or the money supply, Congress became the home of passionate debate. Lengthy and powerful speeches were common, and unlike today, they were not made to an empty chamber for the benefit of television cameras. Box 2 provides a glimpse of floor life in the modern House and Senate.

Box Two: Nuts and Bolts

Life on the Floor of Congress

For reasons we explore later in the chapter, members of Congress no longer have the time or inclination to participate in serious debate on the house floor. Even when Congress is in session, the floors of both houses are often virtually empty except for a member delivering a speech and a C-SPAN camera operator taping it. These speeches are not meaningless. They, along with other materials submitted by members, are published in the Congressional Record, the official transcript of congressional activities. The speeches are a source for scholars, lawyers, executive officials, and judges who, for a variety of purposes, need to discern the intent of Congress with regard to the laws it has passed. But the absence of floor debate does reflect the changing role of Congress. Ordinary members are no longer as active in the consideration of laws that do not emanate from their particular committees and subcommittees. The house floor rarely functions as an arena for meaningful deliberation as it did in the great debates over slavery and the tariff in the nineteenth century. Because the Senate is so much smaller than the House, the Senate floor does sometimes provide such an occasion. One hundred senators have a far easier time exchanging views and sharing insights than do 435 members of the House.

Congress at the Center of the Action

An 1856 event in Congress dramatically illustrates that the House and Senate had become the center of national passions and conflicts. In May of that year, Senator Charles Sumner (R-MA) delivered a two-day speech charging that there was a Southern conspiracy to admit Kansas to the Union as a slave state, a speech that he titled "The Crime against Kansas." Among those members of Congress singled out for insult and ridicule was Andrew P. Butler (D-SC). Sumner described Butler as "Don Quixote who had chosen a mistress to whom he has made his vows, and who ... though polluted in the sight of the world, is chaste in his sight – I mean the harlot slavery."

Congressman Preston Brooks (D-SC), a kinsman of Butler's, decided to avenge his family's honor. Brooks approached Sumner, who was seated at his desk mailing copies of the offending speech to his constituents. Calling the speech a "libel on South Carolina, and Mr. Butler, who is a relative of mine," Brooks brought his cane down on Sumner's head, neck, and shoulders, repeatedly and with increasing force, until the cane shattered. Sumner tried to rise from his desk, ripping up the heavy screws that bolted it to the floor. Blinded by blood, he staggered down the center aisle of the Senate chamber.

The South declared Brooks a hero. The North viewed Sumner as a martyr. Southern opposition prevented the two-thirds majority necessary to expel Brooks from the House, but he resigned anyway. South Carolinians immediately sent him back to Washington with triumphant unanimity. Sumner stayed away from the Senate for three years – recuperating, his

SOUTHERN CHIVALRY — ARGUMENT VERSUS CLUB'S.

The 1856 attack on Senator Charles Sumner of Massachusetts on the floor of the Senate by an opposing member of the House of Representatives symbolized the increasing chasm in the nation over the slavery issue.

supporters said; hiding, claimed his enemies. During that time the Massachusetts legislature reelected him as a symbolic rebuke to the "barbarism of slavery." His empty seat in the Senate chamber remained a visible symbol of the deepening sectional divide. The Sumner-Brooks incident was hardly part of the deliberative process that the Founders of the Constitution prescribed for the Congress, but it shows how the national legislature had become the center of American democratic life, a forum that helped draw Americans into struggles about the most fundamental political issues. John Quincy Adams (when he was in the House), Henry Clay, Daniel Webster, John C. Calhoun, and Charles Sumner shaped the debate over slavery, making Congress, as the historian Henry Jones Ford observed, "a school of political education for the nation."

Lincoln was an exception to the decline in presidential authority that took place after Jackson. But even he was hounded by a joint congressional committee on the conduct of the Civil War. His successor, Vice President Andrew Johnson, formerly a senator from Tennessee, had served on that committee, which had constantly criticized Lincoln's initiatives and had often charged that the president had usurped rightful powers of Congress. Only a few hours after Lincoln died, the committee paid a visit to Johnson and expressed its confidence in his willingness to respect congressional prerogatives. But this faith was short-lived. When Johnson, who was far more sympathetic to the South than his predecessor, proved even more resistant than Lincoln to Congress's ambitious plans to remake the defeated Confederacy in the North's image, he was impeached and was saved from conviction by one solitary Senate vote. Johnson survived, but neither he nor his successors were able to restore strength to the presidency.

The Height of Congressional Government

The zenith of congressional power followed from a combination of Republican party rule and the growing strength of party organizations over legislative campaigns and policy making. In Chapter 11, we discuss how the Whigs were replaced by the Republicans as the major opposition party to the Democrats. Republicans became the dominant party in the aftermath of the Civil War. Since most Republicans were former Whigs, they stood for legislative supremacy. Before the rise of the primary system and mass media in the twentieth century, parties controlled nominations of candidates for office as well as the general election contests. This party influence extended to Congress as party leaders – the Speaker of the House and the majority leader of the Senate (although the position of Senate Majority Leader was not formally designated until 1920 [Democrats] and 1925 [Republicans]) – gained control over the committees, the real legislative policy-making bodies. Thus, Congress strengthened itself as an institution and moderated the scuffle of local interests to which it was prone. Party dominance over Congress reached its peak late in the nineteenth century. President Benjamin Harrison, a Republican from Ohio who was elected in 1888, embraced the Republican commitment to legislative supremacy and served as a virtual figurehead during his one term in office.

Party Government

The Republican speaker during Harrison's tenure, Thomas B. Reed of Maine, greatly streamlined the House's chaotic proceedings. Unlike previous celebrated legislators such as Adams, Clay, Webster, and Calhoun, Reed was about process, not substance. He defined a statesman as "a politician who is dead," and he displayed a wit and cynicism that animated a ruthless disregard for obstruction or delay of House business.

House rules required that a majority of members, a *quorum*, be present in order for the House to meet. In an effort to thwart Reed's authority, the minority Democrats sat mute during attendance call, preventing a quorum. Reed counted them present anyway. The Democrats, and even a few Republicans, protested Reed's disregard of members' rights. Nonetheless, he convinced the majority to change the rules so as to give him power to count a quorum and, as head of the *Rules Committee* (see Box 1 on how a bill becomes a law), to determine when and how a bill would be considered. In 1891, the Supreme Court sanctioned the transformation of the House into a more disciplined legislative body by upholding the constitutionality of these and other "Reed rules" aimed at controlling members' behavior.

The Democrats opposed the increase in discipline, contending that the Constitution intended Congress to be a body of individuals representing various localities. Reed countered that "a majority under the Constitution was entitled to legislate, and that, if a contrary practice has grown up, such practice is unrepublican, undemocratic, against sound policy, and contrary to the Constitution." He was expressing the Jacksonian principle that political parties were a critical agent of popular rule and that grassroots party control of Congress upheld the democratic character of American republican government. Before becoming speaker, Reed had written in a national magazine, "Our government is founded on the doctrine that if one hundred citizens think one way and one hundred and one think the other, the one hundred one are right." His view risked an uncompromising majoritarianism that threatened those rights upheld by America's liberal tradition. Democrats suggested as much by nicknaming him "Czar" Reed.

Democrats used Reed's "tyrannical" rules as a major campaign theme in the 1890 congressional elections. After the Democrats won an overwhelming victory, the new Democratic majority in the House repealed most of Reed's rules. But Reed, now in the minority, launched a retaliatory campaign of obstruction designed to persuade Democrats to acknowledge that his procedural innovations had been necessary to allow the House to function. Although many Democrats remained unhappy with the quorum rule and other procedures that centralized power in the House, they eventually surrendered to Reed's obstructionist tactics. As the political scientist Eric Schickler has written, "Reed's own advocacy of reform – while in the minority as well as the majority – contributed to the slowly emerging consensus that majority rule would benefit all members." A similar joining of partisan and institutional interests led to another major institutional development: the House Rules Committee acquired power to police the legislative agenda. By the end of the nineteenth century, the House was a highly centralized institution, dominated by a powerful speaker who could restrict obstructionist tactics on the floor, control committee assignments, and, through the Rules Committee, exercise influence over the legislative agenda.

The Senate tolerated far more independence. Its party leaders were less likely to remove a committee member for disloyalty. The Senate rules allowed "legislative holdups" by which a member could prevent a bill from coming to the floor for full debate. Also, individual senators could *fili-buster*, which means to talk a bill to death. As a result, Senate debate was unlimited until 1917. At that time, at the suggestion of President Woodrow Wilson, the Senate adopted a rule (Rule XXII) that allowed the Senate to end a debate with a two-thirds majority vote – a motion known as *cloture*. Even then, if those senators who wanted to prolong debate had the votes to defeat a cloture motion, they could prolong debate until the bill's supporters agreed to stop seeking cloture. But the Senate of the late nineteenth century had become far less tolerant of unrestricted debate. The Senate still lacked a single leader analogous to the speaker who could take primary responsibility for controlling legislative issues and how they were managed. During Harrison's presidency, however, Finance Committee chairman Nelson Aldrich (R-RI) and other influential Republican senators imposed controls on the Senate that resembled those that Czar Reed had established in the House, controls that created a previously unknown degree of partisan and procedural discipline in the Senate.

Although party control was justified on the basis of majority rule, critics charged that it worked against the interests of the many. The close identification of the Republican party with business made the Congress vulnerable to control by the great corporations that were coming to dominate American politics in the late nineteenth century. The protective tariff became the party's signature policy (see Chapter 6). Laws such as the McKinley Tariff of 1890 strengthened the Republican party's business connections. The identification with business would later become a liability, but during the prosperous times of the late nineteenth century, it was politically advantageous. Congress, under the tight grip of party leadership, did not engage in vital debate over industrial capitalism as it had over slavery. Party organization existed to pass legislation, not discuss it.

The Emergence of Congressional Professionalism

The party model of congressional government soon became obsolete. Acquisition of the Philippines and greater influence over Cuba, brought about by victory in the Spanish-American War in 1898, broadened America's international obligations and muted partisan differences. William McKinley, a former member of the House elected president in 1896, noted how the emergence of the United States as a world power freed the president from collective party responsibility: "I can no longer be called the President of a party; I am now the President of the whole people." Greater attention to foreign affairs expanded executive discretion and diminished the role of lawmaking. In Chapter 8, we examine additional sources of the rise of presidential power and popularity in the early twentieth century, particularly the impact of Progressivism. Through these combined factors, the presidency threatened to displace Congress as the principal agent of popular rule.

Congress's reaction to this executive challenge gave rise to changes that would define legislative politics and governance for most of the twentieth century. It transformed Congress's organization and practices to make legislators policy specialists. Party organization gave way to narrowly focused autonomous committees, which enabled representatives to acquire expertise in programs that served their ambition. They made Congress their career as they functioned as "policy entrepreneurs," that is, formulators and stewards of new policies and programs for their constituencies and for the organized interests with whom they were allied. These changes improved Congress's ability to oversee the activities of the executive branch and to serve local districts and states. But they sapped its vitality as a representative institution capable of forging consensus among the nation's diverse voices. Table 7.2 provides a list of current house and senate committees.

Making a career in Congress also required legislators to have more control over their personal electoral fortunes. Therefore, they supported progressive reforms such as the direct primary, which replaced partisan campaigns with candidate-centered campaigns (see Chapters 11 and 12). They also sought changes in the power structure of Congress to better enable them to influence public policy in ways that would serve their districts and states and thus enhance their prospects for reelection.

A Revolution in the House

The attack on congressional party leadership began in 1910 with a revolt against third-term Speaker of the House Joseph Cannon (R-IL). A disciple of Czar Reed, "Uncle Joe" Cannon managed the House with an iron fist. Cannon was a standpat Republican, meaning that he resisted popular economic and political reforms. His commitment to the protective tariff was particularly unyielding. Like Henry Clay, Cannon made his will prevail over a weak president. He resisted President William Howard Taft's tariff reduction efforts and pushed the Paine-Aldrich tariff, which raised rates on many items, through the House in 1910. But unlike Clay's command during Madison's occupation of the executive mansion, Cannon's dominance of Taft incited a rebellion that stripped the office of much of its influence.

The Progressive Era, discussed in Chapter 4, resulted in a widespread rebellion against the dominant influence that parties exercised over American political institutions. Parties in Congress, Progressives claimed, served

Table 7.2. Congressional Committees

HOUSE
  Agriculture
  Appropriations
  Armed Services
  Budget
  Education and Labor
  Energy and Commerce
  Financial Services
  Foreign Affairs
  Homeland Security
  House Administration
  Judiciary
  National Resources
  Oversight and Government Reform
  Rules
  Science and Technology
  Small Business
  Standards of Official Conduct
  Transportation and Infrastructure
  Veterans' Affairs
  Ways and Means
  House Permanent Select Committee on Intelligence

SENATE
  Standing:
    Agriculture, Nutrition, and Forestry
    Appropriations
    Armed Services
    Banking, Housing, and Urban Affairs
    Budget
    Commerce, Science, and Transportation
    Energy and Natural Resources
    Environment and Public Works
    Finance
    Foreign Relations
    Health, Education, Labor, and Pensions
    Homeland Security and Governmental Affairs
    Judiciary
    Rules and Administration
    Small Business and Entrepreneurship
    Veterans' Affairs
  Special, Select, and Other:
    Indian Affairs
    Select Committee on Ethics
    Select Committee on Intelligence
    Select Committee on Aging

JOINT HOUSE AND SENATE
  Joint Economic Committee
  Joint Committee on Printing
  Joint Committee on Taxation
  Joint Committee on the Library

---

parochial interests, rather than the public interest, and thus thwarted the emergence of a national democracy that could respond effectively to the domestic and international challenges of the modern era. Of these challenges, the power of large corporations, the "Trusts," over politics and government loomed largest. In the wake of the passage of the Paine-Aldrich tariff, Progressive Republicans joined with Democrats to transform the rules of the House. Before the insurgency, the speaker controlled committee appointments to such an extent that he was able to dismiss three insurgent Republican committee chairmen simply because they favored tariff reduction. The revolt stripped the speaker of all major duties except the constitutional rule of presiding officer. He lost much of his ability to dictate how business was conducted in the House, including his power to appoint committee chairs and to control the Rules Committee. Cannon remained speaker. As the militant Progressive George Norris (R-NE) insisted, "We are not making a fight against the man" but "we have done a great deal toward bringing back to the members of the House of Representatives control of that body."

Senate Reform

The Progressive revolt spread rapidly to the Senate, where it was even more ambitious. Protected by six-year terms and indirect election, senators were more insulated from public opinion and, according to reformers, more beholden to big business. This sentiment was fueled by the muckrakers, Progressive journalists who exposed the Senate's inner workings. Particularly damaging was "The Treason of the Senate," a 1906 seven-part exposé in *Cosmopolitan* magazine written by David Graham Phillips. The articles depicted a political machine doing the bidding of the trusts.

Portraits of the "most outstanding" former senators, including Webster, Clay, and Calhoun, hang in the Senate chamber reception room. Significantly, the only Progressive Era senator whose portrait hangs there is Robert La Follette, Sr., (R-WI). His nineteen-year reign as leader of the Senate's insurgent forces began when he was elected in 1906. He was so despised by the leadership that he was denied the minimal courtesies extended to a freshman senator. Instead of being granted a seat on the Committee on Interstate Commerce, a fine vantage point for taking on the railroads, which reformers viewed as the most egregious of the Trusts, La Follette was appointed chair of the Committee to Investigate the Condition of the Potomac River Front. This powerless committee never had a bill referred to it or even held a meeting.

But this effort to humiliate La Follette backfired. With the help of the press, he took his case to the people and aroused popular opposition to corporate power and the Senate leadership that served it. Breaking the unwritten rule that a freshman should be seen but not heard, he launched his reform crusade with a speech supporting the Hepburn bill, a measure to control unfair railroad pricing practices. Protesting his audacity, a large body of senators arose as he began to speak and left the chamber. In the face of this "polite form of hazing," La Follette broke off from his prepared text to proclaim,

> I cannot be wholly indifferent to the fact that Senators by their absence at this time indicate their want of interest in what I may have to say on this subject. The public is interested. Unless this important subject [of railroad abuses] is rightly settled, seats now temporarily vacated may be permanently vacated by those who have the right to occupy them at this time.

Applause from the members of the public seated in the galleries followed La Follette's outburst, causing the presiding officer to threaten to have the galleries cleared.

Between Senate sessions, La Follette appealed directly to the American people in speeches across the nation. Only President Theodore Roosevelt, who also stumped for the Hepburn bill (see Chapter 8), played a more important part in mobilizing support for it. The bill was enacted despite the efforts of Senate leaders to kill it.

La Follette's successful insurgency signaled the emergence of a new kind of senator, one who stood apart, who resolutely attacked parties and private interests, who was celebrated by the press. La Follette's celebrity contributed not only to economic reform but also to the downfall of the most powerful Republican senator, Nelson Aldrich, who like Speaker Cannon was deprived of legislative control by a coalition of Progressive Republicans and Democrats. After Aldrich's retirement from the Senate in 1911, both parties named party floor leaders for the first time. But the party leaders lacked the ability to defeat minority obstruction or to hold the committee system accountable to a common party agenda. Box 3 shows how Senate insurgents continue to influence modern congressional public policy making.

Box Three: Contemporary Politics

The Role of Senate Insurgents

Since Senator Bob LaFollette, congressional policy making has been punctuated by successful acts of insurgency. In the late 1940s and 1950s, both parties in Congress sought to avoid confrontation over civil rights. This reluctance was most pronounced among the Democrats, who controlled all the Southern congressional delegations. A young Democratic senator from Minnesota, Hubert Humphrey, refused to abide by this bipartisan consensus. On the Senate floor, on radio and television, and on lecture tours around the nation, he echoed the earlier cries of the abolitionists railing against the injustices of racial segregation. His efforts, as well as those of a small band of other senators who rallied around him, made it increasingly embarrassing for Congress to avoid the civil rights issue.

In the mid-1960s, another band of Democratic insurgents – including George McGovern of South Dakota, Frank Church of Idaho, and Eugene McCarthy of Minnesota – broke with Democratic president Lyndon Johnson and Democratic leaders in Congress to protest the war in Vietnam. These insurgents played a leading role in legitimizing opposition to the war.

Insurgency is not restricted to Democrats. Despite strong opposition from congressional Republican leaders, John McCain (R-AZ) established himself as the national spokesman for campaign finance reform. Like Senator McCarthy had done in 1968, McCain mobilized popular support for his cause by running for president in 2000. The great popular success of this insurgent campaign prodded a reluctant Congress to pass campaign finance reform in 2002 and an even more reluctant Republican president, George W. Bush, to sign it into law.

The Progressive attack also aroused public sentiment for the direct election of senators. Enacted in 1913, the Seventeenth Amendment provided that senators be elected by voters, not state legislatures. This change further undermined *party discipline* because candidates now had to depend on their own electioneering ability rather than party control of state legislatures.

The Emergence of Committee Government

After the downfall of Cannon and Aldrich, and continuing well into the twentieth century, committees dominated Congress, shaping policy and overseeing the expanding executive branch. They held hearings and wrote legislation in the privacy of their chambers. Their chairs were virtually legislative barons, controlling committee agendas, hiring staff, and scheduling hearings. Party strength remained important because it determined the relative number of Democrats and Republicans on each committee and whether the senior Democrat or Republican would be chair. For example, when Senator Jeffords quit the Republicans, committee chairs and membership majorities shifted to the Democrats. But party leaders did not choose chairs. Instead, a seniority system allocated leadership positions and committee assignments based on length of congressional service.

The seniority system remained in place until 1974. It enabled members of Congress to plan long careers on a particular committee without fear of being removed by party leaders. Individual members, no longer subject to collective partisan responsibility, became policy makers in their own right. They used this influence to benefit constituents, thereby improving their reelection prospects. Thus, committee government reduced the number of competitive districts, and turnover of both House and Senate seats declined.

Committee government made Congress a less representative institution. In the party-dominated system, members of Congress could be disciplined by party leaders and lose cherished committee assignments. The new seniority system ensured that committee chairs would remain in office even if they thwarted congressional majorities, held meetings in secret, and denied access to dissenting groups. Therefore, the task of popular representation fell increasingly to the president, who, as Chapter 8 describes, was becoming more closely tied to public opinion even as Congress became more insulated. The two branches traded constitutional roles. The people looked to the president for democratic innovation, whereas the House and Senate applied restraint.

This institutional reversal profoundly altered the legislative process. Traditionally, legislation had been formulated in consultation with, if not in deference to, congressional party leaders and had been drafted by legislative staff. However, during the early frantic days of Franklin D. Roosevelt's presidency in 1933, the so-called Hundred Days, Congress frequently received its legislation already drawn up by the White House staff, and the legislation was usually passed without substantial change. This willingness to apply a rubber stamp to presidential initiatives was short-lived; indeed, after 1937, a coalition of conservative Southern Democrats and Republicans took effective control of the Rules Committee and several important legislative committees. But the fragmented congressional system could not fully meet the challenge posed by the rise of a dynamic progressive presidency. The modern executive now became the dominant force in lawmaking. This change undermined the very principle of the rule of law: the idea that government was based on a settled, standing body of law. Increasingly, laws became vague blueprints that delegated broad discretionary policy-making power to the president and administrative agencies. Especially in foreign affairs, policy was frequently made through executive orders and administrative rules without the guidance of law.

The primary responsibility for Congress in this revised constitutional order was to oversee administration of public policy. It used committee hearings, investigations, and individual member or staff interrogations to try to hold the executive accountable. Individual legislators developed policy expertise to match the bureaucrats who staffed the burgeoning executive branch. Committee organization mirrored that of departments and agencies. Thus, for example, the Senate Foreign Relations Committee oversaw the State Department; the Labor and Human Resources Committee oversaw the Department of Health and Human Services.

This shift toward *oversight* brought with it a new set of constitutional difficulties. In the late 1940s and early 1950s the most publicized and controversial use of congressional investigations was for the purpose of uncovering domestic subversion. In the late 1940s, as the power of the Soviet Union grew, Americans began to worry about threats to national security posed by communist espionage. Several different members of the House and Senate made use of their leadership positions on committees or subcommittees to launch investigations into domestic communist subversion. The most prominent of these investigators was Senator Joseph McCarthy (R-WI). His inquisitorial methods and blatant disregard for the civil liberties of the subjects of his investigations became so notorious that the term McCarthyism entered the language as a synonym for unfair and obnoxious intrusion into the private lives and political views of citizens. Despite his highly publicized and extensive investigations, McCarthy unearthed few if any serious instances of security breaches. Such breaches did occur and spies were caught and convicted, but not by McCarthy or by his committee's most influential House counterpart, the House Committee on Un-American Activities.

The witch hunt wilted by overreaching itself. Beginning in April of 1954, Senator McCarthy's Subcommittee on Investigations of the Committee on Government Operations began televised hearings on charges of communist subversion in the U.S. Army. Such sustained exposure to McCarthy's bullying tactics, rude behavior, and the weakness of his evidence eroded popular support. A critical moment in McCarthy's political demise occurred when he implied that a young lawyer named Fred Fischer who worked for the law firm of the Army's special counsel, Robert Welch, had communist leanings. Welch replied: "Until this moment, Senator, I think I never gauged your cruelty or recklessness. . . . Have you no sense of decency, sir?" Welch's calm and measured response to McCarthy's brutalities struck a responsive chord. The audience in the gallery burst into applause. McCarthy's day as a popular leader was done. McCarthy's ignominious political demise served as a salutary cautionary tale. His successors have only rarely wielded congressional investigatory power in ways that threaten civil liberties.

The Growth of Committee Staff

The 1946 Legislative Reorganization Act codified and rationalized congressional oversight. It reduced the number of committees and subcommittees and clarified their *jurisdictions*. It made Congress's oversight responsibility explicit and called on it to engage in "continual watchfulness" over the activities of administrative agencies. It provided individual representatives and committees with large staffs, which enhanced Congress's capacity to oversee the bureaucracy. Committee staff grew from 103 in 1891 (forty-one in the Senate and sixty-two in the House) to 483 in 1947 (290 in the House and 193 in the Senate). As of 2006, committee staff exceeded 2000. The total staff of Congress is more than 17,000 persons. An additional approximately 4000 people work for the three congressional support agencies: the General Accounting Office, the Congressional Research Office, and the Congressional Budget Office. As congressional staff continued to expand in the post–World War II era, staff members came to perform a variety of crucial roles. The greatest prestige went to committee, and later subcommittee, staff. They were, and still are, policy specialists. But even they cannot master all the issues that come before their committee, so they reach out to experts from universities, think tanks, and lobbying organizations. The staff's job is largely to synthesize those expert opinions in a manner that makes them comprehensible to the members. Once a subcommittee reaches agreement on specific issues, its staffers produce a draft that is sent up to the full committee. Committee staff perform similar tasks for the committee as a whole and also become involved in negotiating with the staffs of other committees, particularly the Rules Committee, to resolve issues of jurisdiction and scheduling.

Members of Congress also acquired large personal staffs to run their congressional offices in Washington and in their districts. Some staffers were and are primarily involved in legislative matters, keeping an eye on issues of special concern to their boss. Others perform *constituency service*: tracking down lost Social Security checks, coping with immigration problems, and solving other federal bureaucratic snafus. Still others are engaged in more overtly political endeavors, keeping tabs on political developments in the district, providing their bosses with vital political intelligence, mending fences with their supporters, and trying to keep potential rivals off balance.

An Institution in Crisis

Committee government endured not because it enabled Congress to hold the executive accountable or to represent constituents effectively but because it met the political needs of careerist legislators. Members of Congress provided themselves with more institutional power and staff support to initiate individual legislative proposals and scrutinize particular executive actions. But having ceded party leadership to the president, Congress could not pursue a comprehensive program of its own. It delegated much of its constitutional responsibility to make laws to the executive. And despite staff improvement, it still could not adequately perform its oversight responsibilities. Nor could it contend with the president in policy debate and policy making. To the media and public, Congress appeared to be a decrepit feudal institution ruled by defiant committee barons. Because of the seniority rule, these barons often hailed from the least competitive, most insulated parts of the country, disconnecting them from national political trends.

Some committee chairs did have an important influence on public policy during this period. For example, Congressman Wilbur Mills, a Democrat from Arkansas, used his position as head of the Ways and Means Committee from 1958 to 1974 to become one of the most powerful men in the capital. Taxation was one policy that Congress refused to delegate to the executive branch, and the Ways and Means Committee, which had jurisdiction not only over fiscal policy but also Social Security and the national debt ceiling, became a highly prestigious legislative body after the Second World War. Although a conservative Southern Democrat, Mills did not use his position as head of an important committee to obstruct the development of the New Deal welfare state. Fiscally conservative Democrats like Mills reluctantly accepted middle-class entitlements such as Social Security and Medicare that enabled them to distribute generous benefits to constituents. Otherwise, they used their power of the purse to restrain the long-term growth of government. By supporting middle-class entitlements, while fighting for balanced budgets and low taxation, Mills played a critical part in sustaining a fiscally responsible welfare state. As the historian Julian Zelizer has argued, he helped to maintain the presence of a federal government that was compatible with "the nation's anti-statist, individualist, and fiscal values."

Most members of Congress, however, were less inclined to uphold a larger policy agenda – or to protect the legislature's constitutional prerogatives. Under the rule of committee government, individual members emphasized constituency service in overseeing the executive branch; they manipulated bureaucratic power and exploited programs to serve their own districts and states. Little wonder that Thomas "Tip" O'Neill, the powerful Massachusetts Democrat who became speaker in the 1980s, could declare, even as the national government grew, "All politics is local."

Going Along to Get Along

Before he became president, Lyndon Baines Johnson (LBJ) served as Senate majority leader from 1953 to 1960. He and his fellow Texan and Democrat Sam Rayburn were perhaps the two most important congressional leaders of the committee government era. Rayburn served as Democratic leader from 1940 to 1961, all but four of those years as speaker; only Henry Clay enjoyed a longer reign. But LBJ and Rayburn did not dominate their institutions as Cannon and Aldrich had once done. LBJ and Rayburn wielded influence through accommodation and compromise. Positioned between the entrenched power structure of committee government and the dominant presence of the modern presidency, Rayburn and LBJ were saddled with the important but subordinate task of steering the White House's program through a resistant, sometimes indifferent Congress.

The two Texans maintained this accommodating approach even when a president of the opposite party was in power. During Republican Dwight Eisenhower's two terms (1953–1961), they worked to pass his program so long as it did not attempt to dismantle the core programs of the New Deal. The Texans, given their limited power over committee chairs, were comfortable with Eisenhower, whose moderate approach accommodated the dominantly conservative, Southern, congressional power structure. Rayburn's advice to freshmen representatives – "You got to go along to get along" – summed up his and LBJ's relationship to the White House and the committee chairs. This strategy gained LBJ sufficient national prominence to be tapped by John F. Kennedy to run for vice president in 1960.

The Rules Committee Fight

Congress's posture of accommodation and subordination to the president did not extend to issues of civil rights. By 1961, the courageous efforts of African Americans in the South had brought national and international attention to the continuing racial segregation of restaurants, hotels, mass transit, and employment, and yet Congress had taken only very mild action to alter the situation. President Kennedy and northern pro–civil rights members of the House and Senate were in sympathy with the cause of civil rights, but they were also aware of the tremendous obstacle to passage of civil rights legislation posed by a conservative coalition of Southern Democrats and Republicans and by that coalition's control of the Rules Committee, the "traffic cop of the House." The chair of the committee, Howard Smith (D-VA), was one of the most powerful reactionary House barons. Under his leadership, the Rules Committee could frustrate the will of a congressional majority by blocking House debate of any legislation that the majority favored.

In the previous Congress, the Rules Committee had eight Democrats and four Republicans. But two of the Democrats were Southern conservatives who joined the Republicans to block reform legislation. Rayburn proposed adding three new members, two of them Kennedy loyalists, to the committee, which provided an eight-to-seven anti-Smith majority. Rayburn's proposal passed by the narrow margin of 217 to 212. It failed to gain the support of sixty-four Southern Democrats; Rayburn was saved by twenty-two Northeastern Republicans.

This last and greatest battle of Rayburn's (he died of cancer eight months later) was not an attempt to strengthen the party leadership in the House; in fact, it further dispersed power. His major concern was to give the new Democratic president an opportunity to move his program through Congress. As we point out in the next chapter, Rayburn's victory would ultimately benefit his protégé, LBJ, who became president in November 1963 following Kennedy's assassination. Without the weakening of the Rules Committee, Congress might not have enacted LBJ's civil rights and antipoverty programs.

Box Four: Contemporary Politics

Congressional Redistricting and the African-American Vote

Although the House of Representatives has many African-American members, almost none of them come from white majority districts. All senators are elected by non-African-American majorities because no state has an African-American majority. Only three African

Americans have been elected to the Senate since World War II; currently, only one serves in the Senate (see Table 7.3). This evidence would seem to show that that non-African Americans are reluctant to vote for African Americans for Congress. But the evidence is not conclusive. Republican African Americans, most prominently J. C. Watts of Oklahoma, have been elected to Congress from white majority districts. It could be argued that Republicans have been more successful at getting minority members elected in white majority districts because Republican candidates are more conservative and are able to appeal to white voters on that basis. In this view, it is not racism that prevents African Americans from winning congressional elections but rather the political liberalism of the vast majority of African-American congressional office seekers.

Regardless of the cause, the effect of these voting patterns has been that with rare exceptions African Americans win congressional office only when districts are drawn to ensure a heavy African-American voting majority. This result has caused unexpected political tensions, and coalitions have formed around the issue of the racial composition of congressional districts. On the one hand, white Democratic members of Congress value a sizable African-American voting bloc in their district because such voters will reliably support them over their Republican challengers. On the other hand, African-American members of Congress do not want to see the percentage of African-American voters in their districts decline for fear that the remaining bloc will not be sizable enough for them to be reelected. Republican representatives and would-be representatives are eager to concentrate African-American voters, so that the remaining districts will have few such voters and therefore will be easier for the Republicans to win. Consequently, the Republican party has often sided with African-American Democratic representatives and political organizations to oppose dilution of African-American voters, whereas white Democrats have favored it.

Table 7.3. Blacks in Congress, 1971–2006

Congress	Senate	House
110th (2007–)	1	42
109th (2005–2007)	1	42
108th (2003–2005)	1	39
107th (2001–2003)	0	37

Table 7.3. (continued)

Congress	Senate	House
106th (1999–2001)	0	39
105th (1997–1999)	1	37
104th (1995–1997)	1	38
103rd (1993–1995)	1	38
102nd (1991–1993)	0	26
101st (1989–1991)	0	24
100th (1987–1989)	0	23
99th (1985–1987)	0	20
98th (1983–1985)	0	21
97th (1981–1983)	0	17
96th (1979–1981)	0	16
95th (1977–1979)	1	16
94th (1975–1977)	1	15
93rd (1973–1975)	1	15
92nd (1971–1973)	1	12

The Resurgence of Congress

Starting in the early 1970s, the relationship between the president and Congress began to change in response to two constitutional crises provoked by the effort to contain communism. Americans had fought two major wars – in Korea (1950 to 1953) and Vietnam (1955 to 1975) – without congressional authorization, even though the Constitution grants Congress, not the president, the power to declare war. For the war in Korea, authorization was sidestepped because President Harry Truman successfully claimed that military action against North Korea was a "police action" mandated by the United Nations, not a "war" as the Constitution understood that term. For the war in Vietnam, LBJ relied on the Gulf of Tonkin Resolution, which Congress passed in 1964 in response to an alleged North Vietnamese attack on U.S. naval vessels. The resolution was not a declaration of war as such, but it authorized the president "to take all necessary measures to repel any armed attack against the forces of the United States and to prevent further aggression." Careful readers will notice that U.S. military involvement in Vietnam predated the resolution by nine years.

The failure of the United States to achieve "peace with honor" in Vietnam, discussed in more detail in Chapter 8, fostered not only public cynicism about the merits of presidential policies but also a greater inclination by the press to challenge the wisdom and veracity of presidential statements and proposals. Even champions of a strong presidency became concerned about presidential imperialism and more appreciative of Congress's constitutional responsibility to represent public views and to refine and imbed them in settled, standing law.

Republican Richard Nixon won the presidency in 1968 largely because the electorate was frustrated by the Democrats' inability to reduce racial tension and end the war in Vietnam, but he did not receive a decisive mandate to govern. Nixon was the first new president since Zachary Taylor in 1848 to be elected without a party majority in either house of Congress. Nonetheless, he unilaterally extended the Vietnam War and bombed Cambodia, provoking congressional outrage.

This anger was increased by Nixon's sweeping application of the executive's traditional right to impound – that is, refuse to spend – funds appropriated by Congress. Presidential impoundments were traditionally exercised for reasons of economy and efficiency, but Nixon's were an attempt to undermine the legislative process. Congress had appropriated funds to the Office of Economic Opportunity (OEO), the agency that was responsible for leading the war on poverty and that was a symbol of LBJ's Great Society (see Chapter 8). Expressing his determination to challenge Congress for the right to govern, Nixon impounded the money and ordered the acting OEO director to dismantle the agency.

Nixon found to his regret that he could not remake the federal government on his own. In fact, the modern presidency never was imperial. Its power depended on Congress's willingness to delegate domestic and foreign policy authority. Even before Nixon's Watergate scandal, the president and Congress were poised for a constitutional struggle. Indeed, Congress's willingness to remove Nixon in 1974 was in no small part a response to his repeated efforts to circumvent the legislative process.

Watergate

The Constitution enables Congress to impeach members of the other two branches, but neither the executive nor the judiciary may impeach a member of Congress. The power to impeach has seldom been exercised; nonetheless, it has had great political significance. Like the impeachment of Andrew Johnson, the near impeachment of Richard Nixon (only his resignation saved him from this unhappy fate) in response to the Watergate scandal accelerated a resurgence of congressional influence. Congress's showdown with Nixon encouraged it to reassert its independence and to carry out internal reforms that would equip it to act aggressively.

The Watergate scandal was named for the building that housed the Democratic National Committee headquarters, which was broken into by operatives of the Republican Committee to Re-Elect the President during the 1972 presidential campaign. The key issue was whether Nixon knew about the break-in and had tried to cover up his connection to it. The popular film *All the President's Men* gave the mistaken impression that a newspaper, the *Washington Post*, brought about Nixon's downfall. In truth, the Senate Select Committee on Presidential Campaign Activities, known as the Watergate Committee, did so by ordering Nixon to hand over tapes that he had made of his Oval Office conversations and suing him when he refused to do so.

Nixon claimed *executive privilege*, a president's right to withhold information from Congress. Committee chairman Senator Sam Ervin (D-NC) countered that executive privilege could be defended under some circumstances, such as those dealing with national security, but could not be invoked when dealing with possible criminal activities. Stubbornly, Nixon claimed that "inseparably interspersed in the tapes are a great many very frank and very private comments wholly extraneous to the committee's inquiry."

Partisanship gave way to institutional loyalty as even Nixon's staunchest congressional defenders demanded that Nixon produce the tapes. Senator Howard Baker (R-TN), committee vice chairman, who had long been a friend and advisor to the president, contended that the tapes contained material "essential if not vital, to the full inquiry mandated and required by this committee." Baker's and Ervin's engagingly telegenic presences did much to reassure the nation that the confrontation between the president and Congress could be resolved through regular constitutional procedures. Ervin's country-lawyer image and his passionate but calm invocations of the separation of powers made him a folk hero. His judicious committee leadership served to remind the American people of Congress's critical constitutional responsibility to hold the president accountable.

On July 24, 1974, in *U.S. v. Nixon*, the Supreme Court unanimously ruled against the president. Chief Justice Warren Burger, a Nixon appointee, stated that "to read the Article II powers of the President as providing an absolute privilege against a subpoena essential to enforcement of criminal statutes...would upset the constitutional balance of a 'workable government'...and cut deeply into the guarantee of due process of law."

On the heels of the court's decision, the House Judiciary Committee voted to impeach Nixon on August 4, 1974. His chances of surviving a Senate trial suffered when he admitted that the tapes did implicate him in the Watergate cover-up. Also, a gap was discovered in one of the tapes during what appeared to be a crucial conversation about the break-in between Nixon and key aides. Even Nixon's Republican supporters on the Judiciary Committee conceded that the president had virtually confessed to obstruction of justice. On August 8, 1974, Nixon announced to the nation his decision to resign, becoming the first president forced from office. Whatever the president's actual guilt, the public was left with the impression that he had been involved in something foul, and the scandal further jeopardized confidence in the integrity of the office.

Asked in 1959 whether the president or Congress should have "the most say in government," a representative sample of Americans favored the president 61 percent to 17 percent. Watergate shattered that virtual consensus. A similar survey in 1977 showed that 58 percent of Americans believed Congress should have the most say; only 26 percent supported presidential primacy. For the first time since the heady days of Czar Reed and Nelson Aldrich, Congress seemed poised to assume its place as the primary representative institution.

The Watergate scandal provoked Congress to pass a multitude of laws curbing the president's powers, including the Congressional Budget and Impoundment Control Act of 1974, which required the president to obtain Congress's approval before impounding any funds. The act also created budget committees in both houses to coordinate and strengthen legislative involvement in fiscal policy making, and it established the *Congressional Budget Office* to provide Congress with the same level of fiscal expertise that the Office of Management and Budget provides the executive branch (see Chapter 8).

Congress also reasserted itself in foreign affairs. The 1972 Case Act reduced the president's ability to conduct personal diplomacy by requiring that all executive agreements, which are agreements made between heads of state, be reported to Congress. The War Powers Resolution, enacted over Nixon's veto in 1973, reestablished Congress's war powers by requiring the president to consult with Congress, when possible, before committing troops to combat and to submit a report to Congress within forty-eight hours after doing so. After sixty days, troops must be removed unless Congress votes to declare war or approve their continued deployment.

Congressional Reform

Also in the 1970s, Congress passed important procedural reforms to help reestablish itself as an equal governing partner. Both chambers took action to reduce the committee chairs' near dictatorial control over the legislative process. A coalition of liberal Democrats and junior members of both parties enacted the Legislative Reorganization Act of 1970, which required committees to adopt written rules and promoted open meetings. The most important provision of the act provided for recorded votes on floor amendments in the House. This prevented committee chairs from quietly killing amendments. Now that constituents would know how their representative voted on an amendment, committee chairs would no longer be inoculated from public pressure and floor assaults on their legislation.

The attack on the seniority system and the committee chairs it protected shifted power upward to party leaders and downward to subcommittees and individual members. The majority Democratic caucus in the House, in particular, was revitalized as conservative Southerners began to decline in number and liberals gained a clear majority in the party. The caucus enacted a "subcommittee bill of rights" in 1973 that removed from committee chairs the power to select subcommittee chairs and instead allowed that power to be shared by all Democratic members of each committee. Each member of a committee was also given the right to serve on at least one "choice" related subcommittee. Subcommittees were given fixed areas of responsibility, authorization to meet and hold their own hearings, and larger budgets and staffs. Subcommittees replaced committees as the "little legislatures" that dominated the work of Congress. More dramatic devolution occurred in the Senate. The Senate adopted a new staffing policy in 1975 that provided each senator on a committee with additional staff who were independent of the chairmen. In addition, the filibuster, which had been used rather rarely for much of American history, became a routine tool used by individual senators to influence or block entirely pending bills.

This reform movement came to fruition in 1975 with the arrival of the huge freshman class of seventy-four "Watergate babies," elected in the wake of Nixon's resignation. These reform-minded newcomers spearheaded successful efforts in both houses to ensure that chairs of committees would no longer be chosen on the basis of seniority but instead would be elected by secret ballot of the majority party caucus. They pressed the House Democratic caucus to remove three aging Southern committee chairs, the first "violation" of the seniority rule since 1920. Committee chairs were put on notice that "heads would roll" if they did not share power with their committee colleagues and become more responsive to party members. House Republicans also challenged seniority by providing for individual votes on the party's ranking committee members. Although no Senate chairmen or ranking committee members were deposed, the new rules, adopted by both Democrats and Republicans, served notice that chairmen were expected to be more responsive to party members.

Box Five: Nuts and Bolts

Legislative Hearings

One important responsibility of committees and subcommittees is to hold legislative hearings. A legislative hearing can serve a variety of purposes. It is often used as a vital part of legislative deliberation. Subcommittees and committees seeking to obtain a broad representation of public opinion about a bill they are drafting will invite representatives from among the interested parties to come and share their knowledge and opinions. Representatives from the executive branch and governors and mayors are often invited as well.

If the issue at stake is considered newsworthy, the hearing will be covered by the media, which provides an important opportunity to acquaint the mass public with the issue. Hearings vary considerably in terms of the degree to which they are stacked, that is, the diversity of opinions that are presented. Sometimes the subcommittee or committee majority will selectively invite groups who share its point of view and who are likely to make an impassioned case that the media will highlight. In those cases, hearings are really media events staged to increase public attention and support for positions already adopted by the committee or subcommittee majority.

Hearings are not always used for strictly legislative purposes. They can also be used to expose misdeeds and embarrass executive officials or leaders from the private sector or even to conduct witch hunts, as we describe in this chapter's discussion of the McCarthy hearings. In Box 1 in Chapter 6, we discuss the Enron scandal. Much of the specific information about that scandal was provided by congressional hearings at which many of the leading figures in the scandal testified. Congress does most of its work in committee. Hearings can draw well known personalities including other members of Congress, cabinet secretaries, academics, mayors, governors, and actors such as Michael J. Fox and Mary Tyler Moore.

Before his death in 2004, actor Christopher Reeve testified in favor of therapeutic human cloning for stem cell research at a hearing before the Senate Committee on Health, Education, Labor, and Pensions.

This legislative rebellion in the House and Senate was carried out by insurgents whose target was as much the president as it was their more stolid and conservative congressional adversaries. It resulted in a severe challenge to the modern president's preeminence in legislative and administrative matters. As political scientist R. Shep Melnick has written:

> Using subcommittee resources, members initiated new programs and revived old ones, challenging the president for the title of "chief legislator." No longer would Congress respond to calls for action by passing vague legislation telling the executive to do something. Now Congress was writing detailed statutes which not infrequently deviated from the president's program. Subcommittees were also using oversight hearings to make sure that administrators paid heed not just to the letter of legislation but to its spirit as well.

The new vitality that was created by subcommittee government is best illustrated by the outpouring of congressionally initiated environmental, consumer protection, worker safety, and civil rights laws that took place during the 1970s. These initiatives were not the sort of measures one would expect from the keystone of a conservative Washington establishment.

Greater party caucus influence in organizing the House and Senate did not return the speaker and Senate majority leader to the preeminence they lost during the Progressive insurgency, but the two positions did acquire more power to control the federal budget, make committee assignments, and control the flow of legislation. The new budgetary process, in particular, increased centralization in both the House and Senate. It gave the majority party dominant influence over the budget committees and enabled the speaker, in consultation with the Senate's president pro tempore, to appoint the director of the Congressional Budget Office. As Schickler has written, "perhaps the most enduring impact of the budget process is that it has provided a mechanism for even a slim majority in each chamber to enact sweeping changes in the nation's fiscal policy."

The Limits of Congressional Oversight

This reassertion of congressional strength did not fully restore constitutional checks and balances. Aggressive oversight of the executive during the 1970s and 1980s was less a challenge to administrative government than it was an intrusion into its details. Despite Congress's desire to exert greater control over administration, it could not escape the dilemma that the more complex a question is, the harder it is to write general rules to govern it and to anticipate all the practical circumstances that the rules will have to cope with. Even as Congress devoted more resources to investigations and oversight hearings, it increasingly wrote laws that delegated broad authority to executive agencies.

Consider the Clean Air Act, the law that regulates air pollution. As passed by Congress in 1970 and revised in 1977 and 1990, the act requires that standards be set establishing safe levels for different chemical air pollutants. But members of Congress had neither the time nor the expertise to determine what those standards should be, so they did not really try to do so. The law simply states that air quality standards should be set to protect the public health, providing an "adequate margin of safety." The actual responsibility for the difficult and complex decisions about what constitutes a safe level of a particular air pollutant is delegated to the Environmental Protection Agency, an arm of the executive branch.

Congress's legislative activity decreased during the 1970s and 1980s even as its staff apparatus grew dramatically. The total number of bills introduced in the legislature reached its peak in the 1967–1968 session with 22,000 House bills and 4400 Senate bills. In the 1980s, these numbers dropped to 7500 House bills and 3500 Senate bills. Yet professional staff (both committee and personal) increased from around 3000 employees in the House and Senate in 1976 to more than 11,000 in 1986; professional support staff, including the Congressional Research Service and the Congressional Budget Office, ballooned to nearly 30,000. The increase in staff encouraged specialization and hierarchy in the organization of Congress itself. As political scientist Theodore Lowi wrote, "Congress came to resemble the very executive branch it was trying to control." As it became more bureaucratic, Congress risked losing its connection to the people. Rather than disciplining the administrative state, Congress became ever more enmeshed in the administrative web.

Divided Government and Institutional Combat

Congress's involvement in administrative politics was embittered by partisan rancor. Partisanship was relatively weak during the New Deal political era, as each party contained a dissident wing – Southern Democrats and Northeastern Republicans – that could work harmoniously with the opposition. But in the wake of the conflict over issues such as civil rights and national security, the Democrats lost most of their conservative Southern support, resulting in a more unified and left-of-center party. At the same time, the Republican Party became the majority party in the South and lost considerable support in the Northeast, thus becoming more distinctively conservative. The election of Ronald Reagan to the presidency further clarified the differences between the parties on economic issues. Moreover, Reagan's bold challenge to the Soviet Union extended party polarization to national security issues. This partisan realignment tended to move congressional Democrats to the left and Republicans to the right. Liberal Republicans and conservative Democrats became increasingly restive. As political scientists James Ceaser and Andrew Busch have noted, Republican senator Jeffords's shift to being an Independent who caucused with the Democrats, and Georgia Democratic senator Zell Miller's blistering attack on his party's presidential candidate, Massachusetts senator John Kerry, at the 2004 Republican convention, "was a metaphor for the entire process."

From 1980 to 1992, Republicans held the presidency. Democrats controlled the House of Representatives, and from 1986 on, the Senate as well. This partisan divide greatly aggravated relations between the executive and the legislature. Republican efforts to enhance the unilateral powers of the executive and to circumvent legislative restrictions on presidential conduct were matched by Democratic initiatives to burden the executive with smothering oversight by congressional committees and statutory limits on presidential power.

The main forum for partisan conflict was a series of investigations in which the Democrats and Republicans sought to discredit one another. From the early 1970s to the mid-1980s, there was a tenfold increase in the number of indictments brought by federal prosecutors against national, state, and local officials, including more than a dozen members of Congress, several federal judges, and a number of high-ranking executive officials. Divided government encouraged, as the political scientist Morris Fiorina observed, "a full airing of any and all misdeeds, real and imagined."

This heightened legal scrutiny was partly a response to the Watergate scandal. In what became known as the "Saturday night massacre," Nixon fired special prosecutor Archibald Cox, who had been charged with investigating the scandal. To prevent future "massacres," Congress passed the 1978 Ethics in Government Act. It provided for the appointment of independent counsels to investigate allegations of criminal activity by executive officials. Not surprisingly, divided government encouraged the exploitation of the act for partisan purposes. In the 1980s, congressional Democrats were able to demand criminal investigations and possible jail sentences for their political opponents. When Bill Clinton became president in 1992, congressional Republicans turned the table with a vengeance. Political disagreements were readily transformed into criminal charges. Investigations under the special prosecutor statute tended to focus the attention of Congress and the public on scandal and away from legitimate constitutional and policy questions.

Congress's neglect of debate and lawmaking in favor of confrontation with the executive damaged its popular standing, which was further diminished by the role reversal that occurred between the president and Congress regarding "big government." From the 1930s through the 1960s, presidents, not Congress, had been most aggressive in pressing for government expansion. But during the 1970s and 1980s, presidents responded to growing public skepticism about the New Deal and Great Society programs by advocating cutbacks. Congress, however, resisted these efforts, defending not only popular middle-class entitlements such as Social Security but also unpopular welfare programs such as Aid to Families with Dependent Children (AFDC). Consequently, the rise in popular support for Congress that occurred in response to the Vietnam War and Watergate proved short-lived. By early 1975, surveys showed that a majority of Americans disapproved of the way Congress was "handling its job." This public disdain continued through the early days of the Clinton administration, and it peaked in October 1994, when 70 percent of Americans expressed discontent with Congress.

A New Congress

As we point out in Chapter 8, Bill Clinton won the 1992 presidential election because he presented himself as a "New Democrat," an "agent of change" who offered an alternative to both traditional Democratic liberalism and Republican conservatism. He promised a cease-fire in the institutional confrontations that had afflicted executive-congressional relations for more than two decades. But the major political struggle of his first term, the fight to reform healthcare, appeared to violate his pledge to find middle ground between those who championed and those who would dismantle the welfare state.

Clinton promised to challenge the traditional Democratic commitment to *entitlements*, government benefits that are provided as a matter of right, and to instill public programs with a new sense of personal responsibility. But his effort to simultaneously guarantee universal healthcare coverage and contain costs would have created a new entitlement program coupled with an expanded administrative apparatus of grotesque complexity, providing an easy political target for Republicans.

Despite Democratic control of the House and Senate in the 103rd Congress (1993–1994), the healthcare bill died when a compromise measure, negotiated between Senate Democratic leader George Mitchell of Maine and Republican senator John Chafee of Rhode Island, could not win enough Republican support to break a threatened filibuster. Traditionally, the filibuster had been employed by mavericks or regional minorities to obstruct party leaders. Southern Democrats, for example, had frequently resorted to the filibuster in order to kill civil rights legislation. By contrast, this filibuster was orchestrated by the Senate minority leader, Robert Dole (R-KS). The willingness of Republicans to block a major healthcare bill as well as other Clinton initiatives was a mark of the fundamental conflicts that divided the parties in Congress and prevented harmonious relations between the executive and legislature despite Clinton's promise to dampen such discord.

The president and his party paid dearly for these failures in the 1994 elections. The Republicans gained fifty-two House and eight Senate seats, which gave them control of both houses of Congress for the first time since 1954. This partisan shift appeared to confirm that the welfare state was facing a fundamental challenge to its principles and programs, one that had been evident at the presidential level since Nixon's election in 1968. Now, the last bastion of support for big government, the House of Representatives, seemed to give way.

During the 1994 campaign, the second-ranking House Republican, minority whip Newt Gingrich, persuaded more than 300 House candidates to sign a "Republican Contract with America" that promised to restore limited government by eliminating programs, lightening regulatory burdens, and cutting taxes. Although exit polls – surveys of voters after they voted – suggested that few voters had actually heard of the Republican manifesto, Clinton's attack on the contract during the campaign unwittingly served the Republican objective of turning the congressional elections into a national referendum on his presidency and the Democratic party. The president's assault backfired, serving only to abet Republicans in their effort to highlight his failure to transform the Democratic party and to mute partisan division in Washington.

Gingrich's assault on big government indicted Congress no less than Clinton. Even Republicans, Gingrich claimed, had become complicit, selling out their principles to gain government benefits for their constituents. His efforts were aided considerably by the House banking scandal that erupted in 1991 and 1992. Run like an internal credit union in which members' overdrafts were covered by other members' deposits, the House bank was loosely administered, enabling members to extend their credit by tens of thousands of dollars via interest-free loans. The public saw this scandal as further evidence that Congress had become a corrupt agent of big government and its members a privileged class. Speaker Thomas Foley (D-WA) defended the House and dismissed the banking scandal as an aberration. This defense was derided by Gingrich, who saw the scandal as proof that Congress, Republicans no less than Democrats, had been corrupted by the administrative state. Gingrich's attack resonated even with Foley's own constituents, who did not reelect him in 1994, making Foley the first speaker to lose reelection since the Civil War.

The new House Republican majority chose Gingrich to be speaker. Gingrich viewed Congress as part, perhaps the key part, of the corrupt Washington establishment. He set out to reform House rules, promising to restore its constitutional responsibility to foster democratic debate and resolution. The number and size of committees were reduced, as were their staffs. Term limits were imposed on the speaker and on committee and subcommittee chairs. Closed-door hearings and unrecorded votes were prohibited. Gingrich pledged a renewed emphasis on legislative debate that would "promote competition between different political philosophies." Yet the basic thrust of the GOP reforms was to centralize power in the hands of the party leadership. Party leaders strengthened their hold over committee chairmen, who in turn were empowered over subcommittee leaders. For the first time since Cannon was shorn of his powers, the Speaker of the House presumed to command the counsels of government, restoring Congress as the first branch of government. As Gingrich seized control of the legislative initiative during the early months of the 104th Congress, Clinton issued a plaintive reminder that "the President is relevant here."

The Renewal of Institutional Conflict

Although the new Republican majority promised to restore limited government and states' rights, it did not try to dismantle the national state. The Republican contract proposed to strengthen national defense in a form that would require the expansion rather than the rolling back of the central government's responsibilities. Moreover, the GOP's proposals to reduce entitlements for the poor – to reform the AFDC program – and to get government off the back of business demanded the creation of alternative national and welfare regulatory standards. For example, with respect to welfare reform, the Republican proposal called for national requirements to determine eligibility, to attack illegitimacy and teen pregnancy, and to establish work requirements. Finally, congressional Republicans were reluctant to challenge middle-class entitlements such as Social Security

Senator Joseph McCarthy's congressional hearings on communist infiltration into the American government, academia, and Hollywood seriously undermined the protection of civil liberties.

and Medicare, which dwarfed the programs that guaranteed a minimum standard of living to the destitute, thus making unlikely a serious examination of core assumptions of the welfare state. The Republicans tacitly acknowledged that, as FDR envisioned, security guarantees for the aged and sick had acquired quasi-constitutional status, making them immune from political attack.

Despite Gingrich's pledge, combat immediately broke out between the Democratic president and the Republican Congress. The House Republicans quickly revoked their curbs on administrative oversight and immersed themselves once again in the details of executive activity. And they provoked a fierce battle with the president over the budget. Republicans believed that their support of a constitutional amendment to balance the budget, as promised by the Contract with America, would enable them to control Congress for many years. But in the face of stiff resistance from Clinton, the proposed amendment died in the Senate, one vote short of the necessary two-thirds majority.

To recover from that defeat, congressional Republicans advanced a bold plan to balance the budget by 2002. Clinton rejected key specifics of the plan, especially an effort to scale back the growth of Medicare by encouraging beneficiaries to enroll in health maintenance organizations and other privately managed healthcare systems. To pressure Clinton into accepting their budget-cutting priorities, Congress refused to extend government borrowing privileges, thereby shutting down government offices and threatening to put the U.S. treasury into default.

These tactics backfired. Clinton's December 1995 veto of a sweeping budget bill that overhauled Medicare and revised decades of federal social policy roused popular support. Neither the Contract with America nor Speaker Gingrich's bravado had prepared the country for such a fundamental assault on the welfare state. In attacking Medicare and popular educational and environmental programs, Republicans went beyond their 1994 campaign promises. They, not Clinton, appeared to be the radicals in this budgetary brinkmanship. Clinton's triumph not only paved the way for his reelection victory a year later, it also marked the effective end of Gingrich's political dominance. The second session of the 104th Congress that convened in January 1996 was dominated by the president's modest proposals for incremental reform, not the speaker's agenda of reducing the role of Washington in society and the economy.

Impeachment

Gingrich's defeat in the budget battles of the 104th Congress can be attributed in part to his underestimation of the political advantages available to the president. As congressional scholar Ronald M. Peters, Jr., has said,

> A speaker can sometimes win a legislative standoff with a president, but he can rarely win a public-relations battle; otherwise, Uncle Joe Cannon would be enshrined on Mount Rushmore instead of Teddy Roosevelt. When Newt Gingrich underestimated Bill Clinton he underestimated the presidency itself.

Still, Gingrich, a former history professor, had reasons to believe he could win a standoff with the president. The magnitude of the Republican victory in 1994 elections seemed to require presidential concessions. Moreover, the presidency had been weakened since Watergate. Like the period after the Civil War, this period witnessed closely and bitterly divided parties, an aggressive Congress willing to impeach presidents, and public indifference, if not avowed hostility, toward the federal government. But Gingrich underestimated the extent to which the emergence of the United States as a superpower and the advent of mass media had strengthened the tie between the president and the people. Political parties are a critical ingredient of Congress's institutional strength. Gingrich rallied Congress for an attack on Clinton by asserting more partisan control. But the presidency had now gained a status above parties.

The most dramatic test of the president's political resiliency came in the impeachment episode. In early January 1998, Congress authorized independent counsel Kenneth Starr to expand the "Whitewater" inquiry to pursue allegations that the president had had an affair with White House intern Monica Lewinsky, and that he and his friend Vernon Jordan had encouraged her to lie about it under oath. The original inquiry, limited to Bill and Hillary Clinton's involvement in a real estate development in Arkansas called Whitewater, yielded no evidence of wrongdoing. But the extension of Starr's investigation to a sexual scandal led to the first impeachment of an elected president in U.S. history. Clinton not only denied the affair with Lewinsky but accused Starr, a prominent Republican, and his supporters in Congress of orchestrating a slanderous, partisan campaign to weaken the president.

Starr's relentless investigation uncovered evidence that forced Clinton to admit he had had an "improper relationship" with Lewinsky. In September 1998, Starr issued a report compiling a devastating chronicle of the president's adulterous affair and his months of subsequent lies. The report proposed eleven possible grounds for impeachment to the Congress, including charges of perjury and obstruction of justice. The House of Representatives, voting largely along party lines, approved a resolution calling for a full inquiry into possible grounds for impeachment.

Political experts predicted that the Republicans would emerge from the 1998 midterm elections with a tighter grip on Congress and, therefore, on the president's political fate. But the public continued to express overwhelming approval of Clinton's performance in office. Americans appreciated his successful management of the economy and disapproved of Starr's prosecutorial tactics and the Republicans' sensationalization of the prosecutor's findings. Clinton's approval ratings were so high that Republican congressional candidates shied away from the impeachment issue for fear of alienating voters.

Preoccupation with the Lewinsky scandal left the Republicans with nothing else on which to base their 1998 campaign. Their 55-to-45 margin in the Senate was unchanged, and they lost five House seats, which left them a slim 223-to-211 margin. The Democratic gains marked the first time since 1934 that the president's party gained seats in a midterm election and the first time since 1822 that a second-term president's party did so. Ironically, it was not Bill Clinton but his principal political antagonist, Newt Gingrich, who was forced from office. Having lost the support of the House Republicans, Gingrich announced that he was giving up his leadership position and his seat in Congress.

This extraordinary political drama continued as the new speaker, Robert Livingston (R-LA), resigned six weeks later amid revelations that he too had had extramarital affairs. He was succeeded by the more conciliatory J. Dennis Hastert (R-IL), dubbed by the media as "the Accidental Speaker." Defying opinion polls, House Republicans impeached Clinton on charges of perjury and obstruction of justice. In a reversal of constitutional roles, Congress claimed to be the Constitution's protector while the president rested his claim to stay in office on his success as tribune of the people.

Polling indicated that large majorities of Americans continued to approve of Clinton's handling of his job, to oppose a Senate trial, and to proclaim congressional Republicans to be "out of touch with most Americans." Nonetheless, congressional Republicans were determined to proceed despite certain acquittal. After a five-week trial, on February 12, 1999, the Senate rejected the charge of perjury by a vote of fifty-five to forty-five, with ten Republicans voting against conviction; then, with five Republicans breaking ranks, the Senate split fifty-fifty on a second article accusing the president of obstruction of justice. The modern presidency had been sustained. There would be no return to nineteenth-century-style congressional government.

The Republican Congress and George W. Bush: Executive-Centered Partisanship

With the election of George W. Bush to the presidency, the institutional combat that characterized the relations between the executive and Congress for much of the previous three decades gave way to unified Republican government. Bush came to office with the ambition to make his own distinctive mark on the conservative movement; but, as we will see in Chapter 8, he chose to use the Republican Party as the vehicle for realizing that ambition. Unlike Reagan or his father, George W. Bush came to office enjoying Republican control of the Congress and spied the possibility of extending this situation into the future. The dramatic Republican triumph in the 1994 elections, in which the GOP took control of the House and Senate for the first time in forty-two years, meant that Bush was greeted by a militantly partisan and seasoned Republican majority on taking office. Equally important, the Republicans had managed to retain their congressional majorities in spite of, rather than because of, Bush's infinitesimally small victory. As a result, he was far more dependent on his partisan brethren in the legislature than Ronald Reagan had been.

Bush's active recruitment of Republican candidates and diligent fundraising considerably strengthened the party organization. His dramatic intervention in the 2002 midterm elections helped Republicans regain control of the Senate, which they had lost due to the defection of Jeffords. Not only did the 2002 elections mark the first time in more than a century that the president's party had regained control of the Senate at midterm, it also represented the first time since FDR that a president saw his party gain seats in both houses of Congress in a first-term midterm election. Building on the success in the 2002 elections, Bush and his advisors designed and implemented the most ambitious grassroots campaign in the party's history for the 2004 elections. They mobilized an elaborate network of almost a million and a half campaign volunteers concentrated in the sixteen most competitive states. Not only did this network serve as a key to Bush's narrow but decisive victory, it helped add seats to the Republican majorities in the House and Senate (see Box 6).

Box Six: Nuts and Bolts

Apportioning the House of Representatives

Every ten years the congressional seats are reapportioned in response to the population shifts discovered by the Census. The 2002 House elections were the first ones conducted according to the 2000 Census. Because the population grew and the number of House seats, 435, remained the same, the size of each congressional district grew. A total of twelve seats were shifted from one state to another. On the whole, the Census revealed a movement of the population from the North and East to the Southeast, Southwest, and Pacific Coast. More states and regions favorable to the Republicans gained seats than did those favoring Democrats. Within states, apportionment is usually carried out by the state legislature. However, some state legislatures have chosen to delegate that task to an independent commission.

Figure 7.2 shows the apportionment of the U.S. House of Representatives for the 108th Congress.

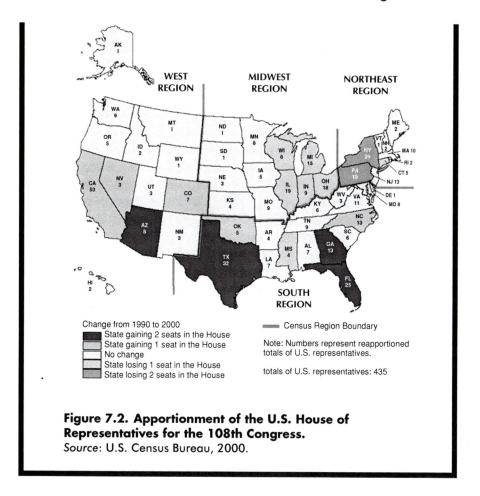

Change from 1990 to 2000
- ■ State gaining 2 seats in the House
- ▨ State gaining 1 seat in the House
- ☐ No change
- ▧ State losing 1 seat in the House
- ▨ State losing 2 seats in the House

▬▬ Census Region Boundary

Note: Numbers represent reapportioned totals of U.S. representatives.

totals of U.S. representatives: 435

Figure 7.2. Apportionment of the U.S. House of Representatives for the 108th Congress.
Source: U.S. Census Bureau, 2000.

Republican congressional candidates and party loyalists rewarded the president for his organizational and financial help with their vigorous support for his controversial tax cuts and for the Iraq War. Republicans in Congress consolidated their influence in a small circle of party leaders and marginalized dissenting voices trying to impede a conservative agenda. Speaker of the House Dennis Hastert had no affinity for the kind of high-stakes political gamesmanship that Gingrich reveled in during his tenure as speaker. But he and the powerful Republican Whip, Tom Delay – whose hard-nosed tactics earned him the moniker, "the hammer" – worked hand in glove with the Bush White House to bring the president's program to fruition. Delay and Hastert made it clear to incumbent and aspiring committee chairs that opposing the party line might very well cost them their positions. The Republican leadership exerted tight control over the House Rules Committee making it very difficult for Democrats to offer alternative legislative proposals – for example, a smaller tax cut than one Republicans advocated. Democrats were increasingly shut out of the final conference committee negotiations needed to reconcile differing House and Senate versions of proposed legislation, which was necessary before it could be enacted into law.

Although Republicans gained only a slim five-seat majority in 2004, Majority Leader Bill Frist (R-TN) seized control of selecting committee members. Wielding this institutional power, Frist sought to strengthen Republican control over the president's judicial nominations. In the wake of the "rights revolution," Senate judicial nomination battles, including those for district and appeals court judges (see Chapter 9), have been especially raw and disruptive. Unable to prevent the Judiciary Committee from bringing controversial conservative nominations to the Senate floor, Democrats resorted to the filibuster to block several of Bush's appeals court nominees. This device for thwarting the majority had rarely been used to block presidential appointments to the courts. Lacking the sixty votes needed to reach cloture, Frist began building a case for changing the rules to prohibit the filibuster of judicial nominations. According to Senate rules, such a change required only a simple majority. However, it was viewed by both supporters and opponents alike to be so radical that both sides referred to it as the "nuclear option." The clash over appeals court nominations became a major public debate, featuring dueling television ads by rival liberal and conservative groups, who saw this battle as a critical prelude to the impending struggle to fill vacancies on the Supreme Court.

This partisan flap over Senate rules pointed to the difficult balancing act Congress, especially the Senate, must play in reconciling liberty and equality. Champions of the filibuster claimed that protecting a minority's right to obstruct judicial nominations was necessary to uphold the Senate's prerogative of advice and consent – a critical role for an institution charged with expressing the "cool and deliberate sense of the community." Those who defended the "nuclear option" indicted the Senate Democrats for thwarting the will of the American public as conveyed in the 2002 and 2004 elections. In the end, a bipartisan group of moderate Democrats and Republicans – referred to as the Gang of 14 – reached an informal agreement to oppose the nuclear option but not to resort to filibusters on judicial confirmations except under "extraordinary circumstances." Those circumstances were not specified, but a sufficient degree of trust was established to forestall a crisis. This temporary cease-fire made a full-scale partisan confrontation over judicial nominations during Bush's second term less likely. At the same time, the episode highlighted the irresolvable tension between party polarization and constitutionalism, between the demands of the majority as voiced in elections and the claims of minority rights sheltered by the complex web of American constitutional government.

The executive-centered approach that the Bush White House pursued, with the strong support of Republican leaders in Congress, raised equally profound constitutional questions. Bush, encouraged by Vice President Richard Cheney, took an expansive view of executive authority to shield his administration's policy deliberations from public scrutiny and to fight the war against terrorism unilaterally. With few exceptions, the Republican controlled Congress deferred to the White House's defense of broad prerogative power.

In 2001, Vice President Richard Cheney chaired a task force to formulate a new energy policy. The administration rejected attempts by several members of Congress and public interest groups to use the Federal Advisory Committee Act, a 1972 law that established openness requirements for advisory boards to the executive, to force the vice president to divulge information about his energy task force, a working group of industry lobbyists and government officials created to formulate national energy policy. Bush officials argued that the Federal Advisory Committee Act was unconstitutional in that it authorized "extreme interference" and "unwarranted intrusion" into executive responsibility. The General Accounting Office (GAO), a legislative agency created to assist Congress in the performance of its constitutional responsibilities, sued the vice president to acquire information about the secret operations of the administration's National Energy Policy Development Group. The constitutional struggle gained heightened political import from the Enron scandal (see Chapter 6), because Enron executives were known to have attended task force meetings and were also very large Bush campaign contributors.

In refusing to release this information, President Bush did not go so far as to claim executive privilege; rather, he argued that in order for the president to obtain the most frank and open advice, he must be able to keep that advice secret, even with regard to who advised him. The GAO acted on its own, without any official support from the speaker or Senate majority leader. But most Democratic members of Congress, and some key Republicans who supported the GAO's position, argued that the president's need for secrecy must be balanced against the public's legitimate interest in openness. As with so many of the conflicts in government, this profound struggle between the two elected branches was ultimately settled by the unelected branch, the judiciary. The administration's position was upheld in the courts. It also successfully defended its position in related suits brought by the Sierra Club and Judicial Watch. The Bush administration's legal victory, if sustained in future litigation (the Supreme Court sent the case brought by the public interest groups back to the Court of Appeals for further adjudication), would amount to an expansion of presidential power to keep information secret. Indeed, with the support of Republican leaders in Congress, exemptions from the Federal Advisory Committee Act were written into the Homeland Security Act, the Medicare Prescription Act, the President's Commission to Strengthen Social Security, and the President's Commission on Intelligence on Weapons of Mass Destruction.

Already executive centered in its approach to politics and policy, the Bush White House, once again buttressed by Republican party leaders in Congress, became even more insulated as it planned and fought the war against terrorism. After the events of September 11, President Bush spoke of a "war on terror," but he felt no obligation to obtain a declaration of war. Congress made little fuss over any such declaration when American forces were deployed against the Taliban and Al Qaeda. But the issue became much more contentious when the administration mobilized for war against Iraq. After much negotiation with congressional leaders, including prominent Senate Democrats, Bush agreed to request a congressional resolution that would grant him authority to attack Iraq. Congress had passed a similar motion that endorsed the Gulf War in 1991. These resolutions fell far short of a formal declaration of war, but they formed a satisfactory compromise.

Despite the intense partisan rancor inspired by Bush's aggressive approach to the War on Terror and his intervention in the 2002 election, both parties continued to agree that the president, rather than the Congress, should assume principal responsibility for the War on Terror. When Congress took up the question of Iraq in October of 2002, Democrats had been divided about whether the country should go to war. But facing a popular president and elections in November, they were anxious to get the war behind them and change the subject to the flagging economy. Many justified their votes by claiming that the Iraqi resolution did not declare war but instead delegated to the president the authority to go to war and to determine its scope and duration. Senator John Kerry, who would become the Democratic nominee for president in 2004, raised substantial arguments against going to war with Iraq, but he voted for the Iraq War resolution because he accepted presidential authority over Congress in foreign affairs. "We are affirming a president's right and responsibility to keep the American people safe," Kerry said, "and the president must take that grant of responsibility seriously." Echoing these sentiments, Senator Hillary Rodham Clinton (D-NY) said in the closing hours of debate that the decision to back the resolution was "the hardest decision I've ever had to make, but I cast it with conviction. I want this president, or any future president to be in the strongest possible position to lead our country, at the United Nations or at war."

Thus, even as Congress became more divided by parties, both Democrats and Republicans were still willing to concede considerable power to the president, especially in matters of national and homeland security. Since Bush's reelection, the Congress, including members of the president's own party, have been much more willing to challenge Bush and his conception of expansive executive power. The growing controversy over the war in Iraq, the Hurricane Katrina debacle, the failed Harriet Miers nomination, the rejection of the White House's plan to "privatize" Social Security, and scandals have eroded Bush's public approval ratings and emboldened legislative resistance to presidential leadership (see Chapter 8).

Nonetheless, in June 2006, the Congress overwhelmingly rejected resolutions in the House and Senate that would have required Bush to start withdrawing troops from Iraq. These measures were put forward by Republican congressional leaders to force Democrats, who had grown increasingly critical of the Iraq War, to go on record in support of resolutions that the Bush administration characterized as the equivalent of surrender to terrorists. Democrats, however, did not take the bait: a resolution that required Bush to bring the troops home immediately failed by a vote of 403 to 3 in the House; the Senate rejected Senator Kerry's proposal to withdraw troops within a year, 86 to 13.

The 2006 congressional elections may well serve to reverse this trend toward increased executive authority. For the first time since 1994, the Democrats regained control of both Houses of Congress. They enjoyed a slim one-vote majority in the Senate and a much healthier twenty-nine seat margin in the House. Immediately after the election, the new House speaker, Nancy Pelosi, the first women to ever hold that office, announced that the House Democrats would push for a phased withdrawal of troops from Iraq. Anticipating Democratic calls for changes in Iraq policy, Bush announced the day after the election that he would replace Defense Secretary Donald Rumsfeld with a man not identified with the current policy, Robert Gates, former Deputy National Security Advisor and Director of the CIA. Although Bush claimed to have a flexible attitude, he flatly rejected the call for troop withdrawals. In February of 2007, the House of Representatives passed a resolution opposing President Bush's decision to send additional troops to Iraq as part of his "surge" strategy, but the resolution was explicitly written to be non-binding on the president. In the Senate, the Republican minority was able to prevent a similar resolution from coming to the floor for a vote. Thus, even as the congressional debate between Democrats and Republicans on the war became more intense, the extent of Congress's power to declare war and oversee national security policy remained unresolved. Such ambiguity raises troubling constitutional questions, but, arguably, it is very much what the Framers intended when they embedded the system of checks and balances into the Constitution.

Conclusion: The First Branch of Government – Representation, Democracy, and Rights

Congress was created to reconcile individual interest – the pursuit of happiness – with national interest in order to build a foundation for government action that combined America's liberal and democratic traditions. With the aid of the extra-constitutional device of political parties, Congress has, on occasion, admirably fulfilled this great responsibility. It has served as the forum for passionate debate about America's rights – during conflicts over such significant issues as the national bank, slavery, big business, and the welfare state. In this way, Congress has played a critical part in strengthening the attachment between the citizenry and the fundamental law, in ensuring, as Jefferson prescribed, that the "Constitution belongs to the Living."

During the ratification of the Constitution, the Anti-Federalists had warned that the American republic risked degenerating into an elected monarchy. Later, this warning was repeated by Jefferson and his fellow Republicans. They believed that representative democracy was based on widespread public discussions that most effectively occur in legislatures and local communities. Such deliberation is undermined by executive dominance. As Alexander Hamilton acknowledged, the benefit of a strong executive is "promptitude of decision," which does not allow for the "differences of opinion and the jarring of parties" that constitute political freedom.

The Anti-Federalists' fear of centralized administration was prescient. Beginning with the Progressive Era, Congress forfeited many of its representative and legislative duties to the president. With Franklin Roosevelt and the New Deal, the president, rather than Congress or the parties, became the principal agent of popular rule. As the Vietnam War and Watergate demonstrated, looking to the White House to solve the nation's problems threatened the very nature of representative democracy. Although Congress was revitalized in the wake of Watergate, the war against terror, including the Iraq War, and the executive-centered, partisan approach to governance embraced by Republicans during the Bush presidency have prompted presidential scholars and public officials to dust off concerns from the 1960s and 1970s about presidential imperialism. Once again, Madison's warning, issued during the first signs of presidential ambition to control foreign affairs, seemed apt: "War was the true nurse of executive aggrandizement."

The subordination of the Congress to the modern presidency has strengthened nationalism but diminished the importance of debate and lawmaking, essential activities of popular rule. At its best, Congress forges a national consensus that bestows legitimacy on government action. Organized by districts and states and separated into two chambers, Congress can debate and enact legislation that fashions public commitments from the diverse interests and voices that constitute American democracy. But it has the defects of its virtues. At certain times in American history, Congress has been prone to fragmentation that thwarts consensus. This discord was especially contentious under committee government, which dominated the House and Senate from the 1920s to the 1970s. In that era, legislators were more likely to be reelected if they channeled benefits from greatly expanded government programs to their constituents. At the same time, committee government detracted from Congress's ability to seek the national interest, which the public came increasingly to identify with the president and the Supreme Court.

Motivated by constitutional and partisan concerns, Congress became more assertive in its relationship to the president after the Nixon administration in the 1970s. This aggressive posture culminated in the Republican-controlled 104th Congress, whose powerful and talented House speaker sought to restore congressional initiative in national affairs and to fulfill the promise of the Reagan revolution to "get government off the backs of the American people." House Speaker Newt Gingrich exploited the renewal of partisan conflict aroused by the Reagan presidency and the persistence of divided government. He enlarged the speaker's role to include mobilizing public opinion and using the powers of government in the service of his Contract with America. But the struggle between the president and the speaker often degenerated into a personal conflict that deflected attention from the constitutional and policy issues at stake. One of Gingrich's failings was to ignore the views of the many Senate Republicans who objected to the budget brinkmanship that led to the shutdown of government services.

Fears abound that the partisan polarization of Congress during the Bush years has further eroded the legislature's institutional capacity. Major policies, such as the 2001 tax cuts, the prescription drug benefit, and Social Security reform, were produced in the White House, which, outside of a small circle of Republican party leaders and Bush loyalists, eschewed meaningful collaboration. Moreover, the centralization of powers in Congress, diminishing the stature and authority of committee chairs, weakened Congress's oversight capacity. Such executive-centered partisanship, critics warn, threatens to transform Congress into an appendage of executive administration.

This chapter began with a discussion of Senator Jeffords's defection from his party and the consequent shift in Senate control from Republicans to Democrats. In 2002, the Republicans capitalized on President Bush's post–September 11 popularity to retake the Senate. Significantly, Jeffords was one of only thirteen senators to support Senator Kerry's resolution to bring U.S. troops home from Iraq within a year. The defeat of moderate Democratic senator Joseph Lieberman in the 2006 Connecticut primary by antiwar candidate Ned Lamont was another dramatic sign that bipartisanship on the war was becoming more difficult as Republican and Democratic positions grew more polarized. A three-term incumbent and the Democratic nominee for vice president in 2004, Lieberman, who strongly supported the Iraq War, won reelection running as an Independent. Just as Jeffords's defection confirmed the more militant conservatism of the Republican party, so Lieberman's independent candidacy ratified the militant liberalism of the Democrats. The polarized politics of the Bush era might seriously compromise Congress's capacity to control the modern executive. Nonetheless, the struggles of Jeffords and Lieberman highlight not only the tensions raised by the competing loyalties that representatives have to their party and to their constituents but also Congress's responsibility to debate national issues. Only by airing differences in domestic and world politics, even as it struggles to identify the national interest, can Congress fulfill its responsibility as the first branch of government, as the constitutional location of democratic confrontations over the proper meaning of the American people's rights and responsibilities.

Chapter Summary

☆ Congress serves both the democratic objective of giving the people a voice in lawmaking and the republican goal of attaining sufficient distance from popular opinion to act deliberatively.

☆ The specific choices the Framers made concerning the methods of selecting congressmen, the size of each house, and what checks to establish between the two houses were all geared toward creating a legislature capable of sustained deliberation and enlightened statesmanship.

☆ The development of a party system was necessary in order to enable Congress to perform its constitutional responsibilities because party provides a mechanism for collective accountability.

☆ In the nineteenth century, Congress functioned as the principal agent of popular rule. The zenith of congressional power followed from a combination of Republican party rule and the growing strength of party organizations over legislative campaigns and policy making.

☆ In the twentieth century, Congress's primacy was challenged by the presidency. During the twentieth and twenty-first centuries, the two branches traded constitutional roles. The people looked to the president for democratic innovation, whereas the House and Senate applied restraint.

☆ In this revised constitutional order, Congress's major responsibility was to oversee the administration of public policy. It used committee hearings, investigations, and individual member or staff interrogations to try to hold the executive accountable.

☆ Party organization gave way to narrowly focused autonomous committees ruled on the basis of seniority. This change improved Congress's ability to oversee the executive branch and to serve local districts and states, but sapped its vitality as a representative institution capable of forging consensus among the nation's diverse voices.

☆ The Watergate scandal provoked Congress to pass a multitude of laws curbing the president's powers, including the Congressional Budget and Impoundment Control Act of 1974, which required the president to obtain Congress's approval before impounding any funds; created budget committees in both houses to coordinate and strengthen legislative involvement in fiscal policy making; and established the Congressional Budget Office to provide Congress with the same level of fiscal expertise that the Office of Management and Budget provides the executive branch.

☆ In the 1970s, Congress also weakened the seniority system and the committee chairs it protected, thus shifting power upward to party leaders and downward to subcommittees and individual members.

☆ Divided government, which occurred between 1980 and 1992, 1994 and 2002, and again in 2006, greatly aggravated relations between the executive and the legislature. Republican efforts to enhance the unilateral powers of the executive and to circumvent legislative restrictions on presidential conduct were matched by Democratic initiatives to burden the executive with smothering oversight by congressional committees and statutory limits on presidential power. In 1994, these roles switched as the Democrats held the presidency and the Republicans recaptured Congress, but the level of rancor grew even higher.

☆ During the period of unitary government, between 2002 and 2006, President George W. Bush and the Republican leadership in Congress made powerful efforts to use party discipline as a means to enable the president to control the legislative agenda.

Major Concepts

cloture
Congressional Budget Office
constituency service
entitlements
executive privilege
filibuster
jurisdictions
oversight
parliamentary democracies
party caucuses
party discipline
party leaders
quorum
Rules Committee
seniority
war hawks

Suggested Readings

Cooper, Joseph, ed. *Congress and the Decline of Public Trust*. Boulder, CO: Westview Press, 1999.

Dodd, Lawrence C., and Bruce Ian Oppenheimer, eds. *Congress Reconsidered*, 7th ed. Washington, D.C.: CQ Press, 2000.

Dodd, Lawrence C., and Richard Schott, eds. *Congress and the Administrative State*. New York: John Wiley, 1979.

Fenno, Richard E. *Congressmen in Committees*. Boston: Little, Brown, 1973.

———. *Home Style: House Members in Their Districts*. Boston: Little, Brown, 1978.

Fiorina, Morris. *Congress: Keystone of the Washington Establishment*, 2d ed. New Haven, CT: Yale University Press, 1989.

Ginsberg, Benjamin, and Martin Shefter. *Politics by Other Means: Politicians, Prosecutors, and the Press from Watergate to Whitewater*, 3d ed. New York: W. W. Norton, 2003.

Hibbing, John R., and Elizabeth Theiss-Morse. *Congress as Public Enemy: Public Attitudes toward American Political Institutions.* New York: Cambridge University Press, 1996.

Jacobson, Gary. *The Politics of Congressional Elections,* 5th ed. New York: Addison-Wesley, 2000.

Mayhew, David. *Congress: The Electoral Connection.* New Haven, CT: Yale University Press, 1986.

Peters, Ronald M., Jr. *The American Speakership: The Office in Historical Perspective,* 2d ed. Baltimore, MD: Johns Hopkins University Press, 1997.

Rohde, David W. *Parties and Leaders in the Postreform House.* Chicago: University of Chicago Press, 1991.

Schickler, Eric. *Disjointed Pluralism: Institutional Innovation and the Development of the U.S. Congress.* Princeton, NJ: Princeton University Press, 2001.

Sundquist, James L. *The Decline and Resurgence of Congress.* Washington, D.C.: Brookings Institution, 2002.

Wilson, Woodrow. *Congressional Government.* Boston: Houghton Mifflin, 1885.

8 The Presidency

First Citizen of American Democracy

This chapter focuses on:

⭐ How the presidency was intended to fit into the constitutional order and how the first, precedent-setting president, George Washington, interpreted his constitutional mandate

⭐ The democratization of the presidential office accomplished by Jefferson and Jackson

⭐ Lincoln's harnessing of the presidency's democratic energy to achieve a "new birth of freedom"

⭐ The rise and flowering of the modern presidency during the Progressive Era and the New Deal

⭐ The role of the mass media and the growing prominence of the president in world affairs in simultaneously strengthening the presidency and making it more politically fragile

⭐ The role of divided government in influencing the president's legislative agenda and policy-making tactics

⭐ George W. Bush's response to September 11, 2001, and how that response has shaped the modern presidency

On September 22, 1993, in the midst of his battle to overhaul the U.S. healthcare system, President Bill Clinton gave a critical speech to a joint session of Congress. The president considered this speech the most important one of his life, the moment at which he would launch a titanic struggle to enact a program that would affect the lives of every citizen and one-seventh of the U.S. economy. Understandably, Clinton felt great pressure as he looked out on the assembled dignitaries; but tension nearly dissolved into panic when he found the wrong speech displayed in the TelePrompTer. He furtively signaled to Vice President Al Gore, sitting behind him on the dais, and then proceeded to improvise. After seven harrowing minutes, the president's aides, notified by the vice president of the mishap, managed to insert the right speech.

Clinton's prepared remarks called for government to "guarantee all Americans a comprehensive package of [healthcare] benefits over an entire lifetime." He brandished a red, white, and blue "health security card" – similar to the Social Security card Americans carry – to symbolize that this plan would be the greatest extension of the welfare state since enactment of Social Security in 1935. The program would mandate employer-paid insurance, provide benefits to non-workers, and create federal purchasing alliances to regulate managed care and control costs.

The president's speech was very well received in the hall. Clinton's pollster, Stanley Greenberg, reported that the Dayton, Ohio, focus group he had convened to provide instantaneous public reaction was also highly favorable to both Clinton's impromptu and planned remarks. The president and his aides would have been shocked to discover that this spine-tingling oratorical episode would prove to be the high point of their battle for healthcare reform. The TelePrompTer gaffe foreshadowed more serious and irremediable problems. Ensuring that "No American Will Go Without Healthcare" was a popular idea. But the complexity of the 1342-page plan and the prospect of government controls on such a large and pervasive industry eventually turned the public and Congress against it. In September 1994, almost a year to the day after Clinton introduced the Health Security Act with such fanfare, Senate majority leader George Mitchell declared the president's bill dead.

Clinton's healthcare debacle illustrates that surveys and focus groups can be a very unreliable basis of support for presidential causes. A president, particularly one as politically gifted as Clinton, can dominate the national political agenda. But a president's ability to shape debate does not necessarily translate into government action. This case also illustrates an uneasy relationship between the people, the president, and the welfare state. Since the Great Depression of the 1930s, Americans have tended to view the national government – and its steward, the president – as the guarantor of economic and social security. They view government entitlements favorably but reject the centralized power necessary to implement those policies. This contradiction poses a profound challenge for public officials, especially for the president.

This chapter charts the development of the American presidency from its roots in the Constitution to the political dominance it has now achieved. The chapter begins with a consideration of how the presidency was intended to fit into the overall constitutional order and how the first, precedent-setting president interpreted his constitutional mandate. Next, the chapter looks at the democratization of the office, especially as it was accomplished by Thomas Jefferson and Andrew Jackson. It discusses how Abraham Lincoln harnessed the democratic energy that was now attached to the office to produce a new public philosophy, a "new birth of freedom" that ended slavery and revised the Constitution to guarantee civil rights. Then the chapter charts the rise of the modern presidency after its post-Lincoln decline, with special attention to the role of the Progressive movement. The focus shifts to Franklin D. Roosevelt and the New Deal to show the flowering of the modern presidency. The chapter describes how the rise of the mass media and the growing prominence of the president in world affairs have both strengthened the presidency and made it more fragile. The last section examines the return of conservatives to the presidency, beginning with Richard Nixon and continuing, with only two interruptions, through to the present. A final discussion on George W. Bush pays special attention to the impact of September 11.

Democracy, Liberalism, and Executive Power

The president is the most important embodiment of national government and the country's leading political figure. In a sense, this has always been so. In their hope to establish self-government on a grand scale, the architects of the American Constitution created the need for such a figure. Ironically, the Anti-Federalists were more clearly aware of this imperative than the Federalists were; they recognized that if the new, more centralized government were to succeed, it needed to cultivate civic affiliation among the people, which meant putting a prominent national personage at the helm. In the words of a leading Anti-Federalist: "In every large collection of people there must be a 'first man,'" a "visible point serving as a common center of government, towards which to draw their eyes and attachment." After the Constitution was ratified, it fell to George Washington (term of office: 1789–1797) to attract the eyes and attachments of the people to the new government, to be the first citizen. All of America's most celebrated presidents would likewise master that role.

The President and Ordered Liberty

The presidency has been buffeted by competing liberal and democratic aspirations. At the time of the founding, this tension was expressed as the incompatibility between a strong executive and rule of the people. Many critics of the Constitution abhorred the establishment of an executive who they believed would inevitably turn into a king disguised by republican robes.

Defenders of the presidency, especially Alexander Hamilton, argued that the executive would refine and enlarge popular opinion, not mute it, and would serve as a critical ingredient of republican government's ambition to protect the people from themselves and to preserve individual freedom from majority whim. James Madison warned that an unrestrained majority would likely carry out "wicked projects," that they would distribute property equally and thus deny individuals the fruits of their own labor. As originally conceived, the president was given a special responsibility to make democracy safe for individual freedom, to protect what Abraham Lincoln (1861–1865) called "the jewel of liberty." Selected by a college of electors, not directly by the people, the executive was expected to restrain popular majorities and provide steady administration of the nation's affairs.

The president's oath sanctified this responsibility to uphold ordered liberty. Although the Constitution prescribes that legislators, judges, and other officials of the national and state governments also take an oath "to support the Constitution," only the executive's oath is included in the document. It charges the president "to preserve, protect, and defend the Constitution," to guard over a system dedicated to restraining unruly majorities and constraining leaders from catering to popular whims and passions.

The President and Popular Leadership

Since Franklin D. Roosevelt (FDR; 1933–1945), the position of executive, originally conceived as the guardian of the liberal order, has become the principal agent of popular rule. FDR ushered in new constitutional principles to protect individuals from market uncertainties and big business abuses. This redefined social contract transformed the president into the champion of a national democracy in which government assumed responsibility for economic and social welfare.

The modern president has become the focus of rising public expectations and the embodiment of popular will. Presidential scholars, public officials, journalists, and talking heads on television all look to contemporary presidents to mobilize public opinion, not to moderate it. They expect the president to overcome rather than uphold constitutional checks and balances. This view of presidential leadership places a premium on rhetorical flair. Like Ronald Reagan (1981–1989), the president is expected to be a Great Communicator. The president must have charisma, radiating the extraordinary charm and popular appeal associated with celebrities.

Charisma implies an ability not just to speak effectively but also to conjure up inspirational imagery. In the 1992 presidential contest, Clinton (1993–2001), the Democratic challenger, showed an ability to communicate effectively with voters. President George H. W. Bush (1989–1993) did not. Commentators across the political spectrum concluded that Bush lost to Clinton because he lacked "the vision thing."

Does the emphasis on charisma and vision in contemporary presidential politics invest America's liberal tradition with democratic energy? Or does it merely foster the illusion of democracy, perverting America's constitutional heritage? The unique ability to influence public opinion gives the president a great opportunity to educate citizens. As Supreme Court justice Felix Frankfurter said of FDR, he "took the people to school" regarding their rights and responsibilities. But charisma emphasizes style over substance. It threatens to divert public attention from the reasoned and sober deliberation necessary to form thoughtful political opinions. It therefore poses grave dangers to liberty and democracy as well as providing opportunities for the exercise of democratic leadership.

The Constitutional Presidency

In "Federalist No. 71," Hamilton said, "when occasions present themselves in which the interests of the people are at variance with their inclinations, it is the duty of the persons whom they have appointed to be the guardians of those interests, to withstand the temporary delusion in order to give them time and opportunity for cool and sedate reflection." Thomas Jefferson (1801–1809), much more suspicious of presidential authority, was no less committed to uphold the liberal tradition, to protect the people's rights, and to represent their enduring principles rather than embody their will. The "cool and deliberate" sense of the Senate and the "firm and independent guidance" of the judiciary would make vital contributions to this constitutional sobriety. But only the president "command[ed] a view of the whole ground," as Jefferson put it, and thus had the greatest responsibility to withstand the temporary delusions of the people so that more cool and sedate reflections could prevail.

The president's authority rested not on public opinion but on powers described or implied in Article II of the Constitution, especially the veto, which is more suited to resisting popular impulses than to advancing them (see Table 8.1). Jefferson argued that "absolute acquiescence in the decisions of the majority [was] the vital principle of republics"; however, this principle presupposed that the House of Representatives and the states, not the executive, were the "surest bulwarks against anti-republican tendencies." Presidents were accountable to public opinion, not merely responsive to it. Indeed, the original Constitution discouraged presidents from going to the people. In "Federalist No. 49," Madison objected to Jefferson's prescription for periodic constitutional conventions because such appeals to the people would "carry an implication of some defect in the government" and "thus deprive the [Constitution] of that veneration which time bestows on everything." As the guardian of the constitutional order, the president would draw authority from this veneration. The president would embody the American liberal tradition, protecting it from the inevitable passionate assaults of democracy.

Making the Presidency Safe for Democracy

American democratic tradition, deeply rooted in colonial life and the fight for independence, did not consider a popular presidency to be its embodiment. Like Jefferson, most ardent democrats viewed the House of Representatives, the states, and the localities as the guardians of the people's will. The ink on the new Constitution was hardly dry before a struggle broke out about how much executive power the American people could tolerate and still consider themselves the ultimate sovereign in this "more perfect Union."

A committee of the House of Representatives wanted to address the president simply as "the President of the United States." But the Senate, at the behest of Vice President John Adams, rejected the House committee's report. Because "titles and politically inspired elegance were essential aspects of strong government," Adams supported the title "His Highness the President of the United States and Protector of Their Liberties." Madison led House opposition to what he took to be the Senate's antirepublican terminology. He was supported by President Washington, who made known his annoyance at Adam's efforts "to bedizen [him] with a superb but spurious title." The Senate proposal was defeated, and Adams was

Table 8.1. Presidential Vetoes

President	Coincident Congresses	Regular Vetoes	Pocket Vetoes	Total Vetoes	Vetoes Overriden
Washington	1st–4th	2	—	2	—
Adams	5th–6th	—	—	—	—
Jefferson	7th–10th	—	—	—	—
Madison	11th–14th	5	2	7	—
Monroe	15th–18th	1	—	1	—
J. Q. Adams	19th–20th	—	—	—	—
Jackson	21st–24th	5	7	12	—
Van Buren	25th–26th	—	1	1	—
W. H. Harrison	27th	—	—	—	—
Tyler	27th–28th	6	4	10	1
Polk	29th–30th	2	1	3	—
Taylor	31st	—	—	—	—
Fillmore	31st–32nd	—	—	—	—
Pierce	33rd–34th	9	—	9	5
Buchanan	35th–36th	4	3	7	—
Lincoln	37th–39th	2	5	7	—
A. Johnson	39th–40th	21	8	29	15
Grant	41st–44th	45	48	93	4
Hayes	45th–46th	12	1	13	1
Garfield	47th	—	—	—	—
Arthur	47th–48th	4	8	12	1
Cleveland	49th–50th	304	110	414	2
B. Harrison	51st–52nd	19	25	44	1
Cleveland	53rd–54th	42	128	170	5
McKinley	55th–57th	6	36	42	—
T. Roosevelt	57th–60th	42	40	82	1
Taft	61st–62nd	30	9	39	1
Wilson	63rd–66th	33	11	44	6
Harding	67th	5	1	6	—
Coolidge	68th–70th	20	30	50	4
Hoover	71st–72nd	21	16	37	3
F. D. Roosevelt	73rd–79th	372	263	635	9
Truman	79th–82nd	180	70	250	12
Eisenhower	83rd–86th	73	108	181	2
Kennedy	87th–88th	12	9	21	—
L. B. Johnson	88th–90th	16	14	30	—
Nixon	91st–93rd	26	17	43	7
Ford	93rd–94th	48	18	66	12
Carter	95th–96th	13	18	31	2
Reagan	97th–100th	39	39	78	9
G. H. W. Bush[a]	101st–102nd	29	15	44	1
Clinton	103rd–106th	36	1	37	2
G. W. Bush	107th–108th	1	—	1	—
Total		**1485**	**1066**	**2551**	**106**

[a] President Bush attempted to pocket veto two bills during intra-session recess periods. Congress considered the two bills enacted into law because of the president's failure to return the legislation. The bills are not counted as pocket vetoes in this table.

Source: Office of the Clerk of the House. Web: http://clerk.house.gov

nicknamed "His Rotundity." The chief executive would have no more august title than "the President of the United States."

Creating a Republican Executive

Washington rejected the substance as well as the trappings of monarchy. Hamilton had argued in "Federalist No. 73" that the president should veto bad laws, but Washington used the veto only against unconstitutional, not unwise, acts of Congress. (The only exception to this rule was Washington's rejection of legislation that would have reduced the size of the army, thus claiming implicitly that presidential deference to Congress was less appropriate in foreign affairs and military policy than in domestic matters.) His caution did not signify weakness. Rather, he sought to win the trust of Congress to ensure against interference with his forceful wielding of power when it was most needed. This trust was secured for the ages by Washington's most important act of self-denial. Washington voluntarily stepped down after completing his second term, although the Constitution did not require him to do so, thereby establishing an enduring precedent for peacefully and lawfully relinquishing presidential power.

Washington also proved that the president was no mere clerk. The Constitution does not empower the president to address the people. Indeed, his duty to preserve the presidency in the face of popular intemperance might be understood to preclude such direct address. Nonetheless, early in his term Washington issued a proclamation honoring Thanksgiving Day. This seemingly innocuous gesture established the tradition of direct popular communication that provides much of the president's power and prestige. Although far more circumspect than Clinton's pleadings for healthcare reform, Washington's proclamation supported his conviction that communication between the nation's first citizen and its people was a vital form of civic education.

Box One: Nuts and Bolts

The President's Cabinet

For the first 100 and more years, the executive branch grew very slowly. For example, although Washington appointed an attorney general, there was no justice department. The chief legal officer of the government worked on his own and had a private practice on the side. Then, as now, the largest civilian federal employer was the post office. The original cabinet departments were treasury, state, and war (renamed the Department of Defense in 1947). Interior was added in 1849, agriculture in 1862, and commerce in 1903. Surprisingly, no new cabinet-level departments were added during the New Deal, but all the departments underwent vast expansion. The Eisenhower administration added the Department of Health, Education, and Welfare (HEW) in 1953. The Department of Transportation was created in 1967. A separate Department of Education was established in 1979, and HEW was reorganized into the Department of Health and Human Services a year later. The Department of Veterans Affairs was created in 1989. Most recently, the Department of Homeland Security was added in 2002.

Washington also defended the president's capacity to manage the executive branch. The Constitution grants the president extensive appointment powers as well as the right to obtain in writing the views of the principal executive officers. But it does not declare the president to be in control of those departments, nor does it give the executive a clear directive to treat employees as subordinates. If Washington had not insisted that all members of the executive branch were in fact his "deputies," the president might have become, as the name suggests, a mere "presider" who ceded actual control over executive affairs to individual department heads acting in conjunction with their senior associates and powerful members of Congress. The heads of the major federal departments are collectively referred to as the president's *cabinet* (see Box 1). The cabinet has no constitutional or even legal status. Individual presidents have treated it differently. Some considered it to be an important forum for deliberation and called many cabinet meetings. Others preferred to deal with individual department heads separately and called few meetings.

The president's power over the cabinet was ratified by a bill, enacted in 1789, which involved the creation of the Department of State. The Constitution requires the president to obtain the advice and consent of the Senate when appointing department heads. Many representatives assumed that, by implication, Senate confirmation was also necessary for the president to fire an executive official. Washington disagreed. Congress allowed the president to fire executive officials on his own, but only after Vice President Adams broke a tie in the Senate. From then on, Congress passed laws to establish the major departments of government that were carefully designed to minimize the legislature's influence in the executive branch. If the president had been a less universally admired and trusted figure than Washington, at least one more senator would probably have voted no, and the deputy theory would not have become part of the unofficial Constitution.

Resisting Executive Authority

During Washington's second term, several western Pennsylvania towns resisted a federal whiskey excise tax and drove away a tax inspector and a federal marshal. Washington summoned troops to quell the uprising, commanding them himself. He risked his prestige to enforce the principle of national supremacy. In the face of a Washington-led army, the rebellion dissolved. The first president understood that to uphold liberty he must uphold the law.

Washington also believed that the executive enjoyed the same clear-cut authority in matters of national security. He determined that the mutual defense treaty with France threatened war with Britain, so he broke it, issuing the 1793 Neutrality Proclamation (see Chapter 4). The Constitution gave the president no authority to dissolve treaties. Washington claimed prerogative power, the right to act where the Constitution is silent or where violating its letter is necessary to ensure its survival.

Presidential Responsibility and Party Conflict

Washington enjoyed such popular support that he was able to suppress factionalism and calm fears of executive dominance, but he left no legacy capable of doing so in the future. Washington understood the presidency to be a non-partisan office, but that conception did not even prevail while he was in office. In 1790, sharp differences arose between Secretary of the Treasury Hamilton and Secretary of State Jefferson that led to party conflict (see Chapter 4). Jefferson and his ally Madison believed that Hamilton's financial scheme, especially his plan to establish a national bank, placed so much power in the hands of the president that it would disrupt the delicate balance between the liberal and democratic features of the constitutional order and put the United States on a path toward a British-style monarchy (see Chapter 6).

Conflict over Presidential Prerogative

Fear of an imperial presidency was aggravated by Washington's Neutrality Proclamation and Hamilton's aggressive defense of it. Hamilton wrote a series of newspaper articles under the pseudonym Pacificus in which he justified extensive discretionary presidential power. He distinguished between the Constitution's grants of legislative authority in Article I, which states, "All legislative Powers herein granted shall be vested in a Congress of the United States," and its general grant of executive authority in Article II, which states, "The executive Power shall be vested in a President of the United States of America" (see Appendix 2 for the full Constitution). The absence in Article II of the words *herein granted*, Hamilton argued, clearly indicated that the executive power of the nation was lodged exclusively in the president, "subject only to the exceptions and qualifications which are expressed in the Constitution." In foreign affairs, wrote Hamilton, explicit constitutional restrictions on presidential power extended no further than the right of the Senate to ratify treaties and Congress to declare war and did not hinder the executive in other foreign policy matters that were "naturally" his domain.

Madison, writing under the name Helvidius – a Roman patriot who had been the victim of tyranny – replied to Hamilton. He denied that foreign policy was "naturally" an executive power. The tasks of foreign policy – to declare war, to conclude peace, and to form alliances – were among "the highest acts of sovereignty; of which the legislative power must at least be an integral and preeminent part." In foreign as in domestic affairs, wrote Madison, republican government confined presidential power to the execution of the laws; otherwise, the executive would acquire legislative power. Such an argument was "in theory an absurdity – in practice a tyranny."

Madison lost the argument. The Neutrality Proclamation established the precedent that the president can act unilaterally in foreign affairs except where the Constitution provides specific exceptions and limitations (see Box 3). But on a more general basis, for the next 100 years Madison's and Jefferson's view of the presidency held sway. The president was constrained by an interpretation of the Constitution that celebrated legislative supremacy and states' rights.

Democratizing the Presidency

As we discuss in Chapter 4, Jefferson's Revolution of 1800 was an exceedingly lawful and merciful one. In his first inaugural address, Jefferson proclaimed: "we are all republicans, we are all federalists." He insisted that his supporters and opponents shared principles more profound than their differences, above all, a commitment to the Constitution itself: "If there be any among us who would wish to dissolve the Union or to change its republican form, let them stand undisturbed as monuments of the safety with which error of opinion may be tolerated where reason is left free to combat it." Jefferson followed this plea for unity by paying homage to Washington as "our first and great revolutionary character" and by pledging to preserve the government in its "whole constitutional vigor."

Yet Jefferson maintained that the strength of the executive office depended not only on its constitutional authority but also on "the affections of the people." He claimed a popular mandate to make the presidency more democratic and more subordinate to Congress, and he celebrated "the state governments in all their rights, as the most competent administrations for our domestic concerns and the surest bulwarks against anti-republican tendencies."

Jefferson made the president look like a democrat. He jettisoned the presidential coach and rode his own horse. At presidential dinners, he flouted distinctions in rank and purposely ignored diplomatic protocol in the reception of foreign envoys. He believed that a presidential appearance before Congress resembled too much a speech from the throne, which would threaten to interfere with the deliberations of the people's representatives. He began the century-long practice of sending the president's annual State of the Union message to Congress in writing to be read aloud by the clerk of the House. These symbolic flourishes went along with a drastic reduction in the size of the national government that would remain until the Civil War. Even today, the United States retains a degree of local self-government, a distrust of elites, and a lack of centralized rule unique among modern representative governments.

Today, the president hardly qualifies as a humble democrat. He flies around the world in his own jet, Air Force One, accompanied by a crowd of staffers ready and able to respond to his every whim. And yet he is still called Mr. President and still required to leave office after, at most, eight years. And, despite the enormity of his responsibilities, relatively speaking, he is modestly paid. Table 8.2 compares the compensation received by the U.S. chief executive officer, the president, to that received by the ten most highly paid corporate chief executive officers.

Presidential Party Building

The Revolution of 1800 could not have occurred without Jefferson's and Madison's sustained party-building efforts during the 1790s. As the beloved author of the Declaration of Independence, Jefferson might well have been elected in 1800 in the absence of party. But without its support and

Table 8.2. Total Compensation for the Year
2004 – Ten Highest Paid Chief Executive Officers
of Corporations and the U.S. President

Colgate Palmolive	$148,000,000
United Technologies	$70,500,000
Lehman Brothers Holdings	$67,700,000
Cendant	$60,000,000
NVR	$58,100,000
Oracle	$40,600,000
Wells Fargo	$37,800,000
Forest Labs	$36,100,000
Bear Stearns	$33,900,000
Apollo Group	$32,800,000
U.S. President	$400,000

Source: Forbes.com (http://www.forbes.com/static/
execpay2004/LIRBNR5.html?).

discipline, he would have either become a prisoner of the status quo or prey to schismatic pressures. Although Andrew Jackson (1829–1837) is usually considered to be the founder of the patronage (spoils) system, it was Jefferson who initiated the replacement of incumbent federal officials with party loyalists. He disciplined his followers by appealing to their party spirit but also by manipulating the supply of patronage. Federal appointments would become the staple of party organization in the nineteenth and early twentieth centuries, thereby adding a practical underpinning to principled loyalties.

Jefferson shared Washington's antipathy to party politics. Once the Republican party triumphed over the Federalists, he expected it to dissolve and non-partisan constitutional government to be restored. Jefferson was a better politician than a prophet. As Madison came to recognize, "the Constitution itself" would be "an unfailing source of party distinctions." The president now derived power directly from the people through a party program. Washington's dream of an executive who stood apart from factions had proved unrealistic.

The Republican party linked the president and the people. Nomination and election by a mass political party made the president both a popular spokesman and accountable to something bigger than the office itself, to a collective organization that enlarged even as it restrained presidential ambition. Although Jefferson's party went into eclipse during the regimes of his successors, it retained a corps of passionate adherents who would later lead the fight to restore and expand it.

Jefferson deemphasized the constitutional powers of his office and chose to govern instead as party leader. He encouraged party discipline in Congress and relied on House and Senate floor leaders to advance his programs. He made extensive use of party caucuses – meetings of leaders from the executive and legislative branches – to formulate policy and to encourage party unity. Secretary of the Treasury Albert Gallatin played an important part in these caucuses; Jefferson himself occasionally presided. Jefferson constructed a highly centralized partisan system within the government, but one that operated for the most part through conference, consultation, and free discussion rather than executive domination.

Presidents, Mass Democracy, and the Union

Andrew Jackson, who viewed himself as a follower of Jefferson, launched a much bolder assault on national institutions and programs than Jefferson did. After his election in 1828, Jackson stopped federal funding of internal improvements – the building of roads and canals – because he saw no constitutional basis for them. The army was reduced. Expenditures shrank. The Bank of the United States, which Jeffersonians had grudgingly accepted, was dismantled, and its deposits were reinvested in selected state banks. In carrying out these reductions, Jackson exercised presidential power more aggressively than did his idol Jefferson. Federalist and Republican presidents had abided by Washington's view that a veto should be cast only if the president believed that a piece of legislation was unconstitutional. But in 1832, Jackson justified vetoing the bank partly on the grounds that the recharter was bad policy.

The Jacksonian assault on national government was carried out in the name of democracy, not liberal individualism. It was intended to strengthen local communities, homes of popular collective action and sources of resistance to the rich and powerful who threatened the economic and political independence of the people. Jackson's actions combined his support for limited government with an abiding commitment to the Union. Jackson gave voice to a new age, to a rising spirit of democratic nationalism that sustained and strengthened the Union in the face of serious sectional conflicts over a new tariff law and slavery. His decisive response to South Carolina's nullification threat, mounted in an effort to compel the federal government to accede to its demands for a lower tariff, was a crucial step in the establishment of American nationhood (see Chapters 4 and 5). Indeed, it is inconceivable that Lincoln could have defeated the much more potent secession threat he faced if Jackson had succumbed to South Carolina.

The Presidency and the New Birth of Freedom

We explain in Chapter 4 that Lincoln's accomplishments were born of a national crisis that threatened to destroy the foundations of constitutional democracy in the United States. The leadership he displayed in navigating the unchartered waters of emancipation and civil war won him the esteem of Americans as their greatest president.

As commander-in-chief, Lincoln seemed more a benign dictator than a democratic leader. The Civil War began while Congress was in recess. For nearly three months, Lincoln acted to resist secession without legislative authorization. He considered his actions to be emergency decisions subject to congressional approval, but only after the fact. He believed that war, especially domestic rebellion, invested extraordinary power in the executive. He also preempted normal judicial functions, suspending the writ of habeas corpus and declaring martial law. But Lincoln did not subvert democracy, he saved it. Although deeply respectful of constitutional regularity and formality, his fidelity to the oath he swore took precedence over any constitutional provision. He powerfully asserted the president's prerogative, the right to go beyond the letter of the Constitution in order to "preserve and protect" it.

Lincoln's presidency provided new and provocative answers to fundamental political questions about the proper role of executive power and how to reconcile the Constitution as a legal document with democratic principles and practice. The true American democratic tradition, Lincoln argued, was represented through his understanding of the Constitution as being inextricably connected to the Declaration of Independence, not through Stephen Douglas's concept of popular sovereignty (see Chapter 4). In tolerating the expansion of slavery, the Democrats had forsaken their Jeffersonian heritage. Their error was compounded by the Supreme Court's 1857 *Dred Scott* decision, authored by the militant Jacksonian Roger Taney, which declared unconstitutional any act of Congress or the territorial legislatures that abolished slavery. Lincoln feared that Douglas's and Taney's doctrines would transform slavery from a necessary evil into a positive good, a moral right, producing "a gradual and steady debauching of public opinion." The consequences of such a change in the public mind would be devastating.

Presidential Leadership and the Republican Party

Lincoln's success involved brilliant party leadership. He presided over a broadly based popular movement, one capable of mobilizing and sustaining support for a difficult and bloody enterprise. He did not reject local democracy but appealed to it in order to fortify the moral principles that made localities part of the nation. Although Lincoln did not found the Republican party, he steered it to success on a national scale, by becoming its first president, and he sustained and nurtured it through its time of testing. He forged the Republican party into a means for overcoming the immoral neutrality symbolized by Douglas's doctrine of popular sovereignty.

Lincoln exploited the spoils system with zeal and skill akin to Jefferson and Jackson. He removed Democrats from office and gave their jobs to Republicans from competing factions, ensuring that the full range of party opinion would be heard. He displayed the same commitment to party unity in selecting and managing his cabinet. He appointed William Seward, the party's leading moderate, as secretary of state, and Salmon Chase, its leading antislavery militant, as secretary of the treasury. When tension between Seward and Chase precipitated a cabinet crisis in 1862, Lincoln was able to maintain the loyalty of both and of the factions they represented. "In the process of managing [his cabinet]," historian Eric McKitrick wrote, Lincoln was "at the same time managing the party and fashioning it into a powerful instrument for waging war. "

Public Philosophy and the Presidency

Lincoln's partisan maneuvers did not distract him from his duty to cultivate a new American public philosophy. During this country's most profound political crisis, he drew America into a contest of opinion about the very meaning of constitutional rights. The 1860 election did not provide him a mandate to resolve these issues. He won a four-way contest, obtaining slightly less than 40 percent of the popular vote and no votes in the South. But his carefully crafted speeches, public letters, and proclamations defined the constitutional purpose of the war and the extraordinary measures taken to preserve the Union. His rhetoric did not invoke the image of military glory. Rather, he stressed the inextricable connection between preservation of America's constitutional heritage and the "new birth of freedom" to be achieved by ending slavery.

At Lincoln's insistence, the Republicans made the Thirteenth Amendment, which emancipated the slaves, "the keystone of its 1864 platform." Reelected by large majorities, Lincoln and congressional Republican leaders pushed the amendment through a reluctant Congress. The Constitution does not require a presidential signature on constitutional amendments, but Congress sent it to the president to sign anyway. This oversight, deliberate or not, testifies to Lincoln's importance as a popular and a party leader. The Thirteenth Amendment was self-consciously based on the Northwest Ordinance, supporting Lincoln's claim that the Northwest Ordinance symbolized the Framers' hostility to slavery (see Chapter 2). Its passage further vindicated Lincoln's position that the Republicans, not the Democrats, were the true heirs of Jeffersonian democracy.

The Republican indictment of slavery, and the constitutional changes stemming from it, brought forth a new, more positive view of liberty that obliged government to ensure equality under the law. Thus, Lincoln and his party lessened the inherent tension between liberalism and democracy. They incorporated the Declaration of Independence into the Constitution by abolishing slavery, promising that American citizens could not be denied the right to vote "on account of race, color, or previous condition of servitude" (the Fifteenth Amendment), and guaranteeing all Americans the "privileges or immunities" of citizenship, "due process," and "equal protection of the laws" (the Fourteenth Amendment). These amendments altered the course of constitutional development. Eleven of the first twelve constitutional amendments limited national government powers; six of the next seven expanded those powers at the expense of the states and localities.

But constitutional change was limited by the Republican party's identification with Jeffersonian principles. Lincoln's understanding of the equality guaranteed by the Declaration was modest when compared with twentieth-century presidents such as Theodore Roosevelt (1901–1909), Woodrow Wilson (1913–1921), Franklin Roosevelt, and Lyndon Johnson (1963–1969). The Republican program was tightly bound by liberalism's commitment to private property, limited government, and administrative decentralization. Allied to local self-government, Republicans did not sanction a constant national government presence in society and economy. They demonstrated their commitment to what Lincoln called "a fair race of life" by ending slavery and enhancing "free labor" through policies such as the 1862 Homestead Act (see Chapter 6). But as the failure of Reconstruction revealed, Republicans were not committed to expanding national administrative power.

The Civil War freed Lincoln to use his powers as commander-in-chief energetically and to deal resolutely with slavery. But war's end caused presidential power to ebb. Lincoln's remarkable leadership did not solve the problems of race nor did it enable expanded executive power to survive the assault on it during the Reconstruction era. "By 1875," the political scientist Theodore Lowi has observed, "you would not know there had been a war or a Lincoln."

Great democratic leadership, however, transcends a president's time. Lincoln's words could not be silenced by an assassin's bullet or by the shame of Jim Crow laws in the South. As president, Lincoln reminded Americans that their democracy was sustained not only by local self-government but also by a civic religion rooted in a common creed. Drawing on the Puritan conception of America as a country with a special mission, a "city upon a hill," Lincoln's speeches challenged the notion that America was conceived as a secular nation, dedicated to a narrow understanding of individual rights. In his first inaugural address, Lincoln appealed "to the better angels of our nature," proclaiming the proposition that "all men are created equal" to be divinely inspired. America was "the last best hope of earth" to secure self-government on a grand scale. That lesson, the moral calling of America's democratic tradition, would never be entirely lost.

Progressive Democracy and the Rise of the Modern Presidency

The so-called modern presidency began to take shape during the Progressive Era, the period of reform spanning the last decade of the nineteenth century and the first two decades of the twentieth century (see Chapter 4). In response to massive economic, cultural, and social changes that occurred during this period, pressures mounted for a more expansive national government and a more systematic administration of public policy. The late nineteenth-century polity, which could accommodate decentralized party organizations, political patronage, and a dominant Congress, began to give way to a new order that depended on consistent and forceful presidential leadership.

Theodore Roosevelt and the Expansion of Executive Power

"In both foreign and domestic affairs," the presidential scholars Samuel and Dorothy Rosenman wrote, Theodore Roosevelt "extended executive authority to the furthest limits permitted in peacetime by the Constitution – if not further." As TR (the first president to be known by his initials) acknowledged in his autobiography, "The most important factor in getting the right spirit in my administration was my insistence upon the theory that the executive power was limited only by specific restrictions and prohibitions appearing in the Constitution or imposed by Congress in its Constitutional powers." The more constricted view of presidential power had rendered the American political system impotent and subject to capture by "special interests." TR proclaimed that the president was "a steward of the people bound actively and affirmatively to do all he could for the people, and not content himself with the negative merit of keeping his talents undamaged in a napkin."

TR's conviction that the president possessed a special mandate from the people made him a self-conscious disciple of Jackson. Unlike Jackson, however, TR wanted to join popular leadership to a greater sense of national purpose. He trumpeted a "New Nationalism" that foretold an unprecedented expansion of government's responsibility to secure the nation's social and economic welfare. The New Nationalism was indebted to Hamilton's original understanding of a great American nation. TR also relied on the defense of a broad discretionary authority for the president that Hamilton articulated to justify Washington's Neutrality Proclamation. Washington, Jackson, and Lincoln had all taken a broad view of presidential authority in times of national crisis. But TR was the first president to apply the Hamiltonian principle to the day-to-day administration of government.

TR turned Hamilton on his head. Hamilton supported an energetic executive because he thought it would curb, not abet, popular influence. TR devoted his energy to social and economic reform. He praised Lincoln's uncompromising defense of the Union, which served the "high purpose" of achieving equality of opportunity: "Men who understand and practice the Lincoln school of American political thought are necessarily Hamiltonian in their belief in a strong and efficient National Government and Jeffersonian in their belief in the people as the end of government." TR conveniently overlooked Lincoln's Jeffersonian acceptance of local self-government and of tight institutional and partisan checks on executive power. TR and the Progressives sought to transform American democracy, to establish the national government – and the president in particular – as "the steward of the public welfare." "In order to succeed we need leaders of inspired idealism," TR proclaimed, "leaders to whom are granted great visions, who dream greatly and strive to make their dreams come true; who can kindle the people with the fire from their own burning souls."

TR vigorously promoted himself as the leader of public opinion. He exploited the newly emerging mass media to make a truly personal impact on American politics. He ushered in what has been called the "rhetorical presidency," an approach to presidential leadership that relied primarily

Theodore Roosevelt proclaimed the executive to be the "steward of the public welfare" and linked a great expansion of popular presidential leadership to energetic government.

on direct communication with the public. TR was an irrepressible, if not always eloquent, speaker and is said to have been the first to describe the presidency as a "bully pulpit. "

The Rhetorical Presidency

The most important policy product of TR's popular appeals was the Hepburn Act of 1906. Although the Interstate Commerce Commission (ICC) had been created in 1887 to regulate transportation, it failed to adequately control the "monster" railroads. TR proposed that Congress give the ICC power to regulate railroad rates and to enforce compliance with its regulations. In the face of opposition from key congressional leaders of his own party, TR appealed "over their heads" directly to the people, who were "masters of both of us." When the Hepburn bill stalled in the Senate, TR left Washington for a long "vacation." Speculation arose that he had given up on rate regulation. To the contrary, TR's trip through the Midwest and Southwest turned out to be a campaign for the Hepburn bill. In Chicago, he called on the federal government "to take an increasing control over corporations." The first step "should be the adoption of a law conferring on one executive body the power of increased supervision of the regulation of the great corporations engaged primarily in interstate commerce of the railroads." The ICC should have "ironclad" powers to set rates. The Chicago speech and similar addresses in Dallas, San Antonio, and Denver received extensive and favorable press coverage.

TR's campaign culminated in his December 1905 annual message to Congress, in which he insisted on the need "to prevent the imposition of unjust and unreasonable rates." Although his message formally addressed Congress, TR had a larger audience in mind. The public pressure that his rhetoric stimulated overcame Senate resistance. The president of the Rock Island railroad confided to Secretary of War William Howard Taft that senators he had counted on for "allegiance," although privately opposed to the Hepburn bill, yielded because the president had "so roused the people that it was impossible for the Senate to stand against the popular demand."

The Hepburn Act marked not only the first significant strengthening of national administrative power to regulate the economy since Washington but also the first time a president successfully forced the hand of Congress through a direct appeal to the people. Jefferson and especially Jackson had sought to establish closer ties between the presidency and the public, but they had worked through their party organizations to do so. Similarly,

Lincoln had relied heavily on the Republican party to mobilize support for the war and his Reconstruction policies. But TR's Republican party was badly divided on the issue of reform, and he believed there was no recourse but to appeal directly to public opinion. This approach conformed to Progressive principles that scorned Congress and parties. TR thus advanced the Progressive cause by establishing the president as the principal agent of popular rule.

TR made great use of the media. Before the 1890s, public debate was dominated by the decentralized party press that had prevailed since the Jacksonian era. But a new medium was brought about through the combination of technological advances and the elimination of patronage that supported "party organ" journalism. TR pioneered the use of mass circulation newspapers and magazines to go over the heads of party leaders and establish direct links with the people.

Third Parties and Presidential Politics

TR called his program the Square Deal, signifying that he sought to forge a middle way between government control and laissez faire. But TR gave up on this middle way when he returned to national politics. The tepid reign of his heir, William Howard Taft (1909–1913), and the Republican party's refusal to support TR in 1912 despite his obvious popular support, led TR to ally himself with the most advanced Progressive activists and their causes. He bolted from the 1912 Republican party convention and accepted the nomination of the newly formed Progressive party. TR's Bull Moose campaign, the most important third-party presidential effort in American history, garnered 27 percent of the popular vote. This excellent showing bolstered the Progressive cause that would later animate the Wilson and FDR presidencies.

The Progressive party platform bore a striking resemblance to the New Deal Democratic platform of 1936. It called for strong national regulation of interstate commerce and for health, unemployment, and old age insurance. Its vision of economic justice, requiring national government oversight of the economy and society, was inextricably linked to comprehensive structural political reform. Those reforms prevented the sort of localist counterrevolution that took place during the previous major effort to centralize national government – Reconstruction.

TR's "direct democracy" program called for direct election of senators, for women's suffrage, and for methods that challenged the very concept of representation, including easier ways to amend the Constitution and to overturn court rulings, mandatory direct primaries, voter initiatives, and referenda. These reforms sought to free representatives from provincial, often corrupt, partisan control of elections and governance and to establish a more direct link between government and public opinion. Direct democracy would make routine what TR achieved through the force of his personality, a presidency that dominated policy and government and that embodied the new aspirations for economic and social justice.

Woodrow Wilson, not TR, was elected president in 1912. Although Wilson's campaign was more conservative than TR's, he agreed not only that the Jeffersonian vision of local democracy and limited national government was no longer compatible with individual liberty but also that concentrated economic power required a greater role for the national government. With the help of his advisor, Louis Brandeis, Wilson articulated a version of Progressivism that was closer to the traditions of the Democratic party. TR's New Nationalism had accepted the evolution of great corporations as inevitable and – with strict public regulation of corporate activities by a powerful national government – as desirable. In contrast, Wilson's New Freedom proposed to reform, rather than discard, the decentralized republic and to restore economic competition via an invigorated antitrust policy rather than greater government control. The election was a decisive rejection of the Republican old guard, whose candidate, Taft, carried only Vermont and Utah. The combined popular vote of Wilson, TR, and the Socialist candidate, Eugene Debs – all advocates of national reform – was more than 75 percent, which emboldened Wilson, who garnered only 41 percent, to press for Progressive social and economic policies as well as expanded executive authority.

Presidential Primaries

In seeking to perfect TR's method of popular leadership, Wilson sought to have presidential and congressional candidates nominated directly by voters, not by conclaves of party leaders (in "smoke filled rooms"). This approach was advanced by popular disgust with the 1912 Republican convention, which refused to nominate TR even though he had dominated the direct primaries held in thirteen states. In the other states, delegates were still chosen by state and local party organizations, which preferred Taft to TR. In his first annual message to Congress, Wilson called for a national primary. This idea made little headway in Congress, but it encouraged Progressives to pursue state-by-state reform. By 1920, twenty-one states enacted presidential primaries. Box 2 explains how Wilson's proposal served as a blueprint for future reform.

Nationalizing the Primary Process

Although neither party has adopted a national primary, the process of presidential selection has become increasingly nationalized. This movement is a consequence of the front-loading of state party primaries and the enormous increase in campaign finance costs created by that process. Every schoolchild knows that if you want the best food, you get to the front of the lunch line. Traditionally, the early nomination contests for both parties were held in small, rural states: New Hampshire and Iowa. The largest states, including California and New York, held their primaries months later. As the early contests became increasingly important media events, they came to be ever more decisive in shaping the eventual nomination outcome. For all intents and purposes, the nominations were decided before many of the big states even held their primaries. In response, the larger states moved up the dates of their primaries, igniting a nasty shoving match over which states get near the front of the nominating "lunch line." Both parties protected Iowa and New Hampshire as the lunch-line leaders, but have allowed the other states to bunch themselves up closer to the front. For the 2008 contest, the Democrats complicated the earliest phase by allowing Nevada to hold its caucus during the week in between the Iowa caucus and the New Hampshire primary and allowing South Carolina to hold its primary the week after New Hampshire. No other state is allowed to hold its primary until the week following the South Carolina primary.

Because candidates must now be prepared to campaign almost simultaneously in several different states, they need sufficient money to buy television time and establish organizations in many locations and media markets. Such huge amounts of cash can only be raised nationally. Therefore, would-be candidates must be capable of appealing to major campaign donors from across the nation well before they ever face a primary voter. More and more, nominating contests have come to resemble the general election itself; the major difference is that they do not take place on a single day but over several different days clumped ever closer together.

Speaking Directly to Congress

Wilson announced in his first inaugural address that presidential rhetoric was the "high enterprise of the new day." In his 1913 address to Congress on tariff reform, he revived the practice, abandoned by Jefferson, of addressing Congress in person. Even TR had not dared to abandon this precedent, which, like the two-term tradition, was viewed as a bulwark against despotism. But Wilson believed that Progressive democracy required the president to take advantage of congressional messages to influence public opinion. The rise of the mass media increased public attention to such events and enabled the president to use them to bring public pressure to bear on Congress. Although die-hard Jeffersonian Democrats resented it, the speech was well received by Congress and the public, aiding Wilson to launch the first successful campaign for tariff reform since before the Civil War. By 1914, all the major elements of Wilson's New Freedom program had been enacted. The president, it seemed, had now supplanted the party system to become the principal agent of popular sovereignty.

The President and Plebiscitary Politics

TR and Wilson believed that just as laissez faire had to give way to a greater sense of national purpose in domestic affairs, so America's isolation had to be abandoned in order to create a better world. In their minds, extending American territory and influence was not imperialistic, it was a way to promote peace and democracy. Practical considerations also prompted a more active foreign policy. The Spanish-American War expanded U.S. territory in the Pacific and Caribbean. To protect it, the United States needed to become more dominant militarily in Central and South America and in the Pacific basin. To do so required that a canal be built across the Central American isthmus so that naval power could move quickly between the Atlantic and Pacific.

Toward the end of World War I, Wilson took the lead in creating an international body, the League of Nations, that would work to preserve the peace. His effort to get the League of Nations treaty ratified aroused intense congressional opposition both because it ignored the warning against forming "permanent alliances with any portion of the foreign world" in Washington's farewell address and because Wilson had not adequately consulted Congress in formulating his plans for the league. To overcome this resistance, Wilson went over the heads of Congress and appealed directly to the people. Congress defeated the treaty, which dealt a major setback to Progressivism and its instrument, the rhetorical presidency.

Wilson was defeated because his opponents were able to show that he was indulging in *plebiscitary politics*; that is, he was trying to govern directly on the basis of public opinion and thereby was undermining such basic constitutional principles as federalism, checks and balances, and the rule of law. The stage for his downfall was set by his campaign in the 1918 midterm elections, in which he urged voters to return Democratic majorities to the House and Senate. TR had accustomed Americans to such efforts, but Wilson's appeal to party loyalty, taking place in the midst of an international crisis, appeared to confirm his opponents' claim that he sought to personally dominate foreign policy, particularly because he had just tried to defeat disloyal Democratic representatives in congressional primary contests.

The Republicans regained control of Congress for the first time since 1912 and made Henry Cabot Lodge of Massachusetts, a leading opponent of the league, the chair of the Senate Foreign Relations Committee. Wilson toured the country trying to mobilize the public behind the league, making increasingly exaggerated claims for the organization and increasingly vituperative attacks against Lodge and his allies. Wilson's intemperance elicited a reaction both against the treaty and against the modern presidency itself. In 1920, Senator Warren Harding (1921–1923), an Old Guard Republican from Ohio, was elected president, in part because of his promises of a "Return to Normalcy."

Harding's election ensured the treaty's defeat. He and his Republican successors, Calvin Coolidge (1923–1929) and Herbert Hoover (1929–1933), were far more circumspect than TR and Wilson about executive authority and popular presidential leadership and were more deferential to Congress and to their party. Hoover did not give the State of the Union address in person; he instead restored the Jeffersonian tradition of submitting it in writing to the clerk of the House.

The Flowering of the Modern Presidency

Wilson's abortive campaign for the League of Nations showed that the presidency was still constrained by a powerful Congress and by a fear of executive power deeply rooted in American political culture. That fear would never be completely overcome, but as we explain in Chapter 4, FDR did make permanent what TR and Wilson had pioneered. Responding to crises at home and abroad, FDR's New Deal grafted a large and powerful national government onto the existing constitutional order, with the presidency at its core. Like previous great presidents, FDR left more than a record of achievement; he bequeathed a constitutional legacy. His legacy was a revised social contract based on an expanded understanding of rights.

FDR's first term was dedicated to formulating the new social contract. To protect those accomplishments, his second term was largely devoted to strengthening the executive office against the decentralizing bulwarks of Jeffersonian democracy: parties, states, and Congress. The successes and failures of this effort defined the contours of modern executive leadership.

The President Challenges the Court

In February 1937, shortly after he was sworn in for his second term, FDR announced the first of three initiatives that would make this second term both contentious and momentous. FDR's first initiative, his court-packing plan, required the president to appoint an additional Supreme Court justice for every existing one who failed to retire within six months of reaching the age of seventy. Six of the nine current justices were seventy or older, which meant that FDR could enlarge the court to fifteen justices, thereby overcoming the court's resistance to New Deal policies.

Jefferson, Jackson, and Lincoln had each fought with the court, but the intensity of the opposition to FDR's plan was unprecedented. Although the new rights that FDR championed had broad popular support, the public was hostile to the plan's audacious aggrandizement of executive power. By controlling the judiciary, the final constitutional barrier to expansion of government and of the presidency would be eliminated.

Humphrey's Executor v. United States and *Schechter Poultry Corp. v. United States*, both handed down on "Black Monday," May 27, 1935, severely constrained presidential authority. *Humphrey* forbade the president from firing members of independent regulatory commissions, a power the court had affirmed in 1926. *Schechter* declared the National Recovery Administration's discretionary powers to be an unconstitutional delegation of legislative authority. Thus, FDR's effort to extend power over the judiciary was more than simply a ploy to amplify his own power or to win disputes over particular policies. It was an effort to regain the powers that he felt the president needed to create and maintain the new economic constitutional order.

Franklin Delano Roosevelt's defeat of Herbert Hoover in the 1932 presidential election set the stage for FDR to revisit the vision of his cousin Theodore Roosevelt. Under FDR, the president became the center of a new constitutional order.

Reorganizing the Executive

FDR's second initiative to strengthen the presidency was the Executive Reorganization Act, also proposed in early 1937. Its purpose was to bolster the institutional support and administrative power of the president, which was quite limited before the 1930s. Many of those officers that are identified with the modern White House – such as chief of staff, director of communications, and national security advisor – did not exist. For better or worse, before FDR, personalities like James Baker, George Stephanopoulos, and Karl Rove were not present in the West Wing. The executive branch included mainly departments and agencies whose secretaries and commissioners composed the cabinet and over whom Congress and party leaders exerted considerable influence.

To make the case for an expanded, professionalized staff, FDR created the President's Committee on Administrative Management, popularly known as the Brownlow Committee after its chair, public administration expert Louis Brownlow. Concluding that "the President needs help," the committee proposed an Executive Office of the President, including a new White House Office and supporting agencies, such as the Budget Bureau, which was then housed in the treasury department. Just as the court-packing plan was designed to remove constitutional obstacles that stood in the way of the modern executive, so the administrative reform program would equip the president with staff and powers to fulfill the new constitutional potential of the executive office.

The President as Party Reformer

The third initiative was FDR's purge campaign. During the 1938 midterm elections, FDR intervened in one gubernatorial and several Senate and House primaries in a bold effort to replace conservative Democrats with 100 percent New Dealers. Although Wilson and Jefferson had dabbled with the idea, no president had ever challenged his own party on such a scale. The press nicknamed FDR's effort the "purge," evoking Adolph Hitler's murder of Nazi dissenters and Joseph Stalin's elimination of suspected opponents within the Soviet Communist party. Although bloodless, FDR's aggressive intervention challenged the very foundation of the party system as a check on presidential ambition.

The Modern Presidency Emerges

FDR's three initiatives were not entirely successful, but they accomplished enough to enable the president and executive agencies to dominate the expanding government. Although the court-packing bill failed, the Supreme Court abruptly ceased overturning New Deal initiatives. Since 1937, it has not invalidated any significant federal statute regulating the economy. Nor has it judged any law (with the exception of the Line Item Veto Act of 1996) to be an unconstitutional delegation of authority to the president. Most of the judicial barriers to national and presidential powers have fallen.

Table 8.3. Executive Office of the President

Council of Economic Advisors
Council on Environmental Quality
Domestic Policy Council
National Economic Council
National Security Council
Office of Administration
Office of Faith-Based and Community Initiatives
Office of Homeland Security
Office of Management and Budget
Office of National AIDS Policy
Office of National Drug Control Policy
Office of Science and Technology Policy
Office of the U.S. Trade Representative
Office of the Vice President
President's Foreign Intelligence Advisory Board
USA Freedom Corps
White House Military Office
White House Office

Source: www.whitehouse.gov/government/eop.html.

After the failure of FDR's original executive reorganization act, a compromise bill was passed in 1939. It created the *Executive Office of the President* (EOP), which contains the White House Office (the so-called West Wing), the nerve center of the modern executive establishment. The act also included the Bureau of the Budget, which later became the *Office of Management and Budget* (OMB). Harry Truman (1945–1953), who succeeded to the presidency when FDR died, added the *National Security Council* (NSC) to the EOP in 1946, followed a year later by the Council of Economic Advisors (CEA).

The 1939 Executive Reorganization Act also enhanced the president's capacity to manage the expanding national bureaucracy. It hastened the development of the administrative presidency, which exercised power on behalf of the president through rule making and policy implementation. The vagueness of Article II of the Constitution had always left the door open for independent presidential action. But the EOP provided an organizational apparatus that presidents could use to short-circuit the separation of powers and accelerate the transfer of power from Congress to the executive. Table 8.3 describes the current EOP.

FDR won only two of his twelve purge attempts, but his very boldness in risking his popularity to defeat certain candidates put his party opponents on the defensive. Moreover, the failure of his purge initiative persuaded FDR that to preserve the New Deal from conservatives in his own party, he would need to run for a third term, something no president had ever done.

A Third Presidential Term

FDR and his political operatives worked quietly behind the scenes to build a "Draft Roosevelt for a Third Term" movement. As one aide put it, they "pistol-whipped" party leaders into accepting the ardent New Dealer and Secretary of Agriculture Henry Wallace as FDR's running mate. This ticket gained the grudging acceptance of the Democratic delegates but not without a last gasp of Jeffersonian resistance. Vice President John Nance Garner and James Farley, chair of the Democratic National Committee, both vied for the nomination. To this day, Garner is the only vice president to challenge the president in a nomination fight. FDR's purge and the precedent-shattering third term enabled FDR to create a party more in his own image. He displaced Jefferson as the patron saint of what was now the majority party.

The powerful political organization that emerged from the New Deal ultimately served to lessen the importance of party politics. Aides to the president displaced party leaders as formulators of policy, organizers of campaigns, liaisons with interest groups, and communicators with the public. Party was no longer the controlling element in presidential elections and governance. Presidents campaigned and governed as the heads of their own personal organizations.

But the purpose of New Deal reform was not to strengthen the presidency for its own sake but to enhance its capacity to foster progressive reform. This objective was most clearly seen in New Deal civil service reform: through executive orders and legislation, FDR extended civil service protection to New Deal loyalists who were brought to Washington to staff the newly created welfare and regulatory state (95 percent of federal service employees were locked in to merit protection by 1941). Traditionally, federal appointments had been used to nourish parties; the New Deal instead built an administrative politics in which federal patronage was doled out on the basis of program, not party, loyalty.

The Ambivalence of Modern Executive Power

FDR was elected president four times; only his death in April 1945 ended his reign. He was the closest that America had ever come to having an elected monarch, an idea Hamilton celebrated and Madison loathed. FDR's death caused many Americans to weep openly and unashamedly for the passing of a great leader. Even so, they hoped never to need such leadership again. The Twenty-second Amendment to the Constitution, which limited presidents to two terms, was ratified in 1951; it made mandatory what Washington had done voluntarily. There would be no more FDRs. But the public did come to hold the president responsible for government action, even for economic and social developments beyond the executive's authority. In the minds of Americans, decentralized American democracy, rooted in the states and localities, was displaced by the president, who came to personify government.

The Importance of the Mass Media

The rise of the mass media greatly intensified the president's personification. Radio enabled presidents to speak directly to the people. Coolidge and Hoover used radio only to make formal pronouncements. FDR's fireside chats were more relaxed and intimate. He built popular support for his programs by explaining them in simple, comprehensible terms.

Dwight Eisenhower (1953–1961) was the first president to appear on television regularly, but John F. Kennedy (1961–1963) was the first to master the new medium. The Kennedy administration staged media events, as political scientist Bruce Miroff has written, that "projected youth, vigor, and novelty, that recast the [presidency] itself as a headquarters for intelligence and masterful will." Convinced that viewers were bored by formal speech making, Kennedy relied more on press conferences. Previous presidents, notably TR and FDR, had used press conferences to cultivate the journalistic fraternity. Kennedy used television to turn them into the visual equivalents of FDR's fireside chats: informal, intimate means for going over the heads of Congress and journalists to reach the public directly. Public opinion surveys gave Kennedy a 91 percent approval rating for his press conference performances. The key was his careful preparation and an ability to appear comfortable and in command on television.

Kennedy's very success compounded the modern president's problems. Even those presidents most gifted in what Hamilton derisively called the "popular arts" have had difficulty meeting rising public expectations. Because they were such effective communicators, Reagan and Clinton were tempted to promise more than they could deliver. As they became increasingly cut off from Congress and party, modern presidents had great difficulty satisfying the very reform demands they helped stimulate. Kennedy's personalization of the presidency greatly accentuated its separation from the other centers of political power.

John F. Kennedy mastered the new medium of television to establish an even closer relationship with the American people.

The Vice Presidency

The personalization of the presidency has had a major impact on the vice presidency as well. Because presidents perform on such a large and prominent stage, they have come to rely on vice presidents to play a more prominent supporting role. This role had shrunk to virtual insignificance during the nineteenth century. Martin Van Buren (1837–1841) was the last incumbent vice president elected president until George H. W. Bush (1989–1993). Other nineteenth-century vice presidents – chosen to provide geographical balance to the presidential ticket – succeeded to the presidency because of the death of the president, but not one of them was elected to a full term. It was not until the election of 1904 that an "accidental" president, Theodore Roosevelt, was elected on his own.

When FDR died, it was obvious that he had failed to fully prepare Vice President Harry Truman to take over. This dilemma created sufficient public anxiety to encourage future presidents to confide more fully in their vice presidents and provide more extensive briefings, particularly about national security. Eisenhower initiated this new relationship by giving Vice President Richard Nixon extensive diplomatic responsibilities. Reagan made Vice President George H. W. Bush head of a task force to provide regulatory relief for business. Clinton put Vice President Al Gore in charge of a major initiative to reform the federal bureaucracy. George W. Bush has relied on Vice President Dick Cheney with regard to a whole raft of domestic and national security matters. Cheney is widely believed to be the most powerful vice president ever.

The Presidency and the National Security State

The modern presidency was created primarily to strengthen the national resolve in terms of domestic programs, but the institutional changes brought by the New Deal reinforced the chief executive's foreign policy role. World War II and the advent of the Cold War irrevocably drew the United States onto the world stage. America's emergence as a world power added greatly to presidential power and prestige but also created new threats and challenges for modern executive leadership.

As early as 1937, FDR began to challenge the mood of isolationism that had dominated the United States since the end of World War I. Whereas the Supreme Court through 1936 had resisted his domestic policy reforms, it abetted his internationalism. In *U.S. v. Curtiss-Wright Export Corporation* (1936), the court upheld a 1934 law authorizing the president to forbid the sale of weapons to countries engaged in armed conflict. This law had been passed with the so-called Chaco War between Bolivia and Paraguay in mind, and FDR quickly forbade arms sales to both countries. Weapons merchants challenged the measure as an unconstitutional delegation of legislative authority to the president. A federal district court agreed, but a near-unanimous Supreme Court held that the president is the government's "sole organ" in international relations, and therefore his actions do not require a specific grant of power from either the Constitution or Congress.

The Curtiss-Wright case established as constitutional doctrine the sweeping defense of the executive's prerogative in foreign affairs that Hamilton had offered in 1793 to defend Washington's Neutrality Proclamation. This principle was reinforced by *U.S. v. Belmont* (1937), which approved the president's right to reach executive agreements with other countries without Senate ratification. These court decisions made it virtually impossible to challenge FDR's increasingly internationalist policies on constitutional grounds. The historian Ellis Hawley has written that "as depression gave way to war, another expansion of presidential power was underway, linked chiefly now to the creation of a national security state rather than a welfare one."

Madison had warned, "War is the true nurse of executive aggrandizement." FDR believed that under conditions of total war, the president was empowered not only to direct military operations abroad but also to manage economic and social affairs at home. To ensure that war production would not be disrupted by labor unrest, he pressured Congress to enact wage and hours legislation. He also took advantage of the war emergency to significantly expand the economic constitutional order. In the first serious effort to extend job protections to African Americans since Reconstruction, FDR established the Fair Employment Practices Committee to prevent racial and other forms of discrimination in the employment of workers in defense industries. Box 3 discusses the president's war powers.

Box Three: Nuts and Bolts

The President's War Powers

Article I of the Constitution grants Congress the power to declare war. Article II anoints the president as commander-in-chief of the military and authorizes executive power. As we point out in the conflict over George Washington's Neutrality Proclamation (see earlier in this chapter), the tensions and possible contradictions inherent in these different grants of power have plagued American politics since the nation began, and they have grown as the presidency has expanded its authority. The Korean and Vietnam Wars were fought without explicit authorization from Congress. The extreme unpopularity of the Vietnam War, aggravated by America's inability to win it, rekindled doubts about granting so much foreign policy discretion to the president. Even a former advocate of greater presidential power, the New Deal historian Arthur Schlesinger, pointed to the Watergate scandal as evidence that "the imperial presidency, created by wars abroad, was making a bold bid for power at home."

In 1973, responding to these growing fears of an "imperial presidency," Congress passed the War Powers Resolution over President Nixon's veto. The act states that during peacetime, the president can deploy troops in hostile actions for only sixty days without obtaining congressional approval. If Congress does not act within that time span, the troops must be removed within thirty days. The constitutionality of the War Powers Resolution has never been tested; no case has come to the Supreme Court. Although presidents continue to deny its constitutionality, when war has threatened they have in fact obtained congressional approval. In 1991, Congress authorized President George H. W. Bush to carry out a United Nations resolution that authorized the use of force to evict Iraq from Kuwait. In 2002, Congress authorized President George W. Bush to take whatever means necessary to ensure the disarmament of Iraq.

The Fragility of the Modern Executive

Of all the post-FDR presidents, Lyndon Johnson (LBJ) most clearly exemplified both the extraordinary prospects and the fragile authority of the modern executive. His greatest achievement came in the struggle for civil rights. More than any of his predecessors, he identified himself with that struggle and enlisted the full force of his rhetorical and legislative gifts in its service. By persuading Congress to enact the 1964 and 1965 civil rights laws, LBJ accomplished what Lincoln could not – statutory protection for African-American political participation, employment opportunity, and access to public accommodations.

The civil rights acts are not just statutes. Like the Social Security Act and the Wagner Act, they are endowed with quasi-constitutional status. Although racial issues remain controversial, the specific rights that these two landmark statutes propound have become as unexceptional as free speech, free assembly, or free practice of religion. Obviously, the enactment of these laws was not all LBJ's doing. He was responding to powerful political and moral pressures exerted by the Civil Rights Movement under the unofficial but inspired leadership of Martin Luther King, Jr. LBJ also built on Kennedy's initiatives, who after a period of indecision had decided to support the civil rights struggle. But LBJ aggressively exploited the political opportunity provided by Kennedy's assassination to press a reluctant Congress to pass the 1964 bill and then availed himself of the huge congressional majority obtained in the 1964 election to pass the 1965 Voting Rights Act.

Taking advantage of this immense electoral victory, Johnson further codified the New Deal vision of a good society. Medicare (1965), which provided healthcare for the elderly, was anticipated by FDR's "economic bill of rights" and Truman's unsuccessful healthcare initiative. Medicaid (1965) gave medical care to the poor. The Elementary and Secondary Education Act (1965) offered educational opportunities for the disadvantaged.

But LBJ was not content to deliver on promises made by Lincoln and FDR. He heralded a Great Society that went beyond the "pursuit of happiness" – as propounded in the Declaration of Independence – to the promise of happiness itself (see Chapter 4). At its most grandiose, the Great Society sought not to enlarge the liberal tradition but to transcend it. LBJ's vision gave rise to a legislative program of remarkable breadth. Policies dedicated to enhancing the quality of American life included pollution reduction, urban redevelopment, consumer protection, and preschool education. These policies of the "spirit rather than the flesh" were also expected to restore a sense of citizenship to political life that had been sapped by bureaucratic indifference and the crass consumerism of mass society.

The Johnson administration launched new social initiatives to foster "participatory democracy." Those people affected by government programs were to be directly involved in policy formulation and implementation. This promise of political self-determination marked a renewal and intensification of the Progressive principle of direct democracy. Participatory democracy was central to LBJ's War on Poverty, which was administered by local community action programs and was required to involve the "maximum feasible participation of residents of the areas and the groups served."

The Great Society did not fulfill its ambitions to supersede the New Deal. Local elected officials threatened by the support given to grassroots movements in their cities and towns appealed to Congress to rein in participatory democracy. The Great Society's hallmarks, those programs that went beyond providing civil and programmatic rights, were killed or gutted. Indeed, by failing in its most grandiose ambitions to restore direct democracy, the Great Society served to increase public skepticism about both the sincerity of governmental intentions and the capacity of government to act effectively.

Presidential Government

Although rhetorically committed to grassroots democracy, LBJ actually increased administrative centralization. His early years in power were the apex of "presidential government." Major policy departures were conceived in the White House, hastened through Congress by the legislative skill of LBJ and his sophisticated congressional liaison team, and administered by new or refurbished executive agencies highly responsive to the president's directives. LBJ also established a personal governing coalition that reached beyond his party.

LBJ overextended himself. The personalized presidency, to which he contributed, proved his undoing. He was a gifted government insider but he lacked the rhetorical skills required to move the wider public. He was unable to cultivate the broad base of popular support that his domestic agenda required. Yet even if he had been a more effective speaker, he would have failed to unite the country because his gargantuan aspirations fractured the nation even as they magnified his burdens. His domination of the political process ensured that he, not Congress, would be blamed if Great Society programs failed. And many of them did, victims of hasty packaging and unrealistic goals.

The war in Vietnam demonstrated even more starkly both LBJ's personal shortcomings and the more troubling aspects of modern presidential government itself. He extended the American commitment in Vietnam because, as a progressive internationalist, he believed that the righteous use of force was necessary in foreign affairs to make the world safe for democracy. Historically, this understanding of America's place in the world had been associated with reform presidents such as TR, Wilson, FDR, Truman, and Kennedy. But the public came to identify Vietnam even more closely and directly with LBJ.

In Korea, Truman could claim to be carrying out the United Nations' dictate. In Vietnam, however, no treaty or other obligations required the United States to intervene. Nor did Congress authorize a "police action" of a magnitude justifying the commitment of 500,000 troops (the size of the American force fighting in Vietnam by the end of 1967). The Johnson administration's claim that such action was authorized by the 1964 Gulf of Tonkin Resolution was highly suspect. In truth, LBJ believed and stated publicly that he had constitutional authority to deploy troops in Vietnam without congressional authorization.

By early 1968, LBJ was trapped, unable to withdraw troops for fear of being damned as the first American president to lose a war, yet lacking the popular support to undertake more aggressive military action. Attacked by

Lyndon Johnson committed his presidency to
the divergent goals of celebrating direct
democracy and dramatically increasing
executive power. His overextended efforts at
home and abroad magnified the dangerous
isolation of the modern presidency.

left and right, he shocked the nation by announcing in a televised address
on March 31, 1968, that he would not seek reelection.

Conservatism and the Modern Presidency

In addition to its specific policy failures, the Great Society left a gnawing
and increasingly pervasive doubt about the capacity of the federal government to achieve its objectives. The New Deal had bequeathed a faith in
the benevolence and the efficacy of Uncle Sam to both intellectuals and
the public at large. Within a decade of the end of the Johnson administration, that faith had largely evaporated. Public mistrust in the presidency
was greatly exacerbated by the Watergate scandal, the subsequent effort to

impeach President Richard Nixon (1969–1974), and Nixon's resignation in 1974 (see Chapter 7).

Continued Welfare State Expansion

Despite growing mistrust of the presidency, the welfare state continued to expand, led by the courts and Congress. But the new environmental, special education, and consumer protection initiatives had a New Deal rather than a Great Society character. These programs involved the writing of checks to individuals, the policing of businesses, or the administering of federal mandates by state and local governments, not ambitious plans to remake American life. Perhaps the single most important expansion was the 1972 amendment to the Social Security Act that pegged Social Security payments to the consumer price index, thereby insulating millions of old age pensioners from the risk of inflation. These regulatory and budgetary changes severely circumscribed presidential power. Because entitlement spending was controlled by formula and because regulatory spending was done mostly by private dollars, these programs did not depend on discretionary federal spending. Presidents could not challenge this spending by cutting the budget; they had to engage in the far more arduous task of revising entitlement formulas and rewriting regulatory statutes.

Challenging the Entitlement State

Ronald Reagan was the only post-FDR president to try to curtail the welfare state. Jefferson and Jackson attacked Hamiltonianism in defense of local self-government. Reagan attacked New Deal neo-Hamiltonianism in the name of personal liberty and private property. Although Reagan's successful 1980 campaign did not result in Republicans' gaining control of Congress, the new president boldly claimed a mandate to cut taxes and spending. Democrats went along. Indeed, they proposed cutting taxes even more. But they opposed many of Reagan's spending reductions. Thus, revenue was reduced far more than spending, which greatly increased the federal deficit, an ironic legacy indeed for a self-proclaimed conservative.

Limits of the Conservative Presidency

Tax reduction may have been all that Reagan could possibly accomplish during his first term. To "get government off the backs of the American people," one of Reagan's stated goals, required a Republican congressional majority. To obtain it, Reagan would need to put his popularity and

Though bold enough to attack the New Deal concept of American national government, Ronald Reagan avoided the type of hard-hitting public debate that could have significantly changed American government.

rhetorical ability in the service of winning votes for Republican congressional candidates.

Forging such partisan loyalty was precisely what FDR accomplished in 1936. Confident of his own reelection, FDR risked alienating voters by demanding that they support Democratic congressional candidates as well. Instead of defusing partisan conflict, FDR crystallized it. He did not take the safe road of simply rehearsing his administration's accomplishments and taking credit for economic recovery. Instead, he castigated New Deal opponents in harsh, provocative terms as "economic royalists" and "privileged princes of the economic dynasty." He turned the election from a personal contest into a partisan conflict, which, given the popularity of the New Deal, he knew he could win.

By contrast, Reagan's 1984 campaign was a marvel of non-partisanship, geared to maximize his personal appeal but drain the election of broader political meaning. Its theme, "Morning in America," provided a soft focus that failed to clarify the choice between Democrats and Republicans. Republicans gained just fourteen House seats, leaving Democrats still in control, and lost two seats in the Senate, retaining a very slim majority. In 1986, Democrats took the upper chamber as well. Failing to gain control of Congress, Reagan had no hope of advancing his agenda during his second term.

The Modern Presidency as a Two-Edged Sword

Although done in the name of limited government, Reagan's approach to reform was as president-centered as that of FDR and LBJ. Reagan challenged liberal policies with acts of administrative discretion that short-circuited the legislative process. Even reductions in environmental and consumer protection were done by administrative action, not legislative change. Reagan had no other option in the short run, but this approach failed to nurture the substantial change in public values and institutions necessary to transform the welfare state. Such a profound reorientation requires the public discussion and debate that elections and congressional deliberation provide. As the Clinton administration recognized, Reagan's administrative quick fixes could be quickly undone.

Winning the Cold War

Ironically, Reagan's greatest accomplishment may have involved an act of perpetuation. Reagan carried the containment policy begun by Truman to fruition by winning the Cold War. He expanded the military buildup begun by Jimmy Carter (1977–1981) in response to the Soviet Union's war in Afghanistan. Reagan's tough talk about the Soviet Union – the "Evil Empire" – steered American policy back to containment and away from the Nixonian detour toward détente. Containment was the policy of exerting continuing pressure on the Soviet Union by stationing troops on its borders and actively preventing its efforts to expand militarily. Containment also involved vast expenditures on defense, much of which was devoted to remaining technologically superior. Détente did not abandon those efforts, but it shifted U.S. diplomatic efforts more in the direction of an accommodation with the Soviets, softening anti-Soviet rhetoric and reducing arms spending. Even before Reagan began his offensive, the Soviets were experiencing severe internal difficulties. But to bring them down, he capitalized on what otherwise might have proved only a temporary setback. The enormity of the economic and technological challenge posed by his military buildup and the staunchness of his rhetoric may have sapped the Soviets of the vigor that otherwise might have proved sufficient for them to stage a comeback.

Despite this extraordinary success, Reagan's foreign policy confirmed the modern presidency's extraordinary isolation and its tendency to ignore constitutional limits. In November 1986, the nation learned that with the president's approval, National Security Council staffers had sold weapons to Iran and that, with or without the president's knowledge, some of the proceeds had been used to assist the Contras, opponents of the socialist Nicaraguan government. Congress had passed the Boland Amendment that expressly forbade arming the Contras, and it would have prohibited selling arms to Iran if it had any inkling such sales were being contemplated. In reaction to the scandal, Reagan's approval rating fell from 67 percent to 46 percent in one month. Although Reagan later reclaimed some of his popularity, his administration never recovered from the institutional estrangement that the Iran-Contra affair instigated. Even members of Congress who supported aid to the Contras regretted Reagan's secrecy; they argued that his long-term efforts to build support for his policies would have been better served by confronting Congress directly, vetoing the Boland Amendment, and taking his case to the nation.

A New Democrat?

In many important respects, Democrat Bill Clinton continued the conservative course charted by his Republican predecessors Reagan and Bush (see Chapter 4). In the presidential primaries, Clinton challenged his party's big government stance; he offered instead a "New Democratic" alternative, a "New Covenant" that promoted personal responsibility and civic virtue. As president, Clinton balanced the budget, initiated no new expensive programs, and signed a very conservative welfare reform law. When he did try to emulate FDR and LBJ, he was rudely rebuked by Congress and the voters. As we discussed at the beginning of this chapter, Clinton's healthcare program was a caricature of the administrative presidency; it was designed behind closed doors by a 630-member task force, and if enacted, it would have created a new government entitlement program and a massively complex bureaucratic apparatus. A Democratic Congress turned it down in 1994. Later that year, the voters signaled their dissatisfaction with Clinton's grandiose ambitions by handing the Democrats the worst congressional elections defeat they had suffered in fifty years.

Clinton recovered from this humiliation to win reelection in 1996. He withstood his impeachment, provoked by the Monica Lewinsky sex scandal, and served out his second term (see Chapter 7). Both of these improbable acts of survival can be explained by the mood of the American electorate in the mid- and late-1990s. Even as they rejected FDR-style reform leadership, the American people remained committed to the New Deal welfare state. Once Clinton shed the programmatic ambition exemplified by his healthcare proposal, his defense of the status quo as embodied by Medicare and Social Security was far more attractive to voters than the Republican threat to curtail them. Likewise, his Lewinsky affair was less troubling to voters than the aggressive and punitive manner in which congressional Republicans and special prosecutor Kenneth Starr hounded him. Liberalism came to Clinton's rescue in two different ways: the voters' devotion to civil liberties made them hostile to Starr's inquisition; and their equal devotion to the programmatic rights pioneered by FDR made them cling to a president who vociferously promised to protect those rights.

Clinton and Foreign Policy

The end of the Cold War left American foreign policy with no clear purpose other than to increase trade. Under Clinton, looming Middle Eastern threats from Al Qaeda and Iraq were downplayed in order to not divert political energy from the negotiation of expanded trade agreements. Clinton supported international human rights and environmental efforts as long as they did not produce American casualties or were not otherwise politically risky. Although the U.S. military intervention in Kosovo killed thousands of Serbs, there were no American battlefield deaths. Clinton signed the Kyoto Accords, designed to lessen global warming. But he did so knowing that the Senate would not ratify the treaty and therefore he would not need to implement the economically costly and politically painful carbon dioxide emissions reductions that the accord called for. Clinton risked his prestige to engage in personal diplomacy that helped achieve the Good Friday Agreement over Northern Ireland. But in the Mideast, similar efforts at personal diplomacy were an abject failure, showing the limits of this technique in the face of truly implacable foes.

The 2000 Election

During the Clinton era, Republicans not only took control of Congress, they also captured the governorships of all the most heavily populated states except California – Texas, New York, Florida, Pennsylvania, Illinois, Michigan, Ohio, New Jersey, and Massachusetts. Recognizing that a defeat of Democratic nominee Al Gore would require them to promote a moderate candidate, these large-state Republican governors united behind Governor George W. Bush of Texas. This display of solidarity shows that even though candidate-centered politics and declining party cohesion emerged as powerful trends after the New Deal, it was still possible, at least for Republicans, to put party well-being above personal ambition. The governors did not choose Bush only because he was the most telegenic among them and came from the largest state. Perhaps his greatest political asset was that he was close to key leaders of the party's more conservative congressional wing, especially Texans Dick Armey and Tom DeLay. This link was especially valuable because Bush's main challenger was expected to be Steve Forbes, who had spent the previous four years bolstering his conservative credentials.

Bush positioned himself perfectly to defeat Forbes, but his most serious challenge came from a moderate and a war hero, Senator John McCain of Arizona. Campaigning as a latter-day Teddy Roosevelt, McCain almost garnered enough independent votes to sufficiently humiliate Bush in the New England primaries and force Bush from the race. Bush survived by moving to the right, and he soundly defeated McCain in South Carolina, where conservative Republicans viewed McCain as a Democrat in war hero's clothing. Bush gained stature among conservatives simply by taking on McCain and defeating him.

As we discuss in more detail in Chapter 9, the 2000 presidential election ended in a virtual tie. For the first time since 1888, the victor did not win the most popular votes, and the outcome in Florida, which provided Bush with his margin of victory, was contested in court and ultimately determined by the U.S. Supreme Court.

The Presidency and September 11

Bush's presidency had a shaky beginning. Like Clinton's claim to be a "New Democrat," Bush's "compassionate conservatism" seemed a weak effort to please all sides. A week before September 11, conservative journalist David Brooks called Bush the political equivalent of Gilligan, the lovable but dopey hero of the 1970s television sitcom *Gilligan's Island*. But Bush found his voice when justifying the war on terrorism. In words reminiscent of FDR, Bush told a joint session of Congress on September 20, 2001, "Freedom and fear are at war. . . . The advance of human freedom, the great achievement of our time, now depends on us. Our nation, this generation, will lift a dark threat of violence from our people and our future. We will not tire, we will not falter, and we will not fail."

Bush's response to September 11 was both a continuation and a departure from the Progressive internationalist tradition that has dominated the modern presidency since TR and Wilson. Like a true Progressive, Bush emphasized that the War on Terror was not only an effort to protect American lives and property but also a "crusade" to protect liberal and democratic values. But he also made clear that the United States was setting its own course, and while it welcomed consultation and assistance from other nations, it would not be deterred by the misgivings of even its closest allies. Wilson had trumpeted the need for a League of Nations to enforce a lasting peace. FDR had invested considerable diplomatic and political capital in working with the wartime allies to found the United Nations. Bush's father, George H. W. Bush, had formed a broad international coalition to prosecute the Persian Gulf War of 1991. But Bush, unlike his father, did not wait to put together a massive allied force to invade Afghanistan. The war was fought and won by U.S. elite forces working in close coordination with missile, drone, and bomber launches and troops from the Northern Alliance. Because Bush did not rely on the Western powers militarily, he had the freedom to offend them verbally. Although Germany and other close allies endorsed the war in Afghanistan, only Britain and Israel supported Bush's contention that beyond Afghanistan, America's goal was to stand vigilant against an "axis of evil" composed of Iraq, Iran, and North Korea.

Bush's new approach to foreign policy was highly controversial within his own official family. It pitted Secretary of State Colin Powell, a committed internationalist, against Vice President Cheney and Secretary of Defense Donald Rumsfeld, who advocated aggressive military action even in the face of allied opposition. Former members of Bush's father's administration, most notably Secretary of State Lawrence Eagleburger and National Security Advisor Brent Scowcroft, spoke out in opposition to Bush's aggressive Iraq policy. Bush's stance was less controversial within the Republican party at large. As we point out in Chapter 7, Republican politicians for the most part backed Bush's verbal aggressions, just as they were pleased with the success of his military tactics. The Christian Right found a godsend in Bush's increasingly unequivocal support for Israel and his "axis of evil" declaration about the "godless" regimes of North Korea and Iraq and the Islamist regime of Iran. The gubernatorial wing's support was indicated by Bush's appointment of former Pennsylvania governor Tom Ridge to the new and crucial post of Secretary of Homeland Security.

Bush's approach created a political dilemma for the Democrats. They could not directly oppose his policies without appearing unpatriotic. But they were less ambivalently progressive than Bush. They treasured close ties with the European allies and were strongly committed to respecting and working through international institutions like NATO and the UN. Democrats were somewhat mollified by Bush's willingness to take his case against Iraq to the UN Security Council and to hold off an attack while he awaited the report of UN arms inspectors, but they sensed that this decision was halfhearted and that Bush would not really allow the UN to deter him from war.

The Democrats' discontent with Bush's approach revealed a deep difference about the importance of "world opinion." This concept is hard to measure, but if it is defined as the professed opinion of leaders around the world and the outpouring of sentiments as expressed by rallies and demonstrations, then it is plausible to conclude that world opinion decisively rejected key aspects of Bush's policy. Although not unconcerned with world opinion, Bush made clear that its influence on U.S. foreign policy was not decisive.

An Expanded Presidency

As we point out several times in this chapter, war expands the power of the presidency. Beginning in spring 2002, Bush and his aides openly pursued the possibility of invading Iraq. Unlike the Gulf War of 1991, this mission would involve a "preemptive" attack and had as its objective the removal of Saddam Hussein from power. In October 2002, Congress passed a resolution that gave Bush the discretion to use military force against Iraq; in November, it created a Department of Homeland Security, the most ambitious reorganization of the government's national security apparatus in a half century.

Congress did not entirely acquiesce to Bush's aggressive assertions of presidential authority. Both Democrats and Republicans criticized the refusal of Tom Ridge, so long as he was director of the White House Office of Homeland Security, to testify before Congress about the president's homeland defense budget. Bush initially resisted the idea of creating another department of government; he created instead a small office by executive order that was housed in the West Wing. The White House claimed that Ridge's office was akin to the National Security Council, a presidential agency whose officials did not have to appear before Congress. Similarly, Attorney General John Ashcroft encountered bipartisan criticism when the administration put some measures in place to crack down on terrorism at home, including military tribunals to try suspected foreign terrorists and a rule allowing investigators to listen in on some lawyer-client conversations. Bipartisan resistance stiffened further toward the end of 2005, buttressed by revelations that the Bush administration had used the highly secret National Security Agency to monitor some domestic communications without judicial review or consultation with Congress.

The Bush administration's determination to fight the War on Terror outside the bounds of conventional legal constraints was a constant source of tension between the White House and Congress. This inter-branch struggle was roiled not only by Bush's policy to use military tribunals to try enemy combatants and the White House's justification for surveillance of overseas phone calls but also by the administration's expansive rules permitting tough interrogation of suspected terrorists. A series of memos from the CIA's general counsel and from the justice department's Office of Legal Counsel gave the government wide-ranging powers to imprison and interrogate terror suspects. In some cases, these powers overrode the Geneva Conventions, the international rules that had governed the treatment of prisoners and civilians during wartime and occupation for the past half century. Since terrorists were not fighting on behalf of an established state or in uniform, the Bush administration argued, they were not covered by the law of war. President Bush approved a permissive set of rules governing interrogation, which allowed the CIA to set up secret detention centers abroad; high-level terrorist suspects were reportedly subject to treatment that approached (or exceeded) torture – for example, techniques like "water-boarding," in which a bound prisoner is held underwater to the brink of drowning.

Withstanding vigorous White House opposition, Congress, led by Senator John McCain, himself a victim of torture as a prisoner of war in Vietnam, enacted the Detainee Treatment Act of 2005. Bush signed this legislation, which prohibited interrogation techniques that, as the bill stated, subjected persons under U.S. control or custody to "cruel, inhuman, or degrading treatment or punishment." But the president appended a statement to his signature, objecting to some of the new law's provisions and explicitly reserving the right to interpret them "in a manner consistent" with his constitutional authority as president and commander-in-chief. Following, indeed wildly exceeding, the practice of his three most recent predecessors – Ronald Regan, George H. W. Bush, and Bill Clinton – Bush used signing statements during his first five years as president to declare that he would not enforce more than 500 provisions of more than 100 laws. In each case, his purpose was to insulate executive power from congressional and judicial oversight, especially in matters pertaining to national and homeland security.

Bush's defense of a largely unchecked "unitary executive" did not go unchallenged. In June 2006, the Supreme Court ruling of *Hamdan v. Rumsfeld* strongly limited the power of the Bush administration to conduct military tribunals for and employ aggressive interrogation techniques on suspected terrorists imprisoned at the U.S. Navy base, Guantanamo Bay, Cuba. Brushing aside administration pleas not to second-guess the commander-in-chief during wartime, a five-justice majority ruled that the tribunals, which were outlined by Bush in a military order of November 13, 2001, were neither authorized by federal law nor required by military necessity, and violated the Geneva Conventions. Consequently, the court ruled, no military commission could try Salam Ahmed Hamdan, the former aide to Osama Bin Laden, captured in Afghanistan, whose case was before the justices, or anyone else, unless the president did one of two things he had refused to do for four years: operate the commissions by the laws of regular military court martial, or ask Congress for specific permission to proceed differently.

Responding to *Hamdan*, Bush had little choice but to press for legislation endorsing his approach to terrorists; however, the White House's efforts to get Congress to narrowly define U.S. obligations under the Geneva Conventions met strong resistance in the Senate, where three respected Republicans – McCain, Lindsay Graham of South Carolina, and John Warner of Virginia, chairman of the Armed Services Committee – rejected the Bush administration's approach not only as unbefitting a free nation but also as an invitation to other countries, including Iran, Syria, and North Korea, to reinterpret international rules regarding the treatment of prisoners as they saw fit if they ever held U.S. soldiers. Anxious to resolve this intra-party dispute before the 2006 elections, the White House and dissident Republicans reached a compromise in September 2006 on legislation that did not formally alter the United States' compliance with the Geneva Conventions but recognized the president's special constitutional responsibilities as commander-in-chief. The White House, for its part, gave up its desire to adopt, with congressional approval, a restricted obligation under Common Article 3 of the Geneva accords. Article 3 requires humane treatment of detainees and prohibits "violence to life and person" such as death and mutilation, as well as cruel treatment and "outrages upon personal dignity." In turn, Congress delegated to the president a dominant role in deciding which interrogation methods are permitted by Article 3 and some discretion to withhold information about the sources of evidence. Most controversially, the Military Commissions Act, which Bush signed into law on October 18, 2006, authorized the use of military tribunals and denied defendants the right of habeas corpus, a hallowed legal protection that compels the government to allow anyone charged with a crime to appear before a civilian judge.

Thus, although the roots of congressional resentment against executive slights ran deep, September 11 and the war against terrorism affirmed the preeminence of the modern presidency. Indeed, the White House and Congress collaborated on a major overhaul of the executive branch that ratified an expansion of the president's authority to protect the country. At the instigation of Congress, Bush proposed to create "a single, permanent department with an overriding and urgent mission: securing the homeland of America, and protecting the American people." Democrats and

Republicans on Capitol Hill looked favorably on Bush's proposal, in part because Congress has much more authority over departments than over a White House office. The president's plan promised to end the protracted struggle about whether Ridge was obligated to testify before Congress concerning his budget and programs. At the same time, the creation of a cabinet department would signify that homeland security had become an ongoing responsibility of the national government. In accepting the idea of a department and urging Congress to authorize it by statute, Bush paved the way for an important expansion of the extraordinary yet fragile authority of the modern presidency. As Box 4 explains, Bush and the Congress also agreed to embark upon a renewed effort to reform the intelligence community.

Box Four: Nuts and Bolts

The Intelligence Community

In the affairs of nations, intelligence means information obtained about the plans and activities of other countries – or foreign organizations, like Al Qaeda – that affect the security and well-being of one's own country. If the intelligence is obtained secretly, it is referred to as covert intelligence. If it regards the intelligence gathering or operations on U.S. soil by foreign powers or organizations, it is called counterintelligence. If it is obtained by spies, it is called human intelligence. If it involves keeping data and documents secure or deciphering data and documents produced by others, it is called cryptology.

September 11 was a massive counterintelligence failure. The perpetrators had been living in the United States for, in some cases, long periods of time, had traveled extensively within its borders, attended flight school, and communicated with one another and yet had remained at liberty to commit their heinous crimes. In the aftermath of September 11 it was discovered that the Federal Bureau of Investigation had indeed possessed important evidence relating to the September 11 plot but had not either acted on the information or shared it with other intelligence agencies.

Since September 11, both the executive branch and Congress have devoted considerable attention to improving the means for obtaining information about terrorist plans and activities and for ensuring that such information is relayed to those in a position to act on it. In 2004 Congress passed and the president signed the *Intelligence Reform and Terrorism Prevention Act* whose purpose was to create better coordination and communication between the various agencies of government that are collectively called the U.S. Intelligence Community. These include Army Intelligence, Central Intelligence Agency, Coast Guard Intelligence, Defense Intelligence Agency, Department of Energy, Department of Homeland Security, Department of State, Department of the Treasury, Drug Enforcement Administration, Federal Bureau of Investigation, Marine Corps Intelligence, National Geospatial-Intelligence Agency, National Reconnaissance Office, National Security Agency, and Navy Intelligence.

The 2004 Act established the new post of Director of National Intelligence (DNI) and designated the DNI as the head of the intelligence community. The DNI also acts as the principal advisor to the president, the National Security Council, and the Homeland Security Council for intelligence matters. In addition, the DNI oversees and directs the implementation of the National Intelligence Program. The president appoints the DNI with the advice and consent of the Senate. The Director is assisted by a Principal Deputy Director of National Intelligence (PDDNI), appointed by the president with the advice and consent of the Senate.

An earlier effort to centralize and coordinate intelligence efforts took place in 1947 when Truman signed the National Security Act, establishing the Central Intelligence Agency (CIA). In 1952, military and civilian cryptologic functions were combined into a single entity, the National Security Agency (NSA). Except for cryptology, the CIA was created expressly to serve as the central provider and coordinator of intelligence activities. However, the NSA Act did not forbid other departments and agencies from performing intelligence and counterintelligence functions. Most notably, the military insisted on retaining its own intelligence capability. In 1961, the Department of Defense reorganized its intelligence efforts to create the Defense Intelligence Agency (DIA) to serve as the principle provider of all forms of military intelligence. Likewise, the Federal Bureau of Investigation (FBI), the investigative arm of the Department of Justice, insisted on retaining its own counterterrorism division. In principle, the DNI heads the defense community, but of the heads of the three major intelligence agencies, only the CIA director reports to the DNI. The DIA remains in the Defense Department and the FBI continues to

> function as a largely autonomous agency within the Department of Justice. The DNI has no direct operational control over either the DIA or the FBI. It remains to be seen whether or not the DNI will actually be able to improve the nation's intelligence capabilities in the face of the continued independence enjoyed by these often rivalrous agencies.

Bush and Congress also placed new responsibilities on the executive for regulating the economy. The collapse of Enron, a huge energy trading corporation, and WorldCom, a leading telecommunications company, amid revelations of fraudulent accounting practices and unethical boardroom scheming caused the stock market and consumer confidence to plummet. Bush lacked the credibility on economic issues that he enjoyed regarding homeland security and the War on Terror. Few presidents have been more closely associated with corporate America than Bush was. Indeed, some critics raised questions about financial dealings by the president and vice president during their years in the oil business.

Anxious to allay doubts about the faltering economy and to protect Republicans in the November 2002 midterm elections, Bush rushed to take charge of efforts, already well advanced in Congress, to reform corporate behavior. Sounding more like TR than like his party's more recent conservative icons, the president gave a tough speech on Wall Street in July 2002, proclaiming that America's "greatest economic need is higher ethical standards – standards enforced by strict laws and upheld by responsible business leaders." Bush announced the creation of a Corporate Fraud Task Force to coordinate federal, state, and local efforts to investigate and prosecute financial crimes.

A few weeks later, Bush signed the Sarbanes-Oxley Act, celebrated as "the most far-reaching reform of American business practices since the time of Franklin Delano Roosevelt." Among other provisions, the act strengthened the Securities and Exchange Commission and formed a Public Accounting and Oversight Board "to enforce professional standards, ethics, and competence for the accounting profession." (See the discussion of Sarbanes-Oxley in Chapter 6.)

Whether these measures prove adequate to right the economy and restore confidence on Wall Street remains to be seen. But they clearly deviate from the prevailing wisdom of the 1980s and 1990s that Washington should interfere as little as possible with securities trading and corporate practices. To shore up his administration's credibility on the economy, Bush

After the War on Terror brought the presidency back to the center of American politics, Bush staked his political credibility on assisting members of his party in their bids for Congress in 2002, such as South Dakota Republican candidate for the Senate Representative John Thune, who eventually won a tight race. Bush's efforts paid off, and the GOP sealed a historic midterm triumph by increasing its majority in the House and taking control of the Senate.

had upheld TR's admonition that presidents must serve as the steward of the public welfare.

Executive Power and the "New" Party System

For much of the history of the modern presidency, executive power and partisanship have appeared to be at odds. The forging of direct ties between the White House and public opinion combined with aggressive executive administration has tended to subordinate partisan loyalty to the personal and programmatic ambitions of the president. According to some scholars, Bush's presidency has defied collective partisan responsibility. As the controversies over spying on terrorist suspects and detention of enemy combatants reveal, the Bush administration has sought to expand the powers of the modern executive office.

At the same time, however, Bush and his top political advisor, Karl Rove, have been unusually committed to building an enduring governing party and partisan coalition. Since the flowering of the modern presidency, in fact, no White House has been so committed to party building. Bush's presidency, in fact, shows how a militantly partisan president can use the expanded powers of the White House for party purposes.

Some commentators claim that the Bush White House's preoccupation with executive power resembles Richard Nixon's presidency. Like Nixon, Bush has emphasized the administrative presidency, consolidating influence in a small circle of advisors in the White House office during his first term and attempting to expand this circle through the appointment of loyalists to head departments and agencies in the second. But whereas Nixon focused on creating a personal machine that marginalized and weakened the Republican Party, Bush has doggedly pursued policies and campaign strategies with a view to strengthening the GOP. Nixon's Committee for the Re-Election of the President (CREEP) operated with complete autonomy from the Republican National Committee (RNC) and set its sights on a personal landslide; the Bush-Cheney reelection effort worked hand-in-glove with the Republican National Committee and the entire campaign was built on the premise of gaining a party victory. The reward for this militant partisanship is that for most of his presidency, Bush has been accorded considerable deference from congressional Republicans.

Indeed, with the steadfast support of Republican leaders in Congress, the Bush White House has mobilized party loyalty and party organization to advance a conservative executive-centered administrative state. This started with Reagan, but Bush has trumped Reagan in his commitment to what might be termed "big government conservatism." The most dramatic example is the Bush administration's foreign policy, especially its controversial "preemption doctrine," used to justify the War in Iraq. The preemption doctrine states that because terrorists strike anywhere and at any time with no warning, it is impossible to wait for evidence of a clear and present danger before taking military action against them. Therefore, offensive measures provide the only prudent defense against terrorist aggression.

Bush-style big government conservatism extends far beyond ambition to homeland security. Rather than curtail New Deal and Great Society entitlements, as the Reagan administration and the Gingrich-led 104th Congress attempted, Bush sought to recast them in a conservative image. His hope has been to cement ties between the Republican Party and groups that have conservative instincts but who, for one reason or another, need government help. For example, religious organizations have felt that they have been unfairly disadvantaged in obtaining federal funds to help those in need.

In response, Bush instituted a "faith-based" initiative to change federal and state regulations to permit private "faith-based" charitable organizations to play a larger role in providing government services to drug addicts, homeless persons, pregnant teenagers, and other disadvantaged members of society. As he had done in Texas, Bush sought to rally conservatives around the idea of making schools better by making them more demanding. Rather than eliminate the Department of Education, as the Reagan administration proposed to do, the Bush administration championed the No Child Left Behind Act, passed in 2001, which holds all schools accountable to standards set by the federal government. In response to pressure from the elderly, he fought for the enactment of an extremely costly expansion to Medicare, the 2003 addition of prescription drugs coverage.

Even Bush's most spectacular domestic policy failure, his doomed effort at the start of his second term to reform Social Security, reflected his commitment to big government conservatism. Unlike Reagan, he did not propose to cut Social Security benefits, but, rather, to "privatize" them by allowing workers under age 55 to divert some of their Social Security payroll taxes into personal retirement accounts. This reform, the White House claimed, would yield a better rate of return on funds dedicated to Social Security benefits and would recast the core New Deal entitlement as a vehicle by which individuals would assume greater responsibility to plan for their own retirement. Yet the federal government would still force people to save, restrict the investment choices they could make, and regulate the pace at which they could withdraw their money in retirement. Lamenting the accelerated growth of national regulations and domestic spending during the Bush years, Christopher DeMuth, the president of the conservative think tank the American Enterprise Institute, has lamented, "The 2001–2005 period marks the transformation of the Republican Party from its traditional role as a win-or-lose guardian of limited government, to that of a majority governing party just as comfortable with big government as Democrats, only with different spending priorities." DeMuth's concerns can only have increased since the 2006 election results, which put Democrats back in control of Congress and therefore made it far more difficult for Bush to press for a traditional conservative agenda.

The Bush administration's party building complemented the cause of big government conservatism. His active recruitment of Republican candidates and diligent fundraising considerably strengthened the national party organization; and his public displays of religiosity and use of strong moral language have served to consolidate a Republican identity of moral and religious conservatism that has energized Republican partisans. Large tax cuts in 2001 and 2003 were equally appealing to the party's economic conservatives. These efforts yielded handsome political benefits during the first six years of the Bush presidency (see Chapter 11). The president's dramatic intervention in the 2002 midterm elections helped Republicans achieve historic victories in the House and Senate. Building on the success in the 2002 elections, Bush and his advisors designed and implemented an ambitious grassroots campaign for the 2004 elections. Indeed, one could argue that they built the first "national party machine" in American history – an elaborate network of campaign volunteers concentrated in the sixteen most competitive states, which was credited as a key to Bush's narrow but decisive victory over his opponent, Senator John Kerry of Massachusetts, in the presidential election, and with helping to increase Republicans' command of the Senate and House. Bush thus surpassed Reagan, whose party leadership never led to Republican majorities in both the House of Representatives and Senate. Indeed, Bush's reelection made him the first president since Franklin Roosevelt to be reelected while his party also gained seats in both the House and Senate – he is the first Republican to win reelection with majorities in the House and Senate since Calvin Coolidge in 1924. Bush's four most recently reelected predecessors – Dwight Eisenhower in 1956, Richard Nixon in 1972, Ronald Reagan in 1984, and Bill Clinton in 1996 – won by much larger margins than he did. But theirs were "lonely landslides" in which the president did well but his party suffered in the congressional elections. In contrast, Bush's 2004 reelection spearheaded a partisan victory.

Bush did not deserve sole credit for the Republican gains. Since the late 1970s, the party had been developing the Republican National Committee (RNC), rather than state and local organizations, into the principal agent of party-building activities. Believing it had been outorganized "on the ground" in the 2000 election, the Republicans devised a mass grassroots mobilizing strategy in 2002. Democrats since the New Deal had relied on auxiliary party organizations such as labor unions to get out the vote. But the Bush White House, working closely with the RNC, created its own organization to mobilize supporters. Depending on volunteers, albeit closely monitored ones, and face-to-face appeals to voters, the Republicans built on their success in 2002 to mount the most ambitious national grassroots campaign in the party's history for the 2004 elections.

After Bush's reelection, the Republican coalition began to show considerable signs of strain: the war in Iraq, the Hurricane Katrina debacle, the failed Harriet Miers Supreme Court nomination (see Chapter 9), and various other scandals eroded Bush's public approval ratings. Important libertarian conservative groups grew increasingly frustrated with Bush's "big government conservatism," which they perceived as an abdication of fiscal and constitutional principles done in deference to the religious and moral concerns of social conservatives. Ironically, at the same time, social conservatives grew frustrated with the administration's willingness to soft-pedal some issues of importance to them, such as abortion and same-sex marriage. The Religious Right and its allies took this to be a pragmatic effort to maintain ties to libertarians and more moderate voters, and to push economic reforms (such as Social Security and bankruptcy reform) that they felt favored business and the rich. Social conservatives have also split from Republican business interests over the issue of immigration reform. Business favored a guest worker program that would accommodate illegal immigrants. Social conservatives preferred a policy emphasizing border security and the removal of undocumented workers.

Bush's poll numbers dropped considerably during his troubled second term, sorely testing the durability of the Republican coalition. But the White House's political troubles would have been even more catastrophic had it not been for the expanded, fiercely loyal Republican party "base" that the president and his political strategists have so assiduously cultivated. The base is composed of those loyal Republicans who participate actively in politics and tend to stay with the party leaders through thick and thin. Bush's favorable ratings, which had dropped to 31 percent in early May of 2006, rebounded to 44 percent by mid-September, buttressed by 86 percent of Republican loyalists who still expressed support for the president.

Instead of focusing on so-called "swing" voters, voters who were still on the fence between the two candidates, the 2004 Bush-Cheney grass-roots organization reached out to "lazy Republicans." These were people predisposed to vote for Republicans at all levels but who needed to be prodded and reminded to go to the polls. In fact, the 2004 campaign may have marked a culmination of sorts in the development of a "new" party system. Before 2004, the "new" national party system had strengthened partisan discipline in Washington, D.C., most notably in Congress, and had been a valuable source of campaign services – especially campaign funds – for candidates. But it had failed to stir the passions and allegiance of the American people, attested to by declining partisan identification and anemic voting rates. In contrast, the 2004 campaign seemed passionate, polarized, and participatory. Thus the Republican "grassroots mobilization" – and earnest Democratic efforts to compete with it – represent the best evidence that a "new" party system has come of age. Significantly, both the Republican grassroots organization and the get-out-the-vote campaign of Americans Coming Together (ACT), the 527 ("shadow party") group that assumed principal responsibility for the Kerry campaign's voter mobilization effort, were organized outside of the regular state and local party organizations (see Chapter 11 for an explanation of 527 organizations). Both camps sought to recruit new insurgent leadership in the states and localities to serve as company commanders in a nationalized party offensive. Beyond its immediate electoral effectiveness, then, the Bush White House's mobilization efforts in 2004 may provide a plausible blueprint for a revitalized party politics that draws more people into the political process and renews linkages between citizens and elected officials.

Although Bush's partisan leadership marks the most systematic effort by a modern president to create a strong national party, the prospects for "a new party system" that can hold the modern presidency to account are still very uncertain. In fact, the "new" party system may turn out to be nothing more than a tool of the modern presidency. As Rove put it, the national parties that have emerged since the 1980s are "of great importance in the tactical and mechanical aspects of electing a president." But they are "less important in developing a political and policy strategy for the White House." In effect, he said, parties served as a critical "means to the president's end."

The Bush-Cheney 2004 campaign sought to frame the choice the voters faced as one between two individuals, George Bush and John Kerry, not one between Republican and Democratic principles. Voters were urged to focus on the questions of character and temperament. Which individual, in the aftermath of September 11, was most likely to manage the imposing tasks of economic and homeland security? The Bush campaign's emphasis on wartime leadership was skillfully tied to national security and traditional values that appealed to Republican partisans (see Chapter 11); but the centrality of presidential leadership tended to emphasize loyalty to Bush rather than to a collective party organization with a past and a future. As Matthew Dowd, the top strategist for the 2004 Bush-Cheney campaign, suggested in a post-election interview, "Leadership is a window into the soul – people want someone they can count on in tough times, and [after September 11] Bush filled this paternalistic role." Given the president's campaign message, the impressive grassroots operation may have been less a means for mobilizing support for shared values and partisan goals than for mobilizing public approval for the president's personal leadership in the War on Terror.

The Democratic campaign, too, emphasized personal administrative competence and strength of character. A central theme of the National Democratic Convention was Kerry's military service. He accepted the nomination with a salute and with the emphatic pronouncement that he was "reporting for duty!" The convention did not emphasize party principles, but focused instead on presenting the Democratic senator as a "plausible alternative" to the incumbent president, one who displayed the "strength required of a leader in post–9–11 America."

Kerry's electoral chances suffered from his "flip-flopping" on the question of his support for the war in Iraq which appeared to defy his campaign's emphasis on his strength of character. But the deciding factor in the election was not his personal indecisiveness but the unwillingness of his party to resist Bush's use of his prerogative power. As we note in Chapter 7, like many Democrats in the Congress, Kerry justified his vote for the Iraqi resolution in 2002 by claiming that it did not declare war, but, instead, delegated to the president authority to go to war and determine its scope and duration. He maintained during the 2004 campaign that he would have cast the same vote even after knowing the facts on the ground in Iraq; after all, he said, "I believe it's the right authority for the president to have." This acceptance of executive aggrandizement badly hamstrung Kerry's effort to challenge Bush on the central issue of the 2004 presidential election.

Although both the Republicans and Democrats engaged in innovative and effective practices in raising campaign funds, getting their message out, and mobilizing voters during the 2004 elections, it remains unclear whether the profound revival of the modern executive's governing authority in the wake of the September 11 attacks has brought a new national party system to fruition or continued the long-term development of a modern presidency that undermines collective partisanship. Ultimately, as Dowd acknowledged, "both parties' organizing force has focused on President Bush – the Republicans in defense of his leadership; the Democrats in opposition – hostility – to it." The 2006 midterm elections confirmed this tendency. It was a victory for the Democrats, but one derived from a campaign based on opposition to a president who, although increasingly unpopular because of the war in Iraq and the ineffective federal response in Louisiana and Mississippi to Hurricane Katrina in August 2005, would not be on the ballot in 2008.

Conclusion: Whither the Modern Presidency?

The presidency was originally conceived as a guardian of constitutional sobriety, as a check against the populist temptations of Congress. During the nineteenth century, it was captured by the mass party system and became a more popular office than the Framers intended it to be. Party constrained the president but also legitimized the office during critical episodes of political development such as the Jacksonian period and the Civil War. Jackson and Lincoln in particular emerged as vital popular leaders, but they did so as rhetoricians and party leaders. Party continued to restrain them.

Beginning in the Progressive Era and culminating in the time of the New Deal, the modern presidency emerged and replaced party and Congress as the principal agent of popular rule. In pursuit of his "economic constitutional order," FDR created a new Democratic majority and condemned his opponents as "Tories" and "economic royalists." But the administrative essence of the New Deal made this party success only a way station on the road to more centralized, executive-dominated politics, a shift greatly augmented by World War II and the Cold War.

This transformation and centralization of the presidency was, to a considerable extent, inevitable and desirable. Without the emancipation of the executive from previous institutional and partisan constraints, the greatest moral triumph of recent American history – ending racial segregation in the South – might not have occurred. This victory shows that modern presidents can combine the best aspects of America's liberal and democratic traditions, that they can, in Lincoln's words, "appeal to our better angels."

In the absence of vital party politics, however, both LBJ and Reagan failed in their hope of becoming great democratic leaders in the tradition of FDR. The tragedy of Vietnam, which deflected LBJ's attempt to build a Great Society, might have been forestalled by a vigilant Democratic party, just as the debacle of Iran-Contra might have been prevented by an alert Republican party. As these disasters illustrate, modern presidents navigate a treacherous and lonely path, subject to a volatile political process that makes great democratic leadership very difficult to achieve.

Clinton's dramatic display of the health identity card on national television showed how dependent he was on arousing public support to pursue his objectives. The failure of his healthcare proposal persuaded him that the grand administrative politics associated with the New Deal and Great Society could not be further expanded. At the same time, it only reinforced his concern to attend closely to public opinion. After 1994, facing a hostile Congress and the crisis of impeachment, Clinton exceeded all his predecessors in measuring and trying to mold public opinion. The White House even polled voters on where the First Family should vacation. Although critical of Clinton's obsession with public opinion, the Bush White House has also made extensive use of polls, albeit the polls are used to figure out how to present ideas to the public rather than as a basis for determining policy. At the dawn of a new century, it appeared that the mastering of public opinion had become an end in itself; contemporary politicians seemed to crave popularity more than greatness.

Perhaps the national parties that have arisen over the past two decades will bind the modern presidency to America's democratic tradition. The current Republican Party and, for much of his tenure, President George W. Bush, have been more committed and better equipped to coordinate campaigns and collaborate on policy than were the Democrats and Bill Clinton. Just as Bush has played a critical part in drawing campaign funds and loyalists to his party, so he has benefited from the steadfast backing of his party members in Congress and party loyalists in the electorate. Without this rock-solid support of his fellow Republicans, Bush's pursuit of a polarizing war in Iraq would have been far more treacherous politically in 2002 and 2004. The traditional decentralized parties, nourished by the patronage system, acted as a gravitational pull against presidential ambition; the national parties sustained not only by the national party committees, but also by advocacy groups, think tanks, and the mass media, encourage presidents to advance bold programs and policies. The rise of more national and programmatic parties deprives partisanship in the United States of some of the tolerance that hitherto has made party loyalty so compatible with the liberal tradition in American politics. It may be, however, as A. James Reichley has written, "that a politics tied more clearly to principles and ideals is more appropriate to the current stage of our national life."

At this point, however, the prospects for a "new" party system are very uncertain. The establishment of the presidency as the "steward of the public welfare" has put a premium on candidate-centered campaigns that showed every sign of reviving as the 2008 presidential nominating process revved into high gear in late 2006, well over a year before the first primary ballot was scheduled to be cast. The modern executive office still summons aspirants whose ambition is best served by acting outside the bounds of party politics. Only by governing independently, as Hamilton wrote in "Federalist No. 72," can presidents pursue "extensive and arduous enterprises for the public benefit." By contrast, Congress cannot be effective, let alone powerful, without the institution of party. A legislature can rival the executive's claim to public confidence only to the extent that it is accountable, which presumes a principle of *collective* responsibility. The rise of the modern presidency, then, encourages each occupant of the White House to exploit the full splendor of the executive office at the expense of public debate and resolution that best take place in the Congress and state legislatures. The War on Terror, the defining issue of George W. Bush's presidency, may offer new confirmation of Madison's warning that "[w]ar is the true nurse of executive aggrandizement." The modern executive establishment, born of war and of New Deal "programmatic liberalism," has subordinated political parties to a more active and better equipped state. But in the absence of strong parties free of presidential domination, that powerful state lacks sufficient means of common deliberation and public judgment without which it cannot adequately cultivate *public* opinion.

Lincoln acknowledged that "public opinion in the country is everything." But to him, public opinion meant more than the sum of individual preferences. It was a body of beliefs that instilled national identity. His characterization of a government "of the people, by the people, for the people" presupposed a moral fabric woven of the country's best possibilities. Lincoln was expressing his faith not only in people's decency but in their dual attachment to liberty and democracy. He trusted in their commitment both to their constitutional heritage, rooted in that great liberal document the Declaration of Independence, and to their political parties that allied democratic passions to liberal principles and engaged them in a continual debate about the meaning of their rights.

Great presidents justified their reform programs in constitutional terms, claiming to restore the proper understanding of first principles even as they attempted to transfuse the Declaration and Constitution with new meaning. But they did so as great party leaders, in the midst of major partisan realignments. Critical partisan elections – leavened by extraordinary presidential leadership – have enabled each generation to claim its right to redefine the Constitution's principles and reorganize its institutions. The burden of the new century is to hold the modern presidency to account, to recapture the understanding of democracy that has made such momentous debate and choice central to the pursuit of America's political destiny.

Chapter Summary

☆ George Washington established crucial precedents regarding the powers of and the limitations on the president, including the following: addressing the people directly, controlling the executive departments, aggressively acting as commander-in-chief of the armed forces, adopting a broad interpretation of his national security responsibilities, and voluntarily retiring at the end of his second term.

☆ Jefferson democratized the presidency in both style and substance by adopting a less regal presentation of self, reducing the size and power of the national government, and increasing the powers of the states. He deemphasized the constitutional powers of his office and chose to govern more as party leader.

☆ Jackson presided over the creation of the first full-fledged political party system and established a critical precedent for the vigorous assertion of presidential leadership in defense of the principle of union. He greatly expanded upon the democratization of the presidency initiated by Jefferson.

☆ Lincoln used the formal powers of the presidency as well as its potential for civic education and party leadership to maintain the Union against the threat of secession. He defended the constitutionality of his actions by arguing that the specific powers the constitution provides are intended to be used in support of the inalienable rights posited in the Declaration of Independence.

☆ Since Franklin D. Roosevelt, the position of executive, originally conceived as the guardian of the liberal order, has become the principal agent of popular rule. The key principle undergirding this new understanding is that the people are entitled to enjoy certain key economic as well as civil and political rights. Such rights differ from the other kinds in that they require positive government action in order to be fulfilled – they are *programmatic* in nature.

☆ The emergence of the United States, in the wake of World War II, as one of only two superpowers, and the intense rivalry between the United States and the Soviet Union that ensued, greatly expanded the power and authority of the president in the realm of foreign and military affairs.

☆ The combined impact of the Vietnam War, the failure of the War on Poverty, and the Watergate scandal was to greatly reduce public trust of and faith in the presidency. But this decline in popular support for the office, and for the national government in general, was not accompanied by any loss of public enthusiasm for the programmatic rights whose fulfillment depended upon a strong, large, and complex public sector.

☆ During the twenty-six-year span from 1980 to 2006, control of the presidency and Congress was divided for eighteen years. Divided government significantly weakened the president's role as legislative leader and encouraged his tendency to govern through a variety of formal and informal methods that did not require legislative approval.

☆ The September 11 catastrophe and the government's response to it affirmed the preeminence of the modern presidency. By defining the threat posed by terrorism as a "war," George Bush was able to make full use of the expanded presidential authority accumulated during World War II and the Cold War.

☆ George W. Bush has made the most systematic and energetic effort of any modern president to create a strong national party. The Bush White House has mobilized party loyalty and party organization to advance a conservative, executive-centered administrative state in support of what might be termed "big government conservatism," which has strong domestic as well as foreign policy principles and objectives.

Major Concepts

cabinet
Executive Office of the President (EOP)
National Security Council (NSC)
Office of Management and Budget (OMB)
plebiscitary politics

Suggested Readings

Arnold, Peri. *Making the Managerial Presidency*, 2d rev. ed. Lawrence: University Press of Kansas, 1998.

Binkley, Wilfred E. *The President and Congress.* New York: Knopf, 1947.

Ceaser, James. *Presidential Selection: Theory and Development.* Princeton, NJ: Princeton University Press, 1979.

Cornwell, Elmer, Jr. *Presidential Leadership of Public Opinion.* Bloomington: Indiana University Press, 1965.

Corwin, Edward. *The President: Office and Powers, 1787–1984*, 5th rev. ed. New York: New York University Press, 1989.

Crenson, Matthew, and Benjamin Ginsberg. *Presidential Power: Unchecked and Unbalanced.* New York: W. W. Norton, 2007.

Karl, Barry D. *The Uneasy State: The United States from 1915 to 1945.* Chicago: University of Chicago Press, 1983.

Landy, Marc, and Sidney M. Milkis. *Presidential Greatness.* Lawrence: University Press of Kansas, 2000.

Lowi, Theodore. *The Personal President.* Ithaca, NY: Cornell University Press, 1995.

Milkis, Sidney M., and Michael Nelson. *The American Presidency: Origins and Development, 1776–2007*, 5th ed. Washington, D.C.: CQ Press, 2007.

Nelson, Michael, ed. *The Presidency and the Political System*, 8th ed. Washington, D.C.: CQ Press, 2005.

Neustadt, Richard. *Presidential Power and the Modern Presidents: The Politics of Leadership from Roosevelt to Reagan.* New York: Free Press, 1991.

Paludan, Phillip S. *The Presidency of Abraham Lincoln.* Lawrence: University Press of Kansas, 1994.

Rudalevige, Andrew. *The New Imperial Presidency: Renewing Presidential Power after Watergate.* Ann Arbor: University of Michigan Press, 2005.

Skowronek, Stephen. *The Politics Presidents Make: Leadership from John Adams to Bill Clinton.* Cambridge, MA: Harvard University Press, 1997.

Tulis, Jeffrey. *The Rhetorical Presidency.* Princeton, NJ: Princeton University Press, 1987.

9 The Judiciary

The Guardians of America's Liberal Tradition

Chapter Overview

This chapter focuses on:

☆ The unique role of an independent judiciary in the American constitutional order and its pivotal importance in balancing claims made on the basis of liberty and of democracy

☆ The meaning, development, and importance of judicial review

☆ The contested meaning of such crucial constitutional principles as *due process of law* and *interstate commerce*

☆ The role of the courts in the post–World War II "rights revolution"

☆ The relationship between federal courts, Congress, and executive agencies

☆ The political implications of the judicial confirmation process

☆ The key intellectual and political divisions within the current Supreme Court

☆ The role of the courts in dealing with constitutional questions raised by the War on Terror

At about ten o'clock in the evening on Tuesday, December 12, 2000, more than a month after election day, the Supreme Court issued a dramatic decision that ended the historic dispute over the presidential election and enabled Republican governor George W. Bush of Texas to become president of the United States. The court's decision was the last act in a legal drama that began the day after the election when Americans awoke to discover that the contest between Bush and his Democratic opponent, Vice President Al Gore, was still undecided. Gore defeated Bush in the popular vote by almost a half million votes but in the Electoral College (see Chapter 3) Gore led Bush by 266 votes to 246 votes, short of the majority needed to win. The outcome would be determined by the vote in Florida, where Bush held a popular vote margin of less than 2000 of the nearly 6 million votes cast. If Florida's 25 electoral votes went to Bush, he would have 271 electoral votes, a bare majority of the 538 total, and would become president despite losing the popular vote.

A discrepancy between the popular and electoral vote had not occurred since 1888, when Republican Benjamin Harrison won despite receiving fewer popular votes than Democrat Grover Cleveland. The 2000 election was a reminder that the Constitution does not provide for majority rule but for republican government, which moderates, or frustrates, majorities in the name of minority rights and local self-government. But the import of this discrepancy was largely disregarded amid the dispute over Florida's votes.

Claiming that machines had failed to count all his votes, Gore called for a hand recount in four counties with high Democratic totals that were controlled by Democratic election commissions. The crux of Gore's legal challenge, supported by the Florida Supreme Court, was that voting machines, and therefore official ballots, were flawed, especially in Democratic counties. A hand count would show the true intent of voters and, in all likelihood, overcome Bush's lead, which had shrunk to 327 votes after the November 10 statewide machine recount required by Florida law for such close elections. As a complex and bitter legal process played out, Americans sought comic relief in stories of how chads, cardboard dots that Florida's voters punched out in casting their ballots, clung stubbornly to ballots, disguising the real intention of voters.

Discerning voter intent was the subject of the Supreme Court decision in *Bush v. Gore*. The court ruled that the Florida Supreme Court order requiring manual recounts of every undervote in Florida (that is, every ballot in the state for which a machine failed to register a vote for president) was unconstitutional. By failing to establish a standard by which counties across the states would judge voter intention, the Florida court violated the Fourteenth Amendment's requirement that states protect the right of individuals to equal protection and due process of the law. Seven of the nine justices agreed that the Florida court had violated basic Fourteenth Amendment rights.

But the Supreme Court divided more closely and bitterly on the second, decisive part of its ruling. By a 5–4 vote, the court ruled that the Florida court had also violated the Constitution in overruling the state legislature. The legislature had invoked a federal law that insulates a state's electors from challenge so long as they are certified by December 12. A proper recount simply could not be conducted by that date, and an attempt to do so violated "the constitutional prerogative of the state legislature to determine how electors are chosen."

Gore conceded. But this surrender did not take place without considerable protest. Justice John Stevens criticized the court's majority for emphasizing the need to certify votes by December 12 rather than enforcing Florida's obligation to determine voter intent. In the interest of "finality," Stevens charged, "the majority effectively orders the disenfranchisement of an unknown number of voters whose ballots reveal their intent – and are therefore legal votes under state law – but were for some reason rejected by ballot-counting machines."

Chief Justice William Rehnquist's majority opinion replied that the Supreme Court's first obligation was to the Constitution, not the voters: "the individual citizen has no federal constitutional right to vote for electors for the President of the United States"; that privilege, according to Article II of the Constitution, exists at the pleasure of the state legislatures. The Florida state legislature had a constitutional right to resolve any controversy over the final selection of electors in order to meet the December 12 deadline imposed by Congress.

In his gracious concession speech, Gore congratulated Bush on "becoming," not on "being elected," the forty-third president of the United States. Gore's distinction hinted at the daunting challenge Bush faced of ruling without a popular mandate. But Bush benefited greatly from the people's faith in the Supreme Court as the proper interpreter, the guardian, of the Constitution. Although many militant Democrats viewed the decision as a crude conservative power play, surveys indicated that most people wanted the courts to decide the contest. They accepted Bush as the legitimate president.

Bush v. Gore revisited the fundamental constitutional debate about the judiciary in relation to the elected branches. This chapter traces the development of that relationship and the strains between liberalism and democracy that it has engendered. It first considers the origins and growth of the judiciary's role in protecting America's liberal tradition against the tide of public opinion. It then describes the court's role in the redefinition of the meaning of rights that has occurred since the New Deal and the political consequences of that redefinition. It concludes by considering whether Americans have become so obsessed with rights and so deferential to the court that they have lost sight of their responsibility as democratic citizens.

Judicial Review and Republican Government

It is hard to imagine public officials and citizens in other representative democracies allowing judges to decide the outcome of a national election. Americans' acceptance of *Bush v. Gore* speaks to the extraordinary power of the independent judiciary to influence virtually every aspect of American political life. This chapter attempts to explain what political scientist David O'Brien calls the "cult of the robe" – how it is that a people with a strong democratic tradition have given so much authority to nine unelected judges. Box 1 lays the foundation for this chapter by explaining a few vital legal concepts.

Box One: Nuts and Bolts

Essential Legal Concepts

The judiciary deals with several different kinds of law. Criminal law provides specific rules by which government punishes criminal offenses. Those offenses are ranked in terms of their severity: a felony is more serious than a misdemeanor. Civil law establishes a framework for overseeing the relationships between private parties, individuals, associations, and firms. When one party believes itself aggrieved by another, it brings a civil action that petitions the judiciary to rule against the other party and provide relief. The party bringing a civil action is called a plaintiff. The other party is the defendant. In criminal cases, the government is the plaintiff. The most common forms of civil actions involve contracts and torts. A contract is a binding agreement between those who sign it, its signatories. A signatory sues when he or she believes that another signatory has violated the terms of the contract. A tort is a harm done to one party by another. If one believes that someone else has done damage to one's property or person, one brings a tort action seeking compensation for that injury.

Public law concerns those cases in which the government or the constitutional rights of citizens are involved. Constitutional law is that form of public law that involves judicial scrutiny of government or private action in terms of whether it violates the Constitution. Most of the cases discussed in this chapter relate to constitutional law. Administrative law relates to the conduct and rulings of administrative agencies in determining whether they are in conformity with the will of Congress and whether the rights accorded to those subject to administrative rulings are being protected. To enter federal court, one must demonstrate that one has standing. Standing is especially important in cases brought against the government. To claim standing, one must show that one has been directly harmed by the entity one is suing; one cannot sue simply to make a political point or because one is sympathetic to the problems of others.

The Constitution does not establish Supreme Court justices as its high priests. Even after the court began to assert that power, it was far from certain that it could withstand opposition from the two elected branches. For much of American history, the court's authority was far more fragile than it is today. In the disputed nineteenth-century presidential elections of 1800, 1824, and 1876, the final decisions were rendered by Congress, not the court. But developments during the twentieth century, especially the expansion of rights, have made the judiciary far more powerful. It is no longer, as Alexander Hamilton once claimed, "the least dangerous branch."

For the most part, the judiciary has acquitted itself well as its power has increased; it has upheld the rights of individuals against intemperate and intolerant majorities. Its moral authority derives especially from the laudable role it played in supporting African Americans' struggle for civil rights. Still, the court's growing influence may have weakened American democracy. As this book repeatedly points out, republican government depends on a balance between America's liberal and democratic traditions. The court's authority has been rooted in America's commitment to natural law, a belief in individual rights that has sustained the liberal tradition in the United States. But liberty also depends on a vigorous democratic tradition that periodically engages the American people in debate and resolution about the meaning of those rights. Liberty is jeopardized by excessive reliance on what Lincoln called "legal right." He insisted that profound public questions, such as slavery, had to be settled in the court of public opinion, not by unelected judges. Otherwise, the people would forfeit their claim to self-government.

Judicial Power

Arguably, the power of the judiciary is the most distinctive characteristic of the American constitutional order. It was often the first thing a foreign visitor noticed about American government. As early as the 1830s, Alexis de Tocqueville observed, "There is hardly a political question in the United States which does not sooner or later turn into a judicial one." American judges, he noted, did not simply interpret an existing body of law, as they did in France or Great Britain; nor were they limited to arbitrating legal disputes. They played a very large part in the development of law and public policy itself.

The power of the American judiciary reaches its height in the Supreme Court's and inferior federal courts' authority to exercise judicial review, the process by which courts determine the constitutionality of laws passed by Congress or actions taken by the president and other public officials. In addition, as revealed in *Bush v. Gore*, the federal judiciary has acquired the power to judge the constitutionality of laws and actions of the states. But the judiciary's power is passive; it can only be exercised when called on to decide a particular case. Box 2 describes the American court system and how a case reaches the Supreme Court.

The Courts

The American judicial system is made up of two parallel systems: federal courts and state courts. State courts vary enormously, as befits the differences in state constitutions. Some states elect their judges, including their state supreme court judges. In other states, the system of district, appeal, and supreme courts more closely mirrors the federal system. Most ordinary civil and criminal matters are handled, under state law, by state courts.

Generally speaking, a case goes to federal rather than state court if the federal government is directly involved, if a federal statute is at issue, if a claim of a violation of the U.S. Constitution is made, or if a civil suit is brought that involves citizens from more than one state. The federal system is composed of three tiers: district courts, appeals courts, and the Supreme Court. District courts are where ordinary civil and criminal federal trials take place. Nationwide, there are ninety-four district courts handling in excess of 200,000 civil cases and 45,000 criminal cases a year. Each state has at least one federal district court. The nation is carved up into eleven separate courts of appeals. There is a twelfth one for the District of Columbia, and the thirteenth is the U.S. Court of Appeals for the Federal Circuit, which specializes in patents and financial claims against the government. Appeals courts deal only with cases brought to them on appeal either from the district courts or federal administrative agencies. The latter type of appeal is the specialty of the D.C. circuit.

The Supreme Court takes cases that arise on appeal from the appeals courts; cases from the highest court of a state; or cases that the Constitution specifically assigns to it, that is, its sphere of original jurisdiction. That sphere includes disputes between the following: a citizen of a state and one of a different state; a state and the federal government; two or more states; or foreign diplomats. The court can refuse to hear any case brought on appeal. For a case to be accepted, at least four justices must agree that it involves "a substantial federal question"; if so, the court issues a writ of certiori – Latin for "made more certain" – which brings the case before the court.

The Supreme Court could not have rendered its momentous verdict in the 2000 presidential election unless Governor Bush and his lawyers chose to bring the case before it. Nonetheless, the courts gain immense political power from their authority to base decisions on the Constitution. Judges are not simply "politicians in black robes." Their ability to operate under the guise of judicial impartiality helps explain their vast influence on American political life.

The Constitution does not expressly give the judiciary power to determine the constitutionality of executive, legislative, or state actions. That authority must be inferred from constitutional arrangements, more particularly from the special status that federal judges are accorded in the original constitutional design. They are chosen by the executive with the advice and consent of the Senate. They serve for life unless they commit an impeachable offense. Many of the Framers took note of this special status, viewing it as a crucial protection of individual rights and the rule of law. George Mason of Virginia believed that the judiciary would be a "restraining power," charged with protecting the fundamental law against the designs of unruly majorities and popular demagogues.

James Madison feared that the president's veto power would provide insufficient protection against unwise measures enacted by Congress unless that check was shared by the judiciary. He wanted to create a Council of Revision in which the judiciary and the executive would jointly review legislation passed by Congress, a council that would serve in effect as a third legislative house. Luther Martin of Maryland opposed the idea; he denied that judges had any special wisdom to participate in public policy making, and he feared it would give too much power to unelected officials. Martin's view won out. The Constitutional Convention defeated every attempt to involve the Supreme Court in the legislative process. As we point out in this chapter, the power of judicial review came into being only after a bitter struggle between the court and President Thomas Jefferson.

Federalists and Anti-Federalists on the Judiciary

The Anti-Federalists feared the judiciary's capacity to restrain democratic impulses. If unaccountable judges decided important moral questions, representative government would become a farce. As Robert Yates of New York, using the pseudonym Brutus, argued: "There is no power above [judges] to control their decisions. There is no authority that can remove them, and they cannot be controlled by the laws of the legislature. . . . Men placed in this situation will generally soon feel themselves independent of heaven itself." Brutus warned that when power was vested in officials so far removed from popular accountability, such power could be contained only by force of arms.

The Federalists denied that the judiciary would endanger the republican character of the Constitution. Alexander Hamilton insisted that the gravity of judicial review would prevent the courts from becoming too powerful; judicial arrogance was to be feared less than judicial weakness. Of the three branches of government, the court least endangered the constitutional prerogatives of the other two and posed the least danger to the rights of the people. Protecting constitutional rights and procedures against popular initiatives would inevitably arouse strong opposition and would occur only if judges were granted life tenure, giving them independence from regular political pressures. Hamilton scoffed at the Anti-Federalists' fears of an imperial judiciary. The court, said Hamilton,

> has no influence over either the sword or the purse; no direction either of the strength or the wealth of society, and can take no resolution whatever. It may be truly said to have neither FORCE nor WILL but merely judgment; and must ultimately depend upon the aid of the executive arm even for the efficacy of its judgments.

The Restraining Role of the Judiciary

The debate between the Federalists and the Anti-Federalists highlighted the judiciary's virtues and the dangers it posed. As Hamilton hoped, it has been a bulwark of liberalism, a defender of individual rights against democratic despotism. The famous nineteenth-century British historian Lord Macaulay, noting the more rapid advance of mass democracy in the United States than in Western Europe and Great Britain, characterized the American political experience as "all sail and no anchor." The absence of a feudal tradition in the United States, and therefore of a restraining aristocracy, made American government too susceptible to the majority and too indifferent to individual rights. Yet, as Tocqueville noted, the Constitution and the judiciary were America's anchor, substituting for an aristocracy in a society with no feudal past. Because feudal aristocracy disappeared in Europe, representative assemblies such as the British parliament or the French assembly were unchecked by any countervailing authority, whereas the American Congress and state legislatures remained disciplined by the judiciary.

In America, legal concepts and practices and appeals to rights dominated not just the courts, but election campaigns, congressional debate, and presidential rhetoric as well. Mass democracy itself, as we pointed out in previous chapters, revolved around legal, constitutional questions regarding polarizing issues such as the national bank, slavery, and the welfare state. Tocqueville noted that legal language "is . . . adopted into common speech; the spirit of the law, born within schools and courts . . . it infiltrates through society right down to the lowest ranks, till finally the people have contracted some of the ways and tastes of a magistrate."

The Judiciary in Defense of the Constitution

Hamilton was not being coy in noting the obstacles to the development of a strong judiciary. Before the adoption of the Constitution, Americans viewed the protectors of their rights to be local governments and elected assemblies, not a non-elected judiciary. Even after the Constitution's adoption, the courts did not immediately obtain authority to interpret the Constitution. The early history of the court was not auspicious. The first chief justice of the Supreme Court, John Jay, answered President George Washington's call to negotiate a treaty with France, but the Jay Treaty proved so controversial that it diminished his reputation for impartiality. That reputation was further damaged by his decision to run for governor of New York twice while serving on the bench. He left the court after winning his second attempt in 1795.

The court's refusal to challenge the constitutionality of the 1798 Sedition Act, which made it a crime to publish anything that could be taken as derogatory about the government, raised doubts about the court's willingness to protect fundamental constitutional rights. As we point out in Chapter 4, the act blurred the distinction between conspiracy and legitimate political opposition and seemed to violate the First Amendment prohibition against any law abridging freedom of speech or press. Its enforcement was marred by partisan intolerance. Most sedition cases were tried in 1800 and were tied directly to that year's presidential election between incumbent Federalist John Adams and Republican Thomas Jefferson. Federal judges, most of them Federalists, were enthusiastic in their prosecution of Republicans who dared to criticize the Adams administration.

The Republicans' jaundiced view of the judiciary's impartiality was reinforced by the Judiciary Act of 1801, enacted just before Jefferson was inaugurated. It created many new federal judgeships that were hurriedly filled via "midnight" appointments by the outgoing Adams administration. The Federalists, having lost control of the other two branches of government, hoped to maintain some governmental control by entrenching a pro-Federalist judiciary protected by life tenure. Among these last-minute appointments was that of staunch Federalist John Marshall as chief justice. This final insult convinced the Republicans to plan a campaign against the judiciary, lest the people's will, as expressed in the 1800 election, be denied.

For Jefferson, the Federalist efforts to exploit and pack the judiciary confirmed Anti-Federalist fears that the courts would not uphold but, rather, destroy liberty. His faith in majority rule animated his war with the judiciary. He did not oppose judicial review, but he insisted that each branch of government, and state governments as well, share equally in deciding matters of constitutionality. The court's constitutional rulings would hold only for specific cases in question and would not obligate the executive or Congress to treat them as legal precedents. The Sedition Act had expired the day before Jefferson took office, but to underscore his fierce opposition to it, he pardoned everyone (mostly Republican newspaper publishers) whom it had convicted. He declared that the law had been unconstitutional, underscoring his conviction that the president as well as the courts had the right to make such a determination.

Marbury v. Madison

These issues of power and principle came to a head in the 1803 case of *Marbury v. Madison*. Adams's secretary of state, John Marshall, in his rush to assume his new duties as chief justice of the Supreme Court, had failed to deliver commissions to seventeen of Adams's last-minute judicial appointments, including one for William Marbury, selected as justice of the peace in the District of Columbia. Marbury's appointment now rested with the new secretary of state, James Madison, who, seeking to prevent it, withheld delivery of the commission. Jefferson supported Madison on the grounds that the previous administration had not fully executed Marbury's commission. Marbury and three others who had been denied their offices petitioned the Supreme Court for a writ of mandamus – a court order to a cabinet official to comply with a legal obligation – that would require Madison to deliver the commission. The court was authorized to issue such a writ by the Judiciary Act of 1789. Jefferson made clear he would order Madison not to comply.

The court lacked the prestige to stand up to a popular president. To order Madison to deliver Marbury's appointment would expose not only the court's impotence to enforce its own rulings but also its fragile standing in the country, because Madison would simply not comply. Yet, to deny Marbury's petition would confirm the constitutional independence of the president and Congress from judicial oversight.

Writing for a unanimous court, Marshall declared that Jefferson and Madison had abused their offices by refusing to deliver an appointment signed by a president, confirmed by the Senate, and sealed by a secretary of state. Jefferson was abrogating a lifetime appointment and thus violating the principal foundation of the judiciary's constitutional independence. Marshall insisted that the protection of constitutional rights required such independence. But after scolding the president, Marshall sidestepped a direct political confrontation by denying Marbury his writ. Marshall did so, however, by exercising and defending judicial review. He ruled that Section 13 of the Judiciary Act of 1789, under which Marbury had brought suit, was unconstitutional. The section gave the Supreme Court *original jurisdiction* in the matter, even though the Constitution insists that the court's jurisdiction is *appellate* in all but a few kinds of cases. In adding to the court's original jurisdiction, the Judiciary Act violated the Constitution.

Marshall's opinion avoided a bitter political controversy that he could not win in such a way as to enlarge the court's power. He gave Jefferson a free hand to bar Federalist appointees from office, but only if the president accepted the court's power to interpret the Constitution. Like Hamilton, Marshall argued that a Constitution embodying the rights and privileges of the American people required an independent judiciary to guard it.

Jefferson did not accept this argument, but Marshall's ruling was so adroit that the president had no way to disobey it. After all, the court had refused Marbury his appointment. In the final analysis, Jefferson's attack on the courts failed because the Republicans were not sufficiently aroused against the judiciary to destroy its independence. Marshall had disarmed them by holding his partisan fire in the service of the court as an institution. By doing so, he displayed just the sort of impartiality the judiciary's special constitutional status called for.

Only a few days after the *Marbury* decision, the Supreme Court sustained repeal of the Judiciary Act of 1801. The court could have challenged Congress's decision to repeal on the constitutional grounds that it eliminated positions occupied by judges entitled to lifetime tenure. The Constitution in Article III, Section 1 seems to say that federal judges cannot be severed unless they commit crimes. Marshall's refusal to overrule Congress further belied the charge that he was a tool of the Federalists. His adroitness did not immediately halt Jefferson's assault on the judiciary. But when the president and his congressional supporters failed in a subsequent effort to remove by impeachment Justice Samuel Chase, the most outspoken Federalist partisan on the bench, Jefferson ended his war with the judiciary. Marshall's moderation enabled the court to survive Jefferson's attack and win the first critical struggle to establish the judiciary's right to interpret the meaning of the Constitution.

The Marshall Court's Achievement

Jefferson's Revolution of 1800 (see Chapters 4 and 8) placed the presidency in the service of democratic rather than liberal principles, which invited a struggle between Republicans and Federalists. Marshall's statecraft preserved the court's impartiality in the face of this great party contest and thereby strengthened its authority and prestige. The court was raised from third-rate power to coequal branch of government and obtained the special constitutional status its champions had sought. With both president and Congress enmeshed in a party struggle, only the judiciary remained above the partisan fray. As Hamilton anticipated, because the court was an independent, small, cohesive body, it could maintain a long-term view, which gave it a decided advantage over a scattered and divided opposition.

Being chief justice gave Marshall several special prerogatives. He cultivated the distinctive qualities of the court and gave it institutional identity and standard procedures for the first time. He led discussion and directed the order of business in private conferences. He either wrote the court's opinions or assigned that task to another justice.

During his time on the Supreme Court, Chief Justice John Marshall wrote a series of opinions that took up the Hamiltonian defense of the national government and established the principle of judicial review.

Getting the Supreme Court to speak with one voice would enhance its prestige. Marshall worked skillfully to forge consensus and to persuade those in the majority not to write their own opinions but to sign on to the "opinion of the court." He wrote an overwhelming number of opinions himself, even when he disagreed with the ruling. As Jefferson and his Republican successors made appointments to the bench, achieving unanimity became more difficult. But the court did not return to the fractious practices that preceded Marshall's arrival. Jefferson's first appointment, Justice William Johnson of South Carolina, persuaded Marshall to appoint someone to deliver the opinion of the court, but to leave the rest of the judges free to voice their dissents. The court still adheres to that procedure. Still, Marshall's firm yet deft hand kept the court from dividing along partisan lines. The example of judicial restraint that he set during his long tenure, which lasted until his death in 1835, enabled the court to fully grasp the role of interpreter of the Constitution.

Nationalism

Its enhanced prestige enabled the Marshall court to moderate some of the Jeffersonian revolution's more extreme tendencies. The Federalists had sought to enhance the Constitution's national character. Jefferson and his allies hoped to strengthen its decentralizing and more democratic parts – Congress and the states. Marshall interpreted the Constitution in a more centralizing direction than the Jeffersonians and their successors, the Jacksonians, were comfortable with. He thereby moderated their inclination toward local self-government and left a nationalist legacy for future generations. Box 3 shows that the Supreme Court still considers cases by the procedures that the Marshall Court established during the early part of the nineteenth century.

Box Three: Nuts and Bolts

How the Supreme Court Considers a Case

When the Supreme Court agrees to hear a case, it accepts briefs both from the contending parties and from outside groups whom the litigants ask to submit amicus curiae, or "friend of the court," briefs. A brief is a written explanation of the legal reasons why the court should rule in a particular way. Then the court schedules oral arguments, during which the two sides present their case directly to the justices and the justices ask questions of the presenting attorneys. The justices then meet in secret conference to discuss the case. After a final vote is taken, the chief justice assigns a justice to write the majority opinion unless the chief justice is on the losing side, in which case the assignment is made by the most senior justice voting with the majority. Every justice is free to write a dissenting opinion, that is, an opinion that opposes the majority, or justices can write opinions that concur with the majority but that offer different reasons than does the majority opinion. (Figure 9.1 indicates the number of opinions rendered by the court.)

At every stage of a case's consideration except the conference, the court is assisted by its clerks. As of 2001, there were thirty-four clerks, each assigned to a specific justice. Because clerking for the Supreme Court is a highly prestigious post, these clerks, who are all law school graduates, usually have outstanding academic records and come from top-ranked law schools. They scrutinize petitions for certiori and make recommendations to the justices they work for. They also do the bulk of the research and help draft the justices' opinions.

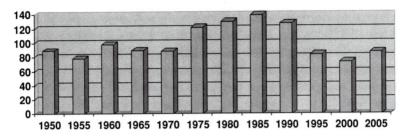

Figure 9.1. Supreme Court Opinions, 1950–2005. The Supreme Court issues few opinions relative to the number of cases it receives. *Source*: The Supreme Court of the United States, 2005. The court's term runs from October 1 to June 30; the year indicated is the closing year of the term.

Marshall's nationalism was displayed, for example, in the national bank controversy that we discuss in Chapters 4 and 6. With Washington's support, the government chartered the Bank of the United States in 1791. The Republicans let it expire in 1811, but some of them, including Jefferson and Madison, had second thoughts after the War of 1812, in which the American military effort was hampered by the national government's reliance on state banks. Consequently, Congress created a second Bank of the United States in 1816 with another twenty-year charter. Continued state-level opposition gave the Marshall court its opportunity to address the constitutional issues raised by the bank controversy in the landmark 1819 case of *McCulloch v. Maryland* (see Chapter 5). Maryland retaliated by enacting a law that imposed a $15,000 tax ($229,000 in 2006 currency) on any bank not chartered by the state. The Bank of the United States, the only financial institution operating in Maryland that was not chartered by the state, and thus clearly the target of the law, refused to pay the tax, and Maryland filed suit against James McCulloch, the cashier of the Baltimore branch of the national bank.

The federal government argued in McCulloch that Maryland's tax on the bank was unconstitutional. Maryland replied that Congress had no power to incorporate a bank, and in any event, states could tax as they willed within their own borders. Speaking for a unanimous court, Marshall upheld the bank's constitutionality and gave the classic statement of the doctrine of national authority. His argument was not new, but he added his own memorable rhetoric and lent the now-considerable prestige of the court to a sweeping concept of nationalism.

Challenging the Jeffersonian notion that the states were the repositories of popular rule, the chief justice responded that the Constitution belonged, as the preamble made clear, to "We, the People": "In form and in substance it emanates from them. Its powers are granted by them, and are to be exercised directly on them, and for their benefit." Although the Constitution limited the powers of the national government, it also clearly established the central authority as "supreme law of the land." It must have the powers to carry out the great responsibilities vested in it. And those means must be understood flexibly, lest the Constitution be laden with the sort of policy detail that would bog down a great experiment in self-rule. "We must never forget it is a constitution we are expounding . . . intended to endure for ages to come," wrote Marshall.

Marshall admitted that the Constitution did not list a bank as one of the enumerated powers. But a bank was a useful tool for powers that the Constitution did enumerate: collecting taxes, borrowing money, regulating commerce, and supporting armies and navies. Therefore, as the Constitution provides, the bank was "necessary and proper" for implementing those powers. The final part of Marshall's opinion followed from this generous interpretation of national sovereignty. Maryland's tax was unconstitutional because the "power to tax involves the power to destroy." To uphold the tax would empower an inferior to destroy a superior.

Jefferson and Madison had come to accept the bank as a necessary evil, so they accepted the court's holding, but they abhorred Marshall's expansive interpretation of national power and the pressure toward governmental consolidation that it created. Marshall's success in tempering the Revolution of 1800 pained Jefferson to the end of his days. In 1819, Jefferson said that "after twenty years' confirmation of the federal system by the voice of the people, declared through the medium of elections, we find the judiciary on every occasion, still driving us into consolidation." Marshall saw no reason why the court should be bound by Jefferson's vision of states' rights; he claimed a "mandate" to uphold the nationalist principles that "We the People" had established in 1787. In deftly positioning itself as the guardian of the people's Constitution, the Marshall court established a tradition of judicial independence and elevated the position of chief justice to a status that would rival the power and prestige of the executive. Table 9.1 lists all the chief justices of the United States and their terms of service.

Table 9.1. Chief Justices of the United States and Their Terms of Service

Chief Justice	Nominating President	Years of Service
John Jay	Washington	1789–1795
John Rutledge	Washington	1795
Oliver Ellsworth	Washington	1796–1800
John Marshall	Adams	1801–1835
Roger B. Taney	Jackson	1836–1864
Salmon P. Chase	Lincoln	1864–1873
Morrison Waite	Grant	1874–1888
Melville Fuller	Cleveland	1888–1910
Edward D. White	Taft	1910–1921
William Howard Taft	Harding	1921–1930
Charles Evans Hughes	Hoover	1930–1941
Harlan Fiske Stone	FDR	1941–1946
Fred M. Vinson	Truman	1946–1953
Earl Warren	Eisenhower	1953–1969
Warren E. Burger	Nixon	1969–1986
William H. Rehnquist	Reagan	1986–2005
John Roberts	George W. Bush	2005–

Nationalism's Limits

Jeffersonian democracy, rooted in legislative supremacy and states' rights, generally prevailed; the court restrained it only marginally. When Congress passed another bill extending the bank's charter, President Andrew Jackson vetoed it, challenging Marshall's interpretation of, and authority over, the Constitution and reopening the question – seemingly resolved by *Marbury v. Madison* – regarding the appropriate authority of the federal courts. Invoking Jefferson, Jackson insisted that in matters of constitutional interpretation, the executive and the legislature must be guided by their own opinions of the Constitution. To rely solely on judicial precedent was to allow for "a dangerous source of authority, and should not be regarded as deciding questions of constitutional power except where the acquiescence of the people and the states can be considered as well settled." Jackson's claim that the popularly elected branches should make constitutional determinations revealed the ongoing tensions between the liberal and democratic traditions in America as well as the institutions that embodied them.

Although Jackson triumphed in the bank fight, Marshall's broad interpretation of national supremacy and judicial review endured, moderating provincial jealousies. In the nullification crisis of 1832, Jackson vigorously rejected South Carolina's refusal to obey a federal statute (see Chapters 4, 5, and 8). In opposition to this virtual threat to secede, his defense of national supremacy received valuable support from the federal judiciary, which had become a focus of public respect and a symbol of union.

Still, as Marshall recognized, the court's uneasy place in a regime dedicated to popular rule required restraint. He rooted judicial authority in American soil by avoiding direct clashes with popular presidents and by fairly arbitrating disputes between the national and state governments. His 1833 opinion in *Barron v. Baltimore* held that the Bill of Rights limited the federal government alone, not the states. The Marshall court strengthened the position of the judiciary in the political system as the principal, if not the sole, guardian of the Constitution, and the power that he established would ripen. Eventually, the judiciary would have enough prestige to directly confront powerful presidents. Nevertheless, the question of whether ultimate authority on matters of constitutionality rests with elected presidents and members of Congress or with the judiciary has arisen again and again in American history and has never been fully resolved.

Dred Scott and the Limits of Judicial Review

No Supreme Court action better displays both the importance and the limited power of the federal judiciary than does *Dred Scott v. Sandford* (1857). This case has been characterized as the court's worst "self-inflicted wound." The court, headed by Chief Justice Roger B. Taney, chosen by President Jackson to replace John Marshall in 1835, weighed in to resolve the issue of slavery in the territories, an issue that had threatened the Union for a decade. Lincoln described the question as a dispute about the morality of slavery. The judiciary's attempt to transform this controversial moral question into a legal one, to take it out of politics, failed miserably. The case not only damaged the prestige of the court, it brought the country to the brink of civil war.

Fearing they would eventually lose if the slavery issue were decided by Congress, proslavery politicians – including President James Buchanan, a Democrat from Pennsylvania who had been elected in 1856 – yearned to have the court settle the issue. Buchanan's deference to the court stemmed from his prior knowledge of what it would decide. Knowing that Taney's decision might have more weight if it included the support of a Northern justice, Buchanan had privately (and highly improperly) urged Justice James Greer, a fellow Pennsylvanian, to side with those who wanted to deny both Congress and the territorial legislatures the right to prohibit slavery. Greer succumbed, giving the court false hope that its opinion would have the appearance of a national, not a sectional, ruling.

Dred Scott had been taken as a slave into Illinois and into the northern part of the Louisiana Purchase. Illinois law forbade slavery. Congress had prohibited slavery in the northern part of the Louisiana Territory in the Missouri Compromise of 1820. Scott, now living in the slave state of Missouri, sued his present owner, arguing that prolonged visits to a free state and territory made him a free man. The case came to the Supreme Court on appeals from the Missouri Supreme Court and the federal appeals court, both of which had ruled against Scott.

The court could have sidestepped the controversial question of whether Congress could bar slavery in the territories by simply affirming the lower court's ruling that Missouri law governed Scott's status. But two antislavery justices, John McClean of Ohio and Benjamin Curtis of Massachusetts, refused to adopt such a narrow position. They threatened to write a sweeping dissent that declared Scott free and that upheld African-American citizenship and Congress's right to prohibit slavery in the territories. In the face of this rebellion, the mostly Southern seven-member majority voted to have Taney write an equally comprehensive proslavery opinion. The majority opinion supported Missouri's contention that Scott was a slave and that the Supreme Court was bound by Missouri law in this case. But the opinion went much further in that it denied that African Americans were citizens in the eyes of the Constitution and stated that they therefore could not sue in federal court. It also declared that Scott's journey to a free territory was meaningless in any case because Congress did not have authority to prohibit slavery in the territories. The Missouri Compromise itself was therefore unconstitutional.

But the "cult of the robe" could not resolve the slavery controversy. Its claim to authoritatively interpret constitutional disputes rested on public perception that its judgments were impartial. In attempting to judge a profound political issue, the court forfeited that claim. "In 1850 the Court enjoyed popular support as nearly unanimous as can ever be expected in a diverse democratic society. It was playing a modest but significant part in the affairs of the nation," the distinguished constitutional scholar Robert McCloskey wrote. "Eight years later, it had forfeited that position and its role in the American polity had become negligible."

The court's diminished influence was confirmed by the triumph of Abraham Lincoln and the Republicans in the 1860 election. Lincoln refused to accept *Dred Scott* as a binding precedent. The great issues that the case raised had to be resolved by the American people. Chief Justice Taney had denied African Americans citizenship on the grounds that the grand words of the Declaration of Independence that "all men are created equal" did not include "the enslaved African race." But Lincoln insisted that the Declaration's meaning, and its relationship to the Constitution, was not a narrow legal issue. It raised the most basic questions about the nature of American rights and responsibilities. Lincoln granted that the *Dred Scott* decision was binding on the parties to the suit, but he would not allow it to determine the future course of slavery policy. If the Supreme Court were going to settle vital political questions, "the people will have ceased to be their own rulers, to that extent, practically resigned their government, into the hands of that eminent tribunal." Lincoln and the Union's triumph in the Civil War ensured that *Dred Scott* would not stand and that the court would not rule the nation.

The Court and Property Rights

The *Dred Scott* decision badly damaged the Supreme Court's prestige. But the judiciary continued to be an important expositor of economic policy. After the Civil War, the rise of industrial capitalism and the political conflicts it provoked established the court as the most important restraining influence on government attempts to regulate the economy. The Republicans' dedication to industrial capitalism enabled them to dominate politics from the 1870s to the 1930s and allowed them to shape the judiciary and mold constitutional law (see Chapters 4 and 11). As it had been during the Marshall era, the judiciary was the "aristocratic" anchor on America's democratic sail, this time as the protector of property rights. Until 1937, the post–Civil War court sought to block economic reform, fearing that the government, state or national, would destroy the free enterprise system.

Slouching toward Laissez Faire

In Chapter 6, we discuss laissez faire, the idea that government should not intervene in the economy. The court codified laissez faire in a series of rulings that interpreted the Constitution as generally forbidding economic regulation. Departing dramatically from Marshall's broad interpretation of the Commerce Clause, the court now interpreted it in a highly restrictive manner. In *United States v. E. C. Knight Co.* (1895), the court gutted the Sherman Antitrust Act (see Chapter 6). That act made it illegal for business to contract, combine, or conspire to create a trust or monopoly for the purpose of restraining free trade and monopolizing interstate or foreign commerce.

E. C. Knight involved the American Sugar Refining Company, which already controlled a majority of American sugar refining companies. It sought to purchase control of four additional ones, including E. C. Knight, and thus acquire 98 percent of refining capacity. The Department of Justice asked for a court order that forbade the purchase, contending that the companies were combining in restraint of trade. The court disagreed, holding that the Sherman Act did not apply to monopolies in manufacturing, because *manufacturing*, no matter how large the companies were or how widely distributed their goods were, was not part of interstate *commerce*. The court confined the term commerce to its most literal meaning, "trade." Manufacturing had only an indirect impact on trade, and regulating it was a matter for the states.

Justice John Marshall Harlan's dissent argued that it was impossible for the states to adequately regulate large manufacturing companies that operated in many states. But this decision was not really about federalism. Taken as a whole, the court's intervention in the economy during the late nineteenth and early twentieth centuries was in defense of private property, not states' rights. Both state and national governments were handcuffed in the service of the principle of laissez faire.

Substantive Due Process

The court demonstrated its disregard for states and localities through its interpretation of the Fourteenth Amendment clause that forbade government from depriving any person of due process of law. Eventually, the court would use this clause to expand civil rights and civil liberties. Before 1937, however, the court used it to restrict state efforts to regulate economic activity. The Due Process Clause, which also appears in the Fifth Amendment, had traditionally been interpreted to mean that government action, national or state, was beyond judicial review so long as fair procedures had been followed. But lawyers and judges who championed laissez faire fastened on the idea of *substantive due process*. This concept declared that intruding on a fundamental right, such as the right of contract, was a violation of due process of law no matter what procedural niceties had been observed. Just what was a fundamental right – the Constitution does not explicitly enumerate a right of contract – was left to the courts.

The most notorious invocation of substantive due process occurred in *Lochner v. New York* (1905). Joseph Lochner, a bakery owner, was convicted of violating a New York law that required bakery employees to work no more than ten hours per day or sixty hours per week. The Supreme Court overruled the conviction on the grounds that this use of New York's police power violated "the right of contract between employer and employees" and was therefore a violation of the Due Process Clause. Contemporary historians of the court rank *Lochner* as second only to *Dred Scott* among its worst decisions. They speak of "lochnerizing" to imply that judges have substituted their own policy preferences for those of the legislature. In this interpretation, historians take their cue from Justice Oliver Wendell Holmes's dissent, which criticized the majority for basing its decision on a dubious economic theory. Surely, Holmes insisted, "the Fourteenth Amendment does not enact Mr. Herbert Spencer's Social Statics."

The sociologist Herbert Spencer's view that government economic policy should be guided by the creed "survival of the fittest" – an application of Charles Darwin's doctrine of "natural selection" – grate on the contemporary conscience. It is hard to appreciate the court's determination to protect the "liberty" of employees to work a twelve-hour day. But its decision was not a complete departure from previous constitutional interpretations. Indeed, as the historian Eric Foner has pointed out, abolitionists and Civil War-era Republicans interpreted the rights of workers to simply mean their freedom not to be a slave, to own their labor, and to be free to sell it. The curious thing about so-called standpat Republicans and many federal judges during the early part of the twentieth century was how tenaciously they clung to these same principles under the radically different economic conditions forty years after the Civil War. Intent on guarding the Constitution from government efforts to protect vulnerable groups, such as bakers, from economic exploitation, the federal judiciary appeared indifferent to the changes brought by the Industrial Revolution.

The judiciary was protected from political attack because most Americans, schooled in the liberal tradition, were likewise slow to make sense of the transformation from a rural republic to an industrial society. And the court did not rule out hours legislation entirely. In *Muller v. Oregon*, three years after *Lochner*, it determined that an Oregon statute regulating the hours of females was a reasonable exercise of the police power because the social and physical characteristics of women put them at a special disadvantage in the struggle for subsistence.

In 1917, the court upheld another Oregon law that set ten hours as the maximum workday for industrial workers, allowing them to work an additional three hours if they were paid time and one-half of their regular wage. The opinion of the court, written by Justice Joseph McKenna, who had voted with the majority in *Lochner*, accepted the defense's argument that the purpose was not to adjust economic relations but to promote the health and safety of the industrial worker. These decisions revealed that the court was not intransigently laissez faire when legislation could be viewed as promoting the morals, safety, and health of the population. Still, the *Lochner* spirit of resistance to economic reform remained strong, and it would harden in the face of the Great Depression and the New Deal reforms that followed.

The Judicial Challenge to the New Deal

The Great Depression, the gravest economic crisis in American history, began in 1929. The New Deal's policies for fighting the Great Depression embodied a new government philosophy, one that rejected laissez faire (see Chapters 4 and 8). These policies were a direct challenge to the court's seventy-year record of protecting economic rights against government intervention. The court – *Dred Scott* excepted – had usually restrained itself during national emergencies. But by 1935, a majority of justices resolved to make a stand against the New Deal.

The four justices who anchored that resistance – James McReynolds, Willis Van Devanter, George Sutherland, and Pierce Butler – were determined to protect the Constitution, no matter how great the public clamor for change. For a time, they were joined by two more ambivalent justices, Owen Roberts and Chief Justice Charles Evans Hughes. The result was that during the term spanning 1935 and 1936, the court struck down more important national laws than in any comparable period in American history, and a number of important state laws as well.

In *Schechter Poultry Corporation v. United States* (1935), the court declared the National Industrial Recovery Act (NIRA) unconstitutional. Schechter operated slaughterhouses in New York City. The company received live chickens from outside the state, slaughtered them, and then sold them to local stores. It was convicted in federal court of violating a number of standards set under NIRA, including hours and wage regulations. The court used *E. C. Knight* as a precedent to claim that such regulation of hours and wages exceeded the national government's commerce power. Moreover, the court claimed NIRA to be an unconstitutional delegation of authority to the executive branch, violating the separation of powers.

The court had never before declared an act of Congress unconstitutional for delegating legislative power to the executive. As such, *Schecter* was a direct challenge to the modern administrative state, whose expansion, in the face of terrifying economic insecurity, seemed inevitable. The decision was unanimous. Even Justice Louis Brandeis, whose righteous anger against big business led his political friends to call him Isaiah, voted with the majority.

President Franklin D. Roosevelt (FDR) voiced his indignation four days later in a news conference. The *Schecter* decision, he said, raised the issue of

> whether in some way we are going to overturn or restore to the federal government the powers which exist in the national governments of every other nation in the world to enact and administer laws that have a bearing on, and general control over, national economic problems. . . .

We have been relegated to a horse-and-buggy definition of interstate commerce.

In *Morehead v. New York, ex rel. Tipaldo* (1936), the court voted 5–4 to overrule a New York law that set a women's minimum wage, reaffirming the Due Process Clause of the Fourteenth Amendment as a barrier to assaults on the liberty of contract. Justice Butler announced an unyielding rule of substantive due process, arguing that "the state is without power by any form of legislation to prohibit, change or nullify contracts between employers and adult women workers as to the amount of wages to be paid." This case created, FDR explained, a "no man's land": it showed that the court majority was opposed to all economic reform regardless of whether it was federal or state.

The Constitutional Revolution of 1937

FDR said nothing further publicly about the court for the rest of that year, not even during his 1936 reelection campaign. But his immense electoral triumph, the biggest victory in the history of the two-party system, must have emboldened him. On February 5, 1937, he proposed the Judicial Reorganization Act, dubbed the "court-packing" bill. It proposed that for every justice within six months of reaching the age of seventy, the president must appoint an additional justice. Six of the nine current justices were seventy years or older, meaning that FDR would be able to enlarge the court to fifteen justices, appointing enough new judges to obtain a solid pro–New Deal majority.

Jefferson, Jackson, and Lincoln had all battled the court. Nevertheless, FDR's plan to pack the court marked an unprecedented challenge to its independence. In spite of his popularity and the controversial nature of the court's decisions, the president's bill encountered serious opposition. Day after day for the next several months, court-packing stories rated banner headlines in the nation's newspapers. The controversy aroused debate in every corner of the country. In Beaumont, Texas, for example, a movie audience cheered rival arguments about the court bill that were shown on the screen.

By the 1930s, the court had become a highly respected, if not revered, institution. But like the Taney court, the Hughes court forgot Marshall's lesson about the need for self-restraint. In this eyeball-to-eyeball confrontation between FDR and the Supreme Court, however, Chief Justice Hughes and Justice Roberts blinked. In *West Coast Hotel v. Parrish* (1937), issued less than two months after FDR's court plan appeared, the court retreated from substantive due process, ruling 5–4 that a Washington state minimum wage

Franklin D. Roosevelt attempted to change the number of justices on the court to ensure a pro–New Deal majority, but his plan was defeated by Congress.

law was constitutional. Justice Roberts switched from the position he had taken in *Tipaldo* just ten months earlier. Because the Washington law protected women, Chief Justice Hughes, writing for the majority, could have resorted to the specific women's exemption articulated in *Muller*. Instead, he defended the general authority of state government to protect all vulnerable citizens against the uncertainties of the market.

Only two weeks later, the court upheld the National Labor Relations Act. In five separate cases, four of which were decided 5–4 (once again, Roberts was the swing vote), the court abandoned the distinction between direct and indirect interstate commerce and between manufacturing and commerce that had been established in E. C. Knight. In *N. L. R. B. v. Jones and Laughlin Steel Corp.*, Chief Justice Hughes returned to Marshall's more robust understanding of the commerce power:

> Although activities may be intrastate in character when separately considered, if they have such a *close and substantial* [emphasis added] relation to interstate commerce that their control is essential or appropriate to protect the commerce from burdens and obstructions, Congress cannot be denied the power to exercise that control.

Just how loosely the majority of justices were willing to define "close and substantial" was revealed in *National Labor Relations Board v. Friedman–Harry Marks Clothing Co.* (1937). In this case, the court ruled against a Richmond, Virginia, clothing company whose production, unlike the Jones and Laughlin steel empire, had only a minimal effect on interstate commerce.

In *Steward Machine Co. v. Davis* (1937), the Supreme Court upheld the New Deal's centerpiece, the Social Security Act. Justice Roberts once again cast the deciding vote in a 5–4 opinion, delivered by Justice Benjamin Cardozo, that sustained the unemployment compensation system despite the act's requirement that state laws meet national standards to be eligible for federal funds. Speaking for six justices, Cardozo also upheld the old age pension system in *Helvering v. Davis* (1937) even though the pensions were funded by a special tax. A year earlier, the court had ruled that using taxes to promote public welfare intruded on the reserved powers of the states and violated the Tenth Amendment, which reserves to the states and the people those powers not delegated to the national government. By upholding the Social Security Act, the court apparently had given up its commitment to so-called dual federalism, an interpretation of the Tenth Amendment that strictly limited the powers of the national government to constitutionally enumerated powers and that viewed the national and state governments as sovereign and equal in their respective spheres of influence.

FDR's triumphant reelection, if not his court-packing plan, must have had some effect on the turnabout by Justices Roberts and Hughes. Whatever the cause, as one contemporary commentator observed tongue-in-cheek, it had the appearance of "the switch in time that saved the nine." FDR, determined to win a complete victory over the Supreme Court, continued his effort to pack the court, but the bill had lost much of its steam. It was defeated, a testament not only to the judiciary's acceptance of the New Deal but also to the unease of Congress, and the American public, with legislation that threatened to destroy what was still a valued institution.

The Hughes court's great escape from FDR's designs was achieved at the cost of abandoning more precedents, in a shorter period of time, than any other court in American history. FDR solidified the court's transformation. As a result of retirements and deaths, he was able to appoint eight justices in the next six years, all of whom were selected less for their distinguished jurisprudence than for their devout loyalty to the New Deal. Thus, despite his plan's defeat, FDR eventually "packed" the court. After winning a third term, he even had the pleasure of replacing his archenemy, Justice McReynolds, who between 1937 and 1941 had dissented from pro–New Deal opinions 119 times. These new appointments caused what historian William Leuchtenburg has called "the constitutional revolution of 1937," a full acceptance of the New Deal constitutional order. Since then, the court has not struck down a single piece of significant economic legislation. Nor has it judged any law (with the exception of the Line Item Veto Act passed in 1996) to be an unconstitutional delegation of authority to the executive.

The Judiciary in Defense of Programmatic Rights

FDR used the term *liberalism* to describe his philosophy of government. By using this term, FDR meant that the New Deal and the modern presidency were to be a liberal as well as a democratic phenomenon, "supplementing," as he put it, the traditional American understanding of rights with a new one (see Chapter 4). Therefore, FDR did not try to weaken judicial power. As he told an aide, the Constitution was not the problem; rather, it was the "manner in which it had been interpreted." FDR was astute enough to recognize that if the court became sympathetic to the new idea of rights he championed, it could help protect liberal programs from inevitable future political attack.

FDR differed from his Progressive predecessors, especially Theodore Roosevelt, who had called for formal constitutional changes to weaken the court's institutional authority. Theodore Roosevelt's Progressive party campaign in 1912 favored submitting court decisions to voter referenda and making it easier to amend the Constitution and thus override judicial interpretations of it. As FDR foresaw, when the Democrats lost the presidency in 1952, liberals became increasingly dependent on the court. With Republican Dwight Eisenhower as president and a coalition of Republicans and Southern Democrats commanding Congress, the judiciary, remade by the constitutional revolution of 1937, became the agent of national political reform.

The cornerstone of liberalism in the nineteenth century was the protection of a realm of private autonomy, especially private property and business corporations, from government. Even the Marshall court's defense of nationalism emphasized the expansion and protection of free enterprise. As political scientist R. Shep Melnick says, contemporary liberalism promises a broader

> security against the vagaries of the business cycle; against the multiple unintended hazards created by a dynamic capitalism; against the prejudices of private citizens and the consequences of three centuries of racism; against the risks of congenital handicaps and inevitable old age; and against the consequences of poverty and of family decomposition.

This new understanding of security forms the basis for the court's novel constitutional interpretations, especially with respect to the Fourteenth Amendment. Many of these new claims on government have also been written into law. The judiciary does not hesitate to supervise wide swaths of the economy and society based on these statutory provisions.

Ending Forced Segregation: The *Brown* Case and the Civil Rights Movement

The modern role of the federal judiciary in the expansion and centralization of government has been most evident in the area of civil rights. The Fourteenth Amendment's promise that no state could deprive American citizens of the "equal protection of the laws" appeared to offer African Americans full citizenship, but that promise had not been fulfilled. The nineteenth-century court upheld the notorious Jim Crow laws in the Southern states that forcibly separated the races and deprived African Americans of equal treatment.

In *Plessy v. Ferguson* (1896), the court invoked the doctrine of "separate but equal," meaning that as long as accommodations of the same quality were provided, it was permissible to segregate according to race. Homer Plessy, a Louisiana resident, boarded a train in New Orleans, having bought a first-class ticket, and took a vacant seat after refusing the conductor's order to sit in the "Colored Only" section. He was arrested and convicted for violating Louisiana's segregation statute. The Supreme Court upheld the conviction, denying that racial segregation was discriminatory. An 8–1 majority insisted that the Louisiana statute did not imply racial inferiority but was a reasonable exercise of state police power to promote the public good.

The "separate but equal" doctrine would stand until the middle of the twentieth century. But Justice Harlan's *Plessy* dissent challenged this tortured interpretation of the Fourteenth Amendment. He insisted that "[o]ur constitution is color-blind" and that therefore it was unconstitutional for a state to base laws on race. He noted that the purpose of the Louisiana law was not to exclude whites from black railroad cars but solely to exclude blacks from white cars, which made a mockery of the state's claim that the law was not racially discriminatory.

Justice Harlan's solitary protest was finally vindicated in *Brown v. Board of Education of Topeka* (1954). This decision was not a total surprise. In the wake of the constitutional revolution of 1937, the Supreme Court indicated that violations of civil rights, rather than "liberty of contract," would now be subject to the most exacting judicial scrutiny. In *Smith v. Allwright* (1944), the court breathed new life into the Fifteenth Amendment guarantee against racial discrimination in voting when it overturned a Texas law barring African-American participation in the Democratic primary.

Brown revitalized the Fourteenth Amendment Equal Protection Clause as a weapon to uphold civil rather than economic rights. This case, which involved segregated elementary schools in Topeka, Kansas, had come to the court in 1951. But in recognition of this case's great historical importance, the justices delayed their decision until after the 1952 presidential election and until they could achieve unanimity. Indeed, Chief Justice Earl Warren's opinion was crafted less to convince legal scholars than to gain public support for a decision that would inevitably engender resistance. Hoping to see the entire *Brown* decision printed in every newspaper, he insisted that "the opinion should be short, readable by the lay public, non-rhetorical, unemotional, and, above all, not accusatory."

Therefore, the court did not produce a richly textured legal analysis. The justices admitted that the historical intent of the Fourteenth Amendment's Framers was inconclusive regarding segregation. Nor did they argue that the amendment justified school desegregation as a remedy for a century of government neglect and oppression. Rather, Brown was rendered on sociological and psychological grounds. It claimed that education had become critical to American democracy, "the foundation of good citizenship." No child could be expected to succeed in life if denied an education, and therefore education had to be provided on equal terms.

The court then moved to consider the deleterious psychological effects that separating the races by law had on black children's motivation to learn. It found that segregation generated "a feeling of inferiority as to their status in the community that may affect the hearts and minds in a way unlikely ever to be undone." Therefore, *de jure segregation* (segregation enforced by law) was a form of discrimination. Regarding public education at least, the justices concluded, "separate but equal has no place." The court's reliance on sociological and psychological grounds rather than on textured constitutional interpretation made it vulnerable to the charge that it was engaged in judicial legislation. Indeed, the *Brown* decision signaled a new era of court activism.

In *New York Times v. Sullivan* (1963), the court used the First Amendment as well as the Fourteenth to strengthen civil rights. A $500,000 libel award was assessed by an Alabama jury against the *New York Times* for publishing an advertisement containing errors about the conduct of L. B. Sullivan, police commissioner of Montgomery, Alabama, with respect to the local Civil Rights Movement. Sullivan claimed that these errors, even if relatively minor and unintentional, damaged his reputation. Many states did allow juries to find newspapers guilty of libel on such grounds.

Again, the court mounted unanimous support for a landmark ruling that reversed the libel verdict. Relying on the First Amendment (the courts were now interpreting the Fourteenth Amendment to permit applying all of the Bill of Rights to the states), Justice Hugo Black expressed the court's support for "open and robust" political debate. Such debate was so important for maintaining democracy as to require legal toleration of error, especially with regard to public officials. Thus, a newspaper was guilty of libel only if misstatements about public officials were published "knowingly" or in "reckless disregard" that they might be false, a severe burden of proof for plaintiffs to shoulder. The court would later include within the definition of "public official" all publicly prominent people regardless of whether they worked for the government. *Sullivan* was not, technically, a civil rights case, but the court was undoubtedly influenced by the civil rights context in which it arose.

Into the Political Thicket: A Right to Fair Representation

The court's aggressive promotion of reform was not limited to civil rights. Beginning with *Baker v. Carr* (1962), the court took up voter apportionment in order to determine whether various sizes and shapes of state, local, and national election districts were fair. Chief Justice Warren considered the court's apportionment decisions to be of even greater importance than its racial segregation decisions. Critics of the Warren Court consider them to be its greatest sin.

Baker involved the Tennessee legislature, which had not reapportioned members' districts since 1901, even as the state's population shifted from rural to urban areas. Charles Baker and several other residents sued, claiming that as urban dwellers they were being denied equal protection of the laws. In previous cases, the most recent being *Colgrove v. Green* in 1946, the court defined the formation of electoral districts as a political question poorly suited to judicial resolution and best solved by the political branches. The court recognized that representation was a complicated matter in the American constitutional order, a means for moderating majority rights in order to protect individual liberty and local self-government. In *Colgrove*, the court found no "discoverable and manageable standard" for resolving the case. The very existence of the Senate, said the court, shows that the Framers of the Constitution considered state boundaries, not simply population, in designing the nation's legislative branch.

Justice William Brennan's majority opinion in the *Baker* case abandoned this restrained position. He understood the Equal Protection Clause as protecting the right of all voters to have their votes count equally. Justice Felix Frankfurter, a militant New Dealer appointed by FDR, dissented; he warned his progressive colleagues that they were committing the same constitutional crime they had once accused their conservative predecessors of perpetrating. Just as the Fourteenth Amendment had been misused to uphold the right of contract and usurp policy responsibility best left to political representatives, so the Warren Court was improperly using it to enter a "political thicket." Denial of franchise because of race, color, religion, or sex was an appropriate matter for constitutional adjudication by the courts, said Frankfurter, but not the relationship between population and legislative representation, which was never a straightforward matter under the Constitution. The judiciary could not reliably adjudicate such disputes impartially because no clear constitutional standard existed. To involve the courts implied that judges were "omnicompetent" and risked "enthroning the judiciary." Appeals for fairer apportionment should be addressed to "an informed, civically minded electorate." Frankfurter wrote, "There is not under our Constitution a judicial remedy for every political mischief. In a democratic society like ours, relief must come through an aroused popular conscience that sears the conscience of people's representatives."

Critics of Frankfurter might argue that malapportioned districts prevent deprived citizens from finding adequate political avenues for registering their grievances. Even some of the Warren court's critics conceded that malapportionment was severe enough in many states, as well as in some congressional districts, to warrant a federal judiciary remedy. But they would have preferred the court to rest its opinion on different constitutional grounds. The political scientist Martha Derthick would have chosen Article IV, Section 4 of the Constitution, which guarantees "every State in the Union a Republican Form of Government." That clause, which had not been invoked since the mid-nineteenth century, could have been applied to cases in which a state legislature's failure to reapportion violated its state constitution and thereby undermined the federal constitution's guarantee. Relying on the Equal Protection Clause of the Fourteenth Amendment "catapulted the federal judiciary" into a "mathematical quagmire" in which the states would be held to a standard of equality that had no place in American constitutional history.

Two years later, in *Reynolds v. Sims* (1964), the court struck down the apportionment system used by most state legislatures for their upper houses. Like the U.S. Senate, state upper houses typically represented smaller units of government, usually counties, of unequal population size. The court rejected this comparison to the Senate because the Senate had merely been a political compromise struck at the Constitutional Convention. The court did not explain why the Senate's status as a compromise made it irrelevant to the case. The court also pointed out that counties, cities, and other local subdivisions, unlike states, had no claim to being sovereign entities.

Chief Justice Warren's majority opinion stated, "Legislators represent people, not trees or acres. Legislators are elected by voters, not farms or cities or economic interests." The only acceptable constitutional standard was "one person, one vote," a principle the court extended to almost all popularly elected, multimember, state decision-making bodies as well as to congressional districts. As Derthick laments,

> legislative districting has been turned into an arcane exercise for computers, consultants, and constitutional lawyers, along with the usual array of incumbents trying to save their seats or party politicians trying to protect or gain majorities. District lines now cut arbitrarily through local places that once would have been respected as such and represented intact.

Neither the promise nor the peril of redistricting has been realized. Justice Frankfurter's fear that judicial involvement in the quagmire of legislative districting would diminish public confidence in the court was not borne out. The court was attacked by some state and federal legislators whose reelection prospects may have been jeopardized by court-mandated reapportionment, but the American people hardly resented the court's effort to equalize the power of voters. Redistricting was supposed to increase political participation, but this did not happen either. As Chapter 12 reveals, American politics rarely produces the sort of passionate debate and activism that the Framers of the Constitution were at pains to temper. By transmuting political into legal questions, the rights revolution born of the New Deal has acted more to dampen than to spark democratic deliberation and debate.

A New Era of Substantive Due Process

Perhaps the best example of how the recent judicial activism has extended the idea of rights in America is the court's creation of, and commitment to, a right of privacy. In *Griswold v. Connecticut* (1965), the court overturned a Connecticut law that made it a crime to sell, use, or counsel the use of contraceptives for birth control. As Justice Potter Stewart put it, this law appeared to be an "uncommonly silly law"; it grated against most Americans' sense of privacy. No language in the Constitution clearly prohibited such a law. Nevertheless, when Planned Parenthood members were charged with breaking it, the Supreme Court struck down their convictions.

In his majority opinion, Justice William Douglas, an ardent New Dealer and judicial activist, granted that the Constitution did not explicitly provide a right of privacy. But the spirit of such a right pervaded the whole document. Specific Bill of Rights guarantees created "zones of privacy" that prohibited the peacetime quartering of soldiers in private houses, unreasonable searches and seizures, and self-incrimination. These specific privacy guarantees cast a broader shadow that created a penumbra, a shadow's outer reach, and protected additional privacy rights, including marital privacy. *Griswold's* creation of a right of privacy proved popular. Although the court's defense of "penumbral rights" was assailed by judicial restraint advocates, most people appreciated the court's defense of the sanctity of marriage and the marital bedroom against a silly and offensive statute.

Much more controversial was the court's extension of privacy rights to abortion in *Roe v. Wade* (1973). *Roe* was arguably the most important court case since *Brown*. It involved an unmarried pregnant woman who sought an abortion in Texas, where abortions were prohibited by law except when the life of the mother was at stake. Justice Harry Blackmun's decision, for a 7–2 majority, did not stress the "penumbra" of privacy rights emanating from the Bill of Rights that the court pronounced in *Griswold*. Rather, the court found, Texas's antiabortion law was unconstitutional because it violated the Fourteenth Amendment's Due Process Clause, a rebirth of the substantive due process doctrine made notorious by *Lochner*. The states' police power, which included the authority to promote health, safeguard medical standards, and protect potential life, violated due process of law if it was used to prevent abortion during the first three months of pregnancy. The *Roe* decision had profound political and policy consequences. It invalidated abortion statutes in forty-six states and gave rise to a pro-life movement that was animated by intense resentment of the court's claim that a fetus was not a "person."

Remarkably, *Roe* was decided by a court led by Chief Justice Warren Burger, who had been appointed by President Richard Nixon in 1969 to replace Earl Warren. During the 1968 campaign, Nixon had strongly opposed the judicial activism of the previous decade. He promised to appoint to the federal bench justices who were "strict constructionists," meaning they would not deviate from the literal meaning of the

The modern form of liberalism found acceptance in the Supreme Court under Earl Warren and continued under Warren Burger as the court waded into controversial issues such as abortion and reapportionment.

Constitution. Justice Blackmun, another Nixon appointee, would severely disappoint the president as well. Indeed, of the four Nixon appointees who participated in *Roe*, only Justice William Rehnquist lived up to Nixon's "conservative" judicial standards. His heated dissent in Roe accused the court of engaging in "judicial legislation" and raised the specter of *Lochner* by suggesting that the Burger court was headed for the same trouble that had discredited the Hughes court and had led to the constitutional revolution of 1937.

But the court's increased activism during the two previous decades had prepared Americans to accept its resolution of major policy questions. Whatever the cogency of its opinions in cases like *Brown* and *Roe*, the court's intervention on behalf of vulnerable individuals and groups did not arouse public anger to the degree that its support for business had done decades before. The *Brown* case was critical to the development of the Civil Rights Movement. Likewise, *Roe* influenced the women's movement to proclaim a "right to choose" in order to press the government to help women forgo childbearing and enter the workforce or, at the least, plan and time their pregnancies.

In spite of Nixon's intentions, the Burger court preserved and frequently expanded the Warren court's liberal decisions, especially with respect to equal protection and right to privacy cases. It issued landmark decisions on busing and sexual discrimination. As the next section shows, even in those areas in which the Burger court sought to limit judicially inspired reform, it did not seriously restrain the activism deeply embedded in the lower courts, which became responsible for much of the day-to-day judicial supervision of constitutional policy.

The Complex Legacy of the *Brown* Decision

As we note in this chapter, the judiciary controls neither purse nor sword. When it was protecting rights such as liberty of contract, the judiciary had only to restrain government. But the Warren and Burger court rulings were about securing rights that could only be provided by government, and therefore they made the court increasingly dependent on other agents of government – lower courts, Congress, and the executive – to implement its will.

Chapter 7 shows that Congress's response to the expansion of national administrative power has been to intervene in the details of administration. By doing so, it has become more like the very bureaucracies it seeks to control. The same is true of the federal judiciary. This transformation began with the *Brown* decision. The Warren court was left with the practical problem of how to end forced school segregation. It waited a year before issuing the so-called *Brown 11* case, *Brown v. Board of Education* (1955), which called for "all deliberate speed" to desegregate schools. Because federal district courts were closer to local conditions, the Supreme Court determined that they should bear the burden of fashioning specific plans for carrying out this mandate.

The Supreme Court's decisions in the *Brown* cases – and the federal district courts' efforts to administer them – needed help from the president and Congress. President Eisenhower disapproved of Warren's opinion in *Brown*. He refused to publicly support the decision, which slowed progress toward racial equality and helped set the stage for a constitutional crisis in Little Rock, Arkansas.

In September 1957, the Democratic governor of Arkansas, Orval Faubus, called up the state National Guard to obstruct a federal court order to desegregate all-white Central High School in Little Rock. Eisenhower's meeting with Faubus on September 14 only seemed to encourage the Arkansas governor's resistance to desegregation. On September 23, nine African-American students were turned away from the school by a howling mob. Eisenhower still did not come out in support of the *Brown* decision. Yet, fearing that to do nothing in the face of Faubus's resistance would encourage every segregationist governor to defy the law, he finally took action to enforce the court order. His delay enabled resistance to grow so great as to require the largest domestic military deployment in decades. On September 24, a contingent of regular army paratroopers was dispatched to Little Rock. The next day Americans saw shocking photographs of troops wielding bayonets in an American city.

The Little Rock incident dramatically underscored the need for presidential and congressional support in order to achieve desegregation. Until 1964, when President Lyndon Johnson and his congressional supporters made that support reliably available, very little actual desegregation took place. Resistant local governments emphasized "deliberate" rather than "speed" in responding to the court's school desegregation edict. After 1964, when the combined authority of all three federal government branches was deployed against the South and its system of Jim Crow, desegregation progress came quickly. Within four years, more Southern schools desegregated than in the previous fourteen years. Box 4 describes the organization of the most powerful of all judicially involved executive departments, the Department of Justice.

Box Four: Nuts and Bolts

The Department of Justice

The Department of Justice is presided over by the attorney general, a member of the president's cabinet. The attorney general is the government's lawyer, defending any agency or department from suits brought against it. He or she is also the main enforcer of federal law and administrative regulations and the chief prosecutor of civil rights and antitrust violations. The second in command of the department is the deputy attorney general, who exercises day-to-day supervision of its several divisions: criminal, civil rights, and antitrust. Each division is headed by an assistant attorney general, who, like the attorney general and the deputy attorney general, is subject to Senate confirmation. Third in the chain of command is the solicitor general, who represents the government in all appellate cases. Therefore, the solicitor general argues the government position in cases before the Supreme Court. The attorney general also appoints U.S. attorneys for every state. These attorneys initiate most prosecutions under federal law. Each U.S. attorney's office is staffed with several assistant U.S. attorneys.

Progress in desegregation was far slower when the objective shifted from simply eliminating legally mandated segregation to remedying the ill effects of past segregation by purposely mixing whites and blacks together. This goal was particularly hard to achieve in locales in which the two races no longer lived in the same neighborhoods. The most controversial remedy that the courts attempted was busing. In *Swann v. Charlotte-Mecklenburg Board of Education* (1971), the court approved massive busing of students as well as a system of attendance zones that was marked by sometimes drastic redrawing of traditional school boundaries. Acknowledging the difficulties that judges faced in designing practical integration plans, the court claimed that the goal was so important that "administratively awkward, inconvenient and even bizarre" solutions could not be avoided.

Busing was successful in communities such as Charlotte, North Carolina, which had large consolidated city-county school districts that allowed judges considerable flexibility in overcoming the legacy of government-sponsored segregation. But elsewhere, busing bred neighborhood violence and white flight to districts unaffected by busing. During the 1970s, the court considered an increasing number of cases outside the South, even locations where there was no history of de jure, or official, segregation.

Police escorted school buses from the Gavin School in south Boston in 1974 amid bitter protests after judicially prescribed school busing was instituted to achieve social desegregation in Boston schools.

In a 1974 Denver, Colorado, case, the court determined that unofficial, *de facto segregation* patterns were unconstitutional if the school board "intended" to separate the races. Such discriminatory intent was shown in other cities including Detroit, Cleveland, and Boston. Remedying de facto segregation in places such as Boston proved very difficult. The Boston metropolitan area encompassed many separate school districts, but the court could prove discriminatory intent only with regard to the city school district. Therefore, busing was confined to the city, which encouraged whites to flee to adjacent suburbs. African Americans were bused to white poor and working-class Boston neighborhoods. As Martha Derthick notes,

> The spectacle of federal judges deciding the most mundane details of local school administration...while ethnic neighborhoods turned into battle zones caused even the most ardent liberals to ponder whether the power of national judges was being appropriately employed.

Because so many whites transferred their children to suburban or private schools, few whites remained in the Boston school system, making racial integration impossible.

Nonetheless, the Supreme Court emerged from the busing controversy with much of its prestige intact. Indeed, the American people accepted the judiciary's supervision of large parts of the economy and society during the 1960s and 1970s. Just as the protracted struggle over school integration had shown the limits of judicial review, so the federal courts' persistent and extensive role in shaping public policy took place in collaboration with Congress and the executive agencies.

Constitutional Policy and Statutory Interpretation

In proposing a civil rights bill in 1961, President John F. Kennedy called it "sound constitutional policy." As law professor Alexander Bickel pointed out at the time, the concept of "constitutional policy" was a novel hybrid of the previously distinct categories of "constitutional law" and "public policy." Significantly, the 1964 Civil Rights Act, like Kennedy's proposal, was justified on the basis of the Commerce Clause. Many Southerners – led by Senator Sam Ervin of North Carolina, who would later become a stalwart defender of the Constitution in the Watergate episode – insisted the act was unconstitutional. These critics claimed that Congress was using the pretense of the commerce power to intrude into matters of strictly local concern. But when the act came before the court in the 1964 case *Katzenbach v. McClung*, the justices upheld it unanimously. As Leuchtenburg has written, this reading of the Commerce Clause, born of the New Deal constitutional crisis, would "make it possible in the 1960s for the government to tell even the most obscure fried chicken shack that it could not discriminate against African-American patrons, because, in the eyes of the Judiciary, its two-bit, off the beaten-track operation was an enterprise in interstate commerce."

Thus, constitutional policy created an institutional partnership between the three branches of the national government that was devoted to the expansion of rights. The enforcement of statutes like the 1964 Civil Rights Act was not left solely to bureaucratic agencies. The courts intervened in the details of administration, developing case law that extensively influenced how constitutional policy was administered. Indeed, the Civil Rights Act is "surprisingly silent," political scientist Melnick observes, on the meaning of the key term *discrimination*: "The most common assumption of the bill's sponsors was 'we mean what the courts have meant.'" No further explanation was needed.

During the 1970s and early 1980s, the courts, Congress, and administrative agencies reinforced each other's activism. The 1964 Civil Rights Act seemed to disallow any form of racial preference, but the courts frequently interpreted it to allow affirmative action, the use of racial classifications to improve access of racial minorities to education, jobs, and other important social goods. In *Griggs v. Duke Power Co.* (1972), the court struck down certain employment criteria used by the Duke Power Company because those practices excluded a disproportionate number of African Americans from the employment pool. Chief Justice Burger's majority opinion held employers responsible for justifying practices that were seemingly fair but had an "adverse impact" on women and minorities.

Griggs stopped just short of interpreting the civil rights law as requiring quotas. Congress did not endorse quotas, but it made no effort to stop courts and agencies from inferring the existence of discrimination based on "nonproportional outcomes." Faced with the difficult choice between merely punishing overt discrimination and requiring racial quotas, Congress made no choice at all, delegating this difficult decision to the courts and the bureaucracy.

Another important example of constitutional policy was the Voting Rights Act of 1965, which asserted expansive federal power to deal with the decades old problem of disenfranchisement of Southern blacks. Just as the Civil Rights Act of 1964 breathed life into the Fourteenth Amendment, likewise did the Voting Rights Act of 1965 (see Chapter 8) invigorate the Fifteenth Amendment guarantee of voting rights for African Americans. It barred the notorious literacy tests that African Americans, but not whites, had to pass in order to be allowed to register to vote and that were often so difficult that no one could pass them. It required all voting law changes in Southern states to be "precleared" by the Department of Justice or the federal courts in order to prevent clever new methods of keeping African Americans from voting. At first, preclearance was only applied to state laws that had an adverse effect (intentional or not) on black registration. Then it was extended to legislative and municipal redistricting as well. Originally, the Voting Rights Act targeted only seven states of the old confederacy. But by the 1970s, it was also being used to secure representation for racial and linguistic minorities nationwide, creating many new safe seats for minority candidates.

The importance of the civil rights acts lay not just in their extensive reach but also in the model they established for other legislation. Emulating them, Lyndon Johnson's Great Society legislation and many laws enacted during the 1970s embodied "statutory rights," meaning rights proclaimed by Congress in statute with no direct reference to the Constitution. Statutory rights included "procedural rights," in which the court held administrative agencies to exacting standards for ensuring "fair representation for all affected interests" (especially those representing "discrete and insular minorities") in the exercise of the discretion Congress had delegated to them. The judiciary's strict scrutiny of administrative procedures and regulations helped convert welfare, consumer protection, and environmental measures into programmatic rights that codified, in many important respects, the New Deal vision of a good society. Once a critical "veto point" that restrained the growth of government, by the end of the 1970s the judiciary had become an unexpected source of political energy for an expansive welfare and regulatory state.

Has the Rights Revolution Run Its Course?

As Chapter 8 indicates, Ronald Reagan was the only president since the New Deal to challenge the growing welfare state. His impact on the federal judiciary is a good measure of both the force and the limitations of the Reagan "revolution." As political scientists Benjamin Ginsberg and Martin Shefter have observed, Reagan "sought not simply to ensure that conservative judges would replace liberal judges on the federal bench, but sought also to stage an intellectual revolution by enhancing the impact of conservative ideas on American jurisprudence." Prominent conservative legal scholars such as Ralph K. Winter and Robert H. Bork of Yale University and Richard Posner of the University of Chicago were appointed to federal appeals courts. In 1986, when Warren Burger retired, Reagan promoted Justice William Rehnquist, the most conservative member of the Burger court, to chief justice and appointed famous conservative jurist Antonin Scalia to take Rehnquist's place as an associate justice. The administration based many of its positions regarding separation of powers, federalism, and competing claims of majority rule and minority rights on Rehnquist and Scalia's legal writings and judicial opinions.

Like Nixon, Reagan promised to appoint strict constitutional constructionists who would not intrude their own public policy preferences when making judicial rulings. But Reagan was much more intent than Nixon on bringing about a full-scale philosophical and political realignment. In that cause, some conservative Republicans opposed judicial restraint; they favored instead an activist court that would restrict the national government's powers and protect property rights, very much like the court had done during the end of the nineteenth century and beginning of the twentieth century.

The Senate Rejects Judge Bork

The culmination of Reagan's efforts to reconstitute the federal judiciary came in 1987, when he nominated Judge Robert Bork to the Supreme Court. (The accompanying Box 5 explains the process by which federal judges are chosen and confirmed.) Bork was perhaps America's leading conservative legal scholar, a brilliant and outspoken critic of recent procedural and programmatic judicial innovations. His appointment almost certainly would have tilted a closely divided court decisively to the right on constitutional issues such as abortion, affirmative action, and criminal law. Stoked by extensive advertising and direct-mail campaigns by progressive and conservative interest groups, the controversy over Bork's nomination was unprecedented in its partisanship and bitterness. The Senate confirmation hearings were nationally televised.

Box Five: Nuts and Bolts

Judicial Confirmation

Federal judges are chosen by the president, who relies heavily on the advice of the attorney general and other members of the president's political inner circle. These designees are almost always from the same party as the president. Judicial nominees come from a variety of legal backgrounds. Many have had previous careers as state judges and prosecutors. Others have been law professors or prominent attorneys. Because these selections must be confirmed by a majority vote in the Senate, its members have a great deal of influence in the selection process. The custom is that the president, before making a judicial nomination, asks for the support of the senators from the prospective nominee's state, if they are of the president's party. This custom is known as senatorial courtesy. The Senate will normally reject a candidate if those senators object.

As the Bork case demonstrates, Senate confirmation has become an increasingly contentious process. The Senate Judiciary Committee hearings provide the stage for the myriad interest groups who seek to influence the Senate vote. Although the most sensational hearings have involved Supreme Court nominees, especially Clarence Thomas and Robert Bork, hearings for appeals court nominees have also proven highly controversial. In 2002, the Senate Judiciary Committee, voting along partisan lines, turned down President George W. Bush's nomination of Albert Pickering, Jr., to the appeals court.

After divisive confirmation hearings in 1987, the Senate ultimately rejected Robert Bork's nomination to the Supreme Court by a wide margin, reflecting dissatisfaction with the Reagan administration's attempt to place well known conservatives on the Court.

It proved critically important that the Democrats had taken control of the Senate in 1986. In five days of questioning before the Judiciary Committee, now dominated by progressive Democrats, Bork was subjected to bitter attack. The Democratic majority derided his promise to restore the Constitution's "original intent." In a resounding defeat for the Reagan administration, Bork became only the fourth twentieth-century Supreme Court nominee to fail to be confirmed by the Senate. No previous nominee had been battered as badly as Bork during his nearly thirty hours of testimony. The vote to defeat him was 58–42, the widest margin of disapproval in the history of Supreme Court nominations.

In part, Bork's rejection testified to widespread public resistance to the Reagan administration's social agenda. Although most voters supported cutting taxes and strengthening national defense, they also favored better political, educational, and economic opportunities for women and African Americans, and they favored abortion rights. As a leading critic of the constitutional and statutory rights advanced by the Warren and Burger courts, especially with respect to affirmative action and abortion, Bork exposed himself to the charge of being "outside the mainstream." The breadth of the opposition to Reagan's social agenda was apparent in the votes against Bork of thirteen Southern Democratic senators and six moderate Republicans.

The fight over Bork's confirmation revived fundamental questions about the Constitution and the court's role in interpreting it. Since the Progressive Era, reformers had insisted that the Constitution was, as Woodrow Wilson put it, a "living document," one that amendments, court rulings, and constitutional policy had made more democratic and protective of new rights. Bork's nomination signaled the rise of political opposition to the rights revolution and the activist court that advanced it. That opposition, which appeared to crest with Reagan's elevation to the White House, viewed social welfare rights as government bounties that undermined individual responsibility and perverted liberty. It sought to revive the nineteenth-century court's commitment to property rights, establish the rights of the unborn, and limit broad interpretations of the Bill of Rights.

After Bork was rejected, Reagan nominated another conservative, Judge Douglas Ginsberg. But Ginsberg was forced to withdraw amid revelations that he had smoked marijuana as a student and as a law professor. Eventually, the administration acquiesced to political reality and nominated the more moderate Anthony M. Kennedy. Reagan's conservative federal judicial appointments strongly influenced court decisions, but not as decisively as the 1937 constitutional revolution had done. The Rehnquist court would curb but not attempt to undo the rights revolution.

We note in Chapter 7 that Republican presidents and the Democratic congressional majority engaged in institutional combat that went beyond mere policy differences in its level of brutality. As Bork's rejection and other nomination battles during the Reagan and Bush presidencies showed, the judiciary was a principal focus of this combat. In addition, Congress fought to reverse court rulings it opposed. The White House fought back to protect them. In 1991, Congress passed an act that nullified court rulings that undercut the minority employment standards established in *Griggs*. *Griggs* put the burden on employers to demonstrate that their employment practices did not have an "adverse impact" on women and minorities. In *Ward's Cove Packing Co. v. Antonio* (1989), the Rehnquist court shifted the burden of proof, requiring plaintiffs to show that employers had no legitimate need for the employment practices under challenge. The new legislation instructed the courts to follow the *Griggs* interpretation of the 1964 Civil Rights Act, not *Ward's Cove*. President George H. W. Bush had vetoed a similar bill in 1990, arguing that it would lead to hiring quotas for minorities and women. But in the wake of the racially charged Senate confirmation hearings over the Supreme Court nomination of Clarence Thomas, a conservative African American, Bush chose to sign a modified version of the bill.

The "Center" Holds

Roe v. Wade, the landmark abortion ruling discussed earlier in this chapter, was perhaps the single greatest cause of conservative condemnation of the court. The 1980 Republican platform singled it out for criticism and promised to appoint justices who would overturn it. The Reagan and Bush administrations tried five times to overturn it and failed. A sixth, more promising opportunity came in 1992 when the Supreme Court heard *Planned Parenthood of Southeastern Pennsylvania v. Casey*. Only one justice who had endorsed *Roe* – Harry Blackmun, author of the original decision – remained on the bench. He had the firm support of one other justice, John Stevens. It seemed that Reagan and Bush had made enough conservative appointments to overrule the controversial abortion decision.

Planned Parenthood concerned a state law that placed conditions on the free exercise of abortion, including obtaining the informed consent of the woman, waiting twenty-four hours after obtaining consent, notifying the husband in advance, and requiring minors to gain consent from at least one parent. Opposing counsels both asked the court to revisit the fundamental question of a right to abortion. The plaintiff argued that upholding the Pennsylvania restrictions amounted to overturning Roe, which would constitute a unique instance of the court withdrawing a fundamental right that had been in place for almost twenty years. Solicitor General Kenneth Starr (who later became independent counsel in the Clinton-Lewinsky scandal) urged the court to repeal *Roe*.

To the surprise of the White House, public, and press, the court once again failed to overturn *Roe*. A five-member majority, including Reagan appointees Sandra Day O'Connor and Anthony Kennedy and Bush appointee David Souter, reaffirmed "the right of women to choose to have an abortion before viability and to obtain it without undue interference from the state." The court upheld the Pennsylvania law, except for the part requiring notification of the husband, on the grounds that the law did not unduly interfere with the right to an abortion. Justice O'Connor's opinion, joined by Justices Kennedy and Souter, provided an alternative to the polarized positions on abortion and has since been the controlling view of the court. It did not confirm that *Roe* had been correctly decided, but it upheld the right to choose on the basis that *Roe* had become settled, standing law, which must be respected by the Supreme Court. Justice Blackmun's earlier principled defense of abortion on Fourteenth Amendment grounds was not mentioned. The right to privacy, Justice O'Connor argued, should be upheld under the principle of *stare decisis*, meaning "let the decision stand." To do otherwise would undermine the legitimacy of the court and threaten the rule of law.

Justice O'Connor's words could be read as the death knell of the Reagan revolution. By relying on liberal precedent, she was blocking conservative efforts to reset the very terms of constitutional government. The doctrine of stare decisis has a long history. After all, if the Supreme Court created every one of its decisions from whole cloth, it would become just another political branch of government. Absent a body of settled, standing law, the court's special place in the constitutional order, as the expositor of law, would be irreparably damaged. Sensitive to the fragile authority of the judiciary, Justice Louis Brandeis once remarked, "Stare decisis is usually a wise policy because in most matters it is more important that the applicable rule of law be settled than that it be settled right." Box 6 describes how the Supreme Court has relied on precedent to deal with a civil liberties issue – pornography on the internet.

Obscenity and the Internet

The internet and the World Wide Web pose new challenges for parents trying to protect their children from exposure to pornography. Because children tend to be far more skilled at "surfing" than their parents are, they can often evade the filtering devices that their parents install. In response to public outrage at the proliferation of pornography on the web, Congress passed in 1996 the Communication Decency Act (CDA). The CDA prohibited deliberate transmission over the internet of obscene or indecent messages in a manner available to any recipient under eighteen years of age. In *Reno v. American Civil Liberties Union* (1997), the Supreme Court overturned the CDA on the grounds that it violated the First Amendment guarantee of free speech: "The CDA lack[ed] the precision that the First Amendment requires when a statute regulates the content of speech" because "in order to deny minors access to potentially harmful speech, the CDA effectively suppressed a large amount of speech that adults had a constitutional right to receive and to address to one another." Congress responded by passing the Child Online Protection Act (COPA). COPA sought to meet the court's objections to the previous legislation by exempting e-mail, limiting coverage to internet communications made for "commercial purposes," and narrowing the definition of prohibited material from "indecent and patently offensive" to "material harmful to minors." Once again, in *Ashcroft v. American Civil Liberties Union* (2001), the civil liberties organization brought suit, claiming that COPA violated the right to free speech.

In a series of cases brought in the 1950s and 1960s, the Supreme Court held that obscene speech is not protected by the First Amendment. But it struggled to establish a clear definition of obscenity. In *Miller v. California* (1973), the court came up with a definition that it has continued to apply ever since. Material is obscene if the average person, applying contemporary community standards, would find that the work, taken as a whole, appeals to the prurient interest, depicts sexual conduct in a patently offensive way, and lacks serious literary, artistic, political, or scientific value. This definition is very hard to apply to something international in scope such as the web because, in the absence of any geographical limitation, it is hard to know how to apply "community standards." Which community is it whose standards apply? In effect, jurors would apply the standards of whatever community is the site of the case being brought under COPA. Smart prosecutors would bring cases in the most conservative communities they could find. The U.S. Court of Appeals for the Third Circuit agreed with the ACLU that the community standards definition should not be applied in such cases. It upheld the district court's injunction against putting COPA into effect.

The Supreme Court, as it had in other pornography cases in which the material under scrutiny was being distributed nationally, refused to admit that nationwide, or even worldwide, dissemination of obscene material undermined the "community standards" definition: "The fact that distributors of allegedly obscene materials may be subjected to varying community standards in the various federal judicial districts into which they transmit their materials does not render a federal statute unconstitutional." Therefore, the court refused to overturn COPA on those grounds. However, it also refused to decide whether COPA's efforts to be more precise and narrowly focused than its predecessor enabled it to escape the charge that it was unconstitutionally vague. The court of appeals had not ruled on that question; the lower court had simply ruled on questions related to community standards. The Supreme Court sent the case back to the court of appeals for a consideration of COPA's constitutionality, and it reserved the right to review the appeals court's subsequent action if it so chose. In the meantime, the court upheld the lower court's injunction against COPA's implementation.

But if government is truly to be based on popular consent, precedent cannot always reign. Sometimes great contests of opinion over the proper meaning of people's rights are required. As the Civil War and the New Deal demonstrate, these contests can create both full-scale political realignments and major constitutional debates that, as Franklin Roosevelt put it, "redefine the social contract." Unlike *Dred Scott* and *Lochner*, *Roe* appeared to be supported by a majority of Americans. Clinton's court appointments, Justices Ruth Bader Ginsburg and Stephen Breyer, backed the pragmatic approach that Justice O'Connor and her allies applied to the abortion controversy. But, as Justice Scalia complained, *Planned Parenthood* required a more intrusive court role in abortion policy. Justice O'Connor's opinion rejected *Roe*'s "strict scrutiny test," which established a strong presumption against any infringement on abortion, at least during the first three months of pregnancy. By replacing "strict scrutiny" with "undue burden," Justice Scalia warned, the court set out an "inherently manipulable" doctrine that would require judges to continually make abortion policy. "Undue burden" committed the courts to determining on a case-by-case basis if a particular restriction created too much hardship for a woman seeking an abortion. In the face of the *Planned Parenthood* decision, the self-restraint displayed by Chief Justice John Marshall and famous dissenters like Justices Holmes and Frankfurter seemed to be forgotten both by ambitious judges and by a rights-conscious people who increasingly looked to the judiciary to resolve thorny, inherently political issues. (See Table 9.2 for a list of the current members of the Supreme Court of the United States.)

Table 9.2. Justices of the Supreme Court (2007)

Name	Year Appointed	Nominated by
John Paul Stevens	1975	Ford
Antonin Scalia	1986	Reagan
Anthony Kennedy	1988	Reagan
David Souter	1990	George H. W. Bush
Clarence Thomas	1991	George H. W. Bush
Ruth Bader Ginsburg	1993	Clinton
Stephen Breyer	1994	Clinton
John Roberts*	2005	George W. Bush
Samuel Alito	2006	George W. Bush

*Roberts was appointed as Chief Justice after the death of William Rehnquist.

The Judiciary in a Partisan Era

As we have noted throughout this book, American politics and government have become more polarized during the past twenty-five years. Once highly decentralized and dependant on patronage, the Democrats and Republicans emerged as national and programmatic parties at the dawn of the twenty-first century. Consequently, the Congress has become significantly more centralized and the president has become more aggressive as a party leader. In both the House and the Senate, party-line voting has become much more common. Indeed, bitter partisanship has destroyed long-established norms of bipartisanship and comity. With George W. Bush's ascent to the White House, and the restoration of unified government in Washington, many scholars and pundits observed, or warned, that a new party system trumped the separation of powers. When Sandra Day O'Connor, the swing vote on the court, stepped down from the bench in March 2006, conservatives expected and liberals feared that the court would also be subject to increased partisan involvement and partisan pressures.

Justice O'Connor, herself, a few weeks after she announced her retirement, gave a speech at Georgetown Law School that expressed her opposition to "judicial reforms driven by nakedly partisan reasoning." She pointed to the experiences of developing and former communist countries where interference with an independent judiciary had allowed dictatorship to flourish. She warned that Americans must be ever-vigilant against those who would strong-arm the judiciary into adopting their preferred policies. Of course, O'Connor had voted with the majority in *Bush v. Gore*, the extraordinary case with which we began this chapter. This was the first time the judiciary had resolved a presidential election, and it led to charges that the court had engaged in a naked partisan power play. But *Bush v. Gore* is best understood not as a partisan political decision but rather as the latest in a line of court decisions, including those dealing with redistricting and abortion, that have substituted judicial authority for public deliberation in resolving profound controversies.

Although members of the Supreme Court disagreed bitterly over the remedy to be applied in *Bush v. Gore* (whether to allow the recount to continue), seven of the nine justices agreed to a novel interpretation of the Fourteenth Amendment that has the potential to greatly increase court intervention in the electoral process. The U.S. Supreme Court deemed that the Florida Supreme Court's recount order was unconstitutional because, by failing to set an adequate standard for evaluating contested ballots, it denied voters the equal protection of the laws. By invoking this broad form of constitutional protection, the court seemed to indicate an unprecedented willingness to enter the political thicket of judging the fairness of elections.

Justice O'Connor, who joined her conservative brethren in halting the recount, was troubled by this audacious application of the Fourteenth Amendment to the presidential selection process. She insisted that the court's opinion include a disclaimer that this decision did not establish a precedent. This disclaimer could be interpreted as judicial modesty, a promise not to intervene routinely in presidential politics, or as judicial activism, an unwillingness to be bound by precedent. Just as the *Planned Parenthood* decision presumed to keep a wrenching issue out of politics, so did the majority opinion in *Bush v. Gore* forestall what would have been a divisive legislative battle to determine the presidential election outcome. A January 2001 Gallup Poll showed that approval of the judiciary fell among Democrats and rose among Republicans, but its overall public approval rating did not change much as a result of its intervention in the 2000 election. The lack of deep-seated public opposition to *Bush v. Gore* indicated that voters preferred a judicial resolution to one forged by either the Florida state legislature or Congress.

The American people have grown increasingly distrustful of politics (see Chapter 12). This distrust has been aroused, and nurtured, by the rights revolution, by the consequent expansion of the administrative state, and by the judiciary's critical role in both these developments. The Rehnquist court did not curtail either the rights revolution or the administrative state; but, as its abortion decisions show, it restrained them. A similar tendency was evident in its decisions about federalism, especially *United States v. Lopez* (1995). In that case, the court decided that the Constitution's commerce power did not entitle Congress to ban concealed handguns near schools (see Chapter 5).

Lopez limited the extent of the commerce power, but Rehnquist's opinion made clear that there was no intent to shrink the commerce power back to its pre-1937 size. He did not revive the distinctions between direct and indi-rect effects, or manufacturing and commerce, that were the foundation of nineteenth-century laissez-faire jurisprudence. Only one justice, Clarence Thomas, dared argue that the court took "a wrong turn in the 1930s." As important as the federalism cases were, they did not involve a funda-mental reevaluation of the relationship between the central government and the states. Rather, they embodied the Rehnquist court's pragmatism. Controlled by its more centrist jurists, the court has sought to oversee that relationship, in effect, on a case-by-case basis.

The justices' ongoing effort to balance rights and state law deeply dis-appointed social conservatives. In 2003, the Supreme Court's decision in *Lawrence v. Texas* overturned an antisodomy law. It reversed an earlier deci-sion involving a Georgia statute that upheld a state's authority to regu-late moral behavior. Anthony Kennedy's majority opinion stopped short of declaring homosexuality a fundamental right. But the court did interpret the Due Process Clause of the Fourteenth Amendment to proscribe laws that condemned homosexual conduct as immoral. Both Justice Kennedy and Justice O'Connor, the author of a concurring opinion, insisted that *Lawrence* did not provide constitutional grounds for constitutionally pro-tecting same-sex marriage. Nonetheless, this case, as Linda Greenhouse, the legal reporter for the *New York Times*, noted, "was [the] background music that suffused" the Massachusetts Supreme Judicial Court decision five months later that "same-sex couples have a state constitutional right to the 'protections, benefits, and obligations of civil marriage.'" The sec-ond paragraph of Massachusetts Chief Justice Margaret Marshall's majority opinion included a quotation from the *Lawrence* decision: "Our obligation is to define the liberty of all, not to mandate our own moral code."

The Rehnquist court thus failed to defend federalism in those instances in which a majority of justices found state law to be discriminatory. Even so, the court showed more concern for the sovereignty of the states than either the Republican Congress or President did. During his first six years in office, President Bush, with the steadfast support of Republican leaders in Congress, sought to advance conservative policy in matters of crime, religion, and, especially, terrorism. These policies require conservative use of, rather than retreat from, national administrative power (see Chapters 7 and 8). The Republican effort to hand the Terri Schiavo case over to the federal courts was a clear example of the party's willingness to jettison federalism concerns when those concerns conflicted with the conservative social agenda. The polarizing fight over Ms. Schiavo, who had suffered severe brain damage in 1990, produced a national debate about the rights of incapacitated people and when their lives should end if they themselves had left no specific instructions. Ms. Schiavo's parents (Mary and Robert

Schindler) had waged a legal battle since 1998 against her husband, who had asked a Florida state court to grant permission to remove her life support. The Schindlers maintained that their daughter was responsive and capable of recovery and tried to win guardianship of her. Although Terry Schiavo could breathe on her own and had periods of wakefulness, Judge George W. Greer of Pinellas-Pasco Circuit Court accepted the testimony of doctors who said she was in a "persistent vegetative state" and incapable of thought or emotion. Judge Greer also found credible Mr. Schiavo's testimony that his wife, although she left no written directive, had said on several occasions that she would not want life-prolonging measures to be used for her.

The Schiavo case did not end with the Florida court's decision. It stirred Congress, which enacted a law days after Ms. Schiavo's feeding tube was removed for the final time on March 18, 2005. That legislation allowed Ms. Schiavo's parents to take their case to the federal courts for a new review. Strongly supported by President Bush, its backers hoped it would lead to a federal court order that Ms. Schiavo's feeding tube be reinserted, giving her parents more time to press their case. But a federal judge in Tampa rejected the Schindlers' argument that their daughter's due process rights had been violated, and the United States Court of Appeals for the 11th Circuit upheld his decision. Judge Stanley F. Birch, Jr.'s appellate court decision admonished President Bush and Congress for acting "in a manner demonstrably at odds with our founding fathers' blueprint for the governance of a free people" – they had sought to impose the will of the federal government, he argued, in a matter better left to individuals, families, and the states.

The Schiavo case fueled conservatives' anger over what they regarded as a runaway judiciary. House Majority Whip Tom DeLay (R-TX), who was instrumental in pushing the emergency legislation that gave the federal courts jurisdiction over Ms. Schiavo's care, attacked the courts for "thumb[ing] their nose at Congress and the president." He declined to rule out the possibility that Congress might impeach the judges involved. Delay's threats against the judiciary, which prompted Justice O'Connor's complaint about "hyperpartisanship" regarding the courts, proved to be idle. The White House and most Republicans in Congress were chastened by polls that consistently showed the public strongly opposed federal intervention in the Schiavo case.

Nonetheless, the controversy further aggravated conflict over President Bush's judicial nominations. As we noted in Chapter 8, the White House and Senate had been engaged in acrimonious battles over judicial nominations, including district and appeals court judges, throughout Bush's presidency. In the wake of the Republican victories in the 2004 elections,

Republican majority leader Bill Frist (R-TN), with the president's encouragement, had explored employing the "nuclear option." This term was a nickname for outlawing filibusters of judicial nominations, a tactic to which Democrats had resorted routinely since the GOP resumed control of the Senate in the 2002 midterm elections. The polarizing struggle over the filibuster was resolved when a bipartisan group of moderates and mavericks – dubbed the Gang of 14 – reached agreement to oppose both the nuclear option and filibusters on judicial confirmations except under extraordinary circumstances. Just how long this uneasy truce would hold remained very uncertain, however. The retirement of Justice O'Connor and the death of Chief Justice William Rehnquist gave President Bush the opportunity to make two appointments to the Supreme Court, and thus perhaps shift its balance of power in a conservative direction. The White House, Congress, and advocates on both the left and right were poised for the renewal of partisan combat over judicial nominations.

Ironically, the most bitter conflict over the court was not between Democrats and Republicans but between President Bush and conservatives in his own party. Bush's first nominee, Appellate Court Justice John G. Roberts, did not cause much controversy. Although Roberts had a conservative record as a member of the Reagan administration's justice department and federal judge, he had not left enough of a paper trail for liberals to exploit. Equally important, Roberts was replacing Chief Justice Rehnquist and the prospect of appointing one conservative, especially one who showed great poise and charm during his Senate confirmation hearings, to replace another did not arouse fierce partisan dispute. Bush's choice to replace Justice O'Connor, the swing vote on many critical decisions, drew much greater scrutiny.

When the president announced that he was nominating White House Counsel Harriet Miers, conservatives responded with a mixture of deep disappointment and angry denunciation. Miers had been Bush's personal lawyer in Texas and a legal advisor to his two gubernatorial campaigns. Although some Democrats dismissed her as a Bush crony, the real anger against her nomination surfaced among conservative activists. They were appalled that the president had passed over a number of proven conservative jurists in favor of a candidate with no known record as a constitutional thinker. Bush expected that the conservative base he had so assiduously cultivated would support his choice. He assured congressional Republicans and conservative activists that Ms. Miers was an Evangelical Christian who would uphold family values. But judicial politics had become too polarized for conservatives to risk an unknown quantity, especially one who was rumored to have moderate views on hot button issues like abortion and affirmative action. After twenty-four days of acrimony, the White House decided to withdraw the Miers nomination and selected Appeals Court Judge Samuel Alito, a proven conservative jurist. "The White House didn't understand the independence of the conservative movement," William Kristol, the editor of the conservative magazine, the *Weekly Standard*, insisted. "What this shows is that for conservatives, the Supreme Court is so central."

The epic battle many pundits predicted over Alito's nomination never materialized. Alito's performance before the Senate, although not quite as impressive as Justice Robert's had been, went over well with the public. (For example, a Gallup Poll taken in January 2006, just before the Senate voted, showed that 54 percent of those surveyed supported Alito's confirmation, while only 30 percent opposed it; 16 percent remained undecided.) Like Roberts, Alito had served in the Reagan administration's justice department. But he left a more substantial paper trail in the form of memoranda that expressed conservative positions on abortion and affirmative action. These opinions, voiced two decades earlier, persuaded liberal activists that Alito could not be trusted on the court. But his modest demeanor, accentuated by tales of growing up as the son of an Italian immigrant family, and his pledge to uphold the law rather than conservative doctrine, made it difficult for congressional Democrats to portray him as so outside the "mainstream" of American politics to justify a filibuster. Significantly, Alito's confirmation was assured when the "Gang of 14" met shortly before the Senate vote and agreed unanimously that the "extraordinary circumstances" stipulation that paved the way for a compromise in the "nuclear option" fight did not apply in this case. The final vote of 58–42 in favor of Alito's confirmation was unusually close and partisan; indeed, only the 52–48 decision to confirm Justice Clarence Thomas in 1991 was closer. But the final verdict was anticlimactic, occurring as it did in the wake of the Democrats' failure to mount enough support for a filibuster. As Republicans celebrated and Democrats lamented what appeared to be the consolidation of a conservative majority on the Supreme Court, liberals conceded that their only hope to influence judicial politics was to become a more effective national political party capable of mounting more successful presidential and congressional campaigns. Their hopes were realized in 2006. Their aggressive and well organized national campaign produced Democratic majorities in both House and Senate capable of blocking judicial nominations they considered to be too conservative.

Whose Court Is It?

It is unlikely, however, that partisanship will trump judicial independence as much as conservatives hope and liberals fear. "What our Constitution has pulled asunder," Melnick insists, "virtually no political party or ideology can unite." Traditionally, the judiciary has been the most difficult branch for parties to tame. The initial term of the Roberts court (President Bush chose Roberts to replace Rehnquist as chief justice) suggests that the court's resistance to party control will continue. As expected, Justices Roberts and Alito generally allied themselves with Justices Thomas and Scalia. But with the departure of Sandra Day O'Connor, Justice Anthony Kennedy, appointed by President Reagan in the wake of the Bork and Ginsberg debacles, positioned himself as the new "swing justice." He cast the deciding vote in a number of important cases in opposition to the conservative positions championed by the White House, the Republican leaders in Congress, and conservative advocacy groups.

Kennedy wrote the majority opinion in the first high profile case of the Roberts court, *Gonzales v. Oregon*, decided in January 2006. The court ruled that former Attorney General John Ashcroft acted without legal authority when he declared that doctors in Oregon who followed the procedures of that state's Death With Dignity Act to help patients commit suicide would lose their federal prescription rights. Without the ability to write prescriptions for those receiving federally provided healthcare – the elderly under Medicare and veterans – doctors would forfeit, as a practical matter, their ability to practice medicine. Oregon voters approved the Death With Dignity Act in 1994 and affirmed it in 1997. The law authorizes doctors to prescribe lethal doses of federally regulated medications that help their mentally competent, terminally ill patients to end their lives. (Through 2004, 325 people had obtained the lethal prescriptions, and 208 had used them.) When the Oregon law first took effect, Ashcroft, then a Senator, urged the Clinton administration to take action against it. Attorney General Janet Reno refused, writing that Congress had not given the executive any authority to do so. Ashcroft then co-sponsored a bill to give the government this authority but it failed to pass.

Still lacking such legal authority when he became attorney general in 2001, Ashcroft invoked the Controlled Substances Act, a 1970 law that established the framework for federal drug policy. He also cited a regulation issued by the justice department that every prescription for a controlled substance "be issued for a legitimate medical purpose." Assisted suicide, Ashcroft claimed, was not a legitimate medical purpose and therefore it was a crime to prescribe drugs in support of it, a position that his successor, Alberto Gonzales, embraced in 2005.

Acknowledging that he was leading the court into "an earnest and profound debate," Justice Kennedy argued that the attorney general's rule was not entitled the deference that the court usually gave to executive interpretations of governing statutes because Congress had not, in fact, given

Ashcroft the authority that he claimed. The Controlled Substances Act proscribed substance abuse and drug dealing, not action taken by medical doctors in pursuance of a state statute. Kennedy's opinion rested on principles of administrative law rather than the Constitution, but it was clearly influenced by the majority's view that the regulation of medical practice belonged, as a general matter, to the states. Kennedy clearly disapproved of the unilateral nature of Ashcroft's action, taken "without consulting Oregon or apparently anyone outside his Department." Justice Kennedy claimed that the justice department was seeking "to effect a radical shift of authority from the States to the Federal government to define standards of medical practice in every locality." The court's opinion did not go so far as to say Congress could not pass a law making assisted suicide a crime, but emphatically declared that the Controlled Substances Act "did not have this far reaching intent to alter the federal-state balance and Congress's role in maintaining it."

Justice Roberts did not write a dissent in the *Gonzales* case, but he joined a dissent written by Justice Scalia. It charged Kennedy and the five justices who signed his opinion with the same sort of case-by-case brokering of a moral debate that characterized many of the decisions that O'Connor delivered on the Rehnquist court. Scalia took issue with the argument that Congress could not have intended to delegate medical judgments of this sort to the attorney general rather than to doctors. The legitimacy of physician-assisted suicide "ultimately rests, not on 'science' or 'medicine,' but on a naked value judgment," Scalia wrote. "It no more depends upon a 'quintessentially' medical 'judgment' than does the legitimacy of polygamy or eugenic infanticide." Although the court gave "lip service to state autonomy," Justice Scalia argued, "its standard for 'legitimate medical purpose' [was] in fact a hazily defined federal standard based on its purposive reading of the [Controlled Substances Act], and extracted from obliquely relevant sections of the Act."

Justice Kennedy's influence also was clear in the most important case of Robert's first term, the historic ruling, *Hamdan v. Rumsfeld*, announced at the end of June 2006, which struck down the military tribunals at the Guantanamo Bay detention camp. Kennedy provided the critical fifth vote. He concurred with Justice Stevens's strongly worded majority opinion that found fault not only with the tribunals but also with President Bush's broader claim that the president has inherent power to execute the War on Terror as he sees fit (see Chapter 7). Roberts did not participate in this case because he had ruled on it a year earlier as an appeals court judge. In that instance, he had voted to uphold the administration's position; thus, he almost certainly would have joined Justices Scalia, Thomas, and Alito in dissent.

The Supreme Court has two recent appointees from the Bush administration, including Chief Justice John Roberts, who inherits William Rehnquist's legacy of reining in the liberalism of the Warren and Burger courts.

The majority decision did not preclude Congress from establishing legal standards that would allow the Bush administration to employ military tribunals and other controversial tactics, such as domestic wiretaps, without judicial search warrants. But, as we note in Chapter 6, congressional efforts to provide standards for prosecuting "enemy combatants" had proved difficult. The White House and Republican Congress had an especially difficult time reaching an accord on legal standards that would comply with the part of the court's ruling that a provision of the international Geneva Conventions, known as Common Article 3, applied to Guantanamo detainees and was enforceable in federal court. Presidential and legislative interpretations of the rights guaranteed by that provision, which requires humane treatment of captured combatants and trials that provide for "a regularly constituted court affording all the judicial guarantees which are recognized as indispensable by civilized people," might be subject to ongoing judicial supervision. In his dissent, Justice Thomas excoriated the majority for presuming to pass judgment on the "military necessity . . . of the Commander in Chief's decision to employ a particular form of force against our enemies." Indeed, the *Hamdan* decision suggested that the court has become less deferential to the president regarding his role as war leader. Judicial intervention in national security policy, once a rare occurrence, might become a more routine affair in the future.

Conclusion: The People's Court

With the retirement of Sandra Day O'Connor from the Supreme Court and the appointment of a more reliable conservative jurist, Samuel A. Alito, to replace her, the court seemed poised to ratify the Reagan "revolution." But if the early days of the Roberts court are any indication, the judiciary will continue to play the role it performed during the Rehnquist era – the arbiter of issues that deeply divided Democratic and Republican activists. As Anthony Kennedy replaced O'Connor at the center of the court, the *New York Times* cheered "the new swing justice in town." At least until the Supreme Court's membership changes again, Kennedy is likely often to have the final word on such deeply divisive issues as abortion, affirmative action, and the prosecution of the War on Terror. More generally, the Supreme Court will adjudicate such issues pragmatically, weighing the facts as well as popular opinion on a case-by-case basis. The control of the Senate by the Democrats since 2006 makes the continuation of this pragmatic approach all the more likely.

Of course, Justice Kennedy may move the center of the court in a more conservative direction. O'Connor was the fifth vote to uphold affirmative action; he dissented. Although both justices have supported *Roe v. Wade*, Kennedy has accepted greater restrictions on abortion rights than did O'Connor while she was on the court. Indeed, in April 2007, in the case of *Gonzales v. Carhart*, Kennedy joined the majority in a 5–4 decision that upheld the federal Partial-Birth Abortion Ban Act, which prohibits a controversial procedure that involves removing the fetus in an intact condition. The banned procedure, known medically as "intact dilation and extraction," is used to terminate pregnancies at about twelve weeks, after the fetus has grown too big to be removed by the suction method that is commonly employed in the first trimester. The *Carhart* case reversed a 5–4 decision seven years earlier, in which Justice O'Connor voted to strike down a similar state law. Kennedy had voted to uphold that state statute, and his steadfast view that *Planned Parenthood* allowed for such restrictions on abortion rights, combined with Justice Alito's vote to uphold the federal law, made the difference in the Roberts court's first consideration of the abortion controversy. *Gonzales v. Carhart* did not overturn *Roe v. Wade* but, as Justice Kennedy noted, it seemed to promise more leniency toward state and federal laws that expressed "respect for the dignity of human life."

Nonetheless, there have been signs that Kennedy is shifting ground on other important issues. For example, soon after his arrival on the court, he joined Justice Scalia's decision, for a 5–4 majority, upholding the constitutionality of the death penalty for juvenile defenders. In 2005, however, he wrote the decision in another 5–4 ruling, *Roper v. Simmons*, reversing his, and the court's, 1989 decision. Kennedy's opinion noted that the American people as well as "the overwhelming weight of international opinion," had turned against the juvenile death penalty. Like the part he played in the court's arbitration of national controversies such as assisted suicide and military tribunals, Kennedy's centrist pragmatic position in the *Simmons* case suggests that his vastly expanded influence may cause him to act more moderately. Justice O'Connor was keenly aware of her position as the swing justice, viewing her place in the court's catbird seat as vesting her with the responsibility to consider the effect of court decisions on public opinion; so Kennedy may likewise consider himself to have a duty to ensure that court decisions remain in line with the views of a majority of Americans. Justice Scalia has been particularly acerbic in attacking his liberal and moderate colleagues for, as he put in his *Simmons* dissent, "proclaiming [themselves] sole arbiter of our Nation's moral standards." But Scalia's views are not shared by the majority of the American public that appears to welcome the judiciary's arbitration of controversies that expose stark differences between liberals and conservatives. A Gallup Poll taken after the first Roberts term found 60 percent approving and 32 percent disapproving of the way the Supreme Court was handling its job – a much more favorable review than President Bush (39 percent approval) and Congress (29 percent approval) received. The public's deference to the court is not merely a reflection of people's growing contempt for politics; it also testifies to the judiciary's special status in American republican government. Cloaked in the robe of impartiality, the courts must not only protect rights but also settle complex boundary disputes between president and Congress and between national and state government. Therefore, as Madison understood and feared, the judiciary will inevitably be drawn into political questions. Although the authority to interpret the Constitution and to call other branches to constitutional account was not explicitly granted in the Constitution, the judiciary's role as interpreter of the law among a population respectful of the rule of law enabled it to assume those powers.

Enraged by the Marshall court's antidemocratic efforts, Madison insisted that such judicial supremacy was improper. And yet the court's imperialistic tendencies have been kept in check both by judicial self-restraint and by the periodic political upheavals that have enabled the people and their representatives to debate and resolve the meaning of the social contract for their own time. In this way, as Lincoln prescribed, the people would decide issues responsibly, without resigning "their Government into the hands of an eminent tribunal." If rights were to trump politics, if the people allowed courts to adjudicate all important political questions, then the republic would lose its democratic character. This prospect is what the country has to fear from incessant rights talk. Unless moderated by the sense of responsibility that comes only from meaningful political participation, the rights revolution could suck the meaning out of American democracy. The country would then be left with a dominant but lifeless liberal tradition.

The question raised by the court's history, as we suggest at the outset of the chapter, is who guards the guardians? In a constitutional system in which so much deference is accorded judges, self-government cannot solely depend on the hallowed but diminished tradition of judicial self-restraint in which judges guard themselves. As Justice Scalia observed regretfully in his *Planned Parenthood* dissent, it is naive to expect a powerful tribunal to curb its own ambition. And yet, the delicate balance between liberty and democracy to which the American republic adheres requires a court that is powerful enough to protect rights but not so powerful as to stifle democracy.

☆ The power and authority of the American Supreme Court and of the federal court system far exceeds that enjoyed by the judiciary in other constitutional democracies.

☆ Neither judicial review nor the supremacy of federal over state law is mentioned in the constitution. Both these principles were established by decisions of the Supreme Court to which the legislative and executive branches and the states acquiesced. Chief Justice John Marshall's leadership was crucial to the establishment of both these critical principles.

☆ The American judicial system is made up of two parallel systems: federal courts and state courts. Most ordinary civil and criminal matters are handled, under state law, by state courts. Generally speaking, a case goes to federal rather than state court if the federal government is directly involved, if a federal statute is at issue, if a claim of a violation of the U.S. Constitution is made, or if a civil suit is brought that involves citizens from more than one state.

☆ The judiciary plays an especially important role in the United States in restraining the threats to liberty posed by mass democracy.

☆ In the late nineteenth century, the Supreme Court relied upon the Fourteenth Amendment's guarantee of due process of law to ensure the sanctity of private property. In the second half of the twentieth century, it relied on the principle of due process to combat racial injustice and to expand the notion of "rights."

☆ During the New Deal, the Supreme Court adopted a very broad definition of the Commerce Clause permitting much greater latitude for the federal government to intervene in policy realms previously reserved for the states.

☆ Rulings of the Warren and Burger courts went beyond securing rights by restraining government to declaring programmatic rights that could only be provided by government. Therefore, the court became increasingly dependent on other agents of government – lower courts, Congress, and the executive – to implement its will.

☆ During the 1970s and early 1980s, the courts, Congress, and administrative agencies reinforced each other's activism.

☆ The increasingly contentious nature of the confirmation process for Supreme Court and federal appeals court justices illustrates the increasing involvement of the courts in politically controversial policy arenas.

☆ A critical line of decisions stretching from redistricting in the 1960s, abortion in the 1970s, and *Bush v. Gore* in 2000 shows the increasing substitution of judicial authority for public deliberation in resolving profound controversies.

Major Concepts

appellate
de facto segregation
de jure segregation
judicial review
original jurisdiction
stare decisis
substantive due process

Suggested Readings

Abraham, Henry. *The Judicial Process*, 7th ed. New York: Oxford University Press, 1998.

_____. *Justices and Presidents*, 3d ed. Lanham, MD: Rowman and Littlefield, 1999.

Ackerman, Bruce. *We the People: Volume I, Foundations*. Cambridge, MA: Harvard University Press, 1991.

Bickel, Alexander. *The Least Dangerous Branch: The Supreme Court and the Bar of Politics*. New York: Bobbs-Merrill, 1963.

Corwin, Edwin S. "The Passing of Dual Federalism." *Virginia Law Review* 36 (February 1930): 1–24.

Derthick, Martha. *Keeping the Compound Republic*. Washington, D.C.: Brookings Institution, 2001.

Fallon, Richard. *The Dynamic Constitution: An Introduction to American Constitutional Law*. New York. Cambridge University Press, 2004.

Foner, Eric. *Reconstruction: America's Unfinished Revolution, 1863–1877*. New York: Perennial, 2002.

Ginsberg, Benjamin, and Martin Shefter. *Politics by Other Means*, 3d ed. New York: W. W. Norton, 2003.

Horowitz, Donald. *The Courts and Social Policy*. Washington, D.C.: Brookings Institution, 1977.

Leuchtenburg, William. *The Supreme Court Reborn*. New York: Oxford University Press, 1995.

McCloskey, Robert, and Sanford Levinson. *The American Supreme Court*, 3d ed. Chicago: University of Chicago Press, 2000.

Melnick, R. Shep. *Between the Lines*. Washington, D.C.: Brookings Institution, 1994.

O'Brien, David. *Storm Center: The Supreme Court in American Politics*, 4th ed. New York: W. W. Norton, 1996.

Rosenberg, Gerald. *The Hollow Hope*. Chicago: University of Chicago Press, 1991.

Shapiro, Martin. *Who Guards the Guardians?* Athens: University of Georgia Press, 1988.

10 Bureaucracy

Chapter Overview

This chapter focuses on:

⭐ Showing how great issues of liberty and democracy are played out in the ordinary bureaucratic and regulatory decisions that affect the lives of ordinary people

⭐ The choices made during America's formative period about how to design and manage bureaucracy and how those choices continue to influence how government is administered

⭐ Political loyalty versus expertise as conflicting means for organizing and staffing the bureaucracy

⭐ The rise of a modern administrative state during the twentieth century and the major schools of thought about how best to reconcile this gigantic bureaucratic apparatus with liberty and democracy

⭐ The bureaucratic response to the War on Terror and the implications of that response for liberty and democracy

Imagine that you are late for a summer job interview. Your anxiety level, already heightened by the possibility of landing a really good position, goes even higher as the slow downtown traffic threatens to keep you from getting there on time. Then the cloud of tension lifts as you find a parking space right in front of your destination. You put a quarter in the meter. Nothing happens. The meter is broken. You quickly scrawl a note and put it on your windshield: "Dear meter checker, this meter is broken."

As you leave the office building an hour later, you are still tense. Was the interview a success? Hard to tell; they said they would get back to you. Stepping onto the curb, you notice that the note on your windshield is gone and has been replaced by a red piece of paper, a $25 parking ticket. The perfect ending to a perfect morning.

Were you the victim of bureaucratic oppression, or was the meter attendant simply doing his or her job? If you challenge the ticket in traffic court, the judge will say that the city's parking regulations clearly state that it is illegal to park at a broken meter, even though both you and the judge know that people do it all the time and often are not ticketed. So you do not bother to protest. Now you have your own story of unfair government treatment to add to the family list: rejection of legitimate deductions by the Internal Revenue Service when your father had a tax audit; denial by the National Science Foundation of the grant application submitted by your graduate student sister, the biotech genius; and refusal of a health permit for the bread-baking business your mother was going to operate from her home kitchen.

Notice that none of these stories involves an elected official. In each case, the perpetrator was a government bureaucrat. For most of us Americans, most of the time, government bureaucracy is the aspect of government we actually encounter. It is where we go to get a driver's license, pay real estate taxes, and register for selective service. It is where the great philosophical issues of liberty and democracy get played out in daily life.

As mad as we get at bureaucracy, in our calmer moments we are forced to admit that we cannot live without it. Our streets would be impassable if parking were not strictly regulated. Government would quickly go bankrupt if tax cheating were permitted. Your mother's customers have a right to expect that the bread they buy was baked under sanitary conditions. How can they have that assurance unless government bureaucrats inspect her kitchen?

Nor is bureaucracy simply a necessary evil. Government employees put men on the moon, caught the Oklahoma City bomber in a matter of days, and saved thousands of lives at the World Trade Center. The challenge of living with bureaucracy is knowing how to organize and control it so as to minimize its assault on liberty and maximize its democratic potential to get the people's business done. This challenge requires charting a course between the two opposing threats to responsible bureaucratic decision making – license and red tape. License means using a privileged governmental position as an opportunity to cheat and steal or to make decisions arbitrarily or capriciously. Newspaper headlines are full of stories of rogue police officers who deal drugs and budget directors who raid their department's funds. Like the fictitious meter attendant who gave you an undeserved parking ticket, these government workers enjoy too much discretion and can deprive others of liberty and property.

Unfortunately, limiting discretion can all too easily produce reams of *red tape*. "Red tape" is the nickname for the multiplicity of regulations and procedures that restrain bureaucratic license by forcing bureaucrats to "go by the book." Sadly, the amount of paperwork and review by superiors that "going by the book" requires of bureaucrats all too often keeps them from making timely decisions and from obeying their own common sense. To deal with the fear that officials will steal from their own agencies, the government has instituted strict procedures regarding who can make what sort of expenditures and under what conditions. At each step in the red-tape ladder, someone is given the opportunity to review and second-guess the decision made at the lower rung. A high school science teacher waits months for a request for new Bunsen burners to make its way first to the school science coordinator, then to the principal, then to the district budget office, and finally to the superintendent of schools. By the time the request is approved, the term is over. Red tape is a terrible source of frustration, but it is not a conspiracy against the public. It is an effort to prevent bureaucratic license. This chapter focuses on how efforts to keep bureaucrats accountable and make bureaucracy effective have dealt with the trade-off between bureaucratic license and red tape.

The United States was born hating bureaucrats. In theory, the American Revolution was fought against the British king. But it was the agents of the king, British soldiers and tax collectors, whose offenses drove the colonists to rebel. From the beginning, less effort was expended to create an efficient and forceful government apparatus than to establish strict methods for limiting bureaucratic license. By European standards, the American bureaucracy has always seemed incompetent. But it is also less intrusive and despotic. In bureaucracy, as in so many other aspects of political life, Americans opted for liberty even at the price of effective government. For most of America's history, this liberty was obtained less by wrapping the bureaucracy in red tape than by simply having less of it. Minimizing government left American public officials, at least in peacetime, with relatively little to do. Their numbers were small. Their tasks were few and simple.

As limited as it was, the federal bureaucracy still needed to be organized and controlled. Choices made during America's formative period about how to design and manage bureaucracy continue to influence it even as the principle of limited government has become less decisive in controlling government's scope and reach. The first section of this chapter describes what those choices were and how they were made. Then the chapter looks at how American bureaucracy transformed itself in the twentieth century, when its numbers and responsibilities multiplied. The next section examines the significance of that transformation as well as the continued importance of the decisions and debates that took place before it. This section is followed by a discussion of contemporary public administration that emphasizes the profound liberal and democratic problems that modern bureaucracy poses and the major efforts to reform it in order to address those concerns. The chapter concludes with a discussion of how the war on terrorism has affected debates about the current and future state of American public administration.

Administering a Limited Government

The Constitution provides only a sketchy account of administration. The "executive power" vested in the president is not defined. The Constitution does not explicitly grant the president control over the heads of executive departments. Rather, it authorizes the president to require their opinion, in writing, on subjects pertaining to their departments. (See Figure 10.1 for a display of current executive departments.) The president is instructed to appoint heads of departments, subject to Senate confirmation. But the power to appoint lesser officials is left unsettled. Congress may choose to let the president make such designations, vest them in the courts, or grant them directly to department heads. The first Congress had to sort out the meaning of these ambiguous constitutional provisions.

The critical moment in the history of American public administration came only three months into the first congressional session. Congress took up the problem of establishing executive departments, beginning with Foreign Affairs (later to become the Department of State). The key question was whether departmental control would be shared with the president. Some members of Congress argued that the constitutional requirement that the Senate approve department heads implied it should also approve a presidential decision to remove them.

James Madison supported giving the president exclusive removal power on democratic grounds. Citizens did not vote for department heads, but they did vote for the president. If the president could not fire executive

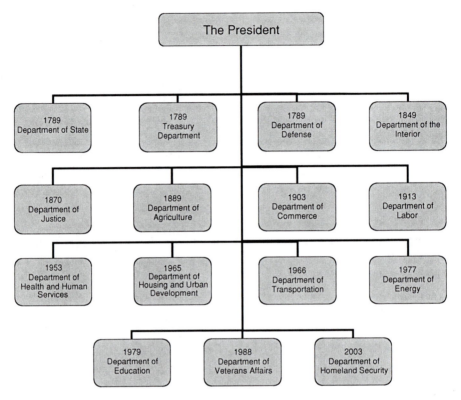

Figure 10.1. Cabinet (Executive) Departments. The Constitution does not explicitly detail the president's relationship to the cabinet or to other federal agencies. The president today is viewed as the chief administrator in the American system. *Source:* U.S. Office of Management and Budget, 2000.

officials, those officials would feel free to ignore the president's instructions. It would be impossible to hold them publicly accountable for their actions. Congress eventually accepted this argument. Although it would later try to challenge the president's administrative preeminence, it never regained this crucial aspect of administrative power that it gave away at the outset. As a result, the heads of executive departments were considered assistants to the president and a chain of command was established within the executive branch with the president at the top.

Although he had been a general, President George Washington did not attempt to impose military discipline on the executive branch. He relied on the character of the men he appointed. He recognized that local post offices and land offices were the only points of federal government contact that most citizens would ever have. He took pains to appoint to these offices people of superior moral character who enjoyed the respect and affection of their neighbors. Thus, he could not only ensure the reliability of the federal service but also enhance the reputation of the federal government as a whole among the citizenry at large.

Despite the lack of an extensive administrative apparatus, the small size of the federal bureaucracy enabled the president to keep track of administrative performance. Traditional social arrangements were still strong. Most communities had an upper class to whom the rest of the people paid deference and respect. It was from this stratum of "gentlemen" that Washington recruited his administrators, and he relied on them to serve as effective ambassadors of the federal government to their hometowns.

Defending the Country

National defense is a fundamental governmental obligation. But from the standpoint of liberty, national security is the most troubling of all governmental functions. Soldiers are supposed to respect civilian authority. But they have the guns. Their ostensible superiors, the politicians, have only words. The colonies had been forced to abide garrisons of British troops and suffer their swaggering arrogance. It became an American article of faith that standing armies were synonymous with oppression.

This antipathy had to be reconciled with the recognition that the new nation faced grave security threats. Despite signing a peace treaty, the British retained strategically located military installations in North America from which they could very plausibly stage a new invasion. The United States had hostile relations with several Indian nations, and many frontier settlers faced great risks from Indian raids.

Providing for national security without threatening individual freedom was the nation's first great administrative challenge. Its approach to this problem would come to typify its approach to public administration in general. It rose to the challenge of protecting its citizens, but it did so grudgingly and in the least intrusive manner possible.

The first impulse of the new nation was to adopt non-governmental means, local and state militia, to provide national security. A militia is composed of ordinary citizens prepared to fight in the event of a military emergency. They train and drill on a part-time basis. Unlike soldiers, they are not agents of the government. To the contrary, they stand armed and ready to defend against any threat to their local liberty and security, whether it is posed by marauding Indians, foreign armies, or the national government itself. Support for the militia and hatred of standing armies is at the core of the Bill of Rights. The Second Amendment states that

THE ATTACK ON THE RIOTERS.

Providing for national security without violating the civil liberties of American citizens was an early test of the administrative state. Initial attempts consisted of local militias and volunteers.

"a well regulated militia being necessary to the security of a free State, citizens must retain the right to bear arms." The Third Amendment forbids the quartering of soldiers in any house in peacetime without the owner's permission and allows it during wartime "only in a lawful manner."

Because militias were organized on a community basis by people who have other things to do, they proved better at local defense than at sustaining a full-fledged war against the British. Although militias did participate in the American Revolution, the bulk of the fighting was done by the Continental Army. At war's end, with no immediate threat of foreign invasion, public sentiment was strongly behind disbanding the army and relying once again on the militias. However, it soon became clear that as currently organized, the militias were inadequate for responding to the growing threat of attack by hostile Indians. Congress refused to either strengthen the militia system or provide a full-fledged alternative. It tried to muddle through by authorizing a mixed force of militia and volunteers, providing little in the way of training or organizational guidance.

In 1791, a 1400-person force composed of militia and some hastily recruited volunteers, commanded by General Arthur St. Clair, was annihilated by a smaller army of Miami Indians. In the wake of this catastrophic defeat, Congress endorsed President Washington's request for a 5000-man army composed of regular soldiers to fight the Indians. That new army, under the brilliant leadership of Anthony Wayne, succeeded where St. Clair's poorly organized and poorly trained army had failed.

Wayne's victories convinced Congress to maintain a permanent professional frontier patrol to ward off Indian attack. But it refused to create a permanent standing army comparable in size to the massive European ones. Such an army was the goal of a Federalist faction led by Alexander Hamilton. He cherished this kind of army for many of the same reasons that most Americans opposed it. He greatly feared the possibility of a domestic insurrection egged on by the French, who were threatening an invasion. Only a permanent and powerful army led by a strong and politically sophisticated general, like himself, could ward off those present threats and future ones as well. In 1797, as the threat of war with France grew, Congress acceded to Hamilton's wishes and created a new 12,000-man army. But much to Hamilton's dismay, public support for such an expanded force waned as the war threat receded. It was disbanded in 1800, never having reached more than half of its allotted size.

As this initial effort to keep the nation safe illustrates, America would adopt key trappings of a modern bureaucratic state but only in a reluctant, minimal fashion. When the national security threat emerged, this country opted for a non-bureaucratic alternative, the militia. When that solution proved inadequate, it grudgingly supported a professional army in the war against the Indians and expanded the army in anticipation of war with France. But public support for this new involvement was reluctant and wary. The people clung to their constitutional right to bear arms. When the war threat diminished, the army was reduced in size and banished back to the frontier. It was not allowed to become an alternative power base for those, like Hamilton, who felt that democracy was too unruly to survive in the absence of armed guardians. Even the claims of national security did not lead the public to fully overcome its antipathy toward a strong central state. Box 1 looks at how the current military is recruited and staffed and the challenges that system poses to liberty, equality, and democracy.

Box One: Contemporary Politics

The Military: Liberty, Democracy, Equality, Efficiency

The deaths of American service men and women in Afghanistan and Iraq serve as a stark reminder that the ultimate sacrifice one can make for one's country is to die for it. Throughout American history, a debate has raged about whether this duty should be imposed on citizens or whether it should be shouldered by volunteers. Initially, the Civil War was fought by volunteers, but as personnel needs grew, a draft was imposed. Those drafted could buy a substitute for $300 and thus evade service. The palpable injustice of this exception set off a wave of draft riots in New York City. The riots were instigated by poor Irish immigrants who had no hope of raising the money to escape service. A draft was also imposed to fight the First and Second World Wars and the Korean War. In these instances, resistance to the draft was most notable by its absence. Because of the large troop strengths needed in Western Europe during the Cold War, the draft remained in place throughout the 1950s and was used to mobilize troops for the Vietnam War in the early and mid-1960s. It was abolished by President Richard Nixon soon after he took office in 1969.

Proponents of a draft stress its virtues from the standpoint of liberty and equality. A draft army spreads the risk of death and injury across a wide spectrum of citizens. It is much less likely to usurp civilian government than is an army of professional soldiers. Although drafters are expected to obey military discipline, they are less likely to abide excessive violence and human rights abuses. They stand as an obstacle to military adventurism. Surely, it was no coincidence that the level of opposition to the Vietnam War diminished when the draft was abolished.

In 2003, Congressman Charles Rangel of Harlem urged that a draft be reinstituted in response to the greater military burdens resulting from the war on terrorism. He noted that in the absence of a draft, the responsibility for defending the country falls inordinately on the poor because middle-class young people are not attracted to military service by the financial inducements the military offers.

Defenders of a volunteer force point to its greater efficiency. As war becomes ever more technologically sophisticated, the training and expertise required to be a good soldier rises exponentially. It is not possible to provide that training to citizen soldiers whose length of service is very short. It can only be provided to those who plan to make the military a career.

This debate pits two concepts of civil liberties against one another. A volunteer army frees people from a terrible governmentally imposed burden and thus promotes liberty. A draft army checks military power and thus also promotes liberty. This debate also pits virtues of liberty against those of equality. A draft is supposed to place more equal burdens on all citizens, whereas a volunteer force gives young people the liberty of choosing to serve or not.

Testing the System

The first major test of the American administrative system came in 1800 when, for the first time, an incumbent chief executive (John Adams) was defeated for reelection. Thomas Jefferson's Revolution of 1800 had an enormous impact (see Chapters 4 and 8). But in the area of public administration, this transition of power was more noteworthy for its continuities than for its changes.

In his inaugural address, Jefferson proclaimed, "We are all republicans; we are all federalists," advertising his intention to dampen the partisan rancor that the election and the bitter controversies of the Adams years had engendered. Because the national government had known only Federalist rule during its first twelve years, most of its employees were Federalist sympathizers. Jefferson resisted considerable pressure from his Republican supporters to purge these incumbents wholesale. Instead he adopted a much more moderate approach. He balanced the number of federal employees supporting each party by appointing only Republicans to vacancies until such time as their numbers equaled the Federalists. He would not remove

Federalists from office unless they displayed excessive partisanship in office or outright corruption or incompetence. The only exception to this rule was the removal of those Federalists hastily appointed by Adams in the lame-duck period between his defeat and Jefferson's inauguration.

Because Jefferson refrained from wholesale removal, his effort to give the national bureaucracy a bipartisan cast took place gradually, with a minimum of disruption. And, despite his egalitarian rhetoric, he maintained the Federalist tradition of appointing well educated people with good reputations to federal office. Like Washington, Jefferson expected such people to act honorably and competently in office, and for the most part, those expectations proved reasonable. At this early stage of the nation's political development, good character, rather than the imposition of red tape, was viewed as a satisfactory solution to the problem of bureaucratic license.

The Principle of Rotation

In Chapters 4 and 8, we discuss the crucial democratic changes that occurred during the Jacksonian era, including the expansion of voting rights, the development of a political party system, and the withdrawal of government from previous efforts to place control of the economy in the hands of a privileged few. Nowhere was the impact of this democratic transformation felt with greater force than within the government bureaucracy itself. The creation of a mass electorate challenged the principle of the "rule of gentlemen." The greater political influence of ordinary citizens made them less tolerant of rule by people they no longer considered their betters. They demanded to be governed by people more like themselves. And many of them looked forward to improving their lot by going to work for the government.

Andrew Jackson's first annual message to Congress in 1833 highlighted the threat to democracy that was posed by allowing public officials to remain too long in office:

> Office is considered as a species of property and government, rather as a means of promoting individual interests than as an instrument created solely for the service of the people. Corruption in some and, in others, a perversion of correct feelings and principles, diverts government from its legitimate ends and makes it an engine for the support of the few at the expense of the many.

In Jackson's view, a view that would dominate American government for the next half century, public employment was very different from work in the private sector. Public employees should never view their office as their property or view their job as one to which their skills and their past services entitled them. Rather, they were to consider themselves public servants, meaning that they served at the pleasure of the public. The best way to preserve this spirit of democratic subservience was through rotation in office. A new president should be free to appoint a new team of public officials who reflected the new president's point of view and who would therefore be more responsive to the majority of voters who put that president in office.

This approach came to be nicknamed the "spoils system," but that term is misleading. "Spoils" places the emphasis on the opportunity for enrichment that public office provides. But Jackson's chief concern was party loyalty, not spoils. By appointing only those who shared the outlook of the electoral majority and firing those who did not, he would make the government obey the will of the people. Jackson rejected Jefferson's theory of evenhandedness. He would appoint only Democrats, recognizing that if he were defeated for reelection, his opponents would, and should, appoint only Whigs.

Jackson did not, and could not, wield the spoils system to centralize power in his own hands. As we discuss in Chapter 11, Jackson was beholden to state and local Democratic party leaders. They dictated who was appointed to federal posts in their own bailiwicks. Thus, rotation became a valuable tool for strengthening bonds between citizens and their government. As the tradition of deference to one's social superiors waned, the government needed new means of solidifying its hold on the loyalties and energies of the citizenry. This problem was greatly aggravated by the rapid westward expansion of the country, which increased the emotional as well as the physical distance that separated citizens from the nation's capital. It became even more important to improve the levels of trust and respect for the government that were accorded by the increasingly far-flung citizenry. Ceding control of federal appointments to local Democratic political organizations decreased the psychic distance between Washington and the hinterlands. It gave the national government a friendly, recognizable local face.

Jackson understood that the success of the rotation system required limited government: "The duties of all public officers are, or at least admit of being made, so plain and simple that men of intelligence may readily qualify themselves for their performance." Because government did not do many ambitious and complicated things, it did not need a highly skilled and experienced workforce and therefore its employees could be easily and painlessly replaced. In later years, as government expanded and the demands placed on the bureaucracy grew ever more complex, this basic assumption on which the principle of rotation rested became less and less plausible.

Having established the spoils principle, Jackson did not find it necessary to fire many public employees. Most of the incumbent federal workers had been appointed by presidents he allied with – Monroe, Madison, and Jefferson. In the first eighteen months of Jackson's administration, only about 10 percent of the incumbent workforce was removed. Subsequent changes resulted mainly from death, retirement, or voluntary resignation. Jackson fired only those workers whom he considered politically untrustworthy because they were too closely identified with the John Quincy Adams administration that had preceded his or because they had given him the impression that they considered their office to be their own property. Otherwise, the knowledge that they would be fired if they deviated from Jackson's policies was sufficient to keep most workers loyal and responsive. The great change wrought by Jackson was not the firing of enemies and hiring of friends but the open and proud endorsement of this sort of politics.

The spoils system ended the era of government by the few and initiated the full democratization of American public life. Now, in addition to juries and other purely local activities, the bureaucracy itself would become a schoolroom for democracy, educating hundreds of thousands of Americans in the mundane realities of politics. The greatest compliment paid to this system came with the defeat of Jackson's protégé, Martin Van Buren, for reelection as president in 1840. The new Whig president, William Henry Harrison, while opposing most of Jackson's policies, openly endorsed the principle of rotation in office; he removed thousands of Jacksonians and replaced them with Whig loyalists. At this next stage of the development of American public administration, party discipline replaced good character as the solution to the problem of bureaucratic license. Box 2 describes the current manner in which the transition between presidential administrations takes place.

Box Two: Nuts and Bolts

Administrative Transitions

As a result of the civil service reforms discussed later, the change in personnel that occurs when a new president is elected is now quite small, even when he is of a different party from his predecessor. Only the highest levels of a cabinet department or federal agency are subject to non-competitive appointment, meaning they are chosen by the president or his appointees. At the Environmental Protection Agency, for example, only the administrator, the deputy administrator, the general counsel, the regional administrators, and the assistant administrators are appointed by the president. From the deputy assistant administrators on down, the agency is staffed by permanent civil servants. The political appointees do enjoy some limited discretion in shifting those civil servants around. So, in practice, the highest rung of civil service posts are held by permanent employees whom the political appointees find congenial. In the entire federal government, less than 6000 of the more than 2.7 million civilian posts are filled by non-competitive appointment.

Expanding the Bureaucracy

The spoils system flourished throughout most of the rest of the nineteenth century. As the number of federal jobs expanded, dispensing them in return for political support became an ever more important aspect of party politics. The late nineteenth century was the heyday of congressional dominance of American government (see Chapter 7). Congress, not the president, became the de facto ruler of the public service. Administrative personnel and budget decisions were determined in congressional committee and in coordination with the congressional leadership.

But even as the spoils system was growing in prominence, its democratic luster began to fade. Because Congress was seen less as the voice of public opinion than as the errand boy for powerful business interests, its servant, the bureaucracy, acquired a similarly sinister reputation. Patronage appointees – postal workers, customs collectors, and land agents – were viewed not as public servants but simply as hacks, people who were concerned only with personal gain. The prestige of the federal government faded as it came to be seen as a hotbed of incompetence and favoritism.

Despite its tarnished image, the federal government grew rapidly. Between 1870 and 1880, the number of federal employees doubled, from 53,000 to 107,000. By 1890, it grew an additional 50 percent, to 166,000, and by 1901 it reached 256,000, almost a fivefold increase in thirty years. European immigration, the populating of the Western territories, economic growth, and technical change all conspired to accelerate demands on the public sector. The federal government did not add many new functions during this period. Rather, this explosion of personnel resulted from expansion in the volume of existing types of federal business and from the growing pressure on the political parties and their representatives in Congress to produce more jobs for partisan loyalists.

The growing pressure to produce more patronage jobs resulted in the rapid growth of the federal government toward the end of the nineteenth century. The more dramatic increase in civilian federal employees that began in the 1930s reflects the expansion of the social welfare state created by the New Deal.

The government in Washington was in the happy position of being able to respond to these demands without imposing greater tax burdens. The bulk of federal revenue came from tariffs on imported goods, which grew as the economy grew, providing ample funds to hire more federal workers. The Republican party supported high tariffs in order to protect American industry. For most of the latter half of the nineteenth century, Republicans controlled the presidency and the Senate and often the House of Representatives as well. The Republican party used its great political power and popularity to stand firmly behind a high tariff policy that enabled it to both satisfy its industrial backers and provide employment for its army of party workers.

To prevent administrative growth in the face of these enormous expansionary pressures would have required a determined and principled commitment to small government of the sort displayed by Andrew Jackson. In Chapter 5, we describe Jackson's veto of federal money to build the Maysville Road in Kentucky. That veto bitterly disappointed many of Jackson's Kentucky supporters, who dearly wanted the road. But Jackson cast the veto anyway because he believed that subsidizing a road built entirely within one state exceeded the interstate commerce power of the federal government. Because his commitment to limited government was a principled one, he had to stick to it even when to do so was politically inexpedient.

Although the post–Civil War Republicans were not big government advocates in the modern sense, they did not adopt Jackson's strict construction of the limits on federal power. As a result, the size of the federal government grew dramatically, and with it grew the opportunities for poorly trained and inexperienced workers to abuse their discretion. The spoils system degenerated because subsequent presidents violated the system's original basis on limited government. Party discipline proved inadequate to the task of checking bureaucratic license, setting the stage for a more rule-oriented form of control and the inevitable red tape that reliance on rules and regulations brings about. Box 3 describes the current state of the federal workforce.

The Federal Workforce

Compared to the size of state and local government, the federal workforce is quite small. This is because so many of the labor-intensive aspects of government are performed by state and local workers. Federal employees are largely in the business of issuing regulations and directives regarding the work that those state and local workers will perform as well as writing checks to pay for a portion of that work. The big exceptions to this pattern are the military and the postal service.

However, the real size of the government workforce is severely understated if one looks only at the federal, state, and local payroll. Much of the work of government is carried out by private-sector firms that receive contracts and grants from government. Because the companies that perform this contracting work may also do work for private clients, it is very difficult to know just how much of their time and energy is devoted to the government-inspired portion of their duties. In his book *The True Size of Government*, political scientist Paul Light explores the size and importance of this "shadow government." He estimates the regular civilian government workforce to be in the neighborhood of 1.9 million workers. In addition, there are about 1.5 million military personnel and 850,000 postal workers who are no longer counted as federal employees because they work for quasi-government corporations. However, the size of the workforce increases dramatically if one also includes what Light calls the "shadow" workforce of full-time worker equivalents employed by federal contracts and grants. This shadow workforce adds another 8 million to the total.

Toward a Modern Public Service

Beginning in the 1880s and continuing into the first two decades of the twentieth century, the federal bureaucracy embarked on a period of reform that introduced many of the elements that characterize the contemporary federal service. These elements include competitive examinations for appointment and promotion, deference to expertise and professional training, systematic analysis of issues relating to governmental performance and public policy, and creation of a comprehensive federal budget. These specific changes reflected a new understanding of the mission of public service and the role of public administrators.

Civil Service Reform

The transformation of the public service into a reasonably modern bureaucracy began with the passage of the 1883 Civil Service Act, also called the Pendleton Act. It diminished federal government patronage by expanding the existing but rarely used system of competitive examinations for public posts. It stipulated that appointees would have to be chosen from among those with the highest exam grades. To oversee the examination system and investigate abuses of it, the act created a three-member, bipartisan Civil Service Commission consisting of one Democrat, one Republican, and one independent; these members were appointed by the president, subject to Senate confirmation.

The Pendleton Act was a response to simmering public disgust with the corruption brought about by the slavish responsiveness of bureaucrats to pressure from members of Congress and the corporate forces they represented. That revulsion had been building for decades, yet despite the impassioned pleadings of reform advocates, previous reform efforts had failed. Because civil service reform was aimed directly at the power and prerogatives of congressional representatives, they vigorously opposed it. The catalyst for dissolving congressional resistance was the 1881 assassination of President James A. Garfield by an unsuccessful office seeker. The direct connection between the patronage system and such a heinous crime, the second presidential assassination in less than twenty years, galvanized public outrage and forced a reluctant Congress to commit itself to civil service reform. The Pendleton Act initially was of limited application. Its coverage extended only to employees of the executive branch in Washington or in major customhouses and post offices around the country. The vast majority – all but 14,000 of 131,000 federal officeholders, including many postal workers – were not covered. Nevertheless, the enactment of civil service reform in 1883 was a critical turning point in the history of the American bureaucracy. During the Progressive Era, the presidential administrations of Theodore Roosevelt (1901–1909) and Woodrow Wilson (1913–1921) expanded the coverage of the merit system for hiring, promotion, and tenure to the point at which it included approximately 60 percent of the federal workforce. With the rise of the New Deal, and the consolidation of a modern administrative state, the civil service included about 95 percent of federal workers.

President James A. Garfield was assassinated by a disappointed office seeker in 1881, leading Congress to pass the 1883 Pendleton Act, which reduced patronage and created a modern civil service.

As a result of civil service reform, presidential leadership, previously dependent on patronage-seeking state and local party machines, now required careful attention to administrative management, sometimes to foster economy and efficiency, sometimes to bolster the power of the increasingly active federal government. The new challenge for the president was to take charge of the large and disparate administrative apparatus (see Box 2). For example, of the tens of thousands of employees of the sprawling Department of Health and Human Services, only 156 are political appointees; the rest are civil servants. The creation of an active and competent bureaucracy began with reformers' determination to develop a more efficient system of control; however, the creation of a "modern" state ultimately led to the consolidation of an administrative apparatus that often defied presidential attempts to control it.

A merit-based civil service bears a superficial resemblance to the character oriented approach of the Federalists and Jefferson. Both attempt to choose civil servants on the basis of their talents rather than their politics. But the differences between the two are equally important. Objective examinations can only measure knowledge. They cannot address the issues of probity, empathy, and judgment that are at the heart of the ability to exercise discretion wisely. Among the most important and subtle discretionary virtues is the ability to know when to submerge one's own judgment in favor of that of one's democratically accountable superiors. Sometimes it is right to insist upon the superiority of one's professional expertise and sometimes it is better to let the politicians determine what it is best. Getting a professional degree and scoring well on an examination do not by themselves prepare people for making such difficult decisions. Therefore, neither Congress nor the President has been willing to grant civil servants the breadth of discretion in making decisions that Washington and Jefferson gave to their subordinates. For the most part, federal public administrators are expected to "go by the book," meaning the thousands and thousands of pages of rules, regulations, and guidelines that their superiors have written for them to obey. If, in a particular circumstance, the rigid application of a rule clearly violates common sense – does it really make sense to give someone a ticket if the meter is broken – the civil servant still may feel that violating the rule is more likely to get her into trouble than being accused of applying it too slavishly.

Progressivism and the Science of Administration

During the next three decades, reform efforts widened beyond the appointments process to encompass the very mission of public service and the role of public administrators in pursuing it. This expansion was an aspect of the rethinking of the relationship between government and society undertaken by Progressivism, a new approach to problems of politics and governance aspects (see Chapter 4 for a fuller discussion of Progressivism).

Woodrow Wilson was the first and only political science professor ever elected president of the United States. He, more than anyone else, framed the Progressive understanding of public administration. In his classic essay "The Study of Administration," published in 1887, Wilson explained that the role of public administration had to greatly expand in order to respond adequately to the economic transformation that had begun in the aftermath of the Civil War.

The economy, no longer the domain of small farmers and family businesses, was now dominated by giant monopolies whose new production methods threatened to cause class warfare. According to Wilson, the federal government was the only institution capable of taming these despotic economic powers and diffusing the conflict between management and labor.

Because these new responsibilities were so weighty and difficult, wrote Wilson, they required "an important and delicate extension of administrative functions...which will require no little wisdom, knowledge and experience." Jackson's axiom that administrative tasks could be kept simple enough to be performed by inexperienced amateurs no longer held true. "To straighten the paths of government, to make its business less unbusinesslike, to strengthen and purify its organization and to crown its dutifulness" would require a whole new science, the science of administration.

Underlying this new science was the separation of politics and administration. A more active and expert administrative corps would not threaten liberty and democracy because political control would remain the exclusive domain of popularly elected officials. These politicians would set the broad course of public policy and leave it to expert administrators to implement those policies efficiently and effectively.

Wilson likened the distinction between politics and administration to that between the head of a household and the kitchen staff: "Self-government does not consist in having a hand in everything any more than housekeeping consists necessarily in cooking dinner with one's own hands. The cook must be trusted with a large discretion as to the management of the fires and the ovens." The head of household remains in control because he or she is the one who tells the cooks what sort of food the family likes, provides them with a firm budget for food and kitchen maintenance, and fires them if they make lousy meals. But, having established broad policy principles and performance guidelines, the head of household stays out of the kitchen, enabling the cooks to make full use of their special talents and expertise to put tasty and nutritious food on the table.

Although Wilson and Jackson disagreed fundamentally about how the public service was to be organized and recruited, they both sought to make it more democratic. In Jackson's view, a democratic link was established through frequent rotation of ordinary citizens into administration and by the ties that the spoils system established between administrators and local party organizations. In Wilson's view, elected officials responded to public opinion by establishing specific policies for administrators to carry out. The appetites of the public prescribed the menu plans of elected officials, which, in turn, guided the preparations of the administrators. Thus, Wilson hoped to escape the unhappy choice between red tape and license both by encouraging legislators to perfect their ability to write wise laws and to so thoroughly train and motivate civil servants that they could successfully address the challenges posed by an expanding government.

Progressive Administration

During the Progressive Era, both the study and practice of public administration changed along the lines proposed by Wilson. In 1914, the University of Michigan established the first graduate program in municipal administration. Soon, other state and private universities began to offer degrees in public administration for the purpose of training students for public service careers. The faculties of such programs also did research aimed at establishing a scientific basis for such critical administrative tasks as budgeting, contract compliance, financial auditing, and personnel management. In 1916, the Institute for Government Research, later renamed the Brookings Institution, was created as the first private research institute devoted to the systematic analysis of issues relating to governmental performance and public policy.

In 1887, the Interstate Commerce Commission was created by Congress to regulate railroad rates. Its staff was trained both in economics and in the intricacies of the railroad business. In 1903, a Department of Commerce and Labor was established to bring expertise to bear on issues relating to trade and labor relations. When Wilson became president in 1913, he pressed for the passage of an act that established the Federal Trade Commission, which was charged with protecting competition and eliminating unfair trade practices. Like the other new agencies and departments, it was staffed with economists and lawyers steeped in the complexities of modern industrial organization.

The Department of Agriculture's Extension Service was another Progressive innovation; it established a state-federal partnership to teach farmers how to become more productive. Not only was the extension service staff trained in modern agricultural science, but they were also pioneers in what would later come to be called "technology transfer." The staff, known as extension agents, developed successful educational methods for convincing skeptical, individualistic, and often uneducated farmers to adopt new, complicated, and unorthodox modern farming methods.

Expertise in Action

Progressive reform of administration was particularly noteworthy in the area of natural resource management. The federal government was the nation's biggest landlord. It owned vast tracts of forest and grazing land, particularly in the West. In 1898, Gifford Pinchot was appointed to head a new Bureau of Forestry in the Department of Agriculture that was dedicated to improving forest *conservation*. This conservation program would manage the nation's timber and mineral resources to maximize the benefits they would provide over the long term.

Because the United States had no forestry school, Pinchot had gone to Germany for his professional training. He would later found the Yale School of Forestry. In 1905, authority for managing 60 million acres of western federal forests was transferred from the Department of the Interior to the Bureau of Forestry, renamed the Forest Service. In 1911, the Forest Service was granted authority over all federal forests.

Pinchot was determined that the Forest Service break the mold of corruption and ineptitude that had enveloped federal public administration. He sought to establish an organization in which personnel at all levels were committed to its goals and were competent, energetic, and skillful enough to attain them. Forest rangers received special training and were encouraged to think of themselves as professionals. They were expected to respond to orders from regional and national service headquarters, not to demands of local citizens or politicians living near the forests they were managing. This quasi-military mode of organization was in stark contrast to the Jacksonian mode in which public servants were expected to identify closely with their local community, have no strong sense of professional identity, and remain loyal to their political party leaders, not their bureaucratic superiors. As their distinctive uniforms proudly proclaimed, the forest rangers were an elite corps. The democratic threat posed by such elites within the public service was presumably outweighed by their expertise and dedication.

An Executive Budget

Wilson's principle of separating politics and administration required that elected officials provide broad policy direction for the bureaucracy. Congress was simply too large and unwieldy to provide such guidance, and so, increasingly, that responsibility was borne by the president. The Budget Act of 1921 provided the president with a powerful tool for performing that task. It created the *Bureau of the Budget* (BOB), housed in the treasury department. The chief task of this new agency was to prepare a budget for the entire federal government. It would review the requests of all federal programs and agencies, assemble those requests, and then suggest to the president how the requests should be pared down to keep overall federal spending in balance with expected revenues.

This notion of an executive budget has become so deeply embedded in the operations of the federal government that it is hard to believe that no such organizing principle for federal spending existed for the first 130 years of the republic. Spending decisions had been a haphazard affair in which, for the most part, individual federal departments made up their own budget proposals and took them directly to Congress. Creation of a budget bureau enabled the president to establish spending priorities and maintain some degree of financial control over his administrative subordinates.

Congress still preserved its constitutionally mandated power of the purse. It could choose to modify the president's budgetary proposals or even to ignore them altogether. But the sheer existence of an overall budgetary plan gave the president the initiative in policy planning and enabled him to appear fiscally responsible. Congress was put on the defensive. If it chose to deviate from this comprehensive blueprint, it bore the onus of demonstrating that its alternative was not a "budget breaker. "

Administering Big Government

President Wilson had only limited opportunity to put his vision of a new science of administration into practice. The Great Depression opened far greater possibilities for Wilson's disciple, Franklin Roosevelt (FDR). The depression ushered in the modern era of big government and thus gave FDR a larger canvas on which to impose Progressive notions of administration. These opportunities were further increased by World War II and the Cold War that began in its aftermath.

FDR had considerable administrative experience; he had served as Wilson's assistant secretary of the Navy, and he then succeeded one of the greatest of all Progressive executives, Al Smith, as governor of New York. To implement New Deal innovations in banking, labor relations, social insurance, and many other fields, FDR relied heavily on seasoned administrators who had pioneered similar programs in progressive-minded states such as Wisconsin and New York. The depth of the crisis and the verve of FDR's response to it greatly increased the attractiveness of government service to students and graduates of the most prestigious professional and graduate schools. Not since the early days of the republic had the government been so successful in attracting members of the elite to serve the government in peacetime.

The New Deal

Graduates of Yale, Columbia, and Harvard law schools and departments of economics flocked to Washington to work for new agencies such as the *Securities and Exchange Commission* (SEC), the Federal Deposit Insurance Corporation (FDIC), the National Labor Relations Board (NLRB), and the *Agricultural Adjustment Agency* (AAA) as well as expanded and reinvigorated organizations such as the *Antitrust Division of the Justice Department* and the *Department of the Interior*. Their bosses were often their own former professors. These highly trained professionals were able to apply their knowledge of such arcane subjects as securities and banking law or labor and resource economics to the daunting task of restoring prosperity.

FDR proposed a major reorganization of the executive branch (see Chapter 8). Although Congress did not give him all he asked for, the *Executive*

Reorganization Act of 1939 did significantly expand his ability to manage the increasingly massive and specialized federal bureaucracy. It created the Executive Office of the President (EOP), which provided him with a well staffed nerve center for obtaining information about the activities of the various executive departments and for planning and coordinating them. At the EOP's core was the Bureau of the Budget, which had been transferred to the EOP from the treasury department. The purpose of this reorganization was to fulfill the democratic as well as the scientific promise of Progressive administration. An expert bureaucracy would be rendered accountable to public opinion by providing the representative of public opinion, the president, with sufficient political and managerial tools to control and direct it.

But the New Deal was not simply Progressivism writ large. FDR's approach to putting the unemployed back to work had more in common with the older spoils system. Although it might have been more efficient to simply give money to the unemployed to alleviate their misery and encourage consumer spending, FDR rejected this approach. He was as concerned about the self-respect of the unemployed as he was about their economic condition. Therefore, he determined that the bulk of New Deal relief for the poor would come in the form of jobs. He established a series of job-creating relief agencies; the largest and most successful was the *Works Progress Administration* (WPA), which put millions of people to work in a remarkably short span of time.

Harry Hopkins, head of the WPA, insisted that the WPA create simple jobs that any able-bodied person could do. Skill and expertise were sacrificed to the greater cause of putting Americans back to work. This approach resulted in a lot of wasted effort and misallocation of resources, but it also enabled millions of Americans to hold their heads high. They were not paupers seeking handouts. They were full-fledged Depression fighters, working hard to build a better country. The WPA and its sister agency, the *Civilian Conservation Corps* (CCC), left a brilliant legacy of accomplishment. Common cultural and recreational opportunities were greatly expanded. Parks were built; hiking trails blazed; murals painted; concerts performed. By creating simple jobs on a massive scale, the New Deal relief programs were more in keeping with Jackson's view of democratic administration than with Wilson's view of administration as a science.

FDR distinguished between the permanent bureaucracies he was establishing, which would function along Progressive lines, and the emergency relief agencies, which would be terminated when the economic crisis had passed. The massive spoils system instituted by the WPA and the CCC did not survive the Depression, but they did leave an indelible mark. Before the New Deal, people did not expect the government to help them if they lost

The largest agency of the New Deal, the Works Progress Administration, put millions of Americans to work building parks, roads, and trails.

their jobs. The success of the WPA and the other relief agencies altered those expectations. Congress acknowledged this new understanding of the responsibility of government when it enacted the Full Employment Act of 1946. This act charges the federal government with the specific responsibility of maintaining prosperity.

As we explain in Chapter 8, FDR insulated his most important New Deal reforms from repeal. Even as he increased presidential power by creating the EOP, he tied the hands of future presidents by transforming his policy goals into a new set of rights. By virtue of being "unalienable," these rights-based programs would be buffered from temporary shifts in public opinion and political power. FDR further constrained his successors by extending civil service protections to his federal appointees. As long as they lived, the committed, youthful New Dealers that he appointed to implement these new programmatic rights would remain in charge of the federal bureaucracy.

Thus, FDR's effort to create an administrative state in service to the new programmatic rights was in tension with his desire to strengthen the presidency. This conflict has permeated American government and politics ever since. The democratic principle that policy should bend to the popular will as championed by the president has coexisted uneasily with the liberal principle that rights are immune from change. No wonder those who actually administer public policy wrap themselves in red tape to gain some protection from the crossfire.

Congressional Resurgence

Congress was uncharacteristically passive during the initial emergency phase of the New Deal, but it soon reasserted itself. As Chapter 7 shows, Congress never succeeded in regaining primacy over public policy formulation. It did, however, increase its ability to conduct executive oversight. By threatening to reduce agency appropriations or by exposing agency failures to the glare of publicity, Congress used its powers to conduct investigations, hold hearings, and appropriate funds to exert substantial influence on the day-to-day conduct of the bureaucracy.

The shift away from party control and toward the standing committees and their chairs facilitated these expanded congressional oversight activities. Legislators became careerists, solidifying their hold on their districts by using their committee assignments to oversee executive activities of special concern to their constituents. The *Legislative Reorganization Act of 1946* provided members of Congress with expanded staffs to aid their bureaucratic probes. As members' terms of service lengthened, their own policy expertise and knowledge of departmental folklore often matched, or even exceeded, that of the administrators they were scrutinizing (see Chapter 7).

Iron Triangles

As Congress regained authority, it was able to find new means to fulfill its constitutional responsibility to check executive power. But its intrusion into the workings of administration created new problems of democratic accountability. The committee chairs who increasingly dominated agency life often came from rural Southern districts whose outlook did not mirror national opinion. Their seniority enabled them to deliver valuable goods and services to their districts. They obtained military bases, dams, highways, and other lucrative and job-creating federal "plums." Therefore, even if a majority of constituents disagreed with their representative on important policy matters, they were loath to replace that representative with a newcomer who would have to slowly climb the seniority ladder. As long as committee chairs continued to deliver the goods back home, they were not held accountable for their conduct of administrative oversight activities.

Diffusion of authority in Congress produced a similar effect within the bureaucracy. Bureau chiefs and agency heads found that their budgets, their lifeblood, were controlled as much by congressional committee and subcommittee chairs as by their department heads or the Bureau of the Budget. This dual control opened new doors to the interest-group clienteles of federal agencies. If they lacked influence with the president, they could still obtain favored treatment from the bureaucracy by persuading the relevant congressional committee chair to be their champion.

Interest-group influence was enhanced by Congress's method of assigning and promoting committee members. For the most part, members of Congress could choose their committee assignments. For example, a representative from a tobacco-growing district could be assured of a long and successful congressional career by obtaining a seat on the agriculture committee's tobacco subcommittee. The seniority system guaranteed that a patient representative would eventually rise to be subcommittee chair and thereby exert enormous influence over the Department of Agriculture's tobacco-related decisions.

Political scientists refer to this pattern of mutual influence among members of Congress, bureaucrats, and interest-group leaders as the *iron triangle*. To some extent, the rise of iron triangles was positive and necessary. Ordinary citizens or their representatives cannot be expected to have the same high level of interest and knowledge about tobacco as do those who grow it. The liberties of tobacco farmers are protected by a system that limits and diffuses bureaucratic power and provides them with privileged access to decision making about the matters that most directly affect them. But the iron triangle does pose a serious threat to democratic accountability because it deprives those who do not grow tobacco of the means to express their legitimate concerns about tobacco policy.

Electoral politics also contributed to rising interest-group influence within the executive branch. For example, organized labor provided a great deal of campaign assistance to the Democrats. Therefore, if a Democratic president were elected, the AFL-CIO would expect to have a big say in the choice of the secretary of labor and to depend on that person to articulate the concerns of the labor movement within the councils of the administration. Farmers were less politically predictable. Therefore, the secretary of agriculture, Republican or Democrat, was expected to have close relations with the various influential farm and commodity organizations and to curry their political allegiance.

In the period after World War II, as the scope of government expanded, new departments were created, such as the *Department of Housing and Urban Development*, the *Department of Veterans Affairs*, the *Department of*

Transportation, and the *Department of Health, Education, and Welfare* (later to be divided into the Department of Health and Human Services and the *Department of Education*). To win over the loyalties of influential interests such as teacher organizations and veterans, each party, when it controlled the presidency, tended to appoint cabinet secretaries with strong ties to those clienteles.

The Military-Industrial Complex

World War II's daunting logistical challenges led to an intimate partnership between government and the private sector. Business-government cooperation had also taken place during World War I and the New Deal. Wilson had appointed a famous financier, Bernard Baruch, to work with private business to coordinate and rationalize production of vital supplies such as munitions, vehicles, and ships. During the New Deal, a National Recovery Administration (NRA) was established to foster cooperation between business, labor, and consumer groups in order to stabilize prices and employment. But American involvement in World War I was brief. Baruch's efforts did not outlive the return of peace. The NRA was likewise short-lived. Even before the Supreme Court declared it unconstitutional, it had proved a failure. Because the Cold War followed hard on the heels of victory in World War II, the high level of interaction and cooperation between business and government established during World War II perpetuated itself.

Confronted with the massive challenge of providing supplies, munitions, and transportation to fight a war on two separate fronts, FDR briefly considered nationalizing the war-related sectors of American industry. But he quickly realized that the government lacked sufficient knowledge and the management skill to run those industries. Instead, he relied primarily on voluntary cooperation from private suppliers. Government restricted its involvement mostly to stimulating such cooperation by paying high prices. Even so, a great deal of direct interaction between government and suppliers was necessary to ensure that the right things were being produced in a timely fashion. To facilitate such coordination, suppliers loaned experienced managers to government for the token price of a dollar a year. These "dollar-a-year men" became vital cogs in the war machine, helping to achieve rates of ship, plane, tank, and munitions production that America's enemies had not thought possible.

To hasten production, government contracts were often written on a cost-plus basis, which meant that suppliers could recover their full costs plus a specified percentage of profit. Therefore, war industries had no material incentive to keep costs down. Indeed, the greater their costs, the greater the absolute amount of profit they would obtain. Working for the government for a dollar a year did not cause managers to forget who really paid their salary. Throughout their government service, they retained a strong loyalty to the companies from which they came and to which they would return.

During the Cold War, as the technology of warfare grew in complexity, government came to depend on yet another body of experts, college professors. Grants from the federal government to university physics, chemistry, and engineering departments became a crucial supplement to corporate research and development as a means for stimulating militarily useful scientific discoveries and technological advances. The increasingly close relationship between the Department of Defense, corporations, and universities led to the creation of a "revolving door" by which the military and civilian bureaucrats who issued defense contracts and grants would leave to work for the very companies or universities who had won those awards. In his farewell address, President Dwight Eisenhower, the great American hero of World War II and himself an architect of the Cold War, warned of threats to liberty and democracy posed by this new, increasingly unaccountable "military-industrial complex." Eisenhower recognized that government dependence on outside expertise was undermining the Wilsonian notion of a scientific administration subservient to executive authority.

In the 1960s and 1970s, the federal government continued to expand its adoption of major new responsibilities in such areas as personnel training, mental health, preschool education, medicine, and other forms of social service. This vast and apparently ceaseless expansion greatly heightened concerns about bureaucratic effectiveness and accountability. In the 1970s, exposés of various departments by consumer advocate Ralph Nader and the law students who staffed the various public-interest organizations he inspired (see Chapter 12) found iron triangles everywhere they looked. Fears about the military-industrial complex burgeoned into worries about a "military, agricultural, labor, education, consulting firm, industrial complex" in which organized interests dominated the public sphere, working in tandem with their congressional and bureaucratic allies to bend public policy to serve their selfish purposes.

Administrative Reform

As the federal government became ever more involved in the lives of the citizenry and as concerns grew about the effect of this involvement on liberty and democracy, the pressure to reform bureaucracy became much more intense. Efforts to address the fears and resentments that the expansion of the administrative state had engendered began almost as soon the expansion itself. In their various ways, each of these reform efforts tried to find a way to avoid the cruel choice between license and red tape. The key to understanding the modern administrative state lies in understanding how these various efforts proposed to escape that vexing dilemma and what their actual impact on liberty and democracy has been. Broadly speaking, these reform efforts have been of two different kinds: efforts to perfect scientific, Wilsonian administration; and efforts to replace Wilsonian administration with alternative approaches based on rights, direct democracy, and markets. These alternatives exchanged Wilsonian faith in expertise and hierarchy with their own faith in, respectively, judicial supremacy, public participation, and consumer choice. All these options, Wilsonian and anti-Wilsonian, continue to influence American public administration. At various times over the past forty years, one or another has captured the spotlight.

Perfecting the Science of Administration: Presidential Commissions

Perfecting the Wilsonian approach has been the central theme of several presidential blue-ribbon commissions established to improve administrative management. In Chapter 8, we highlight the Brownlow Committee Report, many of whose recommendations were embodied in the Executive Reorganization Act of 1939. Its successors included a commission headed by former president Herbert Hoover, appointed by President Harry Truman; a second Hoover commission established by President Eisenhower; and a commission led by prominent industrialist Roy Ash, appointed by President Richard Nixon. The common theme of these commissions is that improved public-sector management requires increased executive accountability. As the chief administrator, the president needs better tools to coordinate and evaluate departmental performance. The commissions recommended giving the president additional staff resources. Likewise, the commissions determined that heads of departments need greater flexibility in order to manage their departments effectively and recommended giving them more latitude in reorganizing bureaus and in hiring and firing personnel.

The Ash Council offered the most ambitious reorganization proposal. It concluded that because presidents have so many other responsibilities, they could not possibly exert sufficient supervision over all the departments reporting directly to them. The Ash Council recommended the creation of a "super-cabinet" – consisting of the secretaries of treasury, defense, and state and the attorney general – to whom all "lesser" cabinet officials and otherwise unsupervised federal agencies would report. These four "super-secretaries" would function almost like deputy presidents by exercising vast discretion over their newly enlarged executive domains. Because these secretaries were so few in number and were the president's highest level appointees, the president could keep an eye on them and reasonably expect them to follow presidential orders even without direct supervision. To oversee this new super-cabinet, Congress would have had to establish new "super-committees," thereby reducing the power and importance of existing committees and their leaders. As it had done with previous proposals to alter or relax its grip on executive departments, Congress rejected the Ash Council proposals.

Congress proved more receptive to reform proposals that did not directly threaten its authority. It greatly expanded the president's capacity to oversee and coordinate the executive branch by expanding the EOP and providing the Office of Management and Budget (previously the Bureau of the Budget) with new staff resources to undertake significant managerial responsibilities. It approved a whole host of new White House coordinating bodies including, most prominently, the National Security Council.

The White House now had better tools for agency oversight, but because Congress had refused to strengthen the management of the individual departments, more and more decision making became centralized in the White House. In his classic study, *Bureaucracy*, James Q. Wilson quotes from Undersecretary of Housing and Urban Development Robert Wood on the dangers of this excessive White House involvement.

> Operational matters flow to the top – as central staffs become engrossed in subduing outlying bureaucracies – and policy making emerges at the bottom. At the top minor problems squeeze out major ones, and individuals lower down the echelons who have the time for reflection and mischief-making take up issues of fundamental philosophical and political significance.

No matter how numerous and energetic, White House staffers are not effective substitutes for departmental managers as bureaucratic disciplinarians. Indeed, their own zeal can actually undermine departmental accountability because they pursue issues that are too detailed and complex for them to master. Such second-guessing of minutia gives the illusion of meaningful political control but not the reality of political accountability. This shift of power from executive departments to the lower echelons of the White House staff has not succeeded in escaping the bureaucratic license versus red tape dilemma.

Perfecting the Science of Administration: Budget Reform

As another means for improving political accountability, Wilsonian-style administrative reform sought to transform departmental budgets from control to management devices. As long as the federal government was considered a "necessary evil," the main purpose of departmental budgets was to prevent waste, fraud, and abuse. They enabled departmental managers and congressional overseers to detect overspending and misallocation of funds. This tight control was based on itemization; it prescribed just how much was to be spent for paper clips, fuel oil, typewriter ribbons, and so on. Therefore, the budget functioned as a form of red tape forcing bureaucrats to spend huge time and effort acquiring and justifying the resources they needed to do their jobs. Unfortunately, the information that is vital from a control standpoint is of little help in managing a complex department. What good is it to know how much is being spent without knowing what departmental functions are being served by those expenditures? Between 1932 and 1940, federal expenditures more than doubled, from 4.2 billion dollars to 10 billion dollars. As the New Deal turned the federal government into a vast and complex enterprise, the inadequacy of existing budgetary techniques became increasingly apparent.

The Coast Guard provides a good illustration of the practical changes required to make budgeting a management tool. Initially, its budget was simply an itemized account of expenditures – fuel, salaries, uniforms, and so on. By shifting to a function-based budget, the Coast Guard was able to determine what it was spending on each of its operational responsibilities – vessels, aircraft, repair, and maintenance. Knowing what it cost to perform specific tasks allowed the Coast Guard to develop measures of performance and make comparisons between performance and cost. For example, if routine engine maintenance could be done for $5000 and a particular repair facility was spending $6000 to do it, management had gleaned valuable information upon which to base a review of that facility's work practices.

In Executive Order 8248, FDR indicated his support for the management approach. He ordered the BOB, now a part of his executive office, to

> keep the President informed of the progress of activities by agencies of the Government with respect to work proposed, work actually initiated, and work completed, together with the relative timing of work between the several agencies of the Government: all to the end that the work programs of the several agencies of the executive branch of the Government may be coordinated and that the monies appropriated by the Congress may be expended in the most economical manner possible to prevent overlapping and duplication of effort.

To effectively implement this order, the BOB staff was increased tenfold.

Perfecting the Science of Administration: The Budget as a Planning Tool

After World War II, to further increase political accountability, an effort was made to expand budgeting into a planning tool. Planning in this sense meant a sustained effort by government to consider how public policy could most effectively be used to improve well-being over the long term. Congress had denounced New Deal planning initiatives as "socialistic." However, Congress's acceptance of a permanent responsibility to maintain full employment, combined with the onset of the Cold War, forced it to modify its previous hostility toward planning.

America's Cold War strategy was premised on the idea of containment. This doctrine meant avoiding direct military confrontation with the Soviets while preventing their territorial expansion. It required massive defense expenditures over a long period of time. For the first time in American history, defense became the single largest element of the federal budget even though the nation was not at war. These sums were so vast, and the military and diplomatic objectives they served were so complex and dynamic, that budgetary planning was unavoidable. To keep spending in check, priorities had to be chosen. Because the hope was that these increasingly sophisticated weapons systems would never be used, their effectiveness could not be known for sure. Therefore, very expensive decisions about which ones to buy, and even which ones to try to develop, had to be made in the face of great uncertainty.

To assist in making these hard decisions, budgetary analysts borrowed new analytic tools from economics and mathematics. *Operations research* uses math to estimate how best to coordinate personnel, materials, and equipment to achieve a designated objective. In principle, it is as useful for planning the Normandy invasion as it is for organizing and staffing an airline's ticket counters. *Cost-benefit analysis* provides numerical estimates of the price to be paid for achieving a particular objective and the rewards to be reaped by accomplishing it. Because neither costs nor benefits can be known for sure, cost-benefit analysis uses mathematical probability theory to try to take those uncertainties into account. These techniques enabled planners to more carefully specify in advance how much it would actually cost to achieve various objectives and thereby enabled them to establish priorities among those goals.

The key difference between planning budgeting and management budgeting lies in how budgetary categories are set up. Management budgeting categories are defined by the work the agency performs. In our Coast Guard example, categories were established on the basis of air surveillance, ship cruises, and repair and maintenance. Planning budgeting categories are created on the basis not of the activities themselves but of the objectives to be achieved. For the Coast Guard, these categories would be search and rescue, navigational assistance, and law enforcement. This change is crucial because, from a planning perspective, the most important question is not how best to fly planes or repair ships but rather how to ensure that useful tasks like helping maritime vessels to navigate safely and catching smugglers are being performed effectively and efficiently.

Planning budgeting also permits comparisons across agency lines. If the Coast Guard is spending $200,000 to catch each drug smuggling boat and the *Drug Enforcement Agency* (DEA) is spending $300,000 to accomplish the same result, it is more efficient to shift more of this responsibility from the DEA to the Coast Guard. Or, if that is politically impossible, the DEA can at least be encouraged to adopt the Coast Guard's surveillance and enforcement techniques.

Planning budgeting can even serve as a means for choosing among public policy objectives. If, for example, the Forest Service can cut the risk of flooding in a specified area in half by spending 1 million dollars to reduce soil erosion by planting additional trees, and the Army Corps of Engineers can accomplish the same degree of flood control by building a dam that costs 10 million dollars, a strong budgetary argument can be made for adding 1 million dollars to the Forest Service soil conservation budget rather than providing 10 million dollars to the corps to build the dam.

Planning budgeting is very difficult because both cost and benefit estimations are hard to calculate and subject to tremendous uncertainty. In addition, the executives charged with making these estimates often have a strong prior opinion about whether a proposed project deserves to be funded. The Tennessee Valley Authority (TVA), for example, was committed to luring industry to the Tennessee Valley by providing very cheap electricity. Its analysis of its proposed Tellico Dam showed that the benefits of the dam far exceeded the costs. But those who opposed the dam claimed that the benefits estimates were wildly inflated. Critics doubted that new industry would move to the remote areas adjacent to the dam regardless of low electricity rates, and they doubted that tourism would increase significantly because the region already had many fish-laden reservoirs created by previous TVA dams. The TVA analysts were not lying, but their agency's strong desire to build the dam naturally inclined them to make optimistic assumptions about the benefits to be reaped, whereas opponents of the dam likewise tended to rely on pessimistic benefits assumptions.

Despite its flaws, planning budgeting is a crucial democratic instrument. At a minimum, it forces both advocates and opponents of proposed expenditures to specify what they expect the costs and benefits to be and to explain and defend the assumptions behind those estimates. Because these analyses must be made public, they can be scrutinized and exposed by skeptical budget bureau officials, congressional staffers, interest-group representatives, and journalists. In the absence of such quantification, the democratically responsible members of government, in deciding whether to fund a proposed project, have little to go on other than their own biases and a desire to please their friends. In this case, freeing up the budgetary process from "red tape" to enable it to function as a planning device has improved the capacity of the executive to be held democratically accountable. Box 4 gives an example of how a thorough assessment of the costs and benefits of an important federal policy helps decision makers to assess its value.

Box Four: Contemporary Politics

The Costs and Benefits of the Clean Air Act

The Clean Air Act, enacted in 1970 and amended in 1977 and 1990, is an ambitious effort to improve the quality of the air that Americans breathe. It also imposes very large costs on those who create air pollution – public utilities, manufacturers of a variety of products, and automobiles. Despite the importance of clean air, until quite recently there was no systematic attempt to measure its costs and benefits. In 1999, the Environmental Protection Agency issued a comprehensive cost-benefit estimate. This analysis is perhaps the most ambitious effort ever to use quantitative methods to judge the value of a major domestic policy initiative.

Using complex computer-modeling techniques, the study estimated that in 2010 the Clean Air Act will prevent 23,000 premature deaths; 170,000 asthma attacks; 67,000 incidences of chronic and acute bronchitis; 4,100,000 lost work days; 22,000 respiratory-related hospital admissions; and 42,000 cardiovascular hospital admissions. The study estimated that the value of the illnesses prevented and deaths avoided would be 110 billion dollars. The detailed estimate of the costs of achieving the air pollution reductions that produced these benefits was only 27 billion dollars, providing a ratio of benefits to costs of almost four to one.

The study had to make many assumptions and guesstimates regarding both the cost and benefit numbers that it arrived at. To some extent, the errors produced by that guesswork should cancel each other out. What makes the study both impressive and relevant to policy deliberation is the great size of the difference between the costs and the benefits. Regardless of how many errors and false assumptions went into the analysis, it is hard to believe, given the great skill and care with which the analysis was undertaken, that the direction of the results could be wrong and that the costs of providing clean air actually exceed the benefits. Cost-benefit analysis is not yet a surgically precise tool. But, as the clean air study shows, cost-benefit analysis can make a significant contribution to the assessment of public policy when it can show that costs and benefits differ by great orders of magnitude.

Perfecting the Science of Administration: NEPA

The most ambitious effort to implement a planning approach to decision making was not aimed at the federal budget per se. The National Environmental Policy Act of 1970 (NEPA) required that an agency proposing a new project submit an *Environmental Impact Statement* (EIS). The EIS contains a cost-benefit analysis of the proposal, of alternative approaches, and of doing nothing. It provides the public with a richer picture of what the array of choices actually are. And it pressures the agency to broaden its consideration of possible options before it fixes on a particular one. It serves as a counterweight to the natural tendency of public officials to stick with the tools and techniques most familiar to them; it requires that they think about other possibilities. Of course, those officials who are rigidly devoted to a particular approach will treat the EIS as nothing more than red tape and will rig their cost and benefit assumptions to ensure that the final result mirrors their initial biases. No planning process can protect against stubbornness. But even in this extreme case, EIS red tape ensures that assumptions will be exposed to public scrutiny. If agency officials approach the EIS process in good faith, they might surprise themselves by discovering that their cherished ways of doing things are not the most efficient or effective ways to get the job done.

The promise of planning budgeting and environmental impact statements has not been fully realized. Planning advocates both in and outside of government blame Congress. Its continuing desire to exert maximum control over the day-to-day operations of agencies and its willingness to ignore cost-benefit data that refutes the claims of constituents stand in the way of effective planning and management. But this clash between executive planning and congressional intervention is not simply irrational. The ongoing struggle between the executive and the legislature has deep constitutional roots. If the Framers had wanted to maximize the ability of administrators to plan and manage, they would not have created the strong legislative checks on the executive that they deemed so essential to the preservation of liberty.

Americans, to a far greater extent than citizens of other modern democracies, continue to mistrust government and prefer private to public problem solving. In the budgetary context, this skepticism is reflected in Congress's continued emphasis on minute control of executive expenditures. Senator William Proxmire (D-WI) insisted on reviewing even the smallest line-item expenditures of the defense department because it enabled him to uncover "$100 hammers" and "$1,000 toilet seats" that served as evocative symbols for his crusade against waste, fraud, and abuse in defense contracting. His creation of the Golden Fleece Award in 1975, which was given to the most egregious example of government waste, made him a hero among taxpayers.

Alternatives to Scientific Administration: Maximum Feasible Participation

The effort to find an alternative to, rather than to perfect, scientific public administration was part of a broader skepticism about the oppressive potential of government, indeed of all large and complex institutions, that surfaced during the 1960s. Initially, this new way of thinking had its greatest impact on the universities and on efforts to combat urban poverty. But it eventually came to encompass the whole question of how public policy should be carried out.

In the early 1960s at the University of California, Berkeley, the protest slogan was "don't bend, spindle, or mutilate." This slogan referred to the warnings printed on the computer cards that students used to register for courses. It symbolized student antipathy toward the growing regimentation and impersonality of university life.

Social scientists diagnosed problems of ghetto dwellers in similar terms. Like students, the urban poor had no voice in decisions that controlled their lives, and they were looked down on by bureaucrats who viewed them as "clients," not people. No wonder both groups felt alienated, that they did not see themselves as belonging to or playing a meaningful part in society. President Lyndon Johnson's *War on Poverty*, launched in 1964, sought to combat poverty by attacking poor people's social and political deficits. His intention was to fight alienation by encouraging political participation. In colleges throughout the country, students fought their way onto student life and curriculum committees that were previously the sole domain of deans and professors. In urban and rural areas, the poor were included in the planning and implementing of new education, training, and economic programs that fought poverty.

The major weapons of the War on Poverty were community action programs (CAPs) with boards elected by the poor. CAPs funneled federal money and technical assistance to poor people, who would direct and control how those resources were spent. CAPs were mandated to promote the "maximum feasible participation" of the poor in all their projects and programs.

The War on Poverty was successful in many ways, but not in promoting civic participation. Voter turnout at CAP board elections was abysmally low, as was participation in other program planning activities. Nor did it serve as a check on bureaucratic license. Favoritism and corruption were far more rampant among these community boards than among the bureaucracies they replaced. If alienation was indeed the root cause of poverty, it was too deep to be alleviated by mere opportunities and invitations to participate.

Although the great optimism surrounding "maximum feasible participation" has not survived, the War on Poverty did leave a permanent mark on public administration. Public participation is now a hallmark of virtually all federal initiatives. Before the 1960s, federally sponsored projects were planned and implemented with very little attention paid to their local impact. Now, community hearings are held before a project is begun; citizen representatives are included on advisory committees that scrutinize the project's progress; and proposed revisions are subjected to further community hearings. Superfund, the law that mandates the cleanup of toxic waste sites, even provides people who live near a site with funds to commission their own scientific studies of proposed cleanup plans so that they need not rely on data spoon-fed to them by government or industry.

This greater openness has forced bureaucrats to pay more attention to citizen concerns but it has created as many democratic problems as it has solved. The views that surface at community meetings and public hearings are those of the people most directly affected by a proposed project; these views may or may not resemble the views of the public at large. The sensitivities to local public opinion that are built into these new participatory processes make it much less likely that communities will have unwanted prisons, highways, or dump sites imposed on them. But if state or national majorities favor these projects as useful means to deter crime, alleviate traffic congestion, or ensure safe treatment of hazardous waste, then the ability of a smaller public to block them frustrates the broader democratic will.

Since the 1970s, many public projects have fallen victim to the NIMBY syndrome. NIMBY is an acronym for "not in my backyard." Faced with living next door to a drug addiction clinic or a halfway house for teenage delinquents, homeowners have learned how to use public participation processes to force governments to locate such facilities elsewhere. Of course, when a feasible alternative site is found, the public participation process begins afresh, setting in motion a new struggle to ensure that the facility is not built "in my backyard." NIMBY efforts do not always succeed. Many prisons, highways, and drug treatment centers have indeed been built since the 1970s. But even when it does not entirely succeed in flouting the popular will, NIMBY extracts a great democratic cost. Knowing that a particular project will evoke NIMBY opposition, government officials have a strong incentive to site the project in communities that are not well organized politically. This tendency encourages the concentration of noxious facilities in those areas that are most politically vulnerable. Thus, NIMBY creates new forms of inequality. It imposes restrictions on bureaucratic decision making that push in a decidly antidemocratic direction.

Affirmative Action

Another approach to making the bureaucracy more democratically responsive was to ensure that its personnel included a sufficient number of the racial minorities who were so often its clients. Because women and racial minorities were underrepresented in the federal civil service, the federal government embarked upon a policy of *affirmative action* to increase their numbers through special means for government service recruitment. The concept of affirmative action was first officially endorsed by President Johnson in 1965. In 1971, President Nixon ordered affirmative action programs for workers on federally funded projects. Individual states and municipalities also embarked upon affirmative action hiring programs for similar reasons.

Affirmative action has succeeded as a policy for integrating the federal workforce. Minority participation in the federal government workforce now exceeds minority participation in the civilian workforce as a whole. Supporters of affirmative action argue that the increase in minority personnel has indeed created greater responsiveness toward and empathy for the minority populations that various departments serve. Critics do not dispute the desirability of employing more minority members. However, they criticize the government for going beyond affirmatively recruiting minorities to favoring minority applicants who have lower civil service test scores than whites. They resort to the same arguments in favor of objective, test-based hiring that the earlier generation of civil service reformers used against defenders of the spoils system.

Alternatives to Scientific Administration: The Courts

In the 1970s, progressives became disappointed with the president, and they looked to the courts for leadership (see Chapters 8 and 9). Progressive reformers were dissatisfied with Wilsonian efforts to make the bureaucracy more efficient, effective, and responsive to the president; they were also unhappy with the more open and democratic Jacksonian approach. So they sought to establish a bureaucracy that was more faithful to the law and to the law's interpreter, the judiciary.

Earlier efforts to use the courts to improve bureaucracy had a conservative, not a progressive, intent. In the wake of the New Deal, people who were subject to the New Deal's vastly more aggressive regulatory efforts demanded limits on bureaucratic discretion. In 1946, Congress passed the *Administrative Procedures Act* (APA) to increase judicial oversight of the bureaucracy. The act states that people who have suffered a "legal wrong" or have been "adversely affected or aggrieved by agency action within the meaning of the relevant statute" may seek redress in court. The court can overturn an agency decision if it finds that the decision was "arbitrary or capricious" or lacked "substantial evidence."

But the courts did not treat the APA as an invitation to second-guess agency decision making. In divining the meaning of "arbitrary and capricious" and "substantial evidence," judges gave bureaucrats the benefit of the doubt. As long as the fact-finding, analysis, and rule-writing procedures employed by an agency were fair and consistent, the court resisted asking whether the agency had made the right decision. In the absence of demonstrated bias, egregious evasion of the intent of the law, or willful ignorance of the facts, the courts deferred to the superior expertise of the bureaucrats.

This deference receded in response to what the court took to be foot-dragging by state and local agencies in their pursuit of racial equality. Here, the pressure for hemming in bureaucratic discretion came not from conservative business interests but from civil rights organizations and their liberal allies. As we discuss in Chapter 9, *Swann v. Charlotte-Mecklenburg Board of Education* propelled judges into the details of administration. In Charlotte, and then in cities across the nation including

Denver, Cleveland, and Boston, judges became de facto school administrators, involving themselves in the details of drawing school boundary lines and bus schedules.

The civil rights issue presented the federal judiciary with an especially compelling argument for second-guessing the bureaucracy. After all, Southern state agencies had for decades been the enforcers of racial inequality. Could these agencies now become the primary agents enforcing racial equality without considerable ongoing federal scrutiny and pressure? But in 1971, federal courts overturned decisions by two *federal* agencies, neither of which was in the same suspect category as a Southern school department. The courts did not find violations of procedure. Rather, they ruled that the agencies had failed to abide by the intent of the law even though that intent had not been spelled out by Congress.

In *Environmental Defense Fund v. Ruckelshaus* (1971), a federal appeals court overruled a decision by the Environmental Protection Agency (EPA) that the pesticide DDT was not an "imminent hazard." The court acknowledged that the law allows the EPA administrator to define "imminent hazard." It justified its intrusion not on the grounds of demonstrated agency bias or superior judicial expertise but rather on its understanding of the responsibility of the judiciary as the guardian of fundamental rights, which EPA's action jeopardized: "courts are increasingly asked to review administrative action that touches on fundamental personal interests in life, health and liberty. These interests have always had a special claim to judicial protection." Because "life, health and liberty" were at stake, the court felt justified in stepping over its normal bounds and substituting its understanding of what Congress meant by "imminent hazard" for that of the agency.

Another important court case, *Citizens to Preserve Overton Park Inc. v. Volpe* (1971), involved Overton Park, a 342-acre city park in Memphis, Tennessee. The U.S. Department of Transportation (DOT) approved federal funds to build a six-lane section of I-40 that would destroy twenty-six acres of the park. Opponents formed a group called Citizens to Preserve Overton Park Inc. They sued the government, claiming that the DOT had violated section 138 of the 1968 Federal Aid to Highways Act, which states "the Secretary of Transportation shall not approve any program or project which requires the use of any publicly owned land from a public park...unless there is no feasible and prudent alternative."

Rerouting the highway to avoid the park would significantly increase its costs. Therefore, the secretary of transportation concluded that there was no prudent alternative. The Supreme Court overturned his decision on the grounds that Congress could not have meant the word "prudent" to mean "less costly" because it would always be cheaper to route a highway through publicly owned parkland than to buy up commercial or residential property for that purpose. If "prudent" meant "cheaper," stated the court, section 138 was meaningless. Therefore prudent *must* mean the same thing as "feasible." Was there some other practical alternative for routing the highway even if it involved greater disruption of businesses and homeowners and much greater cost? If so, the court said, the secretary of transportation could not use prudence as an excuse for failing to choose that alternative.

But if "prudent" and "feasible" mean the same thing, why did Congress include both words? It seems that in this case the true intent of Congress is impossible to divine. In such ambiguous circumstances, the court was willing to substitute its judgment for that of the secretary of transportation based on the same principle of guardianship that the appeals court had invoked in the DDT case. Parkland is very scarce. Private interests and even bureaucrats cannot be relied on to protect it. Therefore, the courts must step in to protect the public interest from greed and bureaucratic inertia.

As with previous efforts to rationalize or democratize bureaucratic decision making, the effort to impose greater judicial control has had only a limited impact. A mere fourteen years after *Overton Park*, the Supreme Court dramatically shifted course. In *Chevron U.S.A., Inc. v. NRDC* (1984), it retreated from its claim to be able to divine congressional intent. In this case, the court allowed an agency to "reasonably" interpret legislative intent so long as Congress has not clearly and expressly revealed it. Since *Chevron*, federal courts for the most part have been less aggressive in challenging exercises of bureaucratic discretion than they were in the 1970s. Nonetheless the "guardian" approach has left its mark. Public agencies are far more sensitive to the threat of legal challenge than they were before. The line between judicial deference and judicial second-guessing remains fuzzy, and bureaucrats are still fearful of having their decisions overturned in court. This perceived need to defend oneself against the claim that one acted illegally puts even greater pressure on bureaucrats to demonstrate the slavish devotion to rules and procedures that goes by the name of red tape.

Alternatives to Scientific Administration: Deregulation

Whatever their differences, advocates of Wilsonian efforts to perfect administration and advocates of alternatives such as public participation and judicial review all share the Progressive faith in a large and powerful federal government. Beginning in the 1970s, a different perspective, highly skeptical of federal intervention and bureaucratic activism, gained prominence. It sought to substitute free-market competition for regulatory and bureaucratic discretionary intrusiveness and red tape.

The competitive approach took three different forms. The strongest form was *deregulation*. Federal and state governments substantially reduced their involvement in the regulation of economic competition. In the 1970s and 1980s (see Chapter 6), Congress passed laws that ended government regulation of interstate trucking, airline scheduling and pricing, and long-distance phone service. It also removed government controls over electric power sales, the commercial activities of banks, and the production of shows by television networks. Several federal agencies were abolished, including the Interstate Commerce Commission, which had set freight rates for railroads and trucking, and the Civil Aeronautics Board, which had regulated airfares. Other agencies, such as the Federal Communications Commission, had their span of responsibilities curtailed.

The premise of economic regulation was market failure, the inability of certain industries to sustain competition. Government corrected market failure by substituting the wisdom and impartiality of its experts. But high prices and lack of technological innovation in regulated industries convinced Congress that the cure for market failure was worse than the disease. Even if there were impediments to free transportation, communications, and energy markets, enterprising competitors could overcome those barriers more easily than they could cope with the inflexibility and timidity of government regulators.

By the new millennium, deregulation had spread so far that virtually no significant sector of the economy remained subject to government-imposed restrictions on competitive behavior. But this success did not spill over into other regulatory spheres. Regulations on air and water pollution, endangered species, wilderness, and occupational safety and health remained and even expanded modestly. Major new regulatory efforts were initiated to protect the rights of the physically disabled. The key word is *rights*. The appeal to rights – to health and safety, to gender equality, to equal opportunity for the mentally and physically disabled, or to a species' right to exist – provided a powerful rationale for government intervention. The same sense of guardianship that led judges to intervene to protect parkland and ban a hazardous pesticide encouraged both Congress and the courts to promote rights-based regulation even as they were terminating regulation aimed at perfecting the market. Box 5 describes the process by which a regulation is enacted.

Box Five: Nuts and Bolts

The Regulatory Process

When Congress writes a law, it normally acknowledges that it is incapable of giving specific direction about how that law is to be implemented. Instead, it writes the law to provide broad guidelines to the administrative agency or agencies charged with devising the specific regulations necessary to put the law into effect. The Administrative Procedures Act details the procedures that an agency must follow in issuing a regulation.

To help ensure consistency of purpose throughout the executive branch and to keep overall costs in check, the Office of Management and Budget (OMB) also actively participates in the process. The initial drafting of a regulation is done by the designated agency. The draft is then scrutinized by OMB. If OMB approves, the agency publishes a notice of the proposed rule in the Federal Register, which enables any interested party to review and criticize the draft. The agency may also choose to hold hearings to obtain even more advice and criticism. It then issues its proposed regulation in the Federal Register and allows thirty to sixty days for comments. It considers the comments and then issues a final draft, which again goes to OMB for review. If OMB approves, the regulation goes into effect and is published in the Federal Register.

Alternatives to Scientific Administration: Privatization

Even after the deregulation tide crested, a milder form of privatization, often called *outsourcing* or *contracting out*, continued to flourish and expand. Outsourcing does not eliminate government involvement in regulation or service delivery, but it restricts government to a supervisory role. Instead of relying on their own personnel to perform the work, agencies contract with the lowest bidder from the private sector. Government has always relied on the private sector for supplies. But in recent years, contracting out has been applied to new realms, including law enforcement, social service delivery, and inspection. For example, a state welfare agency might invite Catholic Charities and other philanthropic organizations to compete for a contract to operate its homeless shelters or its halfway houses for troubled teenagers. In several states, hotel chains such as Marriott bid for the opportunity to build and operate prisons. Some states are experimenting with the hiring of private engineering consulting firms to audit factories to check for compliance with air, water, and hazardous waste pollution control laws.

Privatization takes aim at government, not governance. It implements the policies of the state but removes the public bureaucracy from any role in the actual delivery of services; bureaucracy's role is limited to awarding and supervising contracts with the private suppliers of the services. Privatization rejects the Wilsonian respect for government expertise but accepts the Wilsonian divorce between politics and administration. Unlike deregulation, privatization enables politics, not markets, to make authoritative decisions. But it assumes that real politics should stop at the water's edge of implementation. Because administrators have no role in important policy decisions, it is safe to award administrative responsibilities to the lowest bidder.

Vouchers occupy a middle ground between the high level of government control involved in contracting out and the removal of government authority represented by full-fledged deregulation. The pioneer voucher program, for feeding poor people, was begun by the U.S. Department of Agriculture (USDA). The USDA shifted from directly supplying food commodities to issuing *food stamps* that recipients could take to the grocery stores to obtain food at substantial discounts. Since the food stamp program was begun in the 1960s, it has grown into one of the largest of all aid programs for the poor. As a substitute for public housing, the federal Department of Housing and Urban Development is experimenting with rent vouchers that poor people can give to private landlords in lieu of cash. The most controversial of all voucher schemes, pioneered by the city of Milwaukee, Wisconsin, enables parents to remove their children from the public schools by distributing education vouchers they can spend at private schools.

Vouchers do not represent complete privatization because government retains some control over the purpose for which they are spent. But that control is quite limited. When government provided poor people with surplus food, it had some degree of influence over the nutritional content and variety of what recipients ate. People who qualify for food stamps eat pretty much what they choose. Government controls public school curricula and personnel practices. Vouchers give parents wide latitude in choosing what their children learn and by whom they are taught. Vouchers greatly expand the liberty of recipients but at the price of reducing democratic political control over how disadvantaged children are educated and whether they receive adequate nourishment.

A Third Way: Reinventing Government

Advocates of privatization and vouchers share the low opinion of public servants held by advocates of greater public participation and more stringent judicial review. They believe that bureaucrats are, at best, automatons; at worst, fools, slackers, and tools of powerful interests. This negative view was challenged by the most recent major attempt at administrative reform, President Bill Clinton's initiative of "reinventing government."

Clinton's reinvention task force report placed the blame for governmental failure on the hamstringing of the bureaucracy by the imposition of too many rules and by excessive intervention by Congress, not on the bureaucrats themselves:

> The federal government is filled with good people trapped in bad systems, procurement systems, financial management systems, information systems . . . effective, entrepreneurial governments transform their cultures. They empower those who work on the frontlines to make more of their own decisions and solve their own problems.

Once again the pendulum had swung back in the direction of risking bureaucratic license as the price for avoiding red tape.

Clinton's reinventing government program sought to restore to bureaucrats the discretion that previous reformers had removed. The idea of empowerment was not exactly the same as Wilson's notion of expertise. It was based more on a faith in the creativity and common sense of bureaucrats than on their specialized knowledge. But the program did share Wilson's belief that if politicians formulated sensible policies, bureaucrats were sufficiently talented and public spirited to effectively administer them. True to Clinton's commitment to a "third way" between excessive reliance on and contempt for government, reinvention sought to both check and strengthen government all at the same time.

The reinvention initiative was a response to both dissatisfaction with previous reform efforts and the specific political circumstances faced by the new Clinton administration. Clinton was the first Democrat elected in sixteen years. Like other modern Democratic presidents, he viewed government as a vital instrument for progress. But he came to power at a time of profound skepticism of it. Ronald Reagan had claimed that "government is the problem." Although George H. W. Bush was less hostile to government, he had suffered politically for reneging on his "no new taxes" pledge in order to pay for more government. Clinton recognized that in order to promote an ambitious policy agenda, he had to convince the public that government could indeed be made to function more efficiently and effectively. When, five years later, the Brookings Institution issued a "Reinventing Government Report Card," it gave Clinton an A for effort, acknowledging that no previous president had been as committed to the task of improving the machinery of government. To make his proposals credible, Clinton was frank in acknowledging the depth of the problem.

> The Defense Department owns more than $40 billion in unnecessary supplies. The Internal Revenue Service struggles to collect billions in unpaid bills . . . ineffective regulation of the financial industry brought us the savings and loan debacle. Ineffective education and training programs jeopardize our competitive edge. . . . We spend $25 billion a year on welfare, $27 billion on food stamps and $13 billion on public housing – yet more Americans fall into poverty every year.

The report coupled defense of bureaucratic discretion with a call for making public agencies more "customer driven." The obstacle, the report indicated, was not the bureaucrats who served these "customers," but the excessive red tape that prevented bureaucrats from serving them well. But the report begged the question of who the customers of public administration actually were. For the most part it seemed to consider the customers to be those people who made use of agency services or who were subject to regulation and inspection. But what about the rest of America? Public agencies are also meant to do the bidding of citizens who do not benefit directly from government agencies; such citizens don't necessarily want agencies who are charged with inspecting restaurants or controlling air pollution to be too cozy with their "customers."

Reinvention's most noteworthy success was its reduction of the federal workforce. Between 1993 and 2000, the federal civilian workforce declined by 426,200 positions to the lowest total since the Kennedy administration. Virtually every civilian agency was also cut back. Reducing the size of the federal government does not necessarily make it more efficient and may well hamper its effectiveness. But in view of the pressure on Clinton to show that he would not emulate previous Democratic administrations by swelling bureaucracy, this reduction was a considerable political, if not administrative, accomplishment.

The federal government also succeeded in reducing the cost of supplies, although the reinvention task force's claim of a 12.3-billion dollar savings was viewed by some experts as high. Likewise, customers of

Holiday travelers in 2006 felt the effects of the U.S. Department of Homeland Security's tightened restrictions, as spokesperson Lara Uselding displayed a properly packed bag with three-ounce or smaller containers among confiscated household items at O'Hare Airport, Chicago.

some agencies, meaning people who regularly interact with those agencies, reported great service improvements. But the success of reinvention's broader objectives has proven impossible to judge, because the objectives are either too vague or too subject to diverse and potentially contradictory interpretation.

Homeland Security

Whatever momentum had been established during the 1980s and 1990s toward shrinking the federal government was halted and reversed by

September 11. Before September 11, 2001, the nation's antiterrorism effort resembled the early republic's effort to provide military security through militias. Airport security was supervised by state and local governments and was performed by the airlines themselves. Investigation of biological threats was largely in the hands of local public health departments. In the wake of the attack on the World Trade Center and the Pentagon and the anthrax attacks that took place in the months that followed, the demand for federal intervention drastically increased. The militia phase was over. This devastating attack on the nation's largest city destroyed the comforting illusion that war was something that only happened on foreign soil. The new Department of Homeland Security represented the most ambitious reorganization of the federal government in half a century (since the creation of the Department of Defense). As noted in Chapter 8, President Bush had initially resisted forming another government department. After considerable prodding from Congress, however, the Bush administration agreed to support legislation creating a vast new department to cope with the domestic threat of terror. The Department of Homeland Security (DHS), established in 2003, is the third largest cabinet department in the U.S. federal government after the Department of Defense (DOD) and Department of Veterans Affairs (DVA). As of 2004, it had more than 180,000 employees. Most of those employees are not new, they were transferred to the new department from existing departments including treasury, agriculture, energy, transportation, state, commerce, and health and human services as well as such previously independent agencies as the Federal Emergency Management Agency (FEMA). Table 10.1 lists the agencies that became part of the DHS as a result of the 2003 reorganization.

The centralized approach to homeland security, which DHS embodies, poses grave problems for American liberty. It blurs the distinction between civil and military matters, which the Constitution strives to maintain, and it also greatly aggravates the difficulties that stem from the bureaucratic license–red tape trade-off. These problems cannot easily be remedied because they stem from the very nature of the threat that terrorism poses. The terrorists who perpetrated the September 11 attacks and who continue to plan destructive acts on U.S. soil are not ordinary criminals. They go back and forth between their safe harbors abroad and their targets in the United States taking advantage of technical and financial assistance from terror networks around the globe. Protection of U.S. citizens from terror attack cannot rely on local police or even be viewed as a purely police activity. It needs to call upon a full array of national and international police, military, counterespionage, and border patrol authorities. It therefore militarizes policing and centralizes protection

Table 10.1. Agencies of the Department of Homeland Security

Border and Transportation Security
U.S. Customs Service
Immigration and Naturalization Service
Federal Protective Service
Transportation Security Administration (TSA)
Federal Law Enforcement Training Center
Animal and Plant Health Inspection Service
Office for Domestic Preparedness
Federal Emergency Management Agency (FEMA)
Strategic National Stockpile and the National Disaster Medical System (HHS)
Nuclear Incident Response Team
Domestic Emergency Support Teams
National Domestic Preparedness Office
Science and Technology
Chemical, Biological, Radiological, and Nuclear (CBRN) Countermeasures Programs
Environmental Measurements Laboratory
National Bio-Weapons (BW) Defense Analysis Center
Plum Island Animal Disease Center
Information Analysis and Infrastructure Protection
Federal Computer Incident Response Center
National Communications System
National Infrastructure Protection Center
Energy Security and Assurance Program
U.S. Secret Service
U.S. Coast Guard

---

of the homeland to an unprecedented degree. Unfortunately, a force capable of defending the homeland against the especially dangerous and difficult-to-detect threat of terror is inevitably one with the potential to deprive innocent citizens of their liberties. Thus, the persistence of an international terrorist movement threatens both the safety of Americans and, as a result of what it takes to combat terror, their liberties as well.

A crucial means for diminishing the threat to liberty posed by heightened homeland security is to make sure that those responsible for protecting the public are not granted too much license. As one stands in interminable airport security lines, one is tempted to scream, "I am not a terrorist, can't you tell." Indeed, efforts are underway to expedite security for those who fly regularly and can show evidence that they pose no risk. But a decent respect for civil liberties precludes one from advocating security measures that target "suspicious persons." The whole spirit of the Constitution, and especially the Bill of Rights, speaks against giving bureaucrats license to decide whom to search and whom to ignore. The courts and the president have spoken out against "profiling," the singling out of specific religious and ethnic groups for more careful and intrusive searches. The alternative to letting the airport security screeners single people out is to treat everyone the same, and so we endure the long lines and intrusive searches that stem from regarding every airline traveler as a potential terrorist.

Conclusion

This chapter has chronicled the difficulties of making the bureaucracy effective, accountable, and respectful of American liberties, all at the same time. It has shown how at different eras in American political development different methods for accomplishing these goals have been relied upon including choosing people of good character, rotation in office, civil service examinations, professionalism, executive oversight, congressional oversight, judicial review, private sector competition, and public participation. Although none of these approaches has "solved" the problems bureaucracy poses for liberty and democracy, especially the bureaucratic license-red tape trade-off, each one has made a critical contribution to enabling Americans to enjoy the public benefits that national administration provides without succumbing to bureaucratic despotism.

The key to appreciating the successes as well as the failures of these attempts to reconcile administration, liberty, and democracy is to place the issue in a constitutional perspective. The Constitution does not rely on any one means for protecting American freedom – rather it provides a complex mix of separation of powers, federalism, and limited government. Likewise, coping with the bureaucracy requires a mix of different methods and approaches that are consonant with constitutional principles, the most fundamental of which is limited government. The Constitution does not view government as an all-purpose problem solver. Therefore, it teaches Americans to limit their expectations about what bureaucrats can or should do for them. It also enables each of the three branches to challenge the discretion of bureaucrats via congressional oversight, judicial review, and intervention by an arm of the Executive Office of the President, respectively. Each of these approaches has severe limitations. But, taken as a whole, they succeed in making bureaucrats responsive to democratically chosen representatives and executives and to the judiciary.

The Constitution is also compatible with the other useful means employed to check or improve bureaucracy. Free enterprise is a principle that can and has been usefully applied to doing the public's business. Having to compete with private companies to provide various services forces bureaucrats to strive to cut costs to improve service or risk losing their jobs and funding. Public participation requirements also serve to reduce bureaucratic insularity by forcing bureaucrats to answer questions and respond to criticisms posed by ordinary citizens in open meetings. Because the Constitution does not establish a federal government monopoly over education and training, the way is open for a wide variety of state, local, and private educational efforts to flourish. A great legacy of the Progressive movement has been the establishment of schools of public policy and public administration, both public and private, whose mission is to improve the understanding and skills of those who seek public service careers. Scandals still occur, but the overall trend in public management at all levels of government has been in the direction of greater professionalism and probity. And, because these training centers are not themselves arms of the federal government, they can criticize and propose alternatives to the policies and methods of the incumbent administration to an extent that would be unthinkable if they were themselves under government control.

Chapter Summary

☆ License and red tape are the two greatest obstacles to responsible bureaucratic decision making.

☆ By European standards, the American bureaucracy has always seemed incompetent. But it is also less intrusive and despotic. In bureaucracy, as in so many other aspects of political life, Americans opted for liberty even at the price of effective government.

☆ Choices made during America's formative period about how to design and manage bureaucracy continue to influence it even as the principle of limited government has become less decisive in controlling government's scope and reach.

☆ Providing for national security without threatening individual freedom was the nation's first great administrative challenge. Its approach to this problem would come to typify its approach to public administration in general.

☆ The so-called spoils system was designed to enhance the power of political parties and diminish the antidemocratic threat posed by government centralization and elite rule.

☆ The transformation of the federal public service into a modern bureaucracy began with the passage of the 1883 Pendleton Act, which substituted competitive examinations for patronage in the allocation of administrative jobs.

☆ The New Deal drew heavily upon Progressive ideas to put in place the modern administrative state.

☆ The Great Depression, World War II, and the Cold War were major stimulants of the expansion of the modern administrative state.

☆ The postwar expansion of the administrative state increased concern about the impact of a vast public bureaucracy on liberty and democracy and efforts to reform it. These reform efforts were of two different kinds: efforts to perfect scientific, Wilsonian administration; and efforts to replace Wilsonian administration with alternative approaches based on rights, direct democracy, and markets.

☆ September 11 greatly heightened concern about homeland security leading to a vast expansion of administrative power directed toward diminishing the threat of terrorism and to the most ambitious bureaucratic reorganization in half a century, the creation of the new Department of Homeland Security.

Major Concepts

Administrative Procedures Act (APA)
affirmative action
Agricultural Adjustment Agency (AAA)
Antitrust Division of the Department of Justice
Bureau of the Budget (BOB)
Civilian Conservation Corps (CCC)
conservation
cost-benefit analysis
Department of Education
Department of Health, Education, and Welfare
Department of Housing and Urban Development
Department of the Interior
Department of Transportation
Department of Veterans Affairs
deregulation
Drug Enforcement Agency (DEA)
Environmental Impact Statement (EIS)
Executive Reorganization Act of 1939
food stamps
iron triangle
Legislative Reorganization Act of 1946
operations research
red tape
Securities and Exchange Commission (SEC)
War on Poverty
Works Progress Administration (WPA)

Suggested Readings

Arnold, Peri. *Making the Managerial Presidency: Comprehensive Organization Planning, 1905–1996,* 2d ed. Lawrence: University Press of Kansas, 1998.

Cook, Brian. *Bureaucracy and Self-Government: Reconsidering the Role of Public Administration in American Politics.* Baltimore, MD: Johns Hopkins University Press, 1996.

Derthick, Martha. *Agency under Stress: The Social Security Administration in American Government.* Washington, D.C.: Brookings Institution, 1990.

_____. *Policymaking for Social Security.* Washington, D.C.: Brookings Institution, 1979.

Kaufman, Herbert. *The Forest Ranger: A Study in Administrative Behavior.* Baltimore, MD: Johns Hopkins University Press, 1960.

Landy, Marc K., Marc J. Roberts, and Stephen R. Thomas. *The Environmental Protection Agency: Asking the Wrong Questions from Nixon to Clinton,* 2d exp. ed. New York: Oxford University Press, 1994.

Moynihan, Daniel P. *Maximum Feasible Misunderstanding: Community Action in the War on Poverty.* New York: Free Press, 1970.

Selznick, Philip. *TVA and the Grass Roots: A Study in Politics and Organization.* Berkeley: University of California Press, 1984.

Skowronek, Stephen. *Building a New American State: The Expansion of National Administrative Capacities, 1877–1920.* New York: Cambridge University Press, 1982.

White, Leonard. *The Federalists: A Study in Administrative History.* New York: Macmillan, 1948.

_____. *The Jacksonians: A Study in Administrative History.* New York: Macmillan, 1954.

_____. *The Jeffersonians: A Study in Administrative History, 1801–1829.* New York: Macmillan, 1951.

_____. *The Republican Era: A Study in Administrative History, 1869–1901.* New York: Macmillan, 1958.

Wildavsky, Aaron. *The New Politics of the Budget Process*, 2d ed. New York: Harper-Collins, 1999.

Wilson, James Q. *Bureaucracy: What Government Agencies Do and Why They Do It.* New York: Basic Books, 1989.

A famous saying of Thomas P. O'Neill, Jr., Speaker of the House of Representatives (1977–1988) was that " all politics is local," by which he meant that people's views on the big questions of politics are formed on the basis of what directly affects them, their families, and their communities. It is therefore all the more surprising to notice that the later sections of each of the preceding chapters in Part 3 are dominated by issues relating to questions of global import: the dispute between Congress and the president over the Iraq War, the judicial rights of foreign terrorists, the president's role as commander-in-chief, and the new responsibilities of the federal bureaucracy for protecting the homeland against terror attack. Speaker O'Neill was not wrong to emphasize people's preoccupation with local concerns, it is just that now what affects one's immediate safety and prosperity is inextricably linked to economic, military, and environmental activities occurring thousands of miles away. Today, all politics is global.

The increased sense of American vulnerability to foreign pressures is reminiscent of the early years of the American Republic when political life in the United States was dominated by the threats to its existence emanating from Britain, France, and Spain. The fragile new state was able to survive only because those powers preferred to war among themselves rather than to fully exploit its frailty. But now, American vulnerability is more related to the nation's strength than to its weakness.

The end of the Cold War left the United States as the unchallenged global military power. In 2005, world military spending amounted to approximately 1 trillion dollars and the United States accounted for almost half of that total. It spends ten times as much as the second biggest military spender, the United Kingdom. The United States is also by far the richest country in the world. Its Gross Domestic Product is almost three times the size of its closest rival, Japan. Why should a nation that is so much richer and mightier than any other feel vulnerable?

One source of American vulnerability stems from its dependence on foreign energy. Because it produces so many goods and its population can afford to own and drive so many automobiles, the United States consumes one quarter of the world's oil production. But it produces less than 10 percent of the world total. Therefore, it must import the majority of the oil it needs from abroad. Most foreign oil is located in politically volatile parts of the world: the Middle East, Nigeria, Venezuela, and Russia. If upheavals in those regions and countries radically reduced the availability of oil, the price in the United States and elsewhere would skyrocket, crippling the U.S. and the world economies.

A second source of vulnerability stems from dependence on foreign credit. Currently, the United States owes foreign bondholders – Japan, China, and others – almost two trillion dollars. If those lenders chose to demand their money back, interest rates would have to shoot up to entice them to lend it again. If interest rates rise on one form of debt, government bonds, they will rise on other forms of debt as well because those other forms have to compete with bonds to attract lenders. Therefore, interest rates would rise on consumer credit as well, whether it be in the form of credit cards, installment loans, or any other manner in which people borrow to buy things. Consumer credit is the fuel that makes the American economy hum. American consumers spend vastly more than they earn. They buy flat screen televisions, iPods, SUVs, and trips to Disneyworld on credit. If the U.S. government's foreign creditors decided to call in their loans, heavily indebted American consumers would not be able to keep up with the precipitous rises in interest rates that would ensue. Massive inflation and a huge rise in personal and corporate bankruptcies would follow.

Perhaps these potential economic debacles will never take place. They would prove as disastrous for the producers of oil and for foreign lenders as they would for the United States. Oil producers need foreign sales to keep their populations comfortable and politically calm. Foreign lenders will themselves go bankrupt if their debtors are unable to pay them back. But September 11 gruesomely revealed another form of vulnerability that cannot be avoided, U.S. vulnerability to terrorism.

War on Terror

For all its horrors, terrorism is a very weak form of warfare; indeed, for the most part, it avoids military engagement altogether. Terrorists prey on unarmed civilians because pipe bombs and belts of explosives are no match for determined and well equipped armies. Terrorists' most successful attacks require them to commit suicide. But it is precisely the desire of a rich and powerful country like the United States to enjoy the fruits of its wealth and power that makes it so vulnerable to this weak form of attack. Despite previous airline highjackings and the 1993 bombing of the World Trade Center, Americans chose to continue to enjoy the luxury of living and traveling with minimal intrusion from costly and cumbersome security efforts. When U.S. embassies in Kenya and Tanzania were bombed by

Al Queda in 1998, America contented itself with a perfunctory effort at retaliation, a few missiles lobbed at suspected Al Queda chemical weapons factories in the Sudan and training camps in Afghanistan.

Only the massive devastation of September 11 roused the United States to recognize that wealth and power by themselves created targets for, not protection from, terrorism. By attacking the World Trade Center, Al Qaeda was demonstrating that being the center of the world's commerce and finance was not enough to protect New York City from devastation. To protect itself, the United States would need to engage in levels of heightened vigilance and military commitment ordinarily reserved for a full-scale war. The United States would have to choose between the tragedies and anxieties caused by terror and the arduous, expensive, and ethically dubious undertakings that combating terror involves.

The deepest question the War on Terror raises is whether it is possible to fight terrorists without coming to resemble them. Can civil liberties be retained when the enemy is seeking to take advantage of those liberties to destroy the regime responsible for securing those rights? Can the United States wage war against terror abroad while still maintaining a decent regard for the rights of other people and a capacity to resist the tyrannical temptations that inevitably accompany foreign conquest?

Civil Liberties and Homeland Security

Because terror does not respect the rules of war, fighting it inevitably undermines civil liberties. Terrorists take advantage of the ordinary civilities of life to escape detection. They do not wear uniforms but rather pose as ordinary civilians. They conceal both their deadly purposes and the weapons they use to accomplish those purposes. They use places and forms of organization normally exempted from scrutiny – mosques, charitable foundations – to provide cover for their activities. Therefore, the antiterror effort requires levels of surveillance of ordinary people and of intrusion into the inner workings of religious and philanthropic endeavors that would otherwise not be tolerated.

Because terror activities are so hard to detect, combating them relies heavily on the use of informants. Protecting those informants may mean denying terror suspects the cherished constitutional right to confront one's accuser. There is no simple, reliable means of determining when these moral and constitutional intrusions have gone too far. The terror threat is always open to abuse by those who have other motives for wanting to intrude into the personal and religious activities of ethnic and religious groups they do not approve of and who are willing to fabricate criminal accusations against members of those same groups.

Baghdad not Boston

The September 11 terrorists were all citizens of Middle Eastern countries and their headquarters was in Afghanistan. Perhaps the most fateful and controversial decision made by the Bush administration in the wake of September 11 was to interpret the attacks in New York, Washington, and in the skies above Pennsylvania as constituting a declaration of war by those foreign nations providing safe harbor for terrorists, most importantly Afghanistan. The idea was to take the offensive against terror by fighting it abroad, where terrorists trained and where they planned their attacks, rather than remaining on the defensive waiting for them to strike on American soil. Later, the definition of who constituted the enemy was expanded to include Iraq. The argument was made that American security was best protected by fighting terrorists in Baghdad not Boston.

The case against Iraq had several parts. Iraq was in violation of UN-sanctioned resolutions regarding chemical, biological, and nuclear arms; it had expelled UN arms inspectors. Then, years later, when it readmitted them, it restricted their freedom of access. It stood accused of the mass murder of Kurds and Shiites. The intelligence services of Britain, Egypt, and the United States, among others, provided reports indicating that Iraq possessed weapons of mass destruction and was in contact with Al Qaeda leaders. The rationale for the attack was not simply that the Saddam Hussein regime was evil, which it was, but rather that the evidence of past misbehavior served as a guide for probable future behavior. Given that he had declared himself to be an enemy of the West and was unwilling to submit to UN rules, the September 11 attacks left Saddam with only two choices. He could either ally himself with Al Qaeda, providing them with bases and weapons, or he could do what the leader of another "rogue" state, Moammar Khaddafi, would later do, renounce hostility to the United States and fully open his country to UN weapons inspections. Saddam refused to adopt the second option and therefore he was assumed to be adopting the first.

Opponents of the invasion did not dispute the evil of the Saddam regime, nor initially did they dispute the likelihood that it possessed weapons of mass destruction. Instead, they doubted whether Saddam posed a sufficient threat to the security of American allies to warrant an invasion. They pointed out that whatever his other sins, Saddam was not a radical fundamentalist and would therefore be unlikely to make common cause with Al Qaeda. They felt that given the human and economic costs of invasion, and the deep opposition of most of America's allies, more was to be gained by trying to contain Iraq. They advocated the continued imposition of economic sanctions and a renewed effort to mobilize the world community and world public opinion against it.

The decision to go to war against both Afghanistan and Iraq, neither of whom had declared war on the United States or engaged their national armies against the United States or its allies, raises profound questions about the meaning of liberty and democracy in an international context and about the impact on U.S. domestic life created by this highly aggressive military posture.

Although no enforceable law of war exists, the normal presumption is that a nation should only go to war in the face of imminent danger of attack. The invisibility of the terror threat calls that notion into question. Unlike troops, terrorists do not mass at the border making their presence known to the object of their attack. Terrorists rely on surprise and subterfuge to overcome their inherent military inferiority. Therefore, the United States has insisted that it cannot await unambiguous evidence of an imminent attack. It reserves the right to strike first if it has a strong suspicion that terrorists are preparing to launch an attack. This doctrine is called pre-emption. It was invoked as a rationale for the attack against Iraq. Iraq had not initiated hostilities against the United States nor had it foresworn doing so. The claim was made that the diverse evidence of its ill intentions made it a sufficient threat to warrant attacking it.

Even if the nature of international terror provides a strong rationale for this doctrine, pre-emption poses grave risks to liberty and democracy because it is so easily subject to abuse. Democracy requires that citizens have a say in whether or not they will be called upon to fight and die. In the face of clear and present danger, that choice is so stark that citizens can readily make it. But when the evidence is at best ambiguous, as it is likely to be in any case involving the threat of terror, how is the citizen to make a sensible decision? How is one to know whether indeed one's leaders really do have sound reasons to interpret the ambiguous evidence to mean that war is necessary? Or, are they acting out of motives and ambitions with which the citizen does not sympathize?

This democratic problem is at the heart of the continued controversy about the Iraq War. Supporters of the war stress that because Iraq would not provide full access to its facilities and because it had banned UN inspectors for so long, the reasonable presumption was that Saddam Hussein did in fact have weapons of mass destruction and therefore posed a grave danger to the security of the United States and its allies. As the administration has been forced to admit that its initial intelligence about Iraqi weapons of mass destruction was inaccurate, opponents came to doubt not only the competence of the administration but also its truthfulness and its motives, the facts upon which this interpretation is based. Many believe that those leaders duped the public, withholding and misrepresenting key facts in order to strengthen the case for a war the Bush administration wished to fight but one that was unnecessary and misguided from the point of view of protecting Americans from terror. If those allegations are true, then the Iraq invasion was indeed antidemocratic.

Going It Alone

The United States entered World Wars I and II and the first Gulf War as part of a broad-based alliance of nations. In Korea, it fought on behalf of the UN. The support of the world's leading liberal democratic regimes and of the UN itself substantiated the claim that those wars were being fought in the cause of freedom. The United States has not been able to construct a similarly broad international consensus for the War on Terror. The UN Security Council refused to endorse the attack on Iraq. France and Germany were actively opposed to it. Japan was supportive but Britain and Poland were the only major democratic nations to send troops. In early 2007, Britain announced that it was withdrawing its troops. Instead of leading a worldwide coalition of free nations, many of them blame the United States for endangering freedom by virtue of its unilateral actions. They claim that the United States exaggerated the threat posed by Saddam's regime to provide a spurious rationale for establishing an imperial presence in the Middle East. The Empire of Liberty stands accused of acting like an empire.

"You Break It, You Own It"

Whether or not the United States was justified in attacking Afghanistan and Iraq, it now faces the challenge of helping them reconstitute themselves as decent regimes. If the United States fails to do so, such nations will most likely return to their former policies of providing safe harbor for terrorism. Former Secretary of State Colin Powell called this the "Pottery Barn Rule": "You break it, you own it." As both Iraq and Afghanistan showed, it is far easier for the United States to make use of its extraordinary military weaponry and skilled soldiers to defeat an enemy than it is to reconstruct a stable and law-abiding political order in the conquered territory. In Iraq, the inability of American troops to protect the personal security of ordinary Iraqis led to a complete breakdown of law and order. Criminal gangs and sectarian militias often proved more successful than the U.S.-backed Iraqi government in imposing order and controlling behavior.

Such failures leave the United States with a stark choice. It can either refrain from "breaking" nations that threaten it and accept the risk that those nations will expand the level and scope of the threat they pose to U.S. security or, in line with the Pottery Barn Rule, it can develop more

The recent Iraq War is the most current example of America's struggle to manage its global economic and political dominance with its national interests in security while remaining a cooperative international player and defender of civil liberties at home.

effective means for bringing about the political and economic reconstruction of its enemies. But the Pottery Barn Rule imposes a very heavy financial and moral burden. It requires a vast expansion in the already large military budget in order to provide the vast amounts of troops necessary to perform the policing duties that restoring law and order requires. And, it puts Americans in the morally awkward position of telling other people how to run their affairs and punishing them when they fail to satisfy American standards. This is a level of intrusiveness that is normally imposed only by empires on the peoples they subjugate. The hardest challenge posed by the terror threat is to force America to demonstrate that Jefferson's term, the Empire of Liberty, is not an oxymoron. Somehow, it must learn to act like an empire in the sense of using its great strength to defend a peaceful and decent world order while resisting the illiberal and antidemocratic temptations of empire: to oppress and victimize the weak and the dependent, to ignore and slight its friends, to reduce its citizens to imperial subjects, and to attack when and where it wants to just because it can.

PART FOUR
Political Forces

11 Parties and Elections

This chapter focuses on:

☆ The impact of political parties on liberty and democracy

☆ The origins of the two current major political parties and the creation of a political party system

☆ The role of political party in preserving the Union

☆ The continual efforts to reform political parties to make them more democratic and less corrupt

☆ The makeup of past and present party coalitions

☆ The key issues that currently divide the two parties and that are most critical in determining party identification

In 2001, Michael Bloomberg, a lifelong Democrat, deserted his party to accept the Republican nomination for mayor of New York City and was elected. In statewide and national elections, the city votes overwhelmingly for Democrats, but Bloomberg's predecessor, Rudolph Giuliani, was also a Republican. In July of 2002, Bloomberg named a charter revision commission to recommend amendments to the city charter, one of which would be for the purpose of adopting non-partisan city elections. In a statement accompanying the announcement, Bloomberg explained that *non-partisan elections* had already been adopted by a number of American cities, including Atlanta, Boston, Chicago, Denver, Detroit, and Los Angeles. Instead of *party primaries*, candidates for all city offices would be chosen in a single primary open to all voters. In both the primary and the general election, candidates' names would appear without party label. Bloomberg claimed that abolishing *partisan elections* would "prevent the small number of people who vote in party primaries from determining the course of the election. . . . We should not let party bosses dictate who gets into office." This attack on political parties echoed the decades-old refrain of Progressive reformers that citizens should "vote for the man, or woman, not the party."

Of course, Bloomberg had a practical reason for ending partisan city elections. Because the Republican party is vastly outnumbered in New York City, his reelection chances would improve if he did not have to identify himself with it. His advocacy of non-partisan elections does not necessarily make him a hypocrite. When the rules of the political game change, someone always benefits and someone always loses. Perhaps, in this case, what would be good for Michael Bloomberg would also be good for New York City.

Is Mayor Bloomberg correct in thinking that New York City would be a freer and a more democratic place if it were governed on a non-partisan basis? Supporters of political parties would dispute him. They see political party as an essential means for enabling democracy to operate effectively on a mass scale. They point to the depressing effect that removal of party labels has on voter turnout and the difficulty that voters have in distinguishing between candidates who cannot be identified on the basis of party.

The United States has the oldest continuously operating political *party system* in the world. Every president since 1852 has either been elected to office as a Republican or a Democrat. Both houses of Congress have been controlled either by the Republicans or the Democrats since 1849. During the 1990s, the party cohesion index – which measures the tendency of congressional Democrats to vote the same way as other congressional Democrats and congressional Republicans to vote the same way as other

A former Democrat, New York mayor Michael Bloomberg won the Republican party nomination and called for non-partisan elections in the nation's largest city. He subsequently won reelection in 2005, pictured above.

congressional Republicans – was at its highest level ever. And yet when people talk about "party politics," it is usually in a scornful tone. Many voters register as independents. Although influential political scientists such as V. O. Key, Jr., have stressed the importance of robust political parties for strengthening and maintaining democracy, many voters agreed with Bloomberg that parties are run by "bosses" and that party control of the electoral process stifles the voice of the people.

This chapter examines the mystery of political party and its strong but testy relationship with democracy and liberty. A study of the development of political parties helps the reader to think about whether a democratic republic as big as the United States can function without them and whether the democratic claims made for them are believable. This chapter examines the concept of a party system and the role played by party realignments in enabling ordinary citizens to become involved in crucial constitutional debates. We divide the development of parties into seven periods: the origins of party; the establishment of a party system; the advent of the enduring two-party system; the impact of Populism and Progressivism on political party; the transformation of parties during the New Deal; the resurgence of the Republicans that has taken place since the 1950s; and the current state of the parties, including an assessment of likely future trends. The chapter concludes with a reconsideration of the key democratic and liberal functions that political parties are supposed to perform and some questions about their continued ability to perform them.

When Alexis de Tocqueville examined the American political parties of the 1830s, he called them "small," meaning that there were no deep differences of principle between them. Great parties were nobler because they embodied profound, principled differences. Unfortunately, such differences were so profound that great parties could not coexist. A successful party system more resembles a sports league. The fans cheer and boo vociferously, and some curse when the team loses. But within a short period of time, the fans shrug off defeat and look forward to the next contest.

The sports analogy is imperfect because American political parties do have principled differences, but those differences do not extend to the most essential political questions. Neither great nor small, American parties are best thought of as middle-sized, at least under ordinary circumstances. During times of crisis, however, one or the other party grows in stature, provoking and enabling the citizenry to participate in epochal debates over the meaning and character of the constitutional order. In Chapter 4, we termed these turning points in American political development, "refoundings." It is no coincidence that the way for each of these refoundings was paved by the emergence of a new political party – the Jeffersonian Republicans in the 1790s, the Lincolnian Republicans in the late 1850s – or the rejuvenation of a moribund party – the Jacksonian Democrats in the late 1820s and the New Deal Democrats in the early 1930s. In Chapter 4, we stressed the role of the president in promoting these refoundings. In this chapter, we supplement that view by describing the critical role of party and of presidential party leadership in refoundings.

Parties are built around the effort to win elections. Therefore, a discussion of the impact of political parties on the American political order must also include a consideration of how elections have been and are conducted. As this chapter examines the development of American political parties, it also describes how that development has been influenced by changes in the rules governing elections and in the methods and technologies of electoral campaigning. Box 1 looks at a critical contemporary political issue regarding voting and democracy.

Box One: Contemporary Politics

Go to the Polls or Vote at Home

In a representative democracy, perhaps the most important civic act that most people perform is to vote. If the fraction of people who vote is small, it is very difficult to claim that the candidate elected indeed represents the majority of citizens and that the election was therefore democratic. In Chapter 12, we will discuss the declining levels of voter participation in the United States and the problems that causes. But here we are asking a more fundamental question: why vote? Every once in awhile, an election is so close that an individual voter can really believe that a single vote matters. But, almost always, the margin in an election is large enough to render that conclusion unreasonable. As long as a lot of other people vote, why should I?

One response to this problem is to make voting as easy as possible. All states enable a registered voter to vote by mail, but the procedure for obtaining a mail ballot is often cumbersome and time consuming. In practice, only a small fraction of citizens vote by mail, except in Oregon where almost *everyone* votes by mail. In 1998, voters passed a ballot measure directing all elections to be conducted by mail, commonly called "vote by mail." A voters' pamphlet is mailed to every household in Oregon about three weeks before each statewide election. It includes information about each measure and candidate in the upcoming election. Ballots are mailed to every registered voter fourteen to eighteen days before the election. They fill out the ballot, sign it, and mail it back. Mailed ballots are accepted anytime until 8pm of election day. This means that the voter has the liberty to vote anytime he or she wants over a period of almost two weeks and to do so in the comfort of his or her own home. County election commissions do provide places for voters to vote in person but it is not encouraged and very few do so.

Opponents of electronic voting argue that Oregon has missed the point. The fundamental problem is not that voting is hard but that it appears pointless. They argue that the proper answer is to emphasize the importance of voting as a ritual. People do not go to church, or to parades for that matter, because it is easy. They go because they think they should or because it makes them feel part of something. The problem with voting by mail, or, as some reformers have proposed, computer voting, is not that it is too easy but that it is too private. It is done in isolation. By restricting voting to one day and making people go out in public, the occasion acquires the air of a holiday. At the polls, banners wave; friends greet one another; the airwaves are saturated with speculation about the outcome. Obviously, voters will still not participate if it is too difficult to do so: if they must skip work, if they are confused about the location of their polling place, or if the polling place is too far away. But the appropriate reform would then be to make participation in elections both acceptably easy and very public. Ensure that voters know where to go and what evidence they must produce to prove they are who they say they are. Perhaps election day should be moved to the weekend so that fewer people would have to skip work. It could be held on both Saturdays and Sundays so that no one would have to vote on their Sabbath.

Supporters of the Oregon plan reply that voting by mail need not discourage campaign activities. Bill Bradbury, Oregon's secretary of state, the officer in charge of elections, claims that indeed Oregon experiences as many community activities promoting voting as anywhere. He claims that during the two-week voting period before election day, voters are inundated with ads and mailings and other appeals about the importance of voting. He claims that such activities are more important than the actual trek to the polls in creating a sense of community excitement about voting.

So far, only one other state, Washington, has moved in the vote-by-mail direction. It allows each of its thirty-four counties to decide whether to use polling places or mail voting. Thirty of its thirty-four counties have adopted vote by mail.

There is no real evidence that vote by mail has either discouraged or encouraged voting. Compared to other states, Oregon voter participation is relatively high, but it was high before vote by mail as well. Turnout in a particular election is affected by so many factors – most important, the degree of controversy a particular contest elicits – that it is very hard to tease out the specific impact of mail versus in-person voting. In the absence of substantial evidence, deciding between the two approaches to voting is mostly a matter of playing one's hunch either that voters will respond positively to making voting as easy as possible or that the trip to the polls produces its own incentive to vote.

The Birth of Parties

The United States prides itself on being a constitutional republic and yet its most important political organizations are not even mentioned in the Constitution. All the other key components of the political order – Congress, the executive, the judiciary, and the states – are described in the Constitution, but political parties are not. This omission is no accident. The drafters of the Constitution disagreed about many things, but they all shared Mayor Bloomberg's antipathy to parties. The Framers tried their best to produce a governing blueprint that would make parties unnecessary and difficult to form.

The root of the word party is "part." The Founders were concerned about the "whole." They saw parties as efforts to form majority *factions* that would substitute partial interests for the common good. The elaborate structure of separation of powers and checks and balances in the Constitution was designed to keep such a majority faction from forming. The very idea of the large republic described in "Federalist No. 10" was conceived as a defense against party (see Appendix 3). The republic's size would encourage factions to proliferate and thus would keep any single one from growing large and strong enough to dominate.

The Founders were not of one mind on the subject of democracy. But both those in favor of democracy and those wary of democracy found reasons to oppose party. The Framers who most feared tyranny of the majority believed that party would enable the untutored masses to deprive others of their liberty. The Framers who feared elitism expected defenders of privilege to cunningly use party to manipulate the masses, depriving the people of their liberty and their democratic powers.

And yet, unwittingly, the founding generation created electoral laws that favored the very thing they so desperately opposed, a strong two-party system. The Constitution itself does little to specify how national elections are to be conducted. Presidential electors were to be chosen by the states, but state legislatures were free to choose them as they wished. Likewise, state legislatures were assigned the responsibility of determining the "time, place and manner" of holding elections for senators and members of the House, and they had complete discretion about how to choose their state legislators and governors. Thus, state legislators could have adopted a proportional method for choosing state legislative and congressional representatives. Instead, they carved their states into state legislative and congressional districts, each of which chose a single representative on a plurality basis. *Proportional representation* encourages the growth of several political parties since it does not require a large fraction of the vote to elect at least one representative to office. *Single member districts* favor two parties because only one candidate can win in a single district. Therefore, the "outs" have a strong incentive to band together in support of a single challenger to defeat the incumbent. Awarding victory to the candidate with the most votes, even if the candidate lacks a majority, avoids the need for a runoff election between the two top finishers. Therefore, it deprives smaller parties whose candidates came in third or worse of the political leverage they would have had if one or the other of the top finishers needed their support to gain a majority in the runoff. The decision of almost all states to also award presidential electors on a winner take all plurality basis played precisely the same role in discouraging multiple parties that single member districts and plurality election played in legislative races. These three choices regarding the ground rules for conducting elections are a large part of the reason that with only a few brief exceptions the United States has always had a two-party political system.

The First Party

Despite the Founders' opposition to party, parties began to grow during the very first years of the Republic. By 1800, Thomas Jefferson, the leader of the first full-fledged party – the Republicans – had been elected president. That party was the direct ancestor of the modern-day Democratic party; today's Republican party has other roots. Political parties overcame the fears of the Founders and the obstacles forged by the Constitution because parties provided a very positive, even necessary, function. Rather than undermining the principles of liberty that the Constitution espouses, parties protected those principles. At critical moments in American political development, parties served as vehicles for stimulating and provoking profound public discussion and debate. They have also provided a welcoming political home for millions of Americans – immigrants, poor farmers, industrial workers – who had been otherwise excluded and victimized. Contrary to the Founders' expectations, parties have proven to be vital safeguards of American liberty and democracy. But parties have never entirely shed the disreputable image projected on them by the Founders. Current efforts to weaken parties build on the fears and suspicions about them that are as old as the Republic itself.

James Madison illustrates this profound ambivalence about political parties. He was the author of "Federalist No. 10," but within only a few years of the passage of the Constitution, he changed his mind about political parties. He had assumed that the greatest threat to the Republic came from the people. He feared that a majority would form and deprive others of their liberty. But Madison changed his mind as he watched Secretary of the Treasury Alexander Hamilton – his former partner in the writing of *The Federalist Papers* – strive to amass greater power for the national executive. Madison decided that this centralization of power in the hands of the few was an even greater threat to liberty. The only way to combat this evil was to organize the many to take power away from Hamilton and his cronies, and so the Republican party was born.

Because prevailing opinion was so hostile to party, Madison and Jefferson's party-building efforts were very circumspect. In May of 1791, these two Virginians went on a "botanizing" expedition to the Northeast. Why would Secretary of State Jefferson and Congressman Madison take time out from their important governing responsibilities to look at northern plants unless those flowers and shrubs happened to reside in the backyards of important political personages whose support the two Virginians sought to cultivate? By August of 1791, Jefferson was writing letters to men he had identified as opponents of the Washington administration, urging them to run for Congress. He convinced Madison's friend, Philip Freneau, to start an opposition newspaper in Philadelphia, funded in part through printing contracts with the state department. Madison and Jefferson were both Southerners, Virginians. To create a truly national party, they needed to cement alliances with budding Northern political organizations such as the one Aaron Burr was creating in New York. The bond that these men established between New York and Virginia proved critical to the infant Republican party.

At the same time that an opposition was forming among prominent politicians, ordinary citizens were voicing their indignation at the pro-British tilt of the Washington administration. In more than thirty cities, societies calling themselves "Republican" or "Democratic" arose to support America's sister republic and Revolutionary War ally, France (see Chapter 12 for a full discussion of Democratic-Republican societies). These societies soon died, but their members gravitated to the Republicans and provided the party with new members and leaders. Schooled in the societies' lively debates and discussions, they transferred this same democratic spirit to their party activities.

These different strands of opposition were woven together into the durable thread of party by a single catalytic event – the political furor caused by the Jay Treaty. The treaty was designed to solve a series of outstanding disputes with the British regarding prewar debts, continued British occupation of forts on the Northwest frontier, and the British navy's seizing of sailors aboard American ships. But because the treaty failed to produce full-fledged settlement of most of these outstanding issues, Madison, Jefferson, and their supporters saw it as a virtual capitulation to the British and a sellout of the French.

In the temporary national capital, Philadelphia, an informal committee formed to coordinate opposition to the treaty. For the first time, a major constitutional debate was organized on a party basis. The Constitution grants the power to ratify a treaty exclusively to the Senate. But the power to provide or withhold the funds necessary for implementing the terms of the treaty rested largely with the House of Representatives. By holding up those funds, the House was trying to intrude itself into the treaty-making process. A caucus of all Republican congressmen was convened to pressure them to oppose Washington's request for an appropriation to implement the treaty. Nonetheless, the appropriation passed and the intent of the Constitution was preserved.

In the election of 1796, a coordinated effort was made to defeat the members of Congress who defied the caucus vote and supported the treaty. Of the seven legislators targeted, four were defeated and two reversed their positions. Only one unrepentant incumbent was reelected. This success in punishing disloyalty shows that less than a decade after passage of the Constitution, a political organization had come into being that possessed all the crucial attributes of a political party – a mass membership, an ability to coordinate its activities, and mechanisms for imposing party discipline.

A Test of the Electoral College

The election of 1800 revealed the weakness of the Electoral College as a means for limiting the impact of direct democracy on the choice of a president. The Framers had intended the electors to be independent, exercising their own individual judgment about who would make the best president.

But in 1800, the Republican leaders in the capital coordinated with party organizations in the various states so that electors were selected as instructed agents of the party, pledged to vote for Jefferson. In 1800, most electors were selected by the state legislatures, but by 1824, ordinary voters had the opportunity in most states to elect a slate of electors who were pledged to one or the other party's candidate. And so it has been ever since. Political parties have made the process of Electoral College voting into a strictly mechanical one.

One other feature of the electoral college was formally changed to accommodate parties. In the original Constitution, the electors were to vote for two candidates for president, with the candidate who received the most electoral support, provided it was a majority, becoming president, and the individual who finished second becoming vice president. Such a mechanism made choosing a party ticket very cumbersome, as was demonstrated by the fact that in the 1800 election the Republicans' choice for president (Jefferson) and vice president (Aaron Burr) received the same number of electoral votes, thus throwing the contest to the House of the Representatives. The controversy aroused by the contest in the Federalist-controlled House, which flirted with selecting Burr rather than Jefferson as president, led to the enactment of the Twelfth Amendment to the Constitution, ratified in 1804, which enabled electors to distinguish between presidential and vice presidential candidates. This constitutional recognition of political parties cleared the way for them to nominate and voters to select party tickets.

Presidential Party Leadership

In the Jay Treaty debate, party mechanisms were used to undermine constitutional intent, but Jefferson's presidential party leadership showed that party could also be used to protect the Constitution. He sought to democratize the government, but not at the expense of the rights he himself had declared inalienable in the Declaration of Independence. To accomplish this tricky task, he needed political support both to push his democratizing initiatives and to keep them from being pushed too far. By stressing party unity and imposing party discipline, Jefferson was able to convince his party allies in Congress to greatly curtail government but not to do away with the constitutional checks and balances that protected liberty. Jefferson's Revolution of 1800 abolished all taxes except the tariff, provided for a swift repayment of the national debt, and greatly reduced federal expenditures, but it also left the constitutional governing structure untouched.

Jefferson kept his radical supporters in line through the aggressive application of party discipline. Although the term spoils system is associated with the Jackson administration, this means of rewarding party loyalty was actually instituted by Jefferson. During his first two years in office, Jefferson replaced more than half the federal officeholders with Republican appointees. By the end of his second term, only one-third of the holdover federal officials were still there. Jefferson's ruthless willingness to hire and fire on the basis of party loyalty undoubtedly gave his supporters second thoughts about opposing his plans and policies. When the Republican leader of the House of Representatives, John Randolph, opposed him, Jefferson denied favors to Randolph's allies and rewarded those who broke with Randolph. The rebellion was soon over, and Jefferson's control of the party was reaffirmed.

Although Madison and Jefferson were remarkably successful in creating a political party, they did not believe in the virtues of party; they viewed their party as the "party to end party." By triumphing over Hamilton and his allies, the Republicans hoped to restore the power of the Constitution to direct and control American government. Once proper constitutional government was in place, the need for, and usefulness of, political party would disappear. Jefferson said as much in his first inaugural address when he declared, "We are all republicans; we are all federalists."

By the end of Jefferson's two terms, he had succeeded in converting moderate Federalists into Republicans and in destroying the political power of the Hamiltonians. During the administrations of Madison, Monroe, and John Quincy Adams, the country functioned on a non-partisan basis. In 1820, Monroe was unopposed for reelection. In homage to the lack of partisan rancor, this period of one-party government, which lasted until the election of 1828, was called the "Era of Good Feelings."

The Limits of Non-partisanship

The Era of Good Feelings was hardly that. Instead, it sparked a variety of bad political feelings that are all too likely to arise in the absence of vigorous party life and discipline. Regional rivalries grew and executive accountability declined, as did the authority and legitimacy of the national government. The nation's new capital, Washington, D.C., remained a swampy, desolate place, scarred by its capture by the British during the War of 1812. It had attained none of the symbolic luster possessed by great national capitals such as Paris or London.

In the face of weak central leadership and attachment, sectional differences grew. The West became increasingly disgruntled at the financial dominance of the East and the seeming unconcern of the national government toward the threat posed by the Indians. The South shared the West's resentment of Eastern bankers and was becoming increasingly defensive about mounting Northern opposition to slavery. A division of the country into three or four separate nations seemed a real possibility as public interest in and concern for the idea of American nationhood seemed to ebb.

Within the government itself, the principle of separation of powers was in decline as executives and legislators intermingled their functions, rendering neither accountable. Congress increasingly involved itself in the details of administration. Cabinet officials paid less and less attention to presidential dictates and pursued their own departmental agendas through direct contact with congressional committees. Thus, both the authority of the president and the authority of the leadership of Congress were undermined.

This gradual process of political decline was accelerated by the results of the presidential election of 1824, which cast doubt on the legitimacy of the presidential office itself. Andrew Jackson had won ninety-nine electoral votes to eighty-eight for John Quincy Adams, forty-one for William Crawford, and thirty-four for Henry Clay. Because no candidate received a majority of the electoral vote, the House of Representatives, as specified by the Twelfth Amendment to the Constitution, chose the winner from among the top three finishers – Jackson, Adams, and Crawford. In addition to having the most electoral votes, Jackson was also far ahead in the popular vote. He tallied 153,000 votes, whereas Adams, second in the popular vote, received a mere 109,000 votes. Despite the powerful evidence that Jackson was the popular choice, the House voted to make Adams president. Clay, eliminated as a presidential contender, served as president maker. He used his authority as speaker of the House to obtain votes for Adams. Adams then named Clay secretary of state. Because this position had been the traditional stepping-stone to the presidency since Madison assumed the office in 1809, Clay was virtually anointed as Adams's successor.

A Party System

The 1824 election created a constitutional crisis that pit democratic principles against liberal restraint on popular rule. The House had dutifully abided by the procedure prescribed by the Constitution for selecting the president. No evidence existed that Adams had bribed Clay with the offer of secretary of state. But the result inspired widespread public outrage because, in contrast to all previous presidential elections, the most popular candidate did not win. Just when the spirit of democracy was growing, the constitutional plan for indirect choice of the president was shown to have palpable antidemocratic results. Jackson fanned the flames of public outrage by referring to the verdict as a "corrupt bargain" between Adams and Clay.

As the "victim" of antidemocratic forces, Jackson, already a military hero, became the foremost spokesman for the rapidly expanding popular discontent. Although many hoped that he would serve as the voice of the people, others feared that he would prove to be a demagogue, exploiting his popularity to assume dictatorial powers. This possibility was greatly enhanced by the expansion of the suffrage that had taken place during the previous few decades. By 1828, virtually all white male citizens in the United States were eligible to vote. Martin Van Buren, a senator from New York and the leader of a powerful New York political faction, sought to both take advantage of Jackson's popularity and lessen the demagogic risk to the constitutional order that Jackson posed. Van Buren's idea was to place Jackson at the head of a reinvigorated Jeffersonian party.

After meeting with like-minded politicians from Virginia, Van Buren was able to resurrect the powerful New York-Virginia alliance that had proven so valuable in electing Jefferson. It would support Jackson in exchange for his promise to accept party discipline. Jackson agreed. Although he might well have won anyway, the solid support of New York and Virginia, when added to his strength in the South and West, ensured his victory. Of course, Jackson could easily have reneged on his bargain with Van Buren after the New Yorker had delivered on his part of the deal. But Jackson was a man of honor. And he admired the discipline and sense of purpose embodied by the victorious party, renamed the Democratic party. He authorized the first national major party convention, held in 1832 for the express purpose of lining up support for Van Buren's nomination as vice president, thus ensuring that Van Buren would be his successor.

Jackson made vigorous use of the Democratic party to decentralize and democratize political and economic power. He vetoed the Second National Bank of the United States, which ended the cozy relationship between government and the Eastern economic establishment that the bank had cemented. He reintroduced, indeed championed, the spoils system, using it to enable ordinary people to serve in government (see Chapter 10). Although his enemies decried his aggressive use of presidential power, that power was employed for the purpose of limiting and reducing governmental intrusion. Therefore, on the whole, the democratizing impact of this reborn political party was compatible with the preservation and even the expansion of liberty.

Taming Presidential Ambition

Van Buren was a follower of Jefferson, but unlike Jefferson he did not believe that threats to the integrity of the Constitution would disappear once his party came to power. He recognized the danger of despotism to be a perennial one. The Constitution might provide for the indirect election of the president, but the events of 1824 revealed that the people expected to make the real decision. Nothing could prevent would-be demagogues from making direct appeals to the people and exploiting their own popularity for tyrannical ends. Taming presidential ambition would require buttressing the Constitution with the collective restraint and discipline that only party could impose.

Because the problem of presidential ambition was permanent, the method for coping with it needed to be permanent as well. Although Van Buren's immediate task was to build a party, his long-term objective was to establish a party system. Having witnessed the demise of Jefferson's party, he recognized that one-party rule would eventually turn into no-party rule. The long-term health of a party depended on the existence of a strong and healthy opposition party. Only the continual threat of defeat, and its occasional reality, could keep a party vigorous and cohesive. For a system to endure, it must have rules. Each side must be willing to accept defeat grudgingly, if not gracefully. Neither side must fear that, if they lose, their most cherished values and interests will be destroyed, because under those circumstances neither side will graciously and peacefully accept defeat.

A Two-Party System

Van Buren as the prophet of the party system triumphed at the expense of Van Buren the politician. Having won the presidency in 1836, Van Buren was defeated by William Henry Harrison in 1840. Harrison ran as a candidate of the Whig party, which, as Van Buren had predicted, grew up in opposition to Jackson and the Democrats. The name "Whig" was chosen so as to identify this new party with the English party of the same name that had deposed the autocratic English king James the II in the late seventeenth century. Like their namesake, the new Whigs promised to vanquish the heirs of "King Andrew the First" and remove any trace of the monarchism with which he had endowed the presidency.

To defeat Van Buren, the Whigs used the same partisan techniques that had proven so successful for the Democrats. They staged rallies, published party newspapers, and wielded symbols in an effort to excite and mobilize masses of voters. In this election, the modern notion of an election "campaign" was born. Campaign was a military term, and its application to elections implied that they would now acquire the hard-fought, tactical, and disciplined character associated with warfare. Parties would provide the troops and the logistical support for these political wars. Who better to lead a campaign for the new party against the entrenched Democrats than a military hero?

Harrison was the hero of the battle of Tippecanoe in 1811, in which he defeated the great Shawnee leader Tecumseh. Harrison's combination of military fame and political anonymity made him the perfect candidate to run against Van Buren, who unfortunately had the reputation for being wily and cunning. Nowhere is the American public's antipathy toward party more evident than in its preference for military figures like Harrison, Ulysses S. Grant, and Dwight Eisenhower over seasoned party politicians like Van Buren, Horatio Seymour, and Adlai Stevenson. Unlike Washington, however, who embodied the Founders' fear of factionalism, these military heroes would have to come to terms with political parties, which, by 1840, had substantially modified the working arrangements of constitutional government.

"All Liberals, All Democrats"

Although the Democrats identified more closely with "the common man" and the Whigs had more support among the wealthy, they were not "liberal" and "conservative" parties in the modern sense. They were both liberal in that they both favored free enterprise and protection of private property and they both adhered to the basic principles of the Constitution and the Declaration of Independence – natural rights and limited government. And they were both democratic. The Whigs had abandoned the Federalists' efforts to promote indirect rule. Indeed, by attacking the "monarchic" presidency of Jackson, they claimed to be more democratic than the Democrats.

The Whigs sought to diminish the power of the president but also favored a more active and positive role for the national government. The Democrats had supported the strong presidency of Jackson because they agreed with his project of using powerful executive leadership to decrease the size and scope of the national government. The Whigs favored using government to build canals, roads, and other physical improvements that benefited interstate commerce. And they wanted to raise the tariff on imported products to fund those projects and to protect domestic manufacturers. They also favored the establishment of a national banking and financial system that would provide greater availability and security of credit and facilitate all manner of commercial transactions.

In modern terms, such enthusiasm for activist government would be called "liberal." But the Democrats claimed that these activities were inevitably "illiberal" because they were designed to benefit a select few. Government insiders and their friends would always be better positioned to enjoy the fruits of government-funded projects and to obtain governmentally sponsored bank credit. Democrats believed that the ordinary person had a better chance for equal opportunity in a competitive marketplace than in one dominated by government subsidies and government favoritism.

Although support for the two parties was not evenly spread throughout the country, both parties were truly national in scope. Two of the four Whig presidents who served between 1840 and 1860 were Southerners: John Tyler and Zachary Taylor. Two of the three Democratic presidents during this same period were from the North. In states like New York, Illinois, and Pennsylvania, the two parties were intensely competitive, with frequent alternations in power occurring between them.

A Force for Decentralization

Although created for the purpose of winning presidential elections, the party system that developed in the 1830s actually served to promote political and governmental *decentralization*. Because electoral votes were allocated state by state, the partisan apparatus created to win presidential elections also had to be constructed state by state. In order to maintain the support of the state parties that had brought a president to power, that president had to reward them and be disciplined by them. The spoils system thrived during this period, as state parties demanded what they deemed their fair share of federal jobs.

The dependence of national officeholders on state parties was duplicated by the dependence of state party leaders on local ones. To win statewide elections, party leaders had to rely on local party organizations in cities, towns, and counties to turn out the vote. Therefore, localities held the key to both statewide and national political success and could make powerful demands on higher political authorities. Because the two parties were so evenly matched, they could not afford to ignore even small localities because such seemingly insignificant places might well provide the margin of victory in a close election. This localizing political pressure served as a brake on national political power and a powerful protection of the individuality and diversity of states and localities.

In an era before mass media, local party life was not only a source of spoils but of entertainment as well. Political parties held picnics, rallies, parades, and other public spectacles. These occasions were intended to be light-hearted, even frivolous, but they also served a crucial democratic function. As Tocqueville had remarked, large republics increased an individual's sense of isolation, weakness, and vulnerability. The instinctive reaction to such threatening feelings was to withdraw from public life into the relatively safe private world of self and family. Local party life was sufficiently unthreatening and pleasurable to encourage tentative steps out of the private and into the public realm. Parties provided a link to the wider world of politics that more impersonal and drab governmental entities could not provide, and parties were therefore a critical stimulus for democratic citizenship.

It is easy to exaggerate the ideological coherence of the Whigs and Democrats. In both parties, members disagreed with each other about key policy issues. In such instances, party loyalty owed less to a positive attachment to this or that aspect of the party creed than to common hatred of the enemy. In 1840, the Whigs were held together largely by shared hatred of Andrew Jackson and his "flunky," Martin Van Buren. To this day, a common enemy remains a valuable source of party cohesion. For example, the furor caused by President Bill Clinton's involvement with Monica Lewinsky played itself out politically along party lines. Although many Democrats were appalled by the president's behavior, their anger at what they took to be the unscrupulous tactics employed by the Republicans to force him from office motivated them to fight to save him.

The Positive Impact of Party

A study of the party system that developed during the 1830s and 1840s provides a better understanding of three political problems to which a large democratic republic is prone: despotism, alienation, and sectionalism. One will never know if Andrew Jackson would have become an American Napoleon if he had come to power strictly on his own. But certainly, the strong pressure exerted on him by his party allies worked to curb whatever despotic tendencies he possessed.

As a nation grows in size, it becomes ever more difficult for ordinary citizens to feel a sense of attachment to and participation in the political life of the country. Parties, with roots at the local level and branches extending to the national level, provide people with an accessible means of identification with the broader political realm.

The "part" root of the word *partisanship* does not only apply to parties. Any part of a large nation is prone to feel that its needs are being neglected and that what divides it from the rest of the country is more significant than what binds it. Parties were formed as alliances between states in different regions. Because their chief purpose was to win national elections, they had a strong incentive to find means for overcoming sectional differences. As the Civil War demonstrates, they did not always succeed. But they did serve as a strong countervailing force that acted against such divisive tendencies.

The Parties and Slavery

Because the success of the party system was predicated on bipartisan consensus about fundamental questions, it is not surprising that it failed to cope with a dispute over fundamentals that had plagued the Republic since its inception – the conflict over slavery. Beginning with the Missouri

Compromise of 1820 and continuing until the actual outbreak of the Civil War, both parties sought ways to achieve a compromise over slavery. In this sense, they were continuing in the tradition of the drafters of the Constitution, who had incorporated a series of compromises into the document itself. Both parties contained pro- and antislavery factions. Their desire to survive as national entities, and therefore to paper over their internal differences about slavery, was one of the most important factors that delayed the onset of civil war.

Ultimately, these compromise efforts were unsuccessful. The pressures to admit new states were so powerful that they overwhelmed the capacity of the compromisers in both parties to find means for maintaining a political balance between pro- and antislavery forces. From the mid-1840s onward, regional loyalty came increasingly to outweigh party loyalty. The Democrats gradually shed their democratic and egalitarian concerns to focus themselves on protecting slavery.

This transformation was not necessarily inevitable. A vital opportunity to prevent Southern domination was narrowly missed in 1844. That year, former president Martin Van Buren, who opposed the expansion of slavery, was the front-runner for the Democratic party presidential nomination. The South opposed his nomination because he would not support the annexation of Texas, a move that promised to provide great opportunities for the expansion of slavery. Van Buren came to the convention with a majority of delegates supporting him. But party rules required that the party nominee be supported by at least two-thirds of the delegates. More than a third of the delegates were from the South. Van Buren recognized that his only hope lay in changing the rules so that the nomination would be decided on the basis of a simple majority.

Unlike the nomination itself, changes to convention rules were made on a majority basis. If Van Buren had been able to convince all those who supported him to endorse a change in the two-thirds rule, he would have become the nominee. But he failed to do so. His resolution was defeated by a narrow margin. During the balloting, the South stood fast in its opposition to Van Buren and deprived him of the two-thirds vote he needed. After nine ballots, Van Buren's supporters gave up and the nomination went to a rabid supporter of Texas annexation, James Polk. In the presidential election, Polk defeated the Whig candidate, Henry Clay, and proceeded not only to annex Texas but also to provoke a war with Mexico that resulted in the further acquisitions of New Mexico and California.

History is unpredictable. One cannot say for sure that if Van Buren had been nominated he would have defeated Clay or that even if elected he would have been able to prevent the annexation of Texas on a proslavery basis. But Van Buren did oppose annexation, as did many Whigs, including Abraham Lincoln. It is possible that Van Buren could have delayed annexation until an antislavery means for achieving it was found. Therefore the two-thirds rule, adopted to enable any large bloc of delegates to veto a candidate that the party found unacceptable, may well have changed history. Later in this chapter, we explain that abolition of the two-thirds rule in 1936 played a crucial role in destroying Southern dominance of the Democratic party and enabling it once again to become a truly national party.

The Republicans

If Van Buren had succeeded, the Democrats might have become a powerful party. They would have committed themselves to a great principle – opposition to the expansion of slavery. But, like the Whigs, they failed to do so. Ending slavery required the creation of a new party system that was dominated for several decades by a new party, the Republicans, dedicated to the principle of ending slavery. Although most members of the new party were former Whigs, its leadership included several antislavery Democrats, most notably Salmon Chase of Ohio and Franklin Blair of Missouri. Abraham Lincoln, the first Republican president, had been a loyal Whig. He gave up his former *party identification* with great reluctance and only when it became clear to him that the Whigs were not prepared to lead the attack on slavery's expansion.

As we discuss in Chapters 5 and 12, during the 1860 presidential election and during his presidency, Lincoln gave effective voice to the key Republican principle: incorporation of the ideas of liberty contained in the Declaration of Independence into the principle of union contained in the Constitution. In town squares and community halls throughout the North, a constitutional debate took place along party lines. The 1860 election pitted Lincoln against the man who defeated him for the Senate – the Democratic candidate, Stephen Douglas. Douglas sought to hold the pro- and antislavery factions of his party together by advocating the principle of popular sovereignty, which allowed each new territory to decide for itself whether to adopt a pro- or antislavery state constitution. Lincoln committed his party fully to the principle of no territorial expansion for slavery. He made clear that the constitutional justification for such a radical step was the principle of "unalienable rights" enumerated in the Declaration of Independence. The voter realignment that followed, which granted the Republican party majority status in most parts of the country except the South, was the political outcome of this party-sponsored constitutional reconsideration that gave deeper import to the noble phrase that "all men are created equal."

Lincoln did not succeed through rhetoric alone. He relied on his party to mobilize campaign support for him and to maintain support for his program in Congress. He adroitly manipulated patronage and cabinet appointments to reinforce party cohesion. Most important, during the critical election of 1860 and after, he depended on Republicans to carry on spirited and probing discussions at the state and local level, pressing their constituents to understand and accept the profound principles on which Lincoln was basing his effort to refound the Union.

The Enduring Two-Party System

After the Civil War, the two-party system that had been created in the Jacksonian era solidified itself. Although both parties have undergone vast transformations since then, one or the other of them has won all the presidential elections and controlled the two houses of Congress for the last 150 years. No other nation has demonstrated this degree of political party stability and endurance.

The Republicans: From Great to Middling

By the mid-1870s, the Republicans had descended from a great party to a mid-sized one. Having conquered slavery, they were unable to develop a plausible strategy for integrating the freed slaves into the mainstream of economic and political life. Despite the passage of the Fifteenth Amendment, whose purpose was to enable former slaves to vote, Southern states passed a variety of different laws that negated the amendment's practical impact. For all intents and purposes, Southern African Americans remained unable to vote from the late 1800s until the passage of the Voting Rights Act in 1965. Republican acquiescence to Southern racial segregation permitted the reestablishment of a party system reminiscent of the one that had existed before the Civil War.

The Republicans had no real support in the South. The Democrats were very weak in most of New England and in the Midwest. But elsewhere, vigorous two-party competition existed. Between 1876 and 1896, the Republicans held the upper hand, but not by much. In this period, they won the presidency five times and the Democrats won twice. The Democrats controlled the House of Representatives for most of this period, and the Republicans held the Senate, but by very slim margins.

Party Coalitions

A look at the makeup of the two parties as they existed in the 1870s and 1880s helps to unravel the mystery of party loyalty. The single greatest source of Republican support was the still-fresh memory of the Civil War. The popularity of the party of Lincoln grew enormously after his assassination.

Veterans were particularly staunch in their identification with the party that had successfully prosecuted the war. In the midst of a hotly contested campaign, Republican candidates were known to "wave the bloody shirt," meaning that they would display a Union soldier's uniform, replete with blood stains, to a crowd of veterans and urge them to "vote the way they shot."

The Republican party was closely tied to the dominant Northern religious denominations, all Protestant. To maintain that affiliation, it supported temperance (limits on the sale and consumption of alcohol), Sunday business closings, and opposition to gambling. It also opposed government support for private religious schools because Protestant control of the public schools meant that such aid would mostly be used by Catholics. The Republicans retained the Whigs' pro-business posture. They favored a high tariff on imported goods to protect and encourage American manufacturers, and they supported the subsidy of railroad construction.

As befits a two-party system, the Democrats were, in many respects, the mirror image of the Republicans. Above all, they were the party of the former Confederate states. Their candidates waved gray bloody shirts, reminding white Southerners that it was the Republicans who had invaded their homeland and subjected them to military rule. The South was heavily agricultural. The Democrats opposed the tariff because it made manufactured goods more expensive for farmers to buy, and the party encouraged European countries to impose tariffs on American farm goods. This anti-tariff stand was also helpful in Northern and Western farm areas, but not necessarily helpful enough to overcome the blue "bloody shirt."

The Republicans held such a strong sway over Northern Protestants that the Democrats became the party of Catholics. The flood of immigrants, most of them Catholic, to the great Northeastern cities greatly expanded the strength of the Democratic party in that densely populated region. Because of the strong strain of anti-Catholicism in Protestant America, the Democrats found it a mixed political blessing to become the Catholic party. But as the out party, the Democrats felt compelled to make electoral inroads wherever they could. The two-party system encourages such political entrepreneurship, which pushes the system in a democratic direction. The new immigrants were social outcasts, but their potential voting strength gave the parties, particularly the Democrats, a strong incentive to politically empower them.

Party Identification

The party ties that were forged in the period after the Civil War proved astonishingly durable. The South remained a Democratic bastion for 100 years, as did urban Catholic neighborhoods. Those African Americans who were able to vote, primarily in the North, voted solidly for the party of

Lincoln for the next seventy years. To this day, Northern white Protestants show a strong tendency to vote for the Republicans.

Money and Organization

Post–Civil War industrialization created large new sources of corporate wealth for the parties, particularly the Republicans. And the concurrent wave of European immigration created a huge new reservoir of votes. These two disparate groups – corporations and immigrants – shared one crucial trait in common: they both needed help from government. The railroads wanted subsidies to build new rail lines. Manufacturers wanted high tariffs to fend off foreign competition. Immigrants wanted jobs. Corporations provided huge sums of money to state party organizations capable of delivering the votes of national and state legislators for valued projects and subsidies. The practice of providing material rewards in exchange for votes is known as *patronage*. Party organizations grew strong and prosperous by dispensing these favors in return for money and votes. For example, by the later 1880s, the Republican party in Pennsylvania had 20,000 paid workers and the Republican party in New York had 10,000.

In cities such as New York and Boston, the Democratic party provided jobs for tens of thousands of immigrants and their children. In return, it received the political backing needed for the major public works projects and expanded city services that were the sources of those jobs. The costs of the party organizations were paid for mostly through kickbacks. Those people whom the party helped to receive government jobs or contracts were required to "kick back" a percentage of their profits or their salaries to the party treasury.

Precisely because money and jobs were so highly valued, party organizations proved extremely hard to discipline and control. No sooner would one person assume leadership of a state or city party organization, than others would challenge that person for control of the power and money that such leadership commanded. These challenges fed on the inevitable resentments of those who felt they had not been amply rewarded and by contributors who felt that their needs were not receiving sufficient attention. The demand for jobs and favors was virtually infinite, whereas the supply was limited. Even the most ambitious city politician could not try to raise taxes excessively for fear of driving away the businesses and homeowners whose taxes paid for the expensive, job-rich projects on which that politician's organization depended.

Therefore, to successfully lead a patronage-based party organization, a politician had to learn how to manage disappointment. This type of leadership required both skill and nerve. It involved buoying the hopes of disappointed supporters who remained loyal and of instilling fear into those who threatened to rebel. Because such leadership is always rare, party organizations were frequently in a state of flux. Feuding among rival majority-party factions in a given state or city gave minority-party candidates an unexpected possibility of victory. Thus, Republicans could occasionally exploit feuds within the New York Democratic party to win the mayor's office, and the Democrats could seize a similar opportunity to win the governorship.

Populism, Progressivism, and Parties

In the late nineteenth century, both major parties were, by contemporary standards, conservative. The Democrats remained true to their Jeffersonian roots by advocating limited federal government and opposing efforts to regulate free markets. The Republicans were less committed to states' rights, but they opposed using government to curb corporate power or reduce income disparities. It took a third party – the People's party, known as the *Populists* – to advocate policies that would today be called liberal.

The Populists arose in the economically depressed grain-growing areas of the Midwest. They sought federal laws to protect farmers from the monopoly power of railroads and to reduce the gap between rich and poor. As the agricultural recession worsened, Populist support grew. By the mid-1880s, the Populists had elected governors, senators, and representatives in several Midwestern states and were also gaining strength among Southern farmers. The 1892 People's party platform was a remarkably progressive document. It called for an expanded coinage of silver to inflate the currency, a graduated income tax, a constitutional amendment that mandated civil service reform, and government ownership of railroad, telegraph, and telephone companies. The People's party ticket garnered more than a million popular votes and twenty-two electoral votes.

In 1896, the Democratic party was at a crossroads. It was led by President Grover Cleveland, who had been elected in 1884, lost in 1888, and was then reelected in 1892. Cleveland was a devout believer in limited government. When farmers in Texas, who had been forced to eat their seed corn because their crops had been destroyed by drought, asked the president to give them some of the surplus seed corn being kept in government granaries, he refused, saying, "It is the job of the people to support the government, not the job of the government to support the people."

But Cleveland's views were challenged by Democrats who wanted to come to the aid of economically distressed farmers in Texas and elsewhere. Cleveland's victories had been something of a fluke, due largely to factional feuding among Republicans. The Democrats were still the out party and therefore more open to new political trends and ideas. Populist ideas were making greater inroads among Democrats than among Republicans. Some Democratic politicians, most notably Congressman William Jennings Bryan of Nebraska, were openly courting Populist support.

The 1896 Democratic convention turned into a pitched battle between pro- and anti-Populists. William Jennings Bryan's Cross of Gold speech tipped the balance toward the Populists. In his speech, he depicted the struggle between rich and poor, creditor and debtor, in biblical terms, appealing to the strong religious feeling of many delegates (see Chapter 6 for further discussion). His words electrified the crowd, and Bryan himself was chosen as the Democratic party candidate for president.

Bryan's campaign moved the Democrats in a new direction. Ever since the debate between Jefferson and Hamilton, the party that presumed to speak for the people had been the party most resistant to national power, which it associated with privilege, and most committed to the virtues of local self-government. Preempting the Populists, the Democrats now sought to invoke national power for democratic purposes. Major party adoption of third-party policies and programs has recurred several times since 1896. As we point out later in this chapter when we discuss the 1992 presidential election, the importance of third parties is greater than their lack of success at the ballot box would indicate.

In response to the challenge posed by the fusion of Populists and Democrats, the Republicans rallied behind the theme of stability. Their support of the gold standard was put in the context of a more general defense of the essential soundness of the American economy and the way of life it represented. The two pillars of the Republican platform were sound money and protectionism. Defense of the gold standard resonated not only with the wealthy but also with many industrial workers who feared that silver-generated inflation would lessen the value of their wages. High tariffs also appealed to employer and employee alike. Taxing imported manufacturing products was viewed as the best way to defend American workers and manufacturers against the threat of cheap foreign imports produced by oppressed foreign labor.

Urban workers, shopkeepers, and independent professionals probably agreed with Bryan that, like the farmers, they too were businessmen (see Chapter 6). But all businesspersons do not necessarily see eye to eye. Workers benefited from the low food prices that the farmers were trying to raise. On the whole, the urban non-rich preferred to make common cause with big business than with poor farmers, and they were the decisive force in swinging the 1896 election to William McKinley and the Republicans.

Like the elections in 1832 and 1860, the 1896 election proved to be a realigning election. A great battle over political principles took place between the two parties, and one party, the Republicans, won decisively. For the next thirty-six years, the Democrats won only two presidential elections – Woodrow Wilson's victories in 1912 and 1916 – and they won the 1912 election only because a very popular former Republican president, Theodore Roosevelt, ran as a third-party candidate, which split the Republicans. The Republicans did not simply remain the party of McKinley; they were also strongly influenced by new Progressive thinking and policy reforms. But until the New Deal, Republicans dominated American politics, and their bedrock support for high tariffs and sound money held sway.

The Progressives

The Republican victory in 1896 contained the seeds of the next great change in party politics – the Progressive movement (see Chapter 5). Like the Populists, Progressives favored the curbing of corporate power; they were disturbed by the unchecked growth of large corporations and the monopoly power that those "monsters" came to exercise. But unlike the Populists, Progressives were not primarily farmers. As city dwellers, they feared the growing strength of immigrant-based party organizations, and they resented the graft and corruption that those party organizations engendered.

The Progressive view of democracy denigrated feelings of solidarity in favor of individual reason and respect for expert opinion. It deplored the strong role played by historical attachment, religious affiliation, and symbolism in perpetuating party loyalty. Progressives believed that votes should be cast in response to the specific policy positions taken by parties and candidates rather than on the basis of "irrational" ties. The Progressives therefore favored political regulation designed to curb the power of the political "machines."

The impact of Progressivism might well have been delayed were it not for the assassination of President McKinley, which propelled Vice President Theodore Roosevelt (TR) to the presidency. TR, former governor of New York, was among the most prominent Progressive politicians. Anti-Progressive New York Republicans helped TR secure the vice presidential nomination to get him out of the state. They expected him to do little harm in that largely ceremonial role. To their considerable chagrin, fate placed TR in the most powerful political post in the land.

Because most members of Congress, both Republicans and Democrats, were not Progressives, TR was not able to implement the full Progressive agenda, but he did greatly increase the visibility and popularity of Progressive ideas. When he retired from office in 1909, he manipulated the

Theodore Roosevelt's 1912 Bull Moose campaign was the most successful third-party challenge in the twentieth century.

nomination of his chosen successor, William Howard Taft. Taft won the general election easily, but TR considered Taft's approach too conservative. In 1912, TR tried and failed to win back from Taft the Republican presidential nomination.

Rather than support the Republican nominee, TR formed a third party, the Progressive party, and continued his presidential bid under that label. Free from the need to mollify anti-Progressive Republicans, TR and his new party adopted a much more radical reform agenda. TR did not win. But by depriving Taft of the votes of Progressive-minded Republicans, he ensured the victory of the Democrat, Woodrow Wilson, whom he considered to be the more progressive of the major party candidates. Indeed, Wilson borrowed heavily from the Progressive party platform. For the second time in a generation, a third party had proven to be highly influential in altering the course of American politics. In 1896, the Populists had furthered their cause by joining with the Democrats. In 1912, the Progressives did so by splitting from the Republicans.

Women's suffrage was one of the Progressive party's most celebrated causes. In 1920, the Nineteenth Amendment to the Constitution was adopted guaranteeing women the right to vote. This amendment completed a process that began in 1869 when the territory of Wyoming granted women's *suffrage*. The Utah territory did so the following year. However, in 1887, the U.S. Congress disenfranchised Utah women in the Edmunds-Tucker Bill. In 1890, Wyoming came into the Union as the first women's suffrage state. By 1896, the states of Colorado, Utah, and Idaho also adopted constitutional provisions granting women the right to vote. During the first two decades of the twentieth century, many other states, including New York, Illinois, and California, also enabled women to vote. For many decades, the voting patterns of women did not differ appreciably from that of men. Later in the chapter, we will discuss the "gender gap" that has been detectable in more recent times and how it is best understood.

The Progressive Attack on Party

The Progressive Era perpetuated antiparty attitudes that harkened back to Washington and Jefferson. But just as the earlier antiparty spirit led to the misnamed Era of Good Feelings, this era seems to have produced as many anti- as pro-democratic consequences that affected such issues as non-partisan elections, the spoils system, and primaries.

The Progressives sought to destroy the power of party organizations by draining them of their lifeblood, patronage. Progressives provoked the passage of federal civil service reform laws designed to replace the spoils system with a merit system, a system that awarded government jobs on the basis of examination scores rather than party loyalty.

Although it may be fairer to choose and promote employees on the basis of an objective examination, it makes those jobholders harder to discipline. Elected officials can be disciplined by depriving them of reelection. If bureaucrats serve at the pleasure of elected officials, the public can hold those officials responsible for bureaucratic performance. But if civil servants have no obligation to elected officials and if the officials cannot fire them, the public lacks means for holding bureaucrats accountable. As we point out in Chapter 10, the federal bureaucracy has acquired a reputation for being impersonal and unresponsive.

At the municipal level, Progressives sought to eliminate parties altogether, claiming that there was no "Republican" or "Democratic" way to clean streets or remove garbage, there was only the right way. They prodded many cities to elect local officials on a non-partisan basis.

The whole purpose of non-partisan elections is to remove party label as a guide for voting. Such guidance may be unnecessary in places that are small enough to enable voters to learn a great deal about the candidates for municipal office. But in big cities, such information is not readily accessible to most people. In the absence of a party label to fall back on, voters must rely on other cues that may be even less informative, such as the slickness of campaign advertising and the good looks of the candidate.

To reduce the power of party leaders to designate candidates for state and federal offices, Progressives worked to enable party members to choose candidates directly. Many states instituted primary elections to designate party nominations for governor, senators, representatives, and state legislators. Some states also established presidential primaries.

Primary elections have created democratic difficulties. They often have low turnouts, which means that the choice of candidates is determined by a very small fraction of the eligible electorate. This fraction is not necessarily representative of party identifiers as a whole. Indeed, primary voters tend to be more extreme and passionate in their views and to favor more extreme candidates. By contrast, party leaders have a strong practical incentive to win elections and tend to favor moderate candidates who can appeal to the wider electorate. Therefore, the move from "boss"-dominated nominations to primary elections may have left the bulk of voters, those who do not participate in primaries, with a less satisfying array of choices in general elections.

A later generation of political scientists, led by V. O. Key, Jr., disagreed with the Progressive attack on party. Key pointed out that the world of public policy is an ever-changing and complex one. The ordinary voter is hard put to keep up with the issues, especially since many issues prove to be highly ephemeral. Few individuals have the time, the intellect, and the inclination to make every single important political decision from scratch. Parties are an imperfect guide for people to use in determining how they should vote and what policy positions they should adopt. But an imperfect guide is better than no guide at all. No wonder many people place their trust in the party that seems most solicitous of the particular groups and organizations to which they are most strongly attached.

Voter Turnout

V.O. Key would not have been surprised that the party-weakening Progressive reforms, although aimed at stimulating voter participation by encouraging direct democracy, coincided with the most extreme decrease in electoral participation in American history.

Figure 11.1 makes clear that the decline did not begin with the Nineteenth Amendment. It began in 1896 and continued in 1900, 1904, 1908, and even 1912, despite the interest aroused by the "the Bull Moose" campaign. After a brief spike in 1916, the decline resumed. To this day, voter

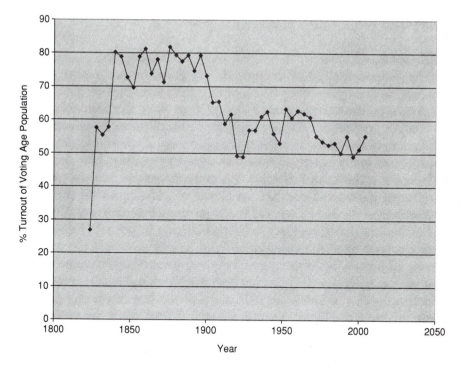

Figure 11.1. Voter Turnout in Presidential Elections, 1824–2004. *Source:* Data from *Vital Statistics in American Politics*, H. Stanley and R. Niemi (CQ Press, 2004), 64.

participation has not returned to the high levels exhibited during the heyday of party dominance in the second half of the nineteenth century.

The New Deal Party System

Woodrow Wilson's presidency, made possible by Republican party schism, did not revive Democratic party fortunes. From 1920 to 1930, Democrats were a minority in both houses of Congress, and they lost three presidential elections in a row. They receded to their pre-Wilsonian status of being the party of the South, the big cities, and little else. The opportunity to reverse their fortunes was provided by the Great Depression, which began with the collapse of the stock market in 1929. Voters responded to this catastrophe by punishing the party in power, giving the Democrats a majority in the House of Representatives in the 1930 election. The presidential victory of Franklin Delano Roosevelt (FDR) in 1932 had little to do with his own popularity and everything to do with Republican Herbert Hoover's inability to make any headway toward improving the economy.

The New Deal Party Coalition

FDR exploited his victory in 1932 to create an enduring majority coalition for the Democrats. His 1936 landslide proved to be yet another critical election that realigned the parties, setting the Democrats on the road to long-term political dominance. From 1936 to 1964, the Democrats won six of eight presidential elections, and they controlled the House and Senate for thirty-two years of a thirty-six-year span. This winning record is unparalleled in the history of American two-party politics. Like prior critical elections, this critical election was more than mere partisan triumph. It reflected widespread popular acceptance of and support for the essential features of the New Deal and the important changes in constitutional understanding that it represented. As we discuss in several chapters, the New Deal redefined the meaning of rights to include a right to economic security. This newfound acceptance by government of an obligation to provide such security was the glue that held the New Deal coalition together. Like the election in 1860, the 1936 election was one in which a political party, this time the Democrats, provoked a debate about the meaning of the rights enumerated in the Declaration of Independence and recast the meaning of those rights in a manner that strengthened the ties between liberty and democracy.

FDR succeeded by retaining traditional Democratic adherents, especially Southern whites, while adding large numbers of new recruits. His greatest weapon was his willingness to spend federal money to help people in need. Even conservative Southerners did not desert him, because they were too dependent on the jobs and other benefits that the New Deal provided. FDR, for his part, refrained from the one provocation that would have caused Southern representatives to bolt: a direct assault on racial segregation.

FDR was one of very few influential Protestant Democrats to support the presidential candidacy of his predecessor as New York governor, Al Smith, a Catholic. FDR did so in 1924, when Smith failed to receive the nomination, and in 1928, when Smith succeeded. Going out on a limb in 1924 to identify with Catholic political aspirations, coupled with his pro-Catholic reputation as governor of New York (1928–1932), enabled FDR to retain the support of Catholic voters, even after Al Smith angrily broke with FDR in 1934. Jews were similarly drawn into the Democratic orbit. FDR's administration was the first to appoint many Jews to important posts, most prominently Henry Morgenthau as secretary of the treasury.

FDR also won over the support of organized labor. Before 1932, labor unions had mostly remained politically neutral in national elections. In the 1932 election, prominent labor leaders such as John L. Lewis, president of the United Mine Workers of America, endorsed Herbert Hoover.

But between 1932 and 1936, the labor movement mushroomed in size. It made inroads in many of America's largest industries, such as steel, mining, and automobile manufacture. Although FDR did not openly support these organizing efforts, he did support section 7a of the National Industrial Recovery Act (NIRA), which unambiguously gave labor unions the right to engage in them. After the NIRA, including section 7a, became law, Lewis and other labor leaders told workers that "FDR wants you to join our union." Although these statements were not literally true, FDR did not repudiate them. As a result, he came to be viewed by labor leaders and members alike as a friend of the laborer, the first president of the industrial age to enjoy such a status (see Chapter 6 for further discussion). In 1936, the labor movement strongly endorsed FDR and provided him with the largest source of his presidential campaign funds.

In the 1930s, African Americans were a small but strategically important segment of the electorate. Their voting strength was concentrated in the biggest cities in such large and politically competitive states as New York, Pennsylvania, and Illinois. A strong turnout of African Americans in a close presidential election could swing a large number of electoral votes from one party column to the other. African Americans had been among the most loyal supporters of the Republican party, the party of Lincoln. FDR pursued cautious racial policies. African Americans participated in New Deal jobs and welfare programs, but not on an equal footing with whites. However, for the first time since Reconstruction, African Americans actually received some help from the federal government. They showed their gratitude by reversing their seventy-year partisan tradition and voting overwhelmingly for FDR in 1936.

In order to ensure an enduring Democratic majority, FDR knew that he had to end the South's ability to veto presidential nominees. Otherwise, Southern conservatism would undermine the party's newfound strength among labor union members and African Americans. At the 1936 convention, when his popularity was at its zenith, FDR stacked the Rules Committee with loyal supporters, and it voted to have nominations determined by a simple majority rather than a two-thirds majority. Had this rule change been in effect in 1844, Martin Van Buren would have been the party nominee. In 1924, the nomination would have gone to Al Smith.

By effecting this rules change, FDR ensured that future Democratic presidential candidates would be in tune with majority party sentiment and would not have to bend to the wishes of a single bloc of delegates. Although it would be another generation before the Democratic party would take up the cause of civil rights, the seeds of that undertaking were sown in the fight over the two-thirds rule that destroyed the South's veto power over the choice of the Democratic party presidential nominee.

With the addition of African Americans, Jews, Catholics, and union members, the Democratic party became the majority party for the first time since the Civil War. It was capable of winning statewide elections in the Northeast, the industrial Midwest, and parts of the Pacific Coast as well as in the "solid" South. The only regions where it did not have a decent chance to win statewide were New England, the non-industrial Midwest, and the Great Plains.

A Party to End Parties

FDR did not seek victory for its own sake. Heir to the Progressive legacy, he sought to exploit the Democrats' large congressional majority to erect a strong and resilient national administrative state. This state would provide on a routine and impartial basis what parties provided on a discretionary basis. Instead of depending on party patronage, people could depend on a social security pension when they got old, unemployment insurance if they were laid off, and welfare payments if they were poor or disabled.

FDR recognized that the new administrative state would weaken political parties, including the powerful one he built and led. But this was a price he was willing to pay. For all his skill as a party builder, his attitude toward party was strikingly similar to that of Jefferson. FDR's New Deal Democratic party would be a party to end party. Once the welfare state he sought to construct was fully in place, FDR believed, parties might well become far less important, if not wither away.

Republican Resurgence

Like Jefferson, FDR was a better politician than he was a prophet. Parties did not wither away. Indeed, the Republicans scored a great political comeback after World War II. As of 1952, the Republicans had not won a presidential election in twenty-four years. They seemed on the verge of suffering the same fate as the Whigs and the Federalists. Instead, they demonstrated a resilience even more impressive than that shown by the Democratic party in the wake of the Civil War. Since 1952, Republicans have won eight presidential elections whereas the Democrats have only won five. The Republicans have never been out of the presidential office for more than eight years. The Democrats were out of office for twelve years, from 1980 until 1992. The Democrats controlled both houses of Congress from 1954 until 1980. Since 1980, Republican congressional fortunes have improved considerably. Republicans have held the Senate for most of the period between 1980 and the present, and they controlled the House of Representatives from 1994 until 2006.

But this rebirth of party strength differed from earlier party resurgences because it happened despite a general weakening of party politics. The Republicans benefited because the Democrats were even more affected by worsening party conditions than they were. Therefore, the relative improvement in Republican fortunes must be examined in the context of this overall party decline.

Eisenhower Republicans

Like the Democrats in 1828 and the Whigs in 1849, the Republicans revived their fortunes by running a military hero, General Dwight David Eisenhower, for president. Eisenhower was the military figure most closely identified with the defeat of the Germans in World War II and had been the architect of the greatest amphibious landing in all of human history, known as D-Day. He was so enormously popular that a group of prominent Democrats, including FDR's son James, had tried to recruit him in 1948 to replace Truman whom they, mistakenly, deemed to be unelectable.

Eisenhower won easily in 1952 and again in 1956. He did not oppose, and thereby tacitly accepted, the key programs of the New Deal, most especially Social Security and the legitimacy of labor unions. And he embraced Truman's cautious but firm internationalist foreign policy that was based on the alliance of the Western powers and resistance to Soviet expansionism. As a result, many independent-minded voters were now willing to consider voting Republican because to do so no longer threatened their economic security, protected by the welfare state, and their security against foreign threat, protected by the Atlantic Alliance. The Republican party suffered its worst post–World War II defeat in 1964 when these moderate "Eisenhower" Republicans deserted the Republican candidate, Senator Barry Goldwater of Arizona, because they viewed him as an opponent of the New Deal and a foreign policy radical.

Suburbs and Sun Belt

In the first half of the twentieth century, population changes, especially increased immigration and the growth of big cities, favored the Democrats. In the second half, the two most important population trends – movement of people from the Northeast and Midwest to the Sun Belt states of the Southeast and Southwest, and from rural and urban areas to suburbs – favored the Republicans. As people moved from cities to suburbs, their partisan ties weakened. Because big-city voters were predominantly Democrats, the Democrats were the primary victims of this ebbing of party loyalty.

Most of the people moving to the Sun Belt were small-town and suburban Northern Republicans. They turned states such as Utah, Colorado, and Arizona solidly Republican and gave them added congressional districts and electoral votes. Florida and Texas, previously solidly Democratic, became competitive two-party states. California became the largest state in the Union and therefore the greatest electoral prize. All four Republicans elected president since Eisenhower – Richard Nixon, Ronald Reagan, George H. W. Bush, and George W. Bush – came from the Sun Belt states of California and Texas.

Feuding Democrats

Republican fortunes were also greatly aided by the feuding among Democrats in 1968 over Lyndon Johnson's conduct of the Vietnam War. Not since the annexation of Texas in 1844 had a foreign policy disagreement proven so divisive. For the first time ever, an incumbent president faced a serious challenge in presidential primaries. Senator Eugene McCarthy, Democrat from Minnesota, ran against Johnson in the New Hampshire primary. Although Johnson narrowly prevailed, the media interpreted McCarthy's impressive showing as a serious setback for Johnson.

In the wake of this "defeat," Johnson withdrew from the race. A three-way contest ensued between Vice President Hubert Humphrey, who defended Johnson's Vietnam policy; Senator McCarthy; and Senator Robert Kennedy of New York, who also opposed the war. McCarthy and Kennedy each won several primaries. The night he won the California primary, Kennedy was assassinated. Although Humphrey had enough delegates to ensure his nomination, many antiwar Democrats refused to endorse him or did so tepidly. Tensions were heightened by the antiwar riots that erupted during the Democratic National Convention in Chicago. The successful Republican candidate, Richard Nixon, profited from the image of Democratic disarray that emerged from Chicago.

In 1972, the feud among Democrats rekindled. The presidential nomination was won by a passionately antiwar candidate, Senator George McGovern of South Dakota. McGovern had chaired a commission created at the 1968 convention to rewrite the party's nominating rules to make them more democratic. The commission did so by establishing complex formulas for choosing convention delegates to ensure that those delegates reflected the full racial and gender diversity of the party's membership. The rules also contained devices to ensure that state and local leaders could not exert the same level of influence over candidate selection that they had in the past. McGovern's bid for the nomination was greatly assisted by the fact that he and his staff understood the rules and his rivals did not. In the wake of 1972, presidential campaigns have become ever more dominated by party primaries. Most states hold primaries in which slates of delegates run pledged to various candidates. Some states hold *caucuses* but these do not resemble the "smoke filled rooms" in which party leaders used to choose delegates. They more closely resemble primaries in the sense that delegates are chosen on the basis of which candidate they are pledged to support not on the basis of their loyalty to local or state party leaders. The nomination is won or lost in the primaries. As a result the national *party conventions* have lost their traditional purpose. They no longer determine who will be chosen, since that decision has already been made. However, as Box 2 shows, they are still an integral part of the presidential election process.

Box Two: Nuts and Bolts

The Political Party Presidential Nominating Conventions

Even though they no longer have an active role in choosing the presidential nominee, the Republican and Democrat presidential nominating conventions retain considerable political importance. They are one of only two occasions during the entire presidential campaign season when many millions of people actually pay attention to the race. The other occasion is provided by the presidential debates. In an age of ten-second sound bites and thirty-second ads, the conventions are an opportunity for the public to have a more lengthy and thorough opportunity to hear why each party and its nominee claim that they should be entrusted with the presidency. In 2004, approximately 48 million viewers tuned in to some part of each of the conventions.

The most important single convention event is the candidate's acceptance speech, which he gives after the roll call of the states and he has been officially nominated. The speech provides a relatively lengthy occasion for the candidate to define himself to the voters and to explain why he is the superior choice.

Second in importance are the speeches that nominate the candidate. The nominators are carefully chosen by the candidate and his staff (not the party leadership) to display the wide range of his support and to ensure that important reasons for supporting him are publicized, reasons that it would be impolitic for the candidate to mention in his own speech. These speeches expand upon the themes that the candidate will later take up in his acceptance speech and also visibly demonstrate that key leaders, representing various elements and factions of the party, are giving him their enthusiastic support.

The other speeches given in prime time are also politically significant because they are an opportunity for less well known, up-and-coming politicians to make an impact on a mass public. These other speeches also provide an opportunity to show that the party is concerned about the various causes and constituencies that these speakers represent.

Off camera, the business of the convention includes determining the party platform and listening to many non-broadcast speeches. These activities are often of great importance to the delegates and the speakers themselves. They are a vital part of the secondary function of the convention, which is to stir up the enthusiasm and improve the morale of party loyalists whose help is desperately needed by the candidate during the campaign. The platforms are a catalog of the various stances on public policy questions that a majority of the party delegates choose to endorse. Candidates are not necessarily bound to support every plank of the platform. As the two parties have come to be more ideologically distinct from one another and more internally cohesive, the platforms have become less politically relevant because the public already has a pretty clear idea regarding what the parties differ about.

As Figure 11.2 shows, there has been a drastic decline in the number of hours that the television networks devote to covering the convention. Until 1976, coverage was complete, or in media jargon "gavel to gavel." Since 1996, it has been limited to approximately three hours a night of only three of the four convention nights. Daytime events are not televised nor is one night. Until 2004, there was a direct relationship between the number of hours that a convention was televised and how many people watched it. But in 2004, television coverage did not expand but overall viewership climbed by almost 3 million viewers.

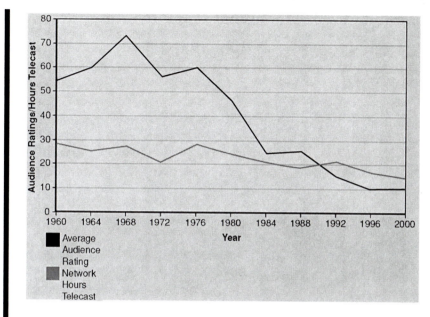

Figure 11.2. Convention Ratings vs. Hours Telecast, 1960–2000.
Source: *Vital Statistics in American Politics*, H. Stanley and R. Niemi (CQ Press, 2000), 64.

Ironically, the rules designed to make the nominating process more democratic and representative resulted in the choice of a candidate who could not obtain the support of key party leaders and coalition members. Organized labor was so offended by McGovern's antiwar stand that the American Federation of Labor, for the first and only time since it was created, refused to endorse the Democratic nominee. Chicago mayor Richard Daley and many other party leaders extended only pro forma support. McGovern suffered the worst defeat of any modern Democratic presidential candidate. He was the first Democratic presidential candidate since the Civil War not to carry the South. Indeed, he did not win a single Southern state. In every presidential election since 1976, Republicans have won the South. In both 2000 and 2004, George W. Bush carried every Southern state.

The 1972 election proved to be a historic turning point in the relationship between party and foreign policy. Since FDR, the Democrats had been the more aggressively internationalist of the two parties. A favorite Republican slogan was "[t]hey [the Democrats] are the party of war!" Eisenhower and Nixon fought bitter intra-party battles against isolationism. But ever since 1972, it is the Republicans who have been consistently more aggressive in prosecuting first the Cold War and then the War on Terror while the Democrats have fought bitter internal battles over whether to support the North American Free Trade Agreement, the Gulf War, and the Iraq War. A majority of Democratic senators voted against the 1991 resolution endorsing the Gulf War. A majority of Democratic congressmen opposed NAFTA. These two pieces of legislation passed only because of overwhelming Republican support for them. Although a majority of Democratic senators supported the 2002 resolution endorsing the invasion of Iraq, the 2004 Democratic presidential candidate John Kerry made opposition to the war his major campaign theme.

Crime, Welfare, and Taxes

The Republicans put their superior resources to work to publicize a message that, especially during the 1980s, strongly resonated with voters. The Republicans attacked the Democrats for being soft on crime and welfare and for raising taxes. Until the 1960s, crime was considered to be a local problem. But President Johnson and many Democratic mayors and governors responded to the mid-1960s urban riots with what voters perceived as softness. This perception enabled Republicans to turn the crime issue into a national, partisan one by successfully identifying themselves as the law-and-order party.

Federal welfare payments to families with dependent children had been relatively uncontroversial since their inception during the New Deal. But during the 1960s and 1970s, skyrocketing levels of illegitimate births and crime waves in welfare-dependent neighborhoods made welfare policy notorious. Because these policies were identified with the Democrats, they provided an inviting target for the Republicans. Strong opposition to crime and to generous welfare benefits enabled the Republicans to regain the status they had enjoyed in the mid- and late-nineteenth century as the party of hard work, piety, and middle-class virtue.

Ronald Reagan also improved Republican fortunes by devising a new, politically popular approach to taxing and spending. Ever since FDR, the Republicans had been divided into two economic policy factions. Moderate Republicans accepted the Keynesian economic doctrines deployed by the Democrats, meaning that they were willing to live with federal budgetary deficits in times of recession as a means of promoting economic expansion. They preferred to criticize individual Democratic spending programs rather than to attack "big government" in general. Conservative Republicans objected to deficit spending. They wanted large cuts in the federal income tax but demanded equally large cuts in the budget in order to avoid deficit.

Both Republican positions were politically problematic. The moderate approach was virtually indistinguishable from that of the Democrats, whereas the conservative formula required politically popular programs to be cut. Ronald Reagan departed from both strategies. He accepted the use of deficit spending, but only to enable tax cuts. He turned traditional conservatism on its head by first proposing tax cuts and only then asking Congress for the budget cuts to pay for them. Thus, he was able to do the politically popular thing, cut taxes, first. Although some representatives in both parties doubted the prudence of this approach, few were willing to vote against giving money back to the people. Reagan's tax cut plan of 1981 passed Congress overwhelmingly.

Reagan's subsequent proposals to cut programs did not receive the same enthusiastic reception. Although some reductions were passed, spending and revenue remained out of balance. The resulting huge deficits continued to plague the federal government for the next fifteen years. Nonetheless, by putting tax cuts ahead of spending cuts, Reagan had found a successful formula for gaining political popularity while halting the expansion of federal domestic spending. Deficit pressure was insufficient to reduce the budget, but, for a time, it did brake additional spending. Until George W. Bush pressed Congress to add a prescription drug benefit to the Medicare program in 2003, Congress had not passed a single new, expensive, federal domestic program.

New Democrats

In 1992, as in 1912, the Democrats were able to regain the presidency because a third candidate siphoned off Republican votes. Like TR, Ross Perot concentrated his attacks on the Republican incumbent. Perot appealed to voters who considered Reagan and Bush's deficit spending irresponsible, promising to eliminate it. Perot gained 19 percent of the vote, the best showing by a third-party candidate since 1912. He took enough votes away from the Republican George H. W. Bush to enable Bill Clinton to win, even though the Democratic share of the vote was scarcely greater than it had been four years earlier.

Like Woodrow Wilson, Clinton took heed of a third candidate's strong showing. He pledged to reduce the budget deficit. He refused to support expensive programs despite their strong appeal to key Democratic party constituents. The one massive exception to this policy – the Clinton proposal to reform national healthcare – ended in a terrible political defeat in

Congress, which was followed by the disastrous 1994 elections (see Chapter 7). After the elections, which saw the Republicans win control of both the House and the Senate for the first time since 1954, Clinton returned to the centrist themes and policies he touted in his run for the presidency. The combination of spending restraint and a strong economy enabled a steady decline in the deficit. By late in Clinton's second term, there was actually a budgetary surplus.

Clinton declared himself to be a "New Democrat." Like Reagan, he recognized that his party could not thrive without changing its approach. Not only did he strive for a balanced budget, but he also aggressively altered his party's posture on welfare and crime. He promised to "end welfare as we know it." As governor of Arkansas, he rejected clemency appeals from prisoners condemned to die. As president, he sponsored legislation providing federal subsidies to cities and towns to hire additional police. In what was probably the most momentous decision of his presidency, he signed the Republican-sponsored welfare reform bill, even though it was much harsher to recipients than Clinton's own proposal. His antiwelfare rhetoric impelled him to support the Republican bill even though he disagreed with the manner in which welfare reform was to be accomplished.

Sources of Party Decline

These Republican successes took place in a new political atmosphere that robbed parties of much of their strength and significance. Parties became less able to depend on patronage to maintain party loyalty and cohesion. Television diminished the importance of their traditional methods for dominating political campaigns – door-to-door campaigning, rallies, and get-out-the-vote drives. Presidential candidates came to rely less on party organization and more on personal campaign organizations. In addition, the amount of money spent in campaigns rose astronomically and was raised and spent in ways that, on balance, diminished party control.

The New Deal assault on patronage was mirrored at the state and local levels where civil service reform greatly diminished the number of jobs that victorious parties could dispense. Patronage powers did not entirely disappear. Local probate judges, for example, retained the discretion to choose which lawyers to assign to lucrative cases. Highway officials kept considerable freedom in choosing companies to perform profitable highway construction jobs. But the decline in the quantity of patronage sapped party leaders at all levels of a major source of their power.

The direct communication between politicians and the public that mass media enabled meant that party was no longer a mediator between the two. FDR proved a master at using radio to speak intimately to voters; he encouraged them to think of these one-way discussions as "fireside chats." Television connected a face to the candidate's voice and increased the feeling of connectedness between candidate and citizen. The televised presidential debates between John F. Kennedy and Richard Nixon in 1960 demonstrated the power of this new medium. Although Nixon was Kennedy's equal as a speaker, voters were struck by the contrast between his grizzled, harsh face and Kennedy's handsome and serene visage. Kennedy was a Democrat, but the capacity to look good on television and speak with warmth and convictions would benefit candidates from both parties, especially the former movie and television actor Ronald Reagan and the magnetic and empathetic Bill Clinton.

Changes in campaign organizations further weakened the connection between candidates and voters. Since FDR, presidential candidates had increasingly come to rely on their own personal campaign organizations, which made them less dependent on their parties. This trend culminated in 1972, when Richard Nixon stacked his campaign fortunes almost completely on his personal organization – the Committee to Re-Elect the President (CREEP) – rather than relying on the existing Republican party organization. CREEP raised unprecedented sums of money, making the 1972 Nixon campaign by far the most expensive in history. CREEP was also deeply implicated in the Watergate scandal (see Chapter 7). The Democratic party that Van Buren created in the late 1820s demonstrated how party could tame presidential ambition. The unscrupulous behavior of CREEP showed that displacing party with a candidate-dominated campaign organization could give full vent to overweening presidential ambition.

The Role of Money

The scandals associated with CREEP and the 1972 presidential election set in motion a series of reforms in campaign finance whose overall result was to further weaken the parties. This was not the intent of the first of these major changes, the 1974 amendments to the Federal Elections Campaign Act. Indeed, one of the aims of those changes was to strengthen party by limiting the resources and the spending opportunities available to personal campaign organizations like CREEP. The amendments established strict disclosure requirements for campaign donations; set specific limits for those donations; expanded public financing of presidential elections, first established in 1971, to include primaries and nominating conventions as well as the general election; set limits on campaign expenditures; and

Table 11.1. Public Funds in Presidential Campaigns

	Primary Matching Funds	Convention	General
1976	$24,789,566	$4,149,630	$43,640,000
	(15)	(2)	(2)
1980	$31,343,128	$8,832,000	$63,122,304
	(10)	(2)	(3)
1984	$36,519,405	$16,160,000	$80,800,000
	(11)	(2)	(2)
1988	$67,547,821	$18,440,000	$92,200,000
	(15)	(2)	(2)
1992	$42,862,123	$22,096,000	$110,480,000
	(12)	(2)	(2)
1996	$58,538,356	$24,728,000	$152,695,400
	(11)	(2)	(3)
2000	$62,261,374	$29,546,690	$147,733,452
	(10)	(3)	(3)
2004	$28,375,506	$29,848,000	$149,240,000
	(8)	(2)	(2)

Notes: Numbers below dollar amounts are the number of candidates/parties receiving funding.
The third candidate receiving general election funding in 1980 was John Anderson.
In 1996, Ross Perot received partial general election funding as a minor party candidate.
In 2000, the Reform party received partial convention funding and Patrick Buchanan received partial general election funding.
Source: Federal Election Commission, www.fec.gov.

established the Federal Election Commission (FEC) to oversee compliance with the law.

Fueled by the voluntary check off on tax forms (now $3), the Presidential Election Campaign Fund matches up to $250 of each contribution made to eligible primary candidates. In return, the candidates must promise that they will limit spending to a certain amount and follow certain other rules. Then, in the general election season, the presidential candidates receive a lump sum in return for not accepting any further private donations. Table 11.1 shows how much public money was spent in presidential elections from 1976 to 2004.

Contribution limits were set differently for individuals and for Political Action Committees (PACs), which were entities that corporations, labor unions, and other types of organizations were required to establish in order to legally contribute to campaigns. An individual was allowed to donate $1000 to a candidate per primary or general election; $20,000 to any other political committee per year; $5000 to a national party committee per year but no more than $25,000 in total. A PAC was limited to $5000 to a candidate per primary or general election; $15,000 to any other political committee per year; and $5000 to a national party committee. No limit was placed on its total contributions per year.

In *Buckley v. Valeo* (1976), the Supreme Court struck down the expenditure limits contained in the 1974 law. It ruled that because advertising is a form of speech, it was unconstitutional to place limits on how much money a candidate could spend to purchase advertising. This ruling made it impossible to place meaningful limits on television advertising, which increased its centrality in the presidential and congressional campaign process and decreased the relative importance of such campaign devices as leafleting, sign posting, rallies, and other techniques in which parties specialize. The court also struck down a provision that would have limited how much money a candidate could contribute to his or her own campaign thus opening the way for very rich individuals to self-finance their campaigns.

The overall impact of these changes was to greatly increase the importance of money in elections. The enhanced importance of television increased the need to buy air time. Because the Republicans had more successfully identified themselves as the party of business and of low taxes, Republican candidates were generally more successful at raising money than were Democrats. Also, the Republican National Committee, the executive arm of the party, was quicker to deploy sophisticated, computerized, mass-marketing techniques to raise funds. Finally, the weakening connection between grassroots efforts and campaigning lessened the need for presidential candidates to cultivate and involve local and state political organizations; this change particularly benefited Republican candidates such as Nixon and Reagan, who had little difficulty raising a vast amount of funds to fuel their own personal campaign organizations. Democrats, traditionally more reliant on the get-out-the-vote efforts of local unions, civil rights organizations, and other stalwart party coalition members found that these efforts, while valuable, did not compensate for the greater financial resources that the Republican presidential candidates were able to amass.

Despite their overall decline, party organizations continued to serve as an important vehicle for campaign fundraising, particularly because the 1974 amendments to the Federal Elections Campaign Act contained a loophole that enabled parties to raise and spend huge amounts of unregulated campaign funds known as "soft money." The 1974 Federal Elections Campaign Act did not seek to regulate donations to political parties that were used to support state and local campaign efforts. Such non-federal funds came to be known as "soft money" to distinguish them from "hard money," regulated donations to individual candidates and parties. Soft money was intended to be used for get-out-the-vote drives and for campaign paraphernalia such as bumper stickers and lawn signs.

Both parties raised huge sums of soft money, which – according to advocates of campaign finance reform – were used to evade the spirit, but not the letter, of the law. In the most controversial action, national parties funneled large sums of soft money to state parties for TV and radio advertising praising party candidates and attacking their opponents. These ads were not subject to campaign donation limits as long as they did not specifically ask voters to vote for or against a particular candidate. Interest groups evaded donation limits by doing the same thing.

The 2002 Bipartisan Campaign Finance Reform Act (BCRA), commonly known as McCain-Feingold in honor of its senatorial sponsors, was designed to reduce the role of soft money. It banned soft-money contributions to national political parties. All donations to political parties would now be subject to a $25,000 limit per donor. Recognizing that this ban would reduce the money available to carry out campaigns, the act raised the limit on hard-money donations from $1000 to $2000 per candidate per election. Finally, it prohibited corporations, trade associations, public interest groups, and labor unions from financing "electioneering communications" within sixty days of a general election or thirty days of a primary. An electioneering communication was defined as an ad that clearly identified a candidate and targeted his or her state or district, whether or not the ad explicitly asked voters to support or oppose the candidate. No sooner had this law been signed by President Bush than a number of plaintiffs, including the AFL-CIO, the California Democratic party, and the Republican National Committee, filed suits in federal court claiming that the statute violated free speech and the right of political parties to associate freely. In 2003, in *McConnell v. Feingold*, a sharply divided court upheld most features of the McCain-Feingold law. Four years later, in the case of *FEC v. Wisconsin Right to Life*, an equally divided court declared unconstitutional those features of the law that bars corporations, trade associations, citizen groups, and unions from using general funds for broadcast ads that mention the name of a federal candidate within thirty days of a primary election and sixty days of a general election. In the latter decision, Samuel Alito, who had recently replaced Sandra Day O'Connor on the court (see Chapter 11), was the deciding vote. Lifting these restrictions on interest groups reinforced the tendency of campaign finance reform to diminish the importance of political parties in elections.

Indeed, closing the "soft money" loophole had the consequence of creating another, perhaps more perverse one. McCain-Feingold's limit on donations applied only to political parties, not to other types of political advocacy organizations. The two most politically active forms of such organizations are known by the numbers that the Internal Revenue assigns to them for tax purposes, 501(c)4 and 527. 501(c)4 organizations such as NARAL Pro-Choice America, formerly the National Abortion and Reproductive Rights Action League, the National Rifle Association, and other single-issue lobbying groups can spend as much as 50 percent of their resources on election-related activities. A tax-exempt group organized under section 527 of the Internal Revenue Code is free to raise and spend as much money for political activities such as voter registration and mobilization efforts and issue advocacy as it is capable of doing. The only limitation is that this money cannot be spent for the express purpose of telling people to vote for a particular candidate. It can even be used for ads criticizing a candidate as long as the ad does not ask voters to vote for the opponent.

In 2004, 527 organizations were especially active and important. Table 11.2 lists the top fifty 527 organizations in terms of their expenditures on the 2004 congressional and presidential election. Table 11.3 lists the twenty largest contributors to 527 organizations during the 2004 election cycle. Notice that a single labor union, the Service Employees International Union, which endorsed Kerry, gave more than 53 million dollars to 527s, whereas its donations to the Democratic party and to Kerry directly were limited to $5000 each. Likewise, a single individual, George Soros, also a Kerry supporter, gave more than 23 million to 527s, whereas his donation to the Democratic party was limited to $5000 and his donation to the Kerry campaign was limited to $2000.

Two critical events in the 2004 presidential election show just how influential the 527 organizations have become and the degree to which they threaten to supplant not only parties but even the candidates' own campaign organizations. Working under an umbrella organization known as America Votes, a coalition of pro-Kerry 527 organizations – including MoveOn.org and America Coming Together – conducted the most ambitious voter registration drive in U.S. history, targeting the fourteen most politically competitive states. Historically, voter registration has been a quintessential political party activity and yet, in this most hotly contested of presidential elections, the Democratic party effectively outsourced this function to other groups beyond its control.

In a similar vein, arguably the most effective advertising campaign of the 2004 presidential election was conceived of and funded without the involvement of either a party or a candidate organization. The Swift Boat Veterans, a 527 organization, devised a series of ads criticizing John Kerry's war record and his anti–Vietnam War stances that effectively undermined the pro-military theme of the Democratic National Convention and placed Kerry on the defensive at a moment when his attacks on Bush appeared to be gaining traction.

Table 11.2. Expenditures of Top Fifty 527 Organizations, 2004

Committee	Total Receipts	Expenditures
America Coming Together	$79,795,487	$78,040,480
Joint Victory Campaign 2004*	$71,811,666	$72,588,053
Media Fund	$59,414,183	$57,694,580
Service Employees International Union	$48,385,367	$47,695,646
Progress for America	$44,929,178	$35,631,378
Swift Vets & POWs for Truth	$17,008,090	$22,565,360
MoveOn.org	$12,956,215	$21,565,803
College Republican National Committee	$12,780,126	$17,260,655
New Democrat Network	$12,726,158	$12,524,063
Citizens for a Strong Senate	$10,853,730	$10,228,515
Club for Growth	$10,645,976	$13,074,256
Sierra Club	$8,727,127	$6,261,811
EMILY's List	$7,739,946	$8,100,752
Voices for Working Families	$7,466,056	$7,202,695
League of Conservation Voters	$6,049,500	$5,078,116
International Brotherhood of Electrical Workers	$5,010,321	$7,368,841
Democratic Victory 2004	$3,696,869	$2,346,179
Laborers Union	$3,455,921	$3,294,785
America Votes	$3,174,936	$2,769,752
November Fund	$3,151,170	$3,124,718
Partnership for America's Families	$3,071,211	$2,936,666
National Association of Realtors	$2,979,522	$3,002,977
Grassroots Democrats	$2,819,483	$2,592,499
Stronger America Now	$2,790,817	$2,690,989
Democrats 2000	$2,547,677	$1,083,595
Coalition to Defend the American Dream	$1,925,890	$1,610,224
Sheet Metal Workers Union	$1,877,505	$1,897,379
GOPAC	$1,819,112	$2,367,852
Music for America	$1,717,820	$1,590,784
California Republican Convention Delegation	$1,600,750	$1,612,595
Illinois Hospital & Health Systems Assn	$1,420,512	$1,151,188
Safer Together 04	$1,387,727	$1,171,323
National Federation of Republican Women	$1,355,354	$3,462,507
Americans for Progress & Opportunity	$1,306,092	$1,305,667
Ironworkers Union	$1,304,454	$1,225,327
Republican Leadership Coalition	$1,294,950	$1,300,752
Environment 2004	$1,205,849	$1,167,762
Americans United to Preserve Marriage	$1,192,090	$1,056,962
Americans for Better Government	$1,185,174	$1,230,227
Progressives League	$1,175,000	$210,105
Natural Resources Defense Council	$1,112,307	$1,005,283
Young Democrats of America	$1,110,227	$723,781
Public Campaign Action Fund	$1,109,209	$990,056

Table 11.2 (continued)

Committee	Total Receipts	Expenditures
Gay & Lesbian Victory Fund	$1,103,509	$1,374,220
America's PAC	$1,081,700	$1,061,336
Mainstreet USA Inc	$1,060,000	$1,110,002
Save American Medicine	$1,000,200	$935,250
Americans for Jobs, Healthcare & Values	$1,000,000	$994,137
Arts PAC	$898,622	$191,711
Florida Leadership Council	$878,500	$729,516

* Joint Victory Campaign 2004 (JVC) is a joint fund-raising committee run by America Coming Together and the Media Fund. Money raised by JVC is divided between these two beneficiaries. Combining receipts for these three groups would result in double-counting.
Source: Center for Responsive Politics, OpenSecrets.org. Data from Internal Revenue Service, October 3, 2007.

Table 11.3. Twenty Largest Contributors to 527 Organizations in 2006 Election Cycle

Contributor	Total
Service Employees International Union	$53,208,553
Joint Victory Campaign 2004*	$37,104,391
Victory Campaign 2004	$32,915,000
Soros Fund Management	$23,581,000
Peter B. Lewis/Progressive Corp	$22,395,000
Golden West Financial	$13,007,959
Shangri-La Entertainment	$12,631,193
Perry Homes	$8,085,199
Sustainable World Corp/Linda Pritzker	$7,205,000
American Federation of State, County, and Municipal Employees	$5,219,035
Gateway Inc	$5,010,000
Ameriquest Capital	$5,002,000
AG Spanos Companies	$5,000,000
AFL-CIO	$4,843,151
BP Capital	$4,600,000
Sierra Club	$4,382,899
Amway Corp	$4,020,000
Chartwell Partners	$4,001,000
August Capital/Andrew Rappaport	$3,643,400
Alida Messinger Charitable Lead Trust	$3,383,200

* Joint Victory Campaign 2004 (JVC) is a joint fund-raising committee run by America Coming Together and the Media Fund. Money raised by JVC is divided between these two beneficiaries. Combining receipts for these three groups would result in double-counting.
Source: Center for Responsive Politics, OpenSecrets.org. Data from Internal Revenue Service, October 3, 2007.

Parties: Present and Future

Clinton's reversal of Democratic positions on budget balancing, crime, and welfare enabled him to recover from the 1994 congressional election debacle and win reelection in 1996. Deprived of their most popular issues, Republicans made no gains in the 1998 and 2000 elections despite the scandals that plagued Clinton's second term. As of 2000, the partisan balance was the most even in all of American history. The Republicans won the presidential election on the basis of a court contest over Florida's electoral votes while their candidate lost the national popular vote. As we describe in Chapter 7, the Senate majority changed on the basis of the switch of a single Republican senator. The Republicans held only a seven-seat margin in the House of Representatives. In 2002, the Republicans gained two additional Senate seats and six more in the House of Representatives. The 2004 election enabled the Republicans to increase their advantage. Bush defeated Kerry by a 51 percent to 48 percent popular vote margin, and Bush won fifteen more electoral votes than he did in 2000. The Republicans also gained four seats in the Senate and four in the House. But as discussed in Chapter 7, the Democrats won back control of both houses of Congress in 2006. Fifty-four percent of all voters nationwide voted for Democratic congressional candidates while only 46 percent voted for Republicans. This represented a larger margin of victory for the Democrats than the Republicans enjoyed in 2004. As of December 2006, 37 percent of the electorate called themselves Democrats as opposed to only 27 percent who called themselves Republicans. Twenty-seven percent identified themselves as independents.

Like the Republican resurgence that preceded it, this new period of party balance has not brought about any rebound in party strength. The same dominance of media and money that contributed to the earlier decline remains in place. Nonetheless, parties are still integral aspects of American politics. Although the percentage of those who identify themselves with one party or the other has declined, it still outnumbers the percentage of those who call themselves independents. Even in the wake of the soft-money ban, parties continue to raise large sums of money. And parties remain the devices by which all federal and most state officials are nominated for office and by which legislatures are organized. This section examines the factors that account for the current party divide.

It paints a portrait of those who call themselves Democrats and of those who call themselves Republicans. Many important features of these portraits are the same as if they had been painted fifty years ago but many equally important features are strikingly different. Several key features of the two-party portraits can be discerned in Table 11.4, which displays gaps

George W. Bush spoke of "compassionate conservatism" when he accepted the 2000 Republican party nomination for president. Bush attempted to broaden the Republican coalition to attract moderate voters, women, and minorities. Bush regained his party's nomination in 2004, above, and went on to win the election.

in the two-party presidential vote according to a variety of different sociological and geographical categories.

The Fate of the New Deal Coalition

Three of the principle bedrocks of the New Deal Democratic coalition remain in place. African Americans and Jews are the two most loyal Democratic voting blocs. Only 26 percent of African Americans voted for George Bush in 2004, whereas almost 59 percent of white voters voted for Bush. Jews supported Kerry over Bush by a margin of 74 percent to 25 percent. The third bloc that has remained loyal to the Democrats since the 1930s is labor union members and their families. In 2004, 59 percent of those who said they had a labor union member in their family voted for Kerry.

The two most significant defections from the New Deal Democratic coalition have been Catholics and white Southerners. Beginning in 1968, Catholic voters began to migrate to the Republicans. In 2004, even though

Table 11.4. Voter "Gaps" in the 2004 Two-Party Presidential Vote

	% for George W. Bush	% for John F. Kerry	**Gap in Bush Vote**	% of the electorate
Race Gap				
White	58.7	41.3	**31.1**	77.1
Non-white	27.6	72.4		22.9
Religion Gap				
Weekly attendee	61.1	38.9	**16.8**	41.8
Less-than-weekly attendee	44.3	55.7		58.2
Income Gap				
$50,000 a year or more	57.0	43.0	**12.3**	54.5
Less than $50,000	44.7	55.3		45.2
Region Gap				
South, Midwest	55.2	44.8	**8.6**	57.2
Northeast, West	46.6	53.4		42.8
Place Gap				
Suburbs, rural	54.5	45.5	**8.6**	60.7
Large and small cities	46.9	53.1		39.3
Gender Gap				
Male	55.5	44.5	**7.3**	46.0
Female	48.2	51.8		54.0
Generation Gap				
40 or older	53.3	46.7	**4.4**	65.5
Younger than 40	48.9	51.1		34.5
Education Gap				
Some college or less	53.1	46.9	**3.2**	57.9
College degree or more	49.9	50.1		42.7
All	**51.5**	**48.5**	**3.0**	**100.0**

Source: "Introduction – Gapology and the Presidential Vote," by Laura R. Olson and John C. Green, PS, XXXIX, no. 3, July 2006: 444.

the Democratic nominee, John Kerry, was a Catholic, Bush carried the Catholic vote 52 percent to 47 percent. As was mentioned in Chapter 7, Catholics gave the Democrats a modest majority of 56 percent in 2006, demonstrating that they remain a significant "swing" vote. Before the 1965 Voting Rights Act, Southern whites voted overwhelmingly for the Democrats while Southern African American were precluded from voting. Since 1965, Southern African Americans have adopted the Democratic party loyalty of their Northern brethren while Southern whites have moved into the Republican camp. Whereas FDR carried every Southern state in 1936, John Kerry did not carry a single Southern state in 2004. White Southerners have moved into the Republican party in large numbers because they became disillusioned with the national Democratic party's

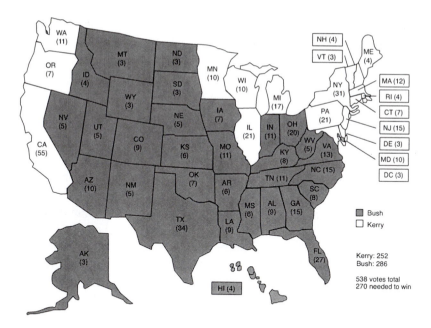

Figure 11.3. Electoral Map of the 2004 Presidential Election.

stand on a wide variety of issues, including affirmative action, school prayer, gun control, and abortion. The conversion of Southern whites from the Democrats to the Republicans is the single most decisive shift of party loyalty in modern times.

Regions

The Northeast, Midwest, and West have traditionally been more politically competitive than the South, but this regional pattern now seems to be changing. A look at the electoral map in Figure 11.3 shows just how stark the regional disparities were in this most recent presidential election.

If the 2004 election is any guide, the only two-party competitive states left in presidential elections are in the Midwest. Although the Midwest is an identifiable region, it shares traits with both the increasingly Democratic and the increasingly Republican regions. Like the Democratic Northeast, the Midwest is highly industrial, has many big cities, and is racially and religiously diverse. Like the Republican South, it is strongly agricultural, has many small cities and towns, and has a large population of funda-mentalist Protestants. For the foreseeable future, the relative strength of the two parties will be determined by the region of the country that is nearest to being a microcosm of the whole: the Midwest. The 2006 elections once again demonstrated the volatility of Midwestern voting. Democrats defeated incumbent Republicans in Ohio and Missouri; added the governorship of Ohio to an impressive list of Midwestern Democratic governors; and picked up House seats in Indiana, Ohio, and Iowa.

Suburbia

Whereas the regions of the country have come to be dominated by one party or the other, an opposite trend is happening in the most heavily populated area of each region, the suburbs. As we discussed before, for most of the twentieth century, the migration to the suburbs that began in the 1920s favored the Republicans. But in the last few decades, many of the largest suburban counties – Orange County in southern California; Westchester, Nassau, and Suffolk Counties near New York City; and Montgomery County near Philadelphia – have gone from being overwhelming Republican to being competitive between the two parties, or, in the case of the New York suburbs, to favoring the Democrats. In 2006, the Democrats captured a number of additional suburban congressional districts in the Northeast and Midwest. On the other hand, many counties that were previously rural have experienced sufficient population growth to be labeled as "suburban." These new suburbs vote overwhelmingly Republican. They were decisive in Bush's victory over Kerry in the key "swing" state of Ohio. Kerry got even more votes in Ohio's major urban areas than expected and held his own in the older suburbs adjacent to Cleveland and Cincinnati. But those gains were more than counterbalanced by the enormous majorities that Bush obtained in the fast growing, newer suburban counties far removed from downtown.

Religion

As we have seen throughout this book, religion has often been a divisive element in American party politics. But, with the exception of African Americans, the electorate divides less over which religion one belongs to than whether one is religious at all. Because most Americans continue to claim to be religious, the Democratic party leadership has sought to erase its image as the secular party. Bill Clinton, Al Gore, and John Kerry publicized their strong religious attachments. Nonetheless, Republicans are much more united in their support of proposals to give federal grants to religious schools and to religious social service providers and less reticent in identifying with religious causes, and they retain the allegiance of non-African-American religious voters accordingly. Indeed, in 2004 being religious was second only to racial identity in terms of its accuracy as a predictor of how someone was going to vote. Those who said they attended church every week voted 61 percent for Bush and only 39 percent for Kerry whereas those who attended less than once a week (which includes those who do not attend at all) voted 46.6 percent for Bush and 53.4 for Kerry.

Gender and Marriage

For the first fifty years that women had the right to vote, they voted for the two parties in the same proportion as men. But, in the last thirty years, women have tended to vote for the Democrats more than men do. In 2004, 55.5 percent of men voted for Bush but only 48.2 percent of women did so. On closer examination, however, the so-called "gender gap" is largely explicable by the far wider "marriage gap." Fifty-eight percent of married people – both men and women – voted for Bush. Fifty-nine percent of all unmarried people voted for Kerry. The role of gender is merely to widen the impact of the marriage gap. Married men voted 60 percent for Bush, unmarried women 62 percent for Kerry. Married women and single men voted more or less as did voters at large.

Income and Education

Income and education are the two most common measures of a person's social standing. At least since the New Deal, poorer, less educated people voted for the Democrats far more than richer, better educated people did. The impact of education and income on party loyalty has not entirely disappeared, but it is no longer as strong or as simple as it used to be. Regarding income, the impact is strongest at the most extreme points of the income distribution. Among the richest fifth of Americans, those whose household income is $92,000 or more, 38 percent call themselves Republicans, 27 percent Democrats and the rest, neither. Among the poorest fifth of Americans, those with annual household income below $19,000, Democrats enjoy a 42 percent to 20 percent advantage. As one gets closer to the middle, the role of income in predicting party loyalty fades. Those whose household income is between $58,000 and $92,000 favor the Republicans, but only by 36 percent to 31 percent. Those who make between $19,000 and $38,000 favor the Democrats by an almost identically narrow margin, 35 percent to 28 percent. Among whites in this income range, the majority now favor the Republicans 33 percent to 29 percent. Among those to be found in the absolute middle, with incomes between $35,000 and $58,000, the electorate is evenly divided – 33 percent favor the Democrats and 32 percent favor the Republicans. Republicans lead among whites, 36 percent to 28 percent.

The relationship between education and party loyalty is quite different. The Democrats win at both extremes. Voters who did not graduate high school as well as those with education beyond college both favor the Democrats. Those in the middle – high school graduates, those with some college education, and those who have graduated college but have not gone on for postgraduate study – all favor the Republicans. Whereas the poorest and least educated Americans favor the Democrats so do the most highly educated. Americans in almost all the other income and education brackets favor the Republicans.

Guns

Forty-three percent of American voters own guns. Sixty-three percent of gun owners voted for Bush. Because gun owners are mostly white and come disproportionately from rural areas, small towns, or less densely settled suburbs, one cannot say for sure that they voted for him because they are gun owners. Nonetheless, 63 percent is such a large number that it does suggest that the Republican tradition of opposing restrictions on gun ownership did contribute to Bush's great success among these voters.

These portraits of party loyalists help us to understand what aspects of a person's private life appear most politically relevant. Despite the great impact of the civil rights laws and major shifts in racial attitudes, race remains the clearest political party divide. A large majority of African Americans are Democrats, a majority of whites are Republicans. Income and education remain important but are only politically decisive at the extremes. Very rich Americans are mostly Republicans, poor ones Democrats. The most educated and the least educated are Democrats. But for the vast bulk of Americans, those who are likely to consider themselves middle class, their party affiliation is not clearly traceable to their level of education and income. Women are somewhat more Democrat-leaning than men, but married women are not. Married men are overwhelmingly Republican, but single men are not. Except among African Americans, church-going people are Republicans, those who go to Starbucks on Sunday morning, not church, are mostly Democrats.

Southerners and those in the Rocky Mountains and Great Plains are mostly Republicans. Easterners and Pacific Coasters are mostly Democrats. But these regional differences are misleading. Southern and Southwestern big cities such as Atlanta and Houston, and university towns like Austin and Chapel Hill favor the Democrats. Many rural areas of Northeastern states favor the Republicans. Region may simply be too broad a category to be helpful. Atlanta and Houston have very large African American populations. Austin and Chapel Hill have large populations of single people, people with postgraduate education, and Sunday morning Starbuckers. Many rural counties in New York or New Jersey are settled mostly by church-going, gun-owning, married whites. The best explanation of regional and state differences in party loyalty is that different regions and states contain differing proportions of churchgoers, married people, and, at least in the cases of the Rocky Mountains and Great Plains, African Americans. Whether one lives in a suburb or not is no longer a good indication of how one will vote because the older suburbs are no longer the exclusive enclaves of married whites and the sort of social pressure that encouraged near universal church going is no longer so strong. Many suburbs are now home to non-whites, non-churchgoers, and single people.

Polarization

Several of the issues that now most divide the two parties are questions of morality and liberty – abortion, gun ownership, and homosexuality, for example. The prominence of these issues may help to explain an otherwise incomprehensible aspect of contemporary partisan politics: its rancorous tone and divisiveness. On most issues, Republicans and Democrats have actually been quite successful in compromising their differences. But these issues of morality and liberty fester. It is very hard to be kind and generous toward partisan opponents whom you believe are murdering unborn children or, alternatively, are trying to deprive you of your right to deal with your own body as you see fit. American politics has always been highly moralistic. Debates over temperance or gambling were at least as moralistic in tone and as passionate as those over abortion or homosexuality. Indeed, what is most striking about all these issues is how the arguments for each side tend to go right past each other. What one side sees as a moral question, the other side defines as one of personal liberty. For example, people who favor legalized abortion do not claim that it is a good thing but rather that women have a right to choose whether to have an abortion. Abortion opponents view abortion as murder and claim that no one has the liberty to commit murder.

Likewise, supporters of gun control claim that guns cause violence. Opponents do not necessarily disagree, but they rest their case primarily on grounds of liberty. They claim that the Second Amendment to the Constitution grants citizens the right to own guns. Similarly, supporters of temperance in the nineteenth century claimed that prohibition of alcohol was necessary to protect family life. Opponents did not defend the positive aspects of alcohol so much as they did their right to drink it if they so wished.

The second characteristic of these issues is that they do not readily lend themselves to compromise. True, issues like the tariff in the late nineteenth century or the minimum wage in the 1930s raised questions of morality and freedom. But economic questions are much easier to bargain over. A tariff can be reduced or increased by a few cents, as can the minimum wage. In the case of abortion policy, however, it is either permissible to destroy a fetus or it is not. Related issues such as parental notification or the permission of the spouse are less absolute in their implications, and supporters and opponents have indeed found room for compromise. But those compromises are tangential. The fundamental difference of principle remains deeply divisive. Likewise, supporters and opponents of gun control have been able to compromise on relatively marginal issues regarding licensing and waiting periods. But on the question of whether citizens have a constitutional right to own a handgun, the two sides remain utterly and bitterly divided.

For the reasons discussed in the previous section, regions differ significantly in their outlook on these highly charged issues, and their congressional delegations differ even more. For example, Rocky Mountain voters are much more opposed to gun control than are voters in the Northeast. And because most Rocky Mountain districts contain anti–gun control majorities, those districts elect anti–gun control representatives, thereby depriving any congressional voice to the significant fraction of dissenting voters in those districts. If congressmen were elected by proportional representation instead of single member districts, the Rocky Mountain delegation would contain a significant minority of pro–gun control congressmen. A similar story could be told about abortion in the Northeast, where the percentage of members of Congress who support abortion is even higher than the percentage of voters who take that position in the region as a whole.

Thus, the growing importance of such hot-button issues as abortion and gun control combines with the single-member-district character of Congress to produce representatives who are more polarized on the issues than is the country taken as whole. These factors, rather than any impressive improvements in the ability of congressional party leaders to discipline members, account for the rise in like-minded voting of representatives of the same party.

Peace and War

The bitterness and *polarization* of modern party politics is also attributable to increasing party difference over questions of peace and war. As we discussed earlier in this chapter, ever since 1972 the Democrats have moved in an antiwar direction. As a result of September 11, 2001, national security has become the paramount issue on voters minds and they increasingly view the two parties as offering distinct and antagonistic approaches to keeping

America safe. As of November 2006, 77 percent of Republicans believed that going to war in Iraq was the right decision for the United States while only 20 percent of Democrats agreed. Independents were more divided, with 38 percent thinking it was the right decision and 47 percent saying it was wrong. Sixty-one percent of Republicans believed the war was going well while only 16 percent of Democrats and 34 percent of independents thought so. In 2006, a majority of Democratic senators supported a resolution to establish a firm timetable for pulling troops out of Iraq. In August of 2006, the most prominent pro-war Democrat, Senator Joseph Lieberman of Connecticut, was defeated in the party primary by a previously unknown antiwar candidate, Ned Lamont. Lieberman won reelection in November of 2006 running as an independent but his primary defeat demonstrates the powerful antiwar antipathy prevalent among Connecticut Democrats.

Expanding the Party Coalition

In their never-ceasing competition to add to their political strength, both parties are constantly on the lookout to add blocs of votes to their side. Because Latinos are the fastest growing ethnically identifiable segment of the population, the parties have been particularly active in pursuing them. Since 1970, roughly 600,000 of the roughly 1,000,000 immigrants who come to the United States each year come from Central and South America. Latinos make up roughly 13 percent of the U.S. population, a percentile that has increased 74 percent over the past sixteen years. However, many Latinos are not citizens and even those who are citizens register to vote in lesser numbers than other groups do. Latinos currently constitute only 8 percent of the electorate. But as they assimilate to life in the United States, this percentage is expected to grow substantially. It is already much higher in several of the most populated states including the three largest – California, New York, and Texas. Although Latinos currently favor the Democrats by a larger percentage, the Republicans believe that the strong religious and family ties and work ethic of Latinos make them very susceptible to Republican appeals. George W. Bush was very successful in winning over Latino voters in his Texas gubernatorial campaigns. In the presidential election of 2000, he did well again among Texas Hispanics but not with Hispanics in California, New York, and Illinois. In the wake of the 2000 election, both parties greatly increased the amount of money and staff devoted to enlisting Hispanic support. For up to two weeks, Republican officials from selected states immersed themselves in Spanish vocabulary and conversation at the Berlitz Language School in Washington.

President Bush, in his role as party leader, has played an active and visible role in the Republican effort. He frequently speaks some Spanish during public appearances. In January of 2002, he held a televised town meeting in California sponsored by the Latino Coalition Foundation, the Ontario Hispanic Chamber of Commerce, and the Latin Business Association. Bush regularly invites Hispanic business owners to the White House, and each year he observes Cinco de Mayo, an important Mexican holiday. The Republican party produces a new Spanish-language television show that airs monthly on Telemundo and Univision affiliates in six cities and feeds stories about Bush to Spanish-language newspapers. The Democrats are involved in similar efforts aimed at protecting and hopefully increasing their current advantage.

In 2004, Bush received 44 percent of the Latino vote, a gain of 8 percentage points from 2000. But these Republican gains evaporated in 2006, when Hispanic support for GOP candidates dropped to 29 percent. Post-election surveys seemed to indicate that the vocal opposition of many congressional Republicans and conservative grassroots activists to a proposed immigration bill that would give an estimated 12 million illegal immigrants a chance at citizenship drove Hispanics back to the Democratic camp. Bush backed citizenship for many individuals who reside in the United States illegally, but House Republican leaders blocked a path to citizenship in the immigration bill, and GOP conservatives, such as Representative John Hostettler of Indiana, who lost his re-election bid, made their opposition a campaign issue. Box 3 describes the tensions that can arise when a political party must choose between investing in expanding its base and in winning elections.

Box Three: Contemporary Politics

Fifty States versus Marginal Seats

In 2005, Howard Dean, the former Vermont governor and contender for the 2004 Democratic presidential nomination, was chosen by the chairs of the state Democratic committees to be the new national Democratic party chair. True to the spirit of his insurgent presidential campaign, Dean sought to reinvigorate the party from the bottom up. He announced a "50 State Strategy" to enable Democrats to win "in every state, ever county and every precinct." In support of this strategy, the Democratic National Committee (DNC) embarked on an expensive effort to hire and fund teams of organizers dedicated to increasing party membership and party activity in all fifty states, including those with few Democrats and no reasonable chance of winning many additional congressional seats or Electoral College votes. The state level organizers were to recruit and train local leaders who, in turn, would recruit more leaders and volunteers until "every single precinct in their area has a trained, effective organization of Democrats dedicated to winning votes for Democrats."

In the fall of 2006, polls showed that the Democrats might be able to win a majority in both Houses of Congress. Leaders of the Democratic House and Senate congressional campaign committees asked Dean to shift money away from the broad fifty-state effort in order to provide more money to close congressional races. They argued that such an infusion might well make the difference between gaining or failing to gain Democratic congressional majorities and that such a victory would mean more to the party than gaining new Democratic adherents in states where the party would still remain in the minority. Dean refused.

The Democrats gained control of both Houses anyway, but this did not silence Dean's critics. James Carville, one of the most prominent of all Democratic party campaign consultants and a chief architect of Bill Clinton's presidential campaigns, demanded that Dean resign his party post. He claimed that Democrats could have picked up as many as fifty House seats, instead of the thirty-one they did win. The reason they did not, he said, was that the Democratic National Committee did not spend some 6 million dollars it could have put into House races against vulnerable Republicans. Carville likened the Democratic takeover of Congress to the Civil War battle at Gettysburg, which the Union army won but then failed to pursue the Confederate army when it retreated. "We should have chased them down," Carville said. Both Dean and Carville sought to rally their supporters to defend their position. Support for Carville came mostly from consultants and elected officials based in Washington. State party leaders backed Dean and he easily held on to his job, but the conflict between those who favored the grassroots party-building strategy and those who want to give priority to winning congressional elections continues to boil.

This dispute reminds us that political parties have various objectives and that those objectives can conflict with one another in crucial ways. Parties are local and state organizations dedicated to electing mayors, state legislators, and governors, *and* national organizations dedicated to winning the presidency and obtaining a majority in Congress. These two roles are often compatible. Strong grassroots organizations can and do help in national elections and control of federal offices can be used to bolster local strength. But they also compete with one another when choices must be made about how and where to spend scarce resources.

Election Strategy

Despite the enormous differences between election campaigns fought at the local, district, state, and national levels, two basic strategic elements are common to them all. To win a close election, a candidate must mobilize his or her "base" and attract "swing" voters. A candidate's base consists of those voters who are assumed to have a strong affinity for him or her. This affinity may arise from any number of sources – ethnicity, religion, geography, or some other point of common identification – but the most stable and durable source is party. Therefore, a great deal of the activity in any partisan campaign involves making sure that all of one's own party members actually come out to vote. Speeches and ads seek to show how loyal a particular candidate is to party principles and how much the other party candidates differ with them. Phone banks and door-to-door canvassing are used to compile lists of reliable party voters and to prod them to go to the polls.

As Republicans learned in 2006, important as it is to mobilize the base, few elections can be won solely by bringing out the party faithful. Candidates also try to devise messages and issue positions that will appeal to those "swing" voters who are not closely identified with either party. Because those who are most politically active are also most closely attached to a party, it is often very hard to tell who those unattached voters actually are. Nonetheless, especially in a close election, candidates and their staffs are compelled to find ways to attract them. In the 2000 election, a large swing vote was thought to consist of "soccer moms," suburban women with school age children torn between their support both for the more fiscally conservative message of the Republicans and the more socially compassionate message of the Democrats. In 2004, a critical swing vote was supposed to consist of "NASCAR dads," blue-collar men whose concerns about wages and job security pushed them toward the Democrats but whose views on national security and social issues turned them toward the Republicans. The key *swing voters* in 2006 appear to have been Catholics and Latinos, both of whom swung toward the Democrats.

Conclusion: Political Parties, Democracy, and Liberty

The contemporary party system both resembles and differs from the one envisaged by Martin Van Buren in the 1830s. Most strikingly, it is still dominated by only two parties, one of which Van Buren himself belonged to. Third parties appear from time to time, but they rarely win. Parties grant the nominations that are the prerequisite for election to almost all major offices. They provide money and people power for election campaigns. And they structure the choice about candidates made by voters. Although Americans often complain that there is not much difference between the two parties, this lament is not true. The typical Republican officeholder has very different opinions about a whole host of issues including abortion, guns, taxes, environmental regulation, relations between church and state, and education than does the Democratic counterpart. Therefore, voters generally have a meaningful choice at election time. It is relatively easy for the public to replace the party in power with the organized and loyal opposition.

Van Buren's vision has been altered in three significant ways. First, he saw party as a device for restraining presidential ambition. But party leaders no longer exert much influence in the actual choice of presidential candidates. Therefore, after the election, the winner is not much beholden to party chieftains. Indeed, the roles are reversed; it is the president who anoints the national party chair and dominates the life of the national party. The two parties are no longer primarily state and local organizations who come together in convention once every four years to choose a president. Now, the party of the president is mostly just another tool for raising money and promoting the president's agenda and prestige with the voters. It is not at all clear what role the other party performs, except to raise money for candidates and wait on tenterhooks for the next presidential election. Parties retain their greatest importance at the legislative level, where they remain the mechanism for determining legislative leadership.

Second, parties were conceived as a means for overcoming sectionalism. Ever since the Virginian Thomas Jefferson chose the New Yorker Aaron Burr as his running mate, parties have sought to encourage national ties and feelings. When they failed to do so in the 1850s, there was civil war. As this chapter mentions, each party is becoming more dominant in particular regions, with fewer and fewer states remaining competitive between them. Although today is not the 1850s and there is no threat to the Union comparable to that posed by slavery, a large republic is always subject to being gradually pulled apart, and parties today seem no longer capable of playing a powerful positive role in pulling America back together.

Third, Van Buren recognized that the essentially local nature of parties provided a second important form of federalism and therefore a second crucial means of protecting the people's liberty against oppressive central authority. Parties are no longer deeply grounded locally, so they cannot play this important role. Equally troubling, they no longer command the loyalty of a very large fraction of the people, and that fraction is growing. Party once provided a means for people to escape the chains of private self-absorption and reach out into the public realm, but it is less and less able to do so.

Parties arose to redress key threats to democracy and liberty that the Constitution could not cope with by itself. If parties are no longer as effective in restraining presidential ambition, reducing regional differences, and combating privatism, some or all of those threats are likely to grow, and new means must be found for curbing them.

Chapter Summary

☆ The Constitution makes no mention of political party, reflecting the Framers' antipathy to political parties.

☆ The Democrats were the first mass political party in world history. They were founded by Jefferson and Madison and significantly revived by Martin Van Buren and Andrew Jackson.

☆ During the 1830s, a two-party system developed based on the electoral competition between them, which led them, at least occasionally, to gain and lose power.

☆ The party system and the decentralized political parties that composed it served as crucial protectors of liberty and promoters of democracy during the nineteenth century.

☆ Lincoln's party leadership was a critical factor in preserving the Union.

☆ In the late nineteenth century, the Democrats moved significantly to the left in the process of co-opting the Populists.

☆ The Progressives sought to destroy the power of party organizations by draining them of patronage. They provoked the passage of federal civil service reform laws designed to replace the spoils system with a merit system.

☆ FDR exploited his victory in 1932 to create an enduring majority coalition for the Democrats. The key components of the New Deal Democratic party were labor, Catholics, African Americans, and big city political organizations in the Northeast and Midwest.

☆ In the second half of the twentieth century, the two most important population trends – movement of people from the Northeast and Midwest to the Sun Belt states of the Southeast and Southwest, and from rural and urban areas to suburbs – favored the Republicans who also benefited from a decrease in Democratic party identification among Catholics.

☆ Parties declined in the latter third of the twentieth century because patronage diminished; television lessened the importance of their traditional methods of electioneering; presidential candidates relied more on personal campaign organizations; and campaign spending increased astronomically.

☆ Contemporary party identification is more tightly bound to issues of religion and foreign policy than to income.

☆ The key swing voters in the 2006 elections were Catholics and Latinos, both of whom swung toward the Democrats.

Major Concepts

Bipartisan Campaign Finance Reform Act (BCRA) of 2002
coalitions
decentralization
factions
partisan versus non-partisan elections
party caucuses
party conventions
party identification
party system
party primaries
patronage
polarization
Populists
Progressives
proportional representation
single member districts
soft money
suffrage
swing voters
voter turnout

Suggested Readings

Aldrich, John. *Why Parties?* Chicago: University of Chicago Press, 1995.

Burnham, Walter Dean. *Critical Elections and the Mainsprings of American Politics.* New York: W. W. Norton, 1971.

Chambers, William Nisbet, and Walter Dean Burnham. *The American Party Systems: Stages of Political Development.* New York: Oxford University Press, 1975.

Epstein, Leon. *Parties in the American Mold.* Madison: University of Wisconsin Press, 1986.

Fiorina, Morris. *Divided Government.* Boston: Allyn and Bacon, 1996.

Hershey, Marjorie Random, and Paul Allen Beck. *Party Politics in America*, 10th ed. New York: Longman, 2002.

Key, V. O. *Politics, Parties, and Pressure Groups*, 5th ed. New York: Thomas Y. Crowell, 1964.

Reichley, A. James. *The Life of the Parties.* Lanham, MD: Rowman and Littlefield, 2000.

Schattschneider, E. E. *Party Government.* New York: Holt, Rinehart, and Winston, 1995.

Wattenberg, Martin P. *The Decline of American Political Parties, 1952–1996.* Cambridge, MA: Harvard University Press, 1998.

12 Public Opinion and Political Participation

This chapter focuses on:

☆ The rise of democratic participation during the first half of the nineteenth century especially as it was expressed through voluntary associations and political parties

☆ Changes in patterns of public opinion formation and participation that took place during and after the Progressive Era, particularly the Progressive emphasis on political reform and the expansion of the role of organized associations

☆ The Civil Rights Movement and the rights-oriented protest movements it spawned

☆ The meaning and importance of "social capital" and the impact of poll-based public opinion and interest-group advocacy on it

☆ The impact of September 11 on public opinion and popular participation

In 1998, Mark Bucher, an Orange County, California, political activist, joined two teachers, Roger Hughes and Kim Jacobsma, in a campaign to pass Proposition 226, the Paycheck Protection Act. It required California unions to obtain annual written permission from each member to use his or her dues for any political purpose. The same restrictions applied to corporations and their employees. It also banned foreign contributions to political campaigns.

Bucher and his political allies did not lobby the California legislature to pass this act. They framed it as an initiative to be approved by the voters. The Progressive movement of the late nineteenth and early twentieth centuries and its commitment to direct democracy had a profound influence on California, which altered its Constitution to allow citizens to enact laws on many important policy matters. Although established with Progressive reform in mind, ballot initiatives became a favorite tactic of conservative activists to challenge the state's progressive establishment. Beginning with Proposition 13, an anti–property tax measure passed in 1978, conservative activists have enacted a number of initiatives that constrain government revenues, reduce welfare benefits for illegal aliens, and prohibit public universities and state agencies from using affirmative action programs in admissions and hiring practices. The popular enthusiasm generated by these measures soon spread beyond California, propelled Ronald Reagan to the White House in 1980, and pushed taxes to the forefront of the national political agenda.

The target of Proposition 226 was the political clout of labor unions, whose *political action committees* (PACs) had been a critical source of support for liberal causes since the New Deal. Bucher belonged to the Orange County Education Alliance, a Christian conservative group that championed school vouchers and supported changes in curriculum, including the teaching of creationism and sexual abstinence. But alliance members found their efforts to win school board seats stymied by candidates backed by the teachers' unions. As one alliance member complained after having lost a race in which the California Teachers' Association (CTA) had spent $77,000 to defeat him, "How can you compete with people who can just pull money out of people's paychecks?"

The fight over local union campaign finance practices escalated beyond the control of Bucher and the CTA. California governor Peter Wilson hoped that striking a blow at union power would help him win the 2000 Republican presidential nomination. Partly because of Wilson's efforts, Proposition 226 became the first critical battle in a campaign led by business and conservative citizen organizations that spread to other states and, eventually, to Congress, which was in the midst of debating an overhaul to federal campaign finance. Wary of early polls that showed considerable voter support for campaign finance reform, the national labor federation, the AFL-CIO, told the press that labor was facing the most serious threat to its existence in a generation, and the organization promised to throw all the unions' resources into the California battle.

Countering the proponents' stress on a worker's right to choose, the unions emphasized the programmatic rights that workers had won since the New Deal (see Chapter 4). One of their television ads began with pictures of a little girl eating a brownie, a child raising his hand in class, and another getting a checkup by a doctor: "Food, quality education, healthcare we can depend on... these protections are guaranteed by California law.... But now big business [and wealthy individuals]... are pushing Proposition 226 to take power away from ordinary citizens.... They claim it protects union members, but [it] would shut working Californians out of the political process."

After an acrimonious five-month campaign, Proposition 226 was defeated, 52 percent to 48 percent. It failed because unions did a better job of mobilizing support than their conservative opponents did. A *Los Angeles Times* exit poll found that one-third of voters were from union households and that two-thirds of them opposed Proposition 226. Supporters spent $6,052,614; opponents spent $23,595,875.

Although this campaign polarized activists across the country, it aroused very little interest among ordinary Californians. The Proposition 226 fight hardly resembled the "pure" democracy that Progressives had celebrated. It was waged by well-heeled *interest groups* who spent lavishly on phone banks and media ads whose messages appeared to confuse voters as much as to educate them. For example, a survey showed that although a majority of Californians polled had voted against Proposition 226, 68 percent agreed with its basic principle, that "unions should be required to get a member's written permission before using his or her dues for political causes." As journalist David Broder wrote, "[T]he larger lesson of Proposition 226 is that the voters were not the source of the initiative campaign; they were its targets. They were not agents of political change; they were closer to being pawns in this interest-group struggle."

We note in Chapter 3 that James Madison opposed "pure democracy" because it was susceptible to mob rule and hostile to property rights. Proposition 226's direct appeal to voters was at odds with the Constitution's efforts to restrain democratic contests over fundamental principles. The Constitution's complex system of divided and separated powers was designed to promote indirect rule, filtering public opinion to "refine and enlarge the public views." But Madison's vision did not entirely prevail. As we point out in Chapter 4, Americans have throughout history engaged in democratic debate about the meaning of liberalism, their rights, and the proper interpretation of constitutional forms. Indeed, the two most critical episodes in American history, the Civil War and the New Deal, were struggles over the aims of the Declaration of Independence and its relationship to the Constitution.

American democracy has been animated in large part by distrust of authority. This lack of faith extends both to the public officials that the Anti-Federalists most feared – presidents, bureaucrats, and judges – and (as the fight over Proposition 226 revealed) to elected representatives as well. As we explain later in this chapter, the Progressive idea of democracy resonated powerfully during the political upheaval of the 1960s and led to the view that the American people should not only choose their representatives but should also have a direct say in the making and administration of public policy.

Direct democracy is now embraced by activists across the political spectrum to advance their causes. The initiative process has become a routine way of making critical government decisions in the twenty-four states that have adopted it. In the 1992 presidential election, Ross Perot, a Texas billionaire, decried the corruption and inefficiency of representative government and proposed creating an "electronic town meeting" that would use the internet to enable voters to examine policy options and record their judgments. He won 19 percent of the popular vote in that presidential election, the best showing by a third-party candidate since 1912.

And yet, as the Proposition 226 story illustrates and as widespread public opinion data substantiates, the more that direct democracy has advanced, the more unhappy Americans have become with their democracy. In part, this dissatisfaction follows from the impersonal nature of ballot *initiatives*, which do not enable citizens to deliberate together and to settle their differences face to face. Moreover, initiatives undermine the role of political associations such as political parties that help individuals make sense of, and participate effectively in, the political process. And direct democracy is now consumed by "rights talk," in which individuals and groups confuse the difference between fundamental freedoms and interests. Contests of opinion are no longer limited to periodic confrontations over matters such as slavery, discrimination, and economic justice; rather, they have become a routine part of political life, constant skirmishes that denigrate the meaning of rights and make the quest for consensus impractical.

This obsession with rights is a prime source of contemporary political difficulty. But individualism and rights discourse are deeply rooted in the American experience, and therefore it does little good to tell Americans to refrain from celebrating their rights. Nevertheless, lessons from the past show that tensions between rights and solidarity can be moderated, if never fully resolved. The politics of rights does not always undermine public spirit. Oftentimes, it stimulates civic participation and helps create civic harmony.

This chapter examines the development of American public opinion and participation, and it pays special attention to the tension between rights and solidarity. The first section looks at the rise of democratic participation during the first half of the nineteenth century and the political associations and social movements that fostered it. The second section focuses on changes in patterns of public opinion formation and participation that took place during and after the Progressive Era, which, as the Proposition 226 story showed, was a particularly crucial moment in the development of contemporary political life. In the third section, the tension between rights and solidarity in modern politics is discussed, and particular attention is paid to the Civil Rights Movement and the other rights-oriented protest movements it spawned. The fourth section describes how these earlier developments have worked to shape the contemporary political landscape into an uneasy combination of poll-based public opinion and interest-group advocacy, and it considers the consequence of a decline in what political scientists call "social capital." The chapter concludes with a reflection on the impact of September 11 on public opinion and popular participation.

The Awakening of American Democracy

The Constitution did not even mention the word citizenship nor provide a right to vote until the Fourteenth Amendment was enacted after the Civil War. Yet, since the Revolution, Americans have claimed the right to participate in politics and have protested when they believed those rights had been denied. The Founders may have moderated, but they did not destroy a sense of entitlement to participate in political life. Indeed, the preamble to the Constitution attributes ultimate authority to "We the People," who "ordain and establish the Constitution for the United States." The Constitution called on the "people" to accept constitutional procedures for delegating authority to representatives who would deliberate in their interest; but the people retained the power and the right to hold those representatives accountable.

Chapter 4 tells the story of how Thomas Jefferson's idea of a "living Constitution" had trumped Madison's hope that law would remain unchallenged and become the political religion of America. Liberalism was not displaced by democracy in 1800; but thereafter, the meaning of rights and the proper institutional arrangements to uphold them would be subject to democratic deliberation and debate.

The Democratic-Republican Societies

The awakening of democratic politics in the 1790s was embodied in the Democratic-Republican societies, which considered themselves extraconstitutional agents of the people. As one proponent argued, "the security of the people against any unwarrantable stretch of power" should not be "confined to the check which a constitution affords" nor to the "periodical return of elections; but rests also on the jealous examination of all the proceedings of the administration."

The Democratic-Republican societies were much more vocal than the Republican party in attacking political elitism. They were the philosophical and political heirs of the Sons of Liberty and Committees of Correspondence that acted as enforcers of republican orthodoxy during the Revolution, but the political context of the 1790s was profoundly different. The Revolution led to the birth of a republic, dedicated to protecting the "natural rights of man." The 1790s revealed that Americans disagreed among themselves over natural rights and what sort of government best upheld them. The Constitution made no provision for such fundamental popular disputes; and Americans still had not settled on regular practices to resolve them.

The controversy stirred by the Democratic-Republican societies came to a head with the Whiskey Rebellion in 1794. Secretary of the Treasury Alexander Hamilton's 1791 financial plan included a tax on whiskey (see Chapter 4). Although it is not clear how much of a direct role these societies played in the rebellion, the increasingly democratic climate of opinion they helped create emboldened those farmers most aggrieved by the tax. This militant opposition was centered in the four westernmost counties of Pennsylvania, where whiskey was so important to the local economy that it was used, like money, as a medium of exchange. The tax was especially detested because it was levied and enforced by what seemed a distant, indifferent federal government.

With support from Democratic-Republican societies in western Pennsylvania, farmers sent petitions to Congress and resisted efforts to collect revenues. A federal marshal and an excise inspector were forced to flee the area, and for two weeks western Pennsylvania was agitated by impassioned meetings, radical oratory, threats to oust all federal authority from Pittsburgh by force, and occasional acts of violence. President George Washington called out the militia of four states and, with Secretary Hamilton and Pennsylvania governor Thomas Mifflin at his side, led an army of 13,000 to confront the rebels. In the face of this massive show of force, the rebellion quickly dissolved.

The Whiskey Rebellion highlighted the tension between democracy and liberalism. The Constitution did not discuss whether and how direct protest in the name of rights against government could be considered legitimate. Washington and the Federalists feared that organizations like the Democratic-Republican societies, formed outside of government, would destroy the republican character of the Constitution. Staunch Federalist George Cabot insisted, "[W]here is the boasted advantage of a representative system . . . if the resort to popular meetings is necessary." This opposition to the very idea of voluntary political association sparked a heated debate on the nature of democracy and representation. The Democratic Society of Philadelphia, which had condemned the Whiskey Rebellion, now championed vigorous public debate: "If the laws of our Country are the echo of the sentiment of the people is it not of importance that those sentiments should be generally known? How can they be better understood than by a free discussion, publication and communication of them by means of political societies?"

The Democratic-Republican societies lost much influence in the face of Washington's denunciation. Their members looked to Jefferson's party as an alternative vehicle for their philosophical and political aspirations. Many members became prominent Republican leaders. Schooled in the societies' freewheeling activities, they helped breathe life into the Republicans' commitment to equality and fraternity.

Democracy Ascendant

Although their defense of the Democratic-Republican societies showed them to be more supportive of popular rule than the Federalists were, Jefferson and Madison did not intend to make direct political action and militant party politics a regular feature of constitutional government. Instead, they attempted to recast constitutional forms to conform more closely with the Anti-Federalist understanding of government. They invested much faith in local and state politics, especially state legislatures, which enjoyed far more intimate contact with constituents than Congress did. As the political historian Michael Schudson has noted, popular interest in state politics expressed itself in controversy over the location of the state capitals. Communities far from the capitals fought to relocate them closer to facilitate sending a full legislative delegation and to communicate more readily with their representatives. Between 1776 and 1812, all thirteen original states considered relocating their state capital, and nine of them did so.

This concern to move government closer to the people was also expressed by electoral reform. Property qualifications for *suffrage* that had begun to erode during the Revolution were gradually dismantled. Delaware eliminated property qualifications in 1792. Maryland followed suit a decade later. Massachusetts, despite the eloquent opposition of John Adams and Daniel Webster, abolished them in 1821. New York did so the same year. Only Virginia held out, clinging to them until 1850. For nearly five decades, residents of its rapidly expanding western counties had clamored to eliminate such restrictions and to redistribute seats in the lower house of the state legislature. Yet Eastern slaveholders resisted such changes, fearing not only the loss of political power but also a populist upheaval that might eventually undermine slavery itself. By 1824, every other state provided suffrage to virtually all white male adults. Box 1 discusses a contemporary political controversy regarding the proper limits of the voting franchise.

Box One: Contemporary Politics

Ex-Felons and the Right to Vote

More than 2 million Americans are currently in prison. The Fourteenth Amendment to the Constitution permits states to deny the vote "for participation in rebellion, or other crime." Forty-eight states make use of this constitutional exception to the right to vote to ban prison inmates from voting. Thirty-three states extend the ban to those on parole and twenty-nine to those on probation. In addition, six states extend the ban to felons who have served their full sentences, regardless of their crime, and seven other states ban only felons who have committed various severe crimes. The *Washington Post* estimates that as of 2004 these various restrictions kept a total of 4.7 million Americans from voting including 13 percent of all African-American men.

Several states are in the process of reconsidering their policy toward felons voting. Those who seek to ease the restrictions focus particularly on ex-felons. They argue that these persons have paid their debt to society and that it is unfair to continue to punish them by restricting their rights. They also point out that society has a stake in fully absorbing ex-felons back into society and that it is counterproductive to stigmatize them by depriving them of a civic duty.

Opponents counter that just because a person finishes a prison term does not automatically signify that they have entirely "paid their debt." They say that those who cause bodily harm to others can never fully pay back that debt and that the very high rate of recidivism (freed prisoners committing crimes once released) shows that most ex-felons will become felons again. At a minimum, they demand that ex-felons demonstrate that they have become useful, law-abiding citizens before the vote is restored to them.

This question has important partisan implications. Ex-felons are disproportionately African-American, tend to have little education, and are likely to be poor. They belong to socioeconomic and racial categories that vote mostly for the Democrats. It is not surprising therefore that Democratic party leaders and elected officials have been in the forefront of the effort to obtain voting rights for ex-felons while Republican leaders have tended to oppose it.

Popular election of governors and the president (through the Electoral College) became standard practice. After 1832, South Carolina stood alone in having its state legislature choose electors. In 1824, six state legislatures selected governors for their states; by 1844, only two did. Local offices also became elective, especially in the West. Illinois and Indiana provided for elected county offices in their first constitutions. The Eastern states were more resistant, but not immune, to this democratizing spirit. New York made many local offices elective in 1821; Delaware in 1831; Pennsylvania in 1838.

Political struggles to expand the franchise displayed a healthy tension between the democratic and liberal traditions. First in the states and later nationally (through the amendment process), a drama played out in which popular will registered at the polls stood in tension with constitutional constraints embodied in written compacts. Democratic practices would weaken constitutional constraints in fits and starts during the nineteenth century, but Americans took their state and national charter documents, and the idea of rights they embodied, very seriously. Significantly, when democratic reforms did come, they were deliberated over in state constitutional conventions.

The Art of Association

During his visit to the United States in the 1830s, the Frenchman Alexis de Tocqueville identified the American habit of forming *voluntary associations* as a distinctive and vital ingredient of American democracy:

There are not only commercial and industrial associations in which all take part, but others of a thousand different types – religious, moral, serious, futile, very general and very limited, immensely large and very minute. Americans combine to give fetes, found seminaries, build churches, distribute books, and send missionaries to the antipodes. Hospitals, prisons, and schools take shape in that way. Finally, if they want to proclaim a truth or propagate some feeling by the encouragement of a great example, they form an association. In every case, at the head of a new undertaking, where in France you would find the government or in England some territorial magnate, in the United States you are sure to find an association.

Tocqueville explained how these organizations – rather than threatening the Constitution, as Washington had feared – strengthened political life by correcting for the Constitution's greatest weakness, its insufficient attention to the conditions nurturing an active and competent citizenry. Echoing Anti-Federalist concerns, Tocqueville warned that "if they did not learn to help each other voluntarily," individuals who were obsessed with their privacy and rights would become helpless, expecting government to do everything for them. By participating in civic associations, the democratic individual would become part of a vital community and learn a sense of responsibility that would counter a "danger that he would be shut up in the solitude of his own heart."

The American Temperance Society, devoted to reducing alcohol consumption, provides a powerful example of how a locally based social movement acquired national power. The society was founded in 1826 and organized on the basis of local chapters. Building on the religious fervor of the Second Great Awakening (see Chapter 4), it appealed to the broad middle class, urging on them intelligent self-control. Having heard that Americans were dedicated only to their material prosperity, the English visitor Edmund Grund was surprised to find that in a single year, the New York Temperance Society gained 50,000 members. Its local chapters printed 350,000 circulars and sent them to every family in the state, inviting each to "abstain from the use of ardent spirits, and to unite with a temperance society." They also printed and distributed 100,000 "Constitutions for Family Temperance Societies," in which the members were "to pledge themselves not only not to use ardent spirits themselves, but not to suffer them to be used in their families, or presented to their friends, or those in their employment, except for medical purposes." Its members also pledged to instruct their children in the ways of abstinence. "They were to agree to place a copy of the [society's] Constitution in their family Bible," to which "their children should be pointed as containing the will of their parents and they were to engage them; as they revered the memory of their parents, sacredly to regard those sentiments."

Although the temperance movement had religious origins and stressed voluntary action, it sought state and national government support. It besieged Congress with petitions asking representatives to promote abstinence. In 1833, Secretary of War Lewis Cass presided over a congressional temperance meeting that adopted a resolution proclaiming Congress's responsibility to aid in protecting public morals. By 1833, the society had 2 million members, out of a national non-slave population of only 13 million. Alcohol consumption had soared after the Revolution and reached a high of four gallons a year per person by 1830, nearly triple present-day levels. By 1845, as the temperance movement gained momentum, consumption dropped to below two gallons a year per person. This success shows how local communities and religion revitalized the American democratic tradition. Although social movements operated outside the formal institutions and practices of the Constitution, they helped galvanize political participation that significantly reduced this space between government representatives and public opinion.

Even as it exercised moral and religious persuasion, the Temperance Society worked to enhance material prosperity. Productive farms and factories required sober laborers. Moreover, temperance societies allowed upwardly mobile Americans – professionals, small business people, and skilled artisans – to improve their social standing. The temperance movement showed that Americans could cultivate mutual responsibility and solidarity without undermining individualism and private property. It fostered civic involvement in a manner compatible with the liberal tradition.

Parties and Elections

Local temperance and other voluntary associations wrote constitutions and bylaws, elected officers, and formed statewide federations governed by annual conventions of locally elected delegates. These practices became models for political parties, which by the 1830s were governed by local, state, and national conventions that nominated candidates, published platforms, and enacted rules for election campaigns.

Political parties reciprocated, helping to sustain the vitality of civic associations by drawing people into political life and cultivating a habit and taste for collective action. The very game of politics, the excitement of competition for votes and the rewards of victory, overcame Americans' natural distaste for working collectively. "A whole crowd of people who might otherwise have lived on their own," Tocqueville noticed, "are taught both to want to combine and how to do so." So one may think of political parties as "great free schools to which all citizens came to be taught the general theory of association."

Participation in elections became a form of self-expression, an assertion of the individual's understanding of his or her rights, but one that took place in concert with other citizens in the collective act of self-government. Voting was not just an opportunity to select public officials. As Philip Nicholas argued on the floor of the Virginia Constitutional Convention of 1829, "it was the right by which man first signifies his will to become a member of Government of the social compact.... Suffrage, is the substratum, the paramount right" on which rested the rights stated in the Declaration of Independence: "the right to life, liberty, and the pursuit of happiness."

By the 1830s, this strong bond between voting and natural rights encompassed virtually every aspect of American life. Club officers, schoolteachers, and team captains were all elected. Democratic principles even penetrated military affairs. Rejecting a standing army as an affront to their egalitarian sensibilities, Americans until the Civil War fought mainly in state militia that selected their own leaders. Foreign visitors, accustomed to the deference accorded leadership in Europe and Great Britain, were startled by the constraints that elections placed on officeholders, corroding the very idea of representation. State legislators, and even members of Congress, were expected to return home after every legislative session to talk with constituents about what they had done and what they would do in the future. "Christ how I hate democracy," moaned a weary North Carolina congressman suffering from the ceaseless chase for public approval.

Andrew Jackson was one of the first political leaders to grasp the new politics that celebrated the ordinary citizen; indeed, his presidency signified its ascendance. For the first time, an inauguration was held outdoors, and ordinary citizens gathered in the capitol to celebrate their hero's rise to power. Jackson's opponents claimed that crowds rushed the new president as soon as he took his oath and that Jackson was forced to escape from the back of the Capitol, only to fight past a wall of people to reach the White House. They claimed the executive mansion was swamped by a mob of 20,000 supporters who "spread filth, smashed glassware, vaulted through windows to get at tubs of whiskey on the lawn, and even obliged a makeshift ring of guards to escort the president to safety." In fact, the large crowd that welcomed Jackson to the presidency was mostly well behaved. Jackson himself thought things went quite well that day. The excitement aroused by his election, he sensed, would empower him to use his office aggressively. Democratic elections not only empowered voters, they gave influence to a new breed of politician who appeared to embody the will of the people.

Local political parties forged a vital link between public officials and voters. Democrats and Whigs drew communities into national political life. Politics became mass entertainment. Parades, glee clubs, massive rallies, and barbecues were used to rouse voters. But entertainment was joined to instruction: parties cultivated new voters, kept issues before them, and brought them to the polls on election day. Even before the Civil War, partisans tended to speak of their organizations as an army, capable of mobilizing its troops repeatedly in an endless series of battles.

Although their organization and practices were decentralized, the two parties orchestrated national campaigns. When Jackson vetoed the Whig-inspired national bank bill, Senator Henry Clay of Kentucky, the Whigs' likely nominee for president in the next election, expected that Democrats from commercial states such as Pennsylvania and New York would abandon Jackson, weakening his reelection prospects. Instead, the Democrats waged a successful national campaign that preached the virtues of Jackson's veto and reestablished the Democratic doctrine of states' rights as the national creed.

Partisan loyalties began with provincial attachments to family, *ethnicity*, and locality. Although political parties mobilized citizens into rival camps, the general election promoted unity. In voting, Americans not only expressed their partisan loyalties but also their birthright as sovereign citizens deciding collectively.

Madison had hoped that improvements in communication and transportation would "dovetail the states" and transform a diverse people into a nation. But democracy, not technology, made America one country. As of November 7, 1848, well before the advent of the transcontinental railroad or the mass media, the United States established a standard presidential election day, and nearly 80 percent of all male citizens voted. European nations relied on ancient traditions and folk spirits to unite them; Americans called on democracy. Walt Whitman, the great poet, declared the rite of selecting presidents "America's choosing day," the Western world's "powerfulest scene and show."

Social Movement Militancy

There were limits to Jacksonian democracy; it denied the right to vote to women, slaves, Indians, and even free African Americans (except in a few states). The Democratic and Whig parties, in fact, sought to avoid divisive issues such as slavery that might splinter their support (see Chapter 11). But the abolitionists made suppression of the slavery issue impossible. Like the temperance movement, abolitionism grew out of the religious revival called the Second Great Awakening. But abolitionists were far more radical, fanning flames that eventually consumed American democracy and fractured the Union.

The movement's militancy was symbolized by William Lloyd Garrison. Once a supporter of the American Colonization Society, which supported gradual abolition and plans to colonize former slaves in Africa, Garrison formulated a new, more radical approach to slavery in the early 1830s. His newspaper, *The Liberator*, advocated immediate, uncompensated emancipation. In what is perhaps the most famous editorial in American history, Garrison told his readers, 60 percent of whom were black, "Urge me not to use moderation in a cause like the present. I am in earnest – I will not equivocate – I will not excuse – I will not retreat a single inch – AND I WILL BE HEARD."

Garrison revolutionized the antislavery movement by linking immediate abolition to African Americans' claim to equal rights. Slavery, he wrote, not only violated the Declaration's "self-evident truth...that all men are created equal," it also exposed America's corruption, crass materialism, shallowness, and irreligion. Calling the Constitution "a covenant with death and an agreement with hell," he burned a copy of it on July 4. No person or conscience, he argued, should participate in the corrupt political system it formed.

Garrison led the American Anti-Slavery Society, whose determined organizers spread antislavery sentiment in the North and challenged slavery's existence in the South. During the years before the Civil War, around 200,000 people, mostly from New England and places like western New York and northern Ohio that were settled by New Englanders, belonged to an abolitionist society.

But the political influence of the American Anti-Slavery Society was limited by its rejection of the Constitution and its ambivalence about the use of force. Its Declaration of Sentiments opposed "physical resistance," but the organization also recognized that the Founders' principles had led them to "wage war against oppressors." The radical nature of abolitionism, resting on a vision of freedom within a biracial society, sparked angry and occasionally violent opposition. A Boston mob seized Garrison in 1835 and paraded him with a rope around his body before he was finally rescued. Another mob burned down the American Anti-Slavery Society's Philadelphia headquarters. In 1837, in Alton, Illinois, the abolitionist editor Elijah Lovejoy was murdered when he tried to protect his printing press from an angry crowd who threw it into the Mississippi River.

At the Young Men's Lyceum Club in nearby Springfield, Illinois, young Abraham Lincoln alluded to the Lovejoy killing in his first important speech. Lyceums, clubs to promote learning and culture, were another form of democratically inspired nineteenth-century voluntary association. Lincoln's subject was the threat that mob violence, aroused by the slavery controversy, posed to America's constitutional tradition. Encouraged by the disdain that champions and enemies of slavery alike had for the Constitution, such violence would expose the America people to popular demagogues who would satisfy their lust for power by destroying the laws that protected individual liberties against unruly majorities. They would gain power "at the expense of emancipating the slaves, or enslaving free people." In the face of this danger, Lincoln invoked Washington, urging that "a reverence for the constitution and laws" become a civic religion, a reverence to serve as a bulwark against immoderate democratic passions.

As Lincoln described, the slavery controversy brought the liberal and democratic traditions, seemingly reconciled by the rise of voluntary associations and the two-party system, once more into fundamental conflict. But not all abolitionists rejected conventional politics. Although the Garrison wing of the abolitionist movement disdained the electoral process, other antislavery militants formed the Liberty party, which garnered 7000 votes in the 1840 presidential election. In 1848, many of them supported the Free Soil party candidate, former president Martin Van Buren, who received over 300,000 votes, about 10 percent of the total. The Free Soil campaign spurred party-building efforts that led to the creation of the Republican party in 1854, with abolitionists forming a principal part of the new party's coalition. The Republican party quickly replaced the Whigs as the Democrats' major rival in a realigned two-party system. Its candidate, Lincoln, won the presidency in 1860. Thus, the abolitionists helped inspire a major party transformation that eventually engaged the entire nation in a virulent yet exalted contest of opinion about the meaning of the Declaration of Independence and its relationship to the Constitution.

Political Debate as Political Theater

The Lincoln-Douglas debates, highlight of the 1858 Illinois Senate race, set the stage for the 1860 presidential election. With the whole nation aroused by the battle over slavery's extension to new territories, the two men received considerable attention. The incumbent Douglas was a national Democratic leader, author of the Kansas-Nebraska Act, and the likely 1860 Democratic presidential nominee. Lincoln, the underdog, had served only one term as a Whig congressman before defecting to the Republicans in 1856. Desperate to gain public attention, Lincoln challenged Douglas to fifty debates. The incumbent reluctantly agreed to just seven, each in a different Illinois congressional district. Those exchanges were a high point in the history of American political deliberation and participation. Thousands listened, for three hours at a time, to Lincoln and Douglas make complex arguments about slavery, the Declaration, and the Constitution. The speakers alternated going first. The opening debater spoke for an hour. His opponent had an hour and a half to reply. The initial speaker then had half an hour to rebut. The opening debate, at Ottawa, a town of 9,000 that was eighty miles southwest of Chicago, attracted at least 10,000 people, who came on foot, horseback, carriage, or Illinois River canal boat. A special seventeen-car train brought visitors from Chicago. Newspapers throughout the country provided extensive coverage. The *New York Times* reported that the Lincoln-Douglas contest was "the most interesting political battle-ground in the Union."

CBS news anchor Dan Rather, criticizing the 1992 Clinton-Bush debates, waxed nostalgic: "When you read the Lincoln-Douglas debates, they jump off the page at you for the depth and substance of the argument. It's exciting, even riveting." Rather gave too much credit to Lincoln and Douglas and went too far in condemning contemporary politics. The debates were not decorous discussions about slavery but were hard-hitting partisan affairs, with audiences shouting encouragement or disapproval of their favorite candidate. As Schudson points out, Douglas's opening remarks at Ottawa were greeted by cries one might hear at a football or hockey game: "Hit him again"; "Put it at him"; "That's it"; and "He can't dodge you." In a world without movies, television, internet, or mass spectator sports, politics was the best show in town. Like many heated political contests at the time, the Lincoln-Douglas debates were part politics and part carnival. Some audience members listened intently to the exchange between two talented statesmen, but many more were there to eat, drink, and socialize.

Lincoln and Douglas took account of their audiences' opinions and prejudices and shaped their arguments accordingly. Douglas's defense of popular sovereignty, in which he advocated that each territory decide for itself by majority vote whether to be slave or free, often degenerated into racism. Illinois was a border state that contained many Southern sympathizers. Douglas began his Ottawa remarks with rhetorical questions that elicited emotional, racist responses: "Do you desire to strike out of our state constitution that clause which keeps slave and free Negroes out of the state, and allow the free Negroes to flow in?" Many spectators shouted: "Never." Such a response was not surprising because the black-exclusion clause Douglas referred to had been enacted in an 1853 popular referendum by a two-to-one margin. Douglas concluded, to resounding cheers, "I am opposed to Negro citizenship in any and every form. I believe this government was made on a white basis."

Lincoln too pandered to his audience. Especially in those debates held in the southern part of the state, Lincoln strongly disavowed any belief in racial equality:

> I will say then that I am not, nor have ever been in favor of, bringing about in any way the social and political equality of the white and black races – that I am not nor ever have been in favor of making voters or jurors of negroes, nor of qualifying them to hold office, nor to intermarry with white people; and I will say in addition to this that there is a physical difference between the white and black races which I believe will forever forbid the two races living together on terms of social and political equality. And inasmuch as they cannot so live, while they do remain together there must be the position of superior and inferior, and I as much as any other man am in favor of having the superior position assigned to the white race.

The contrast between the abolitionist movement and Lincoln's Republican candidacy for the Senate in Illinois highlights the difference between social movements and electoral politics. Garrison and his followers attacked slavery uncompromisingly and showed disdain for the Constitution and politicians who did not share their messianic zeal. Lincoln was a mainstream politician who sought to win a Senate seat in one of the most racially prejudiced Northern states. Ending slavery required not only abolitionist consciousness-raising but also party politicians such as Lincoln who could make ending slavery palatable to the racist white majority.

Although Dan Rather was too uncritical of the debates, he was right to proclaim their greatness. Amid the raucous, emotionally charged atmosphere, Lincoln struggled and succeeded in finding a moral argument that voters could accept. The position he defended consistently proclaimed that slavery was wrong, that it violated America's scripture, the Declaration of Independence. Even when he conceded to white supremacy, Lincoln stood by this position: "I say upon this occasion I do not perceive that because the white man is to have a superior position the negro should be denied everything." Responding sarcastically to Douglas's charge that he advocated interracial marriage, Lincoln told his racist audience that they may not grant African Americans full citizenship, but they must not deny them their humanity.

> I do not understand that because I do not want a negro woman for a slave I must necessarily want her for a wife. My understanding is that I can just let her alone. I am now in my fiftieth year, and I certainly

never have had a black woman for either a slave or a wife. So it seems to me quite possible for us to get along without making slaves or wives of negroes.

From today's perspective, Lincoln's racial views are unenlightened. But in 1850s Illinois, his was an advanced position that put him at risk against a powerful incumbent far more willing to pander to racial prejudice. More important, Lincoln's willingness to participate in party politics, to accept American democracy with all its flaws and prejudices, drew Illinois voters into a thoughtful consideration of slavery, its relationship to the Declaration of Independence, and the meaning of the Constitution.

In the final encounter with Douglas in Alton, where Elijah Lovejoy had been murdered, Lincoln clarified the differences between Douglas and himself and between the parties they represented: "The real issue in this controversy, the one pressing upon every mind, is the sentiment on the part of one class that looks upon the institution of slavery as a wrong, and of another class that does not look upon it as a wrong." Linking the debate with Douglas to the universal principles of the Declaration, and the American Revolution's struggle against King George III, Lincoln reached an oratorical high point that anticipated the exalted statesmanship of his presidency.

> That is the issue that will continue in this country when those poor tongues of Judge Douglas and myself shall be silent. It is the eternal struggle between those two principles – right and wrong – throughout the world. They are the two principles that have stood face to face from the beginning of time; and will ever continue to struggle. The one is the common right of humanity and the other the divine right of kings.

Although November 2, 1858, was a cold, wet, and raw day in Illinois, more voters participated in that election for state legislators than had voted in the 1856 presidential election. In the judgment of most historians, Lincoln won the debates. The judgment of Illinois voters is more difficult to determine. Before the ratification of the Seventeenth Amendment in 1913, members of the U.S. Senate were chosen by the state legislatures, not directly by the voters. But because of the excitement the Illinois Senate race stirred, the candidates for the legislature pledged themselves to support either Lincoln or Douglas. The Republicans, in fact, held a state convention that formally nominated Lincoln for the Senate, only the second time that had happened in the country's history. Republican and Democratic candidates for the legislature won virtually the same number of votes statewide. Nonetheless, because of holdover seats held by Democrats, the Democrats still won control of the state legislature. Consequently, the Democratic majority in the new legislature elected Douglas.

Lincoln was bitterly disappointed, but his impressive campaign caught the attention of Republican leaders and established him as a contender for the 1860 presidential nomination. He had battled the nation's most famous Democrat on at least even terms, clarified the differences between Republicans and Northern Democrats on the "great and durable question of the age," and emerged as a Republican spokesman of national stature. Lincoln's presidential victory, in a rematch with Douglas, showed that American democracy could work, that the provincial, raucous, highly mobilized politics forged on the anvil of Jacksonian democracy was capable of producing a meaningful contest for the soul of the American Constitution. In 1860, 81 percent of the Northern electorate voted for candidates who debated the meaning of the Declaration and the Constitution at the deepest level.

As we point out in Chapter 11, even the Civil War did not diminish democratic energy and party resilience. The 1864 election – in which Lincoln was reelected in a highly competitive race with the Democrat candidate, General George P. McClellan – ensured that the war would continue and that its resolution would put an end to slavery. Lincoln and a Republican Congress were elected on a platform that called for a constitutional amendment abolishing slavery. The Thirteenth Amendment was ratified in 1865. As an 1864 Republican campaign pamphlet proclaimed, the Civil War confirmed "that the Constitution exists for the people . . . and we have a right to modify it to suit our needs according to our will."

A Right to Vote

The Civil War transformed the idea of American citizenship. With the Fourteenth and Fifteenth Amendments, the Constitution for the first time included the words *right to vote*. The Fourteenth Amendment confirmed that the Civil War, as Lincoln promised in the Gettysburg Address, marked "a new birth of freedom" in which African Americans were truly citizens. The amendment did not address the question of political participation directly, but it gave a definition to national citizenship by declaring that "all persons born or naturalized in the United States" were "citizens of the United States and the State wherein they reside."

The Fourteenth Amendment did not resolve the critical matter of how to enforce citizenship rights. Section 2 of the amendment indicated that any state that denied the right to vote to a portion of its male citizens would have its representation in Congress (and thus its number of votes in the Electoral College) reduced in proportion to the percentage of citizens excluded. But the clause would punish only Southern states for preventing blacks from voting; similar practices in the North would be tolerated. For this very reason, abolitionists such as Wendell Phillips saw the Fourteenth Amendment as a "fatal and total surrender." Members of the nascent women's movement, many of whom had participated in the abolitionist struggle, also attacked the amendment, claiming that the use of the word *male* tacitly recognized the legitimacy of excluding women from politics.

Nonetheless, the Fourteenth Amendment demonstrated that the Civil War had reinvigorated a national debate over the meaning of American democracy. Just as Jacksonian politics had expanded political participation for white males, so the Fourteenth Amendment began to extend it to African Americans, renewing efforts to reconcile liberalism's concern for individual rights with the collective aspirations of democracy. Although Lincoln never promised that emancipation would do more than grant African Americans a right to property – to enjoy the fruits of their own labor – more radical Republicans believed that full citizenship must include the right to participate politically.

The Fifteenth Amendment, which forbade federal or state abridgment of voting "on account of race, color, or previous condition of servitude," was intended to enfranchise African Americans. Critics complained that the amendment enabled the national government to usurp the states' power of defining the meaning of citizenship. But abolitionists and militant Republicans insisted that the very idea of "We the People" forged an unbreakable link between freedom and universal suffrage. As Frederick Douglass explained, to deprive African Americans of the vote "would lead us to undervalue ourselves, to put low estimate upon ourselves and to feel that we have no possibilities like other men." In the words of Wendell Phillips, "A man with a ballot in his hand is the master of the situation. He defines all his other rights. What is not already given him, he takes.... The Ballot is opportunity, education, fair play, right to office, and elbow room."

Once Congress approved the Fifteenth Amendment, it easily passed the requisite three-quarters of the state legislatures. Republican state organizations were particularly eager for its ratification in the wake of the unexpected difficulty that the Republican candidate and Civil War hero Ulysses S. Grant had in winning the 1868 presidential election. Enfranchising African Americans would boost Republican fortunes in the South and also in the border, Midwestern, and Mid-Atlantic states. Whatever the motive for its ratification, the amendment signaled to many Americans that the goals of the Civil War had been met. President Grant declared that the amendment "completes the greatest civil change and constitutes the most important event that has occurred since the nation came to life." African Americans jubilantly celebrated, hoping with Frederick Douglass that the amendment's ratification "means that we are placed on an equal footing with all other men . . . and that liberty is to be the right of all." Indeed, a number of former abolitionist groups disbanded on the assumption that now, finally, their work was done.

As we note in Chapter 4, those hopes would be bitterly dashed. The Civil War amendments failed to protect Southern African Americans against discriminatory registration requirements, literacy tests, and white primaries. Leaders of the women's suffrage movement responded with resentment to the continued exclusion of women from voting. Many of these leaders supported Jim Crow in an effort to enlist the backing of Southern women for their cause. Nonetheless, a crucial democratic watershed had been reached. The liberal principles of life and liberty and the democratic principle of equal voting rights had been enshrined in the Constitution.

The Emergence of Modern Democracy

The controversial compromise of 1877 that resolved the disputed 1876 presidential election ended Reconstruction and restored a form of local self-determination to American politics (see Chapter 4). As the slavery issue faded, ideological politics gave way to organizational politics. Congress and the states, not the president, dominated the councils of government. Decentralized, patronage-fed party organizations kept those institutions accountable to local and state party leaders.

Characterized by intense partisan loyalties and locally oriented politics that seemed indifferent to social justice or public policy, the late nineteenth century is often viewed as a provincial and corrupt age. And yet, some political scientists suggest that it offers valuable lessons for contemporary America. In important respects, the democratic tradition flourished; this period witnessed the highest turnout of eligible voters in American history. Nearly 80 percent of the electorate voted in the 1876 presidential contest; only a bare majority did so in 2000. More than three-quarters of the eligible electorate routinely turned out for presidential elections at the end of the nineteenth century; a turnout of 60 percent of the eligible electorate, as was the case in the 2004 presidential contest, signals an unusual surge of voter interest in contemporary American politics. Voting was not viewed simply as an obligation. Americans seemed to really enjoy politics. Local, disciplined party organizations drew people into politics not only with the promise of jobs but with torchlight parades, picnics, and mass meetings.

But despite the Fourteenth and Fifteenth Amendments, democracy was still, for the most part, limited to white males and shaped by party leaders indifferent to the rights of African Americans, Native Americans, and women. *The Wizard of Oz*, Frank Baum's popular 1900 children's novel, reads like an allegory of American political conditions of the time. The wizard, who proclaims mystical powers that will solve the problems of Dorothy and her companions, hides behind a curtain. His false mystique may very well be symbolic of presidents from Grant to William McKinley, who gave the appearance but not the reality of leading. Baum's novel also gave literary expression to growing aspirations for change. Dorothy and her friends the Scarecrow, the Lion, and the Tin Man are forced to look within themselves for solutions to their problems. Similarly, critics of the party system viewed localized democracy as a false form of popular rule that kept people from really taking political responsibility into their own hands.

Progressive Democracy

The assault on the decentralized republic at the end of the nineteenth century was born of protest against the emergence of corporate power. The reformist zeal of the Progressive movement was aimed primarily at taming the "monster" trusts. The rise of giant corporations created the perception that opportunity had become more unequal and that wealth was becoming concentrated. Moreover, many Americans believed that business interests, represented by newly formed associations such as the National Civic Federation, had captured and corrupted parties and public officials. Leaders of both parties were seen as irresponsible "bosses" who served "special interests."

Progressives championed government of people, directly by the people. Reformers fought for the Seventeenth Amendment, ratified in 1913, which provided for direct election of senators, and the Nineteenth Amendment, ratified in 1920, which gave women the right to vote. They also championed measures of "pure democracy," such as the direct primary, initiative, referendum, and *recall*, which would undermine the power of party organizations and give citizens more direct influence over politics and government in the United States. For all their differences, the New Nationalist and New Freedom Progressives that we discuss in Chapter 4 shared a commitment to purifying democracy and viewed the most serious problems in modern America as stemming from "distortions" of the people's voice – by political parties, interest groups, or "robber barons." The direct primary spread from Wisconsin in 1903 to thirty-nine other states by 1913. By 1920, candidates for virtually every local, state, and federal office (except for the presidency) were nominated directly by the voters. By 1914, eleven states had enacted some form of initiative and referendum process.

Progressives did not want merely to empower public opinion but also to educate it. School attendance became mandatory in several states. Because Progressives stressed responsibility rather than rights and community rather than individualism, they also looked to schools as centers of civic activity. They feared that enacting "tools of democracy" such as the initiative, referendum, and recall would be worthless unless used by those citizens who were, as one reformer put it, "aflame with the sense of brotherhood." Direct democracy would not be worth battling for if it degenerated into "a clash of selfish interests." Therefore, Progressive leaders gave support to the social centers movement, which was dedicated to revitalizing public life by recreating in urban life "the neighborly spirit" that Americans knew before they came to live in large, socially fragmented cities.

This movement started in Rochester, New York, where a former Presbyterian Minister, Edward Ward, envisioned public schools at the hub of a revitalized community spirit, "the instrument of that deepest and most fundamental education upon which the very existence of democracy depends." In Rochester, public schools were used as public baths, libraries, theaters, and forums for debate. In 1912, Ward founded the National Community Center Association to help proliferate community centers nationwide. During the 1912 election, both Theodore Roosevelt and Woodrow Wilson celebrated the use of schoolhouses as neighborhood headquarters for political discussion.

The third-party challenge that Theodore Roosevelt (TR) mounted under the Progressive party banner emphasized direct popular participation. In addition to the direct primary, initiative, referendum, and recall, the party platform advocated an easier method to amend the Constitution. Sensing that direct democracy was the glue that held Progressives together, TR's defense of it became bolder throughout that critical election year. Toward the end of September, in a speech in Phoenix, Arizona, TR proclaimed that he "would go even further than the Progressive Platform," applying the recall to everybody, including the President." This struck critics as a far more radical assault on republican government than even the Jacksonians had devised and committed TR to what *The Nation* magazine called "the bald doctrine of unrestricted majority rule."

The Progressive faith in national mass opinion appeared to threaten such valued features of the American liberal tradition as federalism and the separation of powers. Nonetheless, its celebration of the rights of the people resonated with the public at a time when the integrity of local and state governments was being undermined by industrial capitalism. Indeed, the Progressives were able to capitalize on the Jacksonians' democratization of the Constitution. One early Progressive tract stressed this connection between the older idea of local self-government and the Progressive idea of democracy:

> Direct legislation is law-enacting by the electors themselves as distinguished from law-enacting by representatives or by some aristocratic body, or by a single ruler, such as a king, emperor, or czar. In small communities this is accomplished by electors meeting together voting on every law or ordinance by which they are to be governed. In communities too widespread or too numerous for the voters to meet together and decide on the laws by which they are to be governed, Direct Legislation is accomplished by the use of imperative petitions, through what is known as the Initiative and Referendum.

TR finished second to Wilson in the 1912 election, and the incumbent Republican president, William Howard Taft, was a distant third. The Progressives won 27.4 percent of the popular vote and eighty-eight electoral votes. Except for the Republican party of the 1850s, no third-party candidate for the presidency before or after 1912 has received so large a percentage of the popular vote or as many electoral votes. The Progressives, not the Democrats or Republicans, set the tone for this critical political contest. The *San Francisco Examiner*, which supported Wilson, acknowledged that "[t]he People of this country are ready for something new, something different from traditional democratic practices." The Progressive party's support of measures to promote direct democracy "would surely have the attentive hearing of the American public."

The Rise of the Independent Press

Newspapers like the *Examiner* played a critical part in advancing Progressivism. Since the Jacksonian era, public debate had been dominated by local party newspapers that were sustained by patronage. Starting with the clash between Federalists and Republicans, party leaders had given valuable government printing contracts to loyal newspapers. But by the beginning of the twentieth century, the news media was transformed by the elimination of this form of patronage combined with the invention of inexpensive and rapid forms of printing. Insurgent political leaders such as TR and Wisconsin senator Robert La Follette, whom we discuss in Chapter 7, used mass circulation newspapers to go over the heads of party leaders and establish direct links with the public. "In the popular view," the Progressive political philosopher John Dewey wrote, "the press is regarded as the organ of direct democracy. It is the Court of Public Opinion, open day and night, ready to lay down the law for everything all the time."

One group of journalists, whom TR nicknamed "muckrakers," were especially important in transforming the American democratic tradition. Roosevelt derived the term muckraker from the description of the Man with the Muck-Rack in John Bunyan's *Pilgrim's Progress*, a bestselling religious allegory since it had been published in 1684. Just as Bunyan's muckraker could "look no way but downwards" as he cleaned a dirty floor, so the investigative reporters of the Progressive Era were obsessed with exposing the sordid and depressing rottenness of American politics. The muckrakers wrote for new and low-priced mass circulation monthly magazines such as the *Arena* and *McClure's*. As TR's Progressive party ally Senator Albert Beveridge wrote in 1910, "Party lines all over the country have pretty well disappeared." The cause was clearly "the cheaper magazines, which are circulating among the people and which have become the people's literature [producing] almost a mental and moral revolution among the people."

Celebrated muckrakers such as Ida Tarbell and Lincoln Steffens cast a critical eye on big business, prostitution, race relations, and even the churches. But their central theme was the corruption of American political life by an unsavory partnership between corporations and politicians. Embracing the Progressive faith in enlightened public opinion, muckrakers appealed to their readers' consciences. Steffens said that his famous series on the corruption of party politics in major urban areas, first serialized in *McClure's* and eventually published in book form as *The Shame of the Cities* in 1904, was "frankly intended to make people feel guilty for the corruption that riddled their cities" and was part and parcel of the corruption of American democracy.

TR feared that the muckrakers' focus on "vile and debasing" aspects of politics neglected society's constructive elements. His political ally, the fervent reformer Herbert Croly, complained that muckrakers merely stirred resentment, encouraging neither "searching diagnosis" of political and economic problems nor "effective remedial measures." Nevertheless, TR was happy to exploit this "literature of exposure," which reinforced his case for the need to make ordinary people masters over society, government, and the Constitution.

Progressive Reform and Civic Religion

We have noted how American political culture combines a secular belief in religious freedom with a religiosity born of the idea of America as a "city upon a hill" (see Chapter 2). The religious "awakening" of the early nineteenth century aroused social movements such as abolitionism that spurred political reform. Now the Progressives, many of whom were descendants of antislavery crusaders, directed that moral fervor against the sins of the industrial revolution. Their religiosity owed much to the *social gospel movement* that swept through the Protestant churches in the 1890s and early 1900s. Its goal was to ally Christianity with the crusade against poverty, corporate abuses, and political corruption. The Progressive party included many social gospelers in its ranks, lending credence to the claim that the party offered a "fitting medium through which the fervor, the enthusiasm, the devotion of true religion can utter itself in terms of social justice, civic righteousness and unselfish service." TR gave expression to this religious devotion at the Progressive party convention by characterizing his campaign for "pure democracy" as a "Stand at Armageddon" and a "Battle for the Lord."

Observing the reformist speeches punctuated by hymn singing, a reporter marveled that the convention "was more like a religious revival than a political gathering." But in the religious fervor of the delegates, journalists also detected the rumblings of a political revolution, an assault on the political practices of the decentralized republic that had dominated America for nearly a century.

Progressive morality sometimes degenerated into a narrow and intolerant form of evangelical Protestantism (see Chapter 4). But the social gospel was broad enough to embrace reform-minded Catholics, such as Father J. J. Curran who championed the cause of downtrodden Pennsylvania coal miners, and Jews, such as Oscar Straus who was the Progressive party candidate for governor of New York and whom reporters spied singing "Onward Christian Soldiers" at the Chicago convention. The most popular Progressive hymn, in fact, was the "Battle Hymn of the Republic," signifying the reformers' civic religion.

Just as secular reformers praised the whole people, social gospelers likewise proclaimed religious beliefs that downplayed, indeed scorned, particular theological doctrines and denominations. The esteemed social gospeler Walter Rauschenbusch argued, "We have been a wasteful nation. We have wasted our soil, water, our forests, our childhood, our motherhood, but no waste has been so great as our waste of religious enthusiasm by denominational strife. The heed of social service is seen in the fact that as the social spirit rises the sectarian spirit declines." The social gospel thereby invested religious fervor in the Progressive reformers' crusade for a new form of politics that would transform America into a national democracy dedicated to social justice and the common good.

Interest-Group Politics

When TR refused to run again in 1916, the Progressive party wilted. In a sense, its demise was a self-fulfilling prophecy, because its goal was to make party politics less important. It sought to shift political participation from political parties to the national government. In the nineteenth century, one belonged to a party as one belonged to a family or church – and national politics was held accountable to state and local party leaders. The idea and practice of Progressive democracy encouraged individual ties to the nation's capital that rivaled the individual's links to party and community.

But this attempt to create self-government on a grand scale risked weakening the very ties between citizen and government that it was designed to foster. With the decline of local and state parties, government services grew less connected to elected officials and more tied to the administrative agencies and bureaucracies over which voters had little control. Elected representatives, especially the president and members of key congressional committees, remained central to the day-to-day affairs of government, but they were increasingly attentive to interest groups who exerted influence through the leverage of public opinion, lobbyists, and expertise rather than mere election returns.

Political scientists Richard Harris and Daniel Tichenor have documented the rising influence of interest groups during the Progressive Era. Between 1889 and 1899, 216 groups appeared for the first time ever at a congressional hearing. Nearly three times that many, 622, testified for the first time in the first decade of the twentieth century. During the following eight years, more than 1000 new groups testified before congressional committees. Nearly every form of interest group increased during the Progressive Era – professional groups, trade associations, unions, and Progressive-minded citizens' groups. Growth was especially rapid among trade associations and citizens' groups, reflecting the intensity of the struggles between corporations and insurgents over the shape of the American economy during this period.

Because women continued to be denied the vote, women's organizations adopted interest-group methods. While still pressing for women's suffrage, they devoted increasing attention to publicity and lobbying efforts to achieve policy reforms in the areas of child labor, temperance, and protective legislation for working women.

The Decline of Democratic Participation

In their zeal to reduce corruption and set high standards for political participation, the Progressives imposed strict regulations on voting. The secret ballot, called the Australian ballot, swept the country between 1888 and 1896, symbolizing the Progressive ideal of the independent citizen. Similarly, the direct primary, the initiative, and the referendum encouraged

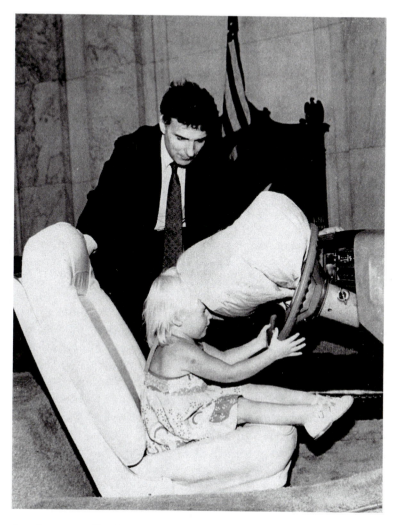

As a lawyer, political activist, and consumer advocate, Ralph Nader was a modern-day muckraker, exposing American car manufacturers' questionable auto safety devices in the 1960s. He became the leader of the public interest movement that used grassroots activism to challenge traditional politics.

citizens to vote their individual consciences. Hoping to make voting decisions more enlightened, to give voice to the whole people, Progressive reformers disdained collective organizations such as the Democratic and Republican parties, formed on personal, family, or community attachments. They also opposed the class-based partisanship – which pitted the working class against the propertied class – that developed in Western Europe and Great Britain during the early part of the twentieth century and that submerged "enlightened" voting decisions in favor of group solidarity. The perverse result of these reforms was to reduce active engagement in the political process. The Progressives' faith in the whole people betrayed them, for it ignored the reality that politics begins with more immediate, particular loyalties. The Progressives' aspiration for a public opinion that transcended family, place, and partisanship was perhaps noble, but it undermined those loyalties and attachments that gave vitality to democracy in the United States. Party organizations had mobilized voters who expressed their partisan and community ties at the polls – the very act of voting was a public exercise that reinforced the civic nature of political participation. Weakening party organization by means of primaries and secret ballots lowered voter turnout. In the presidential election of 1896, 85 percent of eligible citizens, outside the South, voted. In 1924, the total plunged to 53 percent.

In several respects, the Progressive attempt to free voters from partisan, parochial attachments also had the opposite effect. To maximize voter support, party leaders tried to moderate ethnic and religious divisiveness. Reduced party influence coupled with lower electoral turnout made it easier for zealots of various stripes to whip up public enthusiasm for racist and exclusivist policies that were rationalized on the basis of the distinctive virtues of Anglo-Saxon Christianity. Many states expanded their Jim Crow laws. In 1924, the United States abandoned its tradition of open immigration and effectively shut the door against people seeking to escape poverty and oppression in Europe and Asia.

The prime example of Progressivism's encouragement of zealotry was prohibition. Like the temperance movement, this new antialcohol campaign promised a healthier population, fewer abused wives and children, and more responsible working families. But the movement failed to distinguish between these laudable goals and a virulent brand of anti-Catholicism rooted in fundamentalist Protestantism and small-town hostility to the large cities heavily populated by new immigrants. Prohibitionists pointed to the sacramental use of wine by Roman Catholics to prove they were inherently drunkards. Whereas the temperance movement relied principally on voluntary efforts and organizations, Prohibitionism successfully invoked the power of the federal government via the Eighteenth Amendment to the Constitution, which prohibited "the manufacture, sale, or transportation of intoxicating beverages." Although Prohibitionism is no longer a powerful social movement, the question of how and when a voluntary organization's pursuit of its goals tramples on minority rights remains very much alive in contemporary America (see Box 2).

Free Association: Women, Gays, and Expressed Values

In recent years, tensions have emerged between constitutional guarantees of free association and of protection against discrimination. The Supreme Court has interpreted the First Amendment's right of free speech and assembly to mean that private associations can, on the whole, determine who can and cannot join them. But the court has had a difficult time determining how far that right extends. Both the U.S. Junior Chamber of Commerce and the Rotary Club claimed the right to exclude women from membership. The Supreme Court ruled against them on the grounds that freedom of association was not absolute and that protecting women against discrimination superseded that right at least in cases where such discrimination was not central to the organization's purpose.

However, in the case of *Dale v. Boy Scouts of America* (2000), the court supported a private association's right to exclude gays. James Dale, a former Eagle Scout, was assistant scoutmaster of the Monmouth Council, New Jersey, Boy Scout Troop 73. When his local Boy Scout Council discovered that he was an avowed homosexual and co-president of the Rutgers University Lesbian/Gay Alliance, they revoked his membership. Dale sued, claiming that New Jersey's public accommodations law prohibited this form of discrimination against gays. The New Jersey Supreme Court supported Dale, concluding that the Boy Scouts' large size, its non-selectivity, its inclusive rather than exclusive purpose, and its practice of allowing non-members to attend meetings all established that the organization was not "sufficiently personal or private to warrant constitutional protection" of its exclusionary membership policy in the face of the state's compelling interest in eliminating "the destructive consequences of discrimination from our society."

In a 5–4 decision, the U.S. Supreme Court overruled the state court. It determined that the Boy Scouts did have a constitutional right to exclude gay adults from serving as scoutmasters because opposition to homosexuality was one of its "expressed values," as written in a 1978 statement of the Boy Scouts' Executive Committee. In supporting the Boy Scouts, the court took pains to point out that it did not necessarily agree with the ban on gays: "It is not the role of the courts to reject a group's expressed values because they disagree with those values or find them internally inconsistent." Rather, the court insisted that normally groups have a right to exclude people as long as they can demonstrate that such exclusion is not arbitrary but is based on principles that are integral to the group's purpose. The Rotary Club and the Junior Chamber of Commerce failed to achieve that standard with regard to women. The Boy Scouts did attain it with respect to gays.

Debating Democracy

Disappointment with Progressive political reforms led many commentators to question the very idea of mass democracy. In *Public Opinion*, published in 1922, the journalist Walter Lippmann warned that in the "wild and unpredictable environment" of modern America, voters became dupes, as likely to be manipulated by popular demagogues as to be led by responsible politicians. The principal organ of direct democracy, the press, was ill-equipped to enlighten the democratic individual: "The newspaper at the best is a searching light moving restlessly about, bringing an episode here and there into the light." But society cannot be governed by "episodes, incidents, and eruptions." Lippmann proposed to substitute expertise for popular rule. Progressive reformers had embraced a false view of American individualism in proposing to create self-rule on a grand scale. As Tocqueville had argued, Americans would participate in politics only when they perceived that their self-interest was at stake. In modern America, where complex problems were beyond the ken of local communities and where radio, movies, professional sports, and other forms of mass entertainment competed for citizens' attention, Americans felt little urge to get involved in political life.

In the face of Lippmann's withering attack, John Dewey, America's leading public intellectual, sought to resurrect the idea of the whole people. Dewey granted that "pure democracy" had proven thus far to be fool's gold, exposing constitutional government to crass sensationalism and fractious interest-group politics. But instead of a national administrative state to rationalize democracy, as Lippmann advocated, Dewey proposed energizing democracy locally. Dewey did not intend to resurrect pure Jeffersonian democracy, in which localism could degenerate into parochialism. Instead, he proposed to modernize the concept and practice of local self-government so that individual loyalty would shift from the emotionalism of local ties "to the cumulative and transmitted intellectual wealth of the community." Building on the social centers movement, public schools and policy-oriented groups would transform communities into cosmopolitan spheres of civic action: "the Great Community, in the sense of free and full intercommunication," would do "its final work in ordering the relations and enriching the experience of local associations." In the 1960s, this idea of community action would become a key feature of President Lyndon Johnson's Great Society.

The Rise of Rights Consciousness

As we point out in Chapter 4, President Franklin D. Roosevelt (FDR) masterfully revitalized Progressivism under the "liberal" banner. Like TR and New Nationalist reformers, FDR championed mass democracy and national administration and agreed that public opinion would reach fulfillment with the formation of an independent executive power freed from the provincial and corrupt influence of political parties. But FDR's liberalism did not stress majoritarianism. As the very term *liberalism* implied, this new public philosophy was based on respect for rights. FDR championed a new, more expansive understanding of rights wedded to a readiness to use the federal government for important domestic and international purposes and to an inclusive popular nationalism. Unlike Progressivism, this new philosophy did not encourage American nativism. Under its banner, racism slowly gave way, and political support for immigrant exclusion, anti-Catholicism, and anti-Semitism eroded.

FDR gave expression to this more inclusive democracy in a 1936 New York City speech marking the fiftieth anniversary of the Statue of Liberty. Showing none of the concern that Progressives had displayed about "Un-Americanism," FDR celebrated immigration as vital to American democracy. Immigrants, he exulted, "looked to their future, wisely [choosing] that their children shall live in a new language and in the new customs of the people. The realization that we are all bound together by a common future rather than a reverence for a common past helped us build upon this continent a unity not approached in any similar area or population in the whole world."

Unlike European nations, FDR suggested, America was united not by bloodlines but by a belief in common principles, symbolized by the Statue of Liberty, that celebrated the dignity of the democratic individual.

FDR's emphasis on new rights, rather than on Progressive duties, resonated with ordinary citizens, especially in the teeth of a devastating depression. Unlike TR and the leaders of the Progressive party, whose support principally came from white, middle-class voters, FDR and the New Deal Democratic party made strong appeals to blacks and to labor. This appeal was reflected in such New Deal policies as Social Security and the National Labor Relations Act. In 1932, 65 percent of African Americans voted for Republican Herbert Hoover; in 1936, 76 percent voted for FDR. Unions gave FDR and his party vital financial and organizational support for the 1936 election. For the first time since the decline in voting during the 1920s, turnout increased. Of the 6 million new voters, 5 million voted for FDR. Among the poorest Americans, FDR received 80 percent of the vote.

The New Deal coalition, made up of urban workers, ethnic minorities, liberal intellectuals and professionals, and African Americans, did not initially embrace the Democratic party as an organization. Its principal allegiance was to government agencies and programs that embodied the New Deal economic order. Labor-management battles increasingly shifted from the shop floor to the offices of the National Labor Relations Board (see Chapter 4), with whom labor unions developed close ties. The fight for greater economic security also became more enmeshed in administrative politics, as groups such as the American Association of Retired Persons (AARP) established Washington headquarters as vantage points to monitor and lobby social welfare policy. The AARP, launched in 1958 with backing from a teachers' retirement group and insurance company, grew over several decades to 33 million adherents, a membership base that gave it considerable influence over the development of federal legislation affecting seniors.

The Civil Rights Movement and the Rights Revolution

The Civil Rights Movement played a critical part in advancing the new rights-based politics. As we discuss in Chapter 9, *Brown v. Board of Education of Topeka* (1954), which declared school segregation unconstitutional, launched the civil rights struggle that would dominate American politics and government for the next twenty-five years. The Warren court, which rendered this decision, continued the New Deal court's encouragement of citizen groups such as the National Association for the Advancement of Colored People (NAACP), founded in 1909, to turn to the courts to pursue their policy agendas. The NAACP established the Legal Defense and Education Fund in 1939 with a full-time legal staff and eligibility for tax-deductible contributions. NAACP lawsuits against school desegregation finally bore fruit in *Brown*, which helped mold a new form of citizenship that added the courtroom to the voting booth and the administrative agencies as a locus of political participation.

The Civil Rights Movement reverberated well beyond the courtroom, however. The *Brown* decision breathed life into the Equal Protection Clause of the Fourteenth Amendment by confirming the obvious but long contentious point that legal segregation deprived African Americans of full citizenship. But the judiciary could not adequately enforce this principle. Its efforts to do so led to massive resistance and oppression in the South. Laws specifically designed to discourage NAACP activities reduced the organization's membership below the Mason-Dixon line and forced many of its Southern branches to close. Just as discrimination forced the women's movement to develop innovative forms of participation during the Progressive Era, likewise repression helped shift the Civil Rights Movement's focus from litigation to mass organizing.

A bus boycott in Montgomery, Alabama, instigated this transformation. When Rosa Parks refused to give up her seat to a white man, she sparked protests that brought the fight for civil rights into the streets. These protests were carefully organized by civil rights groups that forged a sense of community among African Americans of different education levels and classes. As has been the case throughout American history, religious fervor contributed mightily to democratic protest. Churches were the backbone of the African-American community; they offered a rich culture of song, prayer, and ceremony that helped transform the Civil Rights Movement into a moral crusade. The political struggles of Montgomery were vindicated in 1956 when the Warren court declared bus segregation unconstitutional. Martin Luther King, Jr., a boycott leader, told a mass meeting that this court decision was "not a victory merely for 50,000 Negroes in Montgomery. That's too small. It is not a victory merely for sixteen million Negroes over the United States.... It will be a victory for justice and a victory for good will and a victory for the forces of light."

Unlike the abolitionists, King did not dismiss the Constitution but sought to build on reverence for it. He praised those protesters who conducted sit-ins at segregated lunch counters for "taking our whole nation back to those great wells of democracy which were dug deep by the Founding Fathers in the formulation of the Constitution and the Declaration of Independence. In sitting down at lunch counters, they were in reality standing up for the American dream."

As we discuss in Chapter 2, the idea of an American dream, as "yet unfulfilled," was a constant theme of King's speeches and writings. It permeated his most famous oration, the "I Have a Dream" address heard by more than 250,000 people gathered at the Lincoln Memorial during the 1963 March on Washington. The optimistic national spirit of the 1960s, born of World War II and the prosperity that followed, contributed to the warm reception that greeted King's celebration of the American creed. The communist

The arrest of Rosa Parks for refusing to give up her seat on a bus for a white passenger was the spark that helped launch the modern Civil Rights Movement to make African Americans full citizens.

menace of the Cold War did not dampen this optimism; if anything, it promoted devotion to the principles of freedom and democracy. King proved to be as indispensable an ally of Lyndon Johnson in prosecuting the civil rights revolution as Frederick Douglass had been of Lincoln in the struggle for emancipation.

The New Politics

The Civil Rights Movement inspired a whole array of new social movements and political organizations. By the end of the 1960s, women, gays, environmentalists, consumer advocates, and various ethnic groups were clamoring for new rights and demanding government attention. The growing rights consciousness encouraged Johnson to pursue not just an expansion of the New Deal, but a "Great Society" (see Chapter 4). His pursuit of this vision unintentionally encouraged political movements that would ultimately weaken the presidency. The Great Society helped to empower issue-oriented independents, representing broad causes and movements, who resisted presidential "management" and were less willing to trust administrative agencies.

The new politics that took shape in the wake of the Great Society thus featured a paradox. The new political associations and activists demanded more government programs, yet they deeply distrusted national administrative power charged with putting those programs into effect. The New Deal had combined an activist public philosophy based on rights with a national administrative apparatus designed to secure those rights. These new political movements sought to tear apart what the New Deal had sown together. Public opinion came to reflect this unlikely outlook. As noted in a famous 1967 study by Lloyd Free and Hadley Cantril, the American public had become "ideologically" conservative but "operationally" liberal, meaning that Americans were distrustful of government in general but supported virtually all the particular activities it undertook. By the late 1960s, the public expected the federal government to fight discrimination, improve education, protect the environment, and guarantee healthcare for all. Yet confidence in government had fallen precipitously. In the mid-1960s, three-quarters of Americans thought the federal government could be trusted to do the right thing most of the time. By the mid-1970s, only about one-third shared that view (see Figure 12.1).

Between 1965 and 1975, trust in government fell furthest and most dramatically not among self-described conservatives but among those who called themselves liberals, meaning New Deal liberals. By the twilight of the Johnson years, liberals came to identify big government with the Vietnam War, not social welfare policies. Their antipathy for President Richard Nixon, who continued the war and became embroiled in the Watergate scandal, deepened their hostility to centralized power. A younger generation of activists, born of the civil rights and antiwar movements and calling itself the New Left, condemned the New Deal state as the captive of indifferent bureaucrats, special interests, and imperialists. The New Left celebrated participatory democracy and decentralization. In contrast to the Progressive and New Deal reformers, the New Left generation was intensely suspicious of power. As the political scientist Hugh Heclo explained:

> To be a reformer was to be an activist, but also in a certain sense to be antigovernment. ... Distrust required opening up policy-making to the public view and assuring access for formerly marginalized groups. Confidence in administrative discretion, expertise, and professional independence had to be replaced by contentious public scrutiny, hard-nosed advocacy, strict timetables, and stringent standards for prosecuting the policy cause in question.

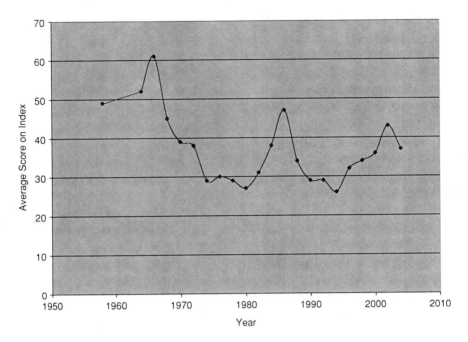

Figure 12.1. Trust in Government Index, 1958–2004. The decline in citizen participation in elections in the last half of the twentieth century coincided with a dramatic decline in trust in the national government.
Source: The American National Election Studies, www.electionstudies.org, 2007.

The Public Interest Movement

The New Left devoted most of its energy to large public protests: marches on Washington, sit-ins, and the like. Beginning in the late 1960s, consumer advocate Ralph Nader became the leading innovator of a new form of politics, known as the public interest movement, that shared many New Left objectives but used different political tactics. Harking back to the muckrakers, Nader and his exposé of the automobile industry, *Unsafe at Any Speed: The Designed-in Dangers of the American Automobile*, energized this new reform movement with revelations of corporate malpractice. When Congress responded by creating the National Highway Traffic Safety Administration (NHTSA) in 1970, Nader and other consumer advocates remained vigilant, constantly criticizing the agency for not regulating the auto industry aggressively enough. This political assault continued even after Jimmy Carter was elected president in 1976 and Nader's protégé, Joan Claybrook, was appointed as the head of NHTSA. This attack on NHTSA and other government agencies, joined by the media and judges, led to the expansion of government programs and to ever more restrictive controls on big business. The public interest movement resolved its ambivalence about centralized power by gaining influence through the exposure of government's failures.

As the political scientist Jeffrey Berry has written, "Leaders of the new [public interest groups] wanted to transcend 'movement politics' with organizations that could survive periods of intense emotion." Unlike the abolitionist and labor movements that lost influence when their causes were embraced by broader governing coalitions, the public interest movement sought to harness the revolutionary fervor of the Civil Rights Movement and the New Left in order to ensure their own survival. Therefore, despite their antiestablishment rhetoric and profound suspicion of centralized power, public interest activists did not try to get rid of bureaucracy. Instead, they made themselves an integral and permanent part of bureaucratic policy making. They fought to establish new agencies such as NHTSA and the Environmental Protection Agency (EPA) and to refurbish existing ones such as the Federal Trade Commission (FTC), which had been created during the Progressive Era but transformed during the 1970s into an aggressive watchdog of consumer rights. These new centers of administrative power were to be responsive to public interest activists. As Nader urged, regulatory bodies were not to be trusted to act for the public, but were to be directed by administrative procedures to enable public participation, "so that agency lethargy or inefficiency could be checked by interested citizen activity."

The attempt to marry administration and democracy led to a fundamental redefinition of rights and citizenship. By the late 1970s, statutory mandates and agency regulations provided for higher levels of citizen involvement in agency affairs. For example, Section 101(e) of the Federal Water Pollution Control Act Amendments of 1972 stated that

> [p]ublic participation in the development, revision, and enforcement of any regulation, standard, effluent limitation, plan or program established by the Administrator, or any State under this Act shall be provided for, encouraged, and assisted by the Administrator and the states.

Congress also fostered public participation by authorizing direct financial aid to citizen groups who participated in specific regulatory actions of certain agencies, most notably the FTC, EPA, and the Consumer Product Safety Commission.

Voter turnout declined dramatically in the second half of the twentieth century. If ordinary citizens find it difficult to muster the interest and time to take part in the relatively simple task of voting, they are most unlikely to participate in the far more complex and lengthy process of bureaucratic rule making. Therefore, the new governmental provisions promoted the participation of these self-proclaimed "public interest" representatives, not the public at large. For example, public participation funds that supported citizen access at the FTC were concentrated among a relatively few organizations. Consumer activists claimed that genuine grassroots participation in agency rule making was impossible because of the high level of expertise required. Federal subsidy was necessary to enable these activists to represent the public and to counter the influence of business and trade groups.

Citizen Suits

Many public interest advocates were lawyers. Therefore, they naturally turned to the courts as allies in their reform efforts. Courts and citizen activists would appear to be strange bedfellows. As we point out in Chapter 9, the Constitution established the judiciary as the guardian of the liberal order, of individual rights against unruly majorities, and gave federal judges life tenure to ensure their independence from public opinion. But the New Deal transformed the meaning of liberalism and the role of the courts. In the 1960s and 1970s, a raft of laws was enacted that couched public policy in terms of entitlements, as statutory rights, thereby inviting the federal judiciary to become a forceful and consistent presence in administrative politics. Lawsuits expanded access to the courts for advocates who claimed to speak for racial minorities, consumers, environmentalists, and the poor. By the 1970s, these *citizen suits* had become a crucial instrument for ensuring democratic control of the bureaucracy and enabling public interest groups to take direct action against lethargic government agencies and unethical corporations.

Joseph Sax, a law professor who educated many public interest lawyers, celebrated citizen suits as "a means of access for ordinary citizens to the process of governmental decision making and a repudiation of our traditional reliance upon professional bureaucrats." Reformers could fight big government and corporations by making innovative legal arguments rather than building political organizations. Of course, "ordinary citizens" could not do this themselves; they had to rely on "public interest" advocates to represent them.

Rights Consciousness and Conservative Movements

The public interest movement gained substantial influence on the policy process, but it did not solidify into an enduring political coalition. Its reliance on lawsuits, media exposure, and single causes was characteristic of what political scientist James Q. Wilson calls "entrepreneurial politics." The movement was dominated by a small number of Washington-based groups. Although it gained numerous supporters through direct mail solicitations, appeals for donations made little demand on the donors' time, energy, and intellect. As one prominent consumer activist, Michael Pertschuck, put it: "We defended ourselves against charges of elitism with strong evidence that the principles we stood for and the causes we enlisted in enjoyed popular, if sometimes passive support. But if we were 'for the people,' for the most part we were not comfortably 'of the people.'"

By the late 1970s, conservative rights talk arose to challenge liberal rights talk. The Christian Coalition, the National Right to Life Committee, and other organizations copied their opponents' legal, publicity, and marketing tactics to oppose court and agency decisions that mandated school busing for racial balance, affirmative action to increase the number of minorities and women in higher education and the workplace, and women's rights to choose to have an abortion. This blossoming of advocacy group politics deepened the paradox of post–New Deal liberalism. The more opportunities that Americans had to directly influence their government, the less they trusted it to do the right thing.

Public Opinion

Despite the serious decline in public participation and civic involvement, political reformers on both the left and the right continue to stress the importance of public opinion and government responsiveness to it. This concern is shared by electoral politicians, who can no longer count on such stable sources of support as party loyalty. They are desperate to find means of gauging voter attitudes in order to gain and maintain power. This hunger has been intensified by technical advances, particularly the development of mass survey techniques that enhance the ability to gauge public opinion.

The Surveying of Public Opinion

George Gallup pioneered the techniques of scientific *sampling* that purport to accurately measure the views of individual Americans. He considered polling to be a vital instrument for improving democracy. It promised a more accurate method than initiatives and referenda for ascertaining the will of the majority. Whereas Walter Lippmann and John Dewey had despaired of mass opinion, viewing it as ignorant and vulnerable to the cynical manipulation of popular demagogues, Gallup saw the *poll* as a way for ordinary citizens to gain control of their representatives. His tri-weekly surveys appeared in newspapers that reached about 8 million readers. Gallup saw scientific surveys as a powerful democratic check on those who claimed to speak on behalf of the public, because surveys provided "barometers of public tolerance" for advocacy groups, whom he derisively termed "marching minorities."

During the 1970s, polling became a huge industry. In 1965, the *New York Times* ran fewer than fifty stories reporting poll results. Ten years later, it ran 500. Since then, other computer-driven innovations have enabled politicians and advocacy groups to make highly targeted direct-mail appeals and to use the internet to solicit funds and public support. Aroused citizens can now almost instantaneously communicate their views to Congress, the White House, and interest groups.

But Gallup and his contemporary disciples have not addressed the deep concerns about mass democracy raised by Lippmann and Dewey. Should surveys that register individual preferences really be considered public opinion? Does public opinion really exist if it has not been nurtured by civic education and deliberation? Can citizenship be reduced to the passive, anonymous response to survey questions? Box 3 discusses how opinion surveys are conducted and what problems they encounter.

Box Three: Nuts and Bolts

The Surveying of Opinion

Public opinion surveys are based on the simple statistical truth that a relatively small sample of a population can provide reliable information about the population as a whole. The information is reliable only if the sample is random, meaning that it does not differ in any important respect from the population. In 1936, the *Literary Digest* poll predicted that the Republican, Alfred Landon, would be elected president. The poll failed to predict FDR's landslide victory in that election because it was based on ballots sent to telephone and automobile owners, who in those days were wealthier than average. The rich were one of the few segments of the population to favor the Republicans in 1936.

Today, pollsters obtain a reliable sample by selecting names at random from the telephone book on the reasonably valid assumption that, these days, people who have telephones are representative of the population at large. The most serious problems that pollsters face now have to do with obtaining responses and framing questions. Bombarded with calls from telemarketers, many people refuse to talk to pollsters. Such technical innovations as caller ID enable people to screen calls and refuse to answer those that come from unfamiliar phone numbers. It is unlikely that people who take calls from pollsters are otherwise identical to people who do not. Therefore, the sample of people who respond to the poll may be significantly different from the sample of people originally picked for the poll.

The framing of questions raises two serious difficulties. First, the poll assumes that people actually have an opinion about the matter at hand. No one likes to seem stupid, and so people often answer yes or no even when they really do not know or care about the question they are being asked. Second, the way in which a question is phrased can significantly determine the response. A person who is asked "Should the government help poor mothers and children?" is far more likely to answer yes than is a person who is asked "Should the government spend more money on welfare?" This result occurs despite the fact that the program known as "welfare" mostly goes to help poor mothers and children.

For these reasons, polls about voting tend to be more reliable than are surveys that measure opinions about policy issues. Especially as the election draws near, people tend to have opinions about the candidates and have decided whom they will vote for. They can answer forthrightly the question "Whom are you going to vote for?" The difficulty that plagues candidate polling has therefore less to do with question framing and more to do with whether the person answering the question will actually vote. Candidates do not want to win polls; they want to win elections. They are only interested in the opinions of real voters. Pollsters try to determine how likely it is that a poll respondent will actually vote by asking such questions as "Did you vote in the last election?" and "Do you know where you have to go to vote?" Ordinarily, these questions are successful in enabling pollsters to limit their sample to real voters. But sometimes a campaign proves so exciting that many "unlikely" voters vote. Or, the race is so dull or dispiriting that even "likely" voters stay home. Under those circumstances, polling, even when conducted close to election day, can prove wildly inaccurate.

The greatest of all American politicians, Abraham Lincoln, claimed that "public opinion is everything" in a democracy. But public opinion as he understood it was more than the sum of individual preferences. It was a body of beliefs that gave identity to a nation. Lincoln's famous characterization of the Constitution as a government "of the people, by the people, for the people" presupposed a moral fabric that affirmed the country's best possibilities. In this affirmation, he was expressing his faith not only in the American people's decency but also in the constitutional heritage and political associations of the United States that allied passionate conviction to moral scruple, cementing "We the People" to the principles of the Declaration of Independence.

Two-Tiered Politics

Political theorist Wilson Carey McWilliams described the uneasy combination of poll-based public opinion and interest-group advocacy as *two-tiered politics*. The first tier, centered in Washington, D.C., is "thick with organized interests, policy advocates, and officials and is characterized by a high level of knowledge about the intricacies of policy and networks of power." Outside the capital's beltway, the second tier, the mass electorate, is "weakly articulated, mostly baffled, and certainly removed from policy deliberations."

As the impeachment trial of President Bill Clinton showed, the second tier is not without political power. When Clinton first admitted to a relationship with White House intern Monica Lewinsky, first-tier Washingtonians – Democrats and Republicans alike – were almost unanimous in the view that he should leave office. In contrast, polls indicated that most Americans did not consider Clinton's peccadilloes to be a violation of the public trust, the sort of action that called for impeachment. They overwhelmingly approved of his presidency even as they impugned his personal character. In the end, the second tier pushed the first tier, at least the Democratic portion, to protect the president.

The second tier was able to triumph because the circumstances were very unusual. The choice to be made was a simple one: should Clinton be removed from office or not? The issue at stake was not highly technical or complicated. It required a moral judgment regarding the president's behavior that the average person was every bit as qualified to make as was a U.S. senator or a newspaper editorial writer. Under ordinary conditions, when the issues are more complex and the choices more subtle, the second tier finds itself far more estranged, confused, and impotent.

"The simple act of voting," political theorist Judith Shklar rightly noted, "is the ground upon which the edifice of elective government rests ultimately." Voting is not just an act to influence government, but an article of faith in the polity, a ritual evoking "We the People." The distinguished jurist Learned Hand once said: "Of course I know how illusory would be the belief that my vote determined anything; but nevertheless when I go to the polls I have a satisfaction in a sense that we are all engaged in a common venture." The second tier's deepening alienation from political life continued to the end of the twentieth century, revealed by the long-term and continuing decline in voter turnout.

By 1964, New Deal liberalism appeared to have overcome the endemic distrust of the central government that was a cardinal principle of traditional rights-based politics: three-quarters of the American public surveyed that year said they trusted government to do the right thing most of the time. Three decades later, only a quarter of Americans were so trusting. Box 4 describes some important social trends, such as the decline of voluntary associations, that account, at least in part, for the disturbing trend of individuals in contemporary America being alienated from their government and from each other.

Box Four: Nuts and Bolts

Social Capital

Political scientist Robert Putnam attributes the growth in public mistrust to the decline of *social capital*. This term, coined during the Progressive Era, refers to the underlying strength of social bonds that make people feel like they are part of a community and encourage them to participate in civic affairs. Invoking Tocqueville, Putnam attributes a great deal of importance to civic action at the local level, especially to voluntary associations that instruct citizens about their rights and about their responsibilities. Voluntary organizations like the League of Women Voters, Parent Teacher association, the Red Cross, the Rotary Club, and the Lions Club teach Americans, obsessed with their privacy and their rights, the practical value of *collective* action.

Membership in such associations, many of which trace their origins back to the beginning of the twentieth century, has fallen off dramatically in the past thirty years. Even recreational activity, a critical source of community adhesion, has become less group oriented. Putnam entitled his book *Bowling Alone* because he originally became concerned about the decline in political capital when he observed that the number of people who go bowling has remained constant

Voluntary organizations teach Americans the value of collective action but have recently experienced a dramatic drop in membership. Here, local Iowa Rotary Club members cook chicken dinners to raise funds for community projects.

over twenty-five years, but the number who visit the alleys to participate in bowling leagues has declined sharply. Putnam has tried to measure the change over time in all manner of social activities that he thinks contribute to social capital. He has found that over the last twenty-five years the average American attends 58 percent fewer club meetings, eats dinner with his or her family 33 percent less of the time, and invites friends over 45 percent less often. Americans sign fewer petitions and go on fewer picnics.

Putnam finds that some of the most plausible explanations for the decline of social capital are not in fact that important. One might think that the decline is due to the fact that Americans move around so much. But, in fact, residential mobility has actually been steadily declining for the last half century. One would also suspect that the increasing time pressure generated by two-career families is to blame. But he finds little evidence to support that hypothesis. Far more important is the fact that so many more Americans live alone. Single and childless people have a much harder time fitting in to the many forms of civic involvement that are organized around schools and family life. Another powerful contributor is the isolating impact of electronic media. Americans spend a much greater percentage of their time watching television than they did twenty-five years ago. And they spend enormous amounts of time using devices like iPods and Xboxes that did not even exist in the recent past. Putnam has not yet been able to assess the full impact of the internet because it has both socially isolating and connecting elements. On the one hand, people use it to communicate with one another via IM, email, and chat groups. On the other, it serves as a purely private entertainment vehicle.

By the end of the twentieth century, something similar had appeared to occur in contemporary political life. Those political associations, such as political parties, that cultivate cooperation and consensus had lost influence on single-issue groups, such as environmental and abortion advocates, that are dedicated to obtaining entitlements for their members. Rights-based groups looked less to political parties and more to bureaucratic agencies and courts to uphold their claims. The parties themselves have lost much of their ability to aggregate interests and engineer compromise. In the 2000 election, Democratic and Republican activists took extreme positions on issues such as abortion and the environment. Because their parties could no longer moderate extremists of left and right, the candidates George W. Bush and Al Gore distanced themselves from both single-issue and party activists and instead sought safe centrist ground on most major issues.

As we discuss in Chapter 9, the 2000 election ended in a deadlock that was ultimately resolved by the Supreme Court. But the election's contentiousness failed to awaken the democratic passions displayed in past critical elections. It bitterly divided first-tier policy activists but not the public at large, many of whom had not even voted. Although the Constitution gives Congress ultimate authority to certify Electoral College votes, surveys have indicated that most people want the courts, not elected representatives, to decide the contest. When disputed presidential elections occurred in 1800, 1824, and 1876, they were settled by Congress, not the judiciary. But twentieth-century developments, especially the expansion of rights, have made the judiciary a more powerful institution, indeed a principal arbiter of the nation's moral standards (see Chapter 9).

The Crisis of Citizenship, the Challenge of September 11, and Partisan Rancor

The dawn of the twenty-first century found citizens less connected with each other and with their government. Then the unspeakable tragedy of

September 11, 2001, appeared to dramatically interrupt democratic decline. In its aftermath, Americans from all walks of life expressed greater interest in public affairs than they had during the 2000 campaign. The percentage of Americans who said they could trust the government to do what is right "just about always" or "most of the time" jumped to 60 percent in polls conducted after September 11, up from 42 percent in 2000. These figures marked the highest level of confidence in government since the high-water mark of the mid-1960s.

In the face of a major crisis, America still seemed blessed with a reservoir of good will and patriotism. But doubts remained about whether this surge of civic interest would endure. Although the Civil War and World War II proved to be galvanizing experiences with long-term consequences, public officials and scholars such as Robert Putnam worried that the civic enthusiasm aroused by a horrific attack on American soil might dissipate unless important changes in political institutions and policies took place. These concerns were justified. Four years after the tragic event of September 11, Americans between the ages of 18 and 25, who experienced the trauma of September 11 at an impressionable age, showed an increased tendency to volunteer for community service as well as discuss and participate in politics. But this increased civic involvement appeared to be limited to the upper middle class. A 2006 report prepared by the Conference on Civic Involvement showed that high school dropouts were considerably less likely to vote, trust government, or do volunteer work than they were three decades ago. Moreover, September 11 seemed to have little or no enduring effects among older generations. Indeed, by the start of 2006, the reservoir of good will that Americans felt toward Washington in the aftermath of national tragedy had largely dissipated: a January 2006 Gallup Poll revealed that only 32 percent of those surveyed said they could trust the government to do what is right always or most of the time, the lowest number recorded in nearly two decades.

September 11 did, indeed, have an enduring effect on America politics and government but not the one that advocates of greater public spirit and commonality had hoped for. As we have noted throughout this volume, the War on Terror, especially when extended with such controversy to Iraq, eventually led to the renewal of the partisan conflict that had shaped American politics before the rise of the temporary spirit of national unity sparked by the tragedy of September 11. President Bush's effort to strengthen the Republican party was aimed at furthering the resurgence of the Republicans as a national, programmatically conservative party that had begun during the Reagan presidency (see Chapter 8).

The 2004 campaign, the first presidential election since September 11, brought intense citizen interest and engagement: turnout increased by nearly 6 percent, an historic, surprising surge in political participation that swamped many polling places and resulted in 60 percent of the eligible electorate voting, the highest turnout since 1968. Moreover, both the Democratic and Republican parties and their allied groups spent a record 2.2 billion dollars on the campaign, including 600 million dollars to fund waves of mostly negative advertising, which began almost a year before election day. As we note in Chapter 8, the 2004 campaign was most distinctive in the way that the battle over the airwaves was linked to innovative grassroots mobilization efforts. This new tactic contributed significantly to the robust voter participation. Although the Republican party had a stronger grassroots operation, both parties built what deserve to be called the first proto–national machines in American politics. They developed sophisticated, effective get-out-the-vote strategies that identified and mobilized their supporters. The 2006 midterm elections continued the trend of increased turnout. More than 80 million voters went to the polls in 2006, a record number for a midterm election.

Paradoxically, even as Americans were bowling alone, they were showing an increasing tendency to vote together. The emergence of strong national party organizations, combined with demographic trends that sorted out Democrats and Republicans in distinct regions, states, and communities, resulted in an impressive increase in party voting. For example, there has been a significant decline in districts splitting their votes between presidential and congressional candidates: in 2004, only fifty-nine congressional districts went in different directions in presidential and House elections; by comparison there were eighty-six such districts in 2000 and more than 100 in both 1992 and 1996. Particularly notable is the way Americans are voting together in increasingly homogenous counties: in 2004, fully 60 percent of the nation's counties gave more than 60 percent of their support to either Bush or his Democratic opponent Senator John Kerry of Massachusetts; the corresponding figure was 53 percent of the counties in 2000, and 38 percent in 1996. This trend continued in 2006 where the bulk of the Democratic gains in the House occurred in districts that had Republican incumbents but which had voted for Gore in 2000 and Kerry in 2004. As William Galston and Elaine Kamarck have observed, the initial reaction to Hurricane Katrina "vividly illustrates the growing intensity of partisan politics." Under normal circumstances, they point out, a natural disaster brings people together, but this did not happen in the wake of the terrible tragedy that devastated New Orleans and other parts of the Mississippi Delta. According to a *Washington Post* poll of September 7, 2005, 74 percent of Republicans but only 17 percent of Democrats approved of President Bush's handling of the crisis; about two in three Republicans rated the federal government's response as good or excellent, compared to only one in three Democrats. (Independents, whose voices became less effective as partisanship intensified, were more evenly divided.)

Most public officials, pundits, and scholars view the division between "red" and "blue" America as a blight on the tradition of constitutional government in the United States. They argue that partisan rancor threatens the division and separation of powers by subordinating the institutional integrity of the three branches of government, as well as the system of federalism, to partisan discipline. Those who scorn the new party system also fear that public opinion has been corrupted. The popular consensus necessary to sustain responsible constitutional government, requiring a citizenry that celebrates individual rights and the separation of church and state, has been eroded by "culture wars" (see Chapter 4). The two Americas, they claim, have been fundamentally divided by issues such as abortion, "intelligent design," and gay marriage.

Nor has the rise in the relative importance of national security issues, relative to social issues, served to heal the breach. As the distinguished political scientist James Q. Wilson lamented, "Denmark or Luxembourg can afford to exhibit domestic anguish or uncertainty over military policy; the United States cannot. A divided America encourages our enemies, disheartens our allies, and saps our resolve – potentially to fatal effect." Yet neither the Republican victory in 2004 nor the increased dissatisfaction with the Iraq War that led to the Democratic resurgence in 2006 has resolved party conflict over the War on Terror. The partisan rancor over Iraq was demonstrated by a survey by the Pew Center conducted in late March of 2007. Although a substantial majority of Americans (59 percent), including most of those calling themselves independents (61 percent), said they wanted their congressional representative to support a bill calling for a withdrawal of U.S. forces from Iraq, the divide between partisan loyalists remains very wide: 77 percent of Democrats favored the withdrawal of all U.S. troops by August of 2008, while only 34 percent of Republicans did so.

The very direct democratic techniques designed by the Progressives to weaken political parties have, in recent elections, been placed at the service of party. In 2004, Republicans placed measures to ban same-sex marriage on many state ballots, all of which passed easily. In the process, some election analysts said, the initiative roused the conservative base to help GOP candidates from President Bush on down. Eight states had ballot measures to ban same-sex marriage in 2006, including Virginia where a critical Senate race took place between the Republican incumbent, George Allen, who supported the measure, and his Democratic challenger, former secretary of the Navy, James Webb, who opposed it.

To counteract this perceived Republican advantage, Democrats hoped to prove that ballot politics could also work for them. In 2006, they put measures to increase the minimum wage, a cause that animated the liberal base, on ballots in six states. Four of these states, Arizona, Ohio, Missouri, and Montana, featured close Senate races, all critical contests in determining which party would control the upper legislative chamber for the next two years. All of the minimum wage initiatives passed easily and in three of the four states that had closely contested Senate races – Missouri, Montana, and Michigan – the Democratic challenger defeated the Republican incumbent. In Missouri, the Democrat, Claire McCaskill, may also have benefited from an initiative on the ballot favoring stem cell research. It passed easily. She supported it and her opponent, incumbent Republican Jim Tallent, opposed it. Thus "direct democracy" hardly displaced partisan polarization in 2006. Instead, party politics was closely linked to advocacy campaigns for ballot initiatives, further intensifying the national partisan divide.

Conclusion: The Virtues of Partisanship

Forgotten amid the routine castigation by scholars, public officials, and pundits of what they deemed to be excessive partisanship was their previous condemnation, during the late 1970s, of the weakening of political parties. The Progressive and New Deal eras had substituted administration for partisan politics in a manner that sucked much of the meaning out of representative government. The fears expressed in the 1970s about the impact of this political decline echoed those expressed 140 years earlier by the great friend and critic of American politics, Alexis de Tocqueville. As Tocqueville saw during the birth of American democracy, the great threat to representative constitutional government was not revolution – a culture war – but an obsession with personal security and private well-being, the lodestar of the administrative state. Tocqueville warned that Americans were tempted to become "so much possessed by a relaxed love of present enjoyments" that they would lose all interest in public affairs and become indifferent, if not avowedly hostile to new ideas and necessary reforms. "If citizens continue to confine themselves more and more narrowly in the circle of domestic interests," he observed, "one can apprehend that in the end they will become inaccessible to those great and powerful emotions that trouble peoples, but develop and renew them." Party polarization was the most effective antidote to such a moral implosion. Although

> the longing to be elected can momentarily bring certain men to make war on each other, . . . in the long term this same desire brings all men to lend each other a mutual support; and if it happens that an election accidentally divides two friends, the electoral system brings

together in a permanent manner a multitude of citizens who would
have always remained strangers to one another. Freedom creates particular hatreds, but despotism gives birth to general indifference.

It remains to be seen, of course, how much the more centralized and programmatic parties of the twenty-first century will engage the American people. But, for better and worse, nationalized parties have begun to penetrate
the electorate. Moreover, heated partisanship is likelier to draw citizens
into the political process than reforms such as the initiative and referendum, which Progressives hoped would encourage greater participation.

Every major shift in domestic and foreign policy in the United States,
beginning with the Jefferson Republicans' vanquishing of the Federalists,
has witnessed intense partisan conflict. Significantly, partisan debate and
resolution about America's role in the world divided the Founders (see
Chapter 4). During the 1790s, in response to President George Washington's Neutrality Proclamation issued during the war between France and
Great Britain, Madison decried Hamilton's claim that foreign policy was
naturally the province of the executive power and thus should be removed
from the normal irrationalities of democratic politics. In the final analysis,
Madison believed, democracy, even a refined and enlarged constitutional
republic, required public debate and judgment that could only take place
in the legislature and other public forums. The tasks of foreign policy – to
declare war, to conclude peace, and to form alliances – were among "the
highest acts of sovereignty"; to relegate such decisions to executive decree
was to destroy the meaning of self-government. Therefore, the relative
insulation from public opinion that took place during the Cold War was
more the exception than the norm of how republican government should
cope with matters of national security. The current conflicts aroused by
September 11 and its aftermath are not necessarily incompatible with the
nation's liberal traditions and its constitutional forms. As the 2006 elections
demonstrated, the existing partisan disputes over Iraq cannot be managed
by discouraging the public from debating the future course of America's
role in the world. Like previous conflicts in foreign affairs that have divided
the country, nation building in Iraq and, more broadly, the viability of the
Bush doctrine's dedication to exporting the principles of the Declaration of
Independence, can only be settled by public debate and resolution. Appealing to a mythic consensus, or hoping for the replenishment of social capital,
will not diminish the partisan disputes that now divide the nation. Seeking
to diffuse them risks embracing the false hope that democratic politics can
be reduced to non-partisan administration – that liberal values can be kept
alive without partisan struggles about their meaning in the development of
American political life.

An alternative to partisanship as a means for stimulating civic involvement might be national service. Nearly 100 years ago, the philosopher William James wrote that reformers had the duty to search for "the moral equivalent of war." One possible solution, he suggested, was to conscript youth into a national service, charged with the responsibility of tackling domestic problems, where "they might get the childishness knocked out of them" and "come back into society with healthier sympathies and soberer ideas." Since John Kennedy, presidents have been attracted to the idea of national service. Indeed, Bill Clinton viewed it as a defining idea of his "New Covenant." But Clinton's AmeriCorps fell far short of James's ambitious proposal. In President George W. Bush's first State of the Union address, he called on Americans not to let the patriotism aroused by the war against terrorism pass away. He urged them to embrace "a new ethic and a new creed" and "to commit at least two years – 4,000 hours over a lifetime – to the service of [their] nation." The president also proposed to launch a new national service organization called USA Freedom Corps to encourage citizens to "contribute to the life of their country." But Bush's plea for national service was overshadowed by more pressing military and administrative concerns. National service has not emerged as an integral part of the war on terrorism. The war has been prosecuted by professional soldiers and technocrats.

In any event, national service does not provide any mechanism for holding the welfare–national security state accountable. Only the collective political discipline provided by strong political parties can accomplish such a demanding political task. In their absence, the long-term trends in the direction of declining social capital and a two-tiered politics are very likely to continue. The resurgence of strong parties would thus offer palpable political benefits, but it would also incur great political costs. Partisanship stirs up democratic interest and activity but endangers rights. The administrative state developed during the New Deal is designed to make people secure and protect their rights, but at the price of fostering political apathy and indifference. After more than 200 years, the problem of reconciling the liberal yearning for rights with the democratic passion for participation remains as difficult as the critics of the Constitution – the Anti-Federalists – feared it would be.

☆ The limits and the proper aims of protest activities have remained a controversial issue throughout American political development.

☆ The American habit of forming civic associations served and continues to serve as a distinctive and vital ingredient of American democracy and a major contributor to its social capital.

☆ Political parties helped to sustain the vitality of civic associations by drawing people into political life and cultivating a habit and taste for collective action. Local political parties forged a vital link between public officials and voters.

☆ Both the temperance movement and abolitionism grew out of the religious revival called the Second Great Awakening.

☆ The Lincoln-Douglas debates demonstrated the potential that political rhetoric contains for illuminating and clarifying the meaning of great public questions, such as the debate over slavery.

☆ Paradoxically, Progressive efforts to make politics more democratic actually contributed to a decline in political participation.

☆ The success of the Civil Rights Movement in forcing an end to government-sponsored racial segregation led to the rise of many other social movements organized on the basis of rights claims including: environmentalism, women's rights, gay rights, and the rights of the disabled.

☆ By the late 1960s, the American public had become "ideologically" conservative but "operationally" liberal, meaning that Americans were distrustful of government in general but supported virtually all the particular activities it undertook. This decline in trust coincided with an equally dramatic decline in political participation.

☆ Despite its antiestablishment rhetoric and profound suspicion of centralized power, the public interest movement, unlike earlier protest movements, did not try to get rid of bureaucracy. Instead, it made itself an integral and permanent part of bureaucratic policy making.

☆ The uneasy combination of poll-based public opinion and interest-group advocacy spawned a two-tiered politics. The first tier, centered in Washington, D.C. is, in the words of Wilson C. McWilliams "thick with organized interests, policy advocates, and officials and is characterized by a high level of knowledge about the intricacies of policy and networks of power." Outside the capital's beltway, the second tier, the mass electorate, is "weakly articulated, mostly baffled, and certainly removed from policy deliberations."

☆ Social capital refers to the underlying strength of social bonds that make people feel like they are part of a community and encourage them to participate in civic affairs. Voluntary organizations are an important means of building social capital.

☆ The continuing impact of September 11 has not been to enhance public spiritedness and commonality. Rather, the War on Terror, especially when extended with such controversy to Iraq, has led to the renewal of the partisan conflict that had shaped American politics before the rise of the temporary spirit of national unity sparked by the tragedy of September 11.

Major Concepts

citizen suits
direct democracy
ethnicity
initiatives

interest groups
political action committees (PACs)
poll
recall
sampling
social capital
social gospel movement
suffrage
two-tiered politics
voluntary associations

Suggested Readings

Broder, David. *Democracy Derailed: Initiative Campaigns and the Power of Money.* Orlando, FL: Harcourt Books, 2000.

Ellis, Richard. *Democratic Delusion: The Initiative Process in America.* Lawrence: University Press of Kansas, 2002.

Gerstle, Gary. *American Crucible: Race and Nation in Twentieth-Century America.* Princeton, NJ: Princeton University Press, 2002.

Keller, Morton. *Affairs of State: Public Life in the Late Nineteenth Century.* Cambridge, MA: Harvard University Press, 1979.

Key, V. O. *Public Opinion and American Democracy.* New York: Knopf, 1961.

Keyssar, Alexander. *The Right to Vote.* New York: Basic Books, 2000.

Lippmann, Walter. *Public Opinion.* New York: Harcourt Brace and Company, 1922.

Miller, William Lee. *Lincoln's Virtues: An Ethical Biography.* New York: Knopf, 2002.

Nye, Joseph, Philip Zelikow, and David King, eds. *Why People Don't Trust Government.* Cambridge, MA: Harvard University Press, 1997.

Putnam, Robert. *Bowling Alone: The Collapse and Revival of American Community.* New York: Touchstone Books, 2001.

Schudson, Michael. *The Good Citizen: A History of American Civic Life.* Cambridge, MA: Harvard University Press, 1999.

Shklar, Judith N. *American Citizenship: The Quest for Inclusion.* Cambridge, MA: Harvard University Press, 1991.

Skocpol, Theda, and Morris Fiorina, eds. *Civic Engagement in American Democracy.* Washington, D.C.: Brookings Institution, 1999.

Verba, Sidney, Kay Schlozman, and Henry Brady. *Voice and Equality: Civic Volunteerism in America.* Cambridge, MA: Harvard University Press, 1996.

Wiebe, Robert. *Self Rule: A Cultural History of American Democracy.* Chicago: University of Chicago Press.

The Sherlock Holmes mystery "Silver Blaze" is about the theft of an expensive racehorse from its stable. During the investigation, Inspector Gregory of Scotland Yard asks if there was any particular aspect of the crime calling for additional study. Holmes replied, "[y]es," and pointed to "the curious incident of the dog in the night-time." Inspector Gregory replied, "The dog did nothing in the night-time." Holmes said, "That was the curious incident."

Perhaps the most surprising incident in the enactment of the landmark education reform law in 2002 was the silence – or silencing – of the principal advocacy groups that had dominated education policy for the past four decades. Since the 1980s, especially, the politics of education, indeed, most social policies, had been roiled by self-styled public interest organizations that contributed significantly to the partisan rancor that we discuss in Chapter 12. Yet the No Child Left Behind Law (NCLB), which dramatically transformed and expanded the role of the national government in secondary and elementary education, was enacted in 2002 with bipartisan support in both congressional chambers and signed by President Bush, even though it included provisions that had long been opposed by powerful constituents in the Democratic and Republican parties. The bipartisan commitment to NCLB resulted in a centralized legislative process that not only silenced liberal and conservative advocacy groups but also preempted debate and deliberation over a policy that overrode an enduring sentiment of American democracy – that education is fundamentally a prerogative of state and local government.

Since the passage of the landmark Elementary and Secondary Education Act of 1965 (ESEA), a signature Great Society reform, the federal government had helped support compensatory education programs for disadvantaged children. "Our society will not be great," President Lyndon Johnson insisted, "until every young mind is set free to scan the farthest reaches of thought and imagination. We are still far from that goal. . . . Poverty must not be a bar to learning, and learning must offer an escape from poverty." Right from the start, however, there were concerns that ESEA funding and regulations did not serve the objectives of the program: schools were neither educating disadvantaged children adequately nor being held accountable for their ineffectiveness. During the 1970s, economic stagflation (a combination of high unemployment and inflation) and middle class flight from inner cities aroused fears about social stability and economic competitiveness. By the 1980s, both liberals and conservatives, as well as key

The No Child Left Behind Act, signed by President Bush in 2002, won bicameral and bipartisan approval, effectively silencing vociferous education advocacy groups, and emboldening the Department of Education to uphold accountability from public schools nationwide.

representatives of the business community, worried that America was losing out to international competitors like Japan and the Soviet Union and that public schools were not preparing the next generation for the economic and security challenges of the late twentieth century.

Nevertheless, presidential and congressional efforts dedicated to raising education standards and holding schools accountable for meeting them were resisted strongly by liberal and conservative advocacy groups. Liberal interest groups such as the National Education Association (NEA), the most powerful lobby for public schools in Washington, and the National Association for the Advancement of Colored People (NAACP) prescribed expanding federal funds for new programs and services, targeted to disadvantaged students, rather than standards, testing, and accountability measures, to meet the crisis in education. In contrast, conservative interests such as the Christian Coalition, the Heritage Foundation, and Empower America fought against expanding, indeed sought to roll back, the federal government's role in education. During the 1980s and 1990s, at the behest of such groups, the Republican party had called for the elimination of the Department of Education.

In spite of the opposition of powerful Democratic and Republican constituent groups, President George W. Bush signed the NCLB into law on January 8, 2002. His signature initiated sweeping changes to the thirty-seven-year-old ESEA and subjected the nation's educators, schools, and school districts to a new principle, *accountability*, which was joined to, if it did not displace, *entitlement* as the cornerstone of reform. NCLB marks an important extension of federal authority over states and local schools, tying federal education funds to new requirements for annual testing of elementary and middle school students while sanctioning districts and schools whose student populations fail to meet specific measures of annual progress on those tests. Although the most powerful liberal and conservative advocacy groups fought against this legislation, NCLB not only survived the legislative process but did so with overwhelming bipartisan support. Buttressed by an alliance between President Bush and liberal icon Senator Ted Kennedy (D-MA), the Senate passed the measure 87–10. The House, where strange bedfellows such as conservative Ohio Republican John Boehner and liberal California Democrat George Miller joined forces, endorsed NCLB by a 381–41 vote.

Early press coverage celebrated this uncommon bipartisanship in support of a major reform measure. Feel-good stories applauded Bush, Kennedy, Boehner, Miller, and other key congressional leaders as they barnstormed the country in a tour that featured smiling teachers and school children, as well as pointed, but good-natured jokes about homework and testing.

The passage of NCLB owed much to a shift in public opinion. Polls taken during the 1990s revealed that although clear majorities of those surveyed favored increased federal funding of schools, they opposed simply throwing money at education problems. Most citizens believed that in order to improve student and school performance, increased funding had to be tied to more rigorous national standards, testing, and other accountability measures.

In response to this change in the public mood, Democrats in the 1990s, led by Bill Clinton, and Republicans in 2000, led by Bush, ultimately accepted positions on education that went against the preferences of strong constituent groups within their parties. The Clinton administration successfully steered through Congress the 1994 reauthorization of ESEA, which required, for the first time, that all states create performance-based accountability systems for schools by 2000. The law failed, however, to give the federal government any meaningful way to enforce these provisions, and most states failed to comply. NCLB both built on and greatly expanded the reformist objectives of the 1994 legislation. It creates stern federal directives regarding test use and consequences; puts federal bureaucrats in charge of approving state standards and accountability plans; sets a single, nationwide timetable for boosting achievement; and prescribes specific remedies for underperforming schools – and the children in them.

Although a partial response to the concerns of leading politicians in both parties and public opinion, the revolutionary features of NCLB were not arrived at by open deliberations. The final product was crafted by a highly centralized process dominated by the White House as well as Democratic and Republican party leaders, which kept in the dark, not only liberal and conservative advocacy groups, but also most state and local officials, who would have to administer many features of the legislation. As education specialist Elizabeth Debray has shown, once the legislative conference began, the stage at which differences between the House and Senate versions of the bill are reconciled, education groups were not consulted about the most controversial provisions of the NCLB legislation.

Both parties supported freezing out the interest groups. The bipartisan National Governors Association (NGA) was especially concerned by the leadership's blackout of information about key agreements on testing and accountability. In a letter sent to conferees in late September, the NGA wrote, "as those who bear the greatest responsibility for implementing any changes enacted by Congress, we would hope there would be full consultation with the nation's governors prior to any agreements on key issues." This plea was ignored, however, as the strategic agreement made during the conference to prevent interest groups from learning about the final conference negotiations remained in effect.

The politics of NCLB testifies to the enduring importance of the national administrative state forged by the New Deal and Great Society. Indeed, the Bush administration's strong push for education reform signaled the willingness of a conservative Republican president and key Republican legislators to embrace national administrative power, albeit for partisan objectives. As we have pointed out throughout this book, rather than try to curtail New Deal and Great Society entitlement programs, as the Reagan administration and Gingrich-led 104th Congress attempted to do, Bush, with the steadfast support of Republican leaders in Congress, has sought to recast these programs in conservative form.

With his commitment to No Child Left Behind, Bush sought to mobilize conservatives to make public schools better by demanding more from educators. First and foremost, NCLB advocates were concerned about the nation's achievement gap – primarily the disparity between the performance of white and Asian students, on the one hand, and African-American and Latino students, on the other. The education establishment's willingness to accept sustained low levels of performance among black, Latino, and poor children was repeatedly attacked by Bush during his 2000 campaign as "the soft bigotry of low expectations." In the words of Kati Haycock and

Ross Wiener of Education Trust, one of the few liberal advocacy groups to support NCLB, Bush's education reform program assumed "[t]hat public education can teach, and has a responsibility to teach, almost every student how to read and do math up to a respectable level defined by the state."

Bush's empowerment of the Department of Education to make public schools more accountable by linking federal aid to national standards and measurements of student learning appeared to bestow bipartisan support on an executive-centered administrative state, the embodiment of modern liberalism. Even as partisan rancor over issues such as the Iraq War intensified, the president maintained the support of key Democrats such as Senator Kennedy and Congressman Miller in his effort to reauthorize the NCLB law. Keeping the support of Miller and Kennedy was especially important because when the Democrats regained control of Congress in the 2006 elections, they became the leaders of the education committees in the Senate and House, respectively. Not surprisingly, the push of Bush and his Democratic allies to renew the NCLB in 2007 has met stern resistance. The opposition has been led by state and local officials who are deeply resentful of the federal government's attempt to micromanage their educational systems. Arizona and Virginia are battling the federal government over rules for testing children with limited English. Utah is fighting over whether rural teachers there meet the qualifications established by the law. And Connecticut is two years into a lawsuit arguing that No Child Left Behind has failed to provide states with federal financing to meet its requirements. Furthermore, as educational politics shifted to the bureaucracies and states, advocacy groups and their proponents in Congress, unusually dormant during the original battle over NCLB, began to reassert themselves. As the reauthorization battle ensued, dozens of Republicans in Congress sponsored legislation that would water down the law by allowing states to opt out of its testing requirements yet still receive federal money. On the other side of the political spectrum, ten Democratic senators signed a letter proclaiming that, based on complaints heard from constituents, they consider the law's testing mandates to be "unsustainable" and want an overhaul.

Thus, the transformation of education policy continued the ongoing battle of the past three decades to balance the rights embodied by the entrenched liberal administrative state and democracy sustained by partisan rancor and the widespread, if faint, protests of states and local officials. More telling, Bush and many Republicans' endorsement of nationalizing education might confirm a shift of conflict in American democracy, from a struggle between the champions and enemies of centralized power to a battle between liberals and conservatives for its services.

13 Conclusion

Liberalism and Democracy in the Twenty-first Century

Chapter Overview

This chapter focuses on:

☆ A review of the central aspects of the American constitutional order to highlight its enduring strengths and its gravest weaknesses

☆ The implications of the ongoing tensions between rights and equality – liberalism and democracy – for the future of American self-government

☆ The particular threats to democracy posed by the current combination of expanded programmatic rights, new factional constellations attached to those rights, and the expansion of administrative power required to fulfill those rights claims

Speaking at a 100th birthday party and retirement celebration for Senator Strom Thurmond (R-SC) on December 6, 2002, the Senate Republican leader, Trent Lott (R-MS) said, "I want to say this about my state: When Strom Thurmond ran for president, we voted for him. We're proud of it. And if the rest of the country had followed our lead, we wouldn't have had all these problems over all these years, either." The audience applauded Lott when he said "we're proud" of his state's vote. But when Lott implied that if Thurmond had won, "we wouldn't have had all these problems over all these years," there was an audible gasp, followed by a deafening silence.

Lott was referring to Thurmond's 1948 Dixiecrat party campaign. Bolting the Democratic party, which had included a civil rights plank in its platform, Thurmond, then governor of South Carolina, carried Mississippi, Alabama, Louisiana, and his home state. He declared during the campaign, "All the laws of Washington and all the bayonets of the Army cannot force the negro into our homes, our schools, our churches."

Broadcast live by the cable network C-SPAN, Lott's gaffe reverberated throughout American society. Shocked and angry reaction to his celebration of a segregationist campaign came from conservatives and progressives alike. Rep. John Lewis (D-GA), a leader of the Civil Rights Movement in the 1960s, expressed astonishment: "I could not believe he was saying what he said.... Thurmond was one of the best known segregationists. Is Lott saying the country should have voted to continue segregation, for segregated schools, 'white' and 'colored' restrooms? ... That is what Strom Thurmond stood for in 1948." William Kristol, editor of the conservative magazine *The Weekly Standard*, was no less indignant: "He should remember that [the Republican party is] the party of Lincoln."

In spite of his gaffe, Lott was determined to hold on to his position as Republican leader. He apologized repeatedly and promised to change his positions on matters such as affirmative action. Although John Lewis ultimately accepted his apology, Lott's remorse was rejected as insincere by most other civil rights activists. They noted that Lott had made similar remarks about the Dixiecrat campaign in the past and had voted against establishing a national holiday in honor of Martin Luther King and against the reauthorization of the Voting Rights Act, measures that even Thurmond, who switched to the Republican party in 1964, had come to support. Lott's fate was sealed by a stern rebuke from President George W. Bush. Appearing before a largely African-American audience in Philadelphia, Bush declared, "Recent comments by Senator Lott do not reflect our country." He added, in an emphatic tone, that the Senate leader's words on the segregated past were "offensive" and "wrong." The following week Lott resigned as majority leader. His relieved colleagues replaced him with the more moderate senator William Frist of Tennessee.

694   American Government

The depth of the antagonism toward Lott was due to the memories that his statement revived of Southern resistance to equal rights for African Americans. Lott was a Southern conservative and a Republican. Southern conservatives had used classical liberal arguments about limited government and federalism to defend racial segregation. The godfather of modern conservatism, Barry Goldwater, the Republican presidential candidate in 1964, voted against the landmark civil rights law enacted that year. Goldwater justified his vote by proclaiming that the rights this legislation presumed to fulfill did not justify the dangerous increase in government control it portended. But such a defense of limited government rang hollow in the face of the racial apartheid that denied African Americans a full share of citizenship. As the African-American writer Shelby Steele, himself a classical liberal, argued, Lott had to resign in order to demonstrate that modern conservatism was free of the taint of racism that had haunted it for so long. The "slow march of conservative [classical liberal] principles back to mainstream respectability" and its defense of individual responsibility in areas such as affirmative action, welfare reform, and educational accountability, Steele contended, was "still so fragile that conservatives themselves must be absolutely innocent of racism."

By defending Thurmond's racist record, Lott failed to heed the wisdom of another Mississippian, the novelist William Faulkner, who wrote, "The past is never dead. It's not even past." More than class, race has been a serious fault line in American politics; indeed, race always has been central to debates about the proper role of American government in addressing inequalities that have resulted from the discriminatory actions of both public officials and private citizens. Racism had left such a deep stain on America's claim to being the land of liberty and democracy that many Americans, and not just African Americans, were unable to forgive Lott for seeming to endorse it. Lott learned to his regret that the way people think about current politics is heavily dependent not only on their own past experiences but also on those of their parents and grandparents and on the collective memory of the groups they identify with. The various encounters with American political development discussed in this book have each sought to discern patterns in the complex interweaving of recollections from the past, concerns about the present, and hopes for the future that come together to form real political life.

Events that occurred in the immediate aftermath of Lott's downfall illustrate another major theme of this book: the uneasy relationship and ongoing tensions that exist between rights and equality – liberalism and democracy. After examining those events, this chapter questions the implications of such ongoing tensions for the future of American self-government. To better understand those implications, this chapter reviews the central aspects of the American constitutional order to highlight its enduring strengths and its gravest weaknesses. The chapter concludes with a return to the question that Benjamin Franklin asked more than 200 years ago: Can a republic such as ours endure?

Democracy and Liberalism in Contemporary America: The Case of Affirmative Action

Soon after Lott stepped down, the White House announced that it was filing a legal brief in support of the plaintiffs who were challenging the University of Michigan's affirmative action programs regarding undergraduate and law school admissions. Students at the University of Michigan were admitted to the undergraduate college based on the number of points they received on a scale of 150. Minority students received an automatic bonus of twenty points and therefore would be admitted in preference to white students who scored as many as nineteen points higher than the minority students did. The Michigan Law School set a loose target for enrolling a critical mass of minority students, roughly 10 percent to 12 percent.

President Bush charged that "the Michigan policies amount to a quota system that unfairly rewards or penalizes prospective students, based solely on their race. . . . Our Constitution makes it clear that people of all races must be treated equally under the law." Bush acknowledged the importance of ethnic, racial, and economic diversity and praised the innovative ways that some states have diversified their student bodies without resorting to racial preferences. For example, when Bush was governor of Texas, the state launched a plan that guaranteed acceptance into its public universities to all students who graduated in the top 10 percent of their high school class, regardless of whether the school was urban, suburban, ghetto, or barrio. The president rejected the Michigan formula as a "quota system." Plans, Bush said, that "use race to include or exclude people from higher education and the opportunities it offers are divisive, unfair, and impossible to square with the Constitution."

The president's supporters argued that his stand on affirmative action was of a piece with his defense of racial tolerance in the Lott episode. Both reflected his classical liberal understanding of freedom. As one supporter described that view: "If you make it in life, wherever you come from, whatever your creed or appearance, you are welcome. . . . Conversely, if you failed, you are on your own." This stern doctrine was supported by the president's national security advisor, Condoleezza Rice, an African-American woman raised in segregationist Alabama in the 1950s. Rice experienced racism from the white community, yet rose to become a leading academic and public official. She has received the American Inspirations

Award, confirming her as one of the nation's leading minority role models. Rice's argument about the Michigan case drew on her experience as provost of Stanford University. She was "absolutely opposed to quotas," yet managed to increase the number of black faculty at this prestigious university from thirty-six to forty-four. As one conservative columnist characterized her, "She does not believe in giving blacks a free hand up the ladder. She believes they should work as she did and that nothing else is consistent with their dignity as Americans."

Opponents of the president's position posed an alternative view of the relationship between affirmative action and freedom. The Senate minority leader, Senator Tom Daschle (D-SD), warned that Bush's approach would have "sweeping repercussions, setting back rights for minorities and women." The University of Michigan president, Mary Sue Coleman, told ABC's *Good Morning America* program that Michigan's undergraduate admissions plan was not a quota system, even though race was a factor in deciding which students were admitted. No admissions places were set aside for minority students, Coleman explained. Applicants got extra points for belonging to an underrepresented racial or ethnic minority. But such diversity points also went to applicants who came from underrepresented parts of the state such as the largely white Upper Peninsula, to athletes, and to men in the nursing program. Given the legacy of racism in the United States, Coleman insisted, Michigan would not be justified in ignoring the claims of minorities in its attempts to attract a diverse student body.

Whereas Rice embraced Bush's classical liberal position, another member of the administration – Colin Powell, the then secretary of state, who is African-American – defended Michigan's plan. Powell did not elaborate on this rare acknowledgment of dissent with the president, but he had made known his disdain for conservative attacks on affirmative action in a speech at the Republican National Convention in 2000:

> We must understand the cynicism that exists in the black community. The kind of cynicism that is created when, for example, some of our party miss no opportunity to roundly and loudly condemn affirmative action that helped a few thousand black kids get an education, but you hardly heard a whimper from them over affirmative action for lobbyists who load our federal tax codes with preferences for special interests.

The dispute over affirmative action continues the long tradition of Americans to debate the meaning of their rights. Although the Declaration of Independence and Constitution remain sacred documents of the country's civic religion, such reverence for fundamental principles and institutions has long competed with Thomas Paine's admonition that "[w]e have it within our power to begin the world over again." The celebration of natural – individual – rights threatens to deny the importance, if not the authority, of deliberation and resolution, the stuff of a vital democratic community. And yet Paine's notion that Americans could remake the world encouraged periodic democratic renewals – "refoundings." These great contests of public opinion enabled each generation to claim the right to redefine the Constitution's principles and reorganize the government. This refusal to accept tradition as lifeless parchment enabled Americans to connect their celebration of rights to active engagement in defining and protecting them. In this way, Americans have made practical Thomas Jefferson's elusive ideal that the Constitution "belongs to the living."

The affirmative action controversy – connected to a broader conflict over the meaning of rights – revealed that the uneasy but essential relationship between liberalism and democracy endures, that the never-ending task of balancing rights and equality continues in contemporary America. But the debate over affirmative action, even when joined to other issues such as voting rights and welfare reform, has not aroused a popular struggle of the magnitude of previous contests over civil rights and liberties. This debate was played out not in the streets, the ballot box, or the halls of Congress, but in federal court. Unlike Presidents Abraham Lincoln or Franklin D. Roosevelt (FDR), President Bush did not give speeches that "took the public to school" to explain how his policy position was rooted in fundamental principles. Instead, the White House stated its position in a complex legal brief.

The administration claimed that the Michigan procedures violated the Fourteenth Amendment's Equal Protection Clause because there were other, "race-neutral" means of achieving racial diversity. Nothing in the Constitution prevented public universities from achieving that "laudable goal" by promoting "experiential, geographical, political, or economic diversity." Race-based policies were not inherently unconstitutional, however – they could be justified if shown to be "necessary." The government "may not employ race-based means without first considering race-neutral alternatives and employing them if they would prove efficacious," the brief stated. But this position acknowledged that racial criteria could be used if race-neutral methods failed to achieve diversity. In fact, the Bush administration embraced diversity as a public obligation: "measures that ensure diversity, accessibility and opportunity are important components of government's responsibility to its citizens." As Rice, who acknowledged that she had benefited from affirmative action during her career at Stanford University, insisted, "It is important to take race into consideration if you must, if race-neutral means do not work."

The Bush brief gave the impression of legal hairsplitting; nonetheless, the administration's stand could have important policy consequences. If the court ruled against the Michigan plan, public universities that used racial criteria in their admissions policies would have to assume a greater burden in defending them. But the debate over affirmative action did not so clearly involve a principled struggle over the meaning of rights – the Bush administration granted that the government had an obligation to promote racial diversity even as it insisted that it should seek indirect avenues to achieve that objective. Moreover, nine unelected judges, not the people or their representatives, would render a judgment in this dispute.

Legal battles waged on principles, such as *Brown v. Board of Education of Topeka* (1954), surely can infuse the Constitution with new vitality. But recent court disputes over morally charged issues such as civil rights, affirmative action, and abortion have involved federal judges in policy decisions that would seem more appropriate for a legislature or administrative agency (see Chapter 9). The African-American journalist Clarence Page was critical of Bush's position in the Michigan case but conceded the court's authority to resolve the issue: "It is healthy for all of us in the long run to have the courts review affirmative action from time to time, see how well it is working – and modify it."

In the past, the health of the republic was thought to be served when great issues that affected economic or civil rights were settled in the court of public opinion, through the regular course of elections. Otherwise, Lincoln warned, "the people will have ceased to be their own rulers, having to that extent practically resigned their government into the hands of an eminent tribunal." But the expansion of rights in the wake of the New Deal and the Great Society tended to blur the line between rights and interests as well as between natural liberties and program entitlements. Neither the opponents nor the champions of affirmative action denied that the government had an obligation to promote diversity; the political struggle came down to the best means by which this purpose could be achieved. The subordination of fundamental political disputes about racial discrimination to legal maneuvers over the social value of diversity might help build a popular consensus for affirmative action. At the same time, leaving such disputes to the courts risks distracting the public's attention from what is really at issue in disputes over affirmative action: the tension between redressing the legacy of racial and sexual discrimination in America and the obligation of the government to uphold the right of individual men and women to have their employment and educational qualifications judged on the merits.

Few observers of the Michigan case were surprised when the Supreme Court decided the issue on narrow grounds. In a pair of decisions issued in June 2003, the judiciary pronounced a qualified endorsement of affirmative

The ongoing affirmative action controversy at the University of Michigan, recently inflamed again by Proposition 2, highlights the tensions between rights and equality, popular opinion and judicial edict, democracy and liberalism. University president Mary Sue Coleman vows to continue to fight for diversity on campus.

action in higher education: "race-conscious" admissions policies were acceptable as long as they were not so inflexible as to constitute a quota system. In the first case, *Grutter v. Bollinger*, a 5–4 majority upheld the University of Michigan law school's approach to enrolling a "critical mass" of

African Americans, Latinos, and Native Americans, an approach in which the school considered each case individually and set no explicit quota. The court's opinion, written by Justice Sandra Day O'Connor, rejected the Bush administration's contention that race should be taken into consideration in admitting a diverse student body only as a last resort, that is, if "race-neutral" means failed to work. Speaking for the majority, O'Connor endorsed the law school's position that "race unfortunately still matters" and deferred to its determination, "based on experience and expertise, that a 'critical mass' of underrepresented minorities is necessary to further its compelling interest in securing the educational benefits of a diverse student body."

At the same time, in the case of *Gratz v. Bollinger*, a 6–3 majority rejected as too mechanistic Michigan's undergraduate affirmative action program because it gave members of "underrepresented" groups an automatic 20-point admission bonus on the 150-point scale to rank applicants. Unlike the law school policy that the court upheld, the procedures employed by the Office of Undergraduate Admissions did not "provide for a meaningful individualized review of applicants."

The court's justices thus brokered the affirmative action issue before them: they backed the president's claim that inflexible racial admissions policies denied individuals equal access to higher education while emphasizing that, until equality between black and white citizens is established throughout the nation, race-conscious policies would be tolerated. Specifically, O'Connor wrote, "We expect that 25 years from now the use of racial preferences will no longer be necessary." This target was not binding, but it was sure to be cited as the court continued its tortured efforts to strike a balance between equality and liberty. Critics of the court's decision, however, lamented that the potential for a principled debate between conservatism and liberalism – between classical and modern liberal understandings – was lost amid the flurry of legal briefs and the court's narrow interpretation of the facts on the merits of specific cases.

The aftermath of the Supreme Court's *Grutter* and *Gratz* decisions offered a more direct political test of whether conflict over affirmative action rose to the level of constitutional politics or had become a mere disagreement over what means best achieved a widely accepted value, equality of opportunity for minorities and women. In 2006, Jennifer Gratz, the lead plaintiff in *Gratz v. Bollinger*, launched a campaign for Proposition 2, a ballot measure that would amend Michigan's constitution. Proposition 2 declared that the state could "not discriminate against, or grant preferential treatment to, any individual or group on the basis of race, sex, color, ethnicity, or national origin for public employment, education, or contracting purposes." Gratz enlisted the help of Ward Connerly, the

African-American businessman and anti–affirmative action activist from California who had led successful initiative battles that enacted anti-affirmative action measures in California, in 1996, and Washington, in 1998. But Connerly and his political allies had lost two contests since then, in Houston, Texas, and Florida. Proposition 2 was viewed as a critical fight in the protracted national struggle over special programs for minorities and women.

Democratic officials, from Governor Jennifer Granholm on down, opposed Proposition 2, as did leaders of the large Arab population, the Jewish community, and the United Auto Workers. So too did the Republican candidate for governor, Dick DeVos, and the great majority of the business community. Voters, however, were less settled in their opinions of affirmative action programs. Opinion surveys showed that they subscribed to the Supreme Court's view, and that of leaders from both political parties, that diversity did not infringe on, but served individual freedom. Yet they were against affirmative action when it was cast in racial terms. In the end, race trumped diversity. Overall, Proposition 2 won a decisive 58 percent majority; however, the divide between male and female voters, and, to an even greater extent, whites and blacks, was significant. CNN reported that a survey of around 2000 voters as they left polling places showed that almost two-thirds of men supported the proposition, while only a slight majority of women did. Two-thirds of the white voters questioned wanted to end affirmative action, compared with only one in seven black voters.

The Michigan vote highlights how affirmative action remains a polarizing issue in American life – how racial politics continues to be a principal source of the ongoing struggle over the proper meaning of rights. It remains to be seen, however, whether the Michigan verdict will reignite a national debate over whether or not affirmative action is an appropriate remedy for intractable inequalities. A day after Michigan approved Proposition 2, a pro-affirmative action group, aptly called By Any Means Necessary, filed a federal lawsuit challenging the measure as unconstitutional. Separately, Mary Sue Coleman, the president of the University of Michigan, pledged "to consider every legal option available" to continue to fight for diversity on campus. No one should be surprised, lawyers predicted, if it takes a dozen years to sort out the lawsuits that Proposition 2 would inspire.

The Future of Self-Government

The struggle over rights in contemporary America raised anew the question of whether it was possible, as the Framers of the Constitution claimed, to promote self-government on a grand scale. Their radical assertion flew in the face of the traditional view that democracy requires a high level of trust

in one's fellow citizens, trust that only a small, closed, relatively homogenous society can cultivate. The Anti-Federalists supported this traditional
view, which presupposed limits to the scale and diversity of political life.
They opposed ratification of the Constitution because it threatened to
destroy liberty by undermining an active and competent citizenry.

The *Federalist Papers* reversed this traditional equation of a closed society
that had a free and open political system; instead, it supported an open,
diverse society that had a more closed political system that imposed severe
checks on democracy. The *Federalist Papers* held that a large commercial
society – inhabited by a cosmopolitan citizenry – was more likely to protect the differences of faculties and opinions of a free people. The Framers
did not believe in complete cultural diversity and unlimited rights – a just
republic had to reside in a political culture that believed in natural rights
and the sanctity of contract. But the Framers prescribed what James Madison called a "system of filtration" that could "refine and enlarge the public
views." They sought to craft a constitutional system that followed the principles of the Declaration of Independence, which taught that interests could
be compromised but that the rights of "life, liberty, and the pursuit of happiness" were sacred and must be inoculated from interests and democratic
sentiments.

Reflecting on the legacy of the Framers' work with the benefit of more
than 200 years of hindsight, the historian C. Vann Woodward saw much
to celebrate. America managed to ally nationalism with diversity in a fashion that is the envy of the world. Although far from complete, Woodward
concluded, America's tolerance of ethnic, religious, and racial differences
was remarkable, especially compared to the conflict and violence that fractured Eastern Europe after the Soviet Union collapsed. Ethnic diversity
smoldered under the threat of a communist regime and exploded once the
force that had imposed authority was lifted. In contrast, American ethnic
and cultural identities flourished in the wake of the rights revolution, with
civil and women's rights activists celebrating their separate identities and
their contributions to national achievement and American civilization.

But, as we have suggested throughout this book, the costs of these gains
threaten to become excessive. Woodward warned that the strident celebration of rights and multiculturalism could destroy America's capacity to
assimilate and integrate diverse cultures. He deplored efforts to change the
United States from "a transformative nation with an identity all its own"
to a nation that preserves or revives old identities, that thinks and acts in
groups, in "a quarrelsome sputter of enclaves, ghettos, and tribes." Such
a nation, said Woodward, would abandon the national ideal of *e pluribus
unum* (one from many) and would celebrate *pluribus* over *unum* (its separate
identities over nationhood). Just as sectional conflicts over economic issues,

slavery, and civil rights tore at the fabric of national unity in the nineteenth century, so the celebration of group rights risks fracturing contemporary America.

Can a renewed sense of national identity be found in America's constitutional tradition – in a revival of the enduring commitment to a balance between liberalism and democracy? Or does the "disuniting of America," as the historian Arthur Schlesinger, Jr., described it, mark the failure of a constitutional order that celebrated rights and gave short shrift to democratic deliberation and choice? The Anti-Federalist Cato (see Chapter 3) warned that to "enlarge the circle" of political life as far as conceived by the Constitution would inevitably result in the loss of "the ties of acquaintance, habits, and fortune" that nurtured civic attachments, that made a rights-conscious people a country. The mass party system – an institutional elaboration of the Anti-Federalists' concerns – periodically brought the Declaration of Independence and constitutional forms into question by drawing them into mass popular upheavals over the meaning of rights. These "refoundings" – the Jeffersonian Revolution of 1800, Jacksonian democracy, the Civil War, and the New Deal – allowed Americans and their representatives to revisit the fundamental principles of the Declaration and reset the terms of constitutional government, to renew their sense of themselves as citizens. Such major political transformations have been America's finest yet most dangerous moments. The explosion of rights and advocacy groups at the dawn of the twenty-first century and the tendency to shift the conflicts they have created to the courts rather than the political area threatens to preempt the sort of polarizing struggles over different understandings of liberalism that have been pivotal to American political development in the past. The danger is that the clash of rights in a large cosmopolitan society may render any meaningful sense of collective responsibility impractical.

The Enduring Constitutional Legacy

In a sense, the problems that appear to afflict contemporary American government and politics testify to the Constitution's success. If Madison and his colleagues could visit America today, they would find that many of their hopes for the American republic have been fulfilled. In "Federalist No. 10" (see Appendix 3), Madison identified two features of the American Constitution that would distinguish it from "pure" democracy and make it possible to balance liberty and equality: representation, by which the people delegate governing responsibility "to a small number of citizens elected by the rest"; and a large republic that would give rise to so many factions that they would be unable to form a stable tyranny of the majority. These two distinguishing characteristics of republican government are still the most familiar features of American political life. "Ambition counteracts ambition" in the relationship between the national and the state governments as well as among the president, Congress, and the courts. And a large and diverse society gives rise to a multitude of narrow factions that compete for influence in Washington as well as in the state capitals.

The American republic came into its own after the Civil War, when the supremacy of the Union was secured. Henry Adams's classic novel, *Democracy*, which depicts political life at the end of the nineteenth century, suggests how enduring the basic features of political life have been over the past century. Adams's heroine, Madeline Lightfoot Lee, a New York socialite, decides to spend a winter in Washington despite the warnings of her New York friends, who fear that she will sorely miss the cultural advantages of her native city. It is not culture, however, but the free and passionate play of political ambition that attracts her to the nation's capital. "What she wished to see," Adams wrote, "was the clash of interests, the interests of 40 millions of people and a whole continent centering on Washington; guided, restrained, controlled, or unrestrained and uncontrollable, by men of ordinary mould; the tremendous forces of government and the machinery of society at work. What she wanted was power." Although the size and complexity of American society have certainly increased since *Democracy* was published in 1880 (now, the interests of 300 million people clash in Washington, D.C.), the scene described by Adams is not very different from the accounts written today about American government in the *Washington Post* or the *New York Times*.

The Absence of Class Conflict

By establishing a large republic, the Framers hoped to avoid class conflict, which they believed would inevitably lead to mob rule. The sheer multiplicity of interests that America contained would make it harder for cohesive classes to form. The checks and balances that operated between the different levels and branches of the government would further discourage the creation of a tyrannical majority. This combination of a large republic and a complex governing system was supposed to produce a tolerant, pluralistic republic that would avoid the twin evils of previous experiments in self-rule: incompetence and majority tyranny. As the distinguished jurist Learned Hand once put it, "The spirit of liberty is the spirit which is not sure it is right."

The Constitution would cultivate this spirit of tolerance by the way it treated the problem of factionalism. It would discourage the tendency in popular governments for a majority faction to impose its will on society, to disregard the rights of individuals and minorities. As Madison argued in "Federalist No. 51" (see Appendix 4), "Whilst all authority in it [government] will be derived from and dependent on the society, the society itself will be broken into so many parts, interests, and classes of citizens, that the rights of individuals, or the minority, will be in little danger from interested combinations of the majority." The persistence of local self-government, decentralized political associations, and virulent sectional conflicts over slavery and monetary policy postponed the question of whether Madison's experiment in self-rule was viable. But with the Civil War, its aftermath, and the rise of industrial capitalism, constitutional government entered a new phase.

In large part, modern American politics has proven Madison prophetic. Despite all the important changes brought by the Progressive Era, the New Deal, and the Great Society, his hope for a highly diverse, tolerant society has largely been realized. The pluralistic nature of American political society and the relative inattention to class differences that it fosters marks what is most distinctive about the United States compared to other representative democracies. Progressive reformers hoped to strengthen self-government by transforming localized democracy into direct rule of the people, who would not have to suffer the interference of decentralizing institutions and associations. Progressives believed that a modern version of "pure democracy" – cultivated by direct primaries, referenda, and civic associations – would instill a greater sense of community among "We the People." Critics warned that Progressives would unleash an unlimited majoritarianism that would violate the Constitution's promise to protect individual freedom against the vagaries of public opinion. But, contrary to the hopes of militant Progressive reformers who sought to substitute a strong national community for the individualism of the past, the "voice of the whole people" would eventually embrace a new understanding of rights, one that presupposed national government protection of individual men and women from the uncertainties of the marketplace, the abuses of big business, and the discriminatory practices of public and private institutions.

Franklin Roosevelt's New Deal played a critical part in linking this new public responsibility to constitutional principles. The economic crisis of the 1930s and the emergence of a strong labor movement sharpened political conflict along class lines. In 1936, FDR attacked his critics in the business community in harsh and provocative terms, condemning them as "economic royalists" who "hid behind the flag and Constitution" with the intention of imposing a "dictatorship of the overprivileged." But New Deal principles and programs were not really class-based. Rather, FDR promised to overthrow an economic monarchy (a privileged class) in the name of the commoners. In a nation where nearly everyone considers oneself a commoner, the breadth of this appeal was enormous.

FDR also provided a means for Americans to affiliate with the New Deal based on an enduring understanding of rights. He enlisted New Deal supporters in a war against privilege: "Necessitous men," Roosevelt insisted, "were not free men." This cause was not limited to industrial workers and the impoverished, he claimed, but a challenge to the entire people. "There is a mysterious cycle in human events," he noted in his 1936 speech accepting renomination. "To some generations much is given. Of other generations much is expected. This generation has a rendezvous with destiny."

Like the New Deal, the Civil Rights Movement did not polarize America along class lines. As the struggle over affirmative action illustrates, the social movements of the 1960s evolved into the public-interest groups of the 1970s that tended to fight their battles in courts and administrative agencies rather than in more democratic venues. By discouraging popular participation, the recourse to bureaucracy and courts further diminished the role of class conflict and class-based politics.

Tellingly, the programmatic rights of the New Deal that have been most immune from political challenge are middle-class entitlements such as Social Security and Medicare. Similarly, the most vulnerable programs have been those aimed at diminishing poverty. In 1996, Congress enacted and President Bill Clinton signed a landmark welfare reform bill: the Personal Responsibility and Work Opportunity Reconciliation Act. This law terminated the open-ended entitlement to cash benefits that had been guaranteed to single mothers under the old welfare system. Now, no one can receive a monthly welfare check for more than five years in a lifetime, except in hardship cases as defined by the states. States are allowed to impose even shorter time limits, and some have done so. The most important part of the act proposed, as Clinton put it, to "re-create the Nation's social bargain with the poor." The law required welfare recipients to go to work, or be involved in activities leading to work, within two years after beginning to receive benefits. In August 2006, a decade after the government transformed the welfare system, the Bush administration and a Republican-controlled Congress enacted new rules that forced states to impose tougher work requirements and to reduce the length of time people on welfare could devote to trying to shed drug addictions, recover from mental illnesses, or get an education.

Thus, welfare programs have discouraged class identity and sought to promote individual responsibility. Defenders of the American welfare state claim that when compared to those in most other advanced industrial democracies, it makes individuals less dependent on a centralized bureaucracy and fosters a more dynamic marketplace. Americans tolerate more economic inequality, they acknowledge, but achieve greater overall levels of prosperity. Compared to other advanced industrial democracies, Americans enjoy higher rates of home ownership, easier access to consumer credit, and more opportunity to attain a college education.

By the end of the twentieth century, however, the growing tendency to emphasize personal responsibility in social policy began to take its toll not only on the least advantaged Americans but also on the middle class. Even the market-friendly magazine *BusinessWeek* conceded, in the wake of President's Bush proposal to "privatize" Social Security, that many middle-class Americans had begun to worry that "the country's web of public and private social protections [was] fraying." As the political scientist Jacob Hacker has argued, Bush's Social Security scheme would mark the culmination of a post-1970s trend toward "risk privatization," in which government programs and private sector benefits, subsidized by government regulations and tax benefits, have come to cover a declining portion of economic uncertainty faced by citizens. For example, as part of a restructuring wave that began in the 1970s, corporations vying to compete globally had steadily shifted costs and responsibility for pensions and healthcare to their employees. In the face of this "privatization," the Bush Social Security plan, which would allow individuals under fifty-five years of age to set up private accounts that would be subject to the vagaries of the stock market, received little support from Democrats or Republicans. Indeed, surveys showed that a large percentage of Americans wanted more, not less "socialization" of risk, especially in the area of healthcare.

With their victory in the 2006 midterm elections, Democrats spied a renewed consensus to guarantee individual men and women security against the uncertainties of the marketplace. They promised to address the growing anxiety about a global economy by pushing for programs that would increase the minimum wage, expand healthcare coverage, and help Americans defray the cost of higher education. Nonetheless, the commitment to government-provided security has not at all eclipsed the enduring faith in markets and the exceptional fear of centralized power that characterizes American political culture. The national consensus that prevails today in support of American economic regulation and middle-class entitlements falls well short of European-style social democracy. The failure of the Clinton administration to enact its healthcare program, which would have guaranteed all Americans minimum coverage, confirmed the limited nature of the welfare state in America compared to those in Great Britain and Western Europe. Ralph Nader's 2000 presidential campaign under the banner of the Green party scorned the limited character of American entitlements and called for programs, such as national health insurance, that would dedicate the national government to the attainment of economic and social equality. But Nader received less than 5 percent of the popular vote, far less than the Green party obtained in European nations such as

Germany. The absence of a strong socialist party highlighted the critical difference between the United States and other advanced industrial democracies during the twentieth century. The limited impact of the Green party and other contemporary social democratic movements on the United States during the twenty-first century signifies the enduring and exceptional resistance in the United States to government programs that heavily impinge on business or redistribute wealth.

Paradoxically, the obsession with rights and "statism" in the United States has not limited the size of government. Nor has the concern to exact reciprocal responsibility from the poor translated, as President Ronald Reagan once promised, into an effort "to get the government off the backs" of the American people. Indeed, as we have noted throughout this book, Bush has sought to put a Republican cast on the era of big government. Even as they bickered over the details of social and welfare programs, Bush and most Democrats reached accord on the creation of a mammoth new cabinet department, the Department of Homeland Security (DHS). DHS extended the national presence into some of the most basic state and local functions, including police, public safety, and public health. Moreover, the president and a leading modern liberal, Senator Edward Kennedy (D-MA), joined hands in pushing through Congress the most important education bill since the 1965 Elementary and Secondary Education Act. Combining progressive liberal demands for more spending and conservative insistence on standards, the No Child Left Behind Act, which became law in 2002, involves Washington more deeply than ever before in the management of local schools. Although classical liberals once promised to eliminate the Department of Education, the Bush administration was prepared to enforce national education standards and oversee reading and math tests for students in the third through eighth grades. Finally, the Bush White House, with steadfast support from Republican leaders in Congress, added an elaborate and expensive prescription drug program to Medicare in 2003. Although the Democrats have been highly critical of this program for giving too much influence to the insurance and pharmaceutical industries, there is no prospect that it will be scaled back once they take control of the House and Senate in January 2007. To the contrary, Democrats speak of expanding the government's control over prescriptions by empowering it to negotiate lower drug prices and fill the gaps in existing coverage.

Both contemporary conservatives and liberals thereby embrace big government and accept programs that are dedicated to economic and national security. Yet for all the changes in America over the past century, its enduring features are impressive. Madison's hope that the Constitution would spawn a republic dedicated to the individual pursuit of happiness seems to have been largely fulfilled. The persistence of a rights-conscious people who look to groups to contest for their interests in a complex system of checks and balances is a remarkable testament to the practical wisdom of the Framers of the American Constitution.

New Factionalism

Since the constitutional founding, of course, major developments in American government have taken place. As the Trent Lott story illustrated, contemporary American politics is a complex blend of the old and the new. A multitude of diverse interests prevail and exercise power: in that way, American government seems timeless. Nonetheless, there does seem to be something new about the factionalism of contemporary American politics. A new factionalism, if not a new political system, shapes contemporary American political life.

Madison believed that factions tempered by the essential features of republican government – size, diversity, and institutional fragmentation – would act as veto points, delimiting the role of government. He and Thomas Jefferson insisted that individual freedom required a limited national presence at home and abroad; as Jefferson put it with respect to the freedom of religion, liberty required building a "wall of separation" between government and society. They opposed Hamilton's ambition to build a constitutional foundation for a powerful national government – an administrative republic – that would encourage commercialism domestically and protect America's interests in the world. They feared that if America became a great empire in the tradition of Rome or Great Britain, the country would depart from the values celebrated in the Declaration of Independence. If the United States was to be a "city upon a hill," the public responsibilities and civic feeling would have to emerge from the provinces, to grow out of a strong sense of individual self-reliance and local self-government. Like Hamilton, Jefferson and Madison were committed to classical liberalism, but they believed that liberty could flourish only in a setting in which individuals could enjoy economic and political independence.

This vision of government was celebrated by Jefferson's Revolution of 1800, which Jefferson and Madison viewed as rededicating the country to the Revolution and the Declaration of Independence. Jefferson's first inaugural address was a clarion call of republican simplicity that would endure well into the twentieth century. He stated the advantages of American citizens, who were "separated by nature and a wide ocean from the exterminating havoc of one quarter of the globe" and who had the good fortune to possess "a chosen country, with room enough for our descendants to the hundredth and thousandth generation." These natural advantages,

Jefferson believed, would be maintained only by a minimalist government that did not squander them: "a wise and frugal government, which shall restrain men from injuring one another, which shall leave them free to regulate their pursuits of industry and improvement, and shall not take from the mouth of labor the bread it has earned."

Jefferson's vision of minimalist government endured until the New Deal. Americans clung to it, professing a belief in what President Herbert Hoover called "rugged individualism," even in the face of serious economic and social injustice at home and imperialist threats abroad. Before the 1930s, factions sprang up around a few problems – foreign trade, internal improvements, disposition of public lands, and veterans' benefits. The traditional idea of individual rights was sorely tested by the conflagration over slavery during the 1860s and the disruptive conflicts aroused by industrial capitalism during the turn of the twentieth century. But classical liberalism proved malleable enough to survive wide disagreements over economic and political issues. With the domestic and international crises of the 1930s and 1940s, however, rugged individualism gave way to a new individualism in which the national government promised its citizens, in FDR's description, "freedom from want" and "freedom from fear."

Thereafter, the clash of ambition and interests in the United States assumed a new form. Unlike uncompromising abolitionists, such as Wendell Phillips, the New Dealers did not denigrate interests. Unlike militant Progressive reformers, such as President Theodore Roosevelt, FDR and his political allies did not reject rights in the name of national obligation and responsibility (see Chapter 4). Rather, a new understanding of rights emerged, an understanding that political scientists call "programmatic" because government must create programs to secure those rights. The clearest example of such a programmatic right is the establishment of Social Security, which created a right to economic security. Medicare and Medicaid, by providing medical coverage to the old and the poor, have gone a long way toward establishing a right to healthcare. These new rights gave rise to a constellation of interests. Factional organizations bloomed as they sought to influence government to protect and promote the particular interests they represented. For example, organized associations of doctors, hospitals, nurses, insurance companies, pharmaceutical manufacturers, and health maintenance organizations are all active in seeking to craft healthcare policy in a manner that will benefit their constituents. In political scientist Hugh Heclo's apt description, "modern" factionalism shares with the old a "rich and complex variety of economic interests and ideological commitments"; the main difference is that the new factionalism "has shaped itself around a government presence that is doing so much more in so many different areas of life."

As political scientist James Q. Wilson has observed, the expansion of the new factionalism has been aided by the lowering of the "legitimacy barrier," meaning the constitutional hurdle that must be crossed to justify a transfer of decisions from the private to the public realm. The problems associated with poverty, old age, illiteracy, illness, and physical disability are not new. What is new is that citizens now believe they have a right to protection against such problems and therefore that government has an obligation to provide such protection. The New Deal's redefinition of the social contract prepared the country for such a change, but its full potential was realized in the 1960s, when rights were expanded to programs that went beyond a commitment to economic security – to causes such as civil rights, environmentalism, and consumer protection. As a result, the separation of powers and federalism can no longer be counted on to limit government. Today, the different branches of state and federal government have each become opportunity points for initiating new policies as much as veto points for keeping policies from being enacted. Because the public expects and desires to have its problems solved by government, elected officials at all levels compete with one another to devise public policies to satisfy those desires and expectations. Although the Constitution offers many different means for limiting government, those means are not, in and of themselves, sufficiently strong to prevent democratic demands from going beyond those limits.

The Expansion of National Administrative Power

The rise of new factionalism has had a profound effect on American political institutions. It has gone hand in hand with the expansion of national administrative power. The redefinition of liberalism during the 1930s led to a strengthening of the presidency and an expansion of the bureaucracy. When FDR announced that "the day of enlightened administration has come," he meant that Congress should pass laws that delegated broad policy responsibility to the executive branch. Furthermore, federal judges should adopt an expansive reading of the constitutional powers of the national government and readily defer to policy decisions of the president and administrative agencies.

But this expansion of administration has not been confined to the president and the bureaucracy. The constitutional system of checks and balances – the cunning of Madison – made such a dramatic centralization of government power impossible. Congress and the courts remained central to the work of contemporary American political life, even as government programs expanded. Especially during the 1960s and 1970s, members of the House, Senate, and federal judiciary aggressively began to oversee the activities of the president and executive agencies. Widespread fears that the Vietnam War and the Watergate scandal had spawned an "imperial presidency" caused Congress and the courts to respond by becoming suspicious of, if not avowedly hostile to, the modern executive. Aided by popular support and the emergence of self-styled public interest groups, Congress and the judiciary began to participate routinely in administrative politics. The institutional reforms implemented in Congress during the 1970s (see Chapter 7), which devolved policy responsibility to subcommittees and increased the size of congressional staff, were compatible with the attention being paid by legislators to policy specialization. Similarly, the judiciary's decreasing reliance on constitutional decisions in its rulings affecting the political economy and its emphasis on interpreting statutes to determine the responsibilities of executive agencies are characteristic of the courts' role as co-director of the administrative state.

Consequently, Congress and the judiciary became more assertive in restricting presidential power during the final three decades of the twentieth century but at the cost of looking and acting more like bureaucracies. The emergence of big government did not lead to presidential imperialism but to a fragmented and often contentious struggle among the branches of government for administrative control. The states, too, increased their institutional capacity after the 1970s, creating agencies to administer policy in matters such as environmental protection and education that mirror, and are closely tied to, those at the national level.

The first six years of the Bush administration appeared to subordinate national administration to a renewed sense of partisanship that joined legislative to executive power and aroused rancorous conflict not only over social issues such as same-sex marriage, but also over matters of national security (see Chapters 7 and 8). Although it is unlikely that this partisan rancor will disappear with the restoration of divided government in 2007, contemporary partisan disputes now seem inextricably tied to disagreements over how to use national administrative power. Put simply, conservatives have embraced the national security state while liberals have devoted more exclusive attention to the welfare state. Nonetheless, just as contemporary liberals have sought to renew their commitment to national security by emphasizing, as John Kerry stressed during his presidential campaign, multilateral diplomacy, so conservatives have attempted to come to terms with the welfare state through think tank–vetted provisions – provisions such as health security accounts, which encourage individuals to set up tax-free funds to help pay for medical expenses, and Social Security "privatization" – that would recast entitlement programs in a conservative image. Moreover, in the wake of the 2006 elections, there are likely to be more

President Bush delivered his State of the Union address in 2007 with Vice President Dick Cheney and Speaker of the House Nancy Pelosi by his side. Political rancor along party lines may intensify as a strong Republican executive must work with the Democrat-controlled Congress to resolve pressing issues of domestic programs and foreign policy.

bipartisan efforts to buttress domestic entitlements, shore up homeland security, and redeploy the War on Terror.

The new factionalism and the expansion of national administrative power have created a more active and better-equipped national state – one that has gone far to fulfill the rights of the American people. But as our example of affirmative action shows, the expansion of national administration in the service of more extensive liberalism has come at a price. Programmatic liberalism has weakened the associations and institutions that traditionally nurtured common deliberation and public judgment, the activities essential to the cultivation of civic associations. Liberalism has been expanded at the risk of weakening the country's democratic tradition.

We should not rule out, of course, the possibility that a new democratic tradition might be formed. Strong national parties emerged during the 2004 and 2006 elections. They used innovative and effective methods to mobilize their supporters. This suggests that contemporary liberal and conservative activists have the potential to engage the American people in important domestic and foreign policy issues (see Chapter 12). Moreover, as the challenge to the University of Michigan's admission standards implies, efforts on the part of liberals and conservatives to settle such controversial issues as stem cell research, same-sex marriage, and affirmative action in courts and administrative agencies have been countered by the increasing use of ballot measures that involve voters directly in social and economic policy. These initiatives, born of the Progressive Era's faith in "direct democracy," have hardly been models of public debate and deliberation. Taking place at the state and local level, they have shown how federalism still poses an important obstacle to centralized administration; more to the point, the expansion of ballot initiatives has posed important challenges to interest groups that would prefer to deploy administrative tribunals and courts to arbitrate controversial issues in American political life.

It is unlikely, however, that the "new" party system or the expansion of direct democracy in the states will fundamentally displace the factionalism that has shaped American politics during the past half century. The traumatic events of September 11, 2001, and their aftermath are likely to confirm, rather than displace, the role of the national state in the United States. Indeed, the 2006 elections may actually serve not to accentuate partisan discord but as a rejection of it. It may encourage the sort of pragmatic governance that privileges executive administration in foreign affairs and the demand for new rights, and interest groups that champion them, in domestic politics. This "new" factionalism, occurring amid the expansion of national administrative power, might be viewed as perverting Madison's vision of a nation that practiced self-rule on a grand scale. Nonetheless, it has not led to the result Madison most feared, mob rule. Instead, as Chapter 12 indicates, contemporary American government is characterized by a two-tiered politics in which policy change and conflict take place within the national and state capitals among a diverse but small circle of policy activists. Meanwhile, the mass electorate remains largely passive, often baffled, and isolated from the effective discussion of public policy.

According to the political scientist Morris Fiorina, partisanship, at least in its contemporary form, would be unlikely to ameliorate this schism; indeed, it might make things worse (see Chapter 4). The mounting partisan rancor that continued up through the 2006 elections, he has argued, has aroused activists in Washington, D.C., and the state capitals but has failed to engage ordinary citizens. Thus heated partisanship, should it continue into 2007, would present the country with a situation that would be ripe for demagogy and for citizens' mounting disaffection from government.

Still, as noted in the discussion of political participation in the previous chapter, we should be careful not to condemn out of hand the partisan struggles that stir the welfare and national security states. Through much of the course of American political development, political parties have provided a vital connection between government and the people. Although they have been isolated by modern factionalism, Democrats and Republicans have shown the potential in the past six years to increase public participation in policy disputes and to enlist citizen support in the resolution of public problems. It still remains to be seen how much these highly centralized organizations can cultivate the renewal of effective party affiliation and meaningful civic ties. But for all their faults, the national Democratic and Republican parties might offer the best antidote to the disease of centralized administration. At the dawn of a new century, it seems, the main threat to the Framers' scheme is not overheated democracy aroused by class hatred, as Madison feared, but rather the expansion of administrative politics in the name of the peoples' rights that threatens to suck the meaning out of representative government.

Can We Keep It?

As we note in Chapter 3, the deliberations of the Constitutional Convention of 1787 were held in strict secrecy. Consequently, anxious citizens gathered outside Independence Hall when the proceedings ended in order to learn what had been produced behind closed doors. The answer was provided immediately. A Mrs. Powel of Philadelphia asked Benjamin Franklin, "Well, Doctor, what have we got, a republic or a monarchy?" With no hesitation whatsoever, Franklin responded, "A republic, if you can keep it."

This end to the Constitutional Convention is a fitting note on which to conclude our story of American government and politics. Franklin's charge to Mrs. Powel and the American people suggested that the Constitution alone could not protect the inalienable rights of individual men and women. Rather, it established a framework in which "We the People" would take responsibility for protecting the freedoms proclaimed in the Declaration of Independence. Republican government required the people to delegate responsibility for governing to a few representatives whose task it would be to draw out, as Hamilton put it, "the deliberate sense of the community," but ultimate sovereignty rested in the citizens themselves. The ratification contest called on Americans to debate whether the new Constitution was, as it promised, a "more perfect Union" that would protect Americans' rights; likewise, the periodic refoundings that have taken place in this country's history have called on Americans to debate the meaning of their rights, to engage in conflicts that have tested their constitutional soul.

Through these refoundings – the awakening of democracy, a great civil war, and the creation of a strong federal government – citizens have been required to participate actively in the protection of their rights. They have redefined the social contract for their own political time. By balancing rights and democracy, Americans have kept the republic that the Framers left to them. In the wake of the unspeakable horrors of September 11, 2001, the country once again faced profound responsibilities, stirring controversies in domestic and foreign policy about how best to guarantee the security of the homeland. As public officials struggled to come to terms with the tasks of a new century, the challenge for the people was to hold their government accountable and to recapture the understanding of democracy that had made such momentous deliberation and choice so central to the pursuit of America's political destiny. In this rediscovery might come the recognition that liberty requires the art of political association no less than the demand for rights. With this recognition, Americans would have reason to expect a true renewal of America's democratic and liberal traditions.

Chapter Summary

☆ The way people think about current politics is heavily dependent not only on their own past experiences but also on those of their parents and grandparents and on the collective memory of the groups they identify with.

☆ By establishing a large republic, the Framers hoped to avoid class conflict and mob rule. The sheer multiplicity of interests in a large republic would make it harder for cohesive classes to form. The checks and balances that operated between the different levels and branches of the government would further discourage the creation of a tyrannical majority. This combination of a large republic and a complex governing system was supposed to produce a tolerant, pluralistic republic that would avoid the twin evils of previous experiments in self-rule: incompetence and majority tyranny.

☆ Madison's hope for a highly diverse, tolerant society has largely been realized. The pluralistic nature of contemporary America and the relative inattention to class differences marks what is most distinctive about the United States compared to other representative democracies.

☆ The mass party system – an institutional elaboration of the Anti-Federalists' concerns – periodically brought the Declaration of Independence and constitutional forms into question by drawing them into mass popular upheavals over the meaning of rights. These "refoundings" – the Jeffersonian Revolution of 1800, the Jacksonian democracy, the Civil War, and the New Deal – allowed Americans and their representatives to revisit the fundamental principles of the Declaration and reset the terms of constitutional government, to renew their sense of themselves as citizens.

☆ As the affirmative action example illustrates, the current tendency is to resolve great disputes over liberty and democracy in the courts, precluding the great contests of popular opinion that resulted in refoundings. Leaving such disputes to the courts risks distracting the public's attention from what is really at issue when deep principles of liberty and democracy collide, thereby robbing them of their capacity to engage in self-government.

☆ The New Deal succeeded in lowering the "legitimacy barrier," meaning the constitutional hurdle that must be crossed to justify a transfer of decisions from the private to the public realm. Citizens now believe they have a right to protection against such problems as poverty, old age, illiteracy, illness, and physical disability and that government has an obligation to provide such protection. The full potential of this lowering of the legitimacy barrier was realized in the 1960s, when rights were expanded to programs that went beyond a commitment to economic security – to causes such as civil rights, environmentalism, and consumer protection.

☆ The new, programmatic understanding of rights that the New Deal spawned gave rise to new constellations of interests devoted to protecting and expanding those rights. Factional organizations bloomed as they sought to influence government to protect and promote the particular interests they represented. The rise of this new factionalism has gone hand in hand with the expansion of national administrative power.

☆ The particular combination of rights, factionalism, and administrative power that we call *programmatic liberalism* has weakened the associations and institutions that traditionally nurtured common deliberation and public judgment. Liberalism has been expanded at the risk of weakening the country's democratic tradition.

Appendix One: The Declaration of Independence

In Congress, July 4, 1776

The Unanimous Declaration of the Thirteen United States of America

When, in the Course of human events, it becomes necessary for one people to dissolve the political bands which have connected them with another, and to assume, among the powers of the earth, the separate and equal station to which the Laws of Nature and of Nature's God entitle them, a decent respect to the opinions of mankind requires that they should declare the causes which impel them to the separation.

We hold these truths to be self-evident, that all men are created equal; that they are endowed by their Creator with certain unalienable Rights; that among these, are Life, Liberty, and the pursuit of Happiness. That, to secure these rights, Governments are instituted among Men, deriving their just powers from the consent of the governed; That, whenever any Form of Government becomes destructive of these ends, it is the Right of the People to alter or to abolish it, and to institute a new government, laying its foundation on such principles, and organizing its powers in such form, as to them shall seem most likely to effect their Safety and Happiness. Prudence, indeed, will dictate that Governments long established, should not be changed for light and transient causes; and, accordingly, all experience hath shown, that mankind are more disposed to suffer, while evils are sufferable, than to right themselves by abolishing the forms to which they are accustomed. But, when a long train of abuses and usurpations, pursuing invariably the same Object, evinces a design to reduce them under absolute Despotism, it is their duty, to throw off such Government and to provide new Guards for their future security. Such has been the patient sufferance of these Colonies, and such is now the necessity which constrains them to alter their former Systems of government. The history of the present King of Great Britain is a history of repeated injuries and usurpations, all having, in direct object, the establishment of an absolute Tyranny over these States. To prove this, let Facts be submitted to a candid world:

He has refused his Assent to Laws the most wholesome and necessary for the public good.

He has forbidden his Governors to pass Laws of immediate and pressing importance, unless suspended in their operation till his assent should be obtained; and, when so suspended, he has utterly neglected to attend to them.

He has refused to pass other Laws for the accommodation of large districts of people, unless, those people would relinquish the right of Representation in the Legislature; a right inestimable to them, and formidable to tyrants only.

He has called together legislative bodies at places unusual, uncomfortable, and distant from the depository of their public Records, for the sole purpose of fatiguing them into compliance with his measures.

He has dissolved Representative Houses repeatedly for opposing, with manly firmness, his invasions on the rights of the people.

He has refused, for a long time after such dissolutions, to cause others to be elected; whereby the Legislative powers, incapable of Annihilation, have returned to the People at large for their exercise; the State remaining, in the meantime, exposed to all the danger of invasion from without, and convulsions within.

He has endeavored to prevent the population of these States; for that purpose, obstructing the Laws for Naturalization of Foreigners, refusing to pass others to encourage their migration hither, and raising the conditions of new Appropriations of Lands.

He has Obstructed the Administration of Justice, by refusing his Assent to Laws for establishing Judiciary powers.

He has made Judges dependent on his Will alone, for the tenure of their offices, and the amount and payment of their salaries.

He has erected a multitude of New Offices, and sent hither swarms of Officers to harass our people, and eat out their substance.

He has kept among us, in time of peace, Standing Armies, without the Consent of our legislatures.

He has affected to render the Military independent of, and superior to, the Civil Power.

He has combined, with others, to subject us to a jurisdiction foreign to our Constitution, and unacknowledged by our laws; giving his assent to their acts of pretended Legislation:

For quartering large bodies of armed troops among us:

For protecting them by a mock trial, from punishment, for many murders which they should commit on the inhabitants of these States:

For cutting off our Trade with all parts of the world:

For imposing Taxes on us without our Consent:

For depriving us, in many cases, of the benefit of Trial by Jury:

For transporting us beyond Seas to be tried for pretended offences:

For abolishing the free System of English laws in a neighboring Province, establishing therein an Arbitrary government, and enlarging its Boundaries so as to render it at once an example and fit instrument for introducing the same absolute rule into these Colonies:

For taking away our Charters, abolishing our most valuable Laws, and altering, fundamentally, the Forms of our governments:

For suspending our own Legislatures, and declaring themselves invested with power to legislate for us in all cases whatsoever.

He has abdicated Government here, by declaring us out of his Protection, and waging war against us.

He has plundered our seas, ravaged our Coasts, burnt our towns, and destroyed the lives of our people.

He is, at this time, transporting large Armies of foreign Mercenaries to complete the works of death, desolation, and tyranny, already begun, with circumstances of Cruelty and perfidy scarcely paralleled in the most barbarous ages, and totally unworthy of the head of a civilized nation.

He has constrained our fellow Citizens, taken Captive on the high Seas, to bear arms against their Country, to become the executioners of their friends, and Brethren, or to fall themselves by their Hands.

He has excited domestic insurrections amongst us, and has endeavored to bring on the inhabitants of our frontiers, the merciless Indian Savages, whose known rule of warfare is an undistinguished destruction off all ages, sexes, and conditions.

In every stage of these Oppressions We have Petitioned for Redress, in the most humble terms; Our repeated Petitions have been answered only by repeated injury. A Prince, whose character is thus marked by every act which may define a Tyrant, is unfit to be the ruler of free people.

Nor have We been wanting in attention to our British brethren. We have warned them, from time to time, of attempts made by their legislature to extend an unwarrantable jurisdiction over us. We have reminded them of the circumstances of our emigration and settlement here. We have appealed to their native justice and magnanimity, and we have conjured them, by the ties of our common kindred, to disavow these usurpations, which would inevitably interrupt our connections and correspondence. They too have been deaf to the voice of justice and of consanguinity. We must, therefore, acquiesce in the necessity which denounces our separation, and hold them as we hold the rest of mankind, Enemies in War, in Peace Friends.

We, therefore, the Representatives of the United States of America, in General Congress Assembled, appealing to the Supreme Judge of the world for the rectitude of our intentions, do, in the name, and by the Authority of the good People of these Colonies, solemnly publish and declare, That these United Colonies are, and of Right ought to be, Free and Independent States: that they are Absolved from all Allegiance to the British Crown, and that all political connection between them and the State of Great Britain is, and ought to be, totally dissolved; and that, as Free and Independent States, they have full Power to levy War, conclude Peace, contract Alliances, establish Commerce, and to do all other Acts and Things which Independent States may of right do. And, for the support of this Declaration, with a firm reliance on the protection of divine Providence, we mutually pledge to each other our Lives, our Fortunes, and our sacred Honor.

The foregoing Declaration was, by order of Congress, engrossed, and signed by the following members:

JOHN HANCOCK

New Hampshire
Josiah Bartlett
William Whipple
Matthew Thornton

Massachusetts Bay
Samuel Adams
John Adams
Robert Treat Paine
Elbridge Gerry

Rhode Island
Stephen Hopkins
William Ellery

Connecticut
Roger Sherman
Samuel Huntington
William Williams
Oliver Wolcott

New York
William Floyd
Philip Livingston
Francis Lewis
Lewis Morris

New Jersey
Richard Stockton
John Witherspoon
Francis Hopkinson
John Hart
Abraham Clark

Pennsylvania
Robert Morris
Benjamin Rush
Benjamin Franklin
John Morton
George Clymer
James Smith
George Taylor
James Wilson
George Ross

Delaware
Caesar Rodney
George Reed
Thomas McKean

Maryland
Samuel Chase
William Paca
Thomas Stone
Charles Carroll, of Carrollton

Virginia
George Wythe
Richard Henry Lee
Thomas Jefferson
Benjamin Harrison
Thomas Nelson, Jr.
Francis Lightfoot Lee
Carter Braxton

North Carolina
William Hooper
Joseph Hewes
John Penn

South Carolina
Edward Rutledge
Thomas Heyward, Jr.
Thomas Lynch, Jr.
Arthur Middleton

Georgia
Button Gwinnett
Lyman Hall
George Walton

Resolved, That copies of the Declaration be sent to the several assemblies, conventions, and committees, or councils of safety, and to the several commanding officers of the continental troops; that it be proclaimed in each of the United States, at the head of the army.

Appendix Two: The Constitution of the United States of America[1]

We the People of the United States, in Order to form a more perfect Union, establish Justice, insure domestic Tranquility, provide for the common defence, promote the general Welfare, and secure the Blessings of Liberty to ourselves and our Posterity, do ordain and establish this CONSTITUTION for the United States of America.

ARTICLE I

Section 1

All legislative Powers herein granted shall be vested in a Congress of the United States, which shall consist of a Senate and House of Representatives.

Section 2

The House of Representatives shall be composed of Members chosen every second Year by the People of the several States, and the Electors in each State shall have the Qualifications requisite for Electors of the most numerous Branch of the State Legislature.

No person shall be a Representative who shall not have attained to the Age of twenty-five Years, and been seven Years a Citizen of the United

[1] This version, which follows the original Constitution in capitalization and spelling, was published by the United States Department of the Interior, Office of Education, in 1935.

States, and who shall not, when elected, be an Inhabitant of that State in which he shall be chosen.

[Representatives and direct Taxes[2] shall be apportioned among the several States which may be included within this Union, according to their respective Numbers, which shall be determined by adding to the whole Number of free Persons, including those bound to Service for a Term of Years, and excluding Indians not taxed, three fifths of all other Persons.][3] The actual Enumeration shall be made within three Years after the first Meeting of the Congress of the United States, and within every subsequent Term of ten Years, such Manner as they shall by Law direct. The Number of Representatives shall not exceed one for every thirty Thousand, but each State shall have at Least one Representative; and until such enumeration shall be made, the State of New Hampshire shall be entitled to chuse three, Massachusetts eight, Rhode-Island and Providence Plantations one, Connecticut five, New York six, New Jersey four, Pennsylvania eight, Delaware one, Maryland six, Virginia ten, North Carolina five, South Carolina five, and Georgia three.

When vacancies happen in the Representation from any State, the Executive Authority thereof shall issue Writs of Election to fill such Vacancies.

The House of Representatives shall chuse their Speaker and other Officers; and shall have the sole Power of Impeachment.

Section 3

The Senate of the United States shall be composed of two Senators from each State, chosen by the Legislature thereof, for six Years; and each Senator shall have one Vote.

Immediately after they shall be assembled in Consequence of the first Election, they shall be divided as equally as may be into three Classes. The Seats of the Senators of the first Class shall be vacated at the Expiration of the second Year, of the second Class at the Expiration of the fourth Year, and of the third Class at the Expiration of the sixth Year, so that one-third may be chosen every second Year; and if Vacancies happen by Registration, or other wise, during the Recess of the Legislature of any State, the Executive thereof may make temporary Appointments until the next Meeting of the Legislature, which shall then fill such Vacancies.

No Person shall be a Senator who shall not have attained to the Age of thirty Years, and been nine Years a Citizen of the United States, and who

---

[2] Altered by the Sixteenth Amendment.
[3] Negated by the Fourteenth Amendment.

shall not, when elected, be an Inhabitant of that State for which he shall be chosen.

The Vice President of the United States shall be President of the Senate, but shall have no vote, unless they be equally divided.

The Senate shall chuse their other Officers, and also a President pro tempore, in the absence of the Vice President, or when he shall exercise the Office of President of the United States.

The Senate shall have the sole Power to try all Impeachments. When sitting for that purpose they shall be on Oath or Affirmation. When the President of the United States is tried, the Chief Justice shall preside: And no person shall be convicted with out the Concurrence of two thirds of the Members present.

Judgment in Cases of Impeachment shall not extend further than to removal from Office, and disqualification to hold and enjoy any Office of honor, Trust, or Profit under the United States: but the Party convicted shall nevertheless be liable and subject to Indictment, Trial, Judgment and Punishment, according to Law.

Section 4

The Times, Place and Manner of holding Elections for Senators and Representatives, shall be prescribed in each State by the Legislature thereof; but the Congress may at any time by Law make or alter such Regulations, except as to the Places of Chusing Senators.

The Congress shall assemble at least once in every Year, and such Meeting shall be on the first Monday in December, unless they shall by Law appoint a different Day.

Section 5

Each House shall be the Judge of the Elections, Returns and Qualifications of its own Members, and a Majority of each shall constitute a Quorum to do Business; but a smaller number may adjourn from day to day, and may be authorized to compel the Attendance of absent Members, in such Manner, and under such Penalties, as each House may provide.

Each House may determine the Rule of its Proceedings, punish its Members for disorderly Behavior, and, with the Concurrence of two thirds, expel a Member.

Each House shall keep a Journal of its Proceedings, and from time to time publish the same, excepting such Parts as may in their Judgment require Secrecy; and the Yeas and Nays of the Members of either House on any question shall, at the Desire of one fifth of those Present, be entered on the Journal.

Neither House, during the Session of Congress, shall, without the Consent of the other, adjourn for more than three days, nor to any other Place than that in which the two Houses shall be sitting.

Section 6

The Senators and Representatives shall receive a Compensation for their Services, to be ascertained by Law, and paid out of the Treasury of the United States. They shall in all Cases, except Treason, Felony and Breach of the Peace, be privileged from Arrest during their Attendance at the Session of their respective Houses, and in going to and returning from the same; and for any Speech or Debate in either House, they shall not be questioned in any other Place.

No Senator or Representative shall, during the Time for which he was elected, be appointed to any civil Office under the Authority of the United States, which shall have been created, or the Emoluments whereof shall have been increased, during such time; and no Person holding any Office under the United States shall be a Member of either House during his continuance in Office.

Section 7

All Bills for raising Revenue shall originate in the House of Representatives; but the Senate may propose or concur with Amendments as on other bills.

Every Bill which shall have passed the House of Representatives and the Senate, shall, before it becomes a Law, be presented to the President of the United States; if he approve he shall sign it, but if not he shall return it, with his Objections, to that House in which it shall have originated, who shall enter the Objections at large on their Journal, and proceed to reconsider it. If after such Reconsideration two thirds of that House shall agree to pass the bill, it shall be sent, together with the objections, to the other House, by which it shall likewise be reconsidered, and if approved by two thirds of that House, it shall become a Law. But in all such Cases the Votes of both Houses shall be determined by Yeas and Nays, and the Names of the Persons voting for and against the Bill shall be entered on the Journal of each House respectively. If any Bill shall not be returned by the President within ten Days (Sundays excepted) after it shall have been presented to him, the Same shall be a Law, in like Manner as if he signed it, unless the Congress by their Adjournment prevent its Return, in which Case it shall not be a Law.

Every Order, Resolution, or Vote to which the Concurrence of the Senate and House of Representatives may be necessary (except on a question of Adjournment) shall be presented to the President of the United States; and before the Same shall take Effect, shall be approved by him, or being disapproved by him, shall be repassed by two thirds of the Senate and House of Representatives, according to the Rules and Limitations prescribed in the Case of a Bill.

Section 8

The Congress shall have Power To lay and collect Taxes, Duties, Imposts and Excises, to pay the Debts and provide for the common Defence and general Welfare of the United States; but all Duties, Imposts and Excises shall be uniform throughout the United States;

To borrow money on the credit of the United States;

To regulate Commerce with foreign Nations, and among the several States, and with the Indian Tribes;

To establish a uniform rule of Naturalization, and uniform Laws on the subject of Bankruptcies throughout the United States;

To coin Money, regulate the Value thereof, and of foreign Coin, and fix the Standard of Weights and Measures;

To provide for the Punishment of counterfeiting the Securities and current Coin of the United States;

To establish Post Offices and post Roads;

To promote the Progress of Science and useful Arts, by securing for limited Times to Authors and Inventors the exclusive Right to their respective Writings and Discoveries;

To constitute Tribunals inferior to the Supreme Court;

To define and punish Piracies and Felonies committed on the high Seas, and Offenses against the Law of Nations;

To declare War, grant Letters of Marque and Reprisal, and make Rules concerning Captures on Land and Water;

To raise and support Armies, but no Appropriation of Money to that Use shall be for a longer Term than two Years;

To provide and maintain a Navy;

To make Rules for the Government and Regulation of the land and naval forces;

To provide for calling forth the Militia to execute the Laws of the Union, suppress Insurrections and repel Invasions;

To provide for organizing, arming, and disciplining the Militia, and for governing such Part of them as may be employed in the Service of the United States, reserving to the States respectively, the Appointment of the

Officers, and the Authority of training the Militia according to the discipline prescribed by Congress;

To exercise exclusive Legislation in all Cases whatsoever, over such District (not exceeding ten Miles square) as may, by Cession of particular States, and the acceptance of Congress, become the Seat of the Government of the United States, and to exercise like Authority over all Places purchased by the Consent of the Legislature of the State in which the Same shall be, for the Erection of Forts, Magazines, Arsenals, Dock-yards, and other needful Buildings; – And

To make all Laws which shall be necessary and proper for carrying into Execution the foregoing Powers, and all other Powers vested by this Constitution in the Government of the United States, or in any Department or Officer thereof.

Section 9

The Migration or Importation of such Persons as any of the States now existing shall think proper to admit, shall not be prohibited by the Congress prior to the Year one thousand eight hundred and eight, but a tax or duty may be imposed on such Importation, not exceeding ten dollars for each Person.

The privilege of the Writ of Habeas Corpus shall not be suspended, unless when in Cases of Rebellion or Invasion the public Safety may require it.

No bill of Attainder or ex post facto Law shall be passed.

No capitation, or other direct, Tax shall be laid unless in Proportion to the Census or Enumeration herein before directed to be taken.

No Tax or Duty shall be laid on Articles exported from any State.

No Preference shall be given by any Regulation of Commerce or Revenue to the Ports of one State over those of another: nor shall Vessels bound to, or from, one State, be obliged to enter, clear, or pay Duties in another.

No Money shall be drawn from the Treasury, but in Consequence of Appropriations made by Law; and regular Statement and Account of the Receipts and Expenditures of all public Money shall be published from time to time.

No Title of Nobility shall be granted by the United States: And no Person holding any Office of Profit or Trust under them, shall, without the Consent of the Congress, accept of any present, Emolument, Office, or Title, of any kind whatever, from any King, Prince, or foreign States.

Section 10

No State shall enter into any Treaty, Alliance, or Confederation; grant Letters of Marque and Reprisal; coin Money; emit Bills of Credit; make any Thing but gold and silver Coin a Tender in Payment of Debts; pass any Bill of Attainder, ex post facto Law, or Law impairing the Obligation of Contracts, or grant any Title of Nobility.

No State shall, without the Consent of the Congress, lay any Imposts or Duties on Imports or Exports, except what may be absolutely necessary for executing its inspection Laws; and the net Produce of all Duties and Imposts, laid by any State on Imports or Exports, shall be for the use of the Treasury of the United States; and all such Laws shall be subject to the Revision and Control of the Congress.

No state shall, without the Consent of Congress, lay any duty of Tonnage, keep Troops, or Ships of War in time of Peace, enter into any Agreement or Compact with another State, or with a foreign Power, or engage in War, unless actually invaded, or in such imminent Danger as will not admit of delay.

ARTICLE II

Section 1

The executive Power shall be vested in a President of the United States of America. He shall hold his Office during the Term of four years, and together with the Vice President, chosen for the same Term, be elected, as follows:

Each State shall appoint, in such Manner as the Legislature thereof may direct, a Number of Electors, equal to the whole Number of Senators and Representatives to which the State may be entitled in the Congress: but no Senator or Representative, or Person holding an Office of Trust or Profit under the United States, shall be appointed an Elector.

[The Electors shall meet in their respective States, and vote by Ballot for two persons, of whom one at least shall not be an Inhabitant of the same State with themselves. And they shall make a List of all the Persons voted for, and of the Number of Votes for each; which List they shall sign and certify, and transmit sealed to the Seat of the Government of the United States, directed to the President of the Senate. The President of the Senate shall, in the Presence of the Senate and House of Representatives, open all the Certificates, and the Votes shall then be counted. The Person having the greatest Number of Votes shall be the President, if such Number be a Majority of the whole Number of Electors appointed; and if there be more than one who have such Majority, and have an equal Number of Votes, then the House of Representatives shall immediately chuse by Ballot one of them for President; and if no Person have a Majority, then from the five highest on the List the said House shall in like Manner chuse the President. But in chusing the President, the Votes shall be taken by States, the Representation from each State having one Vote, a quorum for this Purpose shall consist of a Member or Members from two-thirds of the States, and a Majority of all the States shall be necessary to a Choice. In every Case, after the Choice of the President, the Person having the greatest Number of Votes of the Electors shall be the Vice President. But if they should remain two or more who have equal votes, the Senate shall chuse from them by Ballot the Vice President.][4]

The Congress may determine the Time of chusing the Electors, and the Day on which they shall give their Votes; which Day shall be the same throughout the United States.

No person except a natural-born Citizen, or a Citizen of the United States, at the time of the Adoption of this Constitution, shall be eligible to the Office of President; neither shall any Person be eligible to that Office who shall not have attained to the Age of thirty-five years, and been fourteen Years a Resident within the United States.

In Case of the Removal of the President from Office, or of his Death, Resignation, or Inability to discharge the Powers and Duties of the said Office, the same shall devolve on the Vice President, and the Congress may by Law provide for the Case of Removal, Death, Resignation, or Inability, both of the President and Vice President, declaring what officer shall then act as President, and such Officer shall act accordingly, until the disability be removed, or a President shall be elected.

The President shall, at stated Times, receive for his Services a Compensation, which shall neither be increased nor diminished during the Period for which he shall have been elected, and he shall not receive within that Period any other Emolument from the United States, or any of them.

Before he enter on the execution of his Office, he shall take the following Oath or Affirmation: – "I do solemnly swear (or affirm) that I will faithfully execute the Office of President of the United States, and will, to the best of my Ability, preserve, protect, and defend the Constitution of the United States."

Section 2

The President shall be Commander in Chief of the Army and Navy of the United States, and of the Militia of the several States, when called

[4] Revised by the Twelfth Amendment.

into the actual Service of the United States; he may require the Opinion, in writing, of the principal Officer in each of the executive Departments, upon any subject relating to the Duties of their respective Offices, and he shall have Power to Grant Reprieves and Pardons for Offenses against the United States, except in Cases of Impeachment.

He shall have Power, by and with the Advice and Consent of the Senate, to make Treaties, provided two-thirds of the Senators present concur; and he shall nominate, and by and with the Advice and Consent of the Senate, shall appoint Ambassadors, other public Ministers and Consuls, Judges of the supreme Court, and all other Officers of the United States, whose Appointments are not herein otherwise provided for, and which shall be established by Law: but the Congress may by Law vest the Appointment of such inferior Officers, as they think proper, in the President alone, in the Courts of Law, or in the Heads of Departments.

The President shall have Power to fill up all Vacancies that may happen during the Recess of the Senate, by granting Commissions which shall expire at the End of their next Session.

Section 3

He shall from time to time give to the Congress Information of the State of the Union, and recommend to their Consideration such Measures as he shall judge necessary and expedient; he may, on extraordinary occasions, convene both Houses, or either of them, and in Case of Disagreement between them, with respect to the Time of Adjournment, he may adjourn them to such Time as he shall think proper; he shall receive Ambassadors and other public Ministers; he shall take care that the Laws be faithfully executed, and shall Commission all the Officers of the United States.

Section 4

The President, Vice President and all civil Officers of the United States, shall be removed from Office on Impeachment for, and Conviction of, Treason, Bribery, or other high Crimes and Misdemeanors.

ARTICLE III

Section 1

The judicial Power of the United States, shall be vested in one supreme Court, and in such inferior Courts as the Congress may from time to time ordain and establish. The Judges, both of the supreme and inferior Courts, shall hold their Offices during good Behaviour, and shall, at stated Times, receive for their Services, a Compensation, which shall not be diminished during their Continuance in Office.

Section 2

The judicial Power shall extend to all Cases, in Law and Equity, arising under this Constitution, the Laws of the United States, and Treaties made, or which shall be made, under their Authority; – to all Cases affecting ambassadors, other public ministers and consuls; – to all cases of admiralty and maritime Jurisdiction; – to Controversies to which the United States shall be Party; – to Controversies between two or more states; – between a State and Citizens of another State,[5] – between Citizens of different States – between Citizens of the same State claiming Lands under Grants of different States, and between a State, or the Citizens thereof, and foreign States, Citizens, or Subjects.

In all Cases affecting Ambassadors, other public Ministers and Consuls, and those in which a State shall be Party, the supreme Court shall have original Jurisdiction. In all the other Cases before mentioned, the supreme Court shall have appellate Jurisdiction, both as to Law and Fact, with such Exceptions, and under such Regulations as the Congress shall make.

The trial of all Crimes, except, in Cases of Impeachment, shall be by Jury; and such Trial shall be held in the State where the said Crimes shall have been committed; but when not committed within any State, the Trial shall be at such Place or Places as the Congress may by Law have directed.

Section 3

Treason against the United States, shall consist only in levying War against them, or in adhering to their Enemies, giving them Aid and Comfort. No Person shall be convicted of Treason unless on the Testimony of two Witnesses to the same overt Act, or on Confession in open Court.

The Congress shall have power to declare the Punishment of Treason, but no Attainder of Treason shall work Corruption of Blood, or Forfeiture except during the Life of the Person attainted.

ARTICLE IV

Section 1

Full Faith and Credit shall be given in each State to the public Acts, Records, and judicial Proceedings of every other State. And the Congress may by

---

[5] Qualified by the Eleventh Amendment.

general Laws prescribe the Manner in which such Acts, Records and Proceedings shall be proved, and the Effect thereof.

Section 2

The Citizens of each State shall be entitled to all Privileges and Immunities of Citizens in the several States.

A Person charged in any State with Treason, Felony, or other Crime, who shall flee from Justice, and be found in another State, shall on demand of the executive Authority of the State from which he fled, be delivered up, to be removed to the State having Jurisdiction of the crime.

No Person held to Service or Labour in one State, under the Laws thereof, escaping into another, shall, in Consequence of any Law of Regulation therein, be discharged from such Service or Labour, but shall be delivered up on Claim of the Party to whom such Service or Labour may be due.

Section 3

New States may be admitted by the Congress into this Union; but no new State shall be formed or erected within the Jurisdiction of any other State nor any State be formed by the Junction of two or more States, or parts of States, without the Consent of the Legislatures of the States concerned as well as of the Congress.

The Congress shall have Power to dispose of and make all needful Rules and Regulations respecting the Territory or other Property belonging to the United States; and nothing in this Constitution shall be so construed as to Prejudice any Claims of the United States, or of any particular State.

Section 4

The United States shall guarantee to every State in this Union a Republican Form of Government, and shall protect each of them against Invasion; and on Application of the Legislature, or of the Executive (when the Legislature cannot be convened) against domestic Violence.

ARTICLE V

The Congress, whenever two-thirds of both Houses shall deem it necessary, shall propose Amendments to this Constitution, or, on the Application of the Legislatures of two-thirds of the several States, shall call a Convention for proposing Amendments, which, in either Case, shall be valid to all Intents and Purposes, as part of this Constitution, when ratified by the Legislatures of three-fourths of the several States, or by Conventions in three-fourths thereof, as the one or the other Mode of Ratification may be proposed by the Congress; Provided that no Amendment which may be made prior to the Year One thousand eight hundred and eight shall in any Manner affect the first and fourth Clauses in the Ninth Section of the first Article; and that no State, without its Consent, shall be deprived of its equal Suffrage in the Senate.

ARTICLE VI

All Debts contracted and Engagements entered into, before the Adoption of this Constitution, shall be as valid against the United States under this Constitution, as under the Confederation.

This Constitution, and the Laws of the United States which shall be made in Pursuance thereof; and all Treaties made, or which shall be made, under the Authority of the United States, shall be the supreme Law of the Land; and the Judges in every State shall be bound thereby, any Thing in the Constitution or Laws of any State to the Contrary notwithstanding.

The Senators and Representatives before mentioned, and the Members of the several State Legislatures, and all executive and judicial Officers, both of the United States and of the several States, shall be bound by Oath or Affirmation to support this Constitution; but no religious Tests shall ever be required as a qualification to any Office or public Trust under the United States.

ARTICLE VII

The Ratification of the Conventions of nine States shall be sufficient for the Establishment of this Constitution between the States so ratifying the same.

Done in Convention by the Unanimous Consent of the States present the Seventeenth Day of September in the Year of our Lord one thousand seven hundred and Eighty seven, and of the Independence of the United States of America the Twelfth. In Witness whereof We have hereunto subscribed our Names.[6]

---

[6] These are the full names of the signers, which in some cases are not the signatures on the document.

George Washington

President and deputy from Virginia

New Hampshire
John Langdon
Nicholas Gilman

Massachusetts
Nathaniel Gorham
Rufus King

Connecticut
William Samuel Johnson
Roger Sherman

New York
Alexander Hamilton

New Jersey
William Livingston
David Brearley
William Paterson
Jonathan Dayton

Virginia
John Blair
James Madison, Jr.

North Carolina
William Blount
Richard Dobbs Spaight
Hugh Williamson

Pennsylvania
Benjamin Franklin
Thomas Mifflin
Robert Morris
George Clymer
Thomas FitzSimmons
Jared Ingersoll
James Wilson
Gouverneur Morris

Delaware
George Read
Gunning Bedford, Jr.
John Dickinson
Richard Bassett
Jacob Broom

Maryland
James McHenry
Daniel of St. Thomas Jenifer
Daniel Carroll

South Carolina
John Rutledge
Charles Cotesworth
 Pinckney
Charles Pinckney
Pierce Butler

Georgia
William Few
Abraham Baldwin

Articles in Addition to, and Amendment of, the Constitution of the United States of America, Proposed by Congress, and Ratified by the Legislatures of the Several States, Pursuant to the Fifth Article of the Original Constitution[7]

AMENDMENT I

Congress shall make no law respecting an establishment of religion, or prohibiting the free exercise thereof; or abridging the freedom of speech,

---

[7] This heading appears only in the joint resolution submitting the first ten amendments, which are collectively known as the Bill of Rights. They were ratified on December 15, 1791.

or of the press; or the right of the people peaceably to assemble, and to petition the Government for a redress of grievances.

AMENDMENT II

A well regulated Militia, being necessary to the security of a free State, the right of the people to keep and bear Arms shall not be infringed.

AMENDMENT III

No Soldier shall, in time of peace, be quartered in any house, without the consent of the Owner, nor in time of war, but in a manner to be prescribed by law.

AMENDMENT IV

The right of the people to be secure in their persons, houses, papers, and effects, against unreasonable searches and seizures, shall not be violated, and no Warrants shall issue, but upon probable cause, supported by Oath or affirmation, and particularly describing the place to be searched, and the persons or things to be seized.

AMENDMENT V

No person shall be held to answer for a capital or otherwise infamous crime, unless on a presentment or indictment of a Grand Jury, except in cases arising in the land or naval forces, or in the Militia, when in actual service in time of War or public danger; nor shall any person be subject for the same offence to be twice put in jeopardy of life or limb; nor shall be compelled in any criminal case to be a witness against himself, nor be deprived of life, liberty, or property, without due process of law; nor shall private property be taken for public use, without just compensation.

AMENDMENT VI

In all criminal prosecutions, the accused shall enjoy the right to a speedy and public trial, by an impartial jury of the State and district wherein the crime shall have been committed, which district shall have been previously ascertained by law, and to be informed of the nature and cause of the accusation; to be confronted with the witnesses against him; to have compulsory process for obtaining witnesses in his favour, and to have the Assistance of Counsel for his defence.

AMENDMENT VII

In suits at common law, where the value in controversy shall exceed twenty dollars, the right of trial by jury shall be preserved, and no fact tried by a jury, shall be otherwise reexamined in any Court of the United States, than according to the rules of the common law.

AMENDMENT VIII

Excessive bail shall not be required, nor excessive fines imposed, nor cruel and unusual punishments inflicted.

AMENDMENT IX

The enumeration of the Constitution, of certain rights, shall not be construed to deny or disparage others retained by the people.

AMENDMENT X

The powers not delegated to the United States by the Constitution, nor prohibited by it to the States, are reserved to the States respectively, or to the people.

AMENDMENT XI [1798]

The Judicial power of the United States shall not be construed to extend to any suit in law or equity, commenced or prosecuted against one of the United States by Citizens of another State, or by Citizens or Subjects of any Foreign State.

AMENDMENT XII [1804]

The Electors shall meet in their respective States and vote by ballot for President and Vice-President, one of whom, at least, shall not be an inhabitant of the same State with themselves; they shall name in their ballots the person voted for as President, and in distinct ballots the person voted for as Vice-President, and they shall make distinct lists of all persons voted for as President, and of all persons voted for as Vice-President, and of the number of votes for each, which lists they shall sign and certify, and transmit sealed to the seat of the government of the United States, directed to the President of the Senate; – The President of the Senate shall, in the presence of the Senate and House of Representatives, open all the certificates and the votes shall then be counted; – The person having the greatest number of votes for President, shall be the President, if such number be a majority of the whole number of Electors appointed; and if no person have such majority, then from the persons having the highest numbers not exceeding three on the list of those voted for as President, the House of Representatives shall choose immediately, by ballot, the President. But in choosing the President, the votes shall be taken by states, the representation from each state having one vote; a quorum for this purpose shall consist of a member or members from two-thirds of the states, and a majority of all the states shall be necessary to a choice. And if the House of Representatives shall not choose a President whenever the right of choice shall devolve upon them, before the fourth day of March next following, then the Vice-President shall act as President, as in the case of the death or other constitutional disability of the President. – The person having the greatest number of votes as Vice-President, shall be the Vice-President, if such number be a majority of the whole number of Electors appointed, and if no person have a majority, then from the two highest numbers on the list, the Senate shall choose the Vice-President; a quorum for the purpose shall consist of two-thirds of the whole number of Senators, and majority of the whole number shall be necessary to a choice. But no person constitutionally ineligible to the office of President shall be eligible to that of Vice-President of the United States.

AMENDMENT XIII [1865]

Section 1

Neither slavery nor involuntary servitude, except as a punishment for crime whereof the party shall have been duly convicted, shall exist within the United States, or any place subject to their jurisdiction.

Section 2

Congress shall have power to enforce this article by appropriate legislation.

AMENDMENT XIV [1868]

Section 1

All persons born or naturalized in the United States, and subject to the juris-diction thereof, are citizens of the United States and of the State wherein they reside. No State shall abridge the privileges or immunities of citizens of the United States; nor shall any State deprive any person of life, liberty, or property, without due process of law; nor deny to any person within its jurisdiction the equal protection of the laws.

Section 2

Representatives shall be apportioned among the several States according to their respective numbers, counting the whole number of persons in each State, excluding Indians not taxed. But when the right to vote at any election for the choice of electors for President and Vice-President of the United States, Representatives in Congress, the Executive and Judicial officers of a State, or the members of the Legislature thereof, is denied to any of the male inhabitants of such State, being twenty-one years of age, and citizens of the United States, or in any way abridged, except for participation in rebellion, or other crime, the basis of representation therein shall be reduced in the proportion which the number of such male citizens shall bear to the whole number of male citizens twenty-one years of age in such State.

Section 3

No person shall be a Senator or Representative in Congress, or elector of President and Vice-President, or hold any office, civil or military, under the United States, or under any State, who, having previously taken an oath, as a member of Congress, or as an officer of the United States, or as a member of any State legislature, or as an executive or judicial officer of any State, to support the Constitution of the United States, shall have engaged in insurrection or rebellion against the same, or given aid or comfort to the enemies thereof. But Congress may by a vote of two-thirds of each House, remove such disability.

Section 4

The validity of the public debt of the United States, authorized by law, including debts incurred for payment of pensions and bounties for services in suppressing insurrection or rebellion, shall not be questioned. But neither the United States nor any State shall assume or pay any debts or obligation incurred in aid of insurrection or rebellion against the United States, or any claim for the loss or emancipation of any slave; but all such debts, obligations, and claims shall be held illegal and void.

Section 5

The Congress shall have the power to enforce, by appropriate legislation, the provisions of this article.

AMENDMENT XV [1870]

Section 1

The right of citizens of the United States to vote shall not be denied or abridged by the United States or by any State on account of race, color, or previous condition of servitude –

Section 2

The Congress shall have power to enforce this article by appropriate legislation.

AMENDMENT XVI [1913]

The Congress shall have power to lay and collect taxes on incomes, from whatever source derived, without apportionment among the several States, and without regard to any census or enumeration.

AMENDMENT XVII [1913]

The Senate of the United States shall be composed of two Senators from each State, elected by the people thereof, for six years; and each Senator shall have one vote. The electors in each State shall have the qualifications requisite for electors of the most numerous branch of the State legislatures.

When vacancies happen in the representation of any State in the Senate, the executive authority of such State shall issue writs of election to fill such vacancies: *Provided,* That the legislature of any State may empower the executive thereof to make temporary appointments until the people fill the vacancies by election as the legislature may direct.

This amendment shall not be so construed as to affect the election or term of any Senator chosen before it becomes valid as part of the Constitution.

AMENDMENT XVIII [1919]

Section 1

After one year from the ratification of this article the manufacture, sale, or transportation of intoxicating liquors within, the importation thereof into, or the exportation thereof from the United States and all territory subject to the jurisdiction thereof for beverage purposes is hereby prohibited.

Section 2

The Congress and the several States shall have concurrent power to enforce this article by appropriate legislation.

Section 3

This article shall be inoperative unless it shall have been ratified as an amendment to the Constitution by the legislatures of the several States, as provided in the Constitution, within seven years from the date of the submission hereof to the States by the Congress.

AMENDMENT XIX [1920]

The right of citizens of the United States to vote shall not be denied or abridged by the United States or by any State on account of sex.

Congress shall have power to enforce this article by appropriate legislation.

AMENDMENT XX [1933]

Section 1

The terms of the President and Vice-President shall end at noon on the 20th day of January, and the terms of Senators and Representatives at noon on the 3d day of January, of the years in which such terms would have ended if this article had not been ratified; and the terms of their successors shall then begin.

Section 2

The Congress shall assemble at least once in every year, and such meeting shall begin at noon on the 3d day of January, unless they shall by law appoint a different day.

Section 3

If, at the time fixed for the beginning of the term of the President, the President elect shall have died, the Vice-President elect shall become President. If a President shall not have been chosen before the time fixed for the beginning of his term or if the President elect shall have failed to qualify, then the Vice-President elect shall act as President until a President shall have qualified; and the Congress may by law provide for the case wherein neither a President elect nor a Vice-President elect shall have qualified, declaring who shall then act as President, or the manner in which one who is to act shall be selected, and such person shall act accordingly until a President or Vice-President shall have qualified.

Section 4

The Congress may by law provide for the case of the death of any of the persons from whom the House of Representatives may choose a President whenever the right of choice shall have devolved upon them, and for the case of the death of any of the persons from whom the Senate may choose a Vice-President whenever the right of choice shall have devolved upon them.

Section 5

Sections 1 and 2 shall take effect on the 15th day of October following the ratification of this article.

Section 6

This article shall be inoperative unless it shall have been ratified as an amendment to the Constitution by the legislatures of three-fourths of the several States within seven years from the date of its submission.

AMENDMENT XXI [1933]

Section 1

The eighteenth article of amendment to the Constitution of the United States is hereby repealed.

Section 2

The transportation or importation into any State, Territory, or possession of the United States for delivery or use therein of intoxicating liquors, in violation of the laws thereof, is hereby prohibited.

Section 3

This article shall be inoperative unless it shall have been ratified as an amendment to the Constitution by conventions in the several States, as provided in the Constitution, within seven years from the date of the submission hereof to the States by the Congress.

AMENDMENT XXII [1951]

No person shall be elected to the office of the President more than twice, and no person who has held the office of President, or acted as President, for more than two years of a term to which some other person was elected President shall be elected to the office of the President more than once.

But this Article shall not apply to any person holding the office of President when this Article was proposed by the Congress, and shall not prevent any person who may be holding the office of President, or acting as President, during the term within which this Article becomes operative from holding the office of President or acting as President during the remainder of such term.

This article shall be inoperative unless it shall have been ratified as an amendment to the Constitution by the legislatures of three-fourths of the several states within seven years from the date of its submission to the states by the Congress.

AMENDMENT XXIII [1961]

Section 1

The District constituting the seat of Government of the United States shall appoint in such manner as the Congress may direct:

A number of electors of President and Vice-President equal to the whole number of Senators and Representatives in Congress to which the District would be entitled if it were a State, but in no event more than the least populous State; they shall be in addition to those appointed by the States, but they shall be considered, for the purposes of the election of President and Vice-President, to be electors appointed by a State; and they shall meet in the District and perform such duties as provided by the twelfth article of amendment.

Section 2

The Congress shall have power to enforce this article by appropriate legislation.

AMENDMENT XXIV [1964]

Section 1

The right of citizens of the United States to vote in any primary or other election for President or Vice President, for electors for President or Vice President, or for Senator or Representative in Congress, shall not be denied or abridged by the United States or any state by reason of failure to pay any poll tax or other tax.

Section 2

The Congress shall have the power to enforce this article by appropriate legislation.

AMENDMENT XXV [1967]

Section 1

In case of the removal of the President from office or of his death or resignation, the Vice President shall become President.

Section 2

Whenever there is a vacancy in the office of the Vice President, the President shall nominate a Vice President who shall take office upon confirmation by a majority vote of both Houses of Congress.

Section 3

Whenever the President transmits to the President Pro Tempore of the Senate and the Speaker of the House of Representatives his written declaration that he is unable to discharge to powers and duties of his office, and until he transmits to them a written declaration to the contrary, such powers and duties shall be discharged by the Vice President as Acting President.

Section 4

Whenever the Vice President and a majority of either the principal officers of the executive departments or of such other body as Congress may by law provide, transmit to the President Pro Tempore of the Senate and the

Speaker of the House of Representatives their written declaration that the President is unable to discharge the powers and duties of his office, the Vice President shall immediately assume the powers and duties of the office as Acting President.

Thereafter, when the President transmits to the President Pro Tempore of the Senate and the Speaker of the House of Representatives his written declaration that no inability exists, he shall resume the powers and duties of his office unless the Vice President and a majority of either the principal officers of the executive departments or of such other body as Congress may by law provide, transmit within four days to the President Pro Tempore of the Senate and the Speaker of the House of Representatives their written declaration that the President is unable to discharge the powers and duties of his office. Thereupon Congress shall decide the issue, assembling within forty-eight hours for that purpose if not in session. If the Congress, within twenty-one days after receipt of the latter written declaration, or, if Congress is not in session, within twenty-one days after Congress is required to assemble, determines by two-thirds vote of both Houses that the President is unable to discharge the powers and duties of his office, the Vice President shall continue to discharge the same as Acting President; otherwise, the President shall resume the powers and duties of his office.

AMENDMENT XXVI [1971]

Section 1

The right of citizens of the United States, who are eighteen years of age or older, to vote shall not be denied or abridged by the United States or by any State on account of age.

Section 2

The Congress shall have the power to enforce this article by appropriate legislation.

AMENDMENT XXVII [1992]

No law varying the compensation for the service of Senators and Representatives shall take effect until an election of Representatives shall have intervened.

Appendix Three: Federalist No. 10 (James Madison)

Among the numerous advantages promised by a well-constructed union, none deserves to be more accurately developed than its tendency to break and control the violence of faction. The friend of popular governments never finds himself so much alarmed for their character and fate as when he contemplates their propensity to this dangerous vice. He will not fail, therefore, to set a due value on any plan which, without violating the principles to which he is attached, provides a proper cure for it. The instability, injustice, and confusion introduced into the public councils have, in truth, been the mortal diseases under which popular governments have everywhere perished, as they continue to be the favorite and fruitful topics from which the adversaries to liberty derive their most specious declamations. The valuable improvements made by the American constitutions on the popular models, both ancient and modern, cannot certainly be too much admired; but it would be an unwarrantable partiality to contend that they have as effectually obviated the danger on this side, as was wished and expected. Complaints are everywhere heard from our most considerate and virtuous citizens, equally the friends of public and private faith and of public and personal liberty, that our governments are too unstable, that the public good is disregarded in the conflicts of rival parties, and that measures are too often decided, not according to the rules of justice and the rights of the minor party, but by the superior force of an interested and overbearing majority. However anxiously we may wish that these complaints had no foundation, the evidence of known facts will not permit us to deny that they are in some degree true. It will be found, indeed, on a candid review of our situation, that some of the distresses under which we labor have been erroneously charged on the operation of our governments; but it will be found, at the same time, that other causes will not alone account for many of our heaviest misfortunes; and, particularly, for that prevailing and increasing distrust of public engagements and alarm for private rights which are echoed from one end of the continent to the other. These must be chiefly, if not wholly, effects of the unsteadiness and injustice with which a factious spirit has tainted our public administration.

By a faction I understand a number of citizens, whether amounting to a majority or minority of the whole, who are united and actuated by some common impulse of passion, or of interest, adverse to the rights of other citizens, or to the permanent and aggregate interests of the community.

There are two methods of curing the mischiefs of faction: the one, by removing its causes; the other, by controlling its effects.

There are again two methods of removing the causes of faction: the one, by destroying the liberty which is essential to its existence; the other, by giving to every citizen the same opinions, the same passions, and the same interests.

It could never be more truly said than of the first remedy that it was worse than the disease. Liberty is to faction what air is to fire, an ailment without which it instantly expires. But it could not be a less folly to abolish liberty, which is essential to political life, because it nourishes faction than it would be to wish the annihilation of air, which is essential to animal life, because it imparts to fire its destructive agency.

The second expedient is as impracticable as the first would be unwise. As long as the reason of man continues fallible, and he is at liberty to exercise if, different opinions will be formed. As long as the connection subsists between his reason and his self-love, his opinions and his passions will have a reciprocal influence on each other; and the former will be objects to which the latter will attach themselves. The diversity in the faculties of men, from which the rights of property originate, is not less an insuperable obstacle to a uniformity of interest. The protection of these faculties is the first object of government. From the protection of different and unequal faculties of acquiring property, the possession of different degrees and kinds of property immediately results; and from the influence of these on the sentiments and view of the respective proprietors ensues a division of the society into different interests and parties.

The latent causes of faction are thus sown in the nature of man; and we see them everywhere brought into different degrees of activity, according to the different circumstances of civil society. A zeal for different opinions concerning religion, concerning government, and many other points as well of speculation as of practice; an attachment to different leaders ambitiously contending for pre-eminence and power; or to persons of other descriptions whose fortunes have been interesting to the human passions, have, in turn, divided mankind into parties, inflamed them with mutual animosity, and rendered them much more disposed to vex and oppress each other than to co-operate for their common good. So strong is this propensity of mankind to fall into mutual animosities that where no substantial occasion presents itself the most frivolous and fanciful distinctions have been sufficient to kindle their unfriendly passions and excite their most violent conflicts. But the most common and durable source of factions has been the various and unequal distribution of property. Those who hold and those who are without property have ever formed distinct interests in society. Those who are creditors, and those who are debtors, fall under a like discrimination. A landed interest, a manufacturing interest, a mercantile interest, a moneyed interest, with many lesser interests, grow up of necessity in civilized nations, and divide them into different classes, actuated by different sentiments and views. The regulation of these various and interfering interests forms the principal task of modern legislation and involves the spirit of party and faction in the necessary and ordinary operations of government.

No man is allowed to be a judge in his own cause, because his interest would certainly bias his judgment, and, not improbably, corrupt his integrity. With equal, nay with greater reason, a body of men are unfit to be both judges and parties at the same time; yet what are many of the most important acts of legislation but so many judicial determinations, not indeed concerning the rights of single persons, but concerning the rights of large bodies of citizens? And what are the different classes of legislators but advocates and parties to the causes which they determine? Is a law proposed concerning private debts? It is a question to which the creditors are parties on one side and the debtors on the other. Justice ought to hold the balance between them. Yet the parties are, and must be, themselves the judges; and the most numerous party, or in other words, the most powerful faction must be expected to prevail. Shall domestic manufacturers be encouraged, and in what degree, by restrictions on foreign manufacturers? [These] are questions which would be differently decided by the landed and the manufacturing classes, and probably by neither with a sole regard to justice and the public good. The apportionment of taxes on the various descriptions of property is an act which seems to require the most exact impartiality; yet there is, perhaps, no legislative act in which greater opportunity and temptation are given to a predominant party to trample on the rules of justice. Every shilling with which they overburden the inferior number is a shilling saved to their own pockets.

It is in vain to say that enlightened statesmen will be able to adjust these clashing interests and render them all subservient to the public good. Enlightened statesmen will not always be at the helm. Nor, in many cases, can such an adjustment be made at all without taking into view indirect and remote considerations, which will rarely prevail over the immediate interest which one party may find in disregarding the rights of another or the good of the whole.

The inference to which we are brought is that the *causes* of faction cannot be removed and that relief is only to be sought in the means of controlling its *effects*.

If a faction consists of less than a majority, relief is supplied by the republican principle, which enables the majority to defeat its sinister views by regular vote. It may clog the administration, it may convulse the society; but it will be unable to execute and mask its violence under the forms of the Constitution. When a majority is included in a faction, the form of popular government, on the other hand, enables it to sacrifice to its ruling passion or interest both the public good and the rights of other citizens. To secure the public good and private rights against the danger of such a faction, and at the same time to preserve the spirit and the form of popular government, is then the great object to which our inquiries are directed. Let me add that it is the great desideratum by which alone this form of government can be rescued from the opprobrium under which it has so long labored and be recommended to the esteem and adoption of mankind.

By what means is this object attainable? Evidently by one of two only. Either the existence of the same passion or interest in a majority at the same time must be prevented, or the majority, having such coexistent passion or interest, must be rendered, by their number and local situation, unable to concert and carry into effect schemes of oppression. If the impulse and the opportunity be suffered to coincide, we well know that neither moral nor religious motives can be relied on as an adequate control. They are not found to be such on the injustice and violence of individuals, and lose their efficacy in proportion to the number combined together, that is, in proportion as their efficacy becomes needful.

From this view of the subject it may be concluded that a pure democracy, by which I mean a society consisting of a small number of citizens, who assemble and administer the government in person, can admit of no cure for the mischiefs of faction. A common passion or interest will, in almost every case, be felt by a majority of the whole, a communication and concert results from the form of government itself; and there is nothing to check the inducements to sacrifice the weaker party or an obnoxious individual. Hence it is that such democracies have ever been spectacles of turbulence and contention; have ever been found incompatible with personal security or the rights of property; and have in general been as short in their lives as they have been violent in their deaths. Theoretic politicians, who have patronized this species of government, have erroneously supposed that by reducing mankind to a perfect equality in their political rights, they would at the same time be perfectly equalized and assimilated in their possessions, their opinions, and their passions.

A republic, by which I mean a government in which the scheme of representation takes place, opens a different prospect and promises the cure for which we are seeking. Let us examine the points in which it varies from pure democracy, and we shall comprehend both the nature of the cure and the efficacy which it must derive from the Union.

The two great points of difference between a democracy and a republic are: first, the delegation of the government, in the latter, to a small number of citizens elected by the rest; secondly, the greater number of citizens and greater sphere of country over which the latter may be extended.

The effect of the first difference is, on the one hand, to refine and enlarge the public views by passing them through the medium of a chosen body of citizens, whose wisdom may best discern the true interest of their country and whose patriotism and love of justice will be least likely to sacrifice it to temporary or partial considerations. Under such a regulation it may well happen that the public voice, pronounced by the representatives of the people, will be more consonant to the public good than if pronounced by the people themselves, convened for the purpose. On the other hand, the effect may be inverted. Men of factious tempers, of local prejudices, or of sinister designs, may, by intrigue, by corruption, or by other means, first obtain the suffrages, and then betray the interests of the people. The question resulting is, whether small or extensive republics are most favorable to the election of proper guardians of the public weal; and it is clearly decided in favor of the latter by two obvious considerations.

In the first place it is to be remarked that however small the republic may be the representatives must be raised to a certain number in order to guard against the cabals of a few; and that however large it may be they must be limited to a certain number in order to guard against the confusion of a multitude. Hence, the number of representatives in the two cases not being in proportion to that of the constituents, and being proportionally greatest in the small republic, it follows that if the proportion of fit characters be not less in the large than in the small republic, the former will present a greater option, and consequently a greater probability of a fit choice.

In the next place, as each representative will be chosen by a greater number of citizens in the large than in the small republic, it will be more difficult for unworthy candidates to practice with success the vicious arts by which elections are too often carried; and the suffrages of the people being more free, will be more likely to center on men who possess the most attractive merit and the most diffusive and established characters.

It must be confessed that in this, as in most other cases, there is a mean, on both sides of which inconveniencies will be found to lie. By enlarging too much the number of electors, you render the representative too little acquainted with all their local circumstances and lesser interests; as by reducing it too much, you render him unduly attached to these, and too little fit to comprehend and pursue great and national objects. The federal Constitution forms a happy combination in this respect; the great and aggregate interests being referred to the national, the local and particular to the State legislatures.

The other point of difference is the greater number of citizens and extent of territory which may be brought within the compass of republican than of democratic government; and it is this circumstance principally which renders factious combinations less to be dreaded in the former than in the latter. The smaller the society, the fewer probably will be the distinct parties and interests composing it; the fewer the distinct parties and interests, the more frequently will a majority be found of the same party; and the smaller the number of individuals composing a majority, and the smaller the compass within which they are placed, the more easily will they concert and execute their plans of oppression. Extend the sphere and you take in a greater variety of parties and interests; you make it less probable that a majority of the whole will have a common motive to invade the rights of other citizens; or if such a common motive exists, it will be more difficult for all who feel it to discover their own strength and to act in unison with each other. Besides other impediments, it may be remarked that, where there is a consciousness of unjust or dishonorable purposes, communication is always checked by distrust in proportion to the number whose concurrence is necessary.

Hence, it clearly appears that the same advantage which a republic has over a democracy in controlling the effects of faction is enjoyed by a large over a small republic – is enjoyed by the Union over the States composing it. Does this advantage consist in the substitution of representatives whose enlightened views and virtuous sentiments render them superior to local prejudices and to schemes of injustice? It will not be denied that the representation of the Union will be most likely to possess these requisite endowments. Does it consist in the greater security afforded by a greater variety of parties, against the event of any one party being able to outnumber and oppress the rest? In an equal degree does the increased variety of parties comprised within the Union increase this security? Does it, in fine, consist in the greater obstacles opposed to the concert and accomplishment of the secret wishes of an unjust and interested majority? Here again the extent of the Union gives it the most palpable advantage.

The influence of factious leaders may kindle a flame within their particular States but will be unable to spread a general conflagration through the other States. A religious sect may degenerate into a political faction in a part of the Confederacy; but the variety of sects dispersed over the entire face of it must secure the national councils against any danger from that source. A rage for paper money, for an abolition of debts, for an equal division of property, or for any other improper or wicked project, will be less apt to pervade the whole body of the Union than a particular member of it, in the same proportion as such a malady is more likely to taint a particular county or district than an entire State.

In the extent and proper structure of the Union, therefore, we behold a republican remedy for the diseases most incident to republican government. And according to the degree of pleasure and pride we feel in being republicans ought to be our zeal in cherishing the spirit and supporting the character of federalists.

Appendix Four: Federalist No. 51 (James Madison)

To what expedient, then, shall we finally resort, for maintaining in practice the necessary partition of power among the several departments as laid down in the constitution? The only answer that can be given is that as all these exterior provisions are found to be inadequate, the defect must be supplied, by so contriving the interior structure of the government as that its several constituent parts may, by their mutual relations, be the means of keeping each other in their proper places. Without presuming to undertake a full development of this important idea I will hazard few general observations which may perhaps place it in a clearer light, and enable us to form a more correct judgment of the principles and structure of the government planned by the convention.

In order to lay a due foundation for that separate and distinct exercise of the different powers of government, which to a certain extent is admitted on all hands to be essential to the preservation of liberty, it is evident that each department should have a will of its own; and consequently should be so constituted that the members of each should have as little agency as possible in the appointment of the members of the others. Were this principle rigorously adhered to, it would require that all the appointments for the supreme executive, legislative, and judiciary magistracies should be drawn from the same fountain of authority, the people, through channels having no communication whatever with one another. Perhaps such a plan of constructing the several departments would be less difficult in practice than it may in contemplation appear. Some difficulties, however, and some additional expense would attend the execution of it. Some deviations, therefore, from the principle must be admitted. In the constitution of the judiciary department in particular, it might be inexpedient to insist rigorously on the principle; first, because peculiar qualifications being essential in the members, the primary consideration ought to be to select that mode of choice which best secures these qualifications; second, because the permanent tenure by which the appointments are held in that department must soon destroy all sense of dependence on the authority conferring them.

It is equally evident that the members of each department should be as little dependent as possible on those of the others for the emoluments annexed to their offices. Were the executive magistrate, or the judges, not independent of the legislature in this particular, their independence in every other would be merely nominal.

But the great security against a gradual concentration of the several powers in the same department consists in giving to those who administer each department the necessary constitutional means and personal motives to resist encroachments of the others. The provision for defense must in this, as in all other cases, be made commensurate to the danger of attack. Ambition must be made to counteract ambition. The interest of the man must be connected with the constitutional rights of the place. It may be a reflection on human nature that such devices should be necessary to control the abuses of government. But what is government itself but the greatest of all reflections on human nature? If men were angels no government would be necessary. If angels were to govern men, neither external nor internal controls on government would be necessary. In framing a government which is to be administered by men over men, the great difficulty lies in this: you must first enable the government to control the governed; and in the next place oblige it to control itself. A dependence on the people is, no doubt, the primary control on the government; but experience has taught mankind the necessity of auxiliary precautions.

This policy of supplying, by opposite and rival interests, the defect of better motives, might be traced through the whole system of human affairs, private as well as public. We see it particularly displayed in all the subordinate distributions of power, where the constant aim is to divide and arrange the several offices in such a manner as that each may be a check on the other – that the private interest of every individual may be a sentinel over the public rights. These inventions of prudence cannot be less requisite in the distribution of the supreme powers of the State.

But it is not possible to give to each department an equal power of self-defense. In republican government, the legislative authority necessarily predominates. The remedy for this inconveniency is to divide the legislature into different branches; and to render them, by different modes of election and different principles of action, as little connected with each other as the nature of their common functions and their common dependence on the society will admit. It may even be necessary to guard against dangerous encroachments by still further precautions. As the weight of the legislative authority requires that it should be thus divided, the weakness of the executive may require, on the other hand, that it should be fortified. An absolute negative on the legislature appears, at first view, to be the natural defense with which the executive magistrate should be armed. But perhaps it would be neither altogether safe nor alone sufficient. On ordinary occasions it might not be exerted with the requisite firmness, and on extraordinary occasions it might be perfidiously abused. May not this defect of an absolute negative be supplied by some qualified connection between this weaker department and the weaker branch of the stronger department, by which the latter may be led to support the constitutional rights of the former, without being too much detached from the rights of its own department?

If the principles on which these observations are founded be just, as I persuade myself they are, and they be applied as a criterion to the several State constitutions, and to the federal Constitution, it will be found that if the latter does not perfectly correspond with them, the former are infinitely less able to bear such a test.

There are, moreover, two considerations particularly applicable to the federal system of America, which place that system in a very interesting point of view.

First. In a single republic, all the power surrendered by the people is submitted to the administration of a single government; and the usurpations are guarded against by a division of the Government into distinct and separate departments. In the compound republic of America, the power surrendered by the people is first divided between two distinct governments, and then the portion allotted to each subdivided among distinct and separate departments. Hence a double security arises to the rights of the people. The different governments will control each other, at the same time that each will be controlled by itself.

Second. It is of great importance in a republic not only to guard the society against the oppression of its rulers, but to guard one part of the society against the injustice of the other part. Different interests necessarily exist in different classes of citizens. If a majority be united by a common interest, the rights of the minority will be insecure. There are but two methods of providing against the evil: the one by creating a will in the community independent of the majority – that is, of the society itself; the other, by comprehending in the society so many separate descriptions of citizens as will render an unjust combination of majority of the whole very improbable, if not impracticable. The first method prevails in all governments possessing an hereditary or self-appointed authority. This, at best, is but a precarious security; because a power independent of the society may as well espouse the unjust views of the major as the rightful interests of the minor party, and may possibly be turned against both parties. The second method will be exemplified in the federal republic of the United States. Whilst all authority in it will be derived from and dependent on the society, the society itself will be broken into so many parts, interests and classes of citizens, that the rights of individuals, or of the minority, will be in little danger from interested combinations of the majority. In a free government the security for civil rights must be the same as that for religious rights. It consists in the one case in the multiplicity of interests, and in the other in the multiplicity of sects. The degree of security in both cases will depend on the number of interests and sects; and this may be presumed to depend on the extent of country and number of people comprehended under the same government. This view of the subject must particularly recommend a proper federal system to all the sincere and considerate friends of republican government, since it shows that in exact proportion as the territory of the Union may be formed into more circumscribed Confederacies, or States, oppressive combinations of a majority will be facilitated; the best security, under the republican forms, for the rights of every class of citizen, will be diminished; and consequently the stability and independence of some member of the government, the only other security, must be proportionately increased. Justice is the end of government. It is the end of the civil society. It ever has been and ever will be pursued until it be obtained, or until liberty be lost in the pursuit. In a society under the forms of which the stronger faction can readily unite and oppress the weaker, anarchy may as truly be said to reign as in a state of nature, where the weaker individual is not secured against the violence of the stronger; and as, in the latter state, even the stronger individuals are prompted, by the uncertainty of their condition, to submit to a government which may protect the weak as well as themselves; so, in the former state, will the more powerful factions or parties be gradually induced, by a like motive, to wish for a government which will protect all parties, the weaker as well as the more powerful. It can be little doubted that if the State of Rhode Island was separated from the Confederacy and left to itself, the insecurity of rights under the popular form of government within such narrow limits would be displayed by such reiterated oppressions of factious majorities that some power altogether independent of the people would soon be called for by the voice of the very factions whose misrule had proved the necessity of it. In the extended republic of the United States, and among the great variety of interests, parties, and sects which it embraces, a coalition of a majority of the whole society could seldom take place on any other principles than those of justice and the general good; whilst there being thus less danger to a minor from the will of a major party, there must be less pretext, also, to provide for the security of the former, by introducing into the government a will not dependent on the latter, or, in other words, a will independent of the society itself. It is no less certain than it is important, notwithstanding the contrary opinions which have been entertained, that the larger the society, provided it lie within a practicable sphere, the more duly capable it will be of self-government. And happily for the *republican cause*, the practicable sphere may be carried to a very great extent by a judicious modification and mixture of the federal principle.

Glossary

Abolitionist The group of political reformers who fought for the abolition of slavery before and during the Civil War.

Administrative Procedures Act (APA) The law, passed in 1946, under which some fifty-five U.S. government regulatory agencies create the rules and regulations necessary to implement and enforce legislative acts.

Affirmative action Government policies or programs that attempt to address past practices of discrimination against historically disadvantaged groups by making special efforts to provide members of these groups with access to educational and employment opportunities.

Agriculture Adjustment Act (AAA) A bill passed by Congress in 1933 that authorized government subsidies for farmers, including paying farmers for not producing goods and thereby regulating supply and prices.

Agriculture Adjustment Agency (AAA) A former U.S. government agency originally established by the Department of Agriculture under the Agricultural Adjustment Act of 1933. In 1945, its functions were taken over by the Production and Marketing Administration.

American Federation of Labor (AFL) One of the first and largest trade federations (organization of trade unions), it joined with the Congress of Industrial Organizations (CIO) in 1955 to form the largest trade federation in the United States, the AFL-CIO.

Anti-Federalists Those who opposed the ratification of the U.S. Constitution. Anti-Federalists favored a weak national government and comparatively stronger state governments.

Antitrust Division of the Justice Department The agency, formed in 1934, that is in charge of the enforcement of antitrust laws.

Appellate jurisdiction Jurisdiction to reevaluate or overturn findings of law, but not fact, previously determined in a lower court.

Articles of Confederation The specific compact among the thirteen original states, adopted in 1781, that formed the first American government.

Atlantic Charter The statement of the United States and its ally Great Britain during World War II that expressed their common commitment to the rights of self-determination and self-government of all nations.

Bicameralism The division of a legislative body into two houses to diffuse the legislative power. For example, the U.S. Congress is divided into two chambers – the House of Representatives and the Senate – that share legislative power.

Bill of Rights The first ten amendments to the U.S. Constitution. The Bill of Rights guarantees specific rights and liberties and was viewed as a significant constraint on the national government's encroachment on those liberties.

Block grants A broad transfer of resources distributed to the states by the federal government for specified activities; also called general grants.

Bonds A debt security in which a citizen agrees to purchase promissory notes (essentially lending the government money) that the government is obligated to pay back with interest at an agreed-upon pay schedule.

Bracket creep The situation in which earners are pushed into higher tax brackets as a result of inflation, even though their purchasing power has not increased.

Bureau of the Budget (BOB) An agency created in 1921 under the Department of the Treasury and charged with helping the president prepare and administer the federal budget. The BOB was moved to the Executive Office of the President in 1939; in 1970, it was reorganized into the Office of Management and Budget.

Cabinet The secretaries, or chief administrators, of the major departments of the executive branch. Cabinet secretaries are appointed by the president with the consent of the Senate. Presently, the secretaries of fifteen executive departments constitute the cabinet.

Cartel An association or group of manufacturers or suppliers formed to maintain high prices and restrict competition.

Central bank A bank that serves and supports other banks. It is usually supported by the government and helps control the monetary supply by issuing currency and regulating loan rates.

Checks and balances A governmental structure that gives different branches or levels of government some degree of oversight and control over the actions of the others so that no government institution exercises a monopoly of power.

Citizen suits A lawsuit filed by members of the public against facilities that violate federal laws and regulations.

Civilian Conservation Corps (CCC) A public works program created in 1933 that put more than three million American young men and adults to work during the Great Depression. The CCC worked to save the U.S. environment, especially forests, on a national scale.

Cloture A parliamentary procedure that brings debate to an end. The U.S. Senate now requires sixty members to force cloture of a debate.

Commercial republic A republican government devoted to the quest for material well-being in accord with a commitment to private property and the free market.

Compact theory The theory that claims the U.S. Constitution resulted from an agreement by the sovereign states. Throughout American history, especially in the nineteenth century, public figures offered compact theory in defense of states' rights.

Congress of Industrial Organizations (CIO) A trade federation formed to meet the needs of industrial unions. It joined with the American Federation of Labor in 1955 to form the largest trade federation in the United States, the AFL-CIO.

Congressional Budget Office (CBO) An agency created by the Congressional Budget and Impoundment Control Act of 1974 and designed to provide Congress with the objective, timely, and non-partisan analyses needed for economic and budget decisions and with the information and estimates required for the congressional budget process. The CBO gives Congress the expertise to evaluate the president's budget that is prepared by the Office of Management and Budget.

Conservation Political action or belief that seeks to keep something in being, usually resources or ecosystems.

Conservative One who wishes to preserve what is thought to be best in established society or appeals for a return to a perceived past ideal; in the United States, a proponent of limited government, individual rights, and private property.

Constituency service The assistance that congressional representatives provide to members of their district who need help with navigating government institutions, especially bureaucratic agencies. Constituency service is often referred to as casework.

Constitution The set of fundamental rules and laws of a nation that form the framework of the relationship between government and the people.

Constitutional refounding A shift in how engaged citizens understood the meaning of the Declaration of Independence and Constitution for their own time.

Constitutionalism A belief in a written constitution as the fundamental law and sacred text of a people.

Continental Congress A gathering of delegates from the thirteen colonies who first assembled in the fall of 1774 in Philadelphia. They deliberated and decided upon matters of the Revolution, including the approval of the Declaration of Independence.

Cooperative federalism A term used to describe the actions of the federal government in distributing large amounts of resources to the states to perform services normally in the purview of the states.

Cost-benefit analysis A technique of constructing a balance sheet of the consequences of a project or activity, including all financial and social costs and benefits.

Council of Economic Advisors Established in 1946, a group of independent, professional economists who advise the president on economic policy.

Covenant A religious commitment to uphold an obligation to God that, if strictly adhered to, will bring prosperity and protection from hardship.

Craft union A workers' union organized around a particular craft or occupation.

De facto segregation Segregation that occurs as a result of a practice but not law, such as segregated neighborhoods and school districts.

De jure segregation Segregation specifically enforced by law, such as the "separate but equal" laws that enforced segregation in the South from the end of the nineteenth century until the enactment of the Civil Rights Act in 1964.

Deficit spending The situation in which a government spends more money than it collects, therefore incurring budget deficits and ultimately debt.

Democracy A system of government that gives power and political authority to the people under a system of majority rule. *Democracy* is Greek for "rule by the people."

Department of Education The agency, formed in 1979, that establishes policy for, administers, and coordinates most federal assistance to education.

Department of Health, Education, and Welfare (HEW) The cabinet-level department created in 1953 that was responsible for protecting the health and welfare of all Americans by providing essential human services. After the creation of the Department of Education in 1979, the HEW became the Department of Health and Human Services.

Department of Housing and Urban Development (HUD) Established in 1965, the cabinet-level department responsible for national policy and programs that address America's housing needs and that enforce fair housing laws.

Department of the Interior Created in 1849, the cabinet-level department responsible for the nation's internal affairs, including the conservation of U.S. natural resources.

Department of Transportation Established in 1966, the cabinet-level department responsible for ensuring an efficient transportation system that meets vital national interests and enhances the quality of life of the American people.

Department of Veterans Affairs The cabinet-level department, created in 1989, that is charted with the responsibility to administer the laws providing benefits and other services to veterans and their dependents and beneficiaries.

Deregulation The opening of a market to competition in a previously regulated industry.

Direct democracy A form of popular rule in which all citizens are expected to participate in lawmaking and administration directly, without representative institutions acting as an intermediary between the people and government.

Direct primary The selection of party candidates through the ballots of qualified voters rather than through nominating conventions that are dominated by party leaders.

Discount rate An interest rate that a borrower pays to the institution or person who loaned the money.

Drug Enforcement Agency (DEA) Created in 1973, a federal agency that is responsible for the administration of federal drug enforcement policies.

Economies of scale The economic principle in which increasing units of a product produced by a firm decreases the cost per unit of that product.

Empire of Liberty Thomas Jefferson's vision of an extended agrarian republic.

Entail The right of individuals to perpetually restrict the inheritance of their estates to lineal descendents or another particular group.

Entitlements Government program benefits that constituents have claimed as a right, such as Social Security and welfare.

Enumerated powers Powers of the government specifically granted by the Constitution.

Environmental Impact Statements (EISs) Reports that are required by the National Environmental Protection Act of 1970; EISs must be prepared by agencies proposing to take any action that will have a major impact on the environment. These reports are subject to review by the Environmental Protection Agency.

Equality An assertion of the innate equal capacity or equal standing of persons in a society.

Equality of opportunity Provision of the same chance to everyone.

Equality of result Provision of the same outcome to everyone.

Ethnicity Membership in a group identified as people who share characteristics such as language, history, culture, upbringing, religion, nationality, and geographical and ancestral origins and place.

Executive aggrandizement The growth in size and ambition of the president in particular and the executive branch in general.

Executive Office of the President (EOP) The advisors, offices, and permanent agencies that perform the major managerial tasks for the president. Created in 1939, the EOP includes the White House Office, the Office of Management and Budget, the Council of Economic Advisors, the National Security Council, and other important agencies that serve the modern presidency.

Executive privilege The claim that presidents and their advisors have the constitutional authority to withhold confidential communications from Congress and the judiciary.

Executive Reorganization Act of 1939 An act that expanded the staff and strengthened the administrative power of presidents. It led to the creation of the White House Office and the Executive Office of the President.

Federal Deposit Insurance Corporation (FDIC) Created in 1933, a government organization that insures deposits made to banks and thus promotes investment.

Federal mandate National laws that direct states, localities, businesses, or individuals to follow federal rules or regulations under threat of civil or criminal penalties or as a condition of receiving federal grants.

Federal Reserve Board (the Fed) Established by the Federal Reserve Act of 1913, a seven-person board of governors that operates as the central bank of the United States.

Federal Trade Commission (FTC) Formed by Congress in 1914, an independent regulatory commission that is authorized to protect small businesses and consumers from unfair competition and deceptive marketing.

Federalism A system of government that divides power between a general, national government and regional or local governments.

Federalist Papers A series of eighty-five newspaper articles – written by Alexander Hamilton, James Madison, and John Jay – that appeared under the pseudonym Publius and that supported the ratification of the Constitution.

Federalists Those who supported ratification of the proposed U.S. Constitution. Federalists favored a much stronger national government than that which existed under the Articles of Confederation.

Filibuster An attempt to obstruct legislative proceedings by prolonging debate. Legislatures often have rules to prevent filibusters by introducing procedures to end debate, such as cloture.

Food and Drug Administration (FDA) Formed by Congress in 1906, an independent regulatory commission designed to ensure the safety of pharmaceuticals and food products.

Food stamps Coupons administered by the Department of Agriculture that can be used to purchase food. Approximately 17.2 million Americans use food stamps.

Full Employment Act A law, passed in 1946, that created the Council of Economic Advisers to assist the president in the development of national economic policy.

Great Society The legislative program of President Lyndon Johnson that was designed to end poverty and improve American quality of life.

Homestead Act of 1862 A law passed by Congress to push westward expansion and to expand economic opportunities for the urban poor; this law enabled settlers to claim up to 160 acres of land if they agreed to settle and live off that land for five years.

Industrial union A union in which workers within an industry, regardless of skill or trade, unite together.

Inflation A rate of increase in the general price level of all goods and services in a country.

Initiative A law that may be proposed to the voters of a state through petition, usually qualified by a minimum number of registered voters' signatures.

Interest groups Non-governmental organizations that seek to advance a particular cause or public policy.

Iron triangle The relationship that can arise between an agency, an interest group, and congressional committees or subcommittees in the formation of public policy; an iron triangle locks out the president and the public.

Jim Crow Laws and social customs created after the abolition of slavery and intended to legitimize and perpetuate racism and segregation within Southern society.

Judicial review The power of the federal judiciary to determine the constitutionality of acts of the executive, the national legislature, or individual states.

Jurisdictions The subjects and categories of legislation that a committee or subcommittee is empowered to consider.

Laissez faire French for "to leave alone"; a belief that individuals should be free to pursue their interests without government intervention.

Legislative Reorganization Act of 1946 An act that sought to give Congress greater control over legislative business and to strengthen its institutional capacity to oversee the activities of the executive branch. It banned the introduction of certain types of private legislation and set standards of germaneness of amendments introduced in House-Senate conference committees. The act also reduced the number of standing committees in both chambers and rearranged committee jurisdictions to reduce overlap and confusion and to make the House and Senate committee systems more similar.

Liberalism The belief that the aim of politics is to preserve individual rights and to maximize individual freedom.

Limited government The belief that government is constituted only to secure basic human rights and should have little power.

Limited liability A type of investment in which the investor is not responsible for company debts and therefore cannot lose more than the amount invested.

Macroeconomics The study of the economic performance of a national economy as a whole.

Magna Carta A signed compact between King John and his lords in 1215 that enumerated the rights and privileges of the English people and set a precedent for future constitutions.

Majoritarianism The doctrine that the majority should rule.

Market failure When the price established in the market does not equal the marginal social benefit of a good and the marginal social cost of producing the good.

Mass democracy The Jacksonian version of democracy that sought to make the Constitution and its institutional arrangements servants of public opinion.

Medicare Enacted in 1965 as an outgrowth of Lyndon Johnson's Great Society, a program of social reform that guarantees medical coverage, administered by the federal government, to all citizens over age sixty-five.

Microeconomics The study of how individual economic units (consumers and producers) operate and interact in the economy.

Middle-class entitlements Benefits from the government that citizens have come to rely upon and expect, such as Social Security and Medicare.

National Environmental Policy Act (NEPA) An act passed by Congress in 1970 that requires federal agencies to consider the impact to the environment that will result from programmatic decisions. Agencies that propose policies that will have a major impact on the environment are required to prepare an Environmental Impact Statement (EIS).

National Industrial Recovery Act (NIRA) A 1933 act that, as an ambitious part of Franklin Roosevelt's New Deal, set up the National Recovery Administration (NRA), which oversaw wages, work hours, and price controls in an attempt to stabilize the economy. The Supreme Court found the NIRA unconstitutional in *Schechter Poultry Corporation v. United States* (1935).

National Labor Relations Act A 1935 act that, as an outgrowth of Franklin Roosevelt's New Deal program of economic reforms, gave unions the right to collectively bargain for labor contracts with employers under the supervision of the federal government.

National Labor Relations Board (NLRB) A government agency created by the Wagner Act of 1935 and designed to oversee collective bargaining elections and to protect workers' rights to bargain collectively.

National Recovery Administration (NRA) An agency that formed committees charged with regulating pay increases, working hours, and price controls. The NRA was formed as part of the National Industrial Recovery Act (NIRA), enacted by Congress in 1933.

National Security Council (NSC) The executive agency established in 1947 to oversee policy, both foreign and domestic, that affects national security; it is composed of the national security advisor; the president; the vice president; the secretaries of state, defense, and the treasury; the attorney general; and other officials invited by the president.

Nationalism A political orientation that rests in a commitment to one's country.

Nationality A feeling of loyalty and solidarity that transcends state borders based on adherence to mutual principles articulated in the Declaration of Independence.

Natural rights Individual human rights based on the belief that all humans are by nature endowed with reason and free will and have sovereignty over themselves.

Negative externalities The costs of an action that accrue to someone other than those who are directly involved in the action.

New Deal The set of policies and programs advocated by President Franklin D. Roosevelt for ending the Great Depression and securing programmatic rights.

New Freedom The Progressive campaign agenda of Woodrow Wilson in the 1912 election that emphasized a moderate use of federal and state powers to promote business competition and responsible government.

New Jersey Plan Introduced by William Paterson of New Jersey at the Constitutional Convention, a plan that was offered as an alternative to the Virginia Plan's blueprint for a strong national government. Its main purpose was to preserve the structure of Congress under the Articles of Confederation – a single house in which each state, regardless of size, would cast one vote.

New Nationalism The Progressive campaign agenda of Theodore Roosevelt in the 1912 election that emphasized the use of strong federal powers to regulate industry and advance social progress.

North American Free Trade Agreement (NAFTA) Signed into law in 1993, a treaty between the United States, Mexico, and Canada that calls for the elimination of customs duties.

Nullification doctrine A form of constitutionalism promoted by John C. Calhoun and South Carolina that contended that a state can, in effect, declare acts of Congress unconstitutional.

Office of Management and Budget (OMB) An agency formed in 1970 to strengthen the president's influence on the preparation and administration of the federal budget; originally called the Bureau of the Budget.

Open market operations The term used to describe the Federal Reserve Board's ability to buy and sell government securities on the open market.

Operations research The application of systematic research techniques to improve government decisions and the delivery of programs. It is designed to assess the impact of a proposed course of action on the accessibility, availability, quality, and sustainability of a program.

Organization of Petroleum Exporting Countries (OPEC) An international organization of eleven developing countries that are heavily reliant on oil revenues as their main source of income. The current members are Algeria, Indonesia, Iran, Iraq, Kuwait, Libya, Nigeria, Qatar, Saudi Arabia, the United Arab Emirates, and Venezuela.

Original jurisdiction The authority of a court, determined by law, to first try the facts of a case before any appeal.

Oversight The ability of Congress to review, monitor, and supervise federal agencies, programs, and policies including the policies and agencies of the executive branch. The authority of Congress to do oversight is derived from its implied powers in the U.S. Constitution.

Parliamentary democracies A form of government that empowers an elected assembly as its principle authority. In this form of government, the executive is elected from the assembly, so the executive and legislative powers are combined.

Party caucuses A gathering of all members of a party. Party caucuses have been used to select candidates for office and to discuss and determine what actions members of Congress or state legislatures will take prior to floor debate.

Party discipline The degree to which party members are unified in Congress or the state legislatures. A system of rewards and punishments fostered strong party discipline on Capitol Hill in the nineteenth century, whereas the advent of a more professional Congress in the twentieth century weakened party discipline.

Party leaders Elite members of a party caucus, including the Speaker, majority and minority leaders, caucus chairs, and whips.

Party realignments Periodic critical elections that bring about major changes in party majorities and government policy, followed by large spans of unified party government.

Party system A stable, competitive, and perpetual system of party government based on enduring cleavages in public opinion.

Path dependency The belief that preceding actions alter what choices are available in the future, or alter the costs and benefits of those choices, so that it is unlikely that the original action will be reversed.

Patronage The granting of favors, such as jobs, contracts, or other privileges, to the friends and supporters of a political party.

Personal Responsibility and Work Opportunity Reconciliation Act (PRWORA) An act, passed in 1996, that reformed the American welfare system by dramatically reducing the role the national government played in distributing welfare benefits, by giving more administrative discretion to the states, and by mandating strict work requirements for beneficiaries.

Plebiscitary politics Politics that are characterized by a direct relationship between public officials and public opinion.

Political action committees (PACs) Organizations that obtain contributions from individuals and distribute donations to candidates for political office.

Political creed Strongly held convictions and guiding principles that underlie a system of political beliefs.

Political culture The central beliefs and convictions of a country that inform the character of its people and institutions.

Poll A type of survey or inquiry into public opinion conducted by interviews with a random sample of individuals.

Popular consent Agreement by the people to the form of government that is in place.

Popular sovereignty The concept that the people are the ultimate source of political authority and that it is the right of the majority to govern themselves.

Prerogative The unquestioned privilege of a sovereign to unilaterally direct the official policy of a state at will.

Price discrimination When a company or producer sells a product or service to one buyer at a price that is different from the price asked of another buyer for an identical product or service.

Primogeniture The feudal inheritance custom that dictates that only the eldest male heir may inherit the lands and property of his father.

Process federalism The theory, established in the Supreme Court case *Garcia v. San Antonio Metropolitan Transit Authority* (1985), that held that the states' sovereign interests are more properly protected by procedural safeguards inherent in the structure of the federal government (for example, equal state representation in the Senate) than by judicially created limitations on federal power.

Programmatic rights New Deal political reforms that created programs considered tantamount to rights, such as Social Security.

Progressive movement A political reform movement in the United States that formed in the late nineteenth and early twentieth centuries. The movement sought to advance democratic reforms and to decrease the power of political machines and corporate trusts.

Progressive tax A tax that increases rates as the citizen's or company's income level increases.

Puritans The group of radical Protestant reformers led by John Winthrop who sought religious freedom from the Church of England and founded the Massachusetts Bay Colony in the early seventeenth century.

Quorum The minimum number of members who must be present to validate the proceedings of a legislature or committee. In the U.S. Congress, the quorum for the Senate and House of Representatives is a simple majority of the members.

Reagan revolution Ronald Reagan's effort to stop or at least slow down the expansion of the federal government and the size of the tax burden.

Recall Process whereby an elected official may be subject to an election, which can lead to loss of office before his or her term of office has expired.

Reconstruction The term used to describe the post–Civil War program to rebuild the Southern states politically (ensuring equal rights for African Americans) and economically (moving from an agrarian, slave-based economy to a modern economy).

Red tape Non-essential bureaucratic procedures, forms, and regulations that add to the cost of dealing with government. Red tape includes anything obsolete, redundant, wasteful, or confusing that wastes taxpayers' time and money.

Referendum The right to refer approval or rejection of new laws enacted by a legislature to the voters through a petition, qualified by a minimum number of registered voters' signatures.

Representative democracy A system of government in which the people elect representatives to make decisions on their behalf. The representatives are then answerable to the people through subsequent elections.

Republic A state without a monarch. James Madison used the term to refer to a representative, or indirect, democracy.

Revolution of 1800 Federalist defeat by the Republicans in the 1800 election that strengthened the democratic character of the Constitution and limited the scope of central government authority.

Right A claim that belongs to an individual naturally and that cannot be violated by any person or society.

Robinson-Patman Act A law, passed by Congress in 1936, that makes it illegal for a supplier to charge lower prices to certain customers simply because they purchase in larger quantities than do other customers.

Rules Committee A standing committee of the U.S. House of Representatives that sets the timetable for when a bill will be considered and under what conditions or rules the debate will take place.

Sampling A process in which the respondents of a poll are chosen randomly by one of several methods. The key component in the scientific sample is that everyone within the designated group has a chance of being selected.

Second Great Awakening A spontaneous religious movement of the 1830s in which groups of Evangelical Christians proselytized throughout the United States. The movement generated an intense national religious revival and aroused popular support for social reforms such as temperance and abolitionism.

Securities and Exchange Commission (SEC) A regulatory agency that scrutinizes the securities industry.

Sedition Act A law passed in 1798 that embodied the Federalist party's desire to limit free speech by making it a crime to defame or show contempt in speech or writing for the Congress, president, or the federal government.

Seniority A convention whereby status, committee assignments, and other resources are allocated in proportion to length of service. Seniority has been an important organizing principle in the U.S. Congress, especially since the beginning of the twentieth century.

Separation of powers The doctrine that political power and governmental functions should be divided among several bodies or branches of government as a precaution against tyranny.

Sharecropping An agrarian economic system that emerged after the abolition of slavery and that involves an agreement in which landowners allow someone to farm a portion of their land in exchange for a specified share of the harvest.

Sherman Antitrust Act An act, passed by Congress in 1890, that prohibits the formation of monopolies, trusts, or any collusion that restricts free trade and open market entry.

Slavery The practice of classifying a group of people as property, with no human rights or privileges, and holding them in bondage to perform manual labor.

Social capital The rules, norms, obligations, reciprocity, and trust embedded in social relations, social structures, and society's institutional arrangements that enable members to achieve their individual and community objectives.

Social gospel movement A movement that emerged during the Progressive Era that sought to instill religious principles and morality into the work and programs of government.

Sovereign immunity A doctrine, based on the Eleventh Amendment to the Constitution, that precludes citizens from suing a state without its consent.

Spoils system The practice in which a new party dismisses the defeated party's government workers and replaces them with its own loyal members as a means of reward and of keeping government administration responsive to party control. The spoils system was critical to politics and government during the nineteenth century; the rallying cry of its champions was "to the victor belong the spoils of the enemy."

Stagflation The economic condition of simultaneous increased unemployment and price inflation.

Stare decisis Latin for "the decision stands"; a convention of the courts to respect past rulings and precedents in determining new case law.

Substantive due process The legal principle that the guarantee of specific rights in the Bill of Rights and the federal Constitution apply to the state governments through the authority of the Fourteenth Amendment's guarantee of due process.

Suffrage A right to vote.

Tariff A tax placed on imported goods that is used primarily as a protection for less competitive domestic industries.

Tax expenditures The elimination or reduction of taxation on benefits, such as healthcare or pensions, that employers provide to employees.

Tories The colonists who continued to support the British crown and to oppose the American war for independence after hostilities had started.

Two-tiered politics Popularized by theorist Wilson Carey McWilliams, the knowledge and involvement gap between the high tier – constituting interest groups, bureaucrats, and public officials – and the low tier of the public at large.

Tyranny of the majority The possibility of a majority encroaching on the basic rights of the minority.

United Automobile Workers (UAW) A trade union, formed in 1935, to represent the interests of automobile workers, including truckers and transporters of goods, but now representing workers in many areas of the economy.

United Mine Workers of America (UMWA) A trade union, formed in 1890, to represent the interests of coal miners.

United Steel Workers of America (USWA) A trade union, formed in 1942, to represent the interests of steelworkers.

Virginia Plan The plan for a strong national government introduced by the Virginia delegation at the Constitutional Convention.

Voluntary association A gathering of individuals who join together voluntarily for a common civic goal.

War hawks A general term used to describe proponents of war (as opposed to doves, who are against war); specifically, the war hawks were a group of Jeffersonian Republicans, led by Henry Clay, who persuaded Congress to support a declaration of war against Britain in 1812.

War on Poverty The set of programs devised by the Lyndon Johnson administration to eradicate poverty.

Whigs The political party that grew up in opposition to the powerful presidency of Andrew Jackson and that generally supported a strong federal government over a more decentralized one based on the prerogative of individual states.

Works Progress Administration (WPA) A New Deal agency devoted to creating jobs for the unemployed.

World Trade Organization (WTO) The global international organization that deals with the rules of trade between nations to help producers of goods and services, exporters, and importers conduct their business.

Annotated Bibliography

1. Introduction: American Government: Rights and Democracy, Consensus and Conflict

Croly, Herbert. *Progressive Democracy*. New York: Macmillan, 1914.
Along with Croly's other important book, *The Promise of American Life*, *Progressive Democracy* is an essential source for understanding the principles and political objectives of the Progressive movement. Croly forcefully attacks the traditional liberal ideas and decentralized practices of American constitutional government and urges the American people to embrace Progressive Democracy, which would combine direct rule of the people and a strong national government.

Du Bois, W. E. B. *The Souls of Black Folk*. New York: Penguin, 1996.
A landmark book of social history and African-American political thought, Du Bois's analysis of the condition of post-Reconstruction black life is both scholarly and rhetorically powerful.

Hamilton, Alexander, James Madison, and John Jay. *The Federalist Papers*. New York: Mentor, 1999.
This series of eighty-five newspaper articles written by Alexander Hamilton, James Madison, and John Jay is perhaps the greatest contribution that America has made to political thought. Both pragmatic and philosophical, these arguments in favor of the ratification of the Constitution lead to a deeper understanding of liberal governance and human nature.

Hartz, Louis. *The Liberal Tradition in America*. New York: Harcourt, Brace, and World, 1955.
Hartz finds that the American political condition is based not upon conflict but upon consensus over the protection of individual rights, social freedom, and social equality. Hartz argues that the lack of a feudal tradition allowed the fundamental tenets of liberalism to gain a stronger hold on Americans than on their European counterparts.

Landy, Marc, and Martin Levin, eds. *The New Politics of Public Policy*. Baltimore, MD: Johns Hopkins University Press, 1995.

773

This work, a collection of essays by some of the leading political scientists, focuses on political institutions and the making of public policy. It emphasizes the importance of rights to policy formation, as evidenced by the rights revolution of the 1960s and 1970s.

Lowi, Theodore. *The End of Liberalism*, 2d ed. New York: W. W. Norton, 1979.
Lowi argues that the modern American political system is shaped by a public philosophy of "interest-group liberalism." Born of the New Deal and reaching its zenith during the 1970s, interest-group liberalism is characterized by the decline of the rule of law and the rise of an administrative state that is dominated by special interests.

McWilliams, Wilson Carey. *The Idea of Fraternity in America*. Berkeley: University of California Press, 1973.
A critique of American literature and, ultimately, liberalism, this book offers penetrating insights into the fragility of community and fraternity in the United States.

Morone, James. *The Democratic Wish: Democratic Participation and the Limits of American Government*. New Haven, CT: Yale University Press, 1998.
Morone argues that American politics is shaped not only by a liberal tradition but also by a democratic wish, an appeal to equality, community, and popular participation. Appeals to "the people" lead to major political transformations that, for a time, defy America's liberal tradition and result in the expansion of national administrative power.

Pierson, Paul. "Increasing Return, Path Dependence, and the Study of Politics." *American Political Science Review* 94, no. 2 (2000).
Pierson has taken the lead in showing how economic theories such as path dependency can help explain important political developments, such as the creation and remarkable resiliency of the Social Security program.

Smith, Rogers M. *Civic Ideals: Conflicting Visions of Citizenship in the United States*. New Haven, CT: Yale University Press, 1999.
Smith argues that beyond a liberal and republican understanding of the American political tradition, the development of the nation has been insidiously influenced by an ascriptive tradition that has defined citizenship by categories of race, gender, sexual orientation, or "culture." Smith argues that as pervasive as appeals to individual rights and political equality have been, deeply rooted nativist, racist, and sexist beliefs have also been powerful and embodied in laws that have denied minorities and women the basic rights of citizenship.

Storing, Herbert, ed. *The Complete Anti-Federalist*. Chicago: University of Chicago Press, 1981.

An understanding of the American founding is impossible without an under-standing of the opponents of the ratification of the U.S. Constitution. This collection of essays, including the letters of the Federal Farmer, Centinel, Brutus, and other leading figures who opposed the ratification of the Constitution, rep-resents the major contributions of the Anti-Federalists, which both by themselves and as the core of Jeffersonian democracy allow for a complete understanding of the American liberal and democratic traditions.

Tocqueville, Alexis de. *Democracy in America*. New York: Perennial Classics, 2000.
    Tocqueville was both an admirer and discerning critic of America, and his work remains one of the most powerful and prescient analyses of American democracy. *Democracy in America* is an important historical account of the Jacksonian era; more generally, it offers penetrating insights into the core beliefs and basic dynamics of American political life.

2. Political Culture

Bailyn, Bernard. *The Ideological Origins of the Revolution*. Cambridge, MA: Belknap Press, 1992.
    Concentrating on the writings of revolutionary pamphleteers, Bailyn examines the various philosophical underpinnings of the revolutionary movement in Amer-ica. Bailyn traces the development of a uniquely American ideology that combined a diverse admixture of classical, Enlightenment, and English political theory into a justification for revolution and a basis for the Constitution.

Du Bois, W. E. B. *The Souls of Black Folk*. New York: Penguin, 1996.
    A classic in American literature and political theory, Du Bois paints a vivid portrait of the culture of racism in America. The process of emerging from "behind the veil" of racism is for Du Bois poignantly ambivalent, as African Americans are forced to reconcile and perhaps lose their own unique culture to the intractable culture of white America.

Garraty, John. *The American Nation: A History of the United States*. New York: Harper and Row, 1968.
    This book provides a good political history of the United States. It is especially effective in linking political developments to social, economic, and cultural trends.

Locke, John. *Two Treatises of Government*. London: Cambridge University Press, 1999.
    A fundamental influence on the American founding, Locke's "Second Treatise" argues for the inalienable rights of men to life, liberty, and property based on the God-given property that each man possesses in his own person. According to Locke, government has no authority to limit these rights and is legitimate only insofar as it protects these rights and exercises power with the consent of the governed.

Maier, Pauline. *American Scripture: How America Declared Its Independence from Britain.* New York: Vintage, 1998.
This book is a thorough and engaging historical study of the writing and early history of the Declaration of Independence. Maier investigates its origins and influences, and examines how it was transformed in the public mind from a formal legal document to the most sacred statement of the American political creed.

Oates, Stephen B. *Let the Trumpet Sound: The Life of Martin Luther King, Jr.* New York: Perennial, 1994.
Using firsthand accounts, Oates develops a portrait of Martin Luther King's character, his views about civil rights, and his mission to overcome segregation and racism in America.

Paine, Thomas. *Common Sense.* New York: Dover, 1997.
Written in 1776, this most famous of the Revolutionary pamphlets is a scalding critique of monarchy as fearful tyranny and a trenchant justification for the separation of America from Great Britain to advance the cause of human liberty.

Smith, Rogers M. *Civic Ideals: Conflicting Visions of Citizenship in the United States.* New Haven, CT: Yale University Press, 1999.
Civic Ideals is an attempt to understand American identity through the political history of citizenship. In examining the legal development of the idea of citizenship, Smith finds an "inegalitarian ascriptive tradition" in American political culture that defines rights on the basis of who is excluded from citizenship, not on the basis of political ideals or a commitment to an American political creed.

Winthrop, John. "A Modell of Christian Charity." In *The Journal of John Winthrop, 1630–1649.* Cambridge, MA: Belknap Press, 1996.
Written in 1630 aboard the *Arabella*, this famous sermon by the leader of the Puritans established the ideas that America would serve as a "citty [sic] upon a hill," a beacon of high moral purpose to the world, and that the Puritans' success depended upon their fidelity to a compact with God to maintain their faith.

Wood, Gordon. "The Democratization of Mind in America," In *The Moral Foundations of the American Republic*, 2d ed., ed. Robert H. Horowitz. Charlottesville: University Press of Virginia, 1979.
Wood argues that the Revolution spawned a celebration of public opinion that diminished the intellectual heritage of the Founding Fathers.

_____. *The Creation of the American Republic: 1776–1787.* Chapel Hill: University of North Carolina Press, 1998.
In this celebrated book on the founding, Wood shows how a powerful democratic tradition both fueled the Revolution and shaped the politics that followed in its wake. Although the Constitution would moderate this democratic fervor, Wood shows that by the early years of the nineteenth century, Americans had embraced

"public opinion" as the vital principle underlying American government, culture, and society.

3. Contesting the Constitution: A Lovers' Quarrel

Bailyn, Bernard. *The Ideological Origins of the Revolution*. Cambridge, MA: Belknap Press, 1992.

Using pamphlets and other historical evidence of colonial America, Bailyn rejects economic and social interpretations of the Revolution. He shows that both opponents and advocates of revolution took the stands they did for ideological reasons.

Bowen, Catherine Drinker. *Miracle at Philadelphia: The Story of the Constitutional Convention, May to September, 1787*. New York: Book of the Month Club, 1966.

This book provides a highly readable account of the Constitutional Convention. Bowen does an especially good job at showing how the intense controversies waged in Philadelphia were influenced by the political and social climate of the time, as well as the personalities of the delegates who participated in the Convention.

Chernow, Ron. *Alexander Hamilton*. New York: Penguin Books, 2004.

This is a superb biography of one of the nation's most important founders. The chapters on the writing and the ratification of the Constitution, and Hamilton's critical, yet uneasy part in forming the "more perfect Union," are very rich and insightful.

Farrand, Max, ed. *The Records of the Federal Convention of 1787*. New Haven, CT: Yale University Press, 1986.

Still a classic of American political history, Farrand's book details, clause by clause, the debate and adoption of the U.S. Constitution, adding insight and historical context to Madison's notes on the federal convention.

Hamilton, Alexander, James Madison, and John Jay. *The Federalist Papers*. New York: Mentor, 1999.

Informed by the belief that societies of men are really capable of establishing good government from reflection and choice, these essays thoroughly explain the logic of the proposed Constitution and defend its revolutionary purpose to create self-rule on a grand scale.

Jensen, Merrill. *The Articles of Confederation: An Interpretation of the Social-Constitutional History of the American Revolution, 1774–1781*. Madison: University of Wisconsin Press, 1970.

Jensen's work explains the origins of the first government of the United States. Jensen details both the social cleavages and interstate conflicts that lay at the heart of the Articles of Confederation and analyzes the debate and ratification of this document.

McDonald, Forrest. *E Pluribus Unum: The Formation of the American Republic, 1776–1790.* Indianapolis, IN: Liberty Press, 1979.
Coming a generation after Charles Beard, McDonald characterizes the Constitutional Convention not as a gathering of landed elite intent on maintaining economic domination but as a collection of interest groups frustrated over their circumstance under the Articles of Confederation.

Rakove, Jack. *Original Meanings: Politics and Ideas in the Making of the Constitution.* New York: Vintage, 1997.
Rakove's interpretation of the Framers' "original intent" calls upon readers to seek history and context as a guide. Rakove concludes that there is no singular "framers' intent" because of the diverse nature of the Founders.

Rossiter, Clinton. *1787: The Grand Convention.* New York: Macmillan, 1966.
This work is a narrative of the Constitutional Convention and the ratification fight that sheds light on the grand politics of the founding.

Siemers, David. *The Anti-Federalists: Men of Great Faith and Forbearance.* Lanham, MD: Rowman and Littlefield, 2003.
This book includes several important Anti-Federalist essays and insightful commentary on the importance of Anti-Federalist thought on the country's political heritage. Siemers shows us that the Anti-Federalists were important "Founders" in their own right.

Wood, Gordon. *The Americanization of Benjamin Franklin.* New York: Penguin Books, 2004.
This biography is a revealing portrait of Franklin. It shows him to be not the iconic, folksy figure of conventional wisdom, but rather a practical and cautious man, deeply loyal to Great Britain, who somehow becomes implicated in the Revolution and the writing of two revolutionary documents: the Declaration of Independence and the Constitution of 1787.

4. Political Development: Crucial Episodes

Ackerman, Bruce. *We the People: Foundations.* Cambridge, MA: Harvard University Press, 1991.

———. *We the People: Transformations.* Cambridge, MA: Harvard University Press, 1998.
These two volumes celebrate and analyze constitutional change in America. Since the founding, Ackerman argues, constitutional transformations have not been orderly and formal; rather, constitutional changes have occurred through passionate yet deliberate acts of "We the People."

Brooks, David. "One Nation, Slightly Divisible." *Atlantic Monthly,* December 2001.

This essay is a fine journalistic account of the cultural differences that divide major metropolitan and small town America. Linking the differences between "Red and Blue America" to geography and lifestyle, Brooks sheds considerable light on the factors that shape contemporary American politics.

Burnham, Walter Dean. *Critical Elections and the Mainsprings of American Politics.* New York: W. W. Norton, 1971.
This book is a classic statement on partisan realignments and the critical role that these episodes have played in the development of the American nation.

Derthick, Martha. *Policymaking for Social Security.* Washington, D.C.: The Brookings Institution, 1979.
This is a classic work on the Social Security program and how it transformed political culture and policymaking in the United States.

Dewey, John. *Individualism, Old and New.* Amherst, NY: Prometheus Books, 1999.
Dewey's philosophical writings had a powerful influence on the Progressive Era and the New Deal. These essays challenge the classical liberal premise that limited government nurtured individual freedom. Dewey argues that government had a critical part to play in allowing individuals to realize their full potential. Combining elements of nineteenth-century liberalism with a commitment to collective action, Dewey helped to inspire and justify a new liberalism – and a new understanding of rights – that required the expansion, rather than the limitation, of government's role in the society and economy.

Fiorina, Morris. *Culure War? The Myth of a Polarized America,* 2d ed. New York: Longman, 2006.
This book is a persuasive critique of the idea that America is deeply polarized over social issues such as abortion and same-sex marriage. Analyzing recent elections and public opinion polls, Fiorina concludes that America is closely, but not deeply, divided. Sharp conflict separates party activists but this conflict among activists has not deeply affected the rank-and-file citizenry.

Fletcher, George P. *Our Secret Constitution: How Lincoln Redefined American Democracy.* London: Oxford University Press, 2001.
Fletcher argues that America experienced a constitutional rebirth during the Civil War, guided by the Republicans and the leadership of Lincoln. For Fletcher, the Civil War was a catalyst for converting the Constitution from a positive law compact of states' rights and limited government into one that respected natural rights and a high national moral purpose.

Gerstle, Gary. *American Crucible: Race and Nation in the Twentieth Century.* Princeton, NJ: Princeton University Press, 2002.
This volume provides a well argued and well written account of racial politics in twentieth-century America. It portrays the tension between the country's celebration of "civic nationalism" (defined as the belief in the "fundamental equality of all

human beings... their right to life, liberty, and the pursuit of happiness... and in a government legitimized by the consent of the people") and the stubborn attachment of many citizens to a competing ideal of America as a white, Protestant country.

Glendon, Mary Ann. *Rights Talk: The Impoverishment of Political Discourse*. New York: Free Press, 1993.
Glendon argues that the shift in American jurisprudence from an emphasis on duty and responsibility to an expansive rights doctrine has debased political discourse and common morality. She calls for an approach to law and political discourse that emphasizes community and social ties rather than rights and entitlements.

Goodwin, Richard. *Remembering America*. New York: HarperCollins, 1995.
A speechwriter for John F. Kennedy and Lyndon Johnson, Goodwin recounts his vast experiences in American government during the turbulent era of the 1960s. Initially an advisor to John F. Kennedy, Goodwin continued in the White House under Johnson, writing some of Johnson's landmark speeches until he became disillusioned with the president's stand on the Vietnam War and his increasingly erratic behavior.

Heclo, Hugh. "The Sixties' False Dawn: Awakenings, Movements, and Postmodern Policy-Making." *Journal of Policy History* 8, no. 1 (1996).
This article is a provocative interpretation of the political culture of the 1960s and its effect on government institutions and public policy. Whereas the Progressive Era and New Deal led to the creation of a modern state, the reforms of the 1960s yielded a postmodern form of politics and policy making that expanded the responsibilities of government, yet undermined its public authority.

Howe, Daniel Walker. *The Political Culture of the American Whigs*. Chicago: University of Chicago Press, 1984.
In a searching examination of the political philosophy and personalities that composed the Whig Party, Walker paints an intricate portrait of mid-nineteenth-century American politics. Having grown spontaneously out of opposition to Andrew Jackson, the Whigs embodied Hamiltonian ideas of using government to motivate economic prosperity, but their limited view of rights led them to collapse under the pressures of the Civil War and secession.

John, Richard. "Affairs of Office: The Executive Departments, the Election of 1828, and the Making of the Democratic Party." In *The Democratic Experiment: New Directions in American Political History*. ed. Meg Jacobs, William J. Novak, and Julian E. Zelizer. Princeton, NJ: Princeton University Press, 2003.
This revealing essay shows how early efforts to build a strong national state, which occupied both Federalists and nationally-inclined Republicans, were pre-empted during the Jacksonian era. John argues that the Jacksonians might not have weakened the presidency, but they certainly undermined national administrative

power. This work is an important statement on the inherent tension between the decentralized, highly mobilized two-party system of the nineteenth century and national administrative power.

Katzelson, Ira. *When Affirmative Action Was White: An Untold History of Racial Inequality in Twentieth-Century America*. New York: W. W. Norton, 2006.
This book argues that the New Deal not only failed to redress forced segregation but gave positive government support to it. Rather than seeing affirmative action developing out of the Civil Rights Movement of the 1960s, Katznelson finds its origins in the New Deal policies of the 1930s and 1940s. Yet the affirmative action of the New Deal rested in FDR's dependence on Southern Democrats who were devoted to preserving a strict racial hierarchy. Consequently, New Deal programs and agencies extended Jim Crow to government benefits and the advantages positive government bestowed on the economy: whites received the full benefit of the New Deal political order while blacks were deliberately left out.

McWilliams, Wilson Carey. *The Idea of Fraternity in America*. Berkeley: University of California Press, 1973.
By tracing the evolution of the idea of fraternity in American public life, McWilliams discovers its essential role in promoting citizenship and national unity. The causes for its dissipation in the modern era and the ebbing sense of community in America are, for McWilliams, an inevitable if lamentable result of an ever-increasing embrace of individual rights and the pressures of industrialization.

Meyers, Marvin. *The Jacksonian Persuasion*. Palo Alto, CA: Stanford University Press, 1960.
Meyers reconsiders the conventional view of Jacksonian democracy as a progressive movement that promoted populism and the rights of the common man, finding it instead to embody a reactionary mind-set of an era that resented the dawning industrialization of America and the increasing centralization of political power that industrialization demanded.

Milkis, Sidney M. *The President and the Parties*. New York: Oxford University Press, 1993.
In this reconsideration of Franklin D. Roosevelt's party leadership and the New Deal, Milkis shows that the New Deal strengthened the Democratic party and partisan politics in the short term, but it eventually gave rise to a modern executive establishment that has supplanted vigorous party politics.

Milkis, Sidney M., and Jerome Mileur, eds. *The New Deal and the Triumph of Liberalism*. Amherst: University of Massachusetts Press, 2002.
In this collection of essays, a group of political scientists and historians reevaluate the legacy of the New Deal. Although the authors disagree in their assessment of the successes and failures of New Deal liberalism, all agree that its implications for American political life were profound – in the realm of foreign as well as domestic affairs.

Morone, James. "The Other America: Notes on Rogers Smith's Civic Ideals." *Studies in American Political Development* 13 (Spring 1999): 186–197.
Part of a forum on Smith's seminal volume on American political culture, this essay offers a penetrating critique of the thesis that a non-liberal tradition animates racial and sexual discrimination in the United States. Morone explains how the exclusive features of liberalism itself lead to discrimination, and he encourages scholars to attend more carefully to the connection between liberal aspirations and illiberal prejudices.

————. *Hellfire Nation: The Politics of Sin in American History.* New Haven, CT: Yale University Press, 2003
This book is a sweeping narrative of the profound effect that sermonizing has had on American political development. Morone views developments through two competing kinds of political religion: a Victorian censoriousness and a Social Gospel communalism. The Victorian impulse – arising from Puritan fears of witchcraft and debauchery – inspires the fervor of nineteenth-century abolitionists and twentieth-century prohibitionists. The Social Gospel – springing from Puritan pledges of mutual love – stirs the visionary hopes behind the New Deal and the Civil Rights Movement.

Schattschneider, E.E. *The Semi-Sovereign People: A Realist's View of Democracy in America* (reissued with a new introduction by David Adamany). Hinsdale, IL: Dryden Press, 1975.
This classic work discusses the importance of party politics, especially with respect to expanding conflict in a way that makes public accountability possible. Schattschneider argues that Americans face a choice between pressure politics, dominated by a small circle of policy elites, and party politics, which subjects policy conflict to popular debate and resolution.

Wiebe, Robert. *Self-Rule: A Cultural History of American Democracy.* Chicago: University of Chicago Press, 1995.
Wiebe's extended essay on the birth, development, and demise of American democracy shows that American democracy in the nineteenth century, even though it excluded white women and all people of color from civic life, nevertheless was a radical, progressive departure from the European experience. This engaging work is an excellent source on the cultural and historical roots of the American democratic tradition.

Wills, Garry. *Lincoln at Gettysburg: The Words That Remade America.* New York: Touchstone, 1993.
In this Pulitzer Prize–winning history, Wills re-creates the moment in which Lincoln wrote a short speech that would forever embody the noble cause for "a new birth of freedom" in the United States. Observing the text from historical and literary perspectives, Wills offers a tremendous resource for understanding Lincoln and the meaning of the Gettysburg address.

5. Federalism

Beer, Samuel. *To Make a Nation: The Rediscovery of American Federalism.* Cambridge, MA: Belknap Press, 1993.

Beer's work rejects the idea of compact theory and defends the idea of the national compound republic as essential to foster the unity of the American people and to preserve American democracy.

Conlan, Timothy. *From New Federalism to Devolution.* Washington, D.C.: Brookings Institution, 1998.

By analyzing the evolution of Republican party doctrine on federalism from Richard Nixon's vision of a "new federalism" to Ronald Reagan's theme of reinvigorating the states with a "devolution revolution," Conlan sheds light on twenty-five years of intergovernmental reform.

Derthick, Martha. *Keeping the Compound Republic.* Washington, D.C.: Brookings Institution, 2001.

Derthick writes a definitive group of essays that analyze and advocate the founding notion of American federalism. This book is an essential source for understanding the origins and historical development of the relationship between the national, state, and local communities in the United States.

Donahue, John D. *Disunited States.* New York: Basic Books, 1997.

Though not an opponent of federalism, Donahue in this work uses comparative analysis to question the effectiveness of the current trend to dismantle federal programs and "devolve" authority for managing such programs to the states.

Elazar, Daniel. *American Federalism: A View from the States,* 3d ed. New York: HarperCollins, 1984.

This classic work reveals the cultural underpinnings of American federalism. Elazar illustrates the distinct cultures that the various states display and suggests that the distinctive culture of the states helps explain why they remain a vigorous and powerful entity in American government.

McDonald, Forrest. *States' Rights and the Union: Imperium in Imperio, 1776–1876.* Lawrence: University Press of Kansas, 2000.

McDonald analyzes the founding of American federalism from its revolutionary origins through the first 100 years of the republic. McDonald favors a strong and clearly defined role for the states, whose power is constantly threatened by the encroachments of the national government.

Peterson, Paul E. *The Price of Federalism.* Washington, D.C.: Brookings Institution, 1995.

Peterson argues that there is a tension between two competing theories of American federalism: functional theory, which delegates responsibilities based on the premise of administrative efficiency and effectiveness, and legislative theory, which leads Congress to dictate how states manage programs.

Walker, David B. *The Rebirth of Federalism: Slouching toward Washington*. New York: Chatham House, 2000.
Walker vigorously defends federalism while suggesting that modern American federalism is too nation-centered, ultimately dysfunctional, and as the title suggests, in need of a rebirth.

6. Political Economy

Chandler, Alfred Dupont. *Scale and Scope: The Dynamics of Industrial Capitalism*. Cambridge, MA: Belknap Press, 1994.
Chandler's work offers a thorough analysis of the development and consolidation of industrial capitalism in the United States, Germany, and England. Chandler argues that large companies were able to succeed by taking advantage of buying and selling on a large scale and doing business over broader territories.

_____. *The Visible Hand: The Managerial Revolution in American Business*. Cambridge, MA: Belknap Press, 1980.
Much like *Scale and Scope*, *The Visible Hand* details the rise of the modern corporation in the late nineteenth and the early twentieth centuries and the transition from market-based economic regulation to government-induced market regulation.

Derthick, Martha, and Paul J. Quirk. *The Politics of Deregulation*. Washington, D.C.: Brookings Institution, 1985.
Using multiple case studies of efforts to roll back regulation, Derthick and Quirk conclude that deregulation is not the result of strong business interests but rather is influenced by political ideology and the current political context.

Friedman, Milton. *Capitalism and Freedom*. Chicago: University of Chicago Press, 1963.
Perhaps the most dominant modern economic theorist and leader of the Chicago "monetarist" school, Friedman offers a vigorous defense of capitalism and the free market.

Hacker, Jacob. *The Divided Welfare State: The Battle over Public and Private Social Benefits in the United States*. New York: Cambridge University Press, 2002.
Hacker shows how the deeply ingrained history of employer-sponsored pensions and health insurance has swung the pendulum toward utilizing private initiatives rather than enhanced federal programs to provide Americans with social benefits. He thus shows that the "American welfare regime" is not smaller per se than those in other representative democracies, but, rather, divided between public and "private" benefits, which the government subsidizes through tax incentives and favorable regulations. The consequences are profound: the American welfare state

is not only less redistributive than those in comparable nations, Hacker argues, but also less subject to public accountability.

———. "Privatizing Risk without Privatizing the Welfare State: The Hidden Politics of Social Policy Retrenchment in the United States." *American Political Science Review* 98, no. 2 (May 2004): 243–260.
Although none of the major entitlement programs have been repealed, Hacker argues, these "entitlements" have been weakened by congressional neglect and an indifferent, if not hostile, administration. Consequently, social benefits no longer "socialize" risk; instead, programs have been "privatized," so that risk now tends to fall on individuals much more than it did two decades ago.

Harrington, Michael. *The Other America*. New York: Touchstone, 1997.
Harrington's description of the cultural determinants of poverty in the United States offers a powerful and tragic tale of the persistence of poverty amid the prosperity of post–World War II America.

Harris, Richard, and Sidney M. Milkis. *The Politics of Regulatory Change: A Tale of Two Agencies*, 2d ed. New York and London: Oxford University Press, 1996.
Harris and Milkis examine the Reagan administration's efforts to roll back social regulations at the Environmental Protection Agency and Federal Trade Commission. This book sheds light on how ideological, historical, and institutional factors contributed to the successes and failures that conservative activists experienced in attempting to dismantle environmental and consumer protection programs.

Hawley, Ellis. *The New Deal and the Problem of Monopoly: A Study in Economic Ambivalence*. New York: Fordham University Press, 1995.
Hawley offers a deeply critical analysis of the New Deal economic programs. He claims that New Deal policies were often logically contradictory and did not lead to economic recovery.

Heclo, Hugh. "Ronald Reagan and the American Public Philosophy." In *The Reagan Presidency: Pragmatic Conservatism and Its Legacies*. ed. W. Elliot Brownlee and Hugh Davis Graham. Lawrence: University Press of Kansas, 2003.
This essay offers a penetrating and provocative analysis of Reagan's rhetoric. Reagan preached America's public philosophy, Heclo argues, thus resuscitating the political importance of its core principles: individualism, private initiative, and limited government. But his views were preached out of context – they lacked a sense of historical development – and thus failed to acknowledge the good and necessary things contemporary American government has come to do. When pushed politically, therefore – for example, in efforts to roll back or revamp entitlements such as Social Security and Medicare – Reagan's political views proved damaging to the Republican party and the conservative movement.

McCoy, Drew R. *The Elusive Republic: Political Economy in Jeffersonian America.* Chapel Hill: University of North Carolina Press, 1996.
McCoy illustrates the theoretical underpinnings of Jeffersonian democracy and shows how eighteenth-century social and economic thought influenced policy during the Jeffersonian era.

McCraw, Thomas K. *Prophets of Regulation: Charles Francis Adams, Louis D. Brandeis, James M. Landis, Alfred E. Kahn.* Cambridge, MA: Harvard University Press, 1990.
McCraw studies four important intellectuals and their thoughts on the political economy to critically examine the problems involved in regulatory reform efforts from the end of the nineteenth century to the contemporary political era.

Mettler, Suzanne. *Soldiers to Citizens: The G. I. Bill and the Making of the Greatest Generation.* New York: Oxford University Press, 2005.
Mettler shows how the Greatest Generation was shaped not only by World War II but also by successful public policy. The G. I. Bill, she argues, helped transform soldiers into citizens who made a vital contribution to America's postwar civic culture.

Savage, James. *Balanced Budgets and American Politics.* Ithaca, NY: Cornell University Press, 1990.
Savage traces the popular support for balanced budgets to republican conceptions of limited government and virtue fostered in Jeffersonian and Jacksonian America.

Sellers, Charles. *The Market Revolution: Jacksonian America, 1815–1846.* New York and London: Oxford University Press, 1994.
Sellers argues that despite Andrew Jackson's efforts to prevent the concentration of economic power, America evolved from an agrarian to a market economy during the antebellum period.

Stein, Herbert. *Presidential Politics: The Making of Economic Policy from Roosevelt to Clinton.* Washington, D.C.: American Enterprise Institute Press, 1994.
Stein describes the last half century of economic policy as a fusion of politics and competing economic philosophies of Keynesianism, monetarism, and supply-side economics.

7. Congress: The First Branch of Government

Bessette, Joseph M. *The Mild Voice of Reason: Deliberative Democracy and American National Government.* Chicago: University of Chicago Press, 1994.
Bessette's work argues that deliberation, fostered by republicanism sewn into America's constitutional fabric and legislative institutions, still dominates legislative action and policy development.

Ceaser, James, and Andrew Busch. *Red Over Blue: The 2004 Elections and American Politics*. Lanham, MD: Rowman and Littlefield, 2005.
This book examines the 2004 presidential and congressional elections cast against long-term developments in party organizations and partisan loyalties.

Dodd, Lawrence C., and Richard Schott. *Congress and the Administrative State*. New York: John Wiley and Sons, 1979.
This work is a historically detailed look at the development of Congress from a strongly party-centered body of preeminent national power to a decentralized, member-based institution. Dodd and Schott argue that this development has been caused primarily by Congress's increasing efforts to control the growth and actions of the federal bureaucracy.

Fenno, Richard E. *Congressmen in Committees*. Berkeley, CA: Institute of Governmental Studies Press, 1995.
Fenno analyzes six congressional committees – appropriations, ways and means, education and labor, foreign affairs, interior, and post office – as unique political systems that imbue members with a certain ethos through the use of structural incentives and punishments.

_____. *Home Style*. New York: Longman, 2002.
Fenno's thorough and descriptive stories of congressional representatives in their districts emphasize the personal nature of congressional politics and the importance of legislators' ability to communicate with their districts about developments in Washington, D.C.

Fiorina, Morris. *Congress: Keystone of the Washington Establishment*, 2d ed. New Haven, CT: Yale University Press, 1989.
Fiorina attributes the decrease in competitive congressional elections and the increase in the benefits of incumbency to the rise of big government and the emergence of Congress as the "keystone" of a "Washington establishment." He argues that members of Congress have sacrificed lawmaking to concentrate on doing casework for the people in their districts.

Ford, Henry Jones. *The Rise and Growth of American Politics: A Sketch of Constitutional Development*. New York: Macmillan, 1898.
Ford argues that America's constitutional structure of separation of powers impeded the development of America as a great nation. He proposes that America adopt a more responsible government, a quasi-parliamentary system in which cabinet-level officials would reside in Congress.

Ginsberg, Benjamin, and Martin Shefter. *Politics By Other Means: Politicians, Prosecutors, and the Press from Watergate to Whitewater*, 3d ed. New York: W. W. Norton, 2003.
Ginsberg and Shefter argue in this fresh look at the timeless struggle between the executive and legislature that the United States is entering an era of post-electoral

politics, with "institutional combat" – that is, media revelations, congressional investigation, and judicial proceedings – replacing elections as the primary tools of political competition.

Jacobson, Gary. *The Politics of Congressional Elections*, 5th ed. Boston: Addison Wesley, 2000.
Jacobson explores the political actions of the modern congressional campaign and finds that incumbency advantage follows from the responsiveness of incumbents to their districts.

Keller, Morton. *Affairs of State: Public Life in Late Nineteenth-Century America.* Cambridge, MA: Harvard University Press, 1979.
Keller masterfully describes the American polity in the second half of the nineteenth century. An invaluable source on machine politics, the political economy, and government institutions during Reconstruction and the Gilded Age, *Affairs of State* also sheds light on the enduring features of American political life.

Lowi, Theodore J. "Presidential Democracy in America: Toward the Homogenized Regime." *Political Science Quarterly* 109, no. 3 (Special Issue 1994): 401–437.
Lowi offers a penetrating account of the constitutional consequences of the modern presidency. The Congress has been able to challenge executive power, he argues, only by becoming more administrative in its organization and practices. As a consequence the rule of law has been sacrificed on the altar of "enlightened" administration.

Mayhew, David. *Congress: The Electoral Connection.* New Haven, CT: Yale University Press, 1986.
One of the first rational-choice analyses of congressional action, Mayhew's book argues that most congressional action can be accounted for by viewing members of Congress as single-minded reelection seekers and by logically inferring congressional action from this assumption.

Melnick, R. Shep. "The Politics of Partnership." *Public Administration Review* 45 (November 1985): 653–660.
This essay provides an insightful analysis of how insurgents revitalized Congress during the 1970s. Congressional reformers did not accomplish this task alone, Melnick argues; they had important "institutional partners" in the bureaucracy and courts, and benefited enormously from alliances forged with investigative journalists.

Phillips, David Graham. "The Treason of the Senate." *Cosmopolitan* XL (March, 1906): 496–596.
This long journalistic piece is a classic exposé of the Senate. Graham's article is a good example of "muckraking" journalism, which played an important part in advancing progressive reforms at the beginning of the twentieth century.

Schickler, Eric. "Institutional Development of Congress." In *The Legislative Branch*, ed. Paul J. Quirk and Sarah A. Binden. New York: Oxford University Press, 2005.
This essay provides a solid introduction to the origins and development of congressional institutions. The article is especially insightful in explaining what factors have led to important reforms in the House and Senate throughout American history.

Wilson, Woodrow. *Congressional Government*. Boston: Houghton-Mifflin, 1885.
Wilson's Princeton dissertation and the book that made him famous shows how Congress dominated constitutional government at the end of the nineteenth century and how this dominance denigrated responsible government. Like Henry Jones Ford, Wilson calls on Americans to adopt a quasi-parliamentary system that would combine legislative and executive power.

Zelizer, Julian. *Taxing America: Wilbur D. Mills, Congress, and the State, 1945–1975*. New York: Cambridge University Press, 2000.
This account of Wilbur Mills's long career in Congress sheds light on the development of middle-class entitlements like Social Security and Medicare, as well as the important role that Congress has played in building the "modern state."

8. The Presidency: First Citizen of American Democracy

Arnold, Peri. *Making the Managerial Presidency: Comprehensive Reorganization Planning 1905–1996*, 2d ed. Lawrence: University Press of Kansas, 1998.
Focusing primarily on presidential task forces and commissions, Arnold describes the objectives and strategies of executive reorganization plans from Theodore Roosevelt to Ronald Reagan. He shows how reformers have viewed executive reorganization as a means to establish a more responsible form of government within the framework of the American Constitution.

Binkley, Wilfred E. *The President and Congress*. New York: Knopf, 1947.
Binkley describes, from the Constitutional Convention to the 1940s, the enduring struggle between the president and Congress for constitutional supremacy.

Ceaser, James. *Presidential Selection: Theory and Development*. Princeton, NJ: Princeton University Press, 1979.
This work examines the philosophical and historical developments that have shaped the presidential selection process. Ceaser provides a penetrating account of how the Framers' hope to establish an executive above partisanship and at a distance from popular passions proved impractical, as the presidency was captured by mass party politics in the nineteenth century and transformed into a leader of mass opinion during the Progressive Era.

Cornwell, Elmer, Jr. *Presidential Leadership of Public Opinion*. Bloomington: IN University Press, 1965.

Cornwell shows how the president's leadership of public opinion in the twentieth century has been critically affected by the White House's relationship with the press and its occupant's ability to exploit the mass media.

Corwin, Edward. *The President: Office and Powers, 1787–1984,* 5th ed. New York: New York University Press, 1984.
Corwin's study of executive power is the classic work on the importance of resting executive power in formal constitutional authority and law.

DeMuth, Christopher. "Unlimited Government." *The American Enterprise Online,* www.taemag.com, December 12, 2005.
This essay expresses a conservative's concern that the presidency of George W. Bush, with the complicity of Republican leaders in Congress, had betrayed the Reagan "Revolution" and its commitment to limiting government. By 2005, DeMuth argues, Republicans no less than Democrats had embraced big government, not only in matters of national security, but in domestic policy as well.

Hawley, Ellis. "The Constitution of the Hoover and F. Roosevelt Presidency during the Depression Era, 1900–1939." In *The Constitution and the American Presidency,* ed. Martin L. Fausold and Alan Shank. Albany: State University of New York Press, 1991.
Hawley offers a perceptive account of the constitutional implications of the Great Depression. The essay is especially helpful in understanding how the modern executive establishment was grafted onto traditional American ideas and political institutions.

Landy, Marc, and Sidney Milkis. *Presidential Greatness.* Lawrence: University Press of Kansas, 2000.
Through a thick description of America's most celebrated presidents, this work probes the philosophical, historical, and institutional dimensions of presidential greatness. It argues that America's great presidents have been extraordinary democratic leaders who have engaged the American people in debate and resolution about the meaning of the Declaration and Constitution.

Lowi, Theodore. *The Personal President: Power Invested, Promise Unfulfilled.* Ithaca, NY: Cornell University Press, 1986.
Lowi argues that modern American politics has forged a direct personal relationship between the president and the people. The personal presidency creates expectations that no president can possible satisfy, tempting presidents to abuse power and causing the American people to lose faith in government.

McKitrick, Eric. "Party Politics and the Union and Confederate War Efforts." In *The American Party System: Stages of Political Development,* ed. William Nisbet Chambers and Walter Dean Burnham. New York: Oxford University Press, 1975.

This is a revealing essay on Lincoln's party leadership. It shows how America's "greatest president" masterfully brokered factions in his cabinet and exploited patronage practices. The powerful Republican party he helped build was one of the most important advantages the Union had over the Confederacy, which proscribed partisanship and, consequently, suffered from chronic fractiousness.

Milkis, Sidney M., and Michael Nelson. *The American Presidency: Origins and Development, 1776–2007*, 5th ed. Washington, D.C.: CQ Press, 2007.
This work probes the constitutional and historical roots of the American presidency. It tells the story of how the institution of the presidency was created and how it has developed over two centuries of history.

Miroff, Bruce. "The Presidency and the Public: Leadership as Spectacle." In *The Presidency and the Political System*, 5th edition, ed. Michael Nelson. Washington, D.C. CQ Press. 1998.
Miroff shows how the rise of the modern presidency combined with the development of television to advance a politics of personality that trumps substance. Much of contemporary politics entails staging "spectacles," or message-laden symbolic displays, that seek to project attractive leadership qualities.

Neustadt, Richard. *Presidential Power and the Modern Presidents: The Politics of Leadership from Roosevelt to Reagan*. New York: Free Press, 1991.
Challenging the received wisdom that the power of the presidents resides in formal constitutional authority, Neustadt argues that presidents exercise influence through their ability to persuade.

Reichley, A. James. "The Rise of National Parties." In *The New Direction in American Politics*, ed. John E. Chubb and Paul E. Peterson. Washington, D.C.: Brookings Institution, 1985.
Reichley was one of the first scholars to identify an important transformation of political parties, from decentralized patronage-based to nationalized programmatic organizations.

Rosenman, Samuel, and Dorothy Rosenman. *Presidential Style: Some Giants and a Pygmy in the White House*. New York: Harper and Row, 1976.
This book provides an accessible, anecdotal history of the modern presidency.

Schlesinger, Jr., Arthur M. *The Imperial Presidency*. New York. Popular Library, 1973.
This book marks a key pivot in the shift from the celebration of the modern presidency to charges that it was developing into an elected monarchy. Schlesinger, a historian who championed FDR's presidency and counseled JFK, feared that Vietnam and Watergate portended executive aggrandizement that would destroy constitutional democracy in the United States.

Skowronek, Stephen. *The Politics Presidents Make: Leadership from John Adams to Bill Clinton.* Cambridge, MA: Belknap Press, 1997.
This excellent work on the presidency's place in American political development demonstrates that presidents are persistent agents of change, continually disrupting and transforming the political landscape and periodically resetting the terms of constitutional government.

Tulis, Jeffrey. *The Rhetorical Presidency.* Princeton, NJ: Princeton University Press, 1987.
Tulis argues that the most fundamental change in American government has been the emergence of the president as popular leader. Whereas the Constitution proscribed popular leadership, Progressive Era reformers prescribed it. Since the beginning of the twentieth century, presidents have increasingly relied on rhetorical appeals to the people to arouse support for their programs and to circumvent the constitutional checks on executive power.

9. The Judiciary: The Guardians of America's Liberal Tradition

Bickel, Alexander. *The Least Dangerous Branch: The Supreme Court at the Bar of Politics.* New Haven, CT: Yale University Press, 1986.
Approaching the court with a skeptical view toward its power, Bickel reinvigorates the debate about the Supreme Court's claim of judicial review and casts new light on the tension between the judiciary's power to check the other powers of government and its potential to bring about minority tyranny.

Derthick, Martha. *Keeping the Compound Republic.* Washington, D.C.: Brookings Institution, 2001.
Cast against the expansion of national administrative power, this set of essays gives a spirited, scholarly defense of federalism. Highlighting redistricting and civil rights cases, Derthick shows how the courts became a senior partner of the administrative state during the 1960s.

Farrand, Max, ed. *The Records of the Federal Convention of 1787.* New Haven, CT: Yale University Press, 1986.
In 1911, historian Max Farrand compiled the first edition of Madison's notes on the Constitutional Convention, and this compilation has since proved to be the authoritative collection. The four volumes include an extensive index that is invaluable to any student researching the arguments behind the Constitution.

Foner, Eric. *Free Soil, Free Labor, Free Men: The Ideology of the Republican Party before the Civil War.* New York and Oxford: Oxford University Press, 1995.
Historian Eric Foner looks beyond emancipation as a cause of the Civil War and emphasizes the importance of the ideological roots of the Republican party and its ability to build support in the North for preserving the Union. Foner demonstrates

that the appeal of the Republican party was based in its dedication to the right of every man to work and enjoy the fruits of his own labor.

Greenhouse, Linda. "Same-Sex Marriage: The Context." *New York Times*, November 19, 2003.
Greenhouse argues that the controversial 2003 Massachusetts Supreme Court case of *Goodridge v. Department of Public Education*, which pronounced the right of same-sex couples to marry, was not created out of whole cloth. Instead, it was "linked in spirit even if not as formal doctrine" with the Supreme Court ruling of *Lawrence v. Texas*, which struck down a Texas criminal sodomy law.

Leuchtenburg, William. *The Supreme Court Reborn: The Constitutional Revolution in the Age of Roosevelt*. Oxford: Oxford University Press, 1996.
In this collection of essays, Leuchtenburg examines the reformation of the Supreme Court in the wake of the political and economic upheaval of the 1930s. Using a diverse number of resources, this volume provides a detailed account of how the character of the Supreme Court changed after the New Deal.

McCloskey, Robert, and Sanford Levinson. *The American Supreme Court*. Chicago: University of Chicago Press, 2000.
In this broad survey of the political development of the Supreme Court, McCloskey and Levinson provide a useful resource for understanding how the Supreme Court has shaped the Constitution since its first claim of judicial review.

Melnick, R. Shep. *Between the Lines: Interpreting Welfare Rights*. Washington, D.C.: Brookings Institution, 1994.
The fragmentation of congressional power and the deferential quality of its legislation have given the courts a powerful seat at the head of administrative government. The story Melnick relates about the courts and Congress during the 1960s and 1970s demonstrates the vulnerability of the administrative state to judicial direction and the hazards of deferring legislative questions to courts and administrative agencies.

O'Brien, David. *Storm Center: The Supreme Court in American Politics*, 3d ed. New York: W. W. Norton, 1993.
Informed by detailed research and personal interviews with several former and current justices, O'Brien's work builds a detailed account of the politics and personalities inside the Supreme Court, illuminating the institutional culture behind the published opinions.

Spencer, Herbert. *Social Statics: The Man Versus the State*, rev. ed. La Vergne, TN: University Press of the Pacific, 2003 (originally published in 1884).
This is the classic work that applies biological theories of evolution to the economy. Spencer coined the phrase "survival of the fittest," adopting Charles Darwin's understanding of "natural selection" to economic relations.

10. Bureaucracy

Arnold, Peri. *Making the Managerial Presidency: Comprehensive Reorganization Planning 1905–1996,* 2d ed. Lawrence: University Press of Kansas, 1998.
Arnold describes how administrative reorganizations – primarily through presidential task forces and commissions – have given form to the bureaucracy. He highlights the conflict between Congress and the presidency over bureaucratic reform and, ultimately, control of national administrative power.

Light, Paul. *The True Size of Government.* Washington, D.C.: Brookings Institution, 1999.
Light reveals the true size of government by exposing the "shadow of government" – non-federal employees who work under federal contracts, grants, and mandates to state and local governments. Light argues that it is in the best interest of government to hide the growth of the federal bureaucracy by "contracting out" the responsibility for managing public programs.

Moynihan, Daniel P. *Maximum Feasible Misunderstanding: Community Action in the War on Poverty.* New York: Free Press, 1970.
An in-depth analysis of the community action programs that were an integral part of the War on Poverty, Moynihan's scathing critique of the programs points to the lack of forethought as to the political obstacles and ramifications of such a "war." He also condemns the programs for bureaucratic incompetence and for centralizing power under the guise of "community action."

Selznick, Philip. *TVA and the Grass Roots: A Study of Politics and Organization,* reprint ed. Berkeley: University of California Press, 1984.
A study of the working strategies of the Tennessee Valley Authority, this book is an important analysis of political ideology and how it is used or set aside when grassroots political organizations confront political realities. It is also noteworthy for illustrating the concept of organization "cooptation."

Skowronek, Stephen. *Building a New American State: The Expansion of National Administrative Capacities.* Cambridge, MA: Cambridge University Press, 1981.
Skowronek's path-breaking work rediscovered the importance of the administrative state born of developments at the end of the nineteenth century and beginning of the twentieth. Grafted onto the decentralized "state of courts and parties" that dominated American politics for the first 100 years of its existence, the administrative state emerged not in the form that characterized national states in Europe, but rather with a sui generis American, fragmented structure.

Wilson, James Q. *Bureaucracy: What Government Agencies Do and Why They Do It,* reproduction ed. New York: Basic Books, 2000.
Building on decades of study, Wilson has written the definitive work on how the bureaucracy developed and currently operates in the United States. He offers numerous examples of bureaucratic behavior to show how national administration has been molded to the counters of American constitutional government.

11. Parties and Elections

Burnham, Walter Dean. *Critical Elections and the Mainsprings of American Politics.* New York: W. W. Norton, 1971.

In making one of the most complete statements of the idea of political realignment, Burnham sees the fulcrum of American democracy turning on periodic "critical elections" that reinvigorate citizen engagement and create new cleavages in public policy that last for a generation.

Ceaser, James. *Presidential Selection: Theory and Development.* Princeton, NJ: Princeton University Press, 1979.

In this well argued and well researched study of American presidential selection, Ceaser reminds readers that the establishment of a party system was part of a conscious attempt by Martin Van Buren to control the ambitions of Andrew Jackson and the power of the presidency.

Key, V. O. *Politics, Parties, and Pressure Groups,* 5th ed. New York: Thomas Crowell, 1964.

With careful attention to the detail and complexity of the party system, Key mounts a classic defense of parties as essential but imperfect political associations. Parties, he shows, provide citizens with a guide to policy and politics that is essential for effective citizenship.

12. Public Opinion and Political Participation

Berry, Jeffrey. *Lobbying for the People: The Political Behavior of Public Interest Groups.* Princeton, NJ: Princeton University Press, 1977.

In an in-depth study of eighty-three national public interest groups, Berry offers an important portrait of the public interest movement and the profound effect it has had on contemporary American government.

Free, Lloyd, and Hadley Cantril. *The Political Beliefs of Americans: A Study of Public Opinion.* New Brunswick, NJ: Rutgers University Press, 1967.

This is the first explicit attempt to measure Americans' ambivalent response to the welfare state, their attempt to reconcile a hallowed devotion to individual rights and the post–New Deal acceptance of big government. Free and Cantril show that few people view themselves as ideological liberals; at the same time, most Americans have come to accept the programmatic commitments born of the New Deal political realignment. Americans thus tend to be ideological conservatives and "operational liberals."

Galston, William, and Elaine Kamarck. *The Politics of Polarization: A Third Way Report.* The Third Way Middle Class Project, October 2005, http://www.third-way.com.

Galston and Kamarck provide a fine-grained study of contemporary partisan polarization and explain why, at least until 2006, this polarization tended to benefit conservative activists and the Republican party.

Lippmann, Walter. *Public Opinion.* New York: Free Press, 1985.
Lippmann's important work casts serious doubt on the Progressive idea of democracy. Concluding that democracy could not depend on enlightened citizenship or the mass media, Lippmann prescribes the empowering of experts to command the state that is emerging in modern America.

McWilliams, Wilson Carey. "Two-Tiered Politics Revisited." In *Seeking the Center: Politics and Policymaking at the New Century*, ed. Martin Levin, Marc Landy, and Martin Shapiro. Washington, D.C.: Georgetown University Press, 2001.
This essay reflects on how the rise of the administrative state has affected representative government in the United States. The expansion of national administrative power, McWilliams argues, has carved a chasm between the interest group politics inside of the Washington beltway and the plebiscitary politics that connects, or fails to connect, it to the mass public. McWilliams argues that the elite-mass divide is foreordained by the Constitution, which deliberately insulates public officials from the views of the many.

Pertschuk, Michael. *Revolt against Regulation: The Rise and Pause of the Consumer Movement*, reprint ed. Berkeley: University of California Press, 1984.
Michael Pertschuk, former chairman of the Federal Trade Commission and consumer activist, writes a compelling memoir. It provides a thoughtful defense of the consumer movement, without which, he fears, business lobbyists and congressional representatives and staffers would ignore the public interest. The challenge for public interest activists, he cautions, is to avoid becoming part of a Washington establishment that has little connection to the American public.

Putnam, Robert. *Bowling Alone: The Collapse and Revival of American Community.* New York: Touchstone Books, 2001.
This study claims that America has suffered a dramatic loss of social capital and offers an analysis of the causes and ramifications of this decline. The book has received both popular and scholarly acclaim. Putnam argues that social capital is necessary for the persistence of strong democratic regimes and that the tendencies of Americans to "bowl alone" (rather than participate in bowling leagues) and to experience life from the solitude of their family rooms are symptoms of the decline of civic culture in contemporary America.

Schudson, Michael. *The Good Citizen: A History of American Civic Life*, reprint ed. Cambridge, MA: Harvard University Press, 1999.
In a sweeping and original look at American political culture, Schudson poses intelligent challenges to those scholars who celebrate the localistic polity of the nineteenth century. He shows not only that there was no "Golden Age" of American democracy but also that self-government has persisted and has even been strengthened in important ways in the wake of the rights revolution.

Shklar, Judith N. *American Citizenship: The Quest for Inclusion.* Cambridge, MA: Harvard University Press, 1991.

Shklar explores the deep philosophical roots of citizenship, highlighting the importance of the right to vote and the right to work as the defining entitlements that enable individuals to gain public respect and equal footing in the American "community."

Tichenor, Daniel J., and Richard Harris. "Organized Interests and American Political Development." *Political Science Quarterly* 117, no. 4 (Winter 2003): 587–612.
     Harris and Tichenor examine the Progressive Era to illustrate that the nationalization of interest-group politics preceded the rise of the bureaucratic state forged on the anvil of the New Deal. They shed new light on the importance of interest groups and the Progressive Era in shaping critical political developments during the twentieth century.

Tocqueville, Alexis de. *Democracy in America*. Chicago: University of Chicago Press, 2000.
     Tocqueville was one of the first scholars to notice the particular prevalence and importance of voluntary associations in the United States. Tocqueville noted the propensity for Americans to join groups and that these groups – religious, moral, and political – offered critical support for democratic practices in a political system obsessed with rights and privacy.

Wiebe, Robert H. *Self-Rule: A Cultural History of American Democracy*. Chicago: University of Chicago Press, 1995.
     Wiebe defends the decentralized republic of the nineteenth century against the critics who view this period as elitist and reactionary. For all its limits and failures, he shows, something important, deserving the name "democracy," was born and flowered during the nation's first one hundred years. Wiebe laments that disdain for local self-government, expressed and embodied in reforms during the Progressive Era, has led to the demise of democracy in the United States.

Wilson, James Q. "The Politics of Regulation." In *The Politics of Regulation*, ed. James Q. Wilson. New York: Basic Books, 1980.
     This is a very insightful examination of the different forms of regulatory politics and the conditions under which these types of regulation are likely to succeed. Building on a number of interesting case studies that appear in the volume, Wilson argues that the received wisdom that economic power shapes regulatory behavior underestimates other important factors, including the force of ideas, which are independent of "interests," that can influence regulatory policies and institutions.

————. "How Divided Are We?" *Commentary* (February 2006).
     Wilson warns that party polarization is not, as many commentators have argued, limited to a small circle of activists in the Washington, D.C. beltway. Rather, partisan differences over social issues and even foreign policy have begun to penetrate society. Wilson acknowledges that sharpened partisanship over domestic issues might be healthy, but he fears the effect it might have in foreign policy.

13. Conclusion: Liberalism and Democracy in the Twenty-first Century

Adams, Henry. *Democracy: An American Novel*, reprint ed. New York: Modern Library, 2003.

Originally published anonymously, *Democracy* is a political novel scathing in its critique of Washington society and its inducements to abuses of political power. The story follows the ambitions of Mrs. Lightfoot Lee, a society widow who comes to Washington to find out about the workings of government, and her eventual relationship with the most powerful member of the Senate.

Heclo, Hugh. "The Emerging Regime." In *Remaking American Politics*, ed. Richard Harris and Sidney Milkis. Boulder, CO: Westview Press, 1989.

Heclo, reflecting on the expansion of administrative government and the weakening of political parties in the twentieth century, observes a new type of Madisonian factionalism that is defining American politics. The scope and authority of modern American government has encouraged countless interest groups to negotiate their own private interests outside the mediating popular controls of parties or elections.

Schlesinger, Arthur M. *The Disuniting of America: Reflections on a Multicultural Society*, rev. ed. New York: W. W. Norton, 1998.

Demonstrating the need for a common identity and shared ideals, Schlesinger criticizes the divisive and alienating effects of radical multiculturalism. Harkening back to the days of cultural integration and the "melting pot" understanding of civic identity, Schlesinger casts doubt on the rightness of the modern trend toward an emphasis on cultural differences.

Wilson, James Q. "American Politics: Then and Now." *Commentary* (February 1979).

Wilson observes a continuing trend toward fewer barriers to governmental action in the interests of protecting individuals from social ills. He sees the American people coming to rely increasingly on government for administrative solutions to what used to be considered private problems outside the bounds of governmental interference.

Woodward, C. Vann. "Meanings for Multiculturalism." In *Multiculturalism and American Democracy*, ed. Arthur M. Melzer, Jerry Weinberger, and M. Richard Zinman. Lawrence: University Press of Kansas, 1998.

Woodward praises the success of the American republic in combining a strong national identity with respect for diversity. While imperfect, the United States has combined diverse peoples into one nation better than perhaps any other. He warns against the excesses of multiculturalism that drive apart national unity and purpose in favor of a narrow and divided society.

Index

AARP. *See* American Association of Retired People

Abbot, Lyman, 153

abolitionism, abolitionists, 16, 54, 87, 117, 145, 642–643

abortion, federal funding, 169–170

ACT. *See* Americans Coming Together

activism, 498, 579, 633

Adams, Abigail, 56

Adams, Henry, 704

Adams, John Quincy, 46, 59, 73, 135, 146, 447, 509, 637

Adams, Samuel, 60

Addams, Jane, 157

Adelphia, 291

administrative law, politics and reform, 492, 528–550

    Congress and, 349

    Federalism and, 218–219

    presidential commissions, 529–530

    Wilsonian, anti-Wilsonian, 529

Administrative Procedures Act (APA), 539, 543

advocacy politics, 686–690

AFBF. *See* American Farm Bureau Federation

AFDC. *See* Aid to Families with Dependent Children

affirmative action, 480, 538–539, 695–696, 697, 698–700, 701

Afghanistan war, 413, 508

AFL. *See* American Federation of Labor

African Americans

    after World War II, 256

    for civil rights, 442

    in Congress, 328–341

    congressional vote and, 339–340

    discrimination against, 3, 650

    Fifteenth Amendment and, 649–650

    Jim Crow laws and, 3, 6, 206–208, 211, 256, 650

    party identification of, 585–586

    political participation, 407

    Republican party support by, 595

    state population and, 53

    statutory protection for, 407

    voting rights, 150–151, 171

Agricultural Adjustment Act, 270

Agricultural Adjustment Agency, 522

Aid to Families with Dependent Children (AFDC), 162, 351

Alito, Samuel A. (Justice), 490, 494

Al Qaeda, 415, 558. *See also* September 11, 2001; War on Terror

American Anti-Slavery Society, 643

American Association of Retired People (AARP), 662

American Colonization Society, 643

American Enterprise Institute, 426

American Farm Bureau Federation (AFBF), 270

American Federation of Labor (AFL), 262–263, 601

American foreign policy, 132–133, 382, 396. *See also* War on Terror

    Al Qaeda and, 415

    Bush and, 417

    civil liberties, homeland security, 558

    Clinton and, 415

    credit dependence, 557

    current perspective, 556–562

    democrats, European allies and, 417

    doctrine of pre-emption, 560

    energy dependence, 556

    Iraq and, 415

    party politics and, 601

    pressure vulnerability, 556

    of Reagan administration, 414

    regime reconstitution, 561–562

    terrorism and, 557

    unilateralism, 561

American heroes, 69–70, 73–74

American politics, 2, 20, 36–37, 41, 173–178, 194, 513, 612

    contemporary, 19–21

    development, 21–23

    path dependency in, 23–24